Studies in Political Economy

Series editor
Norman Schofield, Washington University in Saint Louis,
Saint Louis, MO, USA

More information about this series at http://www.springer.com/series/13366

Norman Schofield • Gonzalo Caballero
Editors

State, Institutions and Democracy

Contributions of Political Economy

Springer

Editors
Norman Schofield
Department of Political Science
Washington University in St. Louis
Saint Louis, USA

Gonzalo Caballero
Faculty of Economics
University of Vigo
Vigo, Spain

ISSN 2364-5903 ISSN 2364-5911 (electronic)
Studies in Political Economy
ISBN 978-3-319-44581-6 ISBN 978-3-319-44582-3 (eBook)
DOI 10.1007/978-3-319-44582-3

Library of Congress Control Number: 2016956209

Printed on acid-free paper

This Springer imprint is published by Springer Nature
The registered company is Springer International Publishing AG Switzerland

Contents

Contributors

Marcos Álvarez-Díaz is an associate professor at the University of Vigo (Spain). He holds a Ph.D., M.Ph., and M.A. in economics from Columbia University (New York, USA). He is the head of the research group on economic modeling and forecasting at the University of Vigo. His work has appeared in several economic journals such as *Applied Economics, Economic Modelling, Tourism Management, Journal of Forest Economics, Ecological Economics*, and *Empirical Economics*, among others. His main area of interest is centered on time series modeling and forecasting using nonlinear techniques.

Joan Barceló is a Ph.D. student at Washington University in St. Louis. His research focuses on the identification of the sources of differences in people's preferences and behavior in the political arena.

Joaquim Filipe Ferraz Esteves de Araújo, Ph.D. in Public Administration, University of Exeter, UK, is an Associate Professor of Public Administration, School of Economics and Management, University of Minho, Braga, Portugal. His interest subjects are Public Management, Public Sector Reform, Local Government, Governance, and Transparency.

Ken Binmore is a mathematician turned economist and philosopher. He was one of the pioneers in the revival of game theory in the 1970s and in experimental economics in the 1980s. He has contributed to bargaining theory, evolutionary biology, and the theory of justice. His books include *Mathematical Analysis, Game Theory and the Social Contract, Natural Justice, and Rational Decisions*. He is currently working on the latter topic. He is an emeritus professor of economics at UCL and holds honorary positions at LSE, Bristol, and Warwick universities. He is a fellow of the British Academy and of the American Academy of Arts and Sciences.

Vani K. Borooah, who was born in India, is emeritus professor at the University of Ulster having been professor in applied economics there from 1987 to 2014. After taking his Ph.D. in 1977 from the University of Southampton, he worked for the next 10 years as a senior research officer at the University of Cambridge's

Department of Applied Economics and, concurrently, was a fellow of Queens College. He is a past president of the European Public Choice Society and of the Irish Economic Association and is also honorary professor of economics at the University of Queensland. He was elected a member of the Royal Irish Academy in 2006. His work has been mainly in the areas of unemployment, inequality, poverty, and economic development.

Elise S. Brezis, professor of economics at Bar-Ilan University, is the head of the Aharon Meir Center for Banking and Economic Policy in Israel. She previously was the head of the statistics division at the Research Department in the Bank of Israel. She holds a Ph.D. in economics from MIT (USA). She has taught at the Sloan School of Management (MIT) and Brandeis and has been a visiting professor at the College de France as well as in South Korea. Her research interests cover a wide range of topics related to economic growth, from R&D to higher education and human capital. She is currently working in the field of elites and economic growth, as well as on the revolving door. She has published articles in leading journals as the *American Economic Review* and the *European Economic Review*. In the field of economic growth, she has developed a theory, coined leapfrogging with the Nobel Laureate Paul Krugman.

Oscar Briones holds a bachelor's degree in political science and sociology and a Ph.D. in "contemporaneous political process" from the University of Santiago de Compostela (Spain). Currently, he is a lecturer at the School of Social Sciences and Communication (University of Vigo), where he teaches political science and public administration at the University of Vigo, and in the master's degree in public administration and institutional leadership. He is also a researcher at the Governance Lab G (Political Science and Public Administration, University of Vigo, Spain) that works on management and public services and governance. He is author of numerous publications in topics such as human resources, negotiation, public policy, and direction and leadership.

Gonzalo Caballero is an associate professor of economics at the University of Vigo, Spain. He received a Ph.D. and a B.Sc. in economics with honors from the University of Vigo and a Ph.D. in political science from the University of Santiago de Compostela. He has been a visiting scholar at the Center for New Institutional Social Sciences, Washington University, in St. Louis, the Center for Advanced Studies in the Social Sciences (Juan March Institute, Madrid), the University of California in Santa Barbara, and the University of California in Berkeley. He has been a visiting professor at Charles University (Prague, Czech Republic), Comenius University (Bratislava, Slovakia), the University of Valencia (Spain), Universita Roma Tre (Italy), Tallinn University of Technology (Estonia), the University of Granada (Spain), and the University of Oulu (Finland). He has published over 50 papers on institutional analysis and political economy in journals such as *Economic Modelling, Journal of Institutional Economics, Ecological Economics, Ocean & Coastal Management, Marine Policy, Environmetrics, Aquaculture Research, Forest Policy and Economics, Trimestre Económico, Brazilian Journal of Political*

Economy, Política y Gobierno, Revista de Estudios Políticos, Economic Analysis Review, Revista Española de Investigaciones Sociológicas, Perfiles Latinoamericanos, CLAD Reforma Democracia, and Revista Española de Ciencia Política, among others. He has written several books and recently coedited five volumes: *Political Economy of Institutions, Democracy and Voting* (Springer, 2011, with Norman Schofield), *Nuevo Institucionalismo: Gobernanza, Economía y Políticas Públicas* (CIS-Madrid, 2013, with Xosé Carlos Arias), *Advances in Political Economy: Institutions, Modeling and Empirical Analysis* (Springer, 2013, with Norman Schofield and Daniel Kselman), *Democracia y Políticas Económicas* (Síntesis, 2015, with F. Toboso), and *The Political Economy of Governance* (Springer, 2015, with Norman Schofield)

Joël Cariolle received his Ph.D. from the CERDI—University of Auvergne (Clermont-Ferrand, France) and is a research fellow at the Foundation for Studies and Researches on International Development (Ferdi, Clermont-Ferrand, France). His work focuses on the political economy of corruption in developing and developed countries, on economic vulnerability in least developed countries, and on regional integration in sub-Saharan Africa. Joël Cariolle also provides technical assistance and coordinates research at FERDI on regional integration in WAEMU and CEMAC areas.

Inmaculada Carrasco is a lecturer of the Economic Policy Unit in the University of Castilla-La Mancha. Holder of a Ph.D. in economics with European mention (1997), since 1991 she has taken up different positions as university teacher. She has a wide experience teaching economic policy subjects (four 5-years periods), and she teaches master's in sustainable economic growth and development. She has taken part in several national and international research groups. Of note is her participation in the Global Entrepreneurship Monitor Project. Her papers have been published in several international journals and monographs. She has been recognized with three 6-years researching terms. Her research has focused on different topics related to economic growth and entrepreneurship such as the study of the relationships among entrepreneurship and economic growth with an ethical point of view, the social economy institutions' entrepreneurial activity, gender and entrepreneurship, and some other aspects related to economic policy.

Adão Carvalho is an assistant professor of economics at the Department of Economics of the University of Evora, Portugal. He is the director of the master's program in public policy and projects at the University of Evora. He has a background in economics and received his Ph.D. in science and technology policy studies from the University of Sussex, UK, in 2002. His research focuses on innovation; science and technology policy; economics of knowledge, with an emphasis on R&D expenditures and R&D policy; and electronic public procurement (e-procurement), with a focus on organizational innovation in municipalities.

Harold D. Clarke is Ashbel Smith Professor, University of Texas at Dallas, former director of social and economic sciences at the National Science Foundation and senior editor of electoral studies. A former principal investigator of the British and

Canadian national election studies, he has coauthored numerous books and articles on voting and elections including *Affluence, Austerity and Electoral Change in Britain* (Cambridge University Press, 2013), and *Austerity and Political Choice in Britain* (Palgrave Macmillan, 2015).

Carmen Córcoles graduated in 1991 in economics and business from university of Alicante with distinction and received her Ph.D. from the University of Castilla-La Mancha (UCLM) in 1997 (best doctoral thesis in public economics, award by Instituto Estudios Fiscales of Spain). Since, 1991 she has taken up different professor positions, and from 2000, she is lecturer of the Economic Theory Unit at the Faculty of Economics and Business in Albacete (UCLM). She has a wide experience teaching different economic theory subjects in degrees of economic and business administration and she also teaches at master's in sustainable economic growth and development. Her research has focused on impact economic analysis for countries and regions with input-output analysis. She has participated in several research projects on this topic, among which we can highlight the estimation of input-output tables of Castilla-La Mancha by indirect methods for Consejo Económico y Social (CLM), the estimation of oil derivative demand for the Spanish National Commission of Energy, and the computable general equilibrium model applied to CO_2 emission calculations for the Spanish economy. From 2000, she is vice-dean at the Faculty of Economics and Business in Albacete.

Jon X. Eguia is an associate professor of economics at Michigan State University, with secondary affiliation to the University of Bristol. He obtained his Ph.D. from the California Institute of Technology in 2007. His fields of specialization are political economy and microeconomic theory. His work on party formation, voting and elections, and information aggregation in financial markets has been published in journals such as the *Journal of Political Economy, the American Journal of Political Science, Games and Economic Behavior*, or the *Journal of Politics*, among others.

Raquel Fernández-González is a postdoctoral fellow at the University of Vigo. She received a extraordinary award by her Ph.D. dissertation at the University of Vigo. Her work has been published in *Marine Policy* and *Revista Española de Ciencia Política*.

Nadia Fiorino is currently associate professor at the University of L'Aquila, where she has been teaching public finance and local public finance since 2001. She received a Ph.D. in economics from the University of Rome "La Sapienza." Her main areas of research are public choice/political economy, public finance, law and economics. She has published in numerous international peer-reviewed journals in economics, such as *Public Choice, International Review of Law and Economics*, and *the Journal of Institutional and Theoretical Economics* among others.

Martin Gregor is associate professor in economics at the Faculty of Social Sciences, Charles University in Prague. His main research fields are applied game theory, microeconomic theory, political economics, and organizational economics.

He has published both in economics (*Journal of Economic Behavior & Organization, Economics Letters, International Tax and Public Finance, Review of Economic Design, The B.E. Journal of Theoretical Economics, Applied Economics*) and political science (*Journal of Theoretical Politics*). Currently, he serves as director of the Institute of Economic Studies at Charles University in Prague, Czech Republic.

Jan Klingelhöfer is a postdoctoral fellow at RWTH Aachen University in Germany. He completed his Ph.D. in economics at the Institute for International Economic Studies in Stockholm in October 2010 and spent 1 year as a Max Weber Fellow at the European University Institute in Florence. His research interests are political economics and macroeconomics.

Jani-Petri Laamanen is a university lecturer in economics at the University of Tampere, Finland. He received his doctorate in economics from the same university. During his doctoral studies, he spent an academic year as a visiting researcher at the Tinbergen Institute Amsterdam. His research interests fall within empirical public and labor economics. Among other things, he has worked on the effects of health-care costs on well-being, tax reporting, the relationship between home ownership and the labor market, and economic growth and subjective well-being.

Elena Labzina is a doctoral student in political science at Washington University in St. Louis. A native of Moscow, she holds a B.Sc. in applied math and computer science from Lomonosov Moscow State University (2007) and an M.A. in economics from New Economic School in Moscow (2010). Also, she took an M.A. in political science from the Central European University in Budapest in 2011. Her research interests include applied game theory, big data, and statistical methods.

John McCombie is professor of regional and applied economics in the Department of Land Economy and director of the Cambridge Centre for Economic and Public Policy at the University of Cambridge, UK. He is fellow and director of studies of economics and land economy at Downing College, Cambridge. He was a founding coeditor of the journal *Spatial Economic Analysis*. He is a fellow of the Regional Studies Association and fellow of the Academy of Social Sciences. He has previously held positions as a specialist advisor to the House of Lords on the European Union Committee Inquiry into the EU Structural and Cohesion Funds, and as an economic consultant to the World Bank and Asian Development Bank. His research interests are regional economics, the causes of regional and national growth rate disparities, economic growth and the balance-of-payments constraint, and economic methodology. He has published widely in such journals as the *Economic Journal, Oxford Economic Papers, Urban Studies, the Cambridge Journal of Economics, Metroeconomica*, and *the Journal of Post Keynesian Economics*. His most recent book, written with Jesus Felipe, is entitled *The Aggregate Production Function and the Measurement of Technical Change* (2013).

José M. Pavía is Quantitative Methods Full Professor at the Department of Applied Economics, University of Valencia, Spain. He is also the director of the "Elections and Public Opinion Research Group" of this University. His areas of interest are diverse and they comprise political issues, election forecasting, statistical (machine) learning, spatial statistics, and sampling. His main research has been published in journals such as *Journal of the American Statistical Association, Environment and Planning A, Journal of the Royal Statistical Society, The Political Quarterly*, or *Revista Española de Investigaciones Sociologicas* and he has served as visiting research in many universities, including *Stanford, Leicester, Durham* or *Carlos III de Madrid.*

Mikko Poutanen is a Ph.D. student and a doctoral researcher at the School of Management at the University of Tampere, Finland, where he also received his master's degree. His research interests are multidisciplinary, including the politics of welfare states and the influence of economic rationale and assumptions on political decision-making. Poutanen currently teaches courses on qualitative research methods. While his primary research language is English, he has also written on international security issues in Finnish in a refereed article.

Roberto Ricciuti is Associate Professor of Economic Policy at the University of Verona (Italy) where he is the Director of the Ph.D. program in Economics and Management. He holds an M.Sc. in Economics from the University of Exeter and a Ph.D. in Economics from the University of Siena (Italy). Previously he was a Lecturer at Royal Holloway University of London (2003/2004), a post-doctoral fellow at the University of Siena (2004/2005), and a Lecturer at the University of Florence (2005/2011). He is also a Research Fellow at CESifo and Honorary Professorial Fellow at the Effective States and Inclusive Development Research Centre at the University of Manchester. He works at the boundaries between economics and political science. His papers have been published on Journal of Peace Research, Public Choice, Journal of Economic Behavior and Organization, Cliometrica, European Journal of Political Economy, Defence and Peace Economics, and International Review of Law and Economics, among others.

Norman Schofield is the Taussig Professor in political economy at Washington University in St. Louis. He has published numerous articles and books in this field and holds Ph.D. degree in economics and political science from Essex University, a Litt. D. from Liverpool University, and a D.Sc. from the University of Caen.

Gilles Serra is assistant professor of politics at CIDE in Mexico. Before coming to CIDE, he earned his Ph.D. degree in political economy and government from the University of Harvard, and he was postdoctoral fellow at Nuffield College at the University of Oxford. His research on Mexican institutions, elections, and reforms has been published in *Electoral Studies, the Journal of Politics in Latin America*, and *Política y Gobierno*. His formal models of political parties and electoral competition have appeared in the *Journal of Politics* and *the Journal of Theoretical Politics.*

Katri Sieberg is a professor in the School of Social Sciences and Humanities at the University of Tampere in Finland. Her research combines approaches from economics and political science to address issues of how and why things work—or don't work. To that end, her research applies game theory and social choice theory to address how people make decisions, game theory and economics to assess the effect of these decisions, and experimental economics to evaluate the underlying theories. One of her key interests is welfare state institutions, with a strong focus on health-care economics.

Luís Soares is a highly experienced professional in Public Administration matters having followed closely the changes in "Public Procurement" model, from a strategic perspective particularly focused on procurement, contracting and strategic sourcing. For that effect in 2011 was appointed Head of a Multidisciplinary Team having coordinated and managed, since then, several areas, namely e-procurement, public policies, projects and economic development. Recently at the University of Evora (PT) he finished a Masters degree on Public Policies and Projects. His research, study and interests aim essentially public procurement in carrying out public policies through the European structural investment funds in a relational and holistic approach.

Marianne C. Stewart is professor in the School of Economic, Political and Policy Sciences at the University of Texas in Dallas. A former principal investigator for the British Election Study, her research interests include voting and elections in Canada, Great Britain, and the United States and public opinion dynamics in mature democracies. She has published widely in leading political science journals and her most recent book is *Austerity and Political Choice in Britain* (London: Palgrave Macmillan, 2015).

Anirudh Tagat is research author at the Department of Economics, Monk Prayogshala, Mumbai. Anirudh holds an M.Sc. in economics from the University of Warwick and consults with the World Resources Institute (WRI) India and Institute of Rural Management, Anand (IRMA). His research interests include cross-cultural differences in decision-making, intra-household bargaining, and experimental economics.

Theis Theisen is professor of economics at the Department of Economics and Finance, School of Business and Law, University of Agder. He has previously worked as director of budget and finance in Aust-Agder County and as consultant in the Norwegian Ministry of Finance. He has also served as member of the board of directors of several private companies and public sector organizations.

Fernando Toboso is professor at the Department of Applied Economics, University of Valencia, Spain. He received his degree in Economics with honors in 1985 and his Ph.D. in Economics in 1990 after spending an academic year at the Public Choice Center, George Mason University, USA. His research interests mainly are in methodological and epistemological issues in economic analysis, and in the organization of policy tasks in federal countries. Special attention is paid to the economic consequences of political and fiscal quasi-federalism in Spain as well as to the influences of different electoral institutions and rules. In all these areas he has authored several articles that have been published in English journals such as the *Cambridge Journal of Economics*, the *Regional and Federal Studies*, the *History* *of Economic Ideas*, the *European Journal of Law and Economics* and the *Journal of Interdisciplinary Economics*, among others. He has also published widely in Spanish academic journals and has contributed with several chapters to Spanish collective books as well as to English ones such as Oppenheimer et al. (2004, M.E. Sharpe), Williams (2005, Sage Publ.), Schofield et al. (2011, Springer). He has served as invited editor for two special issues in economic journals (*Economic Analysis Review*, Chile and *Revista Asturiana de Economía*, Spain). He was also an invited participant, together with Elinor Ostrom, Claude Menard and several other colleagues, to the workshop in honor of the career of Allan Schmid at Michigan State University with a paper that appeared in Batie et al. (2008, Routledge).

Enrique J. Varela, Ph.D. in Government and Public Administration (Ortega y Gasset University Research Institute and the Universidad Complutense of Madrid, Spain), is a Lecturer at the Faculty of Social Sciences and Communication (University of Vigo), where he teaches Political Science and Public Administration at the University of Vigo, Bachelor's Degree in Public Management and Master's Degree in Public Management and Institutional Leadership. He is also an academic coordinator and researcher at the Governance Lab G^3 (Political Science and Public Administration, University of Vigo, Spain) that works on management and public services and governance at local and cross-border level, on which he has published numerous contributions.

Fulvio Venturino obtained his Ph.D. in Political Science from the University of Florence, and at present is Associate Professor at the University of Cagliari. His preferred fields of research are party politics and voting behaviour. He was a member of the Scientific Board of the Italian Society for Electoral Research (SISE) between 2005 and 2010, and is now member of Itanes (Italian National Electoral Studies). In 2011 he launched Candidate and Leader Selection (www.cals.it), a standing group of the Italian Political Science Association (SISP). Recently he has published various book chapters and journal articles on the issue of intra-party democracy in Italy from a comparative perspective.

Paul Whiteley is a professor of government at the University of Essex. His research interests include electoral behavior, public opinion, political parties, political economy, and methodology in the social sciences. He is a fellow of the British Academy and a fellow of the Academy of Social Sciences. He is the author or coauthor of 18 academic books including studies of electoral behavior, party members, and citizenship in Britain. He was director of the Economic and Social Research Council Research Programme on Democracy and Participation from 1998 to 2003 and was the codirector of the British Election Study from 2001 to 2012. He has acted as an academic advisor to the Home Office, to the Department of Education, and to the Speaker of the House of Commons on issues relating to citizenship, participation, and Parliamentary representation. He frequently comments in the media on issues relating to elections and public opinion.

Introduction

The state, institutions, and democracy are a central part of the research agenda of contemporaneous political economy. Politics and economics are interested in understanding the state, institutions, and democracy from an interdisciplinary approach in social science that combines modeling, mathematics, and econometrics with solid theoretical foundations, structural factors, political and economic history, applied studies, and institutional analysis. We are trying to open the "black box" of the state, the institutions, and the democracy in a research program that incorporates diverse types of analysis. Theoretical and applied contributions have been included to improve our knowledge of the issues that have been selected.

This volume includes contributions from authors of papers that were presented at the IV Conference on Political Economy and Institutions, held in Baiona, Spain, December 2015, under the auspices of the University of Vigo and Washington University in St. Louis. Moreover, other chapters have been invited to be included in this volume too. The result is a volume with contributions by economists and political scientists from Europe, America, and Asia. Of course, each chapter in this book went through a review process before publication.

The volume is structured in four parts. Part I presents three chapters on bargaining, lobbying, and state capture. Part II presents six chapters that study elections and voting. Part III includes three chapters on state and public services. Part IV presents four cases of institutional change. Below, we briefly sketch the topics discussed in these chapters.

Part I: Bargaining, Lobbying and State Capture

1. "Bargaining with Outside Options," Ken Binmore (University of Bristol) and Jon X. Eguia (Michigan State University)

   This chapter comments on noncooperative and cooperate approaches to distributive (divide-the-cake) bargaining. We first review the challenges addressed by the seminal literature on two-person bargaining and three-person bargaining.

We then explore more recent developments on dynamic multiplayer bargaining over distributive policies, both over a single decision and over an infinite sequence of decisions with an endogenous outside option.

2. "Lobbying Mechanisms," Martin Gregor (Charles University in Prague)

   The Lobbying Disclosure Act 1995 has generated relatively clean data on the salaries of lobbyists and their staff, which has revolutionized the landscape of the analysis of political influence of special interests. This chapter reviews how the economic theory has reflected the recent shift of attention from campaign contributions to informational lobbying. The survey is an attempt to review the theoretical developments that are relevant to modeling of informational lobbying with explicit informational and game-theoretic microfoundations. The first part covers the early models of influence of special interests and discusses attempts to build explicit informational microfoundations for rent-seeking contests. Next, the single-tool (payments or information) and multiple-tool (payments and information) models of influence are covered. Then, the latter models are broadly divided into lobby-and-pay models and pay-and-lobby models. Specific yet important theoretical questions, namely, variants of information transmission, participation, and interaction of instruments of influence, are covered in detail .

3. "Financial Sector Regulation and the Revolving Door in US Commercial Banks," Elise S. Brezis (Bar-Ilan University) and Joël Cariolle (FERDI)

   This chapter develops an index of the distortions due to the revolving door—the Revolving Door Index. This index focuses on the process by which these distortions arise, by measuring the concentration of revolving door movements among private firms. We motivate this index, through a literature review and a small theoretical model, and illustrate it by an empirical application using data on the five biggest US commercial banks. Our data show that there is a concentration of revolving door movements which mainly benefit Goldman Sachs. This index may have policy implications for improving financial sector regulation.

Part II: Democracy, Participation and Electoral Politics

4. "The Rhetoric and the Reality of Austerity: Electoral Politics in Britain 2010–2015," Paul Whiteley (University of Essex), Harold D. Clarke (University of Texas in Dallas), and Marianne Stewart (University of Texas in Dallas)

   The Conservative victory in the 2015 general election in Britain was a surprise since the polls indicated that a hung Parliament was the most likely outcome with no party having an overall majority. The analysis in this paper confirms the proposition that electorates reward an incumbent party for a good economic performance and punish it for a bad one. Thus, public perceptions of the state of the economy played a key role in explaining the election victory. However, the story is not a straightforward one since we argue that the initial economic policy adopted by George Osborne when he became Chancellor of the Exchequer in 2010 would have almost certainly lost the election for the Conservatives had he not changed course in the middle of the Parliament. The initial policy of austerity was adopted for ideological, theoretical, and electoral reasons but then was effectively abandoned midterm when it failed to stimulate an economic recovery. The paper shows how austerity was defined and pursued and how the government changed strategy in 2012 allowing a recovery from recession to take place. This in turn stimulated economic optimism among the voters which subsequently translated into an election victory in 2015.

5. "Valence and Ideological Proximity in the Rise of Nationalist Parties: Spanish General Elections, 2008 and 2011," Elena Labzina, Joan Barceló, and Norman Schofield (Washington University in St. Louis)

   This chapter investigates the rise of nationalist parties from the Spanish National Elections from 2008 to 2011 by adjusting the classic spatial voting framework. The traditional spatial analysis would suggest that stronger nationalistic preferences and nationalistic voters, party alignment might explain the increase in support for these parties. We argue that the rise of small and nationalist parties can hardly be explained by policy or nationalistic preferences given the spatial understanding of the politics.

   Instead, exogenous valence is the main explanation for the electoral success of the political parties. This paper compares party valences and ideological, and demographic effects on the voting shares in the 2008 and 2011 Spanish National Elections to test our hypotheses. To properly capture the variation in the parties across regions, this paper develops and employs a refinement of the Bayesian adaptation for the varying choice logistic model proposed by Yamamoto (2011). Our findings suggest that the rise of the nationalist parties parallels the rise of the new political parties and not necessarily a shift in nationalistic preferences. Furthermore, we find that the main driver of the shifts in the electoral success across parties and regions is the changes in party-region exogenous valence. This paper provides important implications for the relevance of the non-policy considerations in the understanding of the changes in party support.

6. "Measuring Direct Democracy," Nadia Fiorino (University of L'Aquila), Roberto Ricciuti (University of Verona and CESifo), and Fulvio Venturino (University of Cagliari)

   This chapter provides an empirical analysis aimed at uncovering the economic, political, and social variables that make direct democracy institutions more or less likely. We provide a framework to investigate direct democracy institutions along the lines of constitutional design proposed by Aghion et al. (2004). We analyze a unique dataset where 87 countries are classified through an index of direct democracy (DDI). In applying a number of estimation techniques, we find that direct democracy is mainly correlated with income and education and does not significantly relate to institutional variables like presidential system and majoritarian voting rules.

7. "Political Participation in Rural India: A Village-Level Study," Vani K. Borooah (University of Ulster) and Anirudh Tagat (Department of Economics, Monk Prayogshala, Mumbai)

   This chapter uses village-level data on individual voters to study the factors which determine the probability of whether an individual votes. Is this probability greater for national compared to local elections? And is there evidence that people are more likely to vote today than they were in the past? Allied to these questions is another set of questions relating to the choice of candidates. Needless to say, voting in elections is just one facet of political participation. Another might be attending and participating in political meetings. This is particularly relevant in Indian villages since the Constitution (73rd Amendment) Act of 1993. This made it mandatory for all villages to have a village council (hereafter, Gram Sabha) consisting of all registered voters on the electoral roll of a village. The Gram Sabha was to be entrusted with the power of supervising the functioning of the elected village panchayat and to approve the panchayat's development plan for the village and the associated budget. Consequently, in addition to voting, electors in villages had another form of political participation: they could attend Gram Sabha meetings and also participate in its discussions. This paper also analyzes the factors which determine attendance and participation in such meetings.

   A worrisome feature of the results was the high proportion of married women reporting that they cast their vote according to their husbands' instructions and further that this proportion was impervious to the education level of the women. The results would suggest that the reservation of village panchayat positions (including that of panchayat pradhan or village president) for women was a step in the right direction for the empowerment of women. In contrast, there were no intersocial group differences in participation in Gram Sabha meetings.

8. "Elections with International Relations Dominance," Jan Klingelhöfer (RWTH Aachen University)

   This chapter combines a model of international cooperation with a model of domestic politics with national elections between an incumbent prime minister and a challenger. International cooperation is modeled as a repeated prisoner's dilemma game between two countries who are represented by their prime ministers. I compare three types of equilibria. In the country-specific grim trigger equilibrium, domestic politics does not affect international cooperation, and the standard results for the repeated prisoner's dilemma game apply. The second equilibrium is based on McGillivray's and Smith's (2000) idea of agent-specific punishment. If a prime minister cares sufficiently about staying in office, the threat of replacing him in a primary if he does not cooperate internationally can change a politician's incentives and make a larger maximum equilibrium level of cooperation possible. In the third equilibrium, I introduce the new idea of international dominance. In this type of equilibrium, domestic politics are dominated by considerations of international relations. The only function of the elections becomes either to punish or reward the prime minister for international cooperation. Consequently, the maximum achievable level of international cooperation can be increased, but elections no longer lead to the victory of the candidate preferred by the representative voter.

9. "Electoral Rules and Proportionality in Spain: Estimating the Impact of Some Swedish Rules Through the 2011 Electoral Data," José M. Pavía and Fernando Toboso (University of Valencia)

   As many contributions have shown, the share of seats that political parties get in all elections is partly influenced by the electoral rules in place and particularly by the specific rules influencing how votes get converted into seats. In Spain, a traditional complaint has existed by both the leaders and supporters of some statewide political parties (such as IU or UPyD) who systematically have got a much lower share of seats than their share in total popular votes. This nonproportionality is also evident if we compare the results traditionally obtained by these two small statewide parties with those obtained by nationalist parties such as PVN (Basque Country) or the, now broken, coalition called CiU (Catalonia) that only presents candidates at one region-state and not in all regions-states of Spain. As the Swedish electoral system is known as a quite proportional system that could be implemented in Spain without reforming the Spanish Constitution, the purpose of this chapter consists of estimating how much the share of seats that resulted from the 2011 Spanish general elections would change if we apply some Swedish basic rules upon the raw electoral data, ceteris paribus. Of course, the behavior of voters and members of political parties also matters, and this behavior is not independent of the existing electoral rules, so the purpose of the paper is not to provide predictions.

Part III: State and Public Services

10. "Is There a Doctor in the House?", Jani-Petri Laamanen, Mikko Poutanen, and Katri Sieberg (University of Tampere)

    The option to purchase private health insurance in an otherwise public system seems to offer the best of all alternatives. The public system provides universal coverage, while the private option allows those with more resources to be able to purchase superior services. A closer look at the issue, however, reveals the potential for problems to arise in both the demand for the services and supply of the health-care professionals. We present a simple model of the incentives that the private sector can use to attract doctors in their choices between employment in the public and private sector. We further assess the resulting effects on doctor supply between the two sectors—in terms of numbers and in terms of quality. Our results indicate that without controls, the system can at best develop into a two-class system, in which more and/or better doctors select the private system, leaving inferior doctors in the public sector. As a real-world example of this problem, we appeal to the example of the Finnish health-care system, with its mixture of public and private services, and show how the increase in private coverage has been associated with a decrease in resources for the public system. Our results indicate that this hybrid system is harmful to societal goals.

11. "What Makes People Nursing Home Residents: Individual Need or Municipalities' Supply?" , Theis Theisen (University of Agder)

    In a setting where admissions to nursing homes are strictly rationed, we consider which individuals become nursing home residents. Rationing decisions are taken at the level of municipalities. Using a national sample, we examine the impact on the rationing decision of individual characteristics and characteristics of the municipalities in which individuals live. High age, lack of self-care functionality, and lack of cognitive ability have a positive impact on whether an individual is in a nursing home. Men have a slightly lower incidence of living in a nursing home than women. Municipalities' capacity in the nursing home sector has a strong positive impact on the probability of living in a nursing home.

12. "Civil Service and the Crisis: A comparative analysis of Iberian Countries (2008–2013)," Oscar Briones (University of Vigo), Joaquim Filipe Ferraz Esteves de Araújo (University of Minho), and Enrique J. Varela (University of Vigo)

    The aim of this chapter is to assess the changing working conditions of public employees in order to shed some light on controversial issues concerning public employment models of central government in Spain and Portugal. The trends and reforms have been analyzed to assess the theoretical approaches underpinning policy reform implemented until the year 2013. In short, the aim of this study was to answer the question: Are reforms implemented due to the international financial crisis simply reforms and cuts in public employment, or do these changes entail a widespread far-reaching transformation in the current public employment models of the two Iberian states? Should the answer be the latter, this would signal the death of the civil servant as key actor of the human resource management model of the central government in Spain and Portugal.

Part IV: Cases of Institutional Change

13. "Congressional Negotiations with Costly Voting: Understanding the Reforms to PEMEX in 2006–2008," Gilles Serra (CIDE)

    The state-owned petroleum company in Mexico has played a fundamental role in the economy, but its productivity has been worryingly in decline. Several presidents of Mexico before Felipe Calderón tried to modernize Pemex, but they failed to pass any meaningful legal reform through the Congress. In this chapter I explain why Calderón was successful where other presidents were not. At the same time, I explain why Calderón's successes were not as large as they could have been: indeed, the legal reforms to the Mexican oil industry in 2006–2008 were not as profound as they were expected to be. I claim this was due to the costs that political conditions imposed on congressional negotiations. Irrespective of their preferences, legislators faced punishment by radical political leaders and passionate voters if they supported Calderón's initiatives. At the same time, some pivotal negotiators in the Congress were able to extract significant side payments for their support of government initiatives. To clarify these complex dynamics, I use the traditional concepts from spatial voting theory: I identify the main issues regarding Pemex, the main political agents in charge of reform, and the positions of these agents on those issues. I also propose a modeling innovation to the traditional spatial theory of voting, which consists on considering the punishment that legislators may incur from supporting a bill that they like. With these theoretical tools, I am able to explain the puzzling coalitions that were formed for the 2006 budget law, the 2007 fiscal reform, and the 2008 energy reform. I suggest that these same theoretical tools could be used to understand congressional negotiations in other contexts.

14. "Institutional Change, Specific Investments and Photovoltaic Power Plants: The Empirical Effects of the Energy Policy of Solar Farms in Spain," Marcos Álvarez-Díaz, Raquel Fernández-González, and Gonzalo Caballero (University of Vigo)

    The Spanish government introduced a bonus policy for the installation and exploitation of photovoltaic solar energy before the Great Recession, and it implied the increase of the number of solar farms in Spain. Nevertheless, the government did not adequately take into account the cost of the bonuses for the public treasury and neither did it contemplate the changing macroeconomic scenario derived from the Great Recession since 2008. In fact, the government rectified later and proceeded toward cancelation and elimination of the bonus policy in the photovoltaic sector. This chapter analyzes the process of institutional change and of bonus policies in the Spanish solar energy sector from the point of view of new institutional economics, by performing an empirical analysis on the effects of an energy policy that first announced and established public bonuses for solar parks but which later eliminated them unilaterally. These changes in energy policy had a significant impact on return for investors who had made irreversible investments in solar parks. The empirical analysis concludes the change in the trends of the Spanish solar farm sector in September 2008. The institutional analysis includes the study of the process of institutional change and the legal actions, appeals, and lawsuits that the investors presented at the third party enforcement mechanisms.

15. "The Economic Effects of the Implementation of the Greek Adjustment Plan in the Great Recession," Inmaculada Carrasco (Castilla-La Mancha University), Carmen Córcoles (Castilla-La Mancha University), and John McCombie (Cambridge University)

    In a situation of deep economic crisis such as the present one confronting some European countries, it is necessary to take measures to reduce the dangerous disequilibria that they face. The orthodoxy dictates that it is imperative to undertake strong fiscal consolidation to ensure a recovery in economic activity. The existing debate has tended to focus on the global analysis of such policies.

As a contribution to this literature, in this chapter we provide a multisector and multiregional study of the effects of the fiscal adjustment implemented in Greece in 2012 using an input–output methodology. It allows us to trace the consequences of this fiscal policy for the different Greek economic sectors, as well as for the EU and the rest of the world. This is undertaken using the WIOD (World Input–Output Database). This study concludes that, far from leading to a revival in the Greek economy, the fiscal adjustment has led to a contraction in the health and public administration sectors, as well as the industrial sectors with the last leading to a greater downturn in the economy.

16. "E-procurement and Innovation in the Portuguese Municipalities: When Change is Mandatory," Luís Soares (Câmara Municipal de Castro Verde) and Adão Carvalho (Universidade de Evora)

    Changing the traditional pattern of public procurement for an electronic paradigm is a radical innovation involving major organizational changes, the breaking up of traditional processes and practices, and the obsolescence of knowledge and skills. Going beyond the European Commission's recommendations, in 2009 Portugal pioneered in making e-procurement mandatory in the pre-award phase, in a European context of multiple technical standards and lack of interoperability of electronic platforms across the EU countries. Six years later, when the creation of a European e-procurement single market is a EU mission and a major legislative amendment is under way in Portugal, this study looks at the relationship between e-procurement and innovation in the Portuguese municipalities aiming to understand the extent into which the adoption of e-procurement embraced a real organizational change or, on the other hand, if it just represented a mere adaptation of the usual procurement practices. The study draws on data from an electronic survey to all municipalities in mainland Portugal, and the analysis is mainly descriptive and exploratory. The paradigm shift in public procurement involves major organizational changes, but overall, the results suggest that most municipalities do not have a clear understanding of the innovative scope (depth and diversity) implied by e-procurement. E-procurement shows advantages over the paper-based model, but an unbalanced perception of the innovation dimensions has influenced the implementation of e-procurement and the degree of organizational change.

Part I
Bargaining, Lobbying and State Capture

Bargaining with Outside Options

Ken Binmore and Jon X. Eguia

1 Introduction

We begin by reviewing the theory of two-person bargaining and three-person bargaining over a unit of wealth in the presence of outside options. We then explore the implications and developments in the literature for bargaining games with more than three players, and in particular, for legislative bargaining games in a democratic assembly with many members who decide by majority rule how to divide a unit of wealth, or an infinite sequence of units of wealth.

The Nash bargaining solution applies to bargaining problems between two rational players who have no secrets from each other (Nash 1950). Such solution concepts—characterized by a set of axioms—are classified as being part of cooperative game theory. Cooperative game theory is often mistakenly regarded as a rival to noncooperative theory but Nash saw cooperative and noncooperative game theory as complementary approaches in which the strengths of one approach can buttress the weaknesses of the other.

Cooperative game theory presupposes a preplay negotiation period during which the players come to a binding agreement on how a game is to be played. However, all this preplay activity is packed away in a black box during a cooperative analysis. The strength of the approach is that it is often possible (as in the case of the Nash bargaining solution) to obtain a simple characterization of *what* deal rational players will reach. Its weakness is that it fails to explain *why* rational players will honor the axioms that support one solution concept rather than the axioms

K. Binmore
Department of Economics, University of Bristol, Bristol, UK

J.X. Eguia (✉)
Department of Economics, Michigan State University, East Lansing, MI, USA
e-mail: eguia@msu.edu

N. Schofield, G. Caballero (eds.), *State, Institutions and Democracy*,
Studies in Political Economy, DOI 10.1007/978-3-319-44582-3_1

that support an alternative solution concept (like the Kalai-Smorodinsky (1975) bargaining solution).

1.1 The Nash Program

The Nash program invites us to open the black boxes of cooperative game theory to see whether the mechanism inside really does works in the way the axioms characterizing a cooperative solution concept assume. Nash observed that the details of the negotiation process we will find inside such a black box determine a noncooperative game, in which the moves are everything the players may say or do while bargaining. If we model any bargaining that precedes a game $\mathcal{G}$ in this way, the result is an enlarged game $\mathcal{N}$. A strategy for this negotiation game first tells a player how to conduct the preplay negotiations, and then how to play $\mathcal{G}$ depending on the outcome of the negotiations. Negotiation games must be studied *without* presupposing preplay bargaining, all preplay activity having already been built into their rules. Analyzing them is therefore a task for noncooperative game theory. This means looking for their Nash equilibria, in the hope that the equilibrium selection problem won't prove too difficult when there is more than one equilibrium.

When a negotiation game $\mathcal{N}$ can be solved successfully, we have a way of checking up on what a cooperative solution concept tells us about the rational outcome of $\mathcal{G}$. If a cooperative solution concept says that the result of a rational agreement on how to play $\mathcal{G}$ will be s, then s should also result from solving $\mathcal{N}$ as a noncooperative game. If it does not, then we have a mismatch between our cooperative axioms and the economic environment in which they are being applied.

Two mistakes are commonplace. The first is to conclude that we need not bother with cooperative theory at all. One should instead always undertake the impossible task of modeling all bargaining using noncooperative models. This is impossible because a negotiation game that was sufficiently general to capture each twist and turn that a real-life negotiation might conceivably take would be complicated beyond all imagining. One can only analyze simplified negotiation games—as in Nash (1951) or Rubinstein (1982)—and hope that one is right in thinking that the simplified game captures all the strategic factors that really matter. In practice, Rubinstein's model is usually substituted for the actual negotiation game, but this is a pointless activity since we already know that the Rubinstein game implements the Nash bargaining solution (Binmore 2007). This observation leads to the second mistake, which is to proceed as though we need not bother with noncooperative theory at all. The next section explains why this attitude—which is orthodox in the matching-and-bargaining literature—sometimes leads to the parameters that characterize a bargaining problem being written wrongly into the Nash bargaining solution used to predict its outcome.

2 Outside Options

Nash (1950) models a two-person bargaining problem as a feasible set of payoff[1] pairs on which the players might agree, and a *status quo* payoff pair that represents what each player will get in the event of a disagreement. Sometimes this model is adequate and sometimes not. It is not adequate, for example, when information is incomplete.[2] Nor is it adequate when time matters and the players discount time at different rates.[3] Nor when disagreement can arise in more than one way. We focus here on a simple version of the last case.

Suppose that two disagreement points can be distinguished in a bargaining problem: a deadlock point and a breakdown point. The deadlock point is the payoff pair that would result if the players bargained forever without breaking off the negotiations or reaching an agreement. The breakdown point is the payoff pair that would result if one player were to abandon the negotiations irrevocably with the result that both players take up their best outside option.

The breakdown point and the deadlock point may be the same, but when they are not it is commonplace in studying wage bargaining to identify the status quo in the Nash bargaining solution with the breakdown point. When is this sound modeling practice? Two noncooperative models can be used to examine this question.

Nash's Demand Game In this game, two players make simultaneous take-it-or-leave-it demands (Nash 1951). If the demands are jointly infeasible, all bargaining is over and cannot be resumed. The players will then take up their best outside options (that may include continuing to cooperate with their bargaining partner on the same basis as before they failed to agree on a new contract). Identifying Nash's status quo with the breakdown point then makes sense.

Rubinstein's Alternating-Offers Game But who believes people who say they are making their last and final offer? What prevents your bargaining partner from refusing your offer, and then making a counter-offer before you have the chance to commit to an outside option? This natural feature can be built into Rubinstein's (1982) alternating-offers bargaining model without difficulty (Binmore et al. 1982). If the players discount time at equal rates and the interval between successive offers is sufficiently small, the subgame-perfect equilibrium outcome approximates the Nash bargaining solution for the case when all deals that pay players less than their

[1]A payoff in game theory is a Von Neumann and Morgenstern utility.

[2]If it is common knowledge that the valuations of a risk-neutral buyer and seller of a house are independent and equally likely to be anything between \$2m and \$3m, then the result of optimal bargaining is seriously inefficient. Even when the bargaining process is chosen to maximize the expected surplus that rational bargainers can achieve, the house is sold only when it is worth \$0.25m more to the buyer than the seller (Myerson 1991).

[3]The Nash bargaining solution (which treats the bargainers symmetrically) then needs to be replaced by an asymmetric version (Binmore 2007).

best outside option have been removed from the set of feasible agreements.[4] The status quo in this use of the Nash bargaining solution is placed at the deadlock point, which corresponds to the payoffs the players would receive if all offers were always refused and no outside option were ever taken up.

The alternating-offers game so obviously fits wage bargaining better than the demand game that it remains a wonder that the matching-and-bargaining literature should hold so firmly to the practice of locating the status quo in the Nash bargaining solution at the breakdown point rather than the deadlock point.

3 Three-Player Bargaining

What happens when the conclusion of the preceding section on two-person bargaining with outside options is applied to bargaining among more than two players?

A new problem then arises because deals may now be reached that do not include all the bargainers. We therefore have to determine not only how much each signatory of an agreed contract receives, but also who is excluded from the winning coalition (or coalitions). The latter problem is endemic in political science. Many coalitions might form, but which coalition will actually form as the result of rational bargaining? Unfortunately, noncooperative bargaining models adapted to this problem commonly have multiple equilibria, and so a determinate answer is available only in special cases.

The three-player/three-cake problem studied in Binmore (1986) serves to illustrate the latter issue. Only one of three feasible cakes are available for division at the end of the bargaining session. Each cake is controlled by a different pair of players, as illustrated in Fig. 1 (where the cake Y_{ij} is controlled by players i and j). The aim of player i in the bargaining game is to reach an agreement with another player j which determines that cake Y_{ij} is to be divided and how much each player will then receive. The outvoted third player k then gets nothing. We simplify by placing the deadlock point at the origin. Even though we assume that the players have no external outside options, the breakdown situation is more complicated because the outside option for i when bargaining with j is the payoff that i would receive by abandoning j and making a deal with k.

[4]See Binmore (2007, Chap. 16) for examples. When the players have differing discount rates, an asymmetric version of the Nash bargaining solution applies. There are experimental criticisms of the subgame-perfect equilibrium concept, but the result holds with the much weaker idea of a security equilibrium (Binmore and Herrero 1988). In any case, direct experimentation supports the bargaining conclusion (Binmore et al. 1989).

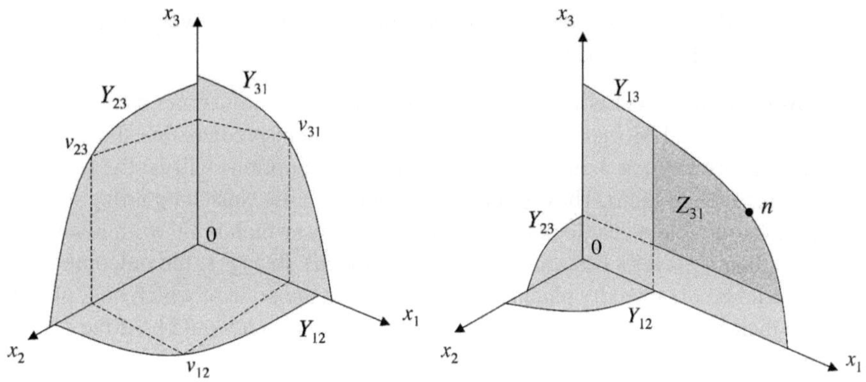

Fig. 1 Three-player/three-cake problem. The deadlock point is placed at the origin, and individual players have no external outside options. However, outside options arise endogenously because when two players make a deal, they always have the alternative of proposing a deal to the third player who will otherwise be left with nothing. The feasible set Y_{ij} is what is available to the coalition $\{ij\}$. The *left diagram* shows a case in which a Von Neumann and Morgenstern triple exists. When such a triple $\{v_{12}, v_{23}, v_{31}\}$ exists, the final outcome is one of its three elements. The *right diagram* shows a case in which no Von Neumann and Morgenstern triple exists. Only one coalition can then form. In the figure, this coalition is $\{31\}$, and the final outcome is the Nash bargaining solution n when the feasible set is Z_{31} and the status quo is 0

3.1 Cooperative Approach

Two distinct cases are identified in Fig. 1.

Von Neumann and Morgenstern Triple The left diagram of Fig. 1 illustrates the case in which a Von Neumann and Morgenstern triple (v_{12}, v_{23}, v_{31}) exists.[5] Suppose that 1 and 2 are bargaining in this case with a view to excluding 3. With the second bargaining model of Sect. 3, they will then agree on the Nash bargaining solution with status quo at the deadlock point 0 for the set Y_{12} with all points that pay 1 or 2 less than their outside options removed. When these outside options are what they would get from v_{23} and v_{31}, this set Z_{12} consists only of the single point v_{12}, which is therefore the deal on which 1 and 2 will agree should they get together to bargain.

An identical argument shows that 2 and 3 will agree on v_{23} if they get together to bargain. Similarly, 3 and 1 will agree on v_{31}. But which of the three two-player coalitions will actually form is left unspecified. In practice, this question

[5]The notion generalizes an idea of Von Neumann and Morgenstern (1944) for zero-sum games, nowadays called a symmetric stable set (Binmore 2007, Sect. 18.4). In such a triple, v_{12} is an efficient point of Y_{12} that assigns the same to 1 and 2 as they would get in v_{31} and v_{23} respectively (and nothing to 3). Similarly for v_{12} and v_{31}.

is determined by historical or accidental factors that may easily vary over time and are not included in the model.[6]

Two Buyers and One Seller The right diagram of Fig. 1 illustrates a case with no Von Neumann and Morgenstern triple. The theory than predicts that the coalition $\{3, 1\}$ will form. When 3 and 1 bargain, their outside options will be the most that 2 can offer each of them. They will therefore agree on the Nash bargaining solution with status quo at the deadlock point 0 for the set Z_{31} (which is Y_{31} with points that pay less than a player's best outside option removed). In Fig. 1, the outcome is *not* what would be obtained by placing the status quo at the point at which both players receive their best outside options. It is exactly the same as it would be if the players had no outside options at all.

A particularly interesting case arises when 1 and 2 are rival buyers, and 3 is the only available seller of a good. The set Y_{12} then contains only the origin. This will make no difference to the preceding result unless Y_{23} in Fig. 1 is enlarged so that 2 can offer 3 more than 3 gets at n. Applying the Nash bargaining solution with status quo at 0 to Z_{31} then results in 3 getting no more than his outside option and 1 getting the rest of what is available. That is to say, 3 sells to 1 at the highest price that 2 is willing to pay, which is the perfectly competitive outcome. The argument that leads to this conclusion is a retelling of the story usually offered when studying Bertrand competition.

3.2 Noncooperative Approach

The results of the previous section are defended in Binmore (1986) using a noncooperative model. Section 3 draws attention to the need to ask whether Nash's Demand Game or Rubinstein's Alternating-Offers Game (or some other game) fits a particular application best. With more than two players, it is necessary to make a further distinction between telephone bargaining models and market bargaining models. The literature commonly appeals to the Telephone Game [as in Chatterjee et al. (1992)] but the Market Game fits many applications better.

Telephone Bargaining Game This game is a direct extension of Rubinstein's Alternating-Offers Game to the three-player/three-cake problem. A player phones one of the other players and they exchange offers until agreement is reached, or else one of the players hangs up (exercises his outside option) and phones the third player, whereupon the situation repeats itself. This model fits applications like the wage-bargaining problem studied by Shaked and Sutton (1984) in which the employer has to bargain with employees one-by-one. He cannot then bring his full bargaining power to bear because an employee will respond to his threat to

[6]Hence the frequent switching of alliances sometimes observed when studying balance-of-power issues?

replace him by observing that the employer will then find himself in exactly the same bargaining situation as at present, but one period later.

But what compels the employer to honor the rules of a Telephone Game? Why does he not find some way of getting his offers to both prospective employees simultaneously, so that they find themselves competing against each other in what effectively becomes an auction? The next model allows players this freedom.

Market Bargaining Game It is easiest to have the players rotate in having the initiative. If a player with the initiative refuses the most recent demands made by *both* his predecessors, he then gets make a demand of his own. Binmore (1986) shows that this Market Game implements all the very natural results described in Sect. 4.1.

4 Many Players: Legislative Bargaining

With more than three players, the n-player version of the Nash bargaining solution can be used, although it is no longer true that it is necessarily implemented by subgame-perfect equilibria of the corresponding Alternating-Offers Game. It is necessary to restrict attention to stationary (Markov) subgame-perfect equilibria for this purpose. More importantly, there is the additional problem that the approach neglects the possibility that coalitions of less than n players might form. Even if they do not form, the fact that they might form will often influence the deal finally reached by the grand coalition of all n players.

Consider, for example, the three-player/four-cake problem (which adds a large fourth cake can be divided among all three players to the three-player/three-cake problem). A greedy player can then be held in check by the prospect of the other two players agreeing on a coalition from which he is excluded. This problem can be solved by applying the three-player Nash bargaining solution to the fourth cake from which all outcomes that give players less than they could get by abandoning the grand coalition for a smaller coalition have been removed.

Unfortunately, combinatorial problems arise when one goes beyond three players. The multiplicity of possible bargaining outcomes already noted in discussing Von Neumann triples then extends not only to determining who will be excluded from a coalition, but also to the overall coalitional structure.

In applications to collective decision-making in legislative assemblies, we need a bargaining theory that can: (a) account for more than three players, and (b) recognize that not all players must participate in the agreement, as in order to advance a policy it suffices to obtain approval from a majority (or a supermajority as determined by the assembly's rules) of legislators. The n-player version of the Nash bargaining solution is then not as appealing in these applications.

Consider a legislative assembly (a Parliament; a Congress; a National, State, Regional or Municipal Assembly) that must make a collective decision of a distributive nature, such as how to allocate an existing budget among various alternative projects. In the simplest case, which most closely resembles two-agent bargaining, each agent is interested in one and only one project and wishes to maximize funds devoted to it, so that agents have purely antagonistic preferences over the division of the budget, without cross-externalities. The standard approach to study this strategic environment is to model it as an infinitely repeated sequential offers game, in which in each round a player is randomly selected to propose an allocation of the budget, players vote simultaneously whether to approve or reject this proposal, and the first proposal to gain a majority of approving votes is implemented. Baron and Ferejohn (1989) showed that in a stationary solution to this game, a proposal passes in the first round and it allocates the whole budget to a minimal winning coalition, with a disproportionately large share for project favored by the first proposer.

While there are other stationary (and many non-stationary) equilibria besides the one described by Baron and Ferejohn (1989), Eraslan (2002) strengthened the result by showing that the payoff to each agent is unique across all stationary equilibria. This payoff uniqueness holds for a more general class of games allowing for unequal discount factors, unequal recognition probabilities and supermajority voting rules [or in fact for any arbitrary definition of the collection of winning coalitions as in Eraslan and McLennan (2013)]. Merlo and Wilson (1995) introduce a budget of stochastic size, which together with a unanimity rule can lead to delays as all players sometimes prefer to wait hoping for the budget to grow; with a stochastic budget and majority rule, there multiple equilibria (Eraslan and Merlo 2002). Eraslan and McLennan (2013) provide an extensive list of references.

Consider the class of coalition formation games in characteristic form (each coalition or subset of agents has an aggregate worth) with transferable utility, in which in each round a proposer is randomly selected to propose a coalition and an allocation of the coalition's aggregate worth among its members, and if all members agree the coalition forms and exits the game, which continues among the remaining players (Okada 1996, 2011). Notice that the legislative bargaining game we have discussed in the previous two paragraphs is a special case in which any majority coalition has aggregate worth of one, and any minority coalition has aggregate worth of zero, and thus we can interpret legislative bargaining games as coalition formation games.

A common feature of the results of all these theories with randomly selected proposers, both the voting-based ones and the coalition-formation ones, is that whoever gets to be the first proposer (or the first proposer in a period with a large budget if the budget is stochastic) is disproportionately advantaged. A question arises: since being the proposer is so important, why would the proposer be randomly selected, and not endogenously chosen by the assembly itself? Note that we can ask the same question about the Telephone game (whoever turns down an offer gets to propose next) or the Market game (players make offers in turns): why would an assembly choose any of these particular protocols, and not others more to its own liking? Inspired by the US Congress, (Breitmoser 2011) assumes that a subset of players (committee members) are sure to be recognized first to make a proposal, in order of seniority; Ali et al. (2014) consider a more flexible setup where the next proposers are somewhat predictable, rather than certain. McKelvey and Riezman (1992) (and later McKelvey and Riezman 1993; Muthoo and Shepsle 2014; Eguia and Shepsle 2015) endogenize proposal rules to explain why seniors are more likely to emerge as early-round proposers: incumbent legislators choose pro-seniority rules in order to gain an electoral advantage in the eyes of constituents. Because a potential challenger—if elected—would have no seniority and the incumbent has seniority, rules that give seniors more power to obtain resources for their districts make incumbents more appealing to their constituents.

A different view is that incumbents can't just vote themselves into a favored status; perhaps being a proposer is a privilege that has to be earned, and each legislator's probability of being recognized as a proposer is proportional to the effort that the legislator invests in gaining agenda power (Yildirim 2007, 2010). The bargaining protocol could also dispense with proposers altogether: in demand bargaining, agents sequentially place budgetary demands, and a receiver (called "formateur" in applications to government formation) decides whether it is worth putting together a majority by satisfying enough of these demands (Morelli 1999). In such demand bargaining models, the payoffs are usually more proportional to the voting weights of the agents, and the receiver is not able to extract as large a fraction of the budget as the proposer in alternating-proposal protocols.

4.1 Bringing in the Outside Option

In many application to private bargaining between two or perhaps three agents as discussed in the previous section, it makes sense that the deadlock and breakdown outcomes would be exogenously given: if buyer and seller (or the buyer, seller, and bank lender) do not agree on how to divide the surplus of a transaction such as a house sale, no transaction occurs and they each get zero surplus. A payoff of zero is then the outside option for each player and both deadlock (indefinite negotiations without resolution) and breakdown (end of negotiations without agreement) lead to this outside option.

In the standard legislative bargaining game with sequential offers (Baron and Ferejohn 1989), legislators have no option to walk out, so the game has no breakdown outcome. With time discount, the deadlock outcome is zero for every player; time discount, like inflation, makes the value of the budget shrinks a little in each period, so that all value ultimately vanishes. But this is not a realistic description of how public finance works: it is more often the case that if legislators do not agree on an allocation of the budget, the previous period's budget is implemented.

Epple and Riordan (1987) pioneered a dynamic model in which players bargain over an infinite sequence of periods, with a new budget to be allocated in each period. In each period, if an offer is turned down, the previous period allocation is implemented. The only exogenous bargaining-failure outcome is the one for the first period; in all subsequent periods, the bargaining failure outcome is endogenous. In this manner, the outside option has been brought inside the model. We may call the endogenous outside option the "reversion" point, "status quo" outcome, or "default policy." It is in any case the outside option—which now varies by period—exercised in case of bargaining failure within a period.

Epple and Riordan's (1987) approach is now mainstream, but it might have been ahead of its time: for nearly two decades it was largely ignored, until Kalandrakis (2004) sparked a flurry of work on dynamic bargaining with an endogenous outside option. The main difference between the two is that Epple and Riordan (1987) use the Market protocol (players take turns to make proposals) whereas Kalandrakis uses the random proposer protocol. Kalandrakis (2004, 2010) constructs a stationary equilibrium in which in each period, the period's proposer gets the whole budget for the period; on the other hand, in a model in which the proposer is always the same, the proposer does not get the whole budget in any period (Diermeier and Fong 2011). Penn (2009) finds that in a model with (exogenous) random proposals, the most frequent outcomes approximately split the budget evenly between a minimal winning majority of agents. Returning to the model with strategic proposals, Bowen and Zahran (2012) construct equilibria that distribute the period budget evenly among a supermajority of the players; allowing for waste, Richter (2014) constructs an equilibrium with a fully egalitarian division of the budget in every period. In laboratory experiments, subjects prefer to allocate the budget evenly within a minimal winning majority, than evenly across all players (Battaglini and Palfrey 2012).

In more recent variations of the legislative divide-the-dollar dynamic bargaining game with an endogenous status quo, Nunnari (2015) introduces a veto player, who appropriates the full budget; Bowen et al. (2014) consider policy bundles that include both discretionary spending (the status quo discretionary spending is exogenous at zero), and mandatory spending with an endogenous status quo; and Jeon (2015) endogenizes the status quo policy and the recognition probabilities to be proposer jointly by letting both be equal to the last period's implemented policy.

If we view multi-player bargaining as a game of dynamic coalition formation, in which the question is to identify the winning coalition that will seize control of the budget, then an endogenous status quo corresponds to a game in which players receive flow payoffs in each period while bargaining takes place, as in Konishi and Ray (2013), Gomes and Jehiel (2005) or Hyndman and Ray (2007). Building on these precedents, Ray and Vohra (2015) seek to unify the cooperative and non-cooperative approaches to coalition formation under their flexible framework of an "Equilibrium Process of Coalition Formation," and they describe (Sect. 5.4) how to use this framework specifically to study bargaining.

Recall that if the outside option is exogenous, as in Baron and Ferejohn's (1989) model of legislative bargaining over a single budget, we obtain a sharp prediction: while there are multiple equilibria, equilibrium payoffs are the same across all equilibria (Eraslan 2002; Eraslan and McLennan 2013).[7] In sharp contrast, if players bargain over an infinite sequence of budgets, with an endogenous status quo, there are multiple stationary equilibria. By 2014, a decade after Kalandrakis (2004), his existence result based on an equilibrium in which the random proposer acts as an ephemeral dictator who obtains all of the period's resources had been supplemented by the construction of other stationary equilibria in which a supermajority (Bowen and Zahran 2012) or all players (Richter 2014) share resources equitably in each period. Anesi and Seidmann (2015) brought the literature full circle—and showed the depth of the equilibrium multiplicity problem—by demonstrating that almost any allocation can be supported in a Markov stationary equilibrium. In particular, any allocation that gives a positive quantity at least to a majority of agents can be sustained.

Anesi and Seidmann's (2015) powerful result leaves us with shattered predictive power. In stark contrast to Eraslan and McLennan (2013) result that in games of bargaining over a single budget the payoff prediction by Baron and Ferejohn's (1989) is unique and robust, Anesi and Seidmann establish the very opposite for bargaining over an infinite sequence of budgets with an exogenous status quo: the result that (almost) anything can happen is robust in a general framework. This "anything goes" prediction, also discussed in Baron and Bowen (2015), closes the research agenda of finding specific equilibria of the now standard dynamic model, but it opens up another: it is not the case that in real world applications anything happens in totally unpredictable fashion (budgets could be burned but are not; and in most assemblies some subsets of members are known to more frequently cooperate and coalesce with each other) and we still wish to explain and predict these coalitional patterns and bargaining outcomes in real world applications.

One might conjecture that we need to include other elements such as public good provision or an ideological dimension into the choice set in order to obtain more realistic predictions. Inspiration could be drawn from instance from Baron et al.'s (2012) model with two-dimensional policies and side payments; or from Battaglini and Coate's (2007, 2008) with public good provision, taxation and debt accumulation.[8]

Dynamic bargaining theories with more general models that allow for preferences over multiple dimensions of ideology, public goods and distributive components, have obtained existence and upper hemi-continuity of the equilibrium correspondence. Unfortunately, they have not shown uniqueness nor tight characterization results, neither in models with a one time policy choice (Banks and Duggan 2000, 2006), nor with an infinitely repeated choice and an endogenous status quo

[7]Notice, however, that experiments only partially support this prediction: while the budget is allocated to a minimal winning coalition as predicted, proposers "do not fully exploit their bargaining power and allocate to their coalition partners a disproportionate share of the pie" (Nunnari and Zapal 2015).

[8]Other theories that include an ideological dimension in a dynamic legislative game but not a distributive one include Baron (1996), Dziuda and Loeper (in press) or Nunnari and Zapal (2015).

as in Duggan and Kalandrakis (2012). The title of Anesi and Duggan's (2015) "Existence and Indeterminacy of Markovian Equilibria in Dynamic Bargaining Games" is self-explanatory and it summarizes the state of the art in dynamic legislative bargaining games with an endogenous status quo.

5 Conclusion

We have reviewed theoretical solutions to bargaining problems with two, three and many players. We highlight how cooperative and non-cooperative approaches relate to each other, the importance of outside options, and how in dynamic models the outside option can become endogenous.

After four decades of research, the basic incentives in static bargaining problems are well understood. Nevertheless, in dynamic applications with an endogenous default outcome, many state-of-the-art theories deliver limited predictive power, as their set of equilibrium solutions is large. The quest for sharper predictions remains an open research agenda.

Acknowledgement We thank Jan Zapal for an instructive discussion.

References

Ali, N., Bernheim, D., & Fan, X. (2014). *Predictability and Power in Legislative Bargaining*. NBER wp 20011.

Anesi, V., & Duggan, J. (2015). *Existence and Indeterminacy of Markovian Equilibria in Dynamic Bargaining Games*. Working paper.

Anesi, V., & Seidmann, D. (2015). Bargaining in standing committees with an endogenous default. *Review of Economic Studies, 82*, 825–867.

Banks, J., & Duggan, J. (2000). A bargaining model of collective choice. *American Political Science Review, 94*, 73–88.

Banks, J., & Duggan, J. (2006). A general bargaining model of legislative policy-making. *Quarterly Journal of Political Science, 1*, 49–85.

Baron, D. (1996). A dynamic theory of collective goods programs. *American Political Science Review, 90*, 316–330.

Baron, D., & Bowen, R. (2015). *Dynamic coalitions*. Working paper.

Baron, D., Diermeier, D., & Fong, P. (2012). A dynamic theory of parliamentary democracy. *Economic Theory, 49*(3): 703–738.

Baron, D., & Ferejohn, J. (1989). Bargaining in legislatures. *American Political Science Review, 83*, 1181–1206.

Battaglini, M., & Coate, S. (2007). Inefficiency in legislative policy-making: A dynamic analysis. *American Economic Review, 97*, 118–149.

Battaglini, M., & Coate, S. (2008). A dynamic theory of public spending, taxation, and debt. *American Economic Review, 98*, 201–236.

Battaglini, M., & Palfrey, T. (2012). The dynamics of distributive politics. *Economic Theory, 49*(3), 739–777.

Binmore, K. (1986). Bargaining and coalitions. In A. Roth (Ed.), *Game-theoretic models of bargaining*. Cambridge: Cambridge University Press.
Binmore, K. (2007). *Playing for real*. New York: Oxford University Press.
Binmore, K., & Herrero, M. (1988). Security equilibrium. *Review of Economic Studies, 55*, 33–48.
Binmore, K., Rubinstein, A., & Wolinsky, A. (1982). The Nash bargaining solution in economic modelling. *Rand Journal of Economics, 17*, 176–188.
Binmore, K., Shaked, A., & Sutton, J. (1989). An outside option experiment. *Quarterly Journal of Economics, 104*, 753–770.
Bowen, R., Chen, Y., & Eraslan, H. (2014). Mandatory versus discretionary spending: The status quo effect. *American Economic Review, 104*(10), 2941–2974.
Bowen, R., & Zahran, Z. (2012). On dynamic compromise. *Games and Economic Behavior, 76*(2), 391–419.
Breitmoser, Y. (2011). Parliamentary bargaining with priority recognition for committee members. *Social Choice and Welfare, 37*(1), 149–169.
Chatterjee, K., Dutta, B., Ray, D., & Sengupta, K. (1992). A noncooperative theory of coalitional bargaining. *Review of Economic Studies, 60*, 463–477.
Diermeier, D., & Fong, P. (2011). Legislative bargaining with reconsideration. *Quarterly Journal of Economics, 126*(2), 947–985.
Duggan, J., & Kalandrakis, T. (2012). Dynamic legislative policy making. *Journal of Economic Theory, 146*(5), 1653–1688.
Dziuda, W., & Loeper, A (in press). Dynamic Collective choice with endogenous status quo. *Journal of Political Economy*
Eguia, J., & Shepsle, K. (2015). Legislative bargaining with endogenous rules. *Journal of Politics, 77*(4), 1076–1088.
Epple, D., & Riordan, M. (1987). Cooperation and punishment under repeated majority voting. *Public Choice, 55*(1–2), 41–73.
Eraslan, H. (2002). Uniqueness of stationary equilibrium payoffs in the Baron–Ferejohn model. *Journal of Economic Theory, 103*(1), 11–30.
Eraslan, H., & Merlo, A. (2002). Majority rule in a stochastic model of bargaining. *Journal of Economic Theory, 103*, 31–48.
Eraslan, H., & McLennan, A. (2013). Uniqueness of stationary equilibrium payoffs in coalitional bargaining. *Journal of Economic Theory, 148*, 2195–2222.
Gomes, A., & Jehiel, P. (2005). Dynamic processes of social and economic interactions: On the persistence of inefficiencies. *Journal of Political Economy, 113*, 626–667.
Hyndman, K., & Ray, D. (2007). Coalition formation with binding agreements. *Review of Economic Studies, 74*(4), 1125–1147.
Jeon, J. (2015). *The Emergence and Persistence of Oligarchy: A Dynamic Model of Endogenous Political Power*. Working paper.
Kalai, E., & Smorodinsky, M. (1975). Other solutions to Nash's bargaining problem. *Econometrica, 45*, 1623–1630.
Kalandrakis, T. (2004). A three player majoritarian bargaining game. *Journal of Economic Theory, 116*(2), 294–322.
Kalandrakis, T. (2010). Minimum winning coalitions and endogenous status quo. *International Journal of Game Theory, 39*(4), 617–643.
Konishi, H., & Ray, D. (2013). Coalition formation as a dynamic process. *Journal of Economic Theory, 110*, 1–41.
McKelvey, R., & Riezman, R. (1992). Seniority in legislatures. *American Political Science Review, 86*(4), 951–965.
McKelvey, R., & Riezman, R. (1993). Initial versus continuing proposal power in legislative seniority systems. In W. Barnett, M. Hinich, & N. Schofield (Eds.), *Political economy: Institutions, competition and representation*. Cambridge: Cambridge University Press.
Merlo, A., & Wilson, C. (1995). A stochastic model of sequential bargaining with complete information. *Econometrica, 63*, 371–399.

Morelli, M. (1999). Demand competition and policy compromise in legislative bargaining. *American Political Science Review, 93*, 809–820.
Muthoo, A., & Shepsle, K. (2014). Seniority and incumbency in legislatures. *Economics & Politics, 26*(1), 13–37.
Myerson, R. (1991). *Game theory: Analysis of conflict*. Cambridge, MA: Harvard University Press.
Nash, J. (1950). The bargaining problem. *Econometrica, 18*, 155–162.
Nash, J. (1951). Non-cooperative games. *Annals of Mathematics, 54*, 286–295.
Nunnari, S. (2015). *Dynamic Legislative Bargaining with Veto Power; Theory and Experiments*. Working paper.
Nunnari, S., & Zapal, J. (2015). *Gambler's Fallacy and Imperfect Best Response in Legislative Bargaining*. Working paper.
Nunnari, S., & Zapal, J. (2015). *Dynamic Elections and Ideological Polarization*. Working paper.
Okada, A. (1996). A noncooperative coalition bargaining game with random proposers. *Games and Economic Behavior, 16*, 97–108.
Okada, A. (2011). Coalitional bargaining games with random proposers: Theory and application. *Games and Economic Behavior, 73*(1), 227–235.
Penn, M. (2009). A model of farsighted voting. *American Journal of Political Science, 53*(1), 36–54.
Ray, D., & Vohra, R. (2015). Coalition formation. In P. Young & S. Zamir (Eds.), *Handbooks in economics: Game theory* (Vol. 4, pp. 239–326).
Richter, M. (2014). Fully absorbing dynamic compromise. *Journal of Economic Theory, 152*, 92–104.
Rubinstein, A. (1982). Perfect equilibrium in a bargaining model. *Econometrica, 50*, 97–109.
Shaked, A., & Sutton, J. (1984). Involuntary unemployment as a perfect equilibrium in a bargaining model. *Econometrica, 52*, 1351–1364.
Von Neumann, J., & Morgenstern, O. (1944). *The theory of games and economic behavior.* Princeton: Princeton University Press
Yildirim, H. (2007). Proposal power and majority rule in multilateral bargaining with costly recognition. *Journal of Economic Theory, 136*, 167–196.
Yildirim, H. (2010). Distribution of surplus in sequential bargaining with endogenous recognition. *Public Choice, 142*, 41–57.

Lobbying Mechanisms

Martin Gregor

1 Introduction

Political influence of special interests is a rich phenomenon, challenging for both theory and empirics. One of the key questions is whether the influence is through the provision of money, information, or both. In the first generation of empirical studies, the monetary channel is examined by looking upon the effect of campaign contributions through Political Action Committees on roll call voting. The results of the roll call voting studies conducted in the United States since 1970s are nevertheless inconclusive. Even descriptive evidence suggests that campaign contributions through Political Action Committees are not as important as direct individual contributions (Ansolabehere et al. 2003).

Gradually, lobbying expenses have been considered a promising alternative measure of political influence. In particular, corporate lobbying expenses have attracted large attention because corporate benefits can be relatively well identified, industries can be classified, and because public concern about its effect is growing (The Economist 2011). Data on lobbying outlays are nonetheless notoriously hard to collect, and except for survey data, for a long time the only extra evidence of lobbying has been participation in interest group associations. Even in developed countries such as the EU countries, the virtual lack of descriptive evidence on lobbying outlays is related to weak or non-existent lobbying regulations (Chari et al. 2010).

The major significant exception is the United States, where the Lobbying Disclosure Act 1995 has generated relatively clean data on the salaries of lobbyists and their staff, prices per reports, and fees for expert consultants. The US data have

M. Gregor (✉)
Institute of Economic Studies, Faculty of Social Sciences, Charles University, Opletalova 26, Prague CZ 110 00, Czech Republic
e-mail: martin.gregor@fsv.cuni.cz

N. Schofield, G. Caballero (eds.), *State, Institutions and Democracy*, Studies in Political Economy, DOI 10.1007/978-3-319-44582-3_2

clearly demonstrated that the magnitude of reported lobbying expenses turns out to be of a higher order than direct payments. Ansolabehere et al. (2003) find for firms with both PACs and a Washington lobby, that the ratio of lobbying expenditures to PAC contributions is 10 to 1. Bennedsen and Feldmann (2002) show that the top 100 contributing interest groups gave a total of $144 million to federal candidates during the 1998 election cycle, and spent over $1 billion on lobbying activities during that period. Lobbying also brings large returns. Richter et al. (2009) measure quid-pro-quo in terms of tax benefits (i.e., tax breaks including R&D credits and tax depreciation schedules) and observe that for each additional $1 spent on lobbying, a mean firm receives $6–$20 in tax benefits. Kang (2016) structurally estimates the average returns to lobbying expenditures in the energy sector in the 110th Congress to be 137–152 %.

Measured by observable spending, lobbying thus represents the single most important channel of political influence of special interests (Ansolabehere et al. 2003; Bennedsen and Feldmann 2002; de Figueiredo and Cameron 2009). By meeting with policy-makers, hiring lawyers and policy experts, submitting briefs and letters, conveying research results and technical information, and engaging in media advertising and PR campaigns, special interests build and maintain influence over policies.

How does the economic theory reflect the massive shift of attention from campaign contributions to informational lobbying? In the 1970s, lobbying of special interests entered economic models through the black box of influence or contest-success functions which were silent on the instrument of influence (Tullock 1980; Becker 1983). This has largely changed over the last three decades, when the proliferation of theories of persuasion contests, disclosure games, strategic communication and evidence production have transformed the landscape of lobbying modeling. Yet, to our best knowledge, progress in this vast area since the reviews by Sloof (1998), Grossman and Helpman (2001) and Winden (2003) has not yet been put into a single treatment.

This survey is an attempt to review those latest developments in lobbying theory that are relevant to modeling of informational lobbying with explicit informational and game-theoretic microfoundations. We proceed as follows: Sect. 2 reflects upon the early models of influence of special interests and discusses attempts to build explicit informational microfoundations for rent-seeking contests. Section 3 classifies the single-tool (payments or information) models of influence. We go beyond Grossman and Helpman (2001) especially by discussing in detail variants of information transmission and showing how lobbying is modeled as a persuasion game with an informational search.

Next, we look into the relation between payments and information. For that purpose, Sect. 4 presents the multiple-tool (payments and information) models of influence, which are broadly divided into *lobby-and-pay* models and *pay-and-lobby* models. To clarify differences in the two modeling traditions in further detail, Sect. 5 reviews the key modeling ingredients and sheds light on the key effects of lobbying mechanisms. Here, we employ the persuasion setting by Kamenica and Gentzkow (2011) to illustrate how payments and information can be combined within a single setting. Section 6 addresses two specific yet important theoretical questions, namely participation and interaction of instruments of influence. Section 7 concludes.

2 Early Models

Our brief tour through early political economy covers models with (explicit or implicit) non-cooperative microfoundations of influence, where the identity of a policy-maker is given and cannot be changed. We thus leave out the large literature on vote functions which looks into how campaign contributions to the policy-makers improve their chances to be elected (e.g., Hillman and Ursprung 1988).

2.1 *Influence Functions*

In early political economy models, the transmission of lobbying efforts into policies is captured by a reduced-form function, namely by postulating an influence function that directly maps effort into influence (e.g., Becker 1983; for a more detailed survey, see van Winden 2003). Axiomatic restrictions on the properties of the production function for influence allow the researchers to study the effects of competition, group size, and changes in influence technology. As a consequence, influence functions bring about several interesting and testable implications, but at the same time avoid (1) consistent modeling of policy-makers' motivations, and (2) characterization of the channels of influence. Instead of developing and calibrating the influence functions, subsequent research switched its attention to building explicit microfoundations of influence, asking why policy-makers respond to evidence, offers and threats, and illuminating how the information is shared between lobbyists and policy-makers in the process of exerting influence.

2.2 *Contests Without Microfoundations*

In parallel to influence functions, the rent-seeking (contest) tradition associated mainly with Tullock (1980) began flourishing to become a lively platform for modeling the political influence of corporations and other interest groups. A *contest* effectively constitutes a special form of an influence function; again, investments in political influence are irreversible, and there is no restriction on how the investments should be interpreted and operationalized. The major difference is that a contest is explicit about how influence is bought (cost function) and exactly how influence affects the policy, namely through the probability of winning a policy rent (a non-divisible prize) or gaining a share of the policy rent (a divisible prize).

Technically, a contest is a mechanism that distributes a policy prize to the contest winner(s). The prize is interpreted as the right to set a certain policy, which in the original interpretation yields a rent to the winner. The valuation of the prize may be player-specific and reflect the net benefits of getting the right relative to not getting the right.[1] The costs of the effort are captured by a separable cost function, and costs are irreversible up-front payments. The probabilities of winning a prize (or shares of the prize) are given by a predetermined contest-success function. Two functional forms are studied most frequently, *Tullock's lottery* and an *all-pay auction*. Both are special cases of a function exhibiting constant elasticity of prize to effort, where Tullock's lottery represents the case of an imperfectly discriminating contest (which is under a common cost of effort equivalent to a simple raffle), while the all-pay auction represents a perfectly-discriminating contest.

The disadvantage of the contest approach is basically threefold. First, like in any model assuming 'influence', contests put the source of influence into a black box. This effort can represent a variety of channels: (1) a pure transfer to politicians in the form of campaign contributions or direct compensation, (2) services provided by an intermediary, for example facilitated access, or (3) investments into the search for valuable evidence. Also, the rent-seeking tradition considers lobbying to be a single activity of exerting pressure, and this is at odds with a more refined approach that defines lobbying exclusively as the search and communication of evidence.

Secondly, the contest does not have well especially competition of more than two lobbies. In particular, the loser's indifference over the winner's identity is an assumption which rules out many competitive environments. Consider for instance standard strictly quasiconcave policy preferences $u_i(x)$ over a single dimension $x \in R$, where the lobby i has a unique and specific bliss point x_i^*. Then, the contest applies if and only if there are only two lobbies. To prove 'if', it is clear that the prize of lobby i is unambiguously $v_i := u_i(x_i^*) - u_i(x_{-i}^*)$ and for her opponent $v_{-i} := u_{-i}(x_{-i}^*) - u_{-i}(x_i^*)$. To prove 'only if', notice that if i is loser and the opponent changes from j to k, then from specificity of bliss points, $x_k^* \neq x_j^*$. From strict quasiconcavity, the prize of lobby i does not change only if $u_i(x_k^*) = u_i(x_j^*)$, which implies either $x_k^* < x_i^* < x_j^*$ or $x_k^* > x_i^* > x_j^*$. Now we repeat the procedure for k being the loser and the identity of the opponent changing from i to j. The prize of lobby k clearly changes, hence the property does not hold for three (or more) lobbies.

Thirdly, it is empirically difficult to determine the shape of the contest-success function. Testing the shape is complicated by the necessity to control for other properties; for example, since the level of outlays depends on the degree of the players' asymmetry, a test for elasticity of effort that uses aggregate spending requires a measure of asymmetry. Even more importantly, the test must control for the possibility of committing to a compromising policy because in the absence of commitment, an increase in discrimination in most cases increases outlays

[1] Typically, the prize is considered a private good, but even collective goods can be covered as long as the net benefit is independent on the winner.

(Epstein and Nitzan 2004), whereas with commitments, total expenditures fall if discrimination increases (Münster 2006). A recent structural estimation of a contest based on lobbying expenditures that tackles endogenous selection bias is Kang (2016).

2.3 *Contests with Informational Microfoundations*

Given evidence about the key role of informational lobbying through production and communication of evidence (Ansolabehere et al. 2003), there is a question whether a contest may be explained by means of production of evidence and informational transmission (Konrad 2009). The agreement within the contest camp is not complete. Epstein and Nitzan (2006b, p. 424) doubt that the contest approach is at all useful for dealing with the role of asymmetric information in politics: 'The contest approach is not useful for dealing with important theoretical topics such as the role of asymmetric information in politics.' (p. 424). Still, a class of activities such as persuasion contests and innovation races can be modeled simultaneously as the transmission of information and the contest.

2.3.1 Persuasion Contests

A typical representative of a persuasion contest is Lagerlöf (2007) who presumes that a policy-maker wants to award a project to an efficient firm. Each firm knows its efficiency, but nothing else. The lobbying firms search for verifiable evidence that would confirm their efficiency, and search outcomes are stochastic. A search is unobservable, so it cannot serve as a signal, and posteriors are conditional only upon the raised evidence. This persuasion contest model is interesting as it may produce non-linearity of total outlays in the number of firms. Skaperdas and Vaidya (2012) model competition between lobbyists in gathering either deterministic or stochastic evidence. The imperfect discrimination of the policy-maker is ensured by assumption. The policy-maker is presumed to follow the presented evidence in accordance with a likelihood-ratio function, which generates the necessary stochastic element that ultimately leads to an imperfectly discriminating contest-success function.

2.3.2 Innovation Races

In the literature on research and labor tournaments, the problem is not to convince a policy-maker of the value of the proposed policy or project, but to generate the value. Consider contestants who competitively search in order to gain extra competence, knowledge or skills that are valuable to a policy-maker. For example, suppose two players compete to be awarded a project, with a government awarding the project to the better proposal. Each player can search for designs, and design proposals are drawn from independent identical distributions. Baye and Hoppe (2003) then offer micro-foundations for a contest-success function with the constant elasticity. Glazer (2008) extends the setup by allowing the government to bargain with those firms that present an equally good design. A channel which affects the shape of the contest is type of the government; Corchon and Dahm (2010) demonstrate how to derive an arbitrary contest-success function for the case of two contestants who have incomplete information about the type of the contest administrator.

Innovation tournament settings yet differ from the standard rent-seeking contests at least in four ways: (1) Investments are productive (used ex post in production), not unproductive (used only ex ante to gain prize). (2) The outcome of investment is a public good and not a private (excludable) prize. (3) Payments to the policy-maker are in the bargaining stage, not in the investment stage. Thus, the policy-maker effectively seizes part of the rent by bargaining, not by contest. (4) The role of the contest is to create and distribute a rent and not only to distribute the rent between the contestants and the policy-maker.

3 Single-Tool Models

3.1 *Payments*

When policy is for sale, the policy-maker either trades the right to set the policy or trades the policy itself.

3.1.1 Trading the Right to Set the Policy

For a single lobby, the distribution of the surplus depends on the trading protocol. For multiple lobbies, contest is a typical mechanism of how the right is assumed to be allocated. It rests on the irreversibility (all-pay) property of payments which is motivated by observing that lobbying and campaign expenditures are submitted by competing parties prior to distribution of the prize, often in order to secure access to the policy-maker. Consider alternatively winner-pay (trading) mechanisms in which only winning lobbyists pay, typically after they are assigned the policy rent. Specifically, we may consider a host of trading (bargaining) protocols and mechanisms, including auctions.

Optimal design is a recurrent topic in this literature. One interesting result is that the revenue-oriented policy-maker may prefer to establish winner-pay to all-pay property even in the case when all payments to produce effort in a contest are cashed in by the policy-maker; alternatively, we could say that a policy-maker may prefer reversibility of payments to irreversibility of payments. Consider three mechanisms for two groups with an identical valuation v: (1) In Tullock's contest with irreversible payments, the government collects $\frac{v}{2}$. (2) In a non-cooperative bargaining protocol where the government alternates take-or-leave offers between the groups with a discount rate $\delta \in (0, 1)$, and in each stage the offer is a Nash bargaining solution for the bilateral bargaining, the subgame-perfect equilibrium gives the policy-maker $\frac{v}{2-\delta}$ (Glazer 2008). (3) In a standard second-price auction, equilibrium bids are even as large as v, and the expected revenue is maximized, $v > \frac{v}{2-\delta} > \frac{v}{2}$.

Epstein and Nitzan (2006b) study the optimal design for a mixed-objective policy-maker. The policy-maker may either organize a standard rent-seeking contest or directly assign the policy rent to a highest-value participant. This design issue becomes even more interesting once the policy-maker additionally has agenda-setting power so that he or she can limit the set of policies that can be implemented by the winner of the contest. This agenda constraint imposed by the policy-maker subsequently affects the valuations of the contestants, and represents another way in which the policy-maker addresses the tradeoff between setting a good policy and raising valuable payments.

3.1.2 Trading the Policy

Suppose it is not the right but the policy itself that is subject to an auction. To determine a policy out of a set of policies, the auction is organized as a (winner-pay) *menu auction* where bids are set contingent on policies and possibly upon other observables (Grossman and Helpman 2001). A winning policy is determined by maximal total bids, and only bids related to the winning policy are collected from the bidders. There is not a single winner who implements a favorable policy, but a single winning policy which is supported by possibly multiple contributors.

3.2 *Information*

Modeling of lobbying as strategic information transmission from a lobby to the policy-maker is motivated by the attempts to provide explicit motivation of the policy-maker, explicitly describe the influence through the effect upon the policy-maker's beliefs, fully describe the structure of the information, and explain influence when there are no commitments on the policy-maker's side.

3.2.1 Costless Communication

At the heart of informational lobbying are messages conveyed by lobbyists to policy-makers. Models of strategic communication can be classified in two key dimensions: (1) *Message cost* matters the most, where in this subsection we consider only costless (pure) communication. Intuitively, pure communication rules out an incentive to give a credible information (signal a type) by exerting a cost. (2) Second, *verifiability* matters substantially; messages are either non-verifiable (cheap talk) or verifiable (hard evidence).[2]

When the lobby communicates non-verifiable messages towards the policy-maker at no cost, we speak of *cheap talk*. The closer aligned are the lobbyist's and policy-maker's preferences, the better cheap talk works. Typically, the content of the costless message is the state of the world, where both lobbyist and policy-maker's optimal policy are correlated with the true state of the world, but the lobbyist's policy is biased. In equilibrium, a costless message on the state, taken literally, serves as a costless signal if the lobbyist's bias is expected to be low. Although full revelation is generally not achieved by cheap talk, the information improves. The credibility of cheap talk messages is further improved in the presence of the opposite lobby that applies counteractive lobbying, and for multidimensional messages (Chakraborty and Harbaugh 2010). For a comprehensive review of the main principles, uses and developments of the cheap talk literature in the context of special interests as well as the general context, see Grossman and Helpman (2001, Chap. 4) and Sobel (2010).

When messages are verifiable but still costless, message space is type-dependent and we speak of *persuasion games* (Milgrom 1981). Verifiability limits how signals (produced evidence) can be treated by the lobby: The lobby can withhold the evidence, but cannot misinterpret or fabricate it. Verifiability appears to be a particularly useful building block of search models where a signal obtained can be interpreted as a piece of hard evidence.

Verifiability normally enhances the credibility of messages and increases the scope for full revelation. More specifically, under monotonicity assumptions (i.e., Receiver's best response increasing in type and Sender's utility preferring higher action than Receiver), any rationalizable equilibrium contains full revelation (Giovannoni and Seidmann 2007). The well-known intuition behind full revelation is that the equilibrium can accommodate maximal skepticism of the policy maker as well as full revelation of the lobby. In the presence of neologism-proofness (i.e., out-of-equilibrium messages taken literally), (Ryan and Vaithianathan 2011) nevertheless show that verifiability not necessarily facilitates full revelation in costless communication settings. Milgrom (2008) reviews the literature on violations of conditions leading to full disclosure; the results on disclosure in markets with unknown quality directly translate to persuasive lobbying.

The drawbacks of strategic communication are the multiplicity of equilibria, difficulty in making robust predictions, and the need to assume extreme sophistication on the part of players to support certain equilibria. For instance, the basic cheap talk embeds no commitments, but a "babbling equilibrium" with no informative message exists always.

[2]Like most of the literature, we cover only the polar cases with zero or infinite 'cost of absorption' of a message. Intermediate cases of positive but finite cost are covered in Dewatripont and Tirole (2005) and the subsequent papers.

3.2.2 Costly Communication

A lobbyist may lend credibility to his or her non-verifiable message (cheap talk) in the situations when provide such a message is costly. Willingness to bear the cost may then signal the lobby's private information, irrespective of the literal content of the message. In pure signaling, the literal content of the message is abstracted from, hence signaling works with a wide range of costly actions, even with those which lack explicit communication. For example, when a company hires a high-caliber lawyer, some information is transmitted even before the lawyer begins to complete his or her lobbying assignment. This is also why costly *signaling*[3] is analyzed as pure *money burning*, where the coordination aspects as present in the cheap talk settings are completely missing.

Costly signaling—through costly messages or more broadly through any costly observable action—is often bounded by parameters. In an exogenous cost signaling, a message with a too-small cost does not convey information credibly, whereas the large cost deters sending a message at all. Only an intermediate cost separates those lobbyists who point to relevant information from those who exploit the opportunity to mislead the policy-maker (Potters and van Winden 1992). Signaling models also exhibit problems typical for information economics: (1) The presence of a costly message in the strategy set may decrease the expected lobbyist's payoff, (2) multiple equilibria and equilibria switches complicate comparative statics, and (3) the pooling equilibria with zero extra information always exist and are hard to rule out by a reasonable equilibrium refinement. For endogenous cost signaling and monotonicity in lobbies' types, it is however fortunately relatively straightforward to obtain the separating equilibrium.

Austen-Smith and Banks (2000, 2002) combine costly actions (money burning) with costless messages (cheap talk) into a single model. The availability of money burning increases the scope for credible cheap talk. With endogenous cost and a single lobby, even full revelation is possible in this combined model. Tovar (2011) extended an endogenous cost-setting and obtained full revelation by assuming that the lobby not only signals at a selected level, but also offers a contribution schedule that is conditional upon all payoff-relevant variables, including the state of Nature.

3.2.3 Production and Communication of Information

Prior to conveying messages, the lobby needs to obtain evidence or signals that can be communicated. The decision to produce (search) supportive evidence can be a strategic decision which can belong in the lobbying activity and an information

[3]Signaling refers to any interaction when a privately informed agent sends signals contingent on his or her type to an uninformed agent. Hence, it contains also cheap talk and disclosure games. In a narrow sense, signaling is used only for setting where utility varies with signals (hence signal costs exist) and where the informed agent's utility is *monotonic* in the signals and actions. Both of these assumptions are violated for typical models of costless communication.

search complements the strategic communication analyzed above. The nature of models that allow for both production and communication of information again depends on verifiability. In *cheap talk* models, production only constitutes a pre-play of cheap-talk subgames. Most of models rather apply verifiable evidence (e.g., Lagerlöf 2007; Henry 2009). The novelty for *hard evidence* is that once a no-evidence message can be reported and the amount of search is unobservable, then the policy-maker faces a more complex inference problem than if the amount of signals is pre-determined.

We will describe the decision on the production of evidence formally; the description will be helpful in the following sections when components of lobbying models are discussed in isolation. Namely, for states of the world in a finite state space $\theta \in \Theta$, let $\Delta(\Theta)$ denote the set of all probability distributions on Θ. A prior is $\mu_0 \in \Delta(\Theta)$. The prior is common to the lobby (Sender) and the policy-maker (Receiver). Policies $d \in D$ are from a compact policy space D. The lobby has a utility function $u(d, \theta)$ and the policy-maker has a utility function $v(d, \theta)$. We denote the policy-maker's optimal set of policies for his/her belief μ as $d^*(\mu)$.

A frequently presented special case is for two states of the world (low and high), $\Theta = \{\theta_l, \theta_h\}$. The probability of a high state is $\mu = \Pr(\theta_h) \in [0, 1]$. The prior probability is $\mu_0 \in [0, 1]$. Consider three policies, $D = \{d_l, d_0, d_h\}$. For each player, the expected payoff of any policy $d \in D$ is a linear combination of the payoffs in each state θ, hence is linear in μ. For convenience, the lobby's preferences over policies is assumed to be invariant to states, such that $0{=}u(d_l) \leq u(d_0) < u(d_h){=}1$.[4] For the policy-maker, a policy d_l is optimal if $\theta = \theta_l$, and a policy d_h is optimal if $\theta = \theta_h$, i.e., $d^*(0) = d_l$ and $d^*(1) = d_h$. A *default policy* d_0 is optimal for priors, $d^*(\mu_0) = d_0$.

Each pair of signal and message technologies (for a definition see Sect. 5.2) induces a Bayes-plausible lottery over the policy-maker's posteriors. Let $\tau(\mu)$ be any *distribution of posteriors* on $\Delta(\Theta)$. Then, for $\tau(\mu)$ to be induced by a persuasion mechanism in a perfect Bayesian equilibrium, the expected posterior probability of each state equals its prior probability, $\int \mu \, d\tau(\mu) = \mu_0$ (Bayes plausibility condition). In our special case, if the lobbying mechanism leads to exactly m posteriors μ_i, $i = 1, \ldots, m$, then the distribution is written $\tau = (p_1, \ldots, p_m)$, and the Bayes-plausibility requires $E_\tau(\mu) = \sum_i p_i \mu_i = \mu_0$.

Now let us specify the values of the persuasion mechanism for the players; this will be crucial for understanding the incentives for lobbying. First, purely for convenience, suppose that some selection criterion ensures that optimal policy $d^*(\mu) = \arg\max_D \int v(d, \theta) d\mu(\theta)$ is a singleton for all posteriors induced by the mechanism. The policy-maker's indirect utility in his/her posterior μ is constructed

[4]The preference structure has important consequences. For monotonic lobby's preferences (invariant to states), a single-dimensional cheap talk is uninformative as all lobby's types would send the *same* message that implements the most favorable policy. Monotonicity therefore restricts the modeler to communication with verifiable evidence and/or to evidence production. In other words, the preference structure (having a conflict or not having a conflict between the lobby's types) is typically related also to the informational structure.

in an upper envelope of the policy-maker's continuous expected payoffs (given by optimal policies $d^*(\mu)$), $V(\mu) := \int v(d^*(\mu), \theta) d\mu(\theta)$.

The lobby's value (*indirect utility*) at a policy-maker's posterior[5] μ is

$$U(\mu) := \int u(d^*(\mu), \theta)\, d\mu(\theta).$$

In our special case with a simple state space and the lobby's state-independent preferences, $U(\mu) = u(d^*(\mu))$. The expected value of the persuasion mechanism for the lobby is $E_\tau U(\mu) = \sum_i p_i U(\mu_i)$. Now, the key thing to see is that inequality $\sum_i p_i U(\mu_i) > U(\sum_i p_i \mu_i) = U(\mu_0)$ requires having $U(\mu)$ *convex at a point* μ_0.[6] In contrast, with concavity, $U(\mu)$ exhibits risk-aversion, and the inequality is opposite.

Thus, the shape of the indirect utility $U(\mu)$ determines the value of communication mechanism for the lobby, and the value is important in either of two ways: Firstly, if the lobby can commit to not communicating, the condition $\sum_i p_i U(\mu_i) \geq U(\mu_0)$ is a necessary condition for lobbying to be informative. Secondly, consider the case when the lobby cannot commit to the absence of communication. (It means, for example, that upon a policy-maker's request for the lobbyist's evidence, the lobby discloses evidence that is favorable to its cause.) Then, the inequality compares the lobby's payoffs in "babbling" vs. informational equilibrium.

The shape of $U(\mu)$ is based on (1) whether the policy-maker's policy $d^*(\mu)$ is concave or convex in μ, and (2) whether the lobby's payoff is concave or convex in d. In our special case, it is normally assumed that the lobby's payoff is convex (or even linear) in d, and the single important property is concavity or convexity of function $d^*(\mu)$. What is important is that for a finite D, $d^*(\mu)$ is a *step function at* μ where the policy-maker changes the policy. These discontinuities make concavities and convexities at points parameter-specific (cf., Dahm and Porteiro 2008b) and also produces discontinuities in the parameters of the persuasion mechanisms such as in the parameters characterizing signal and message technologies. For instance, Bennedsen and Feldmann (2006) separately analyze changes of posteriors that are small enough (weak signals) and large enough (strong signals).[7]

---

[5]Notice that even if the lobby may have a different posterior than the policy-maker, we must use the policy-maker's posterior. The reason is that the value of a mechanism is an ex ante expected value evaluated at μ_0, where information is symmetric, hence the lobby's ex ante belief conditional on learning that the policy-maker will have μ belief must also be μ.

[6]Notice that convexity or quasi-convexity of the lobbyist's (Sender's) payoffs is a recurrent topic in the communication literature (cf., Chakraborty and Harbaugh 2010).

[7]One option to avoid an inconvenient step-wise indirect utility is to let the policy-maker's optimal policy be stochastic in posteriors on fundamentals (Dahm and Porteiro 2008a). For example, suppose the states of the world are characterized by two independent dimensions, a fundamental dimension θ and a policy-maker's type r (e.g., ideology, risk aversion, or relative weights attached to contributions). The policy-maker type is private information that only influences $v(\cdot)$, but no other payoff, and the policy-maker cannot communicate his/her type. A persuasion mechanism is invariant to the policy-maker's type, hence implies a distribution of posteriors where the densities are constant in the type-dimension, and we may let $\mu(\theta) := \mu(\theta, r)$. Then, discontinuity in

Most models of production of evidence impose restrictions on the signal structure, typically parameterized by the number of signals or precision of signals. These restrictions complicate derivation of the lobby's expected value of the mechanism. The calculation becomes much easier in the extreme case of absence of any restrictions. Kamenica and Gentzkow (2011) show that if the lobby can design a communication mechanism arbitrarily, subject only to Bayes-plausibility, then there exists a communication mechanism that improves the lobby's expected utility, hence is preferred to the absence of communication, whenever (1) the default policy d_0 is not the first-best for the lobby and (2) in the neighborhood around prior μ_0, $d^*(\mu)$ is constant. The idea is based on showing that Bayes-plausible persuasion mechanisms implement posteriors in the convex hull of $U(\mu)$, denoted $C(U, \mu)$. The above pair of conditions implies that $U(\mu_0)$ is in the interior of $C(U, \mu)$, hence there is a mechanism that implements a Bayes-plausible convex combination of payoffs in posteriors, $U(\mu)$, such that $E_\tau U(\mu) > U(\mu_0)$. Such *concavification* has been used in a variety of similar communication contexts, e.g., in Brocas and Carrillo (2007).

4 Multiple-Tools Models

Although strategic information transmission literature rightly puts credibility of messages in the forefront of analysis of informational lobbying, it is silent on the interaction with payments. Multiple-tools (or multiple-means) models address the interaction by explicitly modeling the lobby's use of multiple instruments for influence. In this relatively heterogeneous group of papers, timing serves as a key aspect that differentiates between families of multiple-tool games. In the family of *pay and lobby* models, payments are made, and evidence is then presented conditional on the payment. Contributions in the first stage serve as access tickets for lobbying in the second stage. In the family of *lobby and pay* models, evidence is first gathered and presented, and then compensating payments follow.

$U(\mu)$ may disappear, since each $d^*(\mu(\theta))$ is constructed as an expected policy from a continuous distribution of policy-maker types, not as a (deterministic) policy of a single policy-maker with a known type r. An important corollary is that the value of the persuasion mechanism in the presence of uncertainty over the policy-maker's type hinges on concavities and convexities in the distribution $F(r)$. Typically, an assumption of the uniform distribution of the policy-maker's types is applied as in the literature on the communication design. Rayo and Segal (2010) manage to characterize several properties of the optimal communication mechanisms under special assumptions that the policy-maker's action space is binary ($\{d_l, d_h\}$) and that the policy-maker's action is affected by noise to the policy-maker's values, and the noise has a uniform distribution.

4.1 Pay and Lobby

Given natural attention constraints, policy-makers have to allocate scarce access. In classic pay-and-lobby ('money buys access') models, the policy-maker is seen as a *monopolist* who allocates his or her attention by charging access fees (Baron 1989; Snyder 1990; Austen-Smith 1995; Ball 1995; Lohmann 1995). The most typical form is when the fee is a policy-maker's take-it-or-leave-it offer (Austen-Smith 1998), but access can be also subject to a contest or an auction (Cotton 2009). In any case, pre-paid communication is highly attractive for the policy-maker, since it allows the policy-maker to collect access payments (or their fraction) instead of letting the signal be produced by wasteful (money-burning) activities of the lobbies.

The access fee payments are typically associated with campaign contributions, but we may equally consider payments to gate-keeping lobbying intermediaries or any overt or covert compensations. From that perspective, the classic pay-and-lobby models treat intermediaries as delegated gatekeepers who mainly collect access fees and facilitate access[8] and not as autonomous platforms in two-sided markets. The latter is a more recent approach and it is highly relevant especially to modeling many-to-many interactions which are not covered in this survey (Groll and Ellis 2014; Kang and You 2015).

There are two modeling options, depending on whether the lobby has informational advantage over the policy-maker in the moment when she faces the decision to access or not. Both options are seen as relevant (Grossman and Helpman 2001, p. 171). First, if the lobby is privately informed about some aspects of the state of Nature (*interim access*), the access cost serves as an instrument to elicit a separating costly action (i.e., signal).[9] The main difference to costly signaling models is that separation works even for state-independent preferences of the lobby, since verifiability lends credibility to communication in the case of access.

Second, when an access fee is paid well in advance such that a lobby and the policy-maker share common priors (*ex ante access*), the access fee mainly serves to redistribute part of the lobby's surplus from the subsequent communication to the policy maker. In this situation, heterogeneity of lobbies is especially important. For

[8]The body of evidence on the allocation of access through connected intermediaries is growing. Blanes-I-Vidal et al. (2012) measure the value of a political connection for revolving-door lobbyists who were previously congressional staffers. Specifically, by measuring how the exit of a former employer affects their payoff, they observe the premium for connections at above 20 %, and the premium lasts for over 3 years. Bertrand et al. (2014) compare the connection premium with the expertise premium using price tags per report. From price tags per report, the report-level analysis reveals that (1) the premium of having a relevant specialist in the report is 3–5 % and (2) the premium of having a relevant connected lobbyist is 8–10 %. Estimating the value of a lobbyist's political connections from stock markets is another strategy. Gely and Zardkoohi (2001) study firms that retain law firms as lobbyists. The firms show abnormal gains when one of the partners at that firm obtains a federal cabinet position which disappear when anti-lobbying laws are enacted.

[9]Typically, all information is revealed to the lobby. A modified case is when the lobby has only partial advantage of knowing her bias (Austen-Smith 1995; Lohmann 1993).

example, if the policy-maker can discriminate between groups because the lobbies's biases are known, the lobbying groups may separate such that moderate groups never pay but are always listened to, whereas access fee is applied only to extremists (Lohmann 1995).

4.2 *Lobby and Pay*

Informational lobbying (lobby and pay) presumes search and communication in the first stage and payments in the second stage. The second stage is either in the form of extra pressure (Dahm and Porteiro 2008a,b) or in the form of non-cooperative bargaining (Bennedsen and Feldmann 2006). In the former case, the idea is that the policy-maker's posteriors can be modified by buying extra influence. In the latter case, the idea is that if there is a surplus between the lobby and policy-maker associated with a policy change even after strategic information transmission, this surplus can be cashed in by compensating payments. These two different approaches predict different relations between the instruments. A third possibility is lobbying as signaling in the first stage and payments as menu-contributions in the second stage (Tovar 2011). Precisely, the menus of contributions are offered first, then signals are produced and finally payments are made. This setup represents a unique combination of endogenous-cost signaling and common agency in a single framework.

A trading (bargaining) protocol which determines how surplus of a policy change is redistributed between the policy-maker and lobby in the contribution subgame must be defined. In *bilateral bargaining*, an explicit non-cooperative bargaining model derives how the lobby compensates the policy-maker for a policy change (typically, a single take-it-or-leave-it offer made by the lobby is assumed). For several lobbies, each with a different optimal policy, bargaining between the policy-maker and lobbies needs is structured either as a *contest* (see also Sect. 2.2), *auction* (with or without policy commitments; Epstein and Nitzan 2004), *menu-auction* (with or without the policy-maker's private information; Felgenhauer 2010), or as *multilateral bargaining* (e.g., with a sequence of alternate take-or-leave offers; Glazer 2008).

For example, Bennedsen and Feldmann (2006) apply the policy-maker's willingness to pay for single-lobby case, but the lobby's willingness to pay for multiple-lobbies case (by means of a menu auction). Their idea is that a single lobby has strong enough bargaining power to capture the full surplus, whereas competitive lobbying leads to truthful contributions, in which it is the policy-maker who captures the entire surplus. The comparison of single-lobby and multiple-lobbies settings thus has to account for the fact that the bargaining strength of a lobby vis-a-vis policy-maker is not invariant to the number of players.

5 Modeling Ingredients

To understand more exactly about how lobbying influences policy-makers it is essential to review the ingredients of models in the field. Detailed knowledge of the main building blocks gives us a chance to understand the sources of qualitative predictions of the models.

5.1 Players' Instruments and Commitments

5.1.1 Lobby's Instruments

In this review, we restrict our attention only to instruments that target a single policy-maker and policies that differ only in substance and not in other aspects such as durability (cf. Harstad and Svensson 2011). The literature predominantly identifies six instruments of the lobby's political influence:

- *Platform announcement.* If the right to set a policy is sold or auctioned to a single winner, then the competing lobbies may commit to a platform that will be implemented, conditional on winning the right (see Münster 2006). In the competitive case, platform commitments resemble strategic position-taking in electoral competition. Nevertheless, in the context of special interests, the platform announcement never stands alone because the policy-maker has to be compensated for a loss of the policy right; the announcement exists only along with the instrument that is used to win the right (typically a rent-seeking investment or payment to the policy-maker).
- *Signal and message technology.* Both exogenous and endogenous signal structures appear in the literature. For example, in the context of the competitive informational lobbying under endogenous (policy-maker's optimal) access fees, Austen-Smith (1998) considers endogenous noise structures while Cotton (2012) considers exogenous noiseless information structure. Kamenica and Gentzkow (2011) and in a more narrow setup also Rayo and Segal (2010) is a general model that studies the lobby's choice from a *unrestricted* class of communication mechanisms, where the only consistency requirement is Bayes-plausibility. In other words, the lobby selects a *signal technology* and, at the same time, makes a commitment to a *message technology* that maps signals into messages. These are two choices at the same time. Therefore, it is also possible to study in isolation a pure effect of signal technology selection and a pure effect of commitment to a message technology.
- *Communication.* As we have discussed, restrictions on admissible messages matters the most. In cheap-talk games, messages are unverifiable, hence any message is admissible. In persuasion games, messages are verifiable, but presented evidence may be affected by strategically communicating incomplete evidence. Normally, the concealed evidence is not used any further. An exception is Stone

(2011) who argues that concealed evidence may be strategically released into the public domain. Therein, the evidence is only randomly observed by the policy-maker, but the policy-maker is not able to recognize the source of the evidence.

- *Costly action.* The decision to bear a cost of an action may serve as a signal. In pure money-burning settings, the action has a sole signaling function. In pre-paid communication, the costly action (payment for access) has an additional function of securing opportunity to send a message. Thus, communication is complementary to the costly action. An interesting observation is that the lobbies' endogenously determined payments for access fully reveal their evidence even *before* they are allowed to present the verifiable evidence to the policy-maker. The policy-maker thus infers the correct posteriors of the winner's type from the level of contributions, and verification serves only as a confirmatory check (Cotton 2009).
- *Evidence production.* For production of evidence (search/experimenting), its observability associated with existence of monitoring costs is crucial. With an observable search, a no-search subgame is isolated from the subgame containing signals produced by the search. In contrast, unobservable search brings in at least three effects: (1) First, multiple equilibria tend to arise. (2) Second, the policy-maker knows that an extra search is opportunistic (to get better evidence and hide bad evidence), hence anticipates moral hazard. The equilibrium amount of the search tends to increase. (3) Third, the lobby may be subject to pessimistic policy-maker's expectations, called the 'curse of lobbying' or 'trap of information acquisition', which depresses the lobby's value of the persuasion mechanism even below zero (Lagerlöf 1997).
- *Payments.* One of the main properties is whether the payments are contingent upon a policy, rent, or any other observable variable. (Equivalently, the property states whether an upfront-paid contribution is reversible or irreversible.) We can identify four forms of payments, each corresponding to a different mechanism: (1) Policy-contingent compensation in the bargaining stage or in menu auctions. Notice that the shape of the marginal cost of compensation affects concavity vs. linearity in the indirect utility $U(\mu)$ in search games with ex post contributions. For example, Dahm and Porteiro (2008b) have an increasing marginal cost thus additional local concavity, whereas Bennedsen and Feldmann (2006) assume a constant marginal cost. (2) Bids in standard auctions that are paid only by winners. (3) Investments in a contest for a policy rent or in a contest for policy-maker's attention. These payments are irreversible hence not contingent. (4) Tickets for access which are by definition irreversible payments. Paying access tickets serves also a signal in the context of two-level pay-and-lobby games. In a sense, an access ticket is a *double transfer*; both money and information flow from the lobby to the policy-maker.
- *Compensation requirement.* In pay-and-lobby models, the policy-maker commits to not observe the evidence unless the lobby makes a transfer. The commitment is however only unilateral; the lobby cannot commit to not reveal the evidence. In Gregor (2015), also lobbies have outside options in the commitment to not talk. The existence of bilateral outside options and bilateral commitments then

characterizes information transmission as a transaction with evidence, which admit both signs of a transfer. Therefore, one of the potential lobby's instrument is to require an access compensation.

5.1.2 Lobby's Commitments

Commonly, the lobby has significantly less commitment devices at his/her disposal than the policy-maker. Still, three types of the lobby's commitments can be found in lobbying models.

- The first is a commitment to a *policy-contingent payment* that appears in a menu auction (Bennedsen and Feldmann 2006). In Tovar (2011), the payment is also contingent upon the state of the world, and a *state-and-policy-contingent payment* represents the strongest type of the lobby's commitment to an ex post payment. Notice that in an unregulated environment, the lack of the lobby's commitment to pay ex post could theoretically be replaced by a commitment by the policy-maker to return up-front payments to losers.
- In contests, a winner normally realizes his or her first-best policy. Thus, the second type of the lobby's commitment is when contestants commit to realizing a certain compromising outcome (*policy/platform commitment/announcement*). This commitment strategically decreases the opponents' valuations. Epstein and Nitzan (2004) show in a spatial setting that if valuations are endogenous due to the option of policy commitments, the moderation of the aggressiveness of the opponent is a first-order effect to the loss of value from deviating from its own first-best policy. Münster (2006) generalizes by showing that moderation is incomplete for imperfect discrimination and complete for perfect discrimination.
- Finally, we have discussed the lobby's choice from a class of communication mechanisms (Kamenica and Gentzkow 2011; Rayo and Segal 2010). In such a case, the lobby is selecting a *signal technology* and, at the same time, is making a commitment to a *message technology*. Whether this type of the commitment is present in lobbying is open to discussion. Rayo and Segal (2010) motivate the commitment by viewing the sender (i.e., the interest group that lobbies) as a long-run player facing a sequence of short-run receivers (i.e., the policy makers). In such a repeated game, learning arguments support the idea that a patient long-run player is able to develop the Stackelberg leadership. Hence, the commitment seems reasonable to capture long-term interaction of well-organized and stable interests (e.g., unions and corporations) and more volatile decision-makers (e.g., individual legislators with weaker party affiliations).

  The commitment makes a major difference to standard communication (cheap talk, persuasion) where message technology is set to be *ex-post optimal*, not *ex-ante optimal*. The difference naturally leads to a contrasting comparative statics. For instance, in cheap talk, there is more communication if preferences of the lobby and the policy-maker are aligned. This is generally not the case when the communication mechanism is set ex ante. Nevertheless, an ex ante optimal mechanism frequently comprises ex post optimal messages. Kamenica and Gentzkow (2011) show that a fully-revealing message technology is credible if messages are verifiable in the sense of disclosure/persuasion games (Milgrom 1981). In other words, under verifiability assumption, the existence of the lobby's commitment to a message technology is irrelevant.

5.1.3 The Policy-Maker's Instruments

The policy-maker's main roles are assumed to be an ex ante design of an allocation mechanism and an ex post policy-setting.

- *Contest design.* The first generation of rent-seeking contests limited the policy-maker's role to only the distribution of the prize in accordance with the rules of the contest-success function. However, an idea implicit in rent-seeking is that the policy-maker intentionally generates contest prizes because he or she values the benefits associated with the rent-seeking investments. The early contest literature thus focused on *contest design*, but only for a purely revenue-oriented policy-maker.

  To make the policy-maker's decision-making more realistic, one may postulate a policy-maker with a mixed objective who shapes the parameters of the contest. An additional choice of such a policy-maker is to determine whether to use the contest at all or whether to hand out the prize to the highest-valuation group (Epstein and Nitzan 2006a,b). For a mixed-objective policy-maker, another relevant strategic instrument is the presence of policy restrictions that bind the contest winner, change contestants' valuations, and also their efforts. To sum up, before initiating a contest a mixed objective policy-maker solves a number of tradeoffs that are otherwise absent for a purely revenue-oriented policy-maker.
- *Access allocation mechanism.* More broadly, the policy-maker can be a designer of incentives for the lobbies, and may adopt trading mechanisms going beyond contests. The most discussed tradeoff is whether to initiate an auction (winner-pay mechanism) or contest (all-pay mechanism). For example, in Cotton (2009), a single ticket is auctioned in an *all-pay auction* of two interest groups. Each group possesses a private and independent piece of evidence. Payments in this auction reveal both pieces of evidence, hence ex post verification by the policy-maker serves only to confirm the posteriors. Cotton (2009) shows that selling access by means of an all-pay auction is preferred to selling policy rent by means of an all-pay auction, unless the policy-maker's valuation of the policy is significantly lower than the lobbies' valuations. Even more generally, screening combined with the persuasion subgame as constructed in Cotton (2009) is attractive both (1) relative to other means of information transmission (by securing full revelation and raising more funds) and (2) relative to other means of raising funds (by getting a better policy for the policy-maker).
- *Access fee.* In trading protocols, the policy-maker asks a price for access. Typically, the protocols are simple and the policy-maker has a strong bargaining

power; in extreme, the policy-maker is a monopolist who makes a single take-it-or-leave-it offer to a lobby. The offer can be discriminative (lobby-specific) or non-discriminative (all lobbies face an identical fee).

- *Costly information acquisition.* When the policy-maker can acquire costly signals on her own, an interesting feature is that informative messages of lobbies alter incentives to acquire the additional signals. When the signals are close information substitutes, informational lobbying may reduce the net marginal value of an extra signal below zero and consequently may decrease the equilibrium amount of information. In other words, pure informational lobbying may lead to worse informed policy-making than no lobbying (Cotton and Dellis 2016).

5.1.4 The Policy-Maker's Commitments

The literature frequently constrains the ex post policy-maker's actions, hence assumes commitment devices which can be in lobbying context strategic delegation to intermediaries such as aides and connected lobbyists. The most complex commitments are rules of an allocation mechanism (such as a contest), including the promise of using the specific allocation function, the promise to not deteriorate the prize (e.g., instead of the policy right, provide only access), and the promise to not ask for additional side-payments. The incentive of the policy-maker to break a promise varies in parameters, and we may find a variety of potential time-inconsistencies:

- The promise to sell policy may be ex post suboptimal if payments reveal additional information. Consider a symmetric setting with two lobbies and multiple policy choices in the spirit of Bennedsen and Feldmann (2006). If two oppositely extreme groups offer similar amounts, then the policy-maker updates priors very little and prefers the neutral default policy over the lottery of extreme policies. The rules of the policy sale, however, dictate to allocate the policy right to one of the groups. (See also Sect. 5.2.5 on the role of default policy.)
- Cotton (2009) allows the policy-maker choose from two different classes of all-pay auctions. In one, the right to set policy is sold, and in the other, only access is sold. Both are organized exactly in the same way and differ only in the last moment, after payments are collected. The policy-maker has obviously an ex post incentive to switch from policy-sale rules to access-sale rules because it implies a policy improvement without extra cost.
- Time-inconsistency may also be present when the policy-maker sets an agenda in Stage 1 (Epstein and Nitzan 2006b). The policy-maker thereby restricts the set of admissible policies of the winner of the contest and thereby changes valuations and efforts. Once the winner is determined, the policy-maker may have an incentive to lift the restriction and extend the reduced agenda set so that the contest winner can in fact set a better policy both for himself/herself and the policy-maker.

In pure communication literature, the policy-maker's policy is normally non-contractible, and only messages influence policies. The presence of any (message-specific) commitment would substantially alter the game; the policy-maker could commit to skeptical behavior that would force the lobby to exert additional effort. Nevertheless, there are settings where the commitment actually makes no difference. In a simple setup with partial verification, Glazer and Rubinstein (2004) identify the policy-maker's optimal communication mechanism. The optimal mechanism minimizes the policy-maker's probability of mistake subject to three elements: (1) the set of admissible messages of the lobby, (2) which messages will be verified, and (3) the policy-maker's action based on the messages and verification results. In the end, the optimal mechanism is credible, hence the lobby's optimum is to induce such policy-maker's beliefs that make it optimal for the policy-maker to follow exactly as in the prescribed mechanism.

This shows that communication literature considers as relevant also the policy-maker's *commitment to verification*, including random auditing (Cotton 2016). Consider pay-for-access models, where lobbies truthfully reveal evidence by contributions because their equilibrium expectations involve that verification will be undertaken with certainty (Cotton 2009). If verification is costless for the policy-maker, then a commitment to verification is not necessary. But, costless verification is at odds with the assumption that access is rationed due to limited (costly) attention. In contrast, if verification is costly, then ex post verification is time-inconsistent and an announcement to verify must be binding the policy-maker.

5.1.5 The Policy-Maker's Environment

The policy-maker may be restricted not only by its commitments but also by regulations dictated by the exogenous environment. Let us only briefly touch upon the issue of *transparency*. The policy-maker may be subject to the mandatory disclosure of private information which affects equilibrium bids of lobbies in menu auctions. Felgenhauer (2010) examines information asymmetry where it is the government or bureaucracy that disposes of private information, and competing lobbies engage in menu auction contributions. From the policy-maker's perspective, the regime of *secrecy* (no mandatory disclosure of the policy-maker's information) is preferred to *transparency* as it raises the expected equilibrium bids; hence transparency must be imposed by regulation. From the social point of view, however, Felgenhauer (2010) observes that transparency is preferred only if lobbies are sufficiently similar, hence their equilibrium bids do not change the policy-maker's default (socially optimal) policy. If lobbies are sufficiently asymmetric, transparency cannot protect the default policy. In contrast, secrecy provides partial protection to the default policy, since it involves mixed strategies where a default policy is realized with a positive probability.

5.2 *Information*

Communication starts with common priors μ_0 and $\theta \in \Theta$ selected by Nature. Then, we have to distinguish between models with *pure communication* and models of *search and communication*. For pure communication, the lobby exogenously acquires the private signal and a persuasion mechanism directly applies. In search and persuasion models, the lobby makes a decision of whether to acquire a signal or not, and then communicates. Notice that with common priors, the observable lobby's decision to acquire or not to acquire a signal cannot affect the policy-maker's beliefs. Only with asymmetry, search has a signaling effect upon the policy-maker's posteriors. This asymmetry is not present if only a single search is made, but with a sequence of searches, the signaling effect of search per se is in place. To our best knowledge, models with a signaling role of search decisions are yet to be built.

5.2.1 Signal and Message Technologies

A *signal technology* is a family of distributions $\{\pi(s|\theta)\}_{\theta\in\Theta}$ over S, where a signal realized is $s \in S$. A *message technology* is another component of a communication mechanism. For messages $m \in M$, it involves a family of cost functions $c(\cdot|s)$, where the cost of message m after observing s is $c(m|s) \in R^+ \cup \infty$. Often, $M = P(\Theta)$, where $P(\Theta)$ is the set of all subsets of Θ.

Notice how restrictions on message costs serve to define verifiability. In cheap talk games, the cost is zero (or constant), hence signal-independent. For persuasion with verifiable evidence (Milgrom 1981), the signal is perfectly informative, the message space is $M = P(\Theta)$, the message cost is constant if the lobby does not explicitly lie ($s \in m$) and infinity for an explicit lie ($s \in \neg m$). In an honest mechanism, the lobby must tell the 'whole' truth, and nothing but the truth, hence the cost is constant only if the whole truth is revealed ($s = m$), and is infinity otherwise ($s \neq m$). This can be also interpreted such that the signal is directly observable by the policy-maker without need for additional messaging.

How to interpret messages? Traditionally, messages are assumed to have a literal meaning. In cheap-talk, signal technology is perfectly informative for the lobby but it is also assumed that a signal does not involve observable evidence (e.g., logical arguments or documents that cannot be fabricated). Hence, the set of admissible messages is unrestricted. In disclosure/persuasion games, a signal involves observable evidence. The existence of the observable evidence makes the messages verifiable, and the set of admissible messages (i.e., those message that pass the burden of proof) becomes signal-dependent. In such games, notice that a standard message set also includes an 'empty message' defined as the message that implements priors.

Ascribing literal meaning of messages has tremendous consequences with respect to how out-of-equilibrium messages are interpreted by the policy-maker. Consider a case when a privately informed lobby sends an unused out-of-equilibrium message with the meaning: "The world is of type $\theta \in K$." If the message is taken literally by the policy-maker, then he or she would implement policy $d(\mu(K))$. If the lobby's payoff would increase with the policy $d(\mu(K))$ and this increase would be only for $\theta \in K$, then an equilibrium would not be *neologism-proof* (Farrell 1993) and the refinement of neologism-proofness would dictate to eliminate this equilibrium. Nevertheless, the disadvantage of neologism-proofness is that it refines away all equilibria in many settings, including cheap talk, and lacks general existence properties (Sobel 2010). Another possible modification towards literal meaning of messages is to assume communication with a small lying cost.

5.2.2 Production of Evidence

In classic strategic information transmission, involving cheap talk and persuasion games, the lobby exogenously receives a perfectly informative private signal, and the setting can be studied as a case of pure asymmetric information. A different case is when the lobby has no information and must invest in a signal. In particular, two major signaling technologies (a.k.a. search/evidence-production/investigation functions) appear in the literature:

- *Hard evidence*. Signal space includes only two outcomes, truth and no-evidence. For $s = \varnothing$, the only admissible message (not infinite cost) is $m = \varnothing$. For $s = \theta$, the set of admissible messages is $\{\theta, \varnothing\}$. Thus, hard evidence cannot be fabricated, but unfavorable evidence can be presented as a lack of evidence. This setting is also used in search models that use contest with evidence (Lagerlöf 2007). Signal distributions normally feature a common precision level, $\pi(\theta|\theta) = \omega \in [0, 1], \theta \in \Theta$. Thus, in our special case, ex ante probabilities of the realizations of signals $(\theta_l, \varnothing, \theta_h)$ are $(\omega(1 - \mu_0), 1 - \omega, \omega\mu_0)$.
- *Noisy signals*. Signal space does not include no-evidence, but rather noise over all states of the world, $S = \Theta$. In a special case, a common precision is $\pi(\theta|\theta) = \omega \in [0, 1]$. The ex ante probabilities of (θ_l, θ_h) are now $(\omega(1 - \mu_0) + (1 - \omega)\mu_0, \omega\mu_0 + (1 - \omega)(1 - \mu_0))$. (See also Brocas and Carrillo 2007.)

Hard evidence is not necessarily the preferred evidentiary structure for the lobby. Consider our setup where the policy-maker has symmetric preferences and symmetric priors $\mu_0 = \frac{1}{2}$, hence selects $d^*(\mu) = d_l$ if $\mu < \frac{1}{2}$ and $d^*(\mu) = d_h$ if $\mu > \frac{1}{2}$. Recall that the lobby's expected payoff is defined by the probability of getting a favorable policy d_h, $\Pr(d_h)$. For both evidentiary structures, the probability of getting a favorable policy is equal to the probability of delivering favorable evidence, $\Pr(d = d_h) = \Pr(s = \theta_h)$, and the probability of getting an unfavorable policy is equal to the complementary probability, $\Pr(d = d_l) = \Pr(s \in \{\theta_l, \varnothing\}) = 1 - \Pr(s = \theta_h)$. This is because the relevant posterior associated with the favorable evidence satisfies $\mu_h \geq \frac{1}{2}$ (i.e., d_h is implemented), and the relevant posterior associated with unfavorable evidence satisfies $\mu_l \leq \frac{1}{2}$ (i.e., d_l is implemented).

Thus we may compare the structures by studying only the probability of delivering favorable evidence.

For a search with hard evidence, there are three outcomes $(\theta_l, \varnothing, \theta_h)$ with probabilities $(\frac{\omega}{2}, 1-\omega, \frac{\omega}{2})$. The unfavorable evidence θ_l is concealed, and the reported outputs are $(\varnothing, \theta_h)$, with probabilities $(1-\frac{\omega}{2}, \frac{\omega}{2})$. For a noisy signal, there are two outcomes (θ_l, θ_h) with probabilities $(\frac{1}{2}, \frac{1}{2})$, and both are disclosed. As a result, the lobby's expected payoffs in the two structures are $\frac{\omega}{2} \leq \frac{1}{2}$, and the noisy technology is relatively superior to the hard-evidence technology.

5.2.3 Quality

Often, the lobbyists select from the family of evidence-production functions with different precisions ω, where a cost function $C(\omega)$ is convex. The selected precision level may be the lobby's private information. Interestingly, in contests, the quality of the signal is not only subject to the lobby's choice, but may also be *strategically distorted* by the policy-maker. The distortion can be introduced through the delegation of judgment over the lobbying effort to a staff member who commits systematic errors. This echoes the discussion on the stochastic foundations for contest-success functions, where the low elasticity of the prize to relative effort may be due to noise about lobbyists' efforts. In the case of persuasion contests, the effort is represented by the quality of lobbied evidence, and it is the policy-maker's processing of the evidence which decreases the precision of the evidence.

Another issue is whether quality can be interpreted interchangeably as quantity. Lagerlöf (2007), Dahm and Porteiro (2008a) and Henry (2009) interpret the level of precision as *the amount* of lobbying, hence their setups make no distinction between the two aspects. The difference might actually be suppressed for private tests (or an unobservable search), where the outcomes of a search can be jammed into a single message. However, with public tests or observable (repeated) searches, quantity and quality are different features. For example, Brocas and Carrillo (2007) characterize the optimal stopping rule in the flow of public signals (i.e., the optimal quantity) as a function of the quality of a single signal.

5.2.4 Private or Public

The literature differentiates between a *private* production (search/experiment) and *public* search: For a private search, it is possible to withhold evidence and report an empty message. The observability of a search then makes a difference. With an *observable search*, the policy-maker interprets an empty message as both an unsuccessful search (no evidence) and concealed evidence. With an *unobservable search*, an empty message covers not only two but three events at the same time: no search, search without evidence, and search with unfavorable evidence.

When the test is public, evidence cannot be withheld. Imposing a public test (or mandatory disclosure rule) makes not only the search outcome, but also the search itself observable. Thus, analyzing the effect of the public test relative to the private test crucially depends on whether we start with an observable or unobservable search. With an *observable search*, introducing the public test only separates unfavorable evidence from no-evidence. With an *unobservable search*, the public test separates no-search, no-evidence, and unfavorable evidence, and the effects of mandatory disclosure are therefore more complex.

5.2.5 Empty Messages

The literal meaning of an empty message, $m = \varnothing$, is to say nothing but confirm priors. In the absence of a search, an empty message is just one of all admissible messages. With a search and private test, four options arise for the interpretation of the empty message:

1. Consider the absence of a no-evidence outcome ($\varnothing \in \neg S$) and observable search: This is a standard persuasion game preceded by a search in an early stage, where $M = P(\Theta)$. Under verifiability, an empty message has a zero strategic effect, since full disclosure appears (Milgrom 1981; Henry 2009). The idea is that unless private evidence is the worst possible, it is ex post better to separate oneself from all types with worse evidence and pool with all types of better evidence. This 'sharpening' of the messages ultimately leads to the full revelation of the truth.
2. Consider the absence of a no-evidence outcome and unobservable search: An empty message is now used to conceal unfavorable evidence behind a no-search. For example, in Henry (2009), all positive signals are reported, all negative signals are withheld, and the Receiver (policy-maker) understands that the hidden signals are negative. The revelation is incomplete, because the number of positive signals only probabilistically indicates the number of negative signals.
3. Consider the no-evidence outcome ($\varnothing \in S$) and observable search: In addition to unfavorable evidence, an empty message now also captures the existence of a no-evidence outcome. Again, the empty message is ex post always used strategically to conceal bad evidence, namely to conceal bad evidence behind no evidence.
4. Consider the no-evidence outcome and unobservable search: In this most complex case, an empty message jams together no-search, unfavorable evidence, and no-evidence.

We have seen that the empty message especially interacts with the no-evidence search outcome. One effect of having an admissible empty message in the presence of the no-evidence outcome is to bring asymmetry into an otherwise symmetric model. Let us return to a comparison of hard-evidence vs. noisy signal technologies. Consider our special case with a symmetric prior $\mu_0 = \frac{1}{2}$. Start with an observable search for *hard evidence* with a no-evidence outcome, where the precision level is $\omega \in [0, 1]$. The search delivers one of three outcomes, $s \in \{\theta_l, \varnothing, \theta_h\}$. The lobby discloses only two outcomes, $m \in \{\varnothing, \theta_h\}$; unfavorable evidence is hidden by showing no evidence, $m(\theta_l) = \varnothing$. The unconditional probability of obtaining no evidence is $\Pr(\varnothing) = 1 - \omega$.

By Bayes rule, the relevant posteriors are written $\mu_\varnothing := \Pr(\theta_h|\varnothing) = \frac{1-\omega}{2-\omega} \in (0, \frac{1}{2})$ and $\mu_h := \Pr(\theta_h|\theta_h) = 1$. This creates asymmetry in posteriors $(\mu_\varnothing, \mu_h)$ around the prior $\mu_0 = \frac{1}{2}$. The asymmetry is important if there is a default policy d_0 that serves as the policy-maker's insurance against extremes, for instance by providing a state-invariant payoff. In our setting specifically, it is important whether the posterior $\mu_\varnothing$ implements a default policy, $d^*(\mu_\varnothing) = d_0$, or not. If so, then the default policy fully absorbs (neutralizes) the indirect cost of a search associated with posteriors at an empty message, which makes the value of a search positive for the lobby.

In contrast, for a *noisy search without a no-evidence outcome*, a search leads to two outcomes. The relevant posteriors are $(\mu_l, \mu_h) = (\Pr(\theta_h|\theta_l), \Pr(\theta_h|\theta_h)) = (1 - \omega, \omega)$. With symmetric neutralization around $\mu_0 = \frac{1}{2}$, either both posteriors are neutralized, $d^*(\mu_l) = d^*(\mu_h)$, or none of the posteriors are neutralized, $d^*(\mu_l) \neq d^*(\mu_0) \neq d^*(\mu_h)$. Unlike for a hard evidence search, a noisy search (where errors are symmetric) is either uninformative or the indirect search cost cannot be absorbed. In contrast to the comparison in Sect. 5.2.1, this particular aspect makes noisy technology relatively inferior to the hard-evidence technology.

6 Selected Topics

6.1 To Lobby or Not to Lobby

In a sample of lobbying expenditures aiming at tax benefits, Richter et al. (2009) show descriptively that lobbying expenditures follow a skewed, power-law distribution, and only a small fraction of firms actually lobby. There is a host of determinants related not only to the lobbying mechanism but also to the industrial structure. For example, Kerr et al. (2014) find significant evidence that up-front costs associated with entering the political process explain why so few firms lobby, and why lobby status is persistent over time.

To address the participation question, we briefly examine how the structure of the lobbying mechanism and the parameters of the environment affect the decision to participation. One particular motivating piece of evidence is de Figueiredo and Cameron (2009) who explore institutional and political variation across states in the US to deliver that the ideological distance between the lobbying group and the legislature increases outlays; this complies with a standard signaling model with non-verifiable information and endogenous cost where a stronger signal is needed to persuade the legislature if the lobby's bias is larger (Austen-Smith 1995).

6.1.1 Single Lobby

In the context of a single lobby that conducts an observable search, so far we have stressed that the key determinant is the shape of the lobby's expected indirect utility in posteriors, $U(\mu)$. The shape is derived differently with and without subsequent contribution subgames. In the *absence of contribution subgames*, this indirect utility is derived from the policy-maker's policy decision based on his or her upper envelope of the expected utilities of all policies, evaluated at the respective posterior. The existence of policy-switches in μ makes the shape of the lobby's expected indirect utility generally ambiguous. Specifically, conflicting preferences between the policy-maker and lobby imply that the lobby's utility is step-wise at the critical posteriors (i.e., at levels that make the policy-maker change his or her optimal policy), which implies that the utility is neither convex nor concave. With a larger number of policies, the number of policy-switches increases and complexity grows. For instance, some differences between Dahm and Porteiro (2008a) and Bennedsen and Feldmann (2006) stem only from the fact that the former have two policies and a single policy-switch, while the latter allows for three policies and two policy-switches.

With steps in $U(\mu)$, an important variable for the decision to lobby is the *relative* position of the priors to the critical level of posteriors. In our symmetric setting with two policies $\{d_l, d_h\}$, the policy-maker selects $d^*(\mu) = d_l$ if $\mu < 1/2$ and $d^*(\mu) = d_h$ if $\mu \geq 1/2$; the critical posterior that defines a policy-switch is $\overline{\mu} := 1/2$. The incentive to lobby can be found either directly (by calculating expected payoffs) or indirectly (by checking concavity or convexity at the prior level). First, if $\mu_0 > \overline{\mu}$, the lobby never has a strict incentive to lobby since the default policy d_h is his/her first-best policy. Alternatively, we may say that a search brings a negative expected payoff because of concavity at point μ_0 over alternatives $(\mu_\varnothing, \mu_h)$, where $\mu_\varnothing$ is the policy-maker's posterior for an empty message $m = \emptyset$, and μ_h is the policy-maker's posterior for the message $m = \theta_h$. On the contrary, if $\mu_0 < \overline{\mu}$, then the lobby's search for hard evidence with success rate ω implies $\mu_h = 1$, policy $d^*(\mu_h) = d_h$, and gain 1, all with probability $\omega\mu_0$. With probability $1 - \omega\mu_0$, an empty message is presented, and the posterior is $\mu_\varnothing = \frac{(1-\omega)\mu_0}{1-\omega\mu_0} < \mu_0 < \frac{1}{2}$. This implies policy $d^*(\mu_\varnothing) = d_l$, and zero gain. As a result, the lobby's expected payoff is $\omega\mu_0 \geq 0$, and the lobby always lobbies. Notice also that the positive expected payoff of a search is equivalent to convexity at point μ_0 over $(\mu_\varnothing, \mu_h)$.

With subsequent *contribution subgames*, the policy-maker's policy choice in each posterior is affected by contributions offered by the lobby, and the structure of the interaction can be modeled as non-cooperative bargaining. Therein, the additionally important aspects are the existence of surplus, bargaining powers, and transaction costs. Consider our special case and let the policy-maker have value $\alpha r > 0$ from correctly fitting a d_l policy with state θ_l, and $\alpha(1-r) > 0$ from correctly fitting a d_h policy with θ_h, where $\alpha r > 1$. Payoffs from misfits are normalized to zero. Without contributions, the critical level for a policy-switch is $\overline{\mu} := r$. We observe that $d^*(\mu) = d_l$ if $\mu < \overline{\mu}$ and $d^*(\mu) = d_h$ if $\mu \geq \overline{\mu}$. To change a policy from d_l to d_h, the policy-maker has to be compensated by at least $\max\{0, \alpha(r - \mu)\}$, hence the total surplus from the policy change is $S(\mu) := 1 - \alpha(r - \mu)$. If $S(\mu) \leq 0$, there is no compensation. The critical level for compensation to be feasible for the lobby is at $\underline{\mu} := \frac{\alpha r - 1}{\alpha}$. Thus, with contribution subgames, we have (1) no compensation for $\mu \in [0, \underline{\mu})$, (2) positive compensation for $\mu \in [\underline{\mu}, \overline{\mu})$, and (3) no compensation for $\mu \in [\overline{\mu}, 1]$.

Let $\hat{U}(\mu)$ be the lobby's equilibrium payoff in the contribution subgame. First, see that $\hat{U}(\mu) \geq U(\mu)$ since a non-contribution subgame that does not affect the policy-maker's posteriors can always be chosen by the lobby. Second, we have (1) $\hat{U}(\mu) = U(\mu) = 0$ for $\mu \in [0, \underline{\mu})$, (2) $\hat{U}(\mu) \in [0, 1]$ for $\mu \in [\underline{\mu}, \overline{\mu})$, and (3) $\hat{U}(\mu) = U(\mu) = 1$ for $\mu \in [\overline{\mu}, 1]$.

Now, examine the shape of $\hat{U}(\mu)$ in detail. Unless the policy-maker extracts a full surplus, we have $\hat{U}(\mu) > 0$ for intermediate beliefs $\mu \in [\underline{\mu}, \overline{\mu})$. Since zero surplus exists at low beliefs, we have, around $\mu = \underline{\mu}$, and there are points at which $\hat{U}(\mu)$ is *convex*. If the lobby can extract either some but *not all surplus*, then $\hat{U}(\mu) < 1$ for all intermediate beliefs. Thus, at $\mu = \overline{\mu}$, there is a step in $\hat{U}(\mu)$. Therefore, in the neighborhood of $\overline{\mu}$, there are points where $\hat{U}(\mu)$ is *concave*. In other words, unless the lobby extracts full surplus, the step in the lobby's indirect utility exists both with and without contributions. Bennedsen and Feldmann (2006) serve as a good example of how these problems are suppressed: The extra risk-proclivity associated with zero surplus around $\underline{\mu}$ is entirely avoided by assuming a positive surplus for all posteriors. Secondly, the convexity around $\overline{\mu}$ is eliminated by vesting the lobby with full bargaining power.

Alternatively, Dahm and Porteiro (2008a,b) construct the contribution subgame as a unilateral purchase of *extra pressure*. They start with the policy-maker who is expected to set policy d_h with probability μ. (This is the outcome of having a stochastic policy-maker and a uniform distribution of the policy-maker's types, $F(r) = r$.) Hence, in the absence of contributions, $U(\mu) = \mu$, and the lobby is risk-neutral. Their novelty is that extra pressure $\pi \in R^+$ can be purchased at a constant cost $c > 0$. The pressure modifies the posteriors over the states. Specifically, the total 'evidence' in favor of θ_h is $\mu + \pi$, and total 'evidence' in favor of θ_l is $1 - \mu$. As a result, $\hat{U}(\mu) = \Pr(d_h) = \frac{\mu + \pi}{1 + \pi}$. Solving for equilibrium pressure, $\pi^*(\mu)$, we find that pressure decreases and is concave in the posterior μ, and the expected lobby's utility is surprisingly *convex* in the posterior. A lobby becomes risk-loving, independently of the level of posteriors.

To sum up, lobbying by means of search and subsequent persuasion tends to occur with (1) a low search cost, (2) large bargaining power of the lobby in the contribution subgame, (3) an unfavorable status quo that increases gains in the case of success and lowers the indirect cost of a search, and (4) large stakes. Most generally, the decision to lobby depends on whether $\hat{U}(\mu)$ is convex in the relevant posteriors.

6.1.2 Multiple Lobbies

With a competition of heterogeneous lobbies, the participation decision of individual lobbies and the aggregate level of lobbying are potentially separate issues. A parametrical change that motivates one player to increase lobbying may decrease the overall lobbying activity, and vice versa. To start with, focus on the results achieved for a contest over policy rent. This literature has produced a bulk of comparative statics observations on how aggregate and individual lobbying changes with (1) the level of discrimination, (2) contribution caps, (3) player exclusion, and (4) the number of prizes.

A first general result is that, ceteris paribus, perfect discrimination induces more effort for symmetry and imperfect discrimination works better for large asymmetry (Fang 2002; Epstein and Nitzan 2006b; Wang 2010). The explanation goes through the participation-decision of less interested players. The non-participation of an individual contestant has a first-order effect on relaxing the overall contest activity, hence the values of the discrimination parameter that encourages non-participation are excessively high. This issue can be best addressed if both the level of discrimination and relative productivity of efforts can be simultaneously optimized. Then, an all-pay auction with its conditionally optimal relative productivity raises more than any logit contest-success function with its conditionally optimal relative productivity, including Tullock's lottery (Epstein et al. 2011).

The participation of low-valuation lobbying groups may also be encouraged by setting a ceiling to high-level payments. A standard effect of such a cap is to decrease both the highest payments and the total expenditures, hence it represents, from the perspective of the policy-maker, a costly prize redistribution. This property nevertheless varies in the contest success function. While for Tullock's lottery, the aggregate expenditures do fall (Fang 2002), Che and Gale (1998) show that in an all-pay auction, a rigid contribution cap makes the low-valuation lobbyist more proactive, and total expenditures may even rise. Kaplan and Wettstein (2006) argue that a non-rigid contribution cap (i.e., a discontinuous but not infinite marginal cost) re-establishes the result that aggregate contributions decrease in an all-pay auction with a cap. Che and Gale (2006) show that even with a non-rigid cap, the non-intuitive effect of the cap is restored as long as the relative effect of the 'leveling of the playing field' is strong enough. This only confirms the intuition that a too-large asymmetry in contests is, from a revenue-maximization perspective, not desirable. For recent contributions, see also Pastine and Pastine (2010) and Grossmann and Dietl (2012).

In addition to contribution caps, the structure of prizes matters in a contest. Prize redistribution may induce wider participation and stimulate total effort. In a review of multiple-prize contests, Sisak (2009) demonstrates that adding an additional prize to encourage additional participation has ambiguous properties on the individual efforts of contestants. Epstein and Nitzan (2006a) show that sufficiently asymmetrically reducing the prize (valuations) for all players may paradoxically boost total expenditures. For all-pay auctions, Siegel (2009) derives the number of participating players as a linear function of the number of prizes. In a fairly general setting, he shows that increasing the number of prizes and thereby attracting additional players makes existing players weakly worse off.

For the policy-maker, it pays off to stimulate participation even if influence is only through strategic communication. There are two ways how multiplicity of lobbies enhance informativeness of cheap-talk reporting to the policy-maker. First, the policy-maker uses multiple reports as checks and may respond to differences by punishments. Second, the lobby may provide information along a dimension of common interest, and the policy-maker thereby combines the information from multiple lobbies (Sobel 2010). Fully-revealing equilibria exist under relatively weak conditions.

With informational lobbying, the majority of models suggest that the policy-maker can stimulate more intense lobbying competition with a larger number of competitors. In Bennedsen and Feldmann (2006), competition increases the incentive for a search because an unsuccessful search is interpreted against the lobbying group only if the other group is *also* unsuccessful. If contributions are allowed, then this effect represents an information rent to the group with *less informative technology* in the case both groups are unsuccessful. This serves as extra-special motivation for the participation of a weaker player.

An interesting corollary of lobbies' competition arises in settings where lobbies can commit to communication mechanisms (Kamenica and Gentzkow 2011; Rayo and Segal 2010). The role of competition can be incorporated into the design problem by entering the policy-maker's surplus into the lobbies' choice, as a competing lobby tries to outperform its rival by offering a better mechanism to the policy maker. The more competitive is the market, the larger is the weight attached to the surplus. In the limit of perfect competition, the Pareto-optimal communication mechanism is found to be *fully revealing* (Rayo and Segal 2010, Sect. 8A).

When informational lobbying yields a collective benefit but a side-payment gives a private benefit, then non-participation is differently motivated for each of the instruments. Non-participation in lobbying activities is primarily motivated by free-riding, and the total amount of lobbying depends on whether the demand for lobbying benefits exhibits the neutrality or non-neutrality we see in public good games. In contrast, non-participation in contributions is motivated by the absence of a bargaining surplus. An example of the interaction between these two instruments is built in Polk and Schmutzler (2005). They examine a tradeoff of firms that select from collective-good lobbying (industry-specific benefits) and private-good lobbying (firm-specific benefits), and show that the option of the private-good lobbying crowds out the use of the collective-good lobbying.

6.2 *Strategic Substitution and Complementarity*

6.2.1 Theory

Does the possibility of providing direct contributions affect the usefulness of informational lobbying? And vice versa, does lobbying change the effect of direct contributions? In the theoretical literature, the instruments are typically pure or impure *substitutes*. Consider an increase in the bargaining power of a single lobby. In Sect. 6.1, we have seen that it makes a lobby more likely to search. At the same time, the increase in bargaining power implies less payments in each relevant contribution subgame. Overall, we observe less payments and more lobbying, i.e., a substitution effect.

A different story emerges when we study the effects of the deregulation of one instrument upon the equilibrium level of the other instrument. For this purpose, Bennedsen and Feldmann (2006) have built up a setting which allows for 16 configurations of multi-player lobbying: un/observable search, strong/weak signals, with/without contributions, and with/without lobbying. The effects of contributions upon lobbying depend upon the asymmetry of valuations. For symmetry, contributions intensify the competition in terms of the informational search (complementarity). For sufficiently asymmetric lobbies, the introduction of contributions implies that the group with the less effective search technology decides not to participate in info-collection and the decision-maker receives less information (substitution).

To return to our setting with a single lobby, Bennedsen and Feldmann (2006) derive that for observable searches and contributions, lobbying is fully crowded out (pure substitution). Unfortunately, this striking result crucially hinges upon two assumptions: (1) Surplus from attaining the lobby's first-best policy is positive, $S(\mu) > 0$ for $\mu \in [0, 1]$; (2) The policy-maker has zero bargaining power, hence his/her utility is constant with introduction of contributions.

To see crowding-out, denote the equilibrium lobby's compensations in Stage 2 as $C(\mu)$. We know that the policy-maker's indirect utility $W(\mu)$ is derived as an upper envelope of the expected utilities over policies, $W(\mu) := v(d^*(\mu), \mu)$. Since $v(d, \mu)$ is linear in μ for each $d \in D$, the upper envelope from the linear functions is convex. Now, by the two assumptions stated above, $C(\mu) = W(\mu) - W(d_h; \mu)$, and this is the difference between a convex and linear function. As a result, $C(\mu)$ is convex. The lobby's expected utility is $\hat{U}(\mu) = 1 - C(\mu)$. As the difference between a linear and convex function, it is a concave function. With a concave $\hat{U}(\mu)$, the lobby is risk-averse over posteriors and does not lobby. Bennedsen and Feldmann (2006) conclude that lobbying is crowded-out by the introduction of contributions. But notice that if any of the two assumptions is lifted, the chain of reasoning is broken and pure substitution (full crowding out) is no longer present.

To receive complementarity for a single lobby requires a special framework. Dahm and Porteiro (2008a,b) derive complementarity in the case of a single lobby for the high costs of pressure in the contribution subgame. However, this result is derived in the setup with the contribution subgame defined as a pressure subgame, where the shape of $U(\mu)$ depends on the distribution of the policy-maker's types. Hence, it may be potentially fragile to other methods of modeling contribution subgames and to other distributions of the policy-maker's types, as discussed in Sect. 6.1.1.

If a mechanism gives lobbying and payments two different functions, they can be complements even by assumption. For example, in pay-to-play politics, only those who pay the access fee are allowed to present their evidence (Austen-Smith 1995; Lohmann 1995; Cotton 2009, 2012). Or, lobbying facilitates payments to the policy-maker: Damania et al. (2004) suppose that lobbying may be directed at undermining law enforcement so as to make corruption easier.

6.2.2 Selected Evidence

Measuring both payments and information provision is uneasy. Here, we cover only evidence in which bribes are a measure of contributions and political influence is a measure of information provision.

Three studies have recently examined the strategic substitution between corruption and political influence (Campos and Giovannoni 2007; Bennedsen et al. 2011; Kaufmann and Vicente 2011), mainly using the World Bank's World Business Environment Survey. Bennedsen et al. (2011) confirm that the stage of development and maturity of a firm is conducive to lobbying. Firms' characteristics affect corruption and political influence in opposite directions. Large, old, government-owned, and export-oriented firms use more influence than bribes; smaller firms or firms in a fragmented industry choose corruption. When using instruments, the influential firms appear to use less corruption, but corrupt firms are no less influential. To reconcile the two results, they propose the idea of *asymmetric substitutes*: Strong firms have access to both political influence and bribes, whereas weak firms can only resort to corruption. The asymmetric substitution is a challenge to competitive informational lobbying, the main prediction of which is that the competitors with high stakes bribe under almost any condition. Also Chong and Gradstein (2010) confirm that political influence is associated with large firms, especially in countries with a low level of institutional quality. Yet weaker evidence is found for the political influence of state-owned enterprises, exporting firms and firms in competitive industries.

Kaufmann and Vicente (2011) use country-level evidence from the Executive Opinion Survey 2004–2005 of the Global Competitiveness Report of the World Economic Forum. Their definition of legal corruption involves variables that proxy lobbying, such as the *Influence of Well-Connected in Procurement*, *Influence of Legal Contributions to Political Parties*, *Independence of the Judiciary from Influence*, and *Influence on Laws and Regulations-Respondent's Industry*. For illegal corruption, the variables proxy rather direct payments to policy-makers, such as *Illegal Donations to Political Parties*, *Frequency of Bribes in Influencing Laws and Policies*, and *Frequency of Bribes in Procurement*. Their evidence shows that more illegal corruption occurs at low-income levels, low political accountability and high inequality levels. An increase in income inequality, business cycle slumps, structural changes and pro-competitive practices make firms more likely to bribe than lobby.

A disadvantage of this approach is that corruption is comprised of activities targeting the rule enforcers (with only a small portion of political corruption), whereas lobbying is directed towards rule makers (Campos and Giovannoni 2007; Harstad and Svensson 2011). This is not perfectly aligned with our theoretical interest in the production of political influence. Also, the key differences between the instruments are not only be on the cost side and externalities they produce, but also in the qualities of the product, namely the durability of and appropriability of benefits. For example, the fact that lobbying is preferred to corruption by large firms in developed countries may be explained by the barriers to entry and appropriability of lobbying benefits.

7 Conclusions

This review models a policy-maker as a strategic player who benefits both from information and payments provided by special interests. Our main focus is on non-cooperative environment with explicit informational and game-theoretic micro-foundations in which lobbies simultaneously use both information and payments. We demonstrate that the interaction between information and payments primarily depends on whether the lobbying mechanism is *lobby-and-pay*, or *pay-and-lobby*. We focus on the developments in the relevant modeling in the last three decades, and especially examine search, persuasion, and contributions, that on are the cornerstones of the multiple-tools models. Next, the survey presents a variety of modeling components such as policy-makers' and lobbies' instruments, policy-makers' and lobbies' commitments, bargaining protocols, the structure of evidence, message costs, and the (non)observability of a search. We try to highlight at least some consequences of adopting particular modeling choices.

The survey also helps to understand some unexpected features of the lobbying process. For instance, we show that a competitive lobbying contest is often detrimental to contestants. Special interests often gain low or even negative payoffs when lobbying instruments are available and therefore may benefit from regulation of the instruments. First and foremost, competition in a lobbying contest dissipates much of the prize. Contribution caps normally reduce the competition, which redistributes part of the prize from the policy-maker to the lobbies. Secondly, the possibility of concealing evidence generates pessimistic policy-makers' expectations that force lobbyists to make excessive efforts. Mandatory disclosure of reports avoids this information trap and may serve to the benefit of lobbies. Thirdly, if a strategic policy-maker can design access fees to improve information and collect campaign funds at the same time, he or she effectively extracts a huge surplus from a lobby which is generated whenever the policy-maker learns information favorable to the lobby.

The review also presents stylized facts on lobbying, in particular corporate lobbying, generated predominantly from cross-country surveys, lobbying data disclosed in the US since 1995 and event studies (e.g., Borisov et al. 2014). We observe a large benefit-cost ratio for those firms that lobby. Firms resort to relatively few intermediaries who dominate the market with lobbying influence. Only large and connected firms tend to lobby; small firms would rather bribe. The distribution of intermediaries' returns is highly skewed. In terms of instruments for influence, with minor exceptions, lobbying and bribes are substitutes rather than complements. The survey suggests ways how to accommodate these facts with the theory.

We have limited ourselves to one-to-one and many-to-one lobbying interactions, and abstained from the analysis on the intermediation which is typical for many-to-many interactions. Among others, intermediation involves a choice over working alone or hiring an intermediary. The tradeoff is typically attributed to aspects such as specialization, networks, and economies of scale (Johnson 1996), but one idea relevant for political influence is also the lack of transparency associated with intermediation. An even more modern and promising approach to intermediation is a growing body of research on the two-sided market in lobbying (Groll and Ellis 2014; Kang and You 2015).

Acknowledgements I would like to thank participants at ICOPEAI 2015 for their useful comments. An early version of the paper circulated under the title 'Corporate lobbying: a review of the recent literature' (Gregor 2011). Financial support from the Grant Agency of the Czech Republic No. P402/12/G097 is gratefully acknowledged.

References

Ansolabehere, S., de Figueiredo, J. M., & Snyder, J. M. (2003). Why is there so little money in U.S. politics? *Journal of Economic Perspectives, 17*(1), 105–130.

Austen-Smith, D. (1995). Campaign contributions and access. *American Political Science Review, 89*, 566–581.

Austen-Smith, D. (1998). Allocating access for information and contributions. *Journal of Law, Economics, and Organization, 14*(2), 277–303.

Austen-Smith, D., & Banks, J. S. (2000). Cheap talk and burned money. *Journal of Economic Theory, 91*(1), 1–16.

Austen-Smith, D., & Banks, J. S. (2002). Costly signaling and cheap talk in models of political influence. *European Journal of Political Economy, 18*, 263–280.

Ball, R. (1995). Interest groups, influence and welfare. *Economics and Politics, 7*(2), 119–146.

Baron, D. (1989). Service-induced campaign contributions and the electoral equilibrium. *Quarterly Journal of Economics, 104*, 45–72.

Baye, M. R., & Hoppe, H. H. (2003). The strategic equivalence of rent-seeking, innovation, and patent-race games. *Games and Economic Behavior, 44*, 217–226.

Becker, G. (1983). A theory of competition among pressure groups for political influence. *Quarterly Journal of Economics, 98*, 371–400.

Bennedsen, M., & Feldmann, S. E. (2002). Lobbying legislatures. *Journal of Political Economy, 110*(4), 919–946.

Bennedsen, M., & Feldmann, S. E. (2006). Informational lobbying and political contributions. *Journal of Public Economics, 90*, 631–656.

Bennedsen, M., Feldmann, S. E., & Lassen, D. D. (2011). *Lobbying and Bribes: A Survey-Based Analysis of the Demand for Influence and Corruption*. CESifo Working Paper 3496.

Bertrand, M., Bombardini, M., & Trebbi, F. (2014). Is it whom you know or what you know? An empirical assessment of the lobbying process. *American Economic Review, 104*(12), 3885–3920.

Blanes-i-Vidal, J., Draca, M., & Fons-Rosen, C. (2012). Revolving door lobbyists. *The American Economic Review, 102*(7), 3731–3748.

Borisov, A., Goldman, A., & Gupta, N. (2014). *The Corporate Value of (Corrupt) Lobbying*. European Corporate Governance Institute (ECGI) Finance Working Paper No. 423/2014.

Brocas, I., & Carrillo, J. D. (2007). Influence through ignorance. *RAND Journal of Economics, 38*(4), 931–947.

Campos, N., & Giovannoni, F. (2007). Lobbying, corruption and political influence. *Public Choice, 131*, 1–21.

Chakraborty, A., & Harbaugh, R. (2010). Persuasion by cheap talk. *American Economic Review, 100*, 2361–2382.

Chari, R., Hogan, J., & Murphy, G. (2010). *Regulating lobbying: A global comparison*. Manchester: Manchester University Press.

Che, Y., & Gale, I. L. (1998). Caps on political lobbying. *American Economic Review, 88*(3), 643–651.

Che, Y., & Gale, I. L. (2006). Caps on political lobbying: Reply. *American Economic Review, 96*(4), 1355–1360.

Chong, A., & Gradstein, M. (2010). Firm-level determinants of political influence. *Economics and Politics, 22*(3), 233–256.

Corchon, L., & Dahm, M. (2010). Foundations for contest success functions. *Economic Theory, 43*(1), 81–98.

Cotton, C. (2009). Should we tax or cap political contributions? A lobbying model with policy favors and access. *Journal of Public Economics, 93*, 831–842.

Cotton, C. (2012). Pay-to-play politics: Informational lobbying and contribution limits when money buys access. *Journal of Public Economics, 96*, 369–386.

Cotton, C. (2016, in press). Competing for attention: Lobbying time-constrained politicians. *Journal of Public Economic Theory, 18*, 642–665.

Cotton, C., & Dellis, A. (2016, in press). Informational Lobbying and Agenda Distortion. *Journal of Law, Economics, and Organization*. doi:10.1093/jleo/eww005.

Dahm, M., & Porteiro, N. (2008a). Side-effects of campaign finance reform. *Journal of the European Economic Association, 6*(5), 1057–1077.

Dahm, M., & Porteiro, N. (2008b). Informational lobbying under the shadow of political pressure. *Social Choice and Welfare, 30*, 531–559.

Damania, R., Fredriksson, P. G., & Mani, M. (2004). The persistence of corruption and regulatory compliance failures: Theory and evidence. *Public Choice, 121*(3), 363–390.

de Figueiredo, J. M., & Cameron, C. (2009). Endogenous cost lobbying: Theory and evidence. In *CELS 2009–4th Annual Conference on Empirical Legal Studies*. Available at SSRN: http://ssrn.com/abstract=1443559.

Dewatripont, M., & Tirole, J. (2005). Modes of communication. *Journal of Political Economy, 113*(6), 1217–1238.

Epstein, G. S., Mealem, Y., & Nitzan, S. (2011). Political culture and discrimination in contests. *Journal of Public Economics, 95*, 88–93.

Epstein, G. S., & Nitzan, S. (2004). Strategic restraint in contests. *European Economic Review, 48*, 201–210.

Epstein, G. S., & Nitzan, S. (2006a). Reduced prizes and increased effort in contests. *Social Choice and Welfare, 26*, 447–453.

Epstein, G. S., & Nitzan, S. (2006b). The politics of randomness. *Social Choice and Welfare, 27*, 423–433.

Fang, H. (2002). Lottery versus all-pay auction models of lobbying. *Public Choice, 112*(3–4), 351–371.

Farrell, J. (1993). Meaning and credibility in cheap-talk games. *Games and Economic Behavior, 5*(4), 514–531.
Felgenhauer, M. (2010). Transparency and special interests. *Economics Letters, 106*(1), 4–7.
Gely, R., & Zardkoohi, A. (2001). Measuring the effects of post-government employment restrictions. *American Law and Economics Review, 3*, 288–311.
Giovannoni, F., & Seidmann, D. J. (2007). Secrecy, two-sided bias and the value of evidence. *Games and Economic Behavior, 59*(2), 296–315.
Glazer, A. (2008). Bargaining with rent seekers. *Journal of Public Economic Theory, 10*(5), 859–871.
Glazer, J., & Rubinstein, A. (2004). On optimal rules of persuasion. *Econometrica, 72*(6), 1715–1736.
Gregor, M. (2011). *Corporate Lobbying: A Review of the Recent Literature*. IES Working Paper 32/2011. Institute of Economic Studies, Faculty of Social Sciences, Charles University in Prague.
Gregor, M. (2015). To invite or not to invite the lobby, that is the question. *The B.E. Journal of Theoretical Economics, 15*(2), 143–166.
Groll, T., & Ellis, C. J. (2014). A simple model of the commercial lobbying industry. *European Economic Review, 70*, 299–316.
Grossmann, M., & Dietl, H. (2012). Asymmetric contests with liquidity constraints. *Public Choice*, 150, 691–713.
Grossman, G. M., & Helpman, E. (2001). *Special interest politics*. Cambridge, MA: MIT Press.
Harstad, B., & Svensson, J. (2011). Bribes, lobbying, and development. *American Political Science Review, 105*(1), 46–63.
Henry, E. (2009). Strategic disclosure of research results: The cost of proving your honesty. *Economic Journal, 119*, 1036–1064.
Hillman, A., & Ursprung, H. (1988). Domestic politics, foreign interests, and international trade policy. *American Economic Review, 78*, 729–745.
Johnson, P. E. (1996). Corporate political offices in a rent-seeking society. *Public Choice, 88*, 309–331.
Kamenica, E., & Gentzkow, M. (2011). Bayeasian Persuasion. *American Economic Review, 101*, 2590–2615.
Kang, K. (2016). Policy influence and private returns from lobbying in the energy sector. *Review of Economic Studies, 83*(1), 269–305.
Kang, K., & You, H. Y. (2015). Lobbyists as matchmakers in the market for access. Mimeo.
Kaplan, T. R. & Wettstein, D. (2006). Caps on political lobbying: Comment. *American Economic Review, 96*(4), 1351–54.
Kaufmann, D., & Vicente, P. C. (2011). Legal corruption. *Economics and Politics, 23*(2), 195–219.
Kerr, W. R., Lincoln, W. F., & Mishra, P. (2014). The dynamics of firm lobbying. *American Economic Journal: Economic Policy, 6*(4), 343–379.
Konrad, K. A. (2009). *Strategy and dynamics in contests*. Oxford: Oxford University Press.
Lagerlöf, J. (1997). Lobbying, information, and private and social welfare. *European Journal of Political Economy, 13*, 615–637.
Lagerlöf, J. (2007). A theory of rent seeking with informational foundations. *Economics of Governance, 8*(3), 197–218.
Lohmann, S. (1993). A signaling model of informative and manipulative political action. *American Political Science Review, 87*(2), 319–333.
Lohmann, S. (1995). Information, access, and contributions: A signaling model of lobbying. *Public Choice, 85*, 267–284.
Milgrom, P. (1981). Good news and bad news: Representation theorems and applications. *Bell Journal of Economics, 12*, 350–391.
Milgrom, P. (2008). What the seller won't tell you: Persuasion and disclosure in markets. *Journal of Economic Perspectives, 22*(2), 115–131.
Münster, J. (2006). Lobbying contests with endogenous policy proposals. *Economics and Politics, 18*(3), 389–397.

Pastine, I., & Pastine, T. (2010). Politician preferences, law-abiding lobbyists and caps on political contributions. *Public Choice, 145*, 1–21.

Polk, A., & Schmutzler, A. (2005). Lobbying against environmental regulation vs. lobbying for loopholes. *European Journal of Political Economy, 21*, 915–931.

Potters, J., & van Winden, F. (1992). Lobbying and asymmetric information. *Public Choice, 74*, 269–292.

Rayo, L., & Segal, I. (2010). Optimal information disclosure. *Journal of Political Economy, 118*(5), 949–987.

Richter, B. K., Samphantharak, K., & Timmons, J. F. (2009). Lobbying and taxes. *American Journal of Political Science, 53*(4), 893–909.

Ryan, M., & Vaithianathan, R. (2011). Verifiability and neologism-proofness in a Sender-Receiver game. *Journal of Economic Behavior & Organization, 79*(3), 256–262.

Siegel, R. (2009). All pay contests. *Econometrica, 77*(1), 71–92.

Sisak, D. (2009). Multiple-prize contests – the optimal allocation of prizes. *Journal of Economic Surveys, 23*(1), 82–114.

Skaperdas, S., & Vaidya, S. (2012). Persuasion as a contest. *Economic Theory, 51*(2), 465–486.

Sloof, R. (1998). *Game-theoretic models of the political influence of interest groups*. Boston: Kluwer Academic Publishers.

Snyder, J. M. (1990). Campaign contributions as investments: The U.S. House of Representatives 1980–1986. *Journal of Political Economy, 98*, 1195–1227.

Sobel, J. (2010). Giving and receiving advice. Presented at *Econometric Society 10th World Congress*.

Stone, D. F. (2011). A signal-jamming model of persuasion: Interest group funded policy research. *Social Choice and Welfare, 37*(3), 397–424.

The Economist (2011). Money and politics. *The Economist*, October 1st 2011, p. 70.

Tovar, P. (2011). Lobbying costs and trade policy. *Journal of International Economics, 83*, 126–136.

Tullock, G. (1980). Efficient rent-seeking. In J. M. Buchanan, R. D. Tollison, & G. Tullock (Eds.), *Toward a theory of the rent-seeking society* (pp. 97–112). College Station: Texas A&M University Press.

van Winden, F. (2003). Interest group behavior and influence. In C. K. Rowley & F. Schneider (Eds.), *The encyclopedia of public choice* (pp. 118–129). Berlin: Springer.

Wang, Z. (2010). The optimal accuracy level in asymmetric contests. *The B.E. Journal of Theoretical Economics, 10*(1). Art. 13.

Financial Sector Regulation and the Revolving Door in US Commercial Banks

Elise S. Brezis and Joël Cariolle

1 Introduction

The "revolving door" is a practice quite widely in use in the United States, in which heads of state agencies, after completing their bureaucratic terms, are entering the very sector they have regulated. This phenomenon is also frequent in France, where it is coined "*pantouflage*", and in Japan, coined "*amakudari*" (descent from heaven). Research conducted and data collected by the research group *Corporate Europe Observatory* strongly suggest that this process is also significant within EU institutions.[1]

In the last two decades, the revolving door and the intertwining relations between governments and private groups have intensified. The revolving door became so widespread in the financial sector that it has been pointed out by the OECD (2009) and NGO's (Transparency International-UK 2011) as a major cause of the 2008 financial crisis. In its 2009 report on the revolving door and the financial crisis, the OECD therefore stressed the necessity to set appropriate rules and procedures to control conflicts of interest generated by this phenomenon (OECD 2009).[2]

[1] See http://corporateeurope.org/revolvingdoorwatch

[2] See also www.opensecrets.org. on the revolving door inside the US financial sector. See also Transparency International-UK (2011) and Transparency International (2010), which lay down the negative as well as positive effects of the Revolving door.

E.S. Brezis (✉)
Bar-Ilan University, Ramat Gan, Israel
e-mail: Elise.Brezis@biu.ac.il

J. Cariolle
FERDI, Clermont Ferrand, France
e-mail: joel.cariolle@ferdi.fr

N. Schofield, G. Caballero (eds.), *State, Institutions and Democracy*,
Studies in Political Economy, DOI 10.1007/978-3-319-44582-3_3

The revolving door affects the economy through two main channels: a positive one as well as a negative one. On the one hand, this movement of individuals between the public and private sectors may lead to some positive effects and can be desirable. Indeed, the revolving door allows recruiting qualified bureaucrats, and the knowledge the bureaucrat has accumulated while working in the public sector is put in use in their future position.

On the other hand, the revolving door is a recruitment process leading to distortive effects due to strong risk of conflicts of interest and state capture. In fact, in countries where explicit bribes cannot be paid safely, it is an important vehicle for corrupt deals with negative consequences on the economy, leading to lenient regulations which encouraged crisis as in 2008, as emphasized by the OECD (2009) and Transparency International-UK (2011).

The purpose of this chapter is to present a proxy for the distortive effect of the revolving door—the Revolving Door Index (RDI)—in the financial sector. This index will permit to raise awareness on the need of regulating the revolving door process and preventing conflicts of interests that have led to the financial crisis.

The distortive effects of the revolving door stem from the concentration of former regulators in a small number of firms. These "politically-connected firms" through the revolving door will gain significant advantage over their "non-connected" competitors, by benefitting from a wide range of preferential treatments: tailored regulations, lenient regulatory oversight, biased procurement processes, and so on. In fact, the literature widely emphasizes how politically-connected firms can capture regulations and regulatory agencies. As a consequence, our index is derived from a Herfindahl formula, which has the particularity to pinpoint concentration of former regulators among firms. After having defined this index, we calculate it for the top-five US commercial banks.[3]

The chapter is divided in five parts. In Sect. 2, we present the related literature and detail the distortionary effects of the revolving door. The literature stresses that state capture and conflicts of interests induced by the revolving door can take different forms. We more specifically focus on the public resources misallocation and unfair competition between connected and less connected firms. We also focus on how the difference in leniency of regulators towards the various firms can lead to crisis and bubbles.

Section 3 presents a small model illustrating how there can be concentration of revolvers in some specific firms, and how this inequality between firms can affect their profits. We develop the notion of bureaucratic capital, which is a way for public regulators to get high revenues in the private sector, and a way for firms to get influence over regulatory agencies.

In Sect. 4, we develop our Revolving Door Index. In part 5, we propose an empirical illustration of the index using data on the revolving door in the five biggest US commercial banks. Part 6 presents some policy conclusions related to the regulation of the financial sector.

[3] We should underline that this is the first attempt to develop an index related to the revolving door, since we did not find another attempt in the literature to develop such an index.

2 The Literature

The literature on the revolving door, and its effects on the economy, is quite diverse. We divide this literature in three main related subjects: studies addressing firm's performance; those focusing on corruption prevalence; and those documenting distortions created by the revolving door. The rationale behind these different aspects is that the revolving door positively influences firms' market valuation, but this 'over'-value very often results from rent-seeking (including corruption), thereby generating economic distortions in the economy.

2.1 Revolving Door, Political Connections, and Firms' Performances

The literature on the effects of the revolving door on firms' performance is part of a broader literature emphasizing the effects of political connections on firms' performances and aggregate outcomes. It focuses on the value for specific firms of different types of connections, which include campaign contributions (Claessens et al. 2008), personal relationships (Amore and Bennedsen 2013; Johnson and Mitton 2003), political party membership (Khwaja and Mian 2005), and the revolving door (Faccio 2006; Luechinger and Moser 2014).

In emerging and industrialized economies, where relationships linked to kinship, friendship, or ethnicity have been progressively replaced by market-based relationships in economic exchanges (Rajan and Zingales 1998; Andvig 2006), the revolving door is a major source of political connections with significant positive effects on firms' value (Faccio 2006; Cingano and Pinotti 2013; Kramarz and Thesmar 2013; Goldman et al. 2013; Luechinger and Moser 2014).

The revolving door brings value to the firm through two separated types of movements of individuals between public agencies and regulated private entities. The first movement involves regulators (ministers, legislators, high-level officers, advisers) who leave the public sector to enter the private sector they have regulated. The second involves employees of regulated companies entering the government, the Parliament, or key regulatory agencies.

On the theoretical side, the expected effects of the revolving door on firms' value can be derived from the theoretical rent-seeking models emphasizing the allocation of talents between productive activities and unproductive rent-seeking activities (Murphy et al. 1991; Cingano and Pinotti 2013). This literature focuses mainly on the movement from the public sector towards the private one, and stresses that the revolving door may increase firm's performances via two competing channels:

1. *The productive channel or "schooling hypothesis":* the revolving door is used to increase firm's productivity because revolved regulators may be more skilled and familiar with the regulations.

2. *The rent-seeking channel or "quid-pro-quo hypothesis"*: the revolving door is used to capture public resources, through legal and illegal means, and increases the value of the firm without increasing efficiency. Under the quid-pro-quo hypothesis, politically-connected firms through the revolving door therefore benefit from preferential treatments, which are sources of economic distortions.

Do empirical evidences support the prevalence of the rent-seeking or the productive channel?

About the productive channel, except for Lucca et al. (2014) who provide evidence which tend to support the "schooling hypothesis" in the banking sector,[4] most empirical studies tend to invalidate the hypothesis of a productive revolving door process. Cingano and Pinotti (2013), using a sample of Italian firms, have shown that corporate appointments of local politicians do not increase firms' productivity. Kramarz and Thesmar (2013), and Bertrand et al. (2006) show that French firms politically-connected through their CEOs and directors tend to overpay them, are less likely to fire them if they underperform, are associated with poorer accounting performances and excessive employment rates, and make bigger and worse acquisitions. Moreover, Slinko et al. (2005) find that politically-powerful Russian firms adversely affect the performance of small or politically-powerless firms, by getting administrations creating excessive regulation over the latter and by diverting government spending. By contrast, they find that politically-powerless firms invest more and are more productive in regions where the concentration of firms' political power is lower.

About the rent-seeking channel, empirical studies suggest that the revolving door affects the allocation of resources in the economy through three mains areas: (i) public procurement, (ii) access to finance and (iii) tax exemptions.

Regarding public procurement, the revolving door gives firms the power of diverting state resources by biasing public procurement process. Indeed, Goldman et al. (2013) show that, following the 1994 House and Senate election, the presence of former politicians affiliated to the winning (losing) political party at the boards of U.S companies increases (decreases) the total value of awarded public procurement contracts.

In a similar vein, Cingano and Pinotti (2013) show that corporate appointments of local Italian politicians shift public demand toward connected firms, especially in high public expenditure and high corruption provinces, and that this shift reduces public good provision by 20 %.

About the access to finance, a great body of the literature emphasizes that firms using the revolving door are associated with a preferential access to finance (Khwaja and Mian 2005; Boubakri et al. 2012) and are more likely to be bailed out after financial distress (Faccio et al. 2006).

The revolving door also affects benefits from government allocations. Country-level empirical studies suggest that firms engaged in the revolving door are likely

[4]Whose study has received strong criticism from Kane (2014).

to use their influence so as to benefit from tax exemption and subsidy allowance. Slinko et al. (2005) show that politically influential firms in Russia are allowed to accumulate more arrears in tax, supplier, and wage payments than their non-connected counterparts. Faccio (2010) also shows that politically connected firms pay lower tax than other firms.[5]

In summary, the literature supports that politically connected firms through the revolving door are unlikely to be productive, are likely to shape and law and regulations and divert state resources to their own benefit, and to reduce overall productivity in the private and the public sectors.

2.2 *Revolving Door and Corruption*

Transparency International (2011) and the OECD (2009) pointed out that the revolving door may induce various schemes of conflicts of interest, during and after regulators' term in public office, thereby generating unlawful behavior. Moreover, the revolving door is also related to lawful but unethical behavior termed "legal corruption" by Kaufmann and Vicente (2011).[6] Kaufmann has referred this behavior to: "efforts by companies and individuals to shape law or policies to their advantage, often done quasi-legally, via campaign finance, lobbying or exchange of favors to politicians, regulators and other government officials. [...] In its more extreme form, legal corruption can lead to control of entire states, through the phenomenon dubbed 'state capture,' and result in enormous losses for societies."[7]

As an indication of the strong link between the revolving door process and corrupt practices, cross-country analyses (Faccio 2006, 2010) and case studies (Cingano and Pinotti 2013; Slinko et al. 2005) have shown that the differential in economic returns between connected and non-connected firms increases in high corruption environments.

More specifically, connected firms through the revolving door may derive undue advantages by legally and illegally influencing the formulation, adoption, and implementation of law, regulations, and public policies in three different ways:

(i) When firms are connected to (former) Members of Parliaments (MPs), they may influence law and regulations enactment in their favor. Slinko et al. (2005) illustrate the legislative power of connected firms in Russia by detailing the budget law of Kamchatskaya Oblast of 2001, which provides large financial support to a single firm, Akros, among many others. In their attempt to measure

[5]In related empirical studies, Johnson and Mitton (2003) show that Malaysian firms personally tied to the executive have preferred access to subsidies. Adhikari et al. (2006) find similar evidences in Indonesia.

[6]See also Brezis (2013).

[7]See also Kaufmann, D. "Rethinking the Fight Against Corruption", Brookings Opinion, 29/11/2012.

the concentration of the political power of Russian firms, they show that at least 41 % of firms in their sample benefit from legislation biased in their favor. Such biased legislation may offer firms various benefits, such as tax breaks, subsidized loan, and investment credits.

(ii) When firms are connected to (former) ministers and their advisers, they may influence the upstream formulation and implementation of policies and regulations, or take advantage from nonpublic information about the company or on the regulated industry (insider trading). For instance, in the UK, a former Defense minister and his permanent secretary have been disgraced for having taken a job with a Defense firm, AgustaWestland, with which the ministry signed a £1.7 billion contract while they were in office. They have indeed been found to have joined the defense company after having chosen it as a preferred bidder for a Ministry of defense's project, for which no other firms have been invited to bid.[8]

(iii) When firms are connected to (former) high-level officials, they may influence the downstream implementation of regulations. As an illustration, the French "Mediator Affair" involved former officials of the French and European drug agencies prosecuted for unlawful behaviors when they unduly granted the marketing authorization of the Mediator. Indeed, they were accused of getting ludicrous contracts from *Servier*, the pharmaceutical group which commercialized the Mediator, after their leaving the public agencies they worked for. These officials, who became consultants for pharmaceutical industries, are suspected to have monetized this favor in exchange of various lucrative contracts.[9]

2.3 *Powerful Firms, Revolving Door and Economic Distortions*

The literature on revolving door also focuses on the institutional configurations under which it generates economic distortions. Interestingly, the literature on state capture and political influence (Hellman and Kaufmann 2004; Hellman et al. 2003; Slinko et al. 2005) supports that it is the concentration of political power among private firms which is the source of such economic distortions. These studies stress that a concentrated political power results into state capture by influential firms, which not only undermines trust in public institutions and property rights, but is also associated with lower levels of tax compliance, higher levels of bribery, and higher barriers to entry for small or less influential firms.

[8]Jason Groves, "Disgraced Hoon gets top job at defence firm Westland—which landed £1.7 bn contract when he was Defence Secretary" in Dailymail the 18th may 2011, http://bit.ly/jrSdSg

[9]"Mediator: l'enquête sur les conflits d'intérêts s'accélère" *Le Point,* February, 18, 2013, http://www.lepoint.fr/t/1-1629071. See also "Conflit d'intérêts: Aquilino Morelle visé par une enquête préliminaire" in Les Echos, April 22, 2014, http://po.st/lKK8Sx

There have been some attempts to proxy economic distortions generated by the “inequality of influence” within the private sector. Hellman and Kaufmann (2004) propose a survey-based measure of *crony bias* reflecting “the extent to which firm managers believe that there are other actors with more or less influence than their own collective voice on the basic rules shaping their business environment” (Hellman and Kaufmann 2004, p. 101). Slinko et al. (2005) use the regional Herfindahl index of firms’ preferential treatments incorporated into regional laws and regulations, as a proxy of the regional regulatory capture by politically powerful firms in Russia.

Therefore, building on this literature, we hereafter present a small model explaining why some firms use the revolving more than other, and a measure of the risk of state capture induced by revolving door movements, the revolving door index (RDI).

3 The RDI: Theoretical Foundations

We present a small model illustrating how there can be concentration of revolvers in some specific firms, and how this inequality between firms can affect their profits. We develop the notion of bureaucratic capital, which is the way regulators get power over firms.

Indeed, conflicts of interests and State capture stem from the supply by the regulator of bureaucratic capital. Bureaucratic capital is the capital the bureaucrat creates while she is in the public service. The most common type of bureaucratic capital is investing in good relationships with the lower bureaucracy or accumulating a specific knowledge on the ins of the system, which are all valuable lawful behaviors in the future; but it can also consists in unlawful behaviors such as designing unnecessary complex regulations (red tape), regulations tailored to specific private interests, or influencing procurement or subsidy allowance processes towards specific firms.

In this market, the supply of bureaucratic capital is determined by each regulator, while the demand is determined by the firms. This bureaucratic capital will enter in firms’ production function while the regulator is in office and after his term in office when the “revolved bureaucrats” or “revolvers” are hired by the revolving firm, leading to the capture of state resources (including regulations, public contracts, allowances, tax removals, etc.) through lawful and unlawful behaviors. This new market for bureaucratic capital will permit to explain why firms want to pay rents for hiring a previous regulator in their board.

We present some elements of theory explaining how the relative stock of bureaucratic capital brings value to the firm, which may lead to its concentration among few firms. In this configuration, the revolving door generates unfair competition, state capture and therefore distorts economies. Our model sets a monopolistic competition framework, in which regulated financial firms produce differentiated financial services and use bureaucratic capital, supplied by bureaucrats, as input in their production function.

3.1 The Regulators and the Supply of Bureaucratic Capital

The intermediate-goods sector consists of monopolistic firms and in consequence, they are regulated by the regulators. The regulators maximize the present value of their income, while the firms maximize profits.

During her time in office, the regulator regulates and receives an income, but at the same time, she creates *bureaucratic capital*—i.e., networks within public agencies, unnecessary complex regulations, influence in public resource allocation processes, knowledge of the ins-and-outs of the system, and so on. This bureaucratic capital is valuable to the firms in the financial industry, and thus, once she has left the public service, the regulator can cash-in on this bureaucratic capital.

The structure of the model is simple. During her term as a regulator, she acquires bureaucratic capital of size H_i, which costs her effort of size E_i in monetary terms. Extending networks in public offices, creating red-tape, influencing the allocation of public resources, accumulating knowledge of regulations requires efforts, which are costly to the regulator.[10] The amount of bureaucratic capital created by E_i units of effort of the regulator's employment as regulator is monotonically increasing and concave in the total amount of effort given by *h(E)*, with $\partial h/\partial E > 0$ and $\partial^2 h/\partial E^2 < 0$. We therefore assume that the level of bureaucratic capital is a concave function of the amount of effort invested, the same for all bureaucrats, which takes the specific form: [11]

$$H_i\left(E_i\right) = \left[\left(1+\gamma\right)E_i\right]^{1/1+\gamma} \quad \gamma > 0 \tag{1}$$

After leaving her job as regulator, the bureaucrat works for a period of length τ, in the industry that she regulated. She receives in top of her "regular" salary a rent related to the "bureaucratic capital", H_i she has accumulated.

[10] These costs consists of time spent in bureaucratic capital formation, and when unlawful behaviors are undertaken, these costs may encompass ethical costs, the social stigma, the probability of being caught and sanctioned.

[11] We are aware that for some bureaucrats, who are either more social, or with less "ethical values", it is easier to either create connection with other people, or create redundant regulations. For purpose of simplicity, we assume that bureaucrats have the same "production" function of bureaucratic capital, and that these social factors are not linked to ability, since removing this assumption does not affect the results. Moreover, the "effort" which describes either social or ethical costs, are in monetary terms.

The regulator maximizes her lifetime income which consists of (i) earnings which are not related to the creation of bureaucratic capital, denoted Ω, and (ii) of income related to the creation of bureaucratic capital, which equals to the net income she gets when having entered the industry. After passing the revolving door, she will be able to sell her bureaucratic capital, H_i at price q for a number of years τ so that her total income is:

$$V_i = \Omega - E_i + \tau q H_i (E_i) \tag{2}$$

Equation (2) can be rewritten as a function only of the level of bureaucratic capital, by substituting E_i from Eq. (1). We get:

$$V_i = \Omega - \frac{H_i^{1+\gamma}}{1+\gamma} + \tau q H_i \tag{3}$$

From the point of view of the bureaucrat, there is an optimal level of bureaucratic power, $\hat{H}$ she wants to stock, which maximize her income—Eq. (3) and is:

$$\widehat{H}_i = (\tau q)^{1/\gamma} \tag{4}$$

Equation (4) describes the "supply" function of bureaucratic capital by the regulator as an increasing function of the price q. We now turn to discuss the behavior of the firm and its demand for bureaucratic elite.

3.2 *The Demand of Bureaucratic Capital*

The business financial elite is composed of entrepreneurs, who are at the head of intermediate-goods firms j, and who produce goods, x_j, in a monopolistic competitive environment. The output is a function of two factors of production. The first is capital, k_j. Following the standard Romer model, we assume that the production function takes the simple form:

$$x_j = k_j.$$

However, in our model, the output x_j is also function of a second factor of production, which is the level of bureaucratic capital accumulated by the regulator hired by the firm. This increase in the stock of bureaucratic capital H_j results in an increase in production inasmuch firm j has more bureaucratic capital than other firms. If all firms have the same amount of bureaucratic capital—equilibrium situation which happens in the long run—then bureaucratic capital is useless for the firm.[12] So, the production function in sector s takes the form:

$$x_j = k_j \left(\frac{H_j}{H_a} \right)^{\varphi} \quad \varphi > 0 \tag{5}$$

where H_j is the level of bureaucratic capital produced by the regulator of firm j, and H_a is the average level of bureaucratic capital owned by the other firms.

Note that if $H_j = H_a$, then the output is just $x_j = k_j$, no matter the average level of bureaucratic capital. This stems from the rent-seeking hypothesis developed in the literature review according to which the revolving door does not increase production through improved productivity but through rent-seeking. If bureaucratic capital was a productivity factor, it would increase firm j's production, whatever the stock of bureaucratic capital accumulated by its competitors. This comes from the basic idea that, in a given sector, if each firm is as influent as its competitors, then using influence to increase production is useless. Therefore, although having hired a bureaucrat may bring an advantage over other firms from the firm j point of view, it is pure waste from a social point of view.

So, the profit maximization for an intermediate financial firm is:

$$Max\ \pi_j = p_j\left(x_j\right) x_j - rk_j - qH_j \tag{6}$$

where r is the cost of real capital, k_j; and q the cost of the bureaucratic capital H_j, that is the remuneration given to the bureaucrat for bringing bureaucratic capital to the firm.

Each firm maximizes profits by finding the optimal amount of output, x_j and bureaucratic capital H_j. Note that Eq. (6) can be rewritten in the following way:

$$Max\ \pi_j = p_j\left(x_j\right) x_j - rx_j \left(\frac{H_j}{H_a} \right)^{-\varphi} - qH_j \tag{7}$$

According to Eq. (7), firms get higher profits only if bureaucratic capital is unevenly distributed in their industry. In other words, over-performing firms exist because of the industry-level concentration of bureaucratic capital in their hands. This notion of 'inequality' between firms underlies the construction of the revolving door index, which reflects the concentration of revolvers in only a small number of firms.

4 The Revolving Door Index

Following Eq. (7) and in line with the literature on state capture (Kaufmann and Vicente 2011; Slinko et al. 2005; Hellman and Kaufmann 2004), we proxy the distortions created by the revolving door (RD) by measuring the sector concentration of

[12]This model which emphasizes the relative amount of bureaucratic capital is therefore related to the concentration index we present in the next section.

revolvers and RD movements. According to our model, the distortive effects of the revolving door in the economy come from the uneven distribution of bureaucratic capital among firms in the private sector. Therefore, a high concentration of RD movement from firms to public agencies, and from public agencies to firms, indicates that this bureaucratic capital mostly accrue to few firms, thereby inducing a high risk of *state capture*.

In consequence, the Revolving Door Index (RDI) will be derived from a Hirschman–Herfindahl index formula.[13] It measures the sector concentration of revolvers among private firms,[14] and is computed as follow for sector s:

$$RDI_s = 100 \times \frac{\sqrt{\sum_{i=1}^{I}\left(\frac{r_i}{R_s}\right)^2} - \sqrt{1/N_s}}{1 - \sqrt{1/N_s}} \tag{8}$$

The RDI is between 0 and 100. R_s is the total number of revolved regulators in sector s, r_i is the number of revolved regulators in firm i, and N_s is the number of firms in sector s. The higher the index in sector s, the stronger the concentration of revolved regulators, and in consequence, the greater the distortions in sector s.

The RDI is expressed as the ratio of the difference between the actual Herfindahl and that of a competitive sector ($\sqrt{1/N}$), over the difference between the Herfindahl of a monopolistic or monopsonistic sector and that of a competitive sector ($1 - \sqrt{1/N}$). Therefore, in some way this ratio can be interpreted as a share, so that a RDI of size λ would mean that the allocation of bureaucratic capital is λ% of a perfectly concentrated market.

This index does not focus on the total amount of revolvers, and focuses only on the damaging effects of the revolving door by calculating the distortions between firms. We now turn to calculate the RDI for the banking sector.

5 The RDI: Empirical Illustration

We propose an empirical application of the RDI in the context of the US banking sector. US banks have indeed given over the last decades various and striking illustrations of how they used the revolving door to shape regulations to their own interests. We measure the concentration of revolvers—i.e., regulators engaged in the revolving door—among the top five biggest US commercial banks, ranked

[13]This Herfindahl is a rescaled and normalized version of the Herfindahl, and is, used by the UNCTAD to compute its export concentration index (UNCTAD 2013, p. 212): http://unctad.org/en/PublicationsLibrary/tdstat38_en.pdf

[14]We will see in section IV.3. that another declination of the RDI may consist in focusing on public agencies as unit of analysis.

according to their total revenue in 2015: JPMorgan, Bank of America, Citigroup, Wells Fargo, and Goldman Sachs. Some of these large banks, commonly referred as "too-big-to-fail" banks, are known to massively use the revolving door to accumulate bureaucratic capital, and hence represent an interesting (although non representative) sample of firms for RDI calculations.

Raw information on revolvers and revolving door movements is collected from two important websites documenting the movements between the business and the bureaucracy in the US: *Opensecret.org* and *Littlesis.org*. Information on revolvers identity, revolving door movements, the position occupied in public and private offices is compiled, checked, corrected or completed using additional sources of information on revolvers' career: LinkedIn webpage, Wikipedia, newspapers, business websites, SEC files, government agencies websites, and firms' own websites. The Appendix provides additional information on the data collection and treatment methodology. The resulting dataset covers a total of 236 revolvers involved in 299 revolving door movements, undertaken between 1933 and 2015, but mostly occurring in the 2000's.[15]

5.1 *Typology of Revolved Regulators*

Individuals considered as revolvers are current (former) employees in private firms who are former (current) members of a US federal agency: ministry, parliament, or a relevant regulatory agency.[16] We also identify individuals moving from (into) key agencies charged with financial matters: the Treasury, the White House, The Federal Deposit Insurance Company, the Commodity Future Trading Commission, intelligence agencies[17] (FBI, CIA, NSA), the Security and Exchange Commission,

[15]The oldest revolving door movement we documented involves Sidney J. Weinberg, a.k.a "Mr. Wall Street", who was former executive of Goldman Sachs from 1927 to 1969, and who was simultaneously counselor at the White House from 1933 to 1969. See https://en.wikipedia.org/wiki/Sidney_Weinberg

[16]Local or State regulatory agencies—such as the NY housing regulatory agency—as well as foreign agencies—such as the European Central Bank—are therefore excluded from the analysis. However, the examination of the data showed that many firms hire revolvers that at some point of their career joined the Advisory Board of a local Federal Reserve Bank, especially the Federal Reserve Bank of New York, position that can be hold simultaneously with a job in the private sector. Given the many scandals that arose from the leakage Federal Reserve System's secret documents from the NY Fed towards financial firms, we considered individuals holding position in both private firms and local Federal Reserve Banks as revolvers. For similar concerns, we also consider as revolvers the many individuals that have integrated the 2008 Obama Transition Team while keeping their job in the private sector. See Appendix.

[17]Intelligence agencies play a key role in enforcing financial regulation and prosecuting cases of financial malpractices before the courts. The strong interest of financial firms in recruiting members of intelligence agencies can be illustrated by the recent hiring of Patrick Carroll, former FBI agent who headed securities fraud and white collar crime and who locked up Bernard Madoff, by Goldman Sachs. See http://fortune.com/2015/05/26/goldman-sachs-hire-fbi-agent/

the Federal Reserve System, and the US Trade Representative.[18] Therefore, we collected information on revolvers' experience in these key regulatory agencies.

We focus on both private-to-public and public-to-private revolving door movements. While the model emphasizes how revolvers sell their bureaucratic capital after leaving public office, it is also common to see private sector officers cashing in huge exit bonanza before taking public responsibilities.[19] Therefore, three types of revolving door flows are identified:

- *Type 1, public-to-private*: former members of a relevant ministry, administration, or legislature currently hold an executive position in a regulated company.
- *Type 2, private-to-public*: former executives of a regulated company are currently members of a relevant ministry, administration, or legislature.
- *Type 3, two-sided*: when individuals undertake symmetric movements from a private firm to a public agency to the same private firm, or from a public agency to a private firm to the same public agency, they can favour firms both during and after their term in public office. Moreover, given the likelihood of agency capture in this configuration, two-sided RD movements are expected to yield additional value to the firm and are therefore counted threefold: one dummy for the public-to-private sector movement, on dummy for the private-to public-sector movement, and an additional dummy variable indicating this symmetric back-and-forth movement. Therefore, an individual undertaking this revolving door path is associated with three revolving door movements for the company.

We should note that there exists also back-and-forth movements from a given public agency to a private agency and then to another public agency. From our point of view, they are counted twice separately: for each revolved regulator achieving this movement is associated one dummy variable equal to 1 when he has moved from the first public agency to the private financial company, one dummy variable when has moved from the financial company to the other public agency. Therefore, an individual undertaking this revolving door path is associated with two RD movements for the company.

Revolved regulators are also differentiated according to the influence and power of their (former) public sector positions: *Influential revolvers* are those who hold or have held top-level position in the government, in a relevant administration, or who have been members of parliament; while *non-influential revolvers* are those who hold or have held lower-level positions in the government or in a relevant administration.

The Appendix presents a more detailed description on data collection process and on the typology of revolving door movements.

[18]We also considered the US Trade Representative as a finance-related agency because of its key role for banks' implementation in foreign markets, notably through trade agreement negotiations.

[19]See for instance Samantha Lachamn, "Hillary Clinton Backs Bill That Would Ban 'Golden Parachutes' For Wall Street Bankers", The Huff, Aug 31, 2015. http://www.huffingtonpost.com/entry/hillary-clinton-wall-street-golden-parachutes_us_55e44f14e4b0b7a9633974eb

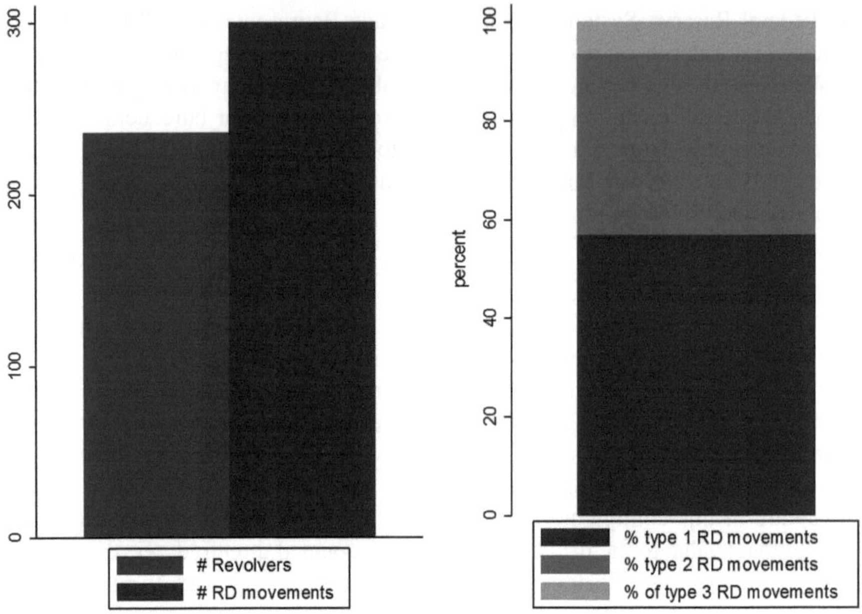

Fig. 1 The revolving door process in the five biggest US commercial banks

5.2 *Anatomy of the Revolving Door: Statistical Highlights*

We now present key statistical highlights on the revolving door process that accrued to the five biggest commercial banks—JPMorgan, Citigroup, Goldman Sachs, Bank of America and Well Fargo—and that occurred over the last 80 years.[20]

Figure 1 shows that there were 236 revolvers engaged in 299 revolving door movements (types 1, 2 and 3), and that most RD movements (57 %) are public-to-private (type 1) ones. Only 6 % of revolving door movements are two-sided. This small share is consistent with the sensitivity of such a revolving door path, which can be interpreted as explicit attempts by firms to capture specific agencies.

Figure 2 plots the distributions of private-to-public sector movements and public to private sector movements over time.[21] Most revolving door movements have occurred between 1990 and 2015. Private-to-public movements display two distribution modes located around 1992 and 2007–2008, while public-to-private movements display one distribution mode located around 2007–2008. Therefore,

[20]The oldest revolving door movement we documented involves Sidney J. Weinberg, a.k.a "Mr. Wall Street", who was former executive of Goldman Sachs from 1927 to 1969, and who was counselor at the White House from 1933 to 1969. He notably advised Presidents Roosevelt, Eisenhower, Johnson. See https://en.wikipedia.org/wiki/Sidney_Weinberg

[21]Two-sided revolving door movements are excluded from the distributions.

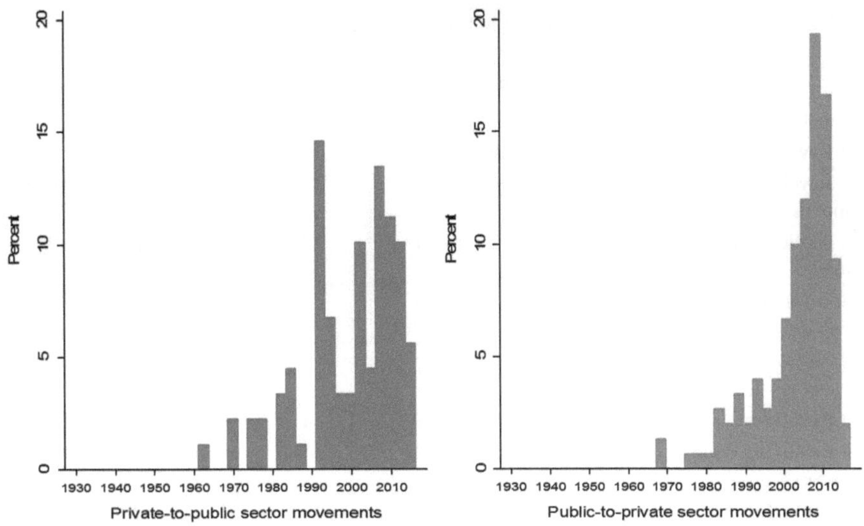

Fig. 2 Time distribution of revolving door movements

the beginning of the last financial crisis is concomitant with an intensity peak in revolving movements.

So as to have a further idea of how big banks are engaged in the RD process, we present a decomposition of the initial stock of revolvers and revolving door movements (Panel A) into sub-movements (see Table 1). This decomposition emphasizes movements of influential revolvers (Panel B), revolvers from key federal agencies (Panel C), and influential revolvers moving from/into key federal agencies (Panel D). We measure the concentration of each RD movement and sub-movement by computing its associated RDI.

Compared to the other firms, Goldman Sachs, and in a lesser extent Citigroup and JPMorgan (hereafter called G-C-J), appear as major beneficiaries of RD movements. This evidence can also be related by their status of "too-big-to-fail" banks which probably make them to be the main demanders on the bureaucratic capital market. As a result, this distribution displays relatively low concentration patterns, with a RDI around 10–15 % (see panel A). We now show that concentration becomes more acute when we break down revolving movements into various typologies.

Indeed, the uptake of bureaucratic capital by G-C-J becomes striking when we restrict the sample to influential revolvers only, when we look at movements involving key federal agencies, and when we focus on two-sided RD movements. In fact, two-sided movements of influential revolvers, particularly influential revolvers from key federal agencies, display the highest concentration scores (of around 26 % and 24 %).

Moreover, the concentration of type-1 RD movements—i.e., public-to-private movements—from key federal agencies (panels C and D) is the one presenting

Table 1 The revolving door breakdown in five major US commercial banks

	JPMorgan	BofA	Citigroup	Wells Fargo	Goldman Sachs	Total	RDI
Panel A—General situation							
# Revolvers	**59**	**29**	**55**	**12**	**81**	**236**	**9.96**
# Revolving door moves	**78**	**36**	**71**	**12**	**102**	**299**	**10.79**
# Public-to-private moves	47	22	41	10	50	**170**	7.96
# Private-to-public moves	26	12	25	2	45	**110**	16.03
# Two-sided moves	5	2	5	0	7	**19**	15.73
Panel B—Influential revolvers							
# Revolvers	**31**	**20**	**28**	**4**	**50**	**133**	**11.96**
# Revolving door moves	**43**	**22**	**42**	**4**	**66**	**177**	**13.15**
# Public-to-private moves	25	14	19	4	32	**94**	9.81
# Private-to-public moves	15	8	19	0	29	**71**	17.48
# Two-sided moves	3	0	4	0	5	**12**	25.70
Panel C—Key Federal Agencies							
# Revolvers	**37**	**16**	**39**	**3**	**58**	**153**	**14.56**
# Revolving door moves	**50**	**21**	**52**	**3**	**77**	**203**	**15.01**
# Public-to-private moves	28	11	30	3	38	**110**	12.97
# Private-to-public moves	18	8	18	0	33	**77**	18.80
# Two-sided moves	4	2	4	0	6	**16**	15.04
Panel D—Influential revolvers from key fed agencies							
# Revolvers	**23**	**14**	**23**	**1**	**40**	**101**	**14.80**
# Revolving door moves	**33**	**15**	**36**	**1**	**54**	**139**	**15.85**
# Public-to-private moves	18	9	17	1	28	**73**	14.40
# Private-to-public moves	12	6	15	0	22	**55**	17.17
# Two-sided moves	3	0	4	0	4	**11**	24.40

the highest divergence from the general situation (panel A). These movements' concentration in panel C significantly increases compared to type 1 RD movements in panel A, and almost double when we focus on type-1 movements of influential revolvers from key federal agencies.

Thus, this brief anatomy of the revolving door among the five biggest US commercial banks show that, despite of the restrictiveness of our sample of firms, the concentration of bureaucratic capital increases when the emphasis is placed on features of the RD expected to yield significant value to the firm—the influence of revolvers, the agency membership, and the direction of revolving door movements; and that these concentration patterns mostly benefit to Goldman Sachs, JPMorgan and Citigroup.

5.3 *Ways Forward*

Our theoretical formalisation of the bureaucratic capital market led us to emphasize the concentration of revolving door movements within the various firms of the banking sector. One drawbacks of our approach is that it partly eludes what is happening within the public sector. The following sub-section tries to lift the veil on the creation of bureaucratic capital within public agencies, which could, *in fine*, enable policymakers to identify effective safeguards against drifting of the revolving door process.

5.3.1 Measuring Agency Capture

In our model, we focus on one agency regulating one specific firm. However, the reality is more complex, and there are many agencies which have a say on the regulation of sectors, especially the financial sector. It is therefore interesting to check the public agencies from which there are RD movements to the banking sector.

Table 2 displays the distribution of revolvers and RD movements from the five biggest US banks among key federal public agencies regulating the financial sector. We observe that among the 299 total revolving door movements, 68 % of RD movements are related to nine agencies. Among these flows, 30 % of RD movements are connected to the Federal Reserve System, 18 % of RD movements are connected to the Treasury, and 12 % of RD movements are connected to the White House.[22]

In consequence, we compute a public-sector declination of the Revolving Door Index, switching the unit of analysis from the firm to the regulatory agency:

$$RDI_a = 100 \times \frac{\sqrt{\sum_{j=1}^{K} \left(\frac{r_a}{R_s}\right)^2} - \sqrt{1/N_a}}{1 - \sqrt{1/N_a}} \qquad (9)$$

The RDI_a is again between 0 and 100. R_s is the total number of revolved regulators in sector s, r_a is the number of revolved regulators in agency a, and N_a is the number of agencies targeted or "captured" by sector s. A high concentration

[22]In terms of revolvers (and not movements), it is slightly lower, see Table 2.

Table 2 The revolving door breakdown in the nine key federal agencies

	White house	Treasury	SEC	Fed system	FDIC	Congress bank and finance committees	CFTC	Intelligence agency	US trade rep	Total	RDI
Panel A—Reference situation											
# Revolvers	**24**	**35**	**12**	**38**	**6**	**18**	**3**	**9**	**8**	**153**	**11.25**
# Revolving door moves	**33**	**48**	**17**	**59**	**7**	**18**	**3**	**10**	**8**	**203**	**14.88**
# Public-to-private moves	19	28	8	20	2	16	1	8	8	110	10.95
# Private-to-public moves	11	16	7	32	5	2	2	2	0	77	25.12
# Two-sided moves	3	4	2	7	0	0	0	0	0	16	**32.80**
Panel B—Influential revolvers											
# Revolvers	**18**	**23**	**11**	**25**	**2**	**6**	**3**	**8**	**5**	**101**	**11.90**
# Revolving door moves	**25**	**36**	**14**	**39**	**2**	**6**	**3**	**9**	**5**	**139**	**16.46**
# Public-to-private moves	15	20	7	14	0	4	1	7	5	73	13.70
# Private-to-public moves	8	12	6	21	2	2	2	2	0	55	22.21
# Two-sided moves	2	4	1	4	0	0	0	0	0	11	**32.95**
Panel C—Systemic revolvers[a]											
# Revolvers	**5**	**11**	**2**	**13**	**2**	**2**	**0**	**4**	**2**	**41**	**18.15**
# Revolving door moves	**6**	**16**	**4**	**23**	**3**	**2**	**0**	**4**	**2**	**60**	**23.74**
# Public-to-private moves	2	8	1	8	1	1	0	4	2	27	19.17
# Private-to-public moves	4	7	2	10	2	1	0	0	0	26	26.10
# Two-sided moves	0	1	1	5	0	0	0	0	0	7	**61.35**

[a] Systemic revolvers are individuals that have worked in at least two of the five banks of our sample

of entry and exit movements of revolvers from specific agencies indicates a high concentration in bureaucratic capital creation, inducing a high risk of *agency capture* by sector *s*.

At first sight, revolving door concentration patterns (RDI values) for the general case is not different from the results in Table 1 (Panel A, bold numbers). We get an RDI of 14.88 for the total and of 32.80 for the two-sided moves. However, when we focus on what we define as systemic revolvers (revolvers that undertook two-sided back-and-forth movements), then the RDI for two-sided moves is of 61.35. This high RDI is due to the fact that the two-sided movements are almost all concentrated within the Fed (see Panel C, last row).

5.3.2 Regulating the Revolving Door

Our index has permitted to pinpoint the loopholes of the revolving door, although we are aware that there is a need for even more data. It is clear that by measuring the sectorial concentration of the revolving door, the RDI is a first step to size up the distortive power of the revolving door, and will permit over time to compare progresses made by the government in implementing safeguards against the risks of conflict of interest associated with promiscuous public and private elites.

The effect of policies and regulations aimed at controlling the revolving door should be reflected in RDI values in various ways. For instance, post-employment restrictions requiring a minimum "cooling-off" period after public office, by slowing down public-to-private and two-sided revolving door flows, should erode the influence of revolved regulators over public decision-making after their term in public office. Their value for captor firms should therefore decrease, as well as the incentives to hire them for rent-seeking purpose. As a consequence, the concentration of public-to-private revolving door flows would be reduced.

Regarding private-to-public revolving door flows (in which the RDI is quite high), pre-employment restrictions preventing former private sector employees from undertaking certain tasks in the public sector should somehow incite captor firms' staff to refrain from entering the public sector. Empowered commissions on civil service, and rules of transparency (such as asset disclosure for parliamentarians and ministers) should also drag down the concentration of revolved regulators by decreasing the value of revolved regulators for rent-seeking firms.

In conclusion, our RDI calculation is a first step to estimate conflicts of interests and state capture induced by the revolving door.

6 Conclusion

In the last decade, the economic literature as well as the media have stressed that the revolving door has negative effects on the economy, and it was even connected to the crisis affecting the financial sectors from 2008 and on.

The literature has stressed that the revolving door process (i) is a major source of political connections for private firms operating in industrialized and emerging economies, (ii) is related to specific corruption risks during the enactment and implementation of laws and regulations, and (iii) adversely affects economic outcomes.

It is quite clear that, unfortunately, regulations of the revolving door process are scarce and when they exist, they are often poorly enforced. Moreover, the revolving door still beneficiates from a great tolerance of the public for it (although decreasing these last years), partly due to a lack of measurement for its prevalence and impact on economies. Indeed, there have been no attempts to use objective data in order to build an actionable and internationally comparable proxy measure of the distortions created by the revolving door process.

This chapter presents an index which permits to quantify the distortionary effects of the revolving door. We first have presented a simple model which is the underlying motivation for this specific formulation of the RDI. In our model, public agents create bureaucratic capital during their term in public office, and the revolving door allows them 'selling' this bureaucratic capital to private firms. In fact, this model stresses that, although having hired a bureaucrat may give an advantage to a given firm over its competitors, it is pure waste from a social point of view. Therefore, the revolving door distorts sectors in which revolvers are unevenly distributed. This is the rationale for our RDI index: a normalized Herfindahl of the concentration of the revolving door movements at the sector level.

As an illustration, we have applied the RDI to the US banking sector, and measured the concentration of revolvers—i.e., regulators engaged in the revolving door—among the top five biggest US commercial banks, commonly referred as "too-big-to-fail" banks. Our data show that the concentration of bureaucratic capital increases when the emphasis is on influential civil servants. Moreover, these concentration patterns mostly benefit to Goldman Sachs, and in a lesser extent to JPMorgan and Citigroup. We also highlight that the Federal Reserve System, the Treasury, and to a lesser extent the White House, are the administrations mostly prone to be captured by banks.

Therefore, the Revolving Door Index (RDI) is an insightful measure of the distortions induced by the revolving door process. It also appeared that the RDI can be used as a tool for assessing the effectiveness of pre and post-employment restrictions, for raising awareness on the need of regulating the market for bureaucratic capital, and therefore for reducing the risk of conflict of interests induced by this process.

Appendix: Methodological Notes

The top five commercial banks are selected according to the *Fortune 500* rankings of commercial banks (with regard to their total revenue). Other famous financial firms strongly involved in the revolving door—such as Fannie Mae, or Freddie Mac—are diversified financial firms and are therefore not included in the sample.

The main raw data sources are on the one hand, the Opensecrets.org website, managed by the Center for Responsive Politics, and on the other hand, Littlesis.org. Opensecrets.org and Littlesis.org provides open-access and documented information on the revolving door process and lobbying in the US political system.[23] Primary raw data on the revolving door in the top five US commercial banks is therefore drawn from these two websites. Information on revolving door career path is then cross-checked, further documented, corrected when necessary, by complementary information drawn from Linkedin, Wikipedia, muckety.org, Beyond.com, zoominfo.com, Bloomberg.com, Businessweek, Business Insider, journal articles and other web sources. When this additional source cannot confirm entry–exit dates in the public and private sectors, dates provided by open secret are taken. If multiple converging additional sources diverge with Opensecrets entry–exit dates, the former are taken into account.

Once data is retrieved and cross-checked, a second round of data collection is undertaken, by searching on google potential additional revolved regulators using the following association of keywords: "name of the company + revolving door", "name of the company + political appointment", "name of the company + lobbyist".

Data Treatment

Revolvers are sorted by the influence and power of their government positions. For those individuals with complex careers and had been in a government position multiple times, the positions that were taken in account are the most influential positions during revolvers' careers.

Influential positions considered are the following:

- Chairman of the Federal Reserve, and New York's Fed.
- Chief of Staff to the White House.
- White House: Assistant to the President, congressional liaison.
- Chief of Staff/Assistant Secretary of Treasury.
- Congressmen.
- Deputy/Director of the National Economic Council.
- Chairman and directors of the Securities and Exchange Commission (SEC).
- Managing Executive of SEC's Division of Enforcement.
- Chief of Staff/Chairman of Commodities Futures Trading Commission.
- Deputy Secretary/Secretary/Assistant Secretary/Under Secretary of US State Department.
- Secretary of Navy.
- Secretary of Treasury.

[23] see for instance Ansolabehere et al. (2003).

- Ambassador.
- Head/Deputy of the Office of the United States Trade Representative.
- Chief of Staff to President's Council of Economic Advisors.
- Director of Office of Management and Budget.
- Director of Congressional Budget Office.
- National Security Advisor.
- Attorney General (Deputy).
- Consul to the President.
- State Governors.
- Chief of Staff to Chairman of the US Consumer Product Safety Commission.
- Director, chief of staff of the Federal Housing Finance Agency.
- Director, chief of staff of the Federal Deposit Insurance Corporation.
- Member of the Congress' Finance Committee.

All other positions in federal agencies, boards or commissions are less influential. Positions in local agencies, commissions or boards are not considered, except for members of advisory boards of local agencies of the Federal Reserve System and chief of staff of State governors, who are recorded as less influential revolvers.

The specific case of the Obama-Biden 2008 transition period: This period allowed many banks' employees integrating Obama transition team without imposing them to leave their position in the private financial sector. We nevertheless consider the membership to this team as less influential position in public office.

Former employees of WaMu, Chase Manhattan Bank, Dime Bancorp and Bank One are considered as part of JP Morgan stock of revolvers. Former employees of Primerica and Travelers group are considered as part of Citigroup stock of revolvers. Former employees of Merrill Lynch and Security Pacific Bank are considered as part of Bank of America stock of revolvers. Former employees of West One Bank are considered as US Bancorp's stock of revolvers.

The Coding of Revolving Door Back-and-Forth Movements

Movements from a given public agency to a private to another public agency are counted twice separately: for each revolved regulator achieving this movement is associated one dummy variable equal to 1 when he has moved from the first public agency to the private financial company, one dummy variable when has moved from the financial company to the other public agency. Therefore, an individual following this revolving door path is counted twice for a given company.

However, back-and-forth movements from a private firm to a public agency to the same private firm, or from a public agency to a private firm to the same public agency, are expected to yield additional value to the firm. They are therefore counted threefold: one dummy for the public to the private sector movement, on dummy for the private to public sector movement, and an additional dummy variable indicating this symmetric back-and-forth movement. Therefore, an individual following this revolving door path is counted threefold for a given company.

References

Adhikari, A., Derashid, C., & Zhang, H. (2006). Public policy, political connections, and effective tax rates: Longitudinal evidence from Malaysia. *Journal of Accounting and Public Policy, 25*, 574–595.

Amore, M. D., & Bennedsen, M. (2013). The value of political connections in a low-corruption environment. *Journal of Financial Economics, 110*, 87–402.

Andvig, J. C. (2006). Corruption and fast change. *World Development, 34*(2), 328–340.

Ansolabehere, S., Figueiredo, J. M., & Snyder, J. M. (2003). Why is there so little money in U.S. politics? *Journal of Economic Perspectives, 17*(1), 105–130.

Bertrand, M., Kramarz, F., Schoar, A., & Thesmar, D. (2006). *Politicians, firms and the political business cycle: Evidence from France* (Working Paper). University of Chicago.

Boubakri, N., Guedhami, O., Mishra, D., & Saffar, W. (2012). Political connections and the cost of equity capital. *Journal of Corporate Finance, 18*, 541–599.

Brezis, E. S. (2013). *Promiscuous elites, the revolving door, and economic growth* (Working Paper series). Israël: Bar-Ilan University.

Brezis, E. S., Paroush, J., & Weiss, A. (2002). *Red tape: Oiling the hinges of the 'revolving door'* (Working Paper series). Israël: Bar-Ilan University.

Brezis, E. S., & Weiss, A. (1997). Conscientious regulation and post-regulatory employment restrictions. *European Journal of Political Economy, 13*, 517–536.

Claessens, S., Feijen, E., & Laeven, L. (2008). Political connections and preferential access to finance: the role of campaign contributions. *Journal of Financial Economics, 88*, 554–580.

Cingano, F., & Pinotti, P. (2013). Politicians at work: The private returns and social costs of political connections. *Journal of the European Economic Association, 11*(2), 433–465.

Faccio, M. (2006). Politically connected firms. *The American Economic Review, 96*, 369–386.

Faccio, M. (2010). Differences between politically connected and nonconnected firms: A cross-country analysis. *Financial Management, 39*(3), 905–927.

Faccio, M., Masulis, M. W., & McConnell, J. J. (2006). Political connections and corporate bailouts. *Journal of Finance, 61*(6), 2597–2635.

Goldman, E., Rocholl, J., & So, J. (2013). Politically connected boards of directors and the allocation of procurement contracts. *Review of Finance, 17*(5), 1617–1648.

Hellman, J., Jones, G., & Kaufmann, D. (2003). Seize the state, seize the day: State capture and influence in transition economies. *Journal of Comparative Economics, 31*, 751–773.

Hellman, J., & Kaufmann, D. (2004). The inequality of influence. In J. Kornai & S. Rose-Ackerman (Eds.), *Building a trustworthy state in post-socialist transition*. New York, NY: Palgrave Macmillan.

Johnson, S., & Mitton, T. (2003). Cronyism and capital controls: Evidence from Malaysia. *Journal of Financial Economics, 67*, 351–382.

Kane, E. J. (2014). Comment on: The revolving door and worker flows in banking regulation by D. Luca, A. Seru, and F. Trebbi. *Journal of Monetary Economics, 65*, 33–35.

Kaufmann, D., & Vicente, P. C. (2011). Legal corruption. *Economics and Politics, 23*(2), 195–219.

Khwaja, A. I., & Mian, A. (2005). Do lenders favor politically connected firms? Rent provision in an emerging financial market. *The Quarterly Journal of Economics, 120*(4), 1371–1411.

Kramarz, F., & Thesmar, D. (2013). Social network in the boardroom. *Journal of the European Economic Association, 11*(4), 780–807.

Laffont, J. J., & Tirole, J. (1996). *A theory of incentives in procurement and regulation*. Cambridge, MA: The MIT Press.

Lucca, D., Seru, A., & Trebbi, F. (2014). The revolving door and worker flows in banking regulation. *Journal of Monetary Economics, 65*, 17–32.
Luechinger, S., & Moser, C. (2014). The value of the revolving door: Political appointees and the stock market. *Journal of Public Economics, 119*, 93–107.
Murphy, K. M., Shleifer, A., & Vishny, R. W. (1991). The allocation of talent: Implication for growth. *The Quarterly Journal of Economics, 106*(2), 503–530.
OECD. (2009). *Revolving doors, accountability and transparency—Emerging regulatory concerns and policy solutions in the financial crisis*. Paris: Public Governance Committee.
Rajan, R., & Zingales, L. (1998). Which capitalism? Lesson from the East Asian Crisis. *Journal of Applied Corporate Finance, 11*, 40–48.
Slinko, I., Yakovlev, E., & Zhuravskaya, E. (2005). Law for sale: Evidence from Russia. *American Law and Economics Review, 7*(1), 284–318.
Transparency International (2010). Regulating the Revolving Door (Working Paper Series), Berlin.
Transparency International. (2011). *Cabs for hire? Fixing the revolving door between government and business*. UK: Transparency International.
United Nations Conference on Trade and Development. (2013). *Handbook of statistics*. New York, NY and Geneva: United Nations.

Part II
Democracy, Participation and Electoral Politics

The Rhetoric and Reality of Austerity: Electoral Politics in Britain 2010 to 2015

Paul Whiteley, Harold D. Clarke, and Marianne Stewart

1 Introduction

Britain experienced its first peace-time coalition government since the 1930s after the 2010 general election. It was put together very hastily and, to the surprise of many people, it survived for the 5 years planned in the original Coalition Agreement between the Conservatives and Liberal Democrats. By 2015 it was widely anticipated in the polls that the Parliament emerging from the general election would also be deadlocked and another possible coalition government formed, but this did not happen. Instead, the Conservatives won a surprising, but narrow election victory, capturing just short of 51 % of the seats in the House of Commons.

We have argued elsewhere that the economic recovery was the most important factor which explains the result (Clarke et al. 2015). The story of the election supports the longstanding proposition in the economic voting literature that incumbent parties are rewarded by the voters for a good economic performance and are punished by a bad one (see for example Key 1968; Lewis-Beck 1988; Norpoth 1997; Lewis-Beck and Stegmaier 2007; Duch and Stevenson 2008; Whiteley et al. 2013). To repeat a famous phrase coined by James Carville, a chief campaign advisor to Bill Clinton in the 1992 US presidential election: 'It's the economy, stupid!'

However, the story is not as straightforward as it seems, since we will argue in this paper that the initial economic policy adopted by George Osborne when he became Chancellor of the Exchequer in 2010 would have almost certainly lost the election for the Conservatives had he not changed course in the middle of

P. Whiteley (✉)
University of Essex, Colchester, UK
e-mail: whiteley@essex.ac.uk

H.D. Clarke • M. Stewart
University of Texas at Dallas, Richardson, TX, USA

N. Schofield, G. Caballero (eds.), *State, Institutions and Democracy*,
Studies in Political Economy, DOI 10.1007/978-3-319-44582-3_4

the Parliament. The original austerity plan embedded in the Coalition Agreement of 2010 (Coalition Programme for Government 2010) derived from a mixture of theoretical ideas about how the economy works and how it should be managed, but also from electoral considerations. When the original strategy looked increasingly like it would fail to deliver it was quietly abandoned and an alternative adopted which was ultimately successful in delivering an election victory. This change of strategy was never announced and indeed has not been acknowledged subsequently following the 2015 general election. So the gap between the rhetoric and the reality of austerity policies continues.

This paper examines three issues: firstly, why the austerity strategy was devised in the first place and what it involved; secondly, why it was abandoned in the midterm of the electoral cycle and a different approach adopted; and thirdly why the new strategy delivered an electoral victory for Conservatives in 2015. The starting point of the analysis is the Coalition Agreement which is a useful benchmark against which to judge the subsequent economic performance of that government. This document was jointly authored by the Conservatives and Liberal Democrats and it identified the aims and objectives of the new government. The agreement described the Government's economic strategy and provides a yardstick for determining how it worked in practice during the life of the Parliament.

2 The Coalition Agreement

After the hung Parliament emerged from the general election of 2010 negotiations between the parties on forming a new government began. It was clear from the beginning that a Liberal Democrat-Conservative coalition would have a comfortable working majority with 364 seats in the House of Commons, whereas a Liberal Democrat-Labour coalition would have been a minority government with only 315 seats. The latter would have needed the support of the Nationalists, the Greens and Northern Irish MPs to obtain a bare majority. So the only real choice of a coalition partner from Liberal Democrat leader, Nick Clegg's, perspective was the Conservatives.

The agreement was signed by both party leaders after a period of about a week of negotiations and the document subsequently published. It had the characteristics of party manifesto setting out policy goals under 31 different headings involving the economy, banking reforms, national security, the NHS and foreign affairs. The most important policy concern related to the economy, which was still being affected by the Great Recession which started after the run on the Northern Rock Bank in 2007. In their respective party manifestoes published prior to the general election the Conservatives and Liberal Democrats were at the opposite ends of the spectrum on the issue of dealing with the ballooning deficit arising from the recession. The former wanted big reductions to be rapidly implemented by large cuts in public expenditure, whereas the latter wanted significantly smaller reductions in spending coupled with tax hikes to be phased in over a longer period.

The Liberal Democrats achieved a lot in their negotiations with the Conservatives and a subsequent analysis showed that many of their policy proposals were adopted by the new government (Quinn et al. 2011). But in relation to the central strategic goal of reducing the deficit the Conservative view prevailed as the following quote from the Coalition Agreement document demonstrates:

> 'We will significantly accelerate the reduction in the structural deficit over the course of a Parliament, with the main burden of deficit reduction borne by reducing spending rather than increasing taxes' (Coalition Programme for Government 2010: 15).

This statement set the tone for the economic policy of the new government.

3 Economic Objectives and Policies from 2010

Initially, the Coalition Agreement specified cuts of £6 billion to non-frontline services in the financial year 2010–2011, while at the same time announcing an emergency budget aimed at further reducing the deficit. This budget planned spending cuts of £32 billion per year by 2014–2015 and a spending review was announced later in the year to work out the details. In addition, an £11 billion reduction in welfare spending and a 2-year freeze in public sector pay were announced. On the taxation side, the budget raised an additional £8 billion in revenue by increasing the value-added tax from 17.5 to 20 % and by increasing the standard and higher rates of Insurance Premium Tax to 6 % and 28 %, respectively, from January 2011 (HM Treasury 2010). Other measures included a bank levy forecast to raise £1.2 billion in 2011–2012 and £2.3 billion in 2012–2013, and an increase in the capital gains tax for the highest earners.

The emergency budget report summarized the plans in the following terms:

> 'The budget and the plans the Government inherited represent a total consolidation of £113 billion per year by 2014–15 and £128 billion per year by 2015–16, of which £99 billion per year comes from spending reductions and £29 billion per year from net tax increases. By 2015–16 77 per cent of the total consolidation will be delivered through spending reductions' (See HM Treasury 2010: 2).

This was a very large fiscal squeeze and, drawing on forecasts from the newly established Office of Budget Responsibility, the Coalition Government claimed that their policies would ensure that public-sector borrowing would decline to 1.1 % of GDP by 2015–2016, the structural deficit would be eliminated by 2014–2015 and a surplus of 0.8 % of GDP would emerge by 2015–2016. They also argued that public-sector net debt would peak at 70 % of GDP in 2013–2014 before declining to 67 % of GDP in 2015–2016. This was a highly ambitious plan which aimed to deal with the deficit within the lifetime of a single Parliament.

It bears emphasis that the economics of the plan were pre-Keynesian in the sense that they prioritized a balanced budget over all else, arguing that this was an essential precondition for economic recovery. Chancellor of the Exchequer George Osborne's views on this issue were set out in a speech delivered in April 2009 before the election:

> The crisis has also exposed two fundamental arguments. The first is whether, when you are already borrowing too much, you should deliberately try to borrow your way out of debt. David Cameron and I have consistently argued against this irresponsible course of action[1]

This meant that the newly formed government embarked on a policy of deflation in a context in which traditional policy-making would have taken the opposite course of action. In fact the previous Labour government led by Prime Minister Gordon Brown had largely pursued the traditional approach in the immediate aftermath of the financial crash and so this was a real break with the past. The new strategy embraced what Keynes had called the 'Treasury view' in response to the Great Depression of the 1930s, and which the famous economist had strongly opposed. There is a puzzle explaining why the Conservatives adopted an essentially pre-Keynesian strategy at this time. From an electoral point of view it was risky, since the economic voting literature clearly indicates that voters are likely to punish parties which preside over recessions.

There are three interrelated factors which help to explain the strategy. First, there are the values and beliefs of Conservative politicians such as David Cameron and George Osborne who were products of the Thatcher era of the 1980s. This was a period when ideas advanced by the economic philosopher Friedrich Hayek about the desirability of a small state and the efficiency of markets, were dominant in the party. Margaret Thatcher had genuinely wanted to reduce the size of the state, thinking this was a necessary precondition for creating prosperity in a world where she saw the private sector as the source of innovation and growth, and state spending and taxation were largely a burden on entrepreneurship and prosperity. Essentially, the new generation of Conservative leaders had imbibed those ideas and looked back at the Thatcher era as a golden age of economic prosperity and electoral success for the party.

Secondly, there was a fundamental failure of macroeconomics to explain the world as it is and therefor to anticipate and subsequently deal with the Great Recession. The unorthodox economist Hyman Minsky was one of the few academics to predict the recession, and as his biographer points out, Minsky explained this failure in the following terms:

> 'The neoclassical approach that provides the foundation for mainstream macroeconomics is applicable only to an imaginary world, an economy focused on market exchange based on a barter paradigm. Money and finance are added to the model as an afterthought—they really do not matter. Because an invisible hand supposedly guides rational individuals who have perfect foresight towards an equilibrium in which all resources are efficiently allocated, there is little role for government to play. The current crisis has shown this approach to be irrelevant for the analysis of the economy in which we live'. (Wray 2016: 60).

'New Classical' economics had emerged as the dominant intellectual force during the 1990s and, in this view, output and employment are determined by the

[1]Quoted in Wren-Lewis (2015: 231).

micro-economic decisions of individuals rather than by macroeconomic policies of governments (Desai 2015). In this approach government has the important task of ensuring that monetary policy works properly and does not stoke up inflation but, apart from that, government should avoid trying to stimulate growth using macroeconomic levers such as spending and taxation and allow entrepreneurs to create jobs and prosperity. This analysis encouraged the belief that if government took care of financial issues such as budget deficits, then individuals would take care of economic growth. George Osborne had accepted these ideas before becoming Chancellor of the Exchequer as is evident from a speech he gave in April 2009 in which he argued for: '[m]onetary policy to keep interest rates low and stimulate the economy ... [f]iscal responsibility to restore confidence and rebuild our battered public finances.'[2]

This strategy meant relying on the Bank of England to keep interest rates low to stimulate economic activity while at the same time squeezing fiscal policy by imposing austerity. It relied heavily on monetary policy and was very skeptical about the role of fiscal policy as a mechanism for recovering from recession. Keynes had pointed out many years ago that one of the problems with this analysis is that it ignores what he called the 'liquidity trap'. This is a situation in which interest rate adjustments become ineffective when they are lowered to near zero because they cannot be lowered any further. It also ignores the point that a severe fiscal squeeze is likely to reduce aggregate demand and therefore prolong the recession rather than restore confidence and produce growth. Needless to say the experience of the Great Recession has prompted a number of economists to temper their enthusiasm for the 'New Classical' path to prosperity, and recent research has confirmed that a fiscal squeeze imposed during a recession is likely to make things worse (Jorda and Taylor 2015).

Philosophical beliefs and economic doctrines aside, there was also an electoral dimension to the drive for austerity. In the 2010 election campaign the Conservatives had made much of the argument that Britain faced imminent bankruptcy and in that respect was in a similar position to Greece and other cash-strapped Portugal, Ireland, Italy, Greece, Spain (PIIGS). This rhetoric was driven by electoral considerations and the need to provide a radical alternative narrative to that of the Labour Party. This narrative enabled both Coalition partners to blame Gordon Brown and Labour policies for the Great Recession. This claim was very wide of the mark in practice since the crash started when a real estate bubble in the US burst and it spread quickly to banks and other financial institutions which themselves had been creating opaque and highly risky financial instruments that proved valueless when the crisis broke (see Tett 2009; Kay 2015). However, the Conservatives' economic argument proved to be a very potent message in the 2010 general election, so much so that echoes of it were still being heard in 2015. It allowed the Conservatives to articulate a clear alternative economic narrative to that of Labour and claim that they had the plan needed to restore prosperity.

[2]Quoted in Wren-Lewis (2015: 231).

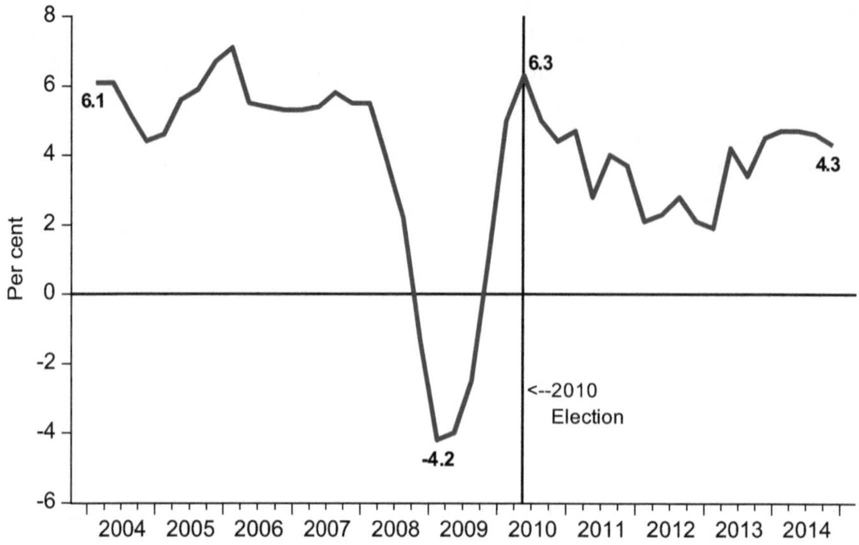

Fig. 1 Percentage growth in gross domestic product, 2004 Q1–2014 Q4

George Osborne's approach of focusing on the size of the budget deficit as the root cause of the problem during the 2010 election was made all the more necessary as a campaign strategy for the Conservatives by the fact that the economy was recovering at that time. The recovery was taking place but the deficit was still enormous, making it easy to focus on the bad news of debt and ignore the good news of growth. Figure 1 shows that income growth had rebounded to a respectable 4.1 % in the last quarter of 2009 and this had much to do with Gordon Brown's leadership in trying to get the political leaders of the G7 countries to co-ordinate their policies to combat the recession. The beggar-my-neighbour policies pursued by leading industrial countries in the 1930s were avoided by ensuring that adequate funds were available and credit did not dry up as a consequence of bank failures. This early recovery was also facilitated by the new policy of 'quantitative easing' adopted by the Bank of England in the autumn of 2008. This is the device of creating money electronically and using it to buy financial assets such as government bonds from private sector institutions like banks and insurance companies. The money received by these institutions then floods into financial markets and ultimately into the wider economy, and so stimulates economic activity. It is a way of providing a monetary stimulus when real interest rates are effectively zero or even negative.

The Bank introduced quantitative easing in the autumn of 2008 at the height of the financial crash, and from March 2009 to January 2010 £200 billion of assets were purchased amounting to some 30 % of government debt held by the private sector and 14 % of GDP. By any standards that was a huge stimulus to the economy (Joyce et al. 2011). The Bank of England's modelling suggested that the effects of these policies were large, raising GDP by 1.5–2 % and increasing inflation by

0.75–1.50 % (Joyce et al. 2011: 201). They help to explain why the economy recovered fairly rapidly at that time.

The budget deficit in 2009–2010 was very high by historical standards, but not so much that it triggered serious problems for government trying to borrow in financial markets. We know this by looking at long-term interest rates in Britain which measure the extent to which British governments can fund their borrowing. If borrowing is so high as to trigger a fear of default then foreign lenders would require a premium on the interest payments they receive in order to compensate them for the extra risks. This would drive long-term interest rates higher something which actually happened to Greece following the Eurozone financial crisis (Higgins and Klitgaard 2011). In fact long-term interest rates declined during this period, largely because Britain was experiencing deflation and also quantitative easing kept rates at a low level.

4 Economic Policy Outcomes: 2010 to 2015

The average quarterly growth of income was 1.55 % between 2004 and the 2010 general election. This included the period of prosperity up to the start of 2008 and the serious recession thereafter, and the modest recovery of 2010. In contrast, from the time of the 2010 general election to the fourth quarter of 2014, incomes increased on average by 0.11 % per quarter, a fraction of the growth in the earlier period. The respected financial journalist, William Keegan explained: 'It had been the slowest recovery from recession on record—slower even than the recovery from the Great Depression of 1929–1931, which took 2 years fewer than in 2008–2014' (Keegan 2014).

Trends in inflation and unemployment are charted in Fig. 2. The figure shows that inflation fell dramatically and unemployment rose rapidly after the onset of the recession in 2008. The economy recovered fairly quickly from deflation by early 2010, but unemployment remained stubbornly above 8 % until well into 2013. After the 2010 general election inflation declined again from late 2011, and at one point in early 2015 it actually reached zero. This highlighted the dangers of deflation, which can be self-reinforcing if consumers put off major purchases as they wait for prices to fall further. Similarly, businesses will postpone investments on the grounds that there might not be a market for their products if consumption spending is stagnant.

The slow recovery of employment during the Coalition years in Fig. 2 is a testament to the duration of the recession. However, from 2013, a fairly rapid decline occurred in unemployment and this, together with rising growth in incomes, allowed the Conservatives and their coalition partner, the Liberal Democrats, to claim that their austerity policies had laid the groundwork for the recovery during the 2015 election campaign.

However, there are reasons for believing that the recovery occurred not because of the austerity policies, but because the George Osborne effectively abandoned them in 2012 when he realized that the economy was—in the words of Labour

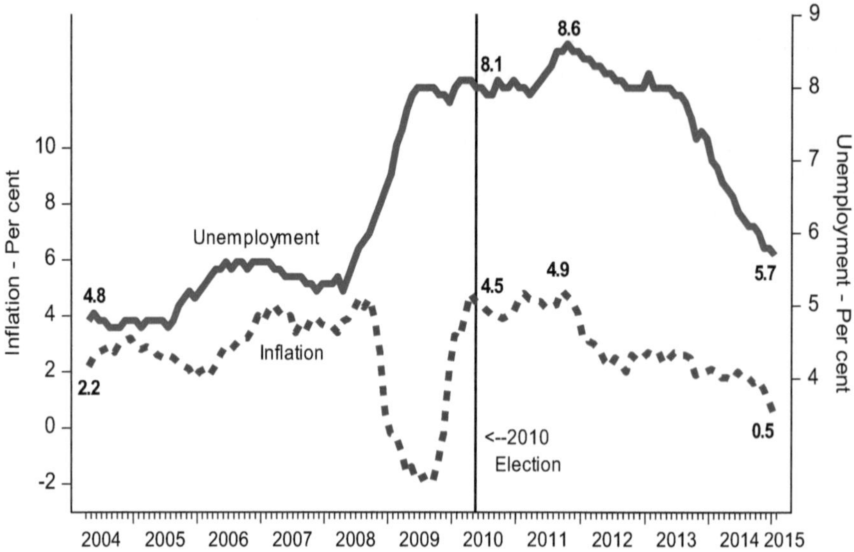

Fig. 2 Trends in inflation and unemployment, April 2004–January 2015

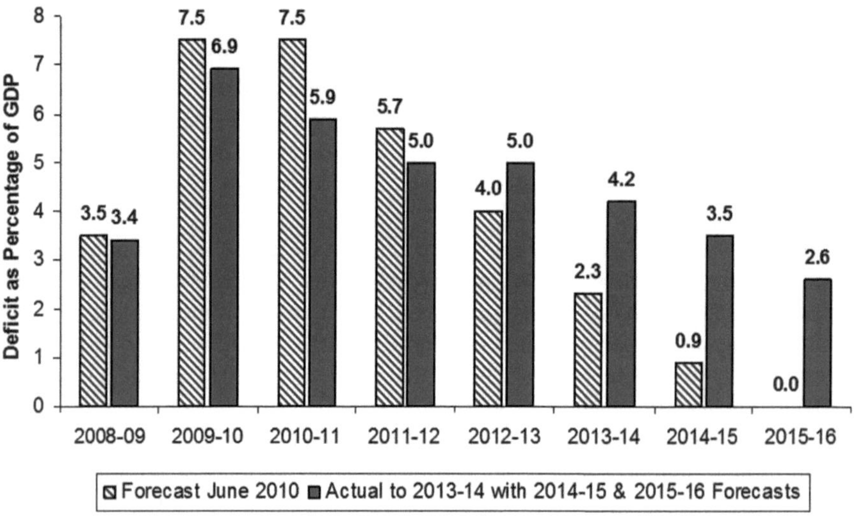

Fig. 3 Forecast and actual budget deficits, 2008–2016

Shadow Chancellor Ed Balls—'flatlining'. Austerity had not produced the recovery that Osborne and his colleagues had advertised. Figure 3 displays the actual and forecast budget deficits published by the Office of Budgetary Responsibility in its first report in June 2010 and then again in December 2014. The figures show the plans for reducing the budget deficit at the start of the Coalition alongside the actual deficit up to the end of the financial year preceding the 2015 general election. It can be seen that at the time of the first OBR report the plan was to cut the deficit in successive years so that it would be reduced to zero by 2015–2016. The outcomes show that the deficit did come down more or less according to plan in each year up to 2012–2013 at which point the decline suddenly halted.

The Figure shows that from 2012 to 2013 onwards the deficit continued to fall but at a much slower rate than originally planned, making the discrepancy between the plan and actual outcome grow each year. Essentially the plan to reduce the deficit to zero by 2015 was scrapped and, subsequently it reached 2.5 % of GDP in that financial year. The change of plan may have had something to do with the so-called 'Omnishambles' budget of 2012 when the Chancellor introduced a 'pasty tax' and a 'caravan tax' which generated loud criticisms and a negative backlash from much of the media. The 2012 budget had a discernable impact on the popularity of the Government in the polls, and may have played a part in triggering a rethink of the original austerity plans (Whiteley et al. 2014).

Of course, there was no announcement of a change, but it seems likely that the continuing high level of unemployment and the growing threat of deflation had changed the government's mind and it decided to embark on what amounted to a disguised fiscal stimulus of slowing down the austerity programme relative to what originally had been planned. The Government had reached the mid-term point of its term of office and was acutely aware that economic recovery had to be given time to work if electoral benefits were to be achieved by 2015. As Fig. 1 shows, the change of policy did restore growth in late 2013 but, from the point of view of reaping electoral rewards, there was an acute problem with the recovery as it related to the ordinary voter. Real wages had stagnated from 2009 and this state of affairs continued well into 2014. This was the longest period of declining real wages since the Great Depression of the 1930s and it had repercussions for economic optimism as the discussion below demonstrates.

This argument suggests that if the original objectives of clearing the deficit by 2015 set out by the Coalition government had actually been pursued according to plan then the economy likely would have continued to flat-line through to the election. This would have neutralized the strongest argument made by the Conservatives in the election campaign, namely that they were responsible for the economic recovery. In the event, the timing of the change of strategy in 2012 was effective from the Chancellor's point of view since it helped to produce an economic revival by 2013. However, the recovery did not percolate through to real wages until very late in the Parliament adding credibility to Labour's claim that it was a recovery designed for the few rather than for the many.

In the next section we examine the political payoffs associated with these policy changes.

5 Policy Performance and Political Payoffs

The performance of the economy and policy delivery in areas such as health care and immigration set the stage for the 2015 general election. The objective performance of the major macroeconomic indicators as charted in Figs. 1 through 3 is one key aspect, but voters' subjective evaluations of this performance is another. As voters considered how they should cast their ballots, they were reacting to what they were learning about the outcomes of the policies being pursued by the Coalition Government. Public judgments about alternative outcomes that might have occurred had Labour been in office also played a significant role. In this section, we study these public reactions to the economic trends using data gathered in the monthly Essex Continuous Monitoring Surveys (ECMS). We begin by mapping people's reactions to the highly consequential changes in economic conditions that occurred during the period between the 2010 and 2015 general elections.

The financial meltdown of 2007–2008 and the major recession that ensued did much to define the policy agenda pursued by the Coalition Government after it took the reins of power in May 2010. Accordingly, we focus first on voters' judgments about the national economy and their own personal financial circumstances. After examining public responses to evolving economic conditions we investigate how these reactions affected voters' judgments about the competence of the political parties and the party leaders—key variables in the valence politics model of electoral choice (see Clarke et al. 2004, 2009; Whiteley et al. 2013). These analyses are prompted by recognition that assessments of the performance of parties and leaders typically have very strong effects on how people vote. In particular, successful management of the economy is often the route to electoral success.

6 The Dynamic Economic Mood

The economy is a quintessential valence issue. This means that there is a widespread consensus among the voters about the objectives of policy, since the voters prefer economic prosperity and low levels of inflation and unemployment to stagnation. The valence model suggests that while there is agreement about goals, there is likely to be disagreement among voters about which party is best at delivering on these widely agreed goals. Economic issues typically rank high on the agenda during election campaigns and people's judgments about a government's economic performance and the likely performance of opposition parties have important effects on the decisions voters make.

After taking office in May 2010, Prime Minister David Cameron and Chancellor of the Exchequer George Osborne clearly believed that their austerity policies would revitalize Britain's struggling economy over the life of a single Parliament. As seen earlier key indicators such as growth rates and unemployment were slow to respond, but eventually growth did return and unemployment began to fall. And, although the

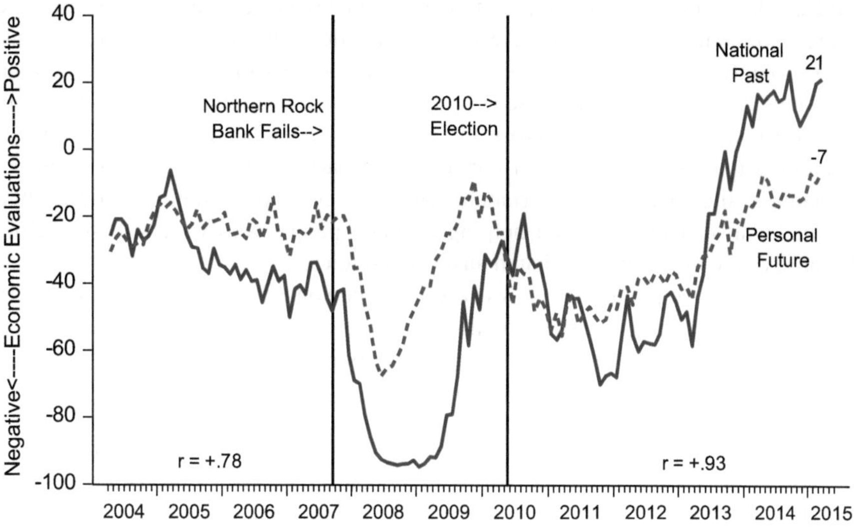

Fig. 4 Evaluations of the national economy and personal financial situation, April 2004–March 2015

Conservatives' ambitious target of eliminating the budget deficit was not reached, the size of the deficit did decrease. Not surprisingly, Cameron and Osborne took every opportunity to insist that their 'long-term economic plan' was responsible for the positive trends. If they could convince voters to accept this argument, then it would very likely secure them an electoral victory in 2015.

However, there was a precondition for the Conservatives' strategy to be successful—the public had to believe that the economy was, in fact, reviving. In this regard, Fig. 4 shows monthly trends in evaluations of the national economy from April 2004 to March 2015.[3] The figure also shows trends in people's expectations about their own personal economic circumstances over this period. Both trends run in tandem, moving sharply downward in the wake of the Northern Rock bank failure in September 2007 and then tracking upwards as the May 2010 general election approached. Almost immediately after the election, national and personal economic evaluations began to fall again. Then, they fluctuated until the summer of 2013 when judgments about the national economy began a sharp rise in a positive direction. Indeed, as Fig. 4 illustrates, by January 2015, evaluations of national economic conditions were more positive than at any time since the spring of 2004.

Personal economic expectations, often considered a key element in the set of forces driving support for British governing parties and their leaders were more sluggish. When public evaluations of the national economy began their take-off in

[3]The survey questions used to measure the variables in the individual level voting model appear in the Appendix.

mid-2013, voters' expectations about their personal financial situations also became more optimistic, but the increase was much smaller than the national evaluations. This prompted some commentators to speculate that the Conservatives' would reap no political benefits from increased optimism about the national economy precisely because it was not translating into a 'feel good' factor at the individual level. Labour strategists quickly picked up on the idea, and party leader, Ed Miliband, began to hammer the Coalition Government with it at every opportunity, charging that the incipient recovery was not helping ordinary people who were still struggling because of the Government's harsh austerity policies.

However, three points are noteworthy. First, personal economic expectations are typically less variable than judgments about the national economy (Clarke et al. 2005), and the 2010–2015 period is a case in point. Second, as Fig. 4 illustrates, personal economic expectations *were* moving upwards from the spring of 2013, so that the correlation between national and personal economic evaluations over the 2010–2015 period was extremely strong ($r = +0.93$). Furthermore the strength of the relationship was greater than it had been before the Coalition government took office ($r = +0.78$). Third, in March 2015—the month before the general election—personal economic expectations reached their highest level since April 2004. Most people may not have been exactly bullish about their personal financial prospects, but they were relatively more optimistic than at any time in the preceding decade. The timing of the recovery in economic expectations could not have been better from the Conservative's point of view.

Analyses indicate that the trend extended to all types of reactions to economic conditions—national and personal, past and future, cognitive and emotional. We can summarize these reactions in a single overall measure of Britain's economic mood. The mood measure, displayed in Fig. 5, followed a distinct U-shaped trajectory over the June 2010–March 2015 period. It fell to its lowest level in the early autumn of 2011, before beginning to revive, at first modestly and then quite dramatically starting in late spring 2013. In fact, in the immediate run-up to the 2105 election, the country's overall economic mood was more positive than it had been in over a decade.

These subjective economic sentiments reflected trends in the objective economy. In this regard, unemployment was a particularly important measure. Monthly levels of unemployment are widely publicized in the press and, as the number of unemployed persons began to fall, Prime Minister Cameron and Chancellor Osborne were quick to claim that the trend was a harbinger of a general economic revival. According to their narrative, the Coalition Government's austerity policies were responsible for the recovery, and as Fig. 5 shows when the unemployment rate receded, the economic mood improved markedly. The statistical relationship is very powerful—the correlation between the two trends is fully –0.93. Good news about the British economy in the form of steadily falling unemployment numbers was being strongly reflected in voters' improving reactions to national and personal economic conditions.

As we will see, there is abundant evidence that the intertwined improvements in objective economic conditions and subjective economic evaluations yielded

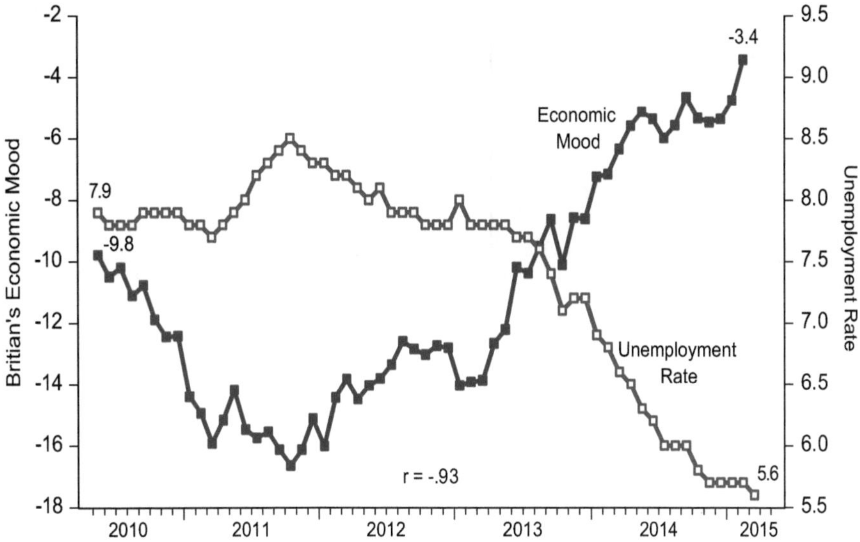

Fig. 5 Britain's economic mood and the unemployment rate, June 2010–March 2015

handsome political dividends for the Conservatives. One indicator is provided by public judgments about which political party is best able to manage the economy. Historically, the Conservatives typically have been seen as more competent economic managers than Labour, a reputation they lost in the early 1990s when John Major's Conservative government badly mishandled the currency crisis and Britain was forced to withdraw sterling from the European exchange rate mechanism. Subsequently, the 'New Labour' governments of Tony Blair and Gordon Brown enjoyed considerable credibility on the economy for several years before the party's competence was severely tarnished by banking crisis and subsequent recession. Despite Gordon Brown's famous claim in December 2008 that he had 'saved the world' from economic calamity, the electorate turned away from Labour in the run-up to the 2010 election.

The extent to which the Conservatives were running ahead of Labour on the economy when the Coalition government came to power is illustrated in Fig. 6. In June 2010 43 % of those surveyed judged that the Conservatives were best able to manage the economy and only 23 % selected Labour. As Fig. 6 also shows, this gap narrowed in early 2011 before widening again. Then, it closed a second time, as key economic indicators such as unemployment worsened and the poorly received March 2012 'Omnishambles' budget signaled that the Coalition Government might not be as capable as it claimed.

However, the economy then began to revive, with the important consequence that the country's economic mood became markedly more positive. In turn, the gap in the parties' economic competence ratings widened once more, and the number of people believing the Conservatives were best on the economy climbed from a low of 25 %

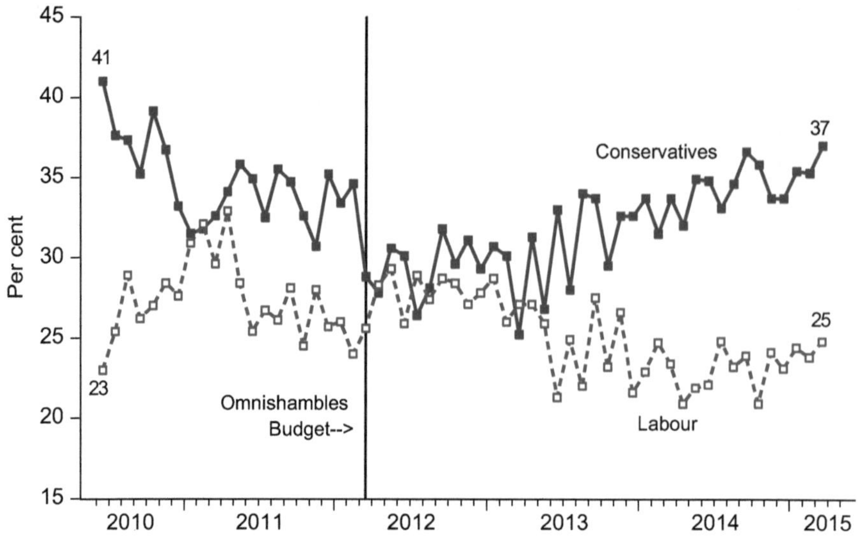

Fig. 6 Party best able to manage the economy, June 2010–March 2015

in March 2013 to 37 per in March 2015. For their part, Labour continued to struggle to refurbish their brand and in the latter month only 25 % judged them to be the best economic managers. Taken together, these data tell a straightforward story, with the Conservatives benefiting from positive trends in key indicators such as growth and jobs. These trends translated into a major improvement in the country's economic mood which, in turn, helped to bolster the Conservatives' image for managerial competence. In sharp contrast, Labour was unable to rebuild its reputation, and as a result, there was a sizable 'economic competence gap' between the two parties when the 2015 election campaign began.

7 Party Choice in 2015

We have seen that public reactions to economic conditions became much more positive as the election approached, but how did this work at the level of the individual voter? In this section we estimate an individual level model of electoral choice by incorporate other variables than make up the valence model into the analysis. The aim here is to get a sense of how important the economy was in that election. The models contain estimates of the effects of the economy and other issues, partisanship, leadership evaluations as well as demographic variables. The modelling provides estimates of voting for the Conservatives, Labour, the Liberal Democrats and UKIP.

Table 1 Logistic models of the conservative vote in the 2015 general election

	Full model	Effects on probability of voting conservative
Conservatives Best at Most Important Issue	0.62***	0.10
Labour Best at Most Important Issue	−0.14	−0.07
Liberal Democrats Best at Most Important Issue	−0.72*	−0.06
UKIP Best at Most Important Issue	0.16	−0.05
Economic Evaluations	0.24**	0.16
Evaluations of Immigration	−0.08	−0.05
Evaluations of National Health Service	0.32***	0.24
Approval of UK Membership of the European Union	−0.01	0.00
Conservative Partisanship	1.35***	0.20
Labour Partisanship	−0.42	−0.06
Liberal Democrat Partisanship	−0.64*	−0.05
UKIP Partisanship	0.03	0.02
Evaluations of David Cameron	0.42***	0.60
Evaluations of Ed Miliband	−0.18**	−0.17
Evaluations of Nick Clegg	−0.02	−0.05
Evaluations of Nigel Farage	−0.10**	−0.09
Occupational Status	0.07	0.01
Graduate	−0.04	0.01
Female	0.41**	0.05
Age	0.02***	0.17
Pseudo R-Square	0.55	

*$p < 0.10$; **$p < 0.05$; ***$p < 0.01$

Table 1 contains the binary logistic model of Conservative voting recorded in the post-election wave of the 2015 panel survey. This measure compares Conservative voters with all others and the various predictors are measured in the pre-election wave of the survey. The details of the measures used appear in the Appendix. Not surprisingly, perceptions that the Conservatives are best at managing the respondent's most important issue have a strong influence on voting for the party. Many of these 'most important issues' are valence variables and often involve economic related issues (Whiteley et al. 2013). Perceptions that the Liberal Democrats are best at handling this issue have a weak negative effect on the Conservative vote. Positive evaluations of the economy and the performance of the NHS both stimulate voting for the party, although positive evaluations of immigration had no effect, in part because very few respondents felt positive about this issue.

Not surprisingly, Conservative partisanship stimulated support for the party, whereas Liberal Democrat partisanship had a weak negative effect. The most important variables were the leadership evaluation measures, with positive evaluations of

David Cameron having a highly significant positive impact on Conservative voting and evaluations of Ed Miliband and Nigel Farage having a negative impact. The exception to this was the Deputy Prime Minister, Nick Clegg, whose evaluations had no impact on Conservative voting. Estimates of the demographic variables show that women and older voters were more likely to support the Conservatives. The goodness of fit of the model as measured by the pseudo R-square statistic is reasonably good at 0.55.

Since log odds coefficients produced by the logistic modelling are hard to interpret, the second column in Table 1 measures the impact of changing a variable from its minimum to its maximum value on the probability of voting Conservative, while holding all other variables at their mean values. These simulations make it possible to evaluate the importance of the different variables in explaining the Conservative vote. They show that the economy was the second most important predictor of Conservative voting among the issue variables, just after evaluations of the National Health Service. The latter is itself a valence issue since more or less everyone wants an efficient, well-run health service. A change in the economic variable from its most pessimistic to its most optimistic scores increased probability of voting Conservative by 16 %. In addition since the 'most important issue' is often related to the economy involving respondent concerns about issues such as 'jobs' and 'prices', the economy really mattered in the election. This boosted the Conservative vote by a further 10 %.

The largest effect of a variable in these simulations was in relation to evaluations of David Cameron. A shift from the minimum to the maximum score on his scale increased the probability of voting Conservative by 60 %. By contrast a similar change in the evaluations of Ed Miliband reduced the probability of voting Conservative by 17 %. The equivalent effect for Nigel Farage, the UKIP leader was 9 %. Conservative partisanship boosted the vote for the party by 20 % and Liberal Democrat partisanship reduced it by 5 %. Table 1 shows that all of the variables in the valence model including partisanship, leadership evaluations and the economy played an important role in explaining the Conservative vote in 2015.

Table 2 contains multinomial logistic model estimates of voting for the opposition parties including Labour, the Liberal Democrats, UKIP and Others, with Conservative voting being the reference category. The estimates tell a similar story to that of Table 1. Labour's support was boosted by partisanship and positive evaluations of Ed Miliband and weakened by positive evaluations of David Cameron, the NHS and the economy. It is noteworthy that evaluation of Nick Clegg and Nigel Farage had no impact on Labour support. But in contrast to Conservative voters in Table 1 Labour did well among the young, though its support was unaffected by gender.

The profile of support for the Liberal Democrats was rather similar to that of Labour; positive evaluations of Nick Clegg increased its vote and positive evaluations of David Cameron reduced it. Interestingly enough positive evaluations of Ed Miliband served to increase support for the party rather than reducing it, suggesting that Liberal Democrat voters saw the Labour leader as being rather similar to their own leader in his appeal. Liberal Democrats support was down

Table 2 Multinomial logistic models of voting for labour, liberal democrats, UKIP and others in the 2015 general election

	Labour	Liberal democrats	UKIP	Others
Conservatives Best at Most Important Issue	−0.83**	−0.92***	−0.16	−1.20***
Labour Best at Most Important Issue	0.24	−0.41	−0.85	−1.47***
Liberal Democrats Best at Most Important Issue	−0.78	0.68	−0.77	−0.61
UKIP Best at Most Important Issue	−0.45	−1.86***	0.51	0.28
Economic Evaluations	−0.31**	−0.33*	−0.34**	−0.16
Evaluations of Immigration	0.08	−0.02	0.14	0.17
Evaluations of National Health Service	−0.52***	−0.40***	−0.20*	−0.52***
Approval of UK Membership of the European Union	0.12	0.04	−0.59***	0.38**
Conservative Partisanship	−1.09***	−1.00***	−1.09***	−2.39***
Labour Partisanship	1.49***	−0.16	0.55	−1.50***
Liberal Democrat Partisanship	0.54	1.35***	0.57	−1.50***
UKIP Partisanship	−0.37	0.11	−0.13	−3.57***
Evaluations of David Cameron	−0.57***	−0.38***	−0.49***	−0.74***
Evaluations of Ed Miliband	0.45***	0.18***	0.12**	0.23***
Evaluations of Nick Clegg	−0.01	0.31***	0.01	0.09
Evaluations of Nigel Farage	−0.02	−0.08	0.50***	0.00
Occupational Status	−0.11	−0.20	−0.14	−0.10
Graduate	0.22	0.29	0.14	0.38
Female	−0.20	−0.70***	−0.07	−0.59**
Age	−0.02***	−0.02**	−0.01	−0.02**
Pseudo R-Square		0.60		

*$p<0.10$; **$p<0.05$; ***$p<0.01$

among women but compared with the Conservatives they gained support among the young.

When comparisons are made between UKIP voting and Conservative voting, not surprisingly positive evaluations of Nigel Farage had a big effect on support for the party while positive evaluations of David Cameron reduced support. Once again Ed Miliband had a positive effect on UKIP support indicating that the Labour leader was not a direct rival for UKIP supporters. The major difference between UKIP and the other parties relates to the issue of UK membership of the European Union. Not surprisingly approval of UK membership had a significant negative impact on UKIP voting, whereas it had no effect on support for Labour or the Liberal Democrats.

Finally the Others category in Table 2 includes the Nationalists in Scotland and Wales and the Greens as well as other minor parties. Interestingly enough, while evaluations of the Conservative and Labour leaders did influence support for the other parties, evaluations of Nick Clegg and Nigel Farage did not. However, in every case attachment to the mainstream parties reduced voting support for these other parties. Clearly partisanship insulates voters from supporting these minor parties. It is interesting to note that economic evaluations did not significantly influence support for other parties in comparison with the Conservatives, but attitudes to the National Health Service were important.

Overall, these results show that the valence model played an important role in explaining support for the Conservatives in the 2015 with attitudes to the economy and to the National Health Service, which is also a valence issue, being of considerable significance. As we have seen the electorate viewed the economy in a more positive light as the election approached. It is important to remember that the effects of economic recovery are also felt via their indirect impact on evaluations of leaders as well as in relation to partisanship. When the economy recovered David Cameron became more popular. Tables 1 and 2 show the direct effects, but when the indirect effects are factored in then the economic revival had an even bigger influence of the Conservative's electoral fortunes in 2015. The losers were Labour, particularly in Scotland, and the Liberal Democrats who were devastated by the loss of 49 of their 57 seats in the House of Commons. The fact that 27 of these seats went to their former Coalition partner was a key factor in explaining why the Conservatives won the election (see Clarke et al. 2015).

8 Conclusion: Mr. Cameron's Magic Horseshoe

Starting in June 2010, the British public mood darkened as the Coalition Government's stringent austerity policy medicine was prescribed and the country's economic misery deepened. Evaluations of the national economy and personal financial circumstances became deeply pessimistic and, for a time, it appeared that the Government would be punished severely in 2015 for its harsh and apparently failed attempt to restore the country's economic well-being. Then, as a consequence of a deft change in strategy in mid-2012 the situation began to change. Statistics on key economic indicators such as growth and employment started to improve and the public's economic mood brightened. The trend accelerated as the 2015 election approached. However the analysis of individual voting testifies to the importance of the economy in that election. It was not the only issue which mattered but it consistently mattered when it came to influencing support for the major parties. The Conservatives gained and Labour, the Liberal Democrats and UKIP all lost ground as the economy revived.

The country's economic mood between June 2010 and March 2015 assumed the shape of a stretched U—a horseshoe that was destined to bring good political fortune for Cameron and the Conservatives. In contrast, the issue of immigration which was consistently very salient during this period did not have a strong effect on the Conservative vote. Labour's reputation for competence had been seriously tarnished by the financial crisis and ensuing 'Great Recession' and, unfortunately for his party and himself, Miliband was unable to restore it, either via policy initiatives or by projecting an image of personal competence. As a result, when the official election campaign began, the Conservatives were positioned to reap political profits from the economic revival and positive mood it had engendered. But this was only because the Chancellor was pragmatic enough to ditch the initial economic strategy once it became apparent that it would not deliver an election victory to his party in 2015.

Appendix: Measurement of Key Variables

Attitudes Towards Membership in the European Union The question is: 'Overall, do you strongly approve, approve, disapprove, or strongly disapprove of Britain's membership in the European Union?' Responses categories are scored: 'strongly approve' = 1, 'approve' = 2, 'disapprove' = 4, 'strongly disapprove' = 5, 'don't know' = 3.

Best Prime Minister The question is: 'Who would make the best Prime Minister?' The response categories are: Ed Miliband = 1, David Cameron = 2, Nick Clegg = 3, Nigel Farage = 4, Don't know = 5. For the analysis in Chapter Three of factors affecting the choice of Cameron/Miliband as best prime minister, the dependent variable is scored: Cameron/Miliband best prime minister = 1, other leader or don't know = 0.

Civic Duty Respondents were asked if they agreed or disagreed with the following statement: 'I would be SERIOUSLY neglecting my duty as a citizen if I didn't vote'. Response categories were scored 'strongly agree' = 5, 'agree' = 4, 'neither agree nor disagree'/don't know = 3, disagree = 2, strongly disagree = 1.

Costs of Political Participation Respondents were asked if they agreed or disagreed with the following statements: (a) 'It takes too much time and effort to be active in politics and public affairs', (b) Most of my family and friends think that voting is a waste of time'. Responses to (a) and (b) were scored 'strongly agree' = 5, 'agree' = 4, 'neither agree nor disagree'/'don't know' = 3, 'disagree' = 2, 'strongly disagree' = 1. The resulting scores were added together to construct a 'costs of political participation' index.

Differential Benefits Provided by Political Parties Respondents were asked to use a 0–10 scale to indicate how much they liked or disliked various parties where 0 means 'strongly dislike' and 10 means 'strongly like'. Missing data were recoded to the mean. Pairwise differences comparing all the parties were computed and averaged.

Economic Mood Questions are: (a) personal retrospective—'How does the financial situation of your household now compare with what it was 12 months ago?'; (b) personal prospective—'How do you think the financial situation of your household will change over the next 12 months?'; (c) national retrospective—'How do you think the general economic situation in this country has changed over the last 12 months?'; (d) national prospective—'How do you think the general economic situation in this country will develop over the next 12 months?' Response categories are: 'get/got a lot better'; 'get/got a little better'; 'stay the same'; 'get/got a little worse'; 'get/got a lot worse'. For purposes of analysis, the response categories are coded: lot better = 5, little better = 4, stay the same/don't know = 3, little worse = 2, lot worse = 1; (e) 'Which, if any, of the following words describe your feelings about the country's general economic situation? (Please tick up to FOUR)'; (f) 'Thinking of the same list of feelings, do any of them describe your feelings about the financial situation of your household? (Please tick up to FOUR)'. The words are: angry, happy, disgusted, hopeful, uneasy, confident, afraid, proud. A word is scored 1 if mentioned and 0 if it is not mentioned. Overall national and personal emotional reactions to economic condition variables are constructed by subtracting the number of negative words mentioned from the number of positive words mentioned.

The six variables (a)–(f) are treated as monthly averages. These scores are subjected to a dynamic factor analysis (see Footnote 4) and the resulting factor scores are used to assess Britain's economic mood each month over the April 2004–March 2015 period. For the individual-level voting analyses, the six variables are subjected to an exploratory factor analysis. This analysis yields a first factor that explains 62.8 % of the item variance, with factor loadings ranging from 0.70 to 0.88. Factor scores are used to measure respondents' economic reactions[4].

Immigration The following questions are used to measure attitudes towards immigration: (a) How well do you think the present government has handled the number of immigrants coming to Britain? Response categories are: (a) 'very well' = 5, 'fairly well' = 2, 'neither well nor badly' = 3, 'fairly badly' = 2, 'very badly' = 1; (b) Which of the following statements comes closest to your view? (i) 'Britain should increase the number of immigrants coming to the country' = 1, (ii) 'The current number of immigrants coming to Britain is about right' = 2, (iii) 'Britain should reduce the number of immigrants coming to the country' = 3, (iv) 'don't know' = 2; (c) 'Using the 0–10 scale, how important a problem is the number of immigrants coming to Britain these days?' (d) 'Do you think the number of immigrants coming to Britain these days is: 'a lot better' = 1, 'a little better' = 2, 'the same' = 3, 'a little worse' = 4, 'a lot worse' = 5, 'don't know' = 3'; (e) 'Which, if any, of the following words describe your feelings about the number of immigrants coming to Britain? (Please tick up to FOUR)'. The words are: angry, happy, disgusted, hopeful, uneasy, confident, afraid, proud. A word is scored 1 if mentioned and 0 if it is not mentioned. Overall emotional reactions to immigration are measured by subtracting the number of negative words mentioned from the number of positive words mentioned.

The four variables (a)–(e) are treated as monthly averages. These scores are subjected to a dynamic factor analysis and the resulting factor scores are used to

[4]See, e.g., David M. Drukker and Richard M. Gates, 'State Space Methods in Stata', *Journal of Statistical Software* 41 (2011), issue #10. http://www.jstatsoft.org/

assess reactions to the NHS each month over the April 2004–March 2015 period. For individual-level voting analyses, the four variables are subjected to an exploratory factor analysis. This analysis yields as single factor that explains 69.6 % of the item variance, with factor loadings ranging from 0.77 to 0.86. Factor scores are used to measure respondents' reactions to immigration.

Interest in 2015 Election The question is: 'How interested are you in the general election that will be held on May 7th this year?' and the scored response categories are: 'very interested' = 4, 'somewhat interested' = 3, 'not very interested' = 2, 'not at all interested, don't know' = 1.

Leader Images are measured using the following question: 'Using a scale that runs from 0 to 10, where 0 means strongly dislike and 10 means strongly like, how do you feel about David Cameron/Ed Miliband/Nick Clegg/Nigel Farage, Nicola Sturgeon, Leanne Wood/Natalie Bennett'? Respondents saying 'don't know' were assigned the mean score.

Most Important Issue The question is: 'What do you think is the most important problem facing the country at the present time?' Using a 'drag and drop' widget, respondents were asked to rank the following issues as most important, second most important and third most important: crime, the economy, education, the environment, Europe, health, housing, immigration, pensions, tax, transport, welfare, inflation, unemployment. 'Don't know' and 'there are no important issues' also were included as response categories.

National Health Service The questions are: (a) 'Do you think the National Health Service these days is: 'a lot better' = 5, 'a little better' = 4, 'the same' = 3, 'a little worse' = 2, 'a lot worse' = 1, 'don't know' = 3'? (b) 'How well do you think the present Government has handled the National Health Service? Response categories are: (a) 'very well' = 5, 'fairly well' = 2, 'neither well nor badly' = 3, 'fairly badly' = 2, 'very badly' = 1; (c) 'Using a 0–10 scale, how important a problem is the National Health Service these days?' (d) 'Which of the following words describe your feelings about the National Health Service? (Please tick up to FOUR)'. The words are: angry, happy, disgusted, hopeful, uneasy, confident, afraid, proud. A word is scored 1 if mentioned and 0 if it is not mentioned. An overall emotional reactions index is constructed by subtracting the number of negative words mentioned from the number of positive words mentioned.

The variables (a)–(d) are treated as monthly averages. These scores are subjected to a dynamic factor analysis and the factor scores are used to assess reactions to the NHS each month over the April 2004–March 2015 period. For the individual-level voting analyses, the four variables are subjected to an exploratory factor analysis. This analysis yields as single factor that explains 51.6 % of the item variance, with factor loadings ranging from 0.58 to 0.82. Factor scores are used to measure respondents' assessments of the performance of the NHS.

Party Best on the Economy The question is: 'With Britain in economic difficulties, which party do you think could handle the problem best—the Conservative

Party, the Labour Party or the Liberal Democrats?' The 'party performance on the economy' variables are a series of 0–1 dummies for the Conservatives, Labour and the Liberal Democrats with 'none' and 'don't know' responses designated as the reference category.

Partisanship Partisan attachments are measured using the first question in the standard BES party identification sequence: 'Generally speaking, do you think of yourself as Labour, Conservative, Liberal Democrat or what?' Party identification variables are a series of 0–1 dummies for Conservative, Labour, Liberal Democrat, UKIP and 'other party' identifications. 'None' and 'don't know' responses are designated as the reference category.

Party Campaign Contacts Respondents in the 2015 ECMS post-election survey were asked: 'Did any of the political parties contact you during recent election campaign?' Those indicating 'Yes' were asked: 'Please indicate all the political parties that have contacted you during the election campaign. Please select all that apply'. Responses to the latter question were recoded into a series of 0–1 dummy variables, e.g., contacted by Greens = 1, not contacted by greens or 'don't know if contacted by Greens = 0.

Personal Political Influence (Political Efficacy) The question is: 'On a scale from 0 to 10, how much influence do you have on politics and public affairs? (where 10 means a great deal of influence and 0 means no influence)'. Missing data are recoded to the mean of valid responses.

Political Knowledge A political knowledge index is constructed by computing the number of correct answers to nine true-false statements. The question is: Please indicate if you think the following statements are 'True or False. If you don't know, please tick Don't know'. The statements are: (a) 'The UK has committed to sending ground troops to fight against ISIS in Iraq' (false), (b) 'The Chancellor of the Exchequer is responsible for setting interest rates in the UK' (false), (c) 'In 2013 over 500,000 new immigrants came to the UK' (true), (d) 'In the UK, the standard personal allowance for income tax is £10,600' (true), (e) 'In their election manifesto the Conservatives promise to hold a referendum on Britain's membership in the European Union by the end of 2017' (true), (f) 'Labour wants to introduce a 'mansion tax' on homes worth over £2 million' (true), (g) 'The minimum voting age for UK general elections has been lowered to 16' (false), (h) 'Any registered voter can obtain a postal vote for a general election by contacting their local council and asking for one' (true), (i) 'The UK currently spends just over one per cent of its gross national income on overseas aid' (false).

Populist Attitudes Respondents were asked if they agreed or disagreed with the following four statements: (a) 'Economic inequality is a major problem in Britain', (b) 'Social injustice is a major problem in Britain', (c) 'Corporate greed is a major problem in Britain', (d) 'British banks are making excessive profits at the expense of ordinary people'. Responses to (a)–(d) are scored: 'strongly agree' = 5, 'agree' = 4, 'neither agree nor disagree'/'don't know' =3, 'disagree' = 2, 'strongly disagree' = 1. An exploratory factor analysis of the four variables explains 70.7 % of the item variance with factor loadings ranging from 0.81 to 0.86. Factor scores from this analysis are used to measure populist attitudes in various multivariate analyses.

Proximities Between Parties and Voters on Tax-Spend Scale Respondents were asked to place the parties and themselves on a 0–10 scale where the end marked 0 means that government should cut taxes a lot and spend much less on health and social services, and the end marked 10 means that government should raise taxes a lot and spend much more on health and social services. Missing data were recoded to the means of the valid scores. The proximity variables for each party were computed the absolute value of respondents' self-placements minus their scores for a given party. For example, if a respondent placed herself at 2 on the scale and the Conservative party at 5, her Conservative proximity score would be abs(2–5) = 3. Since smaller scores indicate closer proximity these scores were multiplied by −1 for the multivariate analyses.

Social Trust The question is: 'Think for a moment about whether people with whom you have contact can be trusted. Use the 0–10 scale again, where 10 means definitely can be trusted and 0 means definitely cannot be trusted'. Missing data are recoded to the mean of valid responses.

Socio-Demographics **Age** is measured as age in years or as a set of 0–1 dummy variables for the following age brackets: 18–25, 26–35, 36–45, 46–55, 56–65; respondents 66 years of age and older are treated as the reference category; **ethnicity** is measured as a 0–1 dichotomy with persons saying they are 'white British' when answering the question To which of these groups do you consider to belong? are scored 1 and all other respondents scored 0; **gender** is a dummy variable with men scored 1 and women 0; **country of residence** is two 0–1 dummy variables for Scotland and Wales with England as the reference category; **social class** is measured by dividing respondents into white collar and blue collar occupations (or former occupations for retired persons), with the white collar group scored 1 and the blue collar group scored 0. In cases where a respondent did not supply requisite occupational information and the respondent had a spouse, the spouse's information was used.

Volunteerism Respondents were asked the following two questions: (a) 'Over the past few years, has anyone asked you to get involved in politics or community affairs?' (b) Over the past few years, have you volunteered to get involved in politics or community affairs? Responses to (a) and (b) were scored: 'yes' = 1, 'no'/'don't know' = 0. The resulting scores were added together to construct a volunteerism index.

Voting Intentions in Monthly ECMS Surveys Respondents are asked: (a) 'If there were a General Election tomorrow, which party would you vote for?' Those saying they 'don't know' are asked: (b) 'Which party would you be most inclined to vote for?' The percentage supporting a party is the sum of (a) and (b).

Voting in the 2015 General Election—Turnout Respondents in the ECMS post-election survey were asked: 'Whenever there is an election, some people decide that they have good reasons not to vote, other people want to vote but are unable to, and some people vote. Thinking of the recent general election on May 7th, which of the following statements best describes you?' (a) 'I definitely did not vote in the May 7th general election', (b) 'I usually vote but decided not to vote this time', (c) 'I really wanted to vote but just wasn't able to', (d) 'I think I voted, but I'm not sure', (e) 'I am absolutely certain that I voted', (f) 'Don't know'. Respondents who indicated that they were 'absolutely certain' that they voted and also gave a score of 10 on a question asked in the ECMS pre-election wave survey concerning the likelihood of voting were considered to have voted in the 2015 general election. For purposes of the multivariate analyses of voter turnout, voters were scored 1 and non-voters were scored 0.

Voting in the 2015 General Election—Party Choice Respondents who were 'absolutely certain; they voted were asked: 'Which party did you vote for in the General Election?' Response categories were: Labour, Conservative, Liberal Democrat, United Kingdom Independence Party (UKIP), Scottish National Party (SNP), Plaid Cymru, Green Party, British National Party (BNP), Other Party.

References

Clarke, H. D., Kellner, P., Stewart, M. C., Twyman, J., & Whiteley, P. (2015). *Austerity and political choice in Britain*. London: Palgrave-Macmillan.

Clarke, H. D., Sanders, D., Stewart, M. C., & Whiteley, P. (2004). *Political choice in Britain*. Oxford: Oxford University Press.

Clarke, H. D., Sanders, D., Stewart, M. C., & Whiteley, P. (2009). *Performance politics and the British voter*. Cambridge: Cambridge University Press.

Clarke, H. D., Stewart, M. C., Ault, M., & Elliott, E. (2005). Men, women and the political economy of presidential approval. *British Journal of Political Science, 35*, 31–51.

Desai, M. (2015). *Hubris: why economists failed to predict the crisis and how to avoid the next one*. New Haven: Yale University Press.

Duch, R., & Stevenson, R. T. (2008). *The economic vote: How political and economic institutions condition election results*. Cambridge: Cambridge University Press.

Higgins, M., & Klitgaard, T. (2011). Saving imbalances and the euro area sovereign debt crisis. *Current Issues in Economics and Finance* (New York, NY: Federal Reserve Bank of New York), *17*, 5.

HM Government. (2010). *The coalition: Our programme for government*. London: HM Government.

HM Treasury. (2010). *Budget 2010*. London: HM Treasury.

Jorda, O., & Taylor, A. M. (2015, February). The time for austerity: Estimating the average treatment effect of Fiscal policy. *The Economic Journal, 126*, 219–255. doi:10.1111/ecoj.12332.

Joyce, M., Tong, M., & Woods, R. (2011). The United Kingdom's quantitative easing policy: Design, operation and impact. *Bank of England Quarterly Bulletin, 51*, 200–212.

Kay, J. (2015). *Other People's money*. London: Profile Books.

Keegan, W. (2014). *Mr Osborne's economic experiment: Austerity 1945–51 and 2010*. London: Searching Finance.

Key, V. O. (1968). *The responsible electorate: Rationality in presidential voting, 1936–1960.* New York, NY: Vintage Books.
Lewis-Beck, M. S. (1988). *Economics and elections: The major western democracies.* Ann Arbor, MI: University of Michigan Press.
Lewis-Beck, M. S., & Stegmaier, M. (2007). Economic models of the vote. In R. Dalton & H. D. Klingemann (Eds.), *The Oxford handbook of political behavior* (pp. 518–537). Oxford: Oxford University Press.
Norpoth, H. (1997). *Confidence regained: Economics, Mrs Thatcher and the British voter.* Ann Arbor, MI: University of Michigan Press.
Quinn, T., Bara, J., & Bartle, J. (2011). The UK coalition agreement of 2010: Who won? *Journal of Elections Public Opinion and Parties, 21*(2), 295–312.
Tett, G. (2009). *Fool's gold.* London: Little Brown.
Whiteley, P., Clarke, H. D., Sanders, D., & Stewart, M. C. (2013). *Affluence, austerity and electoral change in Britain.* Cambridge: Cambridge University Press.
Whiteley, P., Clarke, H. D., Sanders, D., & Stewart, M. C. (2014). The economic and electoral consequences of austerity policies in Britain. *Parliamentary Affairs.* doi:10.1093/pa/gsu015.
Wray, L. R. (2016). *Why Minsky matters: An introduction to the work of a maverick economist.* Princeton, NJ: Princeton University Press.
Wren-Lewis, S. (2015, February). The macroeconomic record of the coalition government. *National Institute Economic Review, 231*, R7.

Valence and Ideological Proximity in the Rise of Nationalist Parties: Spanish General Elections, 2008 and 2011

Elena Labzina, Joan Barceló, and Norman Schofield

1 Introduction

During the last few years, in the aftermath of the bank crisis of 2007, anti-European and right or far-right parties started to gain more and more support across Europe (Bosco and Verney 2012). This reaction seems a natural response to austerity measures and the rise of unemployment in the region. Meanwhile, in some European regions that have a different cultural identity to the dominant identity, a seemingly significant rise of peripheral nationalism has occurred (Gómez Fortes and Cabeza Perez 2013; Brubaker 2011; Rico 2012).

Predictably, rational logic says that the scarcity of resources would likely boost the "unwillingness to share"[1] mentality, especially among those who have more than others. Hence, the rise of local nationalism has been read as a direct consequence to the European economic crisis. In support of this thesis, in few years we have witnessed the promulgation of the Scottish Independence Referendum Act, passed in 2013; followed by the referendum 2014, the continuous attempts by the Catalan parliament to vote for Catalonia's self-determination, and even a surge of the Flemish nationalism in Belgium (Glen 2015).

Common explanations see the rise of nationalist parties as a consequence of the rise of nationalist preferences. However, the rise of nationalist parties can simply

[1]This argument is based on common micro economic logic: that when there is less money in the economy, any distribution toward a more egalitarian state affects the richest regions more severely (Mas-Collel et al. 1995).

E. Labzina (✉) • J. Barceló • N. Schofield
Washington University in St. Louis, Campus Box 1063, One Brookings Drive, St. Louis, MO 63130-4899, USA
e-mail: len4ick@gmail.com; joanbarcelosoler@wustl.edu; schofield.norman@gmail.com

N. Schofield, G. Caballero (eds.), *State, Institutions and Democracy*, Studies in Political Economy, DOI 10.1007/978-3-319-44582-3_5

be part of an overall trend of a rise in support for non-marginal minority parties. In institutional regimes with disproportional electoral systems, non-marginal small parties and nationalist parties (or non-mainstream parties) have been handicapped by strategic voting (e.g., Spain and the UK are clear examples). Thus, non-policy evaluations rather than ideological distance explained their electoral success. However, the effects of the economic crisis on the general confidence towards institutions and major political parties may have favored small and nationalist parties equally.

In this paper, we argue that the rise of small and nationalist parties can hardly be explained by policy or nationalistic preferences by a spatial understanding of the politics. Instead, exogenous valence is the main explanation of the electoral success of political parties. In particular, this affects small and nationalistic parties, which tend to suffer from an exogenous valence disadvantage vis-a-vis mainstream parties due to strategic voting. In addition to this, the rise nationalist parties parallel the emergence of new political parties, and not necessarily a shift in nationalistic preferences.

To test this hypotheses, we implement our refinement of Yamamoto's (2011) *multinomial logistic model for the varying choice sets* to survey data from Spain provided by the *Centro de Investigaciones Sociológicas (CIS)* in 2008 and 2011. From these surveys, we can construct a two-dimensional ideological space for both 2008 and 2011. Thus, the Spanish voters and parties have been assessed along (1) a socio-economic left-right divide, and (2) a central-periphery divide that pits the large parties with the countrywide coverage against parties that advocate either for regionalist issues or for outright secession from Spain. Interestingly, the case of Spain has all the relevant characteristics to test our hypotheses. First, despite Spain's unified rules across regions for parties running for the main Parliament, it has territories with a long history of nationalist identity, including their own languages. Overall, 17 autonomous communities provide a significant ideological variation (Pérez-Nievas and Fraile 2000; Balcells i Ventura 2007). Moreover, for the last 40 years, a process of gradual decentralization has taken place in Spain. Hence, besides a perceived regional self-identification in some regions, all of the regions have a high level of explicitly institutionalized fiscal and political independence (Pérez-Nievas and Fraile 2000).

In addition, electoral results for the General Elections in 2008 and 2011 have proven to be highly variable across regions and across parties. For instance, the *Partido Popular (PP)* gained a substantial result of 49.19 % in Madrid in 2008, while it only achieved a 16.40 and 18.53 % of the vote in *Catalonia* and *Basque Country*, respectively. Meanwhile, the *Partido Socialista Obrero Español (PSOE)* won 39.68 % of the votes in *Madrid* and 45.39 and 38.14 % in *Catalonia* and *Basque Country*, respectively. Similarly, the *PP* and *PSOE* gained 50.97 and 26.05 % in Madrid in 2011, respectively; 20.7 and 29.35 % in Catalonia, and 17.81 and 21.55 % in *Basque Country*. Importantly, in *Basque Country* in 2011, both regional parties, *Partido Nacionalista Vasco (PNV)* and *Amaiur* obtained more votes than the major parties, 27.41 and 24.11 % (del Interior 2015).

Another important consideration is that besides the presence of the strong statewide major parties, *PSOE* and *PP*, there are two non-marginal statewide parties, *Izquierda Unida (IU)* and *Unión, Progreso Y Democracia (UPyD)*, and multiple non-marginal nationalist parties.[2] In contrast to Scotland or Canada, where only one nationalist party exists in each country [namely, the *Scottish National Party (SNP)* in Scotland (Labzina and Schofield 2015), and the *Bloc Quebecois* in Canada (Gallego et al. 2014)], the number of both small and regional or nationalistic parties in Spain provides us with leverage to evaluate the distinctive characteristics of their electoral support. Hence, results based on Spain are more generalizable than in the case of UK or Canada, since they are less specific for particular parties or regions.

The third reason is a clear separation of the central-periphery ideological dimension and socio-economic ideological dimension that started to prevail in the research on regional Spanish politics relatively recently (Dinas 2012). This shows the effect of the peripheral nationalism on the votes separately, and, on the intermediate stage of the spatial analysis, provides a chance to contrast the regions on a two-dimensional ideological scale. Also, this provides a sense of how sensitive the people of various regions are to ideological changes in each ideological dimension. In conjunction with the two-dimensional space, the *(CIS)* provides high quality regular surveys conducted on a large number of individuals. To begin with, these surveys give an opportunity to create balanced ideological scores, capturing various ideological aspects in a condensed form, applying *principal component analysis* to a number of relevant questions. Next, the size of the survey samples helps to overcome the methodological challenge of inapplicability of the *standard multinomial logistic* regression, because the sets of political parties vary across regions. The modification of MNL for the varying individual choice options (VCL) (Yamamoto 2011) requires a decent number of observations for each region.

Lastly, the economic crisis has severely impacted national politics in the recent years, which has immersed the two major parties into a confidence crisis due to economic (management of the economic crisis) and non-economic factors (widespread political corruption scandals). In this scenario, small and regional and nationalistic parties threaten to break the traditional two-party system (see Fig. 1), which, until recently, was thought to be unbreakable due to a sever disproportional electoral system crucially disadvantaged small and nationalistic parties regardless of their policy positions. Altogether, Spain is an ideal case to test our hypotheses.

Our findings suggest that the rise of nationalist parties parallels the emergence of small parties in Spain. Fundamentally, we show that the increase in the support of political parties is largely a function of their exogenous valence. Thus, those small and nationalistic parties that have been more successful in reducing their exogenous disadvantage are more likely to have increased their electoral support between 2008 and 2011. As expected, the rise of nationalist parties does not derive solely from the surge in nationalistic preference, since the party ideological position

[2] Minority Parties: *CiU, IU, UPyD, ERC,Amaiur, PNV, BNG*; majority Parties: *PP, PSOE*; regional parties: *CiU, ERC, Amaiur, PNV, BNG.*

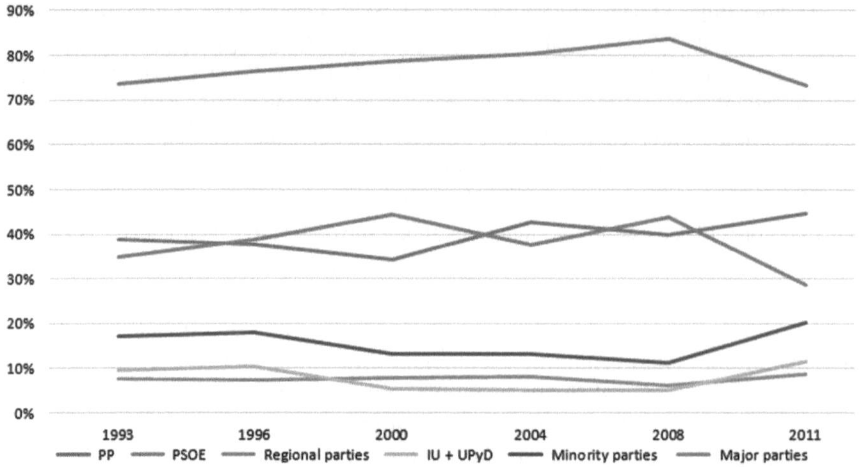

Fig. 1 Voting shares' dynamics: General Spanish Elections 1993–2011

have remained virtually constant between the elections, but from the changes in non-policy considerations.

The outline of this paper is as follows. First, we review the development of the spatial models. In this section, the notion of *valence* is introduced and specified. The second section presents a overview of the methodology. This section contains the most critical details of our final implementation. Next, we present our findings. Finally, we discuss the possible implications and conclude.

2 Background on Spatial Models and Valence in the Context of Spain

This section aims to present the spatial voting model with heterogenous intercepts for each party. This model is one of the last generations in the evolution of proximity voting models. Importantly, the intercepts in this model represent *exogenous party valences* of the parties. In contrast to models in which parties or candidates can take a position in terms of *valence issues* as well (Ansolabehere and Snyder Jr. 2000), the model employed in this paper lets parties maximize their vote shares only through their ideological positions. This work assumes that since parties do not observe their valence fully ex ante—it is defined by the voters—the final electoral positions are not always optimal for the parties. Substantial research has been done on whether the electoral systems in various countries during particular elections are in a local Nash equilibrium, or in a state such that parties have no incentive to even slightly relocate given the position of the other parties (Schofield and Sened 2006). However, the focus of this paper is on voters' perceptions about parties, which are represented in terms of *exogenous valence*. Hence, thinking of the elections as a game between candidate parties and voters, this paper focuses on the voters' side.

To start, historically, the voting models were divided into *spatial models*[3] and *social-psychobiological models* (Bennis et al. 2010; Enelow and Hinich 1984). The spatial models evolved as an adaptation of the unidimensional economic model for competitive markets by Hotelling (1929) to political competition by Downs (1957). The major idea of spatial models is that the voter is a rational actor, and she maximizes her utility by choosing the party or candidate located closest to her in the ideological space. Models of this kind might include uncertainty (Enelow and Hinich 1984); however, the key idea here is that individuals are aware of their electoral first-best knowing the ideological positions of the parties.

The *social-psycho-biological* or *behavioral* models emerged as a response to limitations of rational economic approach. As Stokes (1963) argues in his famous critique on spatial models, many assumptions of the Downs model seem not to reflect actual political competition. Among his crucial comments, he addresses the unidimensionality of political space. He proposes to introduce the second ideological dimension, i.e., *morality* or *religiosity*, in addition to the left-right dimension. Also, crucially, he contrasts *position-issues*, which spatial models mainly describe, to *valence-issues*, which lie in a different space.

This is a significant point, since Stokes addresses extensively the notion of *valence*. In its inception, the author defined *valence-issues* as those "*on which parties or leaders are differentiated not by what they advocate but by the degree to which they are linked in the public's mind with conditions or goals or symbols of which almost everyone approves or disapproves*" (Stokes 1992). Thus, valence issues may be considered to include citizens' evaluations unrelated to parties' policy positions, including parties' and/or candidates' competence, charisma, integrity, psychological affect, etc. Hence, considering ideology as the only rational reason to vote for a party or a candidate, *valence* , in general, may "contain" an irrational component of voters' motivation.

Clarke (2009) presents a somewhat different view on voting models, contrasting spatial against valence models. Following Stokes (1963), to a large extent, probably the most important point he argues explicitly is that valence models "*focus on delivery*". While spatial models, following the Downsian tradition, assume that delivery happens automatically (Clarke 2009), Clarke underlines that in the valence approach "*it might be much more crucial who promises than what policy is promised*".

Meanwhile, substantial research attempted to capture *both* valence and spatial components. Partially, that was because in a dynamic multiparty setting, with a proportional electoral system, the discrepancy between actual positions parties take and the predicted median policy position still lacked a satisfying explanation (Schofield 2003).

Schofield (2003) introduced the probabilistic version of the spatial model using multinomial logistic linear regression. Both of Stokes' (1963) comments mentioned above are included into Schofield's model. Firstly, in most papers,

[3]The spatial models are clearly not restricted to the positional models. Directional models were an important contribution to the voting theory as well (Clarke 2009).

the second "social" dimension is added (Gallego et al. 2014; Schofield 2003). Secondly, *valence* is re-introduced to explain why, given very similar ideological positions, some parties gain more votes than others. Parties with a lower valence are predicted to take more extreme ideological positions. Indeed, if parties are purely vote-motivated, or, in other words, office-seeking, they would be expected to locate near the median, according to the Downsian paradigm. According to Schofield, *valence* can be of two types: *socio-demographic valence*, which is specific for a particular individual—similar to the factors affecting the vote choice in *social-psychobiological* models; and *party valence*, which is specific for a given party (Schofield 2003). Ansolabehere (2000)'s utility voting model is similar to Schofield's (2003) with the distinction that parties take a position in relation to *valence-issues*. Interestingly, given this division, "*party identification*" (Campbell et al. 1966) might be considered a mixture of both types of *valence*.

Having said everything above, what is *valence*? A strict short specification is hardly possible, since no single common view exists. One of the approaches is to assume that its key variables are partisan attachments [*party identification*, (Campbell et al. 1966)], judgements about important issues (Schofield 2003), and party leader/party images (priv. comm.) (Clarke et al. 2011). Clearly, it is difficult to separate these components. Meanwhile, the emphasis on *delivery* of policies (Clarke et al. 2011), which does not contradict that *valence-issues* may be split into components, is crucial for the argument of this paper. In other words, this perspective focuses on the trust in parties. The question whether such trust is justified in relation to regional parties in Spain is beyond the scope of this paper. However, as mentioned in the introduction, some research argues that this is the case (Heller 2002). To conclude this historical overview, Clarke et al. (2011) remarks that the view on *valence* as an *unmoved mover* is incorrect, since *valence* may clearly change. Hence, the fluctuation of the party valence might be considered to reflect changes of trust in the party. This paper employs this view.

In regard to Spain, analysts of Spanish politics tended to pay little attention to the debate on the nation-wide nationalist identity (Núñez 2001) and were focused more on consequences of decentralization and salience of regional nationalism. Hence, two-dimensional spatial models were sometimes used (Albertos 2002), but the common perception was that the socio-economic dimension is significantly correlated with the central-periphery ideological dimension. This belief is still relatively widespread among some researchers who address particularly Catalonia and Basque Country (Dinas 2012). They claim that nationalism and leftist socio-economic political views are strongly interrelated in these regions. Overall, Catalonia and Basque Country have been the center of the research on Spanish politics (Barceló 2014; Fernández and Rodríguez 2006; Martínez-Herrera 2002; Martínez-Herrera and Miley 2010). In this context, some argued that Spanish identity is closer to a valence issue than to a policy issue, since two major parties converged in the defense of "a truly Spanish character" (Bonet et al. 2010). Moreover, little ideological differentiation between the major parties in terms of nationalism led to a lack of empirical approaches to study Spanish nationalism. Nevertheless, some recent work has shown that the time of convergence between PSOE and PP is over. Hence, Spanish politics may start to be influenced by the second ideological dimension

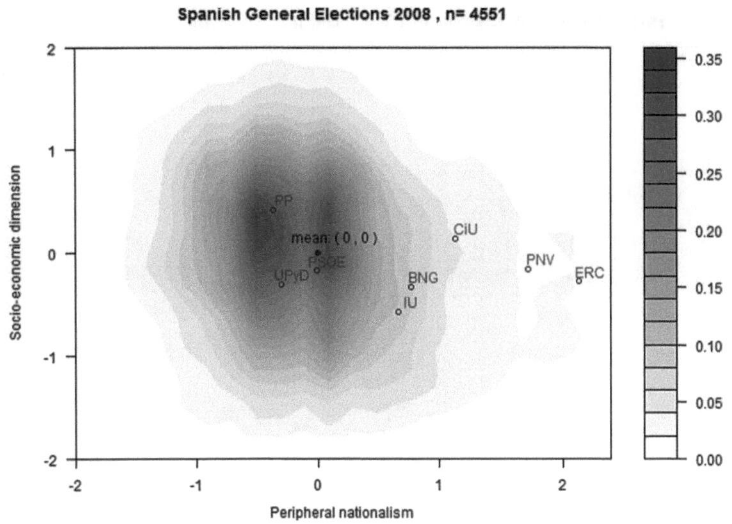

Fig. 2 Density distribution of the individual ideological positions

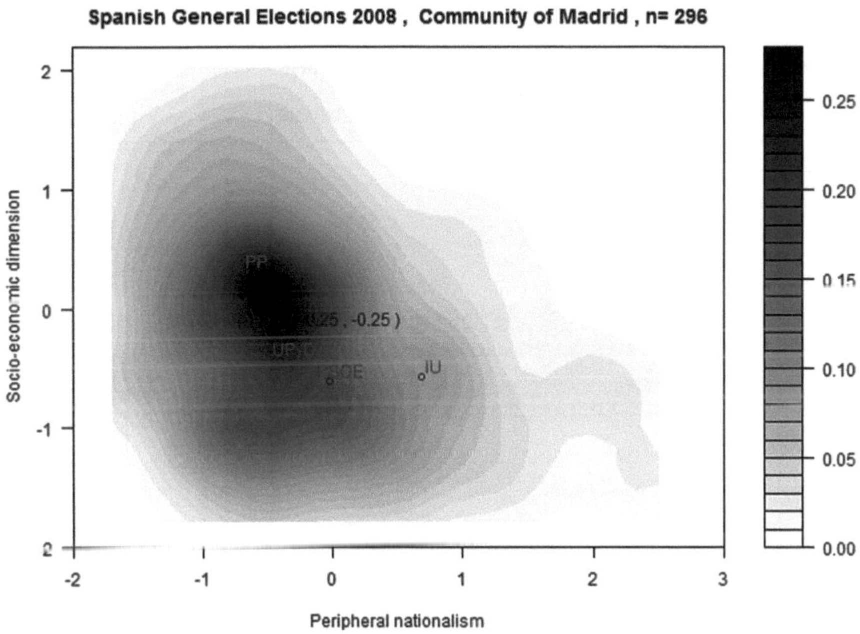

Fig. 3 Density distribution of the individual ideological positions

that merges Spanish identity and decentralization (Bonet et al. 2010; Fernández and Rodríguez 2006; Muñoz 2009). This paper confirms this divergence (Tables 13 and 14, Figs. 2, 3, 4, 5, 6, 7, 8, 9), especially in nationalist regions.

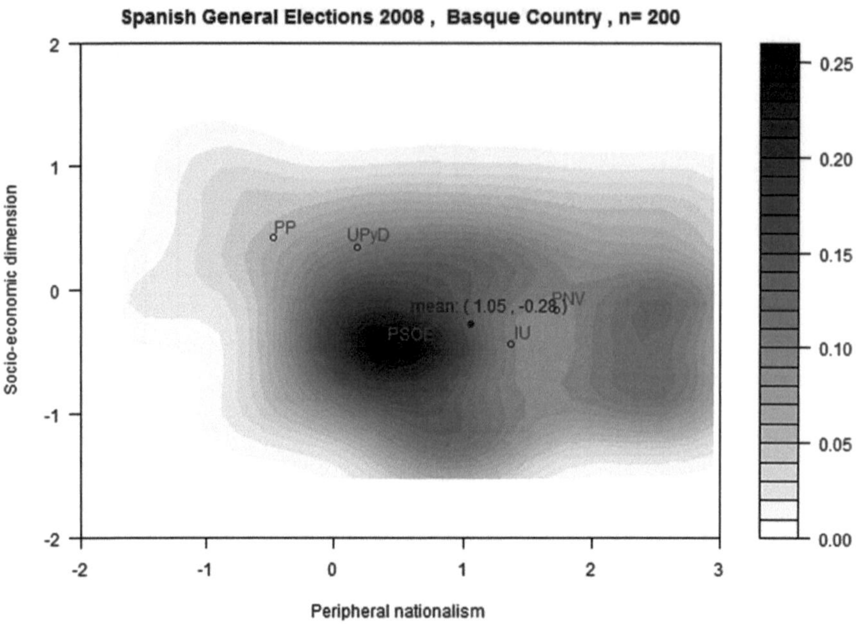

Fig. 4 Density distribution of the individual ideological positions

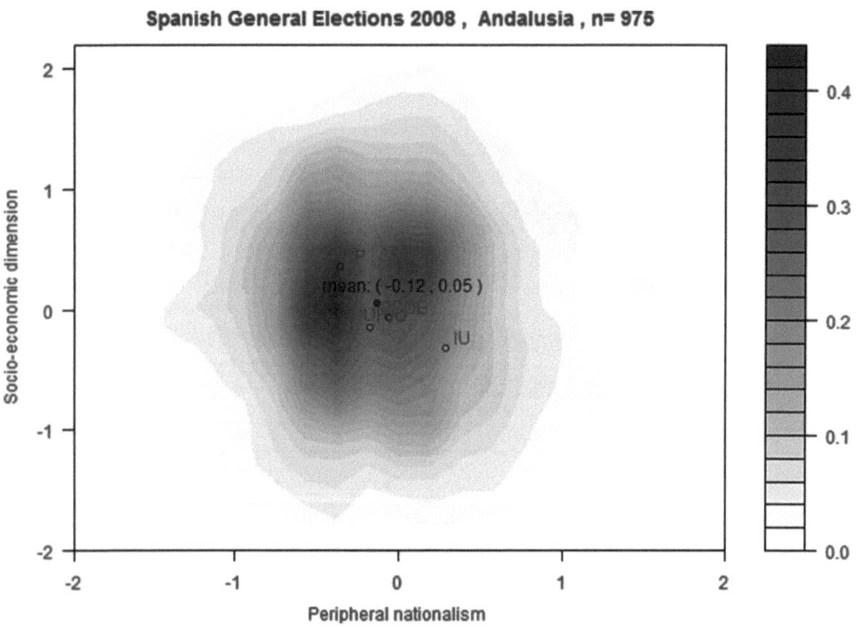

Fig. 5 Density distribution of the individual ideological positions

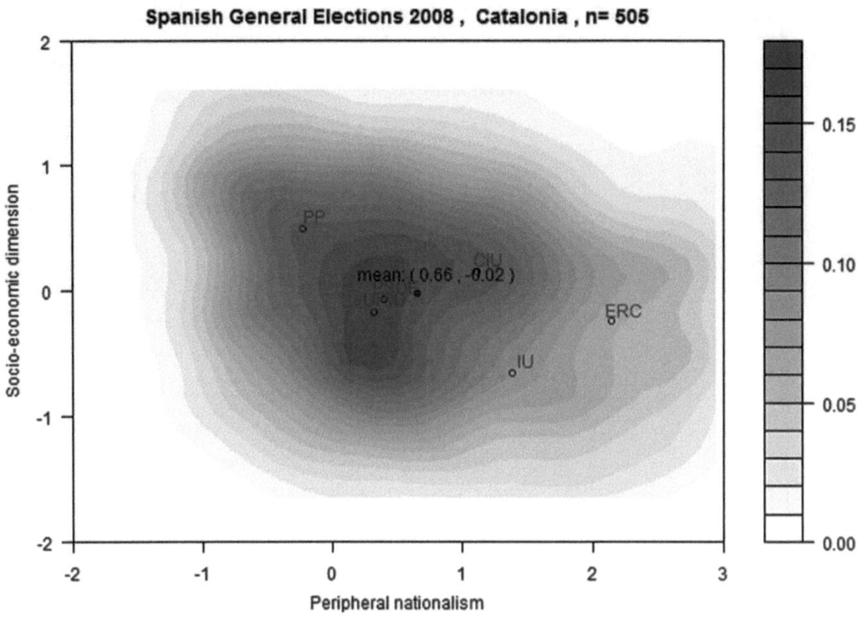

Fig. 6 Density distribution of the individual ideological positions

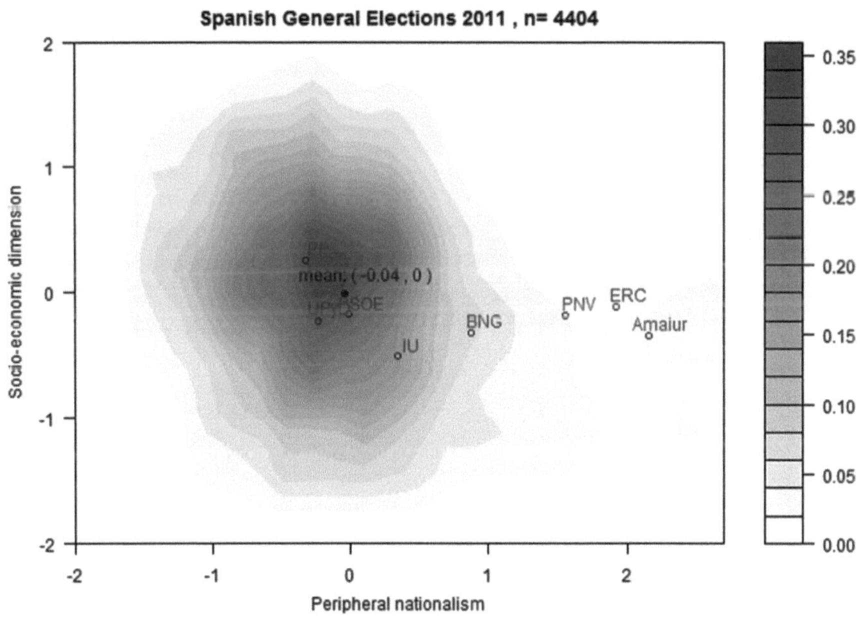

Fig. 7 Density distribution of the individual ideological positions

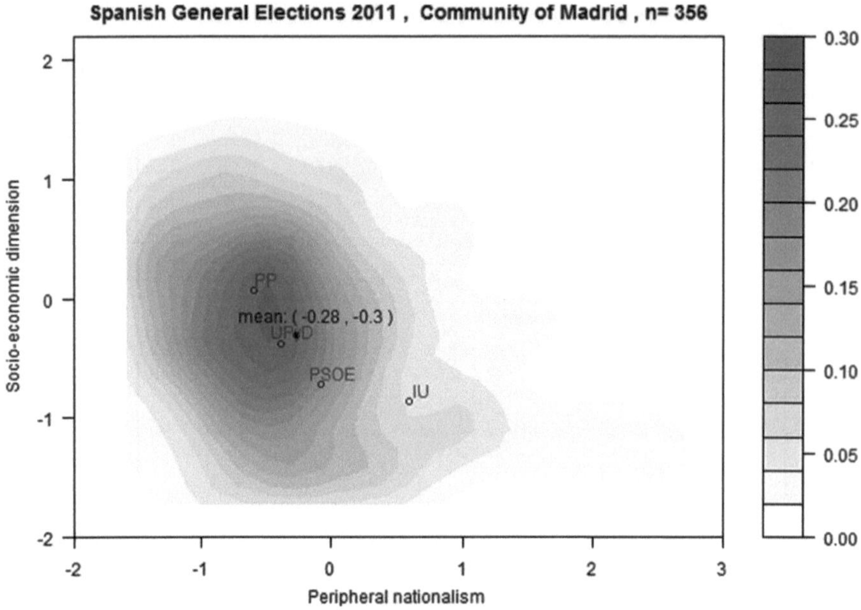

Fig. 8 Density distribution of the individual ideological positions

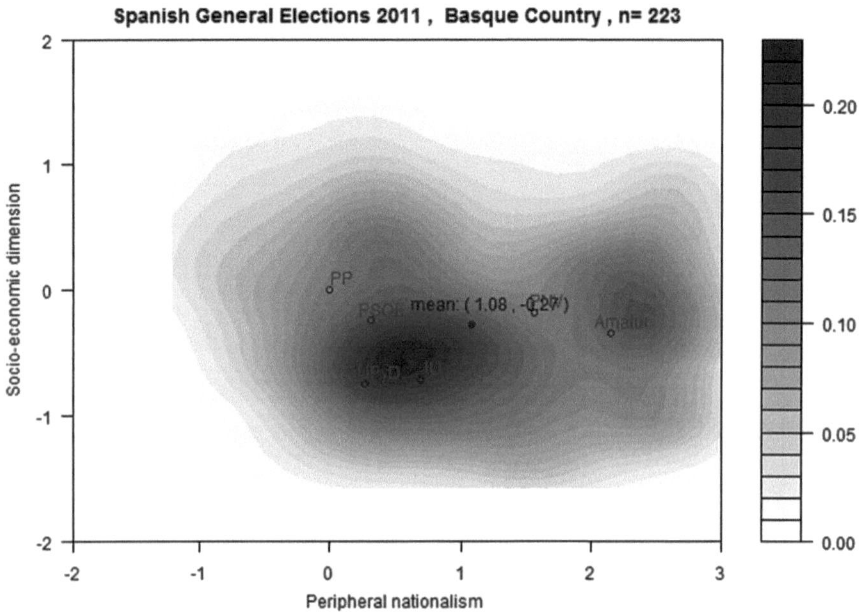

Fig. 9 Density distribution of the individual ideological positions

To sum up, the aim of this work is to show that the source of the increase in voting results of the regional parties between the General Spanish Elections in 2008 and 2011 was a consequence of changes in their *party valence*. Because of parsimonious reasons, this paper employs a modification of a pure spatial voting model with heterogenous intercepts. This model disentangles ideology into the left-right dimension and the central-periphery dimension (e.g., Balcells i Ventura 2007). This paper assumes that *exogenous valence* reflects changes in voters' trust in the ability of the candidate parties to deliver outcomes pursued by the voters.

3 Methodology: Varying Choice Logit

This paper follows Schofield's stream of research spatial voting models and applies a modification of the multinomial logistic regression to explain individual voting choices during the General Elections in Spain in 2008 and 2011. When individuals in the sample select from different sets of party options, the assumption of IIA is counter-factual and requires a modification. This is the case of the Spanish General Elections. For example, a person in Madrid cannot vote for *ERC* or *PNV*. Meanwhile, an individual in Barcelona can vote for *CiU* and *ERC*, but has no option to vote for *BNG*. Everybody in this sample has restricted choices. To overcome this violation of IIA, the paper applies the calibration of Yamamoto's (2011) adjustment for multinomial logistic regression to handle varying choice sets.

Taking the major assumptions from MNL and denoting the utility a voter i gains from voting for the party j, the formal model used in this analysis is defined as:

$$P_i(v = j) = \frac{exp(u_{i,j})}{1 + \sum_{k \in r(i), k \neq m} exp(u_{i,k})} \quad (1)$$

By introducing *the filter (matrix)*, Φ, where $\phi_{r(i)j} = I(j \in r(i))$, the above equation can be simplified:

$$P_i(v = j) = \frac{exp(u_{i,j})}{1 + \sum_{k \in r(i), k \neq m} exp(u_{i,k})} \Longrightarrow P_i(v = j) = \frac{exp(u_{i,j})\phi_{r(i),j}}{1 + \sum_{k \in P, k \neq m} exp(u_{i,k})\phi_{r(i),k}} \quad (2)$$

The later version is almost identical to MNL with the addition of the filter, which makes the implementation in JAGS significantly more accessible.

The papers defines the spatial individual voting utility as:

$$E(u_{i,j}|x_i, z_j) = \mu_j + \mu_{jr(i)} - \beta_{1,r(i)}(x_i^1 - z_j^1)^2 - \beta_{2,r(i)}(x_i^2 - z_j^2)^2, \ \beta_{1,r(i)} \geq 0, \beta_{2,r(i)} \geq 0 \quad (3)$$

The distinctive features of the utility function are the following:

- in addition to the state-level intercept μ_j, the specific regional-level component $\mu_{jr(i)}$ is captured;
- the individual sensitivity along each of the two ideological dimensions is controlled separately, $\beta_{2,r(i)}$ and $\beta_{1,r(i)}$
- the ideological sensitivity varies across the regions.

4 Results

The estimation of the coefficients, representing the exogenous party valences and the spatial ideological sensitivity, of (8) is achieved in two stages. First, the political ideological scores for individuals and parties are constructed based on surveys from *Centro de Investigaciones Sociológicas (CIS)*. Party ideological positions are assumed to be mean ideological positions amongst those individuals in the sample who claimed to have voted for these parties. The following subsection presents the estimation of the ideological scores in detail. Next, ideological scores for individuals and parties are plugged-in the assumed voting utilities, (8), and *multinomial logit regression for the varying choice sets*,[4] (2), is estimated given the utilities. In the estimated model, the political ideological scores are the independent variables and the claimed party voted is the dependent variable.

The second half of this section discusses the results of the estimation of (8). The discussion starts with the review of the obtained ideological spatial coefficients. Then, the paper focuses the exogenous party valences. Because of the space limit of the paper, results are presented only for some regions: the historical regions—*Catalonia*, *Basque Country*, and *Galicia*, and the central *Community of Madrid*, and non-nationalist *Andalusia*. The changes of the exogenous valences of the nationalist parties, *CiU*, *ERC*, *PNV*, *Amaiur*, and *BNG* are of special interest in this section, since they reflect the non-ideological part in the voters' motivation to vote for these parties.

4.1 Political Ideology: Individual and Party Scores

The major variables of the analysis, the individual ideological positions, were derived from a *component factor analysis*[5] estimated for a number of questions

[4]The models for both elections (2008 and 2011) were estimated with the use of the *r package jags*. The following holds for both years. (1) The total number of the iterations in each of the three chains was 12,500 with the first 7500 burned. (2) According to the Raftery-Lewis diagnostic, 2 of 3 chains converged on the probability level of 0.95. (3) The scale reduction factors and the multivariate reduction factor do not exceed 1.1 according to the Gelman-Rubin diagnostic.

[5]Via *the r package factanal*.

coming from the surveys of *Centro de Investigaciones Sociológicas (CIS)* run in 2008 and 2011.[6] The analysis used only the questions aimed at reflecting the socio-economic and nationalist self-evaluations of the individuals in the sample (see Appendix—*Survey Questions*). Two individual ideological scores—the left-right dimension and the central-periphery dimension—were assumed to be the hidden variables best explaining the questions from the sample and having the least possible mutual correlation.[7]

Tables 9 and 10 present the contributions of each question to the calculated individual ideological scores. The results for 2008 and 2011 are very similar, for some variables identical. Therefore most of the following discussion will to address both years at once. Most survey questions contribute to the coordinates in both dimensions in both years. Meanwhile, attitudes to government interventions in the economy and towards people of different origin or culture load only in the second dimension. Also, the nationalist self-identification loads only in the first dimension, so, according to the this analysis, has nothing to do with the right-left scale. This observation confirms the idea that in the modern research on Spanish politics, the socio-economic dimension and the central-periphery dimension tend to become less mutually attached, contrary to the former belief, that only one independent ideological dimension exists in Spain (Amat 2012). However, despite the explicit minimization of the correlation between the axes, as Tables 11 and 12 show, the ideological dimensions still correlate more strongly (0.1 compared to around 0) than in similar CFAs in the spatial voting analysis with social and economic dimensions (Schofield and Sened 2006). The negative correlation points to the fact that in Spain a higher level of peripheral nationalism is associated with more non-conservative, or left, socio-economic views. Overall, the variance in the social-economic axis is slightly lower than that in the central-periphery axis (see Tables 11 and 12). Another interesting observation is that question on the voters' preferred extent of decentralization loads significantly more on the first dimension, even through it is an economic issue, since it concerns the tax system. Also, a higher level of tolerance towards *ETA* loads negatively on the scale of nationalism.

Tables 1 and 2 show the means of the ideological scores grouped by voted parties. As seen, according to the analysis, in both 2008 and 2011, *PP* is the most extreme right party, while *IU*—the most extreme left party. In 2011, *PP* and *IU* converged slightly towards the mean. In terms of the nationalist scale, *ERC* was the most extreme in 2008, while the newly established Basque party *Amaiur* was the most extreme in 2010. Interestingly, all state-level parties have not almost changed their positions between 2008 and 2010, while there has been certain shifts among the

---

[6]The original data were refined in the two steps. First, observations with missing or undefined variable for *party voted* were dropped. Second, for the remaining n = 4551(2008) and n = 4401(2011) the multiple imputation was performed via the *r package mice*.

[7]In the other words, their correlation was minimized, so the basis in the two-dimensional space of these two hidden variable is considered orthogonal.

Table 1 General Elections 2008: ideological means by party

Axis/party	PSOE	PP	IU	UPyD	CiU	ERC	PNV	BNG
Left-right	−0.17	0.42	−0.57	−0.32	0.14	−0.28	0.16	−0.33
Central-periphery	0	−0.37	0.67	−0.30	1.13	2.13	1.72	0.77

Table 2 General Elections 2011: ideological means by party

Axis/party	PP	PSOE	IU	UPyD	CiU	Amaiur	PNV	BNG	ERC
Left-right	0.26	−0.17	−0.51	−0.22	0.16	−0.34	−0.18	−0.11	−0.32
Central-periphery	−0.32	−0.01	0.34	−0.24	1.29	2.15	1.57	1.92	0.88

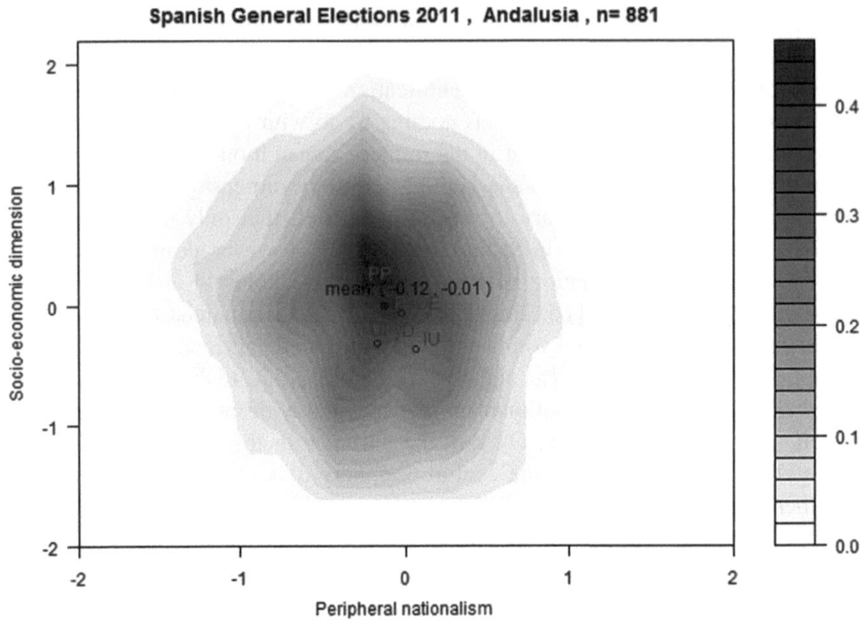

Fig. 10 Density distribution of the individual ideological positions

regional parties in terms of the central-periphery dimensions—*ERC* became less extreme, while *BNG* became more so.

The best way to capture the ideological differences across the regions is to look at the density plots.[8] As Figs. 2 and 7 show, between the General election of 2008 and that of 2011 the electorate's preferences on average converged to the mean. While in 2008, two ideological peaks existed, one of which was significantly to the left of the nationalist mean, in 2011 only one peak was left. The plots for *Basque Country* (Figs. 4 and 9), *Community of Madrid* (Figs. 3 and 11), *Andalusia* (Figs. 5 and 10), and *Catalonia* (Figs. 6 and 11) present the ideological distributions

[8]Means of the scores by region can be found in Tables 13 and 14.

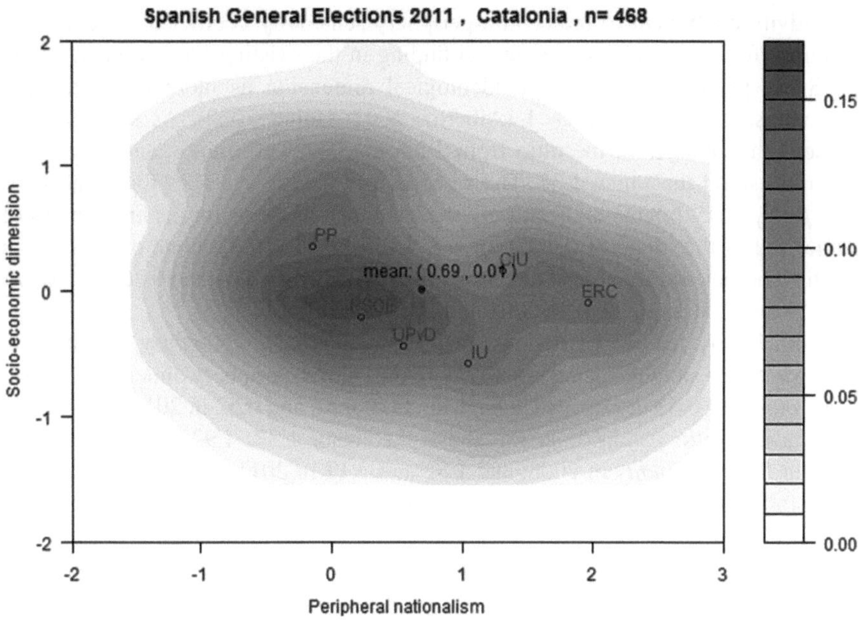

Fig. 11 Density distribution of the individual ideological positions

for the regions. Predictably, *Catalonia* and *Basque Country* exhibit a high level of a peripheral nationalism. Meanwhile, in terms of the socio-economic scale, *Basque country* looks slightly leftist, while Catalonia is almost neutral.

4.2 *Spatial Ideological Sensitivity*

This section elaborates on the spatial component, $-\beta_{1,r(i)}(x_i^1 - z_j^1)^2 - \beta_{2,r(i)}(x_i^2 - z_j^2)^2$, of the individual voting utility (3). This component controls for the political ideology in the voting motivations of the individuals represented with the utility function. Given the model, the part of the voting behavior unexplained by the political ideology is captured with the *exogenous party valence*, $\mu_j + \mu_{jr(i)}$, which is discussed in the following subsection. As mentioned before, the spatial ideological sensitivity coefficients, $\beta_{1,r(i)}$ and $\beta_{2,r(i)}$, reflect how strongly people react to an increase in the ideological distance between them and the parties. The higher these coefficients are the more costly it is in terms of votes for the parties that deviate from the voters' preferences. The ratio of the coefficients, $\beta_{2,r(i)}/\beta_{1,r(i)}$, shows how much more sensitive, by region r(i), the voters are in the socio-economic ideological dimension than to the central-periphery dimension.

Tables 18 and 19 present the estimates for the spatial coefficients for all Spanish regions in 2008 and 2011. Both tables present the ratio of the socio-economic sensitivity coefficient to the central-periphery sensitivity coefficient. These tables confirm, for most regions, the general finding in the existing literature that people in Spain perceive the left-right ideological dimension as more important than nationalism, $\beta_{2,r(i)}/\beta_{1,r(i)} > 1$ (Albertos 2002; Heller 2002). As seen, in most regions the changes in the ratio from 2008 to 2011 were minor, and on average the ratio stood the same, 1.37. The same is true for the averages for $\beta_{1,r(i)}$, 0.76, and $\beta_{2,r(i)}$, 1.05. Interestingly, most of the spatial coefficients for the first dimension either fall in the range of 0.4–0.6 or 0.8–1.0, while for the second dimension the spatial coefficients are almost uniformly distributed from 0.64 and 0.70 in *Navarre*, to 1.59 and 1.56 in *Aragon*, in 2008 and 2011 respectively.

Both highly nationalist regions, *Catalonia* and *Basque Country*, fall into the group with the smaller spatial sensitivity in the central-periphery dimension, 0.57 in *Catalonia* and 0.53 in *Basque Country* in 2008; 0.58 and 0.52 in 2011 respectively, and have a ratio $\beta_{2,r(i)}/\beta_{1,r(i)}$ far above the mean 1.37: 1.92 in *Catalonia* and 2.26 in *Basque County* in 2008; and 1.82 and 2.17 in 2011 respectively. Based on these ratios, *Basque Country* is significantly more electorally sensitive to the moves of the parties along the socio-economic axis than the nationalist axis. However, since $\beta_{1,Catalonia}$ and $\beta_{1,BasqueCountry}$ are close, this is mostly a consequence of the differences of the sensitivity in the left-right ideological dimension, which is significantly higher in *Basque Country* than in *Catalonia*.

Based on the estimates of the spatial ideological sensitivity (Tables 18 and 19), the ideological score means by region (Tables 13 and 14) and the density Figs. 2, 3, 4, 5, 6, 7, 8, 9, it may be concluded than between the General Elections in 2008 and the General Elections in 2011 no significant changes in terms of the political ideology occurred in Spain.

Meanwhile, a more detailed analysis, namely the correlations between the data presented in Tables 13, 14, 18, and 19, might provide certain interesting results (see Table 3) in terms of the relationship between the ideological sensitivity and the mean ideology by region. The most striking observation is that regions with more right-wing ideology are less sensitive to the changes of the positions of the parties along the nationalist ideological dimension. Another important observation is the growth in the correlation between the mean nationalist ideological score and the spatial ideological sensitivity in relation to the nationalist dimension, from the "noisy" score of 0.08 to the more meaningful score of 0.24. Lastly, the magnitude of the change in the ratio β_2/β_1 has a positive correlation with the nationalist views, 0.45, and negative association with the right-wing views, −0.41.

Table 3 Correlations between mean individual ideological scores by region and regional spatial ideological sensitivity

	2008			2011			
Mean regional ideology	β_1	β_2	β_2/β_1	β_1	β_2	β_2/β_1	$\Delta(\beta_2/\beta_1)$
Central-periphery	0.08	−0.18	0.21	0.24	0.16	−0.10	0.45
Socio-economic	−0.43	−0.05	−0.22	−0.45	−0.19	0.13	−0.41

4.3 Exogenous Party Valence

As mentioned in the previous subsection, in this analysis, the *exogenous party valence*, $\mu_j + \mu_{jr(i)}$ reflects the share of voting motivation of the individuals in the sample that could not have been explained with the *spatial ideological component*, $-\beta_{1,r(i)}(x_i^1 - z_j^1)^2 - \beta_{2,r(i}(x_i^2 - z_j^2)^2$, given individual voting utility (3). As shown in the previous subsection, no major changes of political ideology occurred in Spain from the General Elections in 2008 to the General Elections in 2011. Hence the observed changes of the electoral outcomes in 2011 relative to 2008 must be because of the changes of the *exogenous party valence*. The aim of this subsection is to provide evidence for this, pointing out how these changes in *valence* were distributed across parties.

Tables 16 and 17 show the estimates for the *exogenous party valence* for 2008 and 2011 respectively. The first column provides state-level party valences. Other columns provide estimates for the differences between state-level party valence and regional party valence for those regions where this party competed. The blank cells in the table indicate regions where a given party did not run. For both years, *PSOE* was employed as a base category. In 2011 *PP* won the elections, and its state-level valence relative to PSOE increased from −0.42 to 0.59. All other presented parties (expect *BNG*, the *valence* of which fell from −0.99 to −1.94), experienced a rise in the *exogenous valence* as well, similar to that of *PP* relative to PSOE. However, this change is mostly unequal to the change in *PP* valence. Hence, it can be said that the overall distribution of *exogenous party valence* changed between the elections in 2008 and 2011, but PP did not completely "substitute" for the base *PSOE* in valence terms.

Starting from the state-level non-major parties, *UPyD* experienced the most striking increase: its valence grew from −3.72 to −1.81, which is more than double. Meanwhile, this party has a significantly lower valence in *Catalonia* and *Galicia*, by −0.33 and −0.87, respectively, and a higher valence in *Community of Madrid*, by 0.80, in 2011. Interestingly, these regional differences increased substantially from 2008 to 2011. For another non-major state-level party *IU*, the growth of the valence was substantial as well: from −2.42 to 1.23.

Among the regional-level parties, *ERC* experienced the most substantial growth: from −3.03 to −1.90. Strikingly, the regional difference for *ERC*, which competes also in *Valencia*, in *Catalonia*, became huge in 2011—*-1.41* (which is probably why its electoral result did not grow from 2008 to 2010). *CiU*'s valence grew by about the same amount as that of *PP*: from −2.41 to −1.57. *Amaiur* was a new party, so the fact that its valence was about the same as of the winner PP in 2011 is impressive. *PNV* did not experience a significant growth in terms of valence. While its magnitude grew from −0.42 to 0.00, the errors were larger. Lastly, as already mentioned, *BNG* experienced an impressive decrease: from −0.99 to −1.94.

Table 4 Correlations between votes and exogenous party valence

	2008	2011	
	μ_j	μ_j	$\Delta_{2011-2008}\mu_j$
Votes	0.60	0.44	−0.06
$\Delta_{2011-2008}$ votes		0.41	0.39

Table 4 provides a summary of the relationship between votes and *exogenous party valence* for the Spanish General Elections in 2008 and 2010, based on the data presented in Tables 6, 7, 16, and 17. As seen, the correlation between the number of votes and party valence decreased from 2011 to 2008, from 0.60 to 0.44. However, among the parties participating in both elections, there is a substantial correlation between the changes in party valence and the change in the number of votes between the elections, 0.39. Also, the party valence in 2011 and the change in votes are correlated almost the same, 0.41. However, the total number of votes in 2011 and the change in valence are not significantly correlated, –0.06.

The analysis above shows that, despite that the overall effect of the *exogenous party valence* on the number of votes decreased from 2008 to 2011, the changes between the electoral results in 2008 and 2011 is a consequence of the *exogenous party valences* in 2011. However, for one party this effect was especially strong, *UPyD*. For regional parties, this is less clear. Overall, seemingly, a few parties benefited, because of their valence, from the former *PSOE* voters, who did not swing to *PP* in 2011. These parties were the non-marginal state-level parties *UPyD* and *UI* and the regional parties *CiU* and *Amaiur*.

5 Conclusion

The paper has shown that the rise in votes experienced by certain non-marginal minority parties in Spain from the General Elections in 2008 to the General Elections in 2011 is a consequence of an increase in *exogenous party valence*. As said in the introduction, a possible interpretation for this change is an increase in voter trust, meaning, that the minority parties are perceived better than the major parties in terms of their capacity to deliver deserved policy outcomes (Clarke 2009). The shift of a significant number of votes away from the major parties was surprising within the historically established bipartisan political structure of Spain. And, it, probably, signified a general crisis in the political system (Navarro 2014), as may be confirmed by flow of the political events in Spain since 2011.

First of all, a general frustration in the corrupt and inefficient political decisions and political establishment, led to the first demonstration (on May 15, 2011) of the 15-M (or anti-austerity) movement that thereafter organized a substantial number of public demonstrations all over Spain. At the same time, in Catalonia, which "generally never believed in a multinational Spain" (Navarro 2014), huge rallies for self-determination took place. Having reached its peak during a huge rally on 11 September 2014; Catalonia's main intention was to conduct a self-determination referendum. However, this referendum has never taken place since it has been repeatedly declared to be unconstitutional by the Spanish Constitutional court.

Second, as a development of the 15-M movement, a new political force—the party *Podemos*—emerged in 2014. Reflecting the general attitudes during the protests of 2011–2014, *Podemos*, founded by a university professor *Pablo Iglesias*, was a left-wing party with no roots in the old political establishment. Since its appearance, *Podemos* has exhibited a sharp growth in its popularity. An impressive existing achievement of *Podemos* is its successful performance during the country's elections to the European Parliament in 2014 May, just a few months after the party was created. By the end of 2015, the enthusiasm for *Podemos* is decreasing in favor of *Ciudadanos*, a small liberal party that saw a growth in its popularity after its success in the regional Catalan elections of September 2015.

To sum up, the crisis in the voter trust in the performance of the two Spain's mainstream parties *PP* and *PSOE* led to a relative increase in the exogenous party valence of certain minority parties, namely, *UPyD* and, to a smaller extent, *CiU*. In particular, we can see how changes in the exogenous valence of the parties perfectly tracks their electoral success.

Appendix

Survey Questions (The Same in 2008 and 2011)

1. **Multiculturality/immigration issue**

   Some people think it is very positive that people of different origin, culture and religion coexist in the same country (these people would be at the point 0 on the scale). Others think that the presence of migrants can endanger the values and the culture here (these would be at point 10), and there are others who would be at intermediate positions. What place would you stand? (0–10)

2. **Government intervention in economy**

   Some people think they should improve public services and benefits, even if they pay more taxes (these people would be at the point 0 on the scale). Others think it's more important to pay less tax, even if it means reducing public services and social benefits (these would be at point 10), and there are others who would be at intermediate positions. . What place would you stand? (0–10)

3. **Anti-terrorist policy issue**

   Some people think that the only way to stop is defeat ETA policing (these people would be at the point 0 on the scale). Others think that to end ETA also need dialogue (these would be at point 10), and there are others who would be at intermediate positions. What place would you stand? (0–10)
4. **Conservative values scale**

   Some people believe that the key is to defend our traditional religious and moral values (these people would be at the point 0 on the scale), while others think the key is to defend the freedom of the individual to be and believe what you want (these would be at point 10), and there are others who would be at intermediate positions. What place would you stand? (0–10)
5. **Decentralization**

   I will now present some alternative formulas for the organization of the State in Spain. Tell me, please, what do you prefer? (0–4)

   - Just the main state without autonomous regions
   - The main state without autonomous regions as nowadays
   - The main state without autonomous regions more independent than nowadays
   - The main state with autonomous regions having an easy legal option to become independent

6. **Nationalist self-identification**

   Which of the following statements would you say best expresses your feelings? (0–4)

   - I feel only Spanish
   - I feel more Spanish than …
   - I feel as Spanish as …
   - I feel more … than Spanish
   - I feel only …

7. **Proudness to be Spanish**

   To what extent would you say that you are proud to be Spanish: very proud, proud, somewhat proud or not proud? (0–3) (Tables 5, 6, 7, 8, 9, 10, 11 12, 13, 14).

Table 5 Autonomous communities and regions of Spain

cid	Name	Historical nationalities[a]	Observations 2008	Observations 2011
1	Andalusia	✗	1262	1225
2	Aragon	✗	263	236
3	Asturias	✗	128	163
4	Balearic Islands	✗	172	137
5	Canary Islands	✗	356	324
6	Cantabria	✗	99	136
7	Castilla-La Mancha	✗	292	370
8	Castile and Leon	✗	473	472
9	Catalonia	✓	694	696
10	Valencian Community	✗	577	410
11	Extremadura	✗	199	190
12	Galicia	✓	511	525
13	Community of Madrid	✗	374	432
14	Region of Murcia	✗	190	176
15	Navarre	✗	75	147
16	Basque Country	✓	381	362
17	La Rioja	✗	37	81
		6083	6082	

[a]Inherited from the Franco's regime

Table 6 Parties participating in General Elections in 2008

pid	Name	Regional	Provinces	Observations	Percentage	Elections
1	PSOE	✗		2455	53.94	43.75
2	PP	✗		1432	31.47	39.94
3	IU (ICV in Catalonia)	✗		215	4.72	3.77
4	UPyD	✗		66	1.45	1.19
5	CiU	✓	Catalonia	82	1.80	3.03
7	PNV	✓	Basque Country	62	1.36	1.19
8	BNG	✓	Galicia	42	0.92	0.83
6	ERC	✓	Catalona, Valencia	40	0.88	1.16
9	CC	✓	Canary Islands	28	0.53	0.68
10	EA	✓	Basque Country	12	0.23	0.20
11	CHA	✓	Aragon	9	0.17	0.15
12	Na-Bai	✓	Navarra	12	0.23	0.24
13	*Other*			96	1.82	3.04

Table 7 Parties participating in General Elections in 2011

pid	Name	Regional	Provinces	Observations	Percentage	Elections
1	PP	✗		2030	46.09	44.63
2	PSOE	✗		1280	29.06	28.76
3	IU (ICV in Catalonia)	✗		344	7.81	6.92
4	UPyD	✗		220	5.00	4.70
5	CiU	✓	Catalonia	123	2.79	4.17
6	Amaiur	✓	Navarra, Basque Country	71	1.61	1.37
7	PNV	✓	Basque Country	55	1.25	1.33
8	BNG	✓	Galicia	44	1.00	0.76
9	ERC	✓	Catalonia, Valencia	42	0.95	1.06
10	CC	✓	Canary Islands	14	0.32	0.59
11	Compromis Equo	✗		48	1.09	0.51
12	FAC	✓	Canary Islands, Asturias, Valencia	11	0.25	0.41
13	Geroa Bai	✓	Navarra	21	0.48	0.17
14	CHA	✓	Aragon	4	0.09	0.057
15	*Other*			96	2.20	1.60

Table 8 Parties participating in General Elections in 2011

pid	Name	Regional	Provinces	Observations	Percentage	Elections
1	PP	✗		2030	46.09	44.63
2	PSOE	✗		1280	29.06	28.76
3	IU (ICV in Catalonia)	✗		344	7.81	6.92
4	UPyD	✗		220	5.00	4.70
5	CiU	✓	Catalonia	123	2.79	4.17
6	Amaiur	✓	Navarra, Basque Country	71	1.61	1.37
7	PNV	✓	Basque Country	55	1.25	1.33
8	BNG	✓	Galicia	44	1.00	0.76
9	ERC	✓	Catalonia, Valencia	42	0.95	1.06
10	CC	✓	Canary Islands	14	0.32	0.59
11	Compromis Equo	✗		48	1.09	0.51
12	FAC	✓	Canary Islands, Asturias, Valencia	11	0.25	0.41
13	Geroa Bai	✓	Navarra	21	0.48	0.17
14	CHA	✓	Aragon	4	0.09	0.057
15	*Other*			96	2.20	1.60

Table 9 CFA: Factor loadings for 2008

		Central-periphery	Socio-economic	Uniqueness
1	Multiculturality/immigration issue		0.649	0.575
2	Government intervention in economy		0.415	0.826
3	Anti-terrorist policy issue (ETA)	−0.216	0.527	0.676
4	Conservative values scale	0.339	−0.370	0.748
5	Decentralization	0.584	−0.145	0.638
6	Nationalist self-identification	0.582		0.656
7	Proudness to be Spanish	0.670	−0.128	0.535
	SS loadings	1.296	1.050	
	Proportion variance	0.185	0.150	
	Cumulative variance	0.185	0.335	

The χ^2 statistic is 67.54 on 8 degrees of freedom
The p-value for the model with 2 factors is 0.00001

Table 10 CFA: Factor loadings for 2011

		Central-periphery	Socio-economic	Uniqueness
1	Multiculturality/immigration issue		0.636	0.575
2	Government intervention in economy		0.425	0.826
3	Anti-terrorist policy issue (ETA)	−0.225	0.514	0.676
4	Conservative values scale	0.422	−0.228	0.748
5	Decentralization	0.588	−0.136	0.638
6	Nationalist self-identification	0.629		0.656
7	Proudness to be Spanish	0.666	−0.107	0.535
	SS loadings	1.422	0.934	
	Proportion variance	0.203	0.133	
	Cumulative variance	0.203	0.337	

The χ^2 statistic is 21.27 on 8 degrees of freedom
The p-value for the model with 2 factors is 0.00646

Table 11 CFA: correlation matrix for the scores, 2008

	Central-periphery	Socio-economic
Central-periphery	0.654	−0.104
Socio-economic	−0.104	0.585

Table 12 CFA: correlation matrix for the scores, 2011

	Central-periphery	Socio-economic
Central-periphery	0.680	−0.095
Socio-economic	−0.095	0.558

Table 13 Ideological means by region: 2008

cid	Name	Historical nationalities	Nationalist	Left-right
1	Andalusia	✗	−0.12	−0.12
2	Aragon	✗	−0.20	−0.05
3	Asturias	✗	−0.17	−0.16
4	Balearic Islands	✗	0.14	0.08
5	Canary Islands	✗	0.04	0.00
6	Cantabria	✗	−0.13	−0.21
7	Castilla-La Mancha	✗	−0.36	0.15
8	Castile and Leon	✗	−0.38	0.07
9	Catalonia	✓	0.66	−0.02
10	Valencian Community	✗	−0.17	0.05
11	Extremadura	✗	−0.19	0.14
12	Galicia	✓	0.10	−0.04
13	Community of Madrid	✗	−0.25	−0.25
14	Region of Murcia	✗	−0.28	0.27
15	Navarre	✗	0.65	−0.24
16	Basque Country	✓	1.05	−0.28
17	La Rioja	✗	0.01	−0.08
			0.00	0.00

Table 14 Ideological means by region: 2011

cid	Name	Historical nationalities	Nationalist	Left-right
1	Andalusia	✗	−0.12	−0.01
2	Aragon	✗	−0.27	0.27
3	Asturias	✗	−0.24	0.10
4	Balearic Islands	✗	0.01	0.03
5	Canary Islands	✗	0.06	0.09
6	Cantabria	✗	−0.31	−0.06
7	Castilla-La Mancha	✗	−0.31	0.03
8	Castile and Leon	✗	−0.45	0.11
9	Catalonia	✓	0.69	0.01
10	Valencian Community	✗	−0.17	0.04
11	Extremadura	✗	−0.15	0.11
12	Galicia	✓	0.05	0.03
13	Community of Madrid	✗	−0.28	−0.30
14	Region of Murcia	✗	−0.20	0.13
15	Navarre	✗	0.74	−0.11
16	Basque Country	✓	1.08	−0.27
17	La Rioja	✗	−0.27	0.04
			0.00	0.00

Implementation of the VCL

The *varying choice logit* with the individual voting utility function (3), for which Sect. 3 provides a theoretical description, was implemented through the Bayesian approach via Gibbs sampling (Gelman et al. 2013) in the *r package rjags* with R version 3.0.3.

In the beginning of the computational analysis, all estimated coefficients for the formula (3) were assigned the commonly recommended uninformative normal priors with their variances distributed inverse-gamma (Gelman et al. 2013):

$$\beta_{t,r(i)} \sim \mathcal{N}(0, \gamma_\beta),\ t \in \{1, 2\}, \forall i$$

$$\mu_p \sim \mathcal{N}(0, \gamma_{\mu_1}),\ p \in P$$

$$\mu_{p,r(i)} \sim \mathcal{N}(0, \gamma_{\mu_2}),\ p \in P, \forall i$$

$$\gamma_{beta} \sim Inv - Gamma(0.1, 0.1)$$

$$\gamma_{mu_1} \sim Inv - Gamma(0.1, 0.1)$$

$$\gamma_{mu_2} \sim Inv - Gamma(0.1, 0.1)$$

The model graph for the analysis consisted of 591,480 nodes for the data on General Spanish Elections in 2008; and 664,432 for 2011. The total number of the iterations in each of the three chains for each of the analysis was 12,500 with the first 7500 burned. Table 15 presents the deviance statistics for this estimation.

Convergence Statistics

- ***Spanish General Elections in 2008***

  The Gelman-Rubin diagnostic.

  All points estimates for the *potential scale reduction factors* for the parameters did not exceed 1.04, while the upper confidence interval estimates were less than 1.15. For most of the parameters both point estimates and the upper confidence interval were 1.0. *The multivariate potential scale reduction factor* was 1.09.

  The Raftery-Lewis diagnostic.

  Two of three chains converged on the probability level of 0.95.
- ***Spanish General Elections in 2011***

  The Gelman-Rubin diagnostic.

  All points estimates for the *potential scale reduction factors* for the parameters did not exceed 1.07, while the upper confidence interval estimates were less than 1.2.[9] For most of the parameters both point estimates and the upper confidence interval were 1.0. *The multivariate potential scale reduction factor* was 1.09.

  The Raftery-Lewis diagnostic.

  Two of three chains converged on the probability level of 0.95 (Tables 15, 16, 17, 18, 19, 20, 21).

Table 15 Deviance statistics for VCL

	2008	2011
Mean deviance	8338	10,143
Penalty	89.83	108.5
Penalized deviance	8428	10,251

[9]According to the Gelman-Rubin diagnostic, the upper confidence interval for the potential reduction factors for μ_7 is 1.20, for the rest of the coefficients the upper C.I for their potential reduction factor is less than 1.10.

Table 16 Filter matrix (Φ) for the Spanish General Elections in 2008

	PSOE	PP	IU	UPyD	CiU	ERC	PNV	BNG	CC	EA	CHA	Na-Bai
Andalusia	1	1	1	1	0	0	0	0	0	0	0	0
Aragon	1	1	1	1	0	0	0	0	0	0	1	0
Asturias	1	1	1	1	0	0	0	0	0	0	0	0
Balearic Islands	1	1	1	1	0	0	0	0	0	0	0	0
Canary Islands	1	1	1	1	0	0	0	0	1	0	0	0
Cantabria	1	1	1	1	0	0	0	0	0	0	0	0
Castilla-La Mancha	1	1	1	1	0	0	0	0	0	0	0	0
Castile and Leon	1	1	1	1	0	0	0	0	0	0	0	0
Catalonia	1	1	1	1	1	1	0	0	0	0	0	0
Valencian Community	1	1	1	1	0	0	0	0	0	0	0	0
Extremadura	1	1	1	1	0	0	0	0	0	0	0	0
Galicia	1	1	1	1	0	0	0	1	0	0	0	0
Community of Madrid	1	1	1	1	0	0	0	0	0	0	0	0
Region of Murcia	1	1	1	1	0	0	0	0	0	0	0	0
Navarre	1	1	1	1	0	0	0	0	0	0	0	1
Basque Country	1	1	1	1	0	0	1	0	0	1	0	0
La Rioja	1	1	1	1	0	0	0	0	0	0	0	0

Table 17 Filter matrix (Φ) for the Spanish General Elections in 2011

	PSOE	PP	IU	UPyD	Amaiur	CiU	ERC	PNV	BNG	CC	Compromis	FAC	CHA	Geroi-Bai
Andalusia	1	1	1	1	0	0	0	0	0	0	1	0	0	0
Aragon	1	1	1	1	0	0	0	0	0	0	1	0	1	0
Asturias	1	1	1	1	0	0	0	0	0	0	1	1	0	0
Balearic Islands	1	1	1	1	0	0	0	0	0	0	1	0	0	0
Canary Islands	1	1	1	1	0	0	0	0	0	1	1	0	0	0
Cantabria	1	1	1	1	0	0	0	0	0	0	1	0	0	0
Castilla-La Mancha	1	1	1	1	0	0	0	0	0	0	1	0	0	0
Castilla and Leon	1	1	1	1	0	0	0	0	0	0	1	0	0	0
Catalonia	1	1	1	1	0	1	1	0	0	0	1	0	0	0
Valencian Community	1	1	1	1	0	0	0	0	0	0	1	0	0	0
Extremadura	1	1	1	1	0	0	0	0	0	0	1	0	0	0
Galicia	1	1	1	1	0	0	0	0	1	0	1	0	0	0
Community of Madrid	1	1	1	1	0	0	0	0	0	0	1	0	0	0
Region of Murcia	1	1	1	1	0	0	0	0	0	0	1	0	0	0
Navarre	1	1	1	1	1	0	0	0	0	0	1	0	0	1
Basque Country	1	1	1	1	1	0	0	1	0	0	1	0	0	0
La Rioja	1	1	1	1	0	0	0	0	0	0	1	0	0	0

[a]La Rioja did not have enough observations for the program to run and had to be dropped from the analysis

Table 18 General Parliamentary elections in 2008: Spatial ideological coefficients (β_1—the central periphery dimension, β_2—socio-ecomomic dimension)

	Historical region	β_1	β_2	β_2/β_1
Andalusia	✗	0.97	0.67	0.69
		[0.72, 1.21]	[0.52, 0.83]	
Aragon	✗	0.97	1.59	**1.64**
		[0.47, 1.50]	[1.13, 2.10]	
Asturias	✗	1.30	0.92	0.71
		[0.65, 2.03]	[0.47, 1.38]	
Balearic Islands	✗	0.77	0.89	**1.16**
		[0.41, 1.21]	[0.41, 1.50]	
Canary Islands	✗	0.47	0.89	**1.89**
		[0.07, 0.90]	[0.69, 1.27]	
Cantabria	✗	0.40	1.47	**3.68**
		[−0.03,1.15]	[0.68, 2.37]	
Castilla-La Mancha	✗	0.94	0.78	0.83
		[0.65, 1.40]	[0.48, 1.12]	
Castile and Leon	✗	1.18	1.37	**1.16**
		[0.75, 1.62]	[1.04, 1.74]	
Catalonia	✓	0.57	1.09	**1.91**
		[0.47, 0.67]	[0.81, 1.38]	
Valencian Community	✗	0.50	0.96	**1.92**
		[0.30, 0.69]	[0.76, 1.16]	
Extremadura	✗	0.41	1.02	**2.49**
		[−0.35, 1.05]	[0.61, 1.52]	
Galicia	✓	0.99	1.45	**1.46**
		[0.70, 1.32]	[1.12, 1.84]	
Community of Madrid	✗	0.84	1.05	**1.25**
		[0.70, 1.32]	[0.76, 1.38]	
Region of Murcia	✗	0.82	0.76	0.93
		[0.56, 1.24]	[0.43, 1.10]	
Navarre	✗	0.56	0.64	**1.14**
		[0.29, 1.40]	[0.07, 1.34]	
Basque Country	✓	0.53	1.20	**2.26**
		[0.33, 0.86]	[0.57, 1.86]	
Mean		0.76	1.05	1.37
Standard error		0.28	0.29	1.05

N = 4530

Note: The estimates are provided with the credible intervals

Note: Values of $\beta_2/\beta_1 > 1$ are indicated in bold

Table 19 General Parliamentary elections in 2011: Spatial ideological coefficients (β_1—the central periphery dimension, β_2—socio-ecomomic dimension)

	Historical region	β_1	β_2	β_2/β_1	Change 2011–2008
Andalusia	✗	0.98	0.68	0.69	0.00
		[0.74, 1.22]	[0.52, 0.84]		
Aragon	✗	0.89	1.56	**1.75**	0.11
		[0.39, 1.43]	[1.07, 2.06]		
Asturias	✗	1.28	0.95	0.74	0.03
		[0.55, 2.05]	[0.42, 1.49]		
Balearic Islands	✗	0.77	0.88	**1.14**	−0.01
		[0.37, 1.20]	[0.42, 1.40]		
Canary Islands	✗	0.48	0.96	**2.00**	0.11
		[0.10, 0.90]	[0.67, 1.28]		
Cantabria	✗	0.39	1.45	**3.72**	0.04
		[0.37, 1.17]	[0.76, 2.20]		
Castilla-La Mancha	✗	0.94	0.8	0.85	0.02
		[0.45, 1.46]	[0.48, 1.17]		
Castile and Leon	✗	1.23	1.37	**1.11**	−0.05
		[0.80, 1.68]	[1.06, 1.69]		
Catalonia	✓	0.58	1.06	**1.83**	−0.08
		[0.48, 0.69]	[0.78, 1.36]		
Valencian Community	✗	0.46	0.96	**2.09**	0.17
		[0.29, 0.64]	[0.73, 1.21]		
Extremadura	✗	0.4	1.03	**2.58**	0.09
		[−0.24, 1.03]	[0.61, 1.51]		
Galicia	✓	1.01	1.45	**1.44**	−0.03
		[0.70, 1.32]	[1.11, 1.81]		
Community of Madrid	✗	0.86	1.07	**1.24**	−0.01
		[0.58, 1.15]	[0.78, 1.38]		
Region of Murcia	✗	0.82	0.75	0.91	−0.01
		[0.32, 1.42]	[0.43, 1.08]		
Navarre	✗	0.62	0.7	**1.13**	−0.01
		[0.33, 0.98]	[0.03, 1.43]		
Basque Country	✓	0.52	1.14	**2.19**	−0.07
		[0.40, 1.66]	[0.54, 1.76]		
Mean		0.76	1.05	1.37	0
Standard error		0.28	0.28	0.96	−0.09

N = 4346
Note: The estimates are provided with the credible intervals
Note: Values of $\beta_2/\beta_1 > 1$ are indicated in bold

Table 20 General Parliamentary elections in 2008: Exogenous party valence (N = 4346)

	Spain	Catalonia	Basque County	Galicia	Community of Madrid	Andalusia
	μ_j	$\mu_{j,Catalonia}$	$\mu_{j,Basque}$	$\mu_{j,Galicia}$	$\mu_{j,Madrid}$	$\mu_{j,Andalusia}$
PSOE	0.00	0.14	**0.14**	0.36	−0.55	**0.35**
	[0.00,0.00]	[−0.56, 0.83]	**[0.57, 0.85]**	[−0.36, 1.12]	[−1.31, 0.14]	**[0.43, 1.07]**
PP	−0.42	**−0.99**	−0.48	0.58	−0.14	−0.01
	[−0.90, 0.7]	**[−1.71, −0.26]**	[−1.26, 0.30]	[−0.10,1,31]	[−0.87, 0.54]	[0.80, 0.74]
IU	**−2.42**	0.33	0.52	−0.09	−0.17	0.56
	[−3.00, −1.92]	[−0.38, 1.06]	[−0.26,1.34]	[0.92, 0.77]	[−0.99, 0.61]	[−0.22, 1.35]
UPyD	**−3.74**	−0.33	−0.16	−0.23	**0.96**	−0.04
	[−4.35, −3.18]	[−1.29, 0.59]	[−1.30, 0.89]	[1.25, 0.78]	**[0.14, 1.80]**	[−0.90, 0.78]
CiU	**−2.41**	0.00				
	[−3.50, −1.22]	[0.00,0.00]				
ERC	**−3.04**	0.56				
	[−4.38, −1.91]	[−0.51, 1.72]				
PNV	−0.42		0.00			
	[−1.88, 1.044]		[0.00,0.00]			
BNG	−0.99			0.00		
	[−2.51, 0.55]			[0.00,0.00]		

Note: The estimates are provided with the credible intervals
Note: Estimates with the credible intervals not including 0.00 are indicated in bold

Table 21 General Parliamentary elections in 2011: Exogenous party valence (N = 4530)

	Spain		Catalonia	Basque County	Galicia	Community of Madrid	Andalusia
	μ_j	$\Delta\mu_j$	$\mu_{j,Catalonia}$	$\mu_{j,Basque}$	$\mu_{j,Galicia}$	$\mu_{j,Madrid}$	$\mu_{j,Andalusia}$
PSOE	0.00	0.00	0.27	0.36	0.16	−0.42	0.48
	[0.00,0.00]		[−0.30, 0.91]	[−0.31, 1.02]	[−0.49, 0.83]	[−1.08, 0.18]	[−0.13, 1.06]
PP	**0.59**	1.02	−0.46	−0.32	**0.43**	−0.13	0.17
	[0.14, 1.03]		[−1.08,0.20]	[−1.03, 0.37]	**[0.18, 1.06]**	[−0.77, 0.55]	[−0.49, 0.79]
IU	**−1.23**	1.19	0.99	0.01	−0.41	−0.43	0.37
	[−1.71, −0.82,]		[−0.16, 1.14]	[−0.67, 0.81]	[−1.11, 0.32]	[−1.11, 0.24]	[−0.16, 1.18]
UPyD	**−1.81**	1.93	**−0.33**	0.00	**−0.87**	**0.80**	−0.04
	[−2.3, −1.30]		**[−1.86, −0.18]**	[−0.92, 0.75]	**[−1.79, −0.04]**	**[0.14,1.47]**	[−0.34, 1.04]
CiU	**−1.57**	0.84					
	[−2.68, −0.56]						
Amaiur	−0.34	–		0.27			
	[−1.38, 0.74]			[−0.71, 1.24]			
ERC	**−1.90**	2.07	**−1.41**				
	[−3.09, −0.79]		**[−2.53, −0.48]**				
PNV	0.00	0.48					
	[−1.23, 1.35]						
BNG	−1.90	−0.93					
	[3.00, −0.85]						

Note: The estimates are provided with the credible intervals
Note: Estimates with the credible intervals not including 0.00 are indicated in bold
Note: Values of $\Delta\mu_j > \Delta\mu_{PP}$ are underlined

Code: rjags[10]

```
data2008 <-
        structure(list(
             sec=c(...), lr=c(...), vote=c(...),
                 region=c(...), N = 4551, P = 13,
                 R = 17, psec = c(...), plr = c(...),
                 phi=c(...)),
        .Names = c("sec", "lr", "vote", "region",
                "N", "P", "R", "psec", "plr","phi"))

model
{
    for (i in 1:N) {
        for (p in 1:P) {
            v[i, p] <- lambda[p]
                        - beta[1, region[i]] * (sec[i] - psec[p])^2
                        - beta[2, region[i]] * (lr[i] - plr[p])^2)
                        + mu[region[i], p]
            expv[i, p] <- exp(v[i, p]) * phi[region[i], p]
            pv[i, p] <- expv[i, p]/sum(expv[i, 1:P])
        }
        vote[i] ~ dcat(pv[i, 1:P])
    }
    lambda[1] <- 0.00000E+00
    for (p in 2:P) {
        lambda[p] ~ dnorm(0.00000E+00, taul)
    }
    for (r in 1:R)
                for (i in 1:2) {
                        beta[i, r] ~ dnorm(0.00000E+00, tbeta)
                        }
        }

   for (r in 1:R) {
        for (p in 1:P) {
            mu[r, p] ~ dnorm(0.00000E+00, taum)
        }
    }
    taum ~ dgamma(0.1, 0.1)
    taul ~ dgamma(0.1, 0.1)
    tbeta ~ dgamma(0.1, 0.1)
}
```

[10]Without restricting the generality, the *rjags* code is given for 2008.

References

Albertos, J. F. (2002). Votar en dos dimensiones: el peso del nacionalismo y la ideología en el comportamiento electoral vasco, 1993–2001. *Revista Española de Ciencia Política, 6*(1), 153–181.

Amat, F. (2012). Party competition and preferences for inter-regional redistribution in spain. *South European Society and Politics, 17*(3), 449–465.

Ansolabehere, S., & Snyder, J. M. Jr. (2000). Valence politics and equilibrium in spatial election models. *Public Choice, 103*(3–4), 327–336.

Balcells i Ventura, L. (2007). Es el voto nacionalista un voto de proximidad o un voto de compensación? una nueva aproximación espacial al voto en dos dimensiones. *Revista española de ciencia política, 16*, 61–88.

Barceló, J. (2014). Contextual effects on subjective national identity. *Nations and Nationalism, 20*(4), 701–720.

Bennis, W. M., Medin, D. L., & Bartels, D. M. (2010). The costs and benefits of calculation and moral rules. *Perspectives on Psychological Science, 5*(2), 187–202.

Bonet, E., Montiel, S. P.-N., & Hernández, M. J. H. (2010). España en las urnas: Territorialización del voto e identidad nacional en las elecciones de 2008. In *Elecciones Generales 2008* (pp. 331–364). Madrid: Centro de Investigaciones Sociológicas (CIS).

Bosco, A., & Verney, S. (2012). Electoral epidemic: The political cost of economic crisis in southern Europe, 2010–11. *South European Society and Politics, 17*(2), 129–154.

Brubaker, R. (2011). Economic crisis, nationalism, and politicized ethnicity. In J. Fagerberg, D. Mowery, & R. Nelson (Eds.), *The deepening crisis. Governance challenges after neoliberalism*. New York and London: New York University Press.

Campbell, A., Converse, P. E., Miller, W. E., & Donald, E. (1966). *The American voter*.

Clarke, H. D. (2009). The theory of valence politics. In *Performance politics and the British voter* (pp. 31–52). Cambridge: Cambridge University Press.

Clarke, H. D., Scotto, T. J., & Kornberg, A. (2011). Valence politics and economic crisis: Electoral choice in Canada 2008 *Electoral studies*, 30(3):438–449.

del Interior, E. M. (2015). Consulta de resultados electorales: Congreso. http://www.infoelectoral.interior.es/min/. Accessed March 16, 2015.

Dinas, E. (2012). Left and right in the basque country and catalonia: The meaning of ideology in a nationalist context. *South European Society and Politics, 17*(3), 467–485.

Downs, A. (1957). *An economic theory of democracy*: Harper Collins

Enelow, J. M., & Hinich, M. J. (1984). *The spatial theory of voting: An introduction*. CUP Archive.

Fernández, P. A., & Rodríguez, I. S.-C. (2006). gestión o representación?: Los determinantes del voto en contextos políticos complejos. *Estudios/Working Papers (Centro de Estudios Avanzados en Ciencias Sociales)* (220), 1.

Gallego, M., Schofield, N., McAlister, K., & Jeon, J. S. (2014). The variable choice set logit model applied to the 2004 Canadian election. *Public Choice, 158*(3–4), 427–463.

Gelman, A., Carlin, J. B., Stern, H. S., Dunson, D. B., Vehtari, A., & Rubin, D. B. (2013). *Bayesian data analysis*. Boca Raton, FL: CRC.

Glen, D. M. (2015). The European economic crisis and rising secessionism: New demands on the european social model in Scotland, Flanders and Catalonia. In S. Romano & G. Punziano (Eds.), *The European social model adrift: Europe social cohesion and the economic crisis*. Surrey: Ashgate Publishing Company.

Gómez Fortes, B., & Cabeza Perez, L. (2013). Basque regional elections 2012: The return of nationalism under the influence of the economic crisis. *Regional & Federal Studies, 23*(4), 495–505. doi:10.1080/13597566.2013.798650. http://dx.doi.org/10.1080/13597566.2013.798650.

Heller, W. B. (2002). Regional parties and national politics in europe spain's estado de las autonomías, 1993 to 2000. *Comparative Political Studies, 35*(6), 657–685.

Hotelling, H. (1929). Stability in competition. *The Economic Journal, 39*(153), 41–57. ISSN: 00130133.

Labzina, E.,& Schofield, N. (2015). Application of the variable choice logit model to the British general elections of 2010. In *The Political Economy of Governance*. Berlin: Springer.

Martínez-Herrera, E. (2002). From nation-building to building identification with political communities: Consequences of political decentralisation in Spain, the Basque country, Catalonia and Galicia, 1978–2001. *European Journal of Political Research, 41*(4), 421–453.

Martínez-Herrera, E., & Miley, T. J. (2010). The constitution and the politics of national identity in Spain. *Nations and Nationalism, 16*(1), 6–30.

Mas-Collel, A., Whinston, M. D., & Green, J. R. (1995). *Micreconomic theory*.

Muñoz, J. (2009). From national-catholicism to democratic patriotism? democratization and reconstruction of national pride: The case of spain (1981–2000). *Ethnic and Racial Studies, 32*(4), 616–639.

Navarro, V. (2014). Lo que esta pasando en catalunya y en espana. http://www.vnavarro.org/?p=11312. Accessed December 28.

Núñez, X.-M. (2001). What is spanish nationalism today? from legitimacy crisis to unfulfilled renovation (1975–2000). *Ethnic and Racial Studies, 24*(5), 719–752.

Pérez-Nievas, S., Fraile, M. (2000). *Is the nationalist vote really nationalist?: Dual voting in Catalonia 1980–1999* (Vol. 147). Madrid: Instituto Juan March de Estudios e Investigaciones.

Rico, G. (2012). The 2010 regional election in catalonia: A multilevel account in an age of economic crisis. *South European Society and Politics, 17*(2), 217–238. doi:10.1080/13608746.2011.589140. http://dx.doi.org/10.1080/13608746.2011.589140.

Schofield, N. (2003). Valence competition in the spatial stochastic model. *Journal of Theoretical Politics, 15*(4), 371–383.

Schofield, N., & Sened, I. (2006). *Multiparty democracy: Elections and legislative politics*. Cambridge: Cambridge University Press.

Stokes, D. E. (1963). Spatial models of party competition. *The American Political Science Review 57*, 368–377.

Stokes, D. E. (1992). Valence politics. In *Electoral politics* (pp. 141–164). Oxford: Clarendon Press.

Yamamoto, T. (2011). *A Multinomial Response Model for Varying Choice Sets, with Application to Partially Contested Multiparty Elections*. Technical report, Working paper.

Measuring Direct Democracy

Nadia Fiorino, Roberto Ricciuti, and Fulvio Venturino

1 Introduction

The empiricaltheory of democracy, contrasting the "classical" conception, is often said to have been conceived by Schumpeter (1942). Since then, a lot of theoretical and empirical contributes have been added. Most of them are directly related to the approach proposed by the venerable founding father. For this reason, they form the so-called economic theories of politics, strongly based on assumptions of individuals as rational and self-interested decision-makers (Downs 1957; Riker and Ordeshook 1973; Olson 1965). Another strand of research developed since the 1960s' agreeing to completely different theoretical underpinnings. Here the main concepts draw from sociology, political culture being (one of) the most important (Dahl 1971; Lijphart 1968).

The merits and shortcomings of both economic and sociological approaches have been discussed in Barry (1978), and they are not worth to be recalled here. Rather, it deserves attention the fact that both approaches share a point of view: in opposition with the "ancient democracy" (Finley 1985), contemporary democratic regimes are essentially representative (Manin 1997). This point of view drives the researchers' consideration towards the usual paraphernalia of representation: electoral systems (Gallagher and Mitchell 2008; Cox 1997), parties and party systems (Sartori 1976; Katz and Crotty 2005), and parliaments (Fish and Kronig 2009).

N. Fiorino
University of L'Aquila, L'Aquila, Italy

R. Ricciuti (✉)
University of Verona and CESifo, Verona, Italy
e-mail: roberto.ricciuti@univr.it

F. Venturino
University of Cagliari, Cagliari, Italy

N. Schofield, G. Caballero (eds.), *State, Institutions and Democracy*,
Studies in Political Economy, DOI 10.1007/978-3-319-44582-3_6

Therefore, within the studies that address democracy (but also different kinds of regimes), direct democracy has been a neglected issue for a long time. However, scholars have recently become more interested in it. For instance, Lijphart (2012, chapter 12) deals with referendum as a tool requested to change rigid constitutions, and hence exploited by institutional engineering to reinforce the consensual working of proportional democracies. Significantly enough, the examination of referenda by Lijphart is confined in a short "addendum", while the process of constitutional change is mainly referred to the judicial review wielded by special courts. Even Tsebelis (2002) deals somewhat incidentally with the role of referenda. In his theoretical stand, referenda add a veto player to the decisional process of a given polity, namely the median voter of the electorate expressing its point of view through a referendum.

More recently, Aghion et al. (2004) provided a theory of constitutional design that focuses on the optimal degree of insulation of political leaders, which is the trade-off between the stability that allows the government to implement its policy, and the risk of expropriation on citizens that a powerful government may cause. Within this framework we argue that direct democracy institutions signal a non-insulation of political leaders to empirically evaluate some of the circumstances that in the model explain the degree of insulation (i.e., make direct democracy institutions more or less likely), and some others that have been proposed in the political science literature to describe the extent of the democracy. Specifically, we investigate the impact of these elements on a unique dataset consisting of a country index on citizen lawmaking in 87 countries. This index refers both to the availability of direct democracy instruments and to their actual use.

The paper proceeds as follows: in Sect. 2, we posit the theoretical hypotheses to explain the adoption of direct democracy. In Sect. 3, we present the methodology behind the Direct Democracy Index, the indicator we use to measure direct democracy. Section 4 describes the data and specifies the variables used for the empirical analysis. We then present the results in Sect. 5. Section 6 offers some concluding remarks.

2 Direct Democracy: Looking for Explanations

Empirical literature discussing the impact of economic, political and cultural factors on the extent of direct democracy is not developed, probably due to the lack of a formalized theory that explicitly refers to this issue.[1] Starting from de Tocqueville (1835), political theorists have debated the requisites for

[1]The empirical analyses of direct democracy have mainly discussed the relationship between initiatives and referendums and government spending (Matsusaka 1995, 2004; Feld and Matsusaka 2003), and the impact of direct democracy institutions on economic performance (Feld and Savioz 1997; Blomberg et al. 2004; Frey et al. 2001). Most of these studies deal with either Switzerland or the US states.

successful democratic institutions. Building on them, Aghion et al. (2004) have recently considered a problem of constitutional design in which a society has to choose the degree of insulation of its political leader, namely the degree to which a ruler is maintained accountable by citizenship. The idea is that if, once elected, a leader cannot be limited by *ex post* checks and balances, society runs the risk of a tyranny of the majority, or alternatively, of a tyranny of a dictator. The model focuses on this tradeoff between delegation of power and *ex post* controls of policy makers.[2] This framework is used to empirically discuss the determinants of the degree of insulation. They consider two sets of explanatory variables, political institutions and ethno-linguistic fractionalization. Autocrats are more insulated than democratically elected governments. Within democracy, presidential systems are the "most insulated" form of government, while hybrid regimes—such as semi-presidentialism—and parliamentary systems are the least insulated. Overall, the authors find significant evidence that various indices of insulation are positively correlated with measures of ethno-linguistic fractionalization. Thus, highly fragmented (polarized) societies tend to have more "insulated" rulers (less democratic or more presidential). The majority group knows that it cannot dominate the other groups unless its leader is sufficiently insulated.

In terms of the theory drawn in Aghion et al. (2004), referenda represent one of the forms of non-insulation of political rulers, the extreme form of non-insulation closest to the letter of the model being a popular referendum that requires a majority of 100 %. Our analysis builds on their theoretical framework. We focus on direct democracy institutional arrangements only, and extend the investigation to other factors that the literature analyzes as conditions for democracy. These hypotheses fall into three broad categories: economic and demographic, institutional and cultural.

Economic and Demographic Variables Economic theory has investigated the link between democracy and growth, predicting contrasting effects (Przeworski and Limongi 1993; Przeworski et al. 2000). On the one hand, democratic institutions guarantee checks and balances, limiting the possibility that politicians will extract rents from the public budget at the expense of the voters' welfare. On the other hand, an expansion of democracy promotes a redistribution of income from the rich to the poor and may increase the power of interest groups. Evidence that democratization leads to economic growth is quite weak.

We are interested in the reverse channel of such a link, focusing on the impact of economic variables on direct democracy institutions. The hypothesis is loosely

[2]Formally, the political leader has to implement reforms, but voters do not know ex ante whether the executive will reform or just expropriate rents from the voters. This degree of insulation is captured by a (super)majority of individuals (M) that can block the action of the leader (expropriation or reform) once the aggregate shock on preferences is realized. If M is high, only a large majority of voters can block the reform. In contrast, a low M means that, when in office, the leader is kept in check by small fractions of the electorate.

based on Lipset (1959), who discusses a broad category of economic development as determinant of democracy, including indexes of wealth, urbanization and industrialization. The key element of this hypothesis is that richer countries are more willing to promote democratic values and more receptive to norms of tolerance.

Both La Porta et al. (1999) and Alesina et al. (2003) pinpoint ethnic fragmentation as determinant of economic success both in terms of output (GDP growth) and the quality of institutions (measured by the extent of corruption, political freedom, etc.). The results show that the democracy index they use views racial fractionalization as negatively affecting economic success. The polarization of society, as we already emphasized, is also one of the explanatory variables used in the empirical analysis provided by Aghion et al. (2004) to test the model of political insulation. Across the different estimation techniques, ethnic fractionalization seems to increase the probability of ending up in a more autocratic and insulated regime.

Institutional Variables Political economy models (Persson and Tabellini 2003) have investigated the institutions of democratic regimes. This approach sheds light on how alternative institutional arrangements affect the binding force of checks and balances and, therefore, the accountability of the political system. A central feature of this line of research is that effective decision-making power in presidential regimes is split among different politicians, who are separately and directly accountable to voters. Presidential systems are therefore predicted to have less rent extraction than parliamentary ones. Furthermore, the electoral formula may shape rent extraction through the sensitivity of election outcomes to the incumbent's performance. Since incumbents may be more severely punished under plurality rule than under proportional representation, the former may be more effective in deterring rent extraction.

Starting from these hypotheses, we argue that as presidentialism and majoritarian parliamentarism are more accountable to voters, blocking legislation in these systems takes place indirectly and within the institutional structure of delegation of power. Voters are less interested in using direct democracy instruments in the presidential system and under majoritarian rules. These instruments therefore work as corrective devices, substituting other institutional arrangements in securing checks and balances between the bodies of government.

Cultural Variables The link between democracy and cultural factors has been debated in political science since Lipset (1959). Lipset predicts that a better educated population entails better chances for democracy and democratic practices. This positive relationship may exist because education can teach individuals the value of staying politically involved. Subsequent analyses have discussed the role of cultural conditions on democracy. These studies typically use religious affiliation as a proxy for the "dimension" of the culture (i.e., ethics, tolerance, trust), and evaluate democracy simply in terms of government performance. Putnam (1993) analyzes the effect of the provision of public goods, while Landes (1998) is concerned with the flow of people, goods and ideas between countries. Furthermore, many cultural explanations of democratic institutions and policies include a political element, as Landes's emphasis on the use of intolerance for political purposes makes clear. Huntington (1991) claims that the Catholic Church in the 1960s became a powerful force for democratization, probably to maintain its membership levels. Other scholars have turned to the link between education and democracy. Matsusaka (2005) claims that the rising level of education among the population and the decrease of information costs due to the communication technology revolution have dramatically reduced the knowledge advantage that elected officials had over ordinary citizens. The result of these trends is that important policy decisions are shifting from legislatures to the people. Glaeser et al. (2004, 2007) also discuss the link between education and democracy, arguing that schooling teaches people to interact with others and increases the benefits of civic participation. Democracy has a wide potential base of support, but offers weak incentives to its defenders, whereas dictatorship provides stronger incentives to a narrower base. As education increases the benefits of civic participation, it simultaneously raises support for more democratic regimes.

3 An Index of Direct Democracy

Direct democracy is a broad term that encompasses a variety of decision-making processes. They greatly differ according to the institutional design and the political culture prevalent in each country. Measuring direct democracy is not an easy task. Scholars have pursued different solutions. For instance, Scarrow (2001) uses an index based on three dimensions—direct election of executives and head of states, constitutional referenda, legislative referenda and/or direct decision on municipal ordinances—for 23 Western countries since 1970–1999, showing a spread of direct democracy institutions for the whole period. The diffusion of direct democracy tools in 18 presidential democracies in Latin America has been documented by Breuer (2007), who claims that referenda reduce accountability. Anckar (2004) provides a typology of direct democracy in small islands and micro-states. He finds that, in comparison with other democratic countries, micro-states make limited use of the popular initiative and the policy vote, whereas they frequently apply the constitutional referenda. According to his conclusion, the colonial background explains this pattern. Recently Altman (2011) arranged a large dataset of 949 mechanisms of direct democracy in 186 countries. He finds that the use of direct democracy is positively associated with the level of democracy in general, the age of the regime, the type of colonial heritage, and the use of direct democracy in neighboring countries.

This cursory review makes clear that including all tools countries employ to implement direct democracy in a simple classification is complex. An inclusive list would include town meetings, recall elections, initiatives, and various forms of referenda.

We build a Direct Democracy Index (DDI) for the period 2000–2005 referring to initiatives and referenda as already dealt with by several authors. The right of initiative enables citizens to originate legislation, acting as agenda setters bringing together the signatures of a number of endorsers. A referendum instead is a ballot vote on a law already approved by the legislature, which must also qualify for the ballot by receiving a predetermined number of signatures. Citizens are involved in both cases, by signing initiatives or by voting on a referendum.

Our index is based on three sources: Kaufmann (2004) for 43 Western and Central-Eastern European countries, Hwang (2005) for 33 Asian countries, and Madroñal (2005) for 17 Latin American countries. This amounts to 93 cases, but due to lack of data for independent variables our dataset is restricted to 87 countries. To produce our own classification we have principally built on Kaufmann's procedure. He sorts his 43 cases into seven categories, giving each country a specific rating. Each country is classified as: (1) radical democrat; (2) progressive; (3) cautious; (4) hesitant; (5) fearful; (6) beginner; (7) authoritarian. The sources for Asia and Latin America instead use a fourfold ranking. After a careful reading of each country report, we have re-ranked these countries according to the more sensitive Kaufmann's seven-step scale. Finally, we have recoded the original Kaufmann's scores by giving 7 to radical democrats—Switzerland being the only case—and 1 to authoritarianisms. The result of such a procedure is summed up in Table 1.

In implementing the DDI, we try to move from *de iure* circumstances that make referenda and initiatives possible. Rather, we try to rely on a *de facto* measure of direct democracy. This implies that we consider the procedures a political system provides in order to propose, approve, amend, and delete laws through popular initiative and referenda, as well the actual practices of direct democracy and the general political condition a country experiences. This is necessary to avoid fallacies dues to formally existing but emasculated procedures for direct democracy.

Table 1 A classification of political regimes according to the Direct Democracy Index

DDI score	Number of countries	List of countries
1	25	Afghanistan, Armenia, Azerbaijan, Belarus, Bhutan, Bolivia, Brunei, Cambodia, China, Costa Rica, Honduras, Indonesia, Laos, Malaysia, Mexico, Mongolia, Nepal, Nicaragua, Pakistan, Russia, Singapore, Sri Lanka, Thailand, Ukraine, Vietnam
2	18	Albania, Argentina, Bangladesh, Brazil, Chile, El Salvador, Georgia, Guatemala, Kazakhstan, Kyrgyzstan, Macedonia, Maldives, Moldova, Panama, Tajikistan, Turkey, Turkmenistan, Uzbekistan
3	9	Colombia, Croatia, Cyprus, Ecuador, Greece, Iceland, Paraguay, Peru, Venezuela
4	11	Estonia, Finland, Germany, Hungary, India, Japan, Malta, Romania, South Korea, Taiwan, United Kingdom
5	13	Austria, Belgium, Bulgaria, Czech Republic, France, Latvia, Luxembourg, Norway, Poland, Portugal, Spain, Sweden, Uruguay
6	10	Australia, Denmark, Ireland, Italy, Lithuania, Netherlands, New Zealand, Philippines, Slovak Republic, Slovenia
7	1	Switzerland

Sources: Kaufmann (2004), Hwang (2005) and Madroñal (2005)

Consider the case of Belarus. A respectable amount of nine referenda has been held from 1995 to 2004. However, they were deceitfully used by President Alexander Lukashenka to increase his power at the expense of the legislature, and the wanted results have allegedly been obtained by prosecuting political oppositions and harassing the voters in front of the polling stations. Therefore, as shown in Table 1, the country has the lowest DDI score. Remarkably, Altman (2011, 93–94) provides a full list of the "nightmare team", namely those authoritarian countries formally adopting direct democracy, but subjecting its results to the rulers' ultimate control.

A consequence of the methods of measurement used in this field of research is that all indexes are affected by some degree of subjectivity. Yet we believe that this is not a reason to condemn them. Indeed, several measures regularly used in comparative politics are built by recurring to subjective judgments: from Left to Right positioning (Castles and Mair 1984), to the levels of freedom (see Freedom House indices), to the diffusion of corruption (see Transparency International indices).

To validate our measurement of direct democracy we match the DDI just described with other measures of democracy. We thus correlate DDI scores with two of the most renowned indicators to assess democracy, the Freedom House and the Polity IV indexes for our 87 countries. In its original form, FH scores 1 for the highest and 7 the lowest level of freedom. We have rescaled these scores in such a way that 1 stands for low and 7 for high democracy, so that a positive sign is expected for all relationships. The correlations are detailed in Table 2. As expected, all relationships among the three indexes are positive. Moreover, the correlation between DDI and the Polity IV index reach a medium level, while that linking DDI with the Freedom House index is rather high. As a result, our index shows that direct democracy is related to democracy in general, an intuitive information however substantiating the procedure of measurement.

Table 3 details the relationship between direct democracy and levels of freedom as measured by the Freedom House index. Remarkably, countries with a poor level of direct democracy (scores 1–2 on the DDI) show a large array of levels of freedom, spanning from 1 to 7. For example, absence of direct democracy is associated with no freedom (e.g., China and Vietnam), with middle levels of freedom (e.g., Bolivia and Honduras), and with high levels of freedom (e.g., Costa Rica). A mild degree of direct democracy (scores 3–4 on the DDI) is associated with middle (e.g., Paraguay) to high (e.g., Germany and Finland) levels of political freedom, but not

Table 2 Correlation matrix between the DDI and other indexes of democracy

	DDI (2000–2005)	Freedom House (2000–2005)	Polity IV (1999–2004)
DDI	1		
Freedom House	0.73	1	
Polity IV	0.57	0.92	1

Table 3 Cross-tabulation of 87 countries according to their scores on the Freedom House and the DDI indexes, 2000–2005

Direct Democracy Index	Freedom House Index						
	1 (low)	2	3	4	5	6	7 (high)
1 (low)	4	6	3	1	6	4	1
2	2	3	1	2	5	3	2
3				1	3	2	3
4				1		1	9
5							13
6					1		9
7 (high)							1

free countries are present in this category. Finally, higher levels of direct democracy (scores 5–7 on the DDI) are almost exclusively related with higher degrees of freedom (e.g., Australia, Italy, and Switzerland). The Philippines are the only outlier, since they show a higher level of DDI (score = 6) with respect to countries of similar level of freedom (score = 5).

We are now in a position to ask why in some countries direct democracy is more developed than others. Using the index presented in this section, we next investigate which factors promote direct democracy.

4 Model and Data

Using the index presented in the previous section, we now investigate the correlates of direct democracy. We estimate a number of models and specifications. Our first approach is to regress a model that considers demographic, economic, institutional and cultural variables. The model is the following:

$$DDI_i = \alpha_0 + \alpha_1 \mathbf{ECDEM}_i + \alpha_2 \mathbf{INST}_i + \alpha_3 \mathbf{CULT}_i + \varepsilon_i \qquad (1)$$

where *DDI* is the variable defined in the previous Section, **ECDEM** is a vector of economic and demographic variables, **INST** is a vector of institutional variables, **CULT** is a vector of religious and cultural variables, and ε is an error term. **ECDEM** includes the log of GDP per capita in the year 2000, the log of population, the urbanization rate and a measure of ethnic fractionalization and finally the log of infant mortality. **INST** consists of two dummy variables for majoritarian and presidential systems. **CULT** includes the percentages of population that are Catholic and Muslim and the log of school attainment. We always add dummies for Latin American and Asian countries. The variable *DDI* comes from Kaufmann (2004), Hwang (2005), and Madroñal (2005). Data on ethno-linguistic fractionalization are taken from Alesina et al. (2003). Persson and Tabellini (2003) is the source of institutional variables, while data on education come from Barro and Lee (2010). Data on GDP comes from the Penn World Tables. For the year 2000, the remaining

Table 4 Summary statistics

Variable	Mean	Variance	Min	Max
Asia	0.351	0.480	0.000	1.000
DD index (0, 1)	0.428	0.261	0.143	1.000
Ethnic fractionalization	0.339	0.216	0.002	0.796
Latin America	0.176	0.382	0.000	1.000
Log income per capita	7.650	1.318	4.997	10.151
Log infant mortality	3.357	0.844	1.979	5.188
Log population	1.059	0.764	−1.397	3.117
Log school attainment	1.623	0.487	0.177	2.435
Majoritarian	0.536	0.501	0.000	1.000
Number of referendums	1.244	2.670	0.000	15.000
Presidential	0.494	0.502	0.000	1.000
Share of Catholics	36.240	41.214	0.000	97.300
Share of Muslims	14.657	29.430	0.000	99.900
Urbanization rate	60.076	22.002	14.000	100.000

variables are taken from La Porta et al. (1999). Table 4 gives summary statistics for the variables involved in our analysis.

One problem with testing whether income and education affect direct democracy is that these variables might be affected by reverse causation. While cross-country literature does not have developed a way to take care of endogeneity between education and direct democracy,[3] we use the more established latitude as instrument for income, therefore estimating a Two-stage least square model (2SLS) as our baseline.[4] It is typical in the empirical literature to normalize the data in the (0, 1) space although the original data are categories. As a robustness check we re-estimate Eq. (1) with ordered probit.

5 Results

Table 5 reports the 2SLS results of Eq. (1). As income and direct democracy may be endogenously determined, we use the absolute value of the latitude as an instrument. We start with economic and demographic variables: the first column of Table 3 shows that income per capita is positive and significant, meaning that direct

[3]Glaeser and Saks (2006) in analyzing corruption in America utilize historical factors like Congregationalism in 1890 as instrument for the level of schooling. Yet, this kind of instruments is specific for the country they examine, and furthermore they estimate panel data from 1976 to 2002.

[4]Acemoglu et al. (2008) address the same issue concerning democracy in a panel setting, by using past savings rates and changes in the incomes of trading partners.

Table 5 2SLS results

	(1)	(2)	(3)	(4)	(5)	(6)
Constant	−0.145** (0.063)	−0.226** (0.079)	−0.325* (0.202)	−0.796* (0.372)	−0.220* (0.100)	−0.288** (0.137)
Log income per capita	0.090*** (0.020)	0.094*** (0.019)	0.067* (0.035)	0.095* (0.055)	0.092** (0.031)	0.095* (0.039)
Log population	0.021 (0.030)	0.002 (0.028)	0.040 (0.046)	0.029 (0.044)	0.001 (0.033)	
Ethnic fractionalization	−0.205 (0.107)	−0.129 (0.096)	−0.167 (0.135)	−0.198 (0.151)	−0.128 (0.093)	−0.150 (0.113)
Majoritarian		−0.063 (0.045)	−0.043 (0.053)	−0.051 (0.055)	−0.063 (0.039)	
Presidential		−0.072 (0.057)	−0.027 (0.076)	−0.040 (0.094)	−0.072 (0.061)	
Share of Catholics		0.0033*** (0.0006)	0.0026*** (0.0007)	0.0025*** (0.0007)	0.0027*** (0.0007)	0.0029*** (0.0006)
Share of Muslims		−0.0007 (0.0007)	−0.0009 (0.0013)	−0.0014 (0.0018)	−0.0006 (0.0005)	
Log school attainment			0.129* (0.066)	0.155* (0.079)	0.179* (0.096)	0.194** (0.090)
Log infant mortality				0.075 (0.120)	0.099 (0.126)	
Urbanization rate					0.0001 (0.0017)	−0.0019 (0.0021)
Asia	−0.125** (0.055)	0.065 (0.058)	0.121 (0.074)	0.131* (0.071)	0.065 (0.060)	0.078 (0.061)
Latin America	−0.125* (0.063)	−0.231** (0.070)	−0.211* (0.111)	−0.230* (0.124)	−0.233** (0.092)	−0.229*** (0.074)
Obs.	87	79	53	53	50	54
R^2	0.443	0.608	0.678	0.682	0.652	0.665
Overid. p-value	0.312	0.419	0.112	0.228	0.287	0.571
F	14.54***	14.60***	14.95***	13.14***	23.44***	21.75***

Numbers in parentheses are robust standard errors
Log of income per capita is instrumented with the absolute value of the latitude
*, **, and *** denote significance at 10 %, 5 %, and 1 % levels, respectively

democracy is an ordinary good that is consumed more in richer societies. The results did not verify the idea posited by Aghion et al. (2004) that, in more fragmented societies, a group will restrict political liberty to impose control on the other groups. Ethnic fractionalization is negative as the theory predicts, but it is not significant. Both geographical dummies are significantly negative. Adding institutional and religious variables (column 2) strongly improves the model's goodness of fit. While majoritarian voting rule and a presidential system do not appear to cause direct democracy institutions, the share of Catholics is significantly positive, though the size of the coefficient is very small. In the regression shown in column (3), we add the log of school attainment; the education variable reduces the significance of income, but does not change the main results of the model. Furthermore, the education variable is always significant, providing evidence for the link between education and democracy highlighted by Glaeser et al. (2007). The log of infant mortality and the urbanization rate (in columns 4, 5 and 6) are not significant. Overall, the goodness of fit is satisfactory and the joint significance of the variables is quite high.

A robustness check is provided in Table 6, where we estimate Eq. (1) with ordered probit, therefore taking into account the ordinal nature of the data on direct democracy. The most notable difference with respect to Table 5 is the significance of ethnic fractionalization, which has a negative coefficient as the theory of endogenous institutions suggests. Infant mortality and urbanization are also significant. All other variables have basically the same behaviour as the 2SLS estimates. Again, the joint significance of the variables is very high, but the pseudo-R^2 is lower.

As highlighted in the previous section, an important caveat of the result we have presented is that they are based on a subjective index of direct democracy. Table 7 turns to the results of the count data estimates, employing the number of referendums that took place from 2000 to 2005, rather than the Direct Democracy Index, as the dependent variable. The source of these data is the Research Centre on Direct Democracy (2006). The findings do not differ much from the previous estimates. The log of income per capita and the share of Catholics remain positive and significant, although less so than in previous regressions. In contrast, the log of population becomes significantly positive. Log of school attainment, infant mortality and the urbanization rate are all significant. Some problems arise with the geographical dummies. The Latin America dummy is negative but often insignificant, whereas the Asia dummy is negative and sometimes significant, though not at a very high level. Although these results are consistent with the previous ones, we must regard them with care since we cannot control for endogeneity. Furthermore, the number of referenda is too simplistic a measure, failing to account for the quality of the democratic process (plebiscites are a form of direct democracy, but are ineffective at scrutinising the executive power).

Table 6 Ordered probit results

	(1)	(2)	(3)	(4)	(5)
Log income per capita	0.501** (0.134)	0.629*** (0.141)	0.407** (0.228)	0.768* (0.408)	1.226** (0.464)
Log population	0.095 (0.182)	0.011 (0.214)	0.525 (0.284)	0.248 (0.311)	
Ethnic fractionalization	−1.121** (0.541)	−0.805 (0.636)	−1.717* (0.739)	−1.561* (0.921)	−1.859** (0.888)
Majoritarian		−0.347 (0.269)	−0.007 (0.354)	−0.324 (0.387)	
Presidential		−0.382 (0.340)	−0.455 (0.428)	−0.140 (0.503)	
Share of Catholics		0.018*** (0.004)	0.020*** (0.006)	0.019*** (0.006)	0.021*** (0.005)
Share of Muslims		−0.0005 (0.0044)	0.0015 (0.0112)	−0.0024 (0.0122)	
Log school attainment			1.240* (0.682)	1.476** (0.755)	2.358** (0.739)
Log infant mortality				0.637 (0.755)	1.364** (0.673)
Urbanization rate					−0.024* (0.013)
Asia	−0.684* (0.355)	0.318 (0.407)	0.909 (0.577)	0.971 (0.612)	0.830 (0.540)
Latin America	−0.484 (0.311)	−1.355*** (0.526)	−1.345** (0.586)	−1.469** (0.621)	−1.403** (0.550)
Obs.	87	79	53	51	50
Pseudo-R^2	0.165	0.245	0.283	0.284	0.303
Wald	57.83***	104.41***	52.27***	51.38***	57.42***

Numbers in parentheses are robust standard errors
*, **, and *** denote significance at 10 %, 5 %, and 1 % levels, respectively

Table 7 Count data results

	(1)	(2)	(3)
Constant	−2.880** (1.353)	−1.600** (1.024)	−1.833** (0.703)
Log income per capita	0.085** (0.038)	0.309** (0.169)	2.016* (1.085)
Log population	0.061 (0.152)	0.819** (0.309)	1.198** (0.573)
Ethnic fractionalization	0.046 (0.538)	0.607 (0.786)	
Majoritarian	0.129 (0.244)	0.327 (0.306)	
Presidential	0.261 (0.274)	−0.371 (0.525)	
Share of Catholics	0.016*** (0.004)	0.021** (0.008)	0.018* (0.011)
Share of Muslims	−0.015*** (0.005)	−0.044 (0.053)	0.014 (0.021)
Log school attainment		1.158** (0.578)	0.773** (0.390)
Log infant mortality			−2.512* (1.435)
Urbanization rate			−0.067* (0.037)
Asia	−1.044*** (0.387)	−1.624 (1.825)	−2.168* (1.954)
Latin America	−0.864** (0.325)	−0.485 (0.395)	−0.590 (0.515)
Obs.	79	53	50
Wald	52.59***	67.66***	34.91***

Numbers in parentheses are robust standard errors
*, **, and *** denote significance at 10 %, 5 %, and 1 % levels, respectively

6 Conclusions

In this paper we have addressed the issue of the determinants of direct democracy. In doing so, we have exploited a newly assembled dataset that encompasses 87 countries. We have estimated a number of models, with an emphasis on controlling for possible reverse causality effect with direct democracy. Across the many models we assess, direct democracy does not significantly relate to institutional variables like presidential system and majoritarian voting rules, and there is not large evidence supporting the influence of ethnolinguistic heterogeneity. These finding are poorly consistent with the theory of endogenous institutions provided by Aghion et al. (2004). The model of political insulation relates to the general institutional settings (including the role of the judiciary) that within the structure of the delegation of power allow blocking or passing a reform law. We restrict our analysis on two particular institutional arrangements as a form of insulation, specifically referenda and initiative use, which may directly block or pass legislation. It seems that moving from an indirect to a direct form of blocking legislation reduces the importance of racial fractionalization and nullifies the influence of majoritarian electoral rule and of the presidential system. Furthermore, it emphasizes the role of income and education in encouraging direct democracy instruments.

Taken as a whole, our findings seem to suggest that direct democracy institutions are stronger in countries with populations that are richer and more educated. This evidence is consistent with the Lipset's view, and also with the empirical results presented in Glaeser et al. (2004) that development in human capital and in income is likely to improve political institutions. Data also show that political rights and political stability affect direct democracy, indicating that direct democracy comes after some political preconditions are fulfilled. Moreover, the share of Catholics seems to shape direct democracy. We interpret these findings as evidence of the Huntington view on the role of the Catholic Church in what he calls the *third wave of democratization processes* that took place in the last few decades. Starting from the 1960s, the Catholic Church becomes a powerful political force that leaves the conservative position encouraging the authoritarian regimes and the *status quo* in poor countries to promote the development of democratization processes (Huntington 1991). Finally, Latin America tends to be systematically related with less direct democracy.

Further work should address the issue of time, therefore exploring changes of direct democracy in a panel data setting, both with qualitative and quantitative indicators. Furthermore, a distinction between social and economic issues on the one hand and individual rights issues on the other hand needs also to be investigated.

References

Acemoglu, D., Johnson, S., Robinson, J. A., & Yared, P. (2008). Income and democracy. *American Economic Review, 98*, 808–842.

Aghion, P., Alesina, A., & Trebbi, F. (2004). Endogenous political institutions. *Quarterly Journal of Economics, 119*, 565–612.

Alesina, A., Devleeshauwer, A., Easterly, W., Kurlat, S., & Warcziarg, R. (2003). Fractionalization. *Journal of Economic Growth, 8*, 155–194.

Altman, D. (2011). *Direct democracy worldwide*. Cambridge: Cambridge University Press.

Anckar, D. (2004). Direct democracy in microstates and small island states. *World Development, 32*, 379–390.

Barro, R., & Lee, J. W. (2010). A new data set of educational attainment in the world, 1950–2010. *Journal of Development Economics, 104*, 184–198.

Barry, B. (1978). *Sociologists, economists, and democracy*. Chicago, IL: The University of Chicago Press.

Blomberg, S. B., Hess, G. D., & Weerapana, A. (2004). The impact of voter initiatives on economic activity. *European Journal of Political Economy, 20*, 207–226.

Breuer, A. (2007). Institutions of direct democracy and accountability in Latin America's presidential democracies. *Democratization, 14*, 554–579.

Castles, F. G., & Mair, P. (1984). Left–right political scales: some 'Expert' judgments. *European Journal of Political Research, 12*, 73–88.

Cox, G. W. (1997). *Making votes count. Strategic coordination in the world's electoral systems*. Cambridge: Cambridge University Press.

Dahl, R. A. (1971). *Polyarchy*. New Haven, CT: Yale University Press.

de Tocqueville, A. (1835). *Democracy in America*. London: Saunders and Otley.

Downs, A. (1957). *An economic theory of democracy*. New York, NY: Harper & Row.

Feld, L. P., & Matsusaka, J. G. (2003). Budget referendums and government spending: Evidence from Swiss Cantons. *Journal of Public Economics, 87*, 2703–2724.

Feld, L. P., & Savioz, M. R. (1997). Direct democracy matters for economic performance: An empirical investigation. *Kyklos, 50*, 507–538.

Finley, M. I. (1985). *Democracy ancient and modern*. New Brunswick, NJ: Rutgers University Press.
Fish, M. S., & Kronig, M. (2009). *The handbook of national legislatures. A global survey*. Cambridge: Cambridge University Press.
Frey, B. S., Kucher, M., & Stutzer, A. (2001). Outcome, process and power in direct democracy. New econometric results. *Public Choice, 107*, 271–293.
Gallagher, M., & Mitchell, P. (Eds.). (2005). *The politics of electoral systems*. Oxford: Oxford University Press.
Glaeser, E. L., La Porta, R., Lopez-de-Silanes, F., & Shleifer, A. (2004). Do institutions cause growth? *Journal of Economic Growth, 9*, 271–303.
Glaeser, E. L., & Saks, R. E. (2006). Corruption in America. *Journal of Public Economics, 90*, 1053–1072.
Glaeser, E. L., Ponzetto, G., & Shleifer, A. (2007). Why does democracy need education? *Journal of Economic Growth, 12*, 77–99.
Huntington, S. (1991). *The third wave: Democratization in the twentieth century*. Norman, OK: University of Oklahoma Press.
Hwang, J.-Y. (2005). *Direct democracy in Asia: A reference guide to the legislation and practice*. Taiwan: Taiwan Foundation for Democracy Publication.
Katz, R. S., & Crotty, W. (Eds.). (2005). *Handbook of party politics*. London: Sage.
Kaufmann, B. (2004). *Initiative and referendum monitor 2004/2005*. Amsterdam: IRI Europe.
La Porta, R., Lopez-de-Silanes, F., Shleifer, A., & Vishny, R. (1999). The quality of government. *Journal of Law, Economics, and Organization, 15*, 222–279.
Landes, D. (1998). *The wealth and poverty of nations*. New York, NY: W.W. Norton.
Lijphart, A. (1968). Typologies of democratic systems. *Comparative Political Studies, 1*, 3–44.
Lijphart, A. (2012). *Patterns of democracy. Government forms and performance in thirty-six countries*. New Haven, CT: Yale University Press.
Lipset, S. M. (1959). Some social requisites of democracy: Economic development and political legitimacy. *American Political Science Review, 53*, 69–105.
Madroñal, J. C. (2005). *Direct democracy in Latin America*. Madroñal: Mas Democracia and Democracy International.
Manin, B. (1997). *The principles of representative government*. Cambridge: Cambridge University Press.
Matsusaka, J. G. (1995). Fiscal effects of the voter initiative: Evidence from the last 30 years. *Journal of Political Economy, 103*, 587–623.
Matsusaka, J. G. (2004). *For the many or the few: The initiative, public policy, and American democracy*. Chicago, IL: University of Chicago Press.
Matsusaka, J. G. (2005). Direct democracy works. *Journal of Economic Perspectives, 19*, 185–206.
Olson, M. (1965). *The logic of collective action*. Cambridge, MA: Harvard University Press.
Persson, T., & Tabellini, G. (2003). *The economic effects of constitutions*. Cambridge, MA: MIT Press.
Przeworski, A., Alvarez, M., Cheibub, J., & Limongi, F. (2000). *Democracy and development: Political institutions and well-being in the world 1900–1950*. Cambridge: Cambridge University Press.
Przeworski, A., & Limongi, F. (1993). Political regimes and economic growth. *Journal of Economic Perspectives, 7*, 51–69.
Putnam, R. (1993). *Making democracy work: Civic traditions in modern Italy*. Princeton, NJ: Princeton University Press.
Research Centre on Direct Democracy. (2006). *Database on direct democracy*. University of Geneva. www.c2d.unige.ch
Riker, W. H., & Ordeshook, P. C. (1973). *An introduction to positive political theory*. Englewood Cliffs, NJ: Prentice-Hall.
Scarrow, S. E. (2001). Direct democracy and institutional change. A comparative investigation. *Comparative Political Studies, 34*, 651–665.

Sartori, G. (1976). *Parties and party systems: A framework for analysis*. Cambridge: Cambridge University Press.
Schumpeter, J. A. (1942). *Capitalism, socialism and democracy*. New York, NY: Harper & Row.
Tsebelis, G. (2002). *Veto players: How political institutions work*. Princeton, NJ: Princeton University Press.

Political Participation in Rural India: A Village Level Study

Vani K. Borooah and Anirudh Tagat

1 Introduction

If countries have a 'unique selling point' then India's must surely be that, with over 700 million voters, it is the world's largest democracy. Allied to this is the enthusiasm with which Indians have embraced the electoral process. The turnout in Indian national elections has been over 62 % in 10 of the last 15 national elections with 66 % of eligible voters voting the 2014 *Lok Sabha* (Parliamentary) elections; the last time that a US Presidential election came close to matching this was the 60 % turnout in the 1968 election between Nixon and Humphrey.

Against this backdrop, this paper uses village level data for India on *individual* voters to ask what are the factors which determine the probability of whether an individual votes? Is this probability greater for national compared to local elections? And is there evidence that people are more likely to vote today than they were in the past? Allied to these questions is another set of questions relating to the choice of candidates. What are the factors that make for women's autonomy in voting, meaning that they voted without reference to their spouses' instructions? What are the factors which contribute to people voting for candidates who are of their

This paper was presented at the IV International Conference on Political Economy and Institutions (ICOPEAI) at Baiona, Spain, 9–10 December 2015 and we are grateful to the participants for their valuable comments.

V.K. Borooah (✉)
University of Ulster, Room A02, Shore Road, Co. Antrim BT37 0QB, Northern Ireland, UK
e-mail: vkborooah@gmail.com

A. Tagat
Department of Economics at Monk Prayogshala, Mumbai, India
e-mail: at@monkprayogshala.in

N. Schofield, G. Caballero (eds.), *State, Institutions and Democracy*,
Studies in Political Economy, DOI 10.1007/978-3-319-44582-3_7

own caste that is, 'group identity' voting? And, lastly, what are the factors which contribute to people voting for candidates who have a reputation for honesty and fairness?

These specific questions are, in turn, grounded in a number of general hypotheses about people's motivation to vote. Traditional theories of voting are based on an individualistic model of voting. On this view of voting, it is not clear why a rational individual, on a purely cost–benefit basis, would bother to vote: the chances of an individual vote influencing the electoral outcome are infinitesimally small while the costs of voting—taking time off work, standing in a long queue—are real and not insubstantial (Downs 1957). However, given the far from negligible turnout witnessed in elections throughout the world, it is clear that people do take the trouble to vote.

One reason why people vote is because of 'group identity' voting. In the Indian context, Srinivas (1955) coined the term 'vote banks' to mean the exchange of benefits and favours to groups of citizens in return for their political support. Vote banks had three essential features: political parties which, at the time Srinivas was writing, was essentially the Congress party; a village 'middle man', usually a high caste landowner who was a party member and who had agency over groups of voters; and voter groups. There was then a patron-client relationship between party and 'middle man', and the middle man and voters, based on a system of reciprocal favours.

Vote banks go some way towards explaining why people in India turn out to vote in such large numbers. Downs' (1957) argument was based on the belief that the *costs* of voting—gathering information about parties and candidates, registration, time spent to/from/at the polling station—were specific to the voter and were likely to exceed the *benefits* from voting. The latter are in the form of collective goods and their benefit to a specific voter are likely to be zero.[1] However, in the context of 'vote banks', many of the benefits of voting may be private benefits paid to groups of voters for their electoral support and may be quite substantial.

Favours to voters took essentially two forms: the provision of local public goods targeted at particular groups, say a paved road or a school in a locality in which people from a group were concentrated; the provision of private benefits to targeted groups of (usually poor) voters, often in the form of cash payments or gifts in kind like cycles, sewing machines, and illegally supplying below poverty line (BPL) cards to voters who do not qualify for these (Breeding 2011). This raises the interesting question, addressed by Schedler and Schaffer (2007), of how one should distinguish between favours granted through the public purse ('local' public goods) and payments in cash and in kind. Indeed, even when direct payments are made they should not necessarily to be viewed as purely commercial transactions; instead, they may reflect a socio-cultural relationship between the patron and client, embodying

[1]Besley et al. (2012) suggest that, in the context of Indian villages, residents in the Chief Councillor's village had greater access to public goods than residents in other villages.

'obligation and reciprocity' and an egalitarian transfer of resources from rich to poor (Srinivas 1955).

Inglehart (2000) points out that the transition from group identity to individualistic identity is a part of the process of economic development broadly conceived. On this criterion, the importance of the group as a source of votes is decreasing in the Indian polity. Over half a century after Srinivas (1955) formulated his theory of vote banks, Breeding (2011) observed that "while the structure of vote banks remains largely unaltered the meaning of obligation and reciprocity in modern vote banks has completely altered." Indian politics has changed considerably since the days that the Congress was the dominant party. Firstly, the rise in party competition means that there are now many more parties attempting to attract the vote of the same group of voters. Vote banks have thus become an inefficient form of electoral campaigning: parties feel obliged to supply benefits but inter-party competition means that voters feel under no obligation to reciprocate with their votes.

Secondly, the possibility of free-riding has now become greater, particularly so with a stricter enforcement of the secret ballot. The Electoral Commission of India (ECI) has progressively tightened its views on permissible campaigning practices through its *Model Code of Conduct.* At the start of an election period, this Code sets out an elaborate set of parameters within which elections should be conducted; in particular, under this code, the 'payment for votes' is illegal and there are severe restrictions on the use of public resources, particularly by incumbent governments, to 'seek votes'.

Consequently, the reliance of parties in India on vote banks to deliver electoral approval is based more on hope than on expectation and, as these hopes are more often than not belied, parties will begin to see that the cost of maintaining 'vote banks' outweighs their benefits. Overlaying the fickleness of vote banks is the fact that running such client groups can easily cause parties to fall foul of the ECI's strictures and, thereby, risk severe penalties including disqualification.[2] In India today, as Breeding (2011) observes, "vote banks are social displays of wealth on the part of political parties to attract, primarily low-income citizens; they are gestures, historical remnants of a system in which the rules governing the game have changed" (p. 77).

So, in order to explain why the turnout in Indian elections is so high one has to explain why people bother to vote even though their vote may not be decisive. In addition to opportunistic electoral politics, there are several, more general, explanations for this paradox of (not) voting. As Geys (2006) observes, the instrumental theory of voting holds that an action has value only if it affects outcome. Sen (1977) argued that if "outcome" was narrowly defined as serving one's own interest, to the exclusion of any others, then a person acting in such a

[2]As a consequence of employing over two million workers during elections, the ECI's observers are ubiquitous and, since they are drawn from the ranks of those in civilian employment, cannot be easily identified. In addition, the Indian media seizes upon any infractions of the Model Code and affords them considerable publicity.

manner might be ‘rational’ but he would also be a fool. Indeed, Sen (1977) argued that people act out of a myriad motives many of which are unconnected with self-interest. One of these is ‘sympathy’, another is ‘commitment’. Even if it is argued that ‘sympathy’ is just an economic externality, Sen (1977) argues that commitment involves a counter-preferential choice, destroying the crucial assumption that the chosen alternative must be better than the others—“it drives a wedge between personal choice and personal welfare” (p. 329). Consequently, the high turnout in elections “may be guided not so much by expected utility maximisation but by something simpler, *viz.* just a desire to record one’s true preference” (p. 333).

The concept of ‘expressive voting’ elaborates upon, and extends, the view of people voting to record their preference. In terms of ‘expressive voting’, people vote not for instrumental reasons—that is to effect change—but rather to express an opinion or a point of view, regardless of whether that turns out to be the winning opinion. This view has been articulated by *inter alia* Brennan and Lomasky (1993) and Hamlin and Jennings (2011).

All this is not to say that expressive voting cannot be self-interested or not result in change. The 2014 Indian election results, which led to a landslide victory for the Bharatiya Janata Party (BJP) under Narendra Modi, can be interpreted as an expression of the electorate’s distaste for the ineffectual, dynastic government led by the Congress Party. As Banerjee (2014) argues that, “for many Indian voters, voting is not just a means to elect a government…rather the very act of voting is seen by them as meaningful, as an end in itself, that expresses the virtues of citizenship, accountability, and civility that they wish to see in ordinary life, but rarely can.” (p. 3)

For all these reasons this paper analyses the decisions of *individuals*, rather than of groups, on whether to vote and the basis on which to vote. Of course, in making such decisions, individuals are constrained by group identity, whether it is women burdened by the strictures of patriarchy or individuals voting on grounds of caste loyalty. All these issues—women’s autonomy, caste loyalty, and, indeed, the (possibly futile) desire for honest candidates—are central to political participation in rural India. The novelty of this paper is that it addresses them using a unique set of data on individuals living in nearly 250 villages distributed over 17 different Indian states. This enables it to provide *quantitative* answers to questions relating to voting and meetings in contrast to answers based upon *qualitative* responses (for example, Banerjee 2014). The next section describes the data used and the subsequent sections provide the analysis.

Voting in elections is just one facet of political participation. Another might be attending and participating in ‘political meetings’. This is particularly relevant in Indian villages since the Constitution (73rd Amendment) Act of 1993. This made it mandatory for all villages to have a village council (hereafter, *Gram Sabha*) consisting of all registered voters on the electoral roll of a village. The *Gram Sabha* was to be entrusted with the power of supervising the functioning of the elected village *panchayat* and to approve the panchayat’s development plan for the village and the associated budget. Consequently, in addition to voting, electors in villages had another form of political participation: they could attend *Gram Sabha* meetings and also participate in its discussions. This paper also analyses the factors which determine attendance and participation in such meetings.

2 Data and Preliminary Analysis

The data for this paper is from the Rural Economic and Demographic Survey (REDS) of 2006 covering 17 states in India and encompassing 8652 households. Members of these households were asked whether they had voted in the *period* covering the (i) current panchayat election (ii) the previous panchayat election, and (iii) the previous to previous panchayat election. They were also asked the election *level* at which they voted: (i) for the *gramt pradhan* (village president); a ward member of the *panchayat*; (iii) a member of the state legislative assembly (MLA); (iv) a member of the national parliament (MP).

In total, there were 272, 532 *responses* to this question, from 25,995 *individuals*. Of the total of responses, 75 % (204,984) did, and 25 % (66,714) did not, vote. The respondents were also distinguished by religion and caste. So, for example, 78 % of Scheduled Caste (*SC*), and 76 % of Other Backward Classes (*OBC*), respondents voted compared to 74 % of Scheduled Tribe (*ST*), and 74 % of Upper Caste (*UC*), respondents. A test on the difference in proportions of those who voted between persons from the SC and the UC showed that these differences were significantly different from zero for all three election periods: current, previous and previous to previous. However, it was only for local elections that the proportion of persons from the *SC* who said they had voted was significantly different from that of *UC* persons; there was no significant difference between the two groups in the proportions of their members who voted in national elections.

It was hypothesised that an individual's decision to participate in the electoral process would *inter alia* depend upon (a) social; (b) economic; and (c) demographic factors. These factors capture the primary socio-economic characteristics driving electoral participation in rural India. Understanding electoral participation through the perspective of these socio-economic determinants will also help us in identifying the "ideal" type of voter in rural India. Thus, an understanding of who typically votes in elections will be gained.

We used the following *conditioning variables* or factors in our analyses:

(a) **Social factors**:
These include the *social group* to which the household belonged: *SC, ST, OBC, and UC*;

(b) **Economic factors**:
These include the primary *occupation* of the person:

a. Self-employed in agriculture.
b. Self-employed in non-agriculture.
c. Agricultural wage labourer.
d. Non-agricultural wage labourer.

e. Salaried.
f. Family Worker (agriculture and non-agriculture).
g. Household worker.
h. Retired, dependent, or student;

And the *educational level* of the person:

a. Illiterate.
b. Educated up to primary level.
c. Educated up to secondary level.
d. Educated up to higher secondary level or uncompleted college.
e. Educated with a degree or higher.

(c) **Demographic factors**:
These include the person's gender and age.

The equation to be estimated can be expressed as:

$$P(Y_{iv} = 1) = \alpha + \beta_1 X_{iv} + \beta_2 V_v + \varepsilon_{iv} \tag{1}$$

Where y_{iv} is the outcome variable of interest (whether individual i residing in village v voted in the election/participated in a Gram Sabha meeting). α represents unobserved individual and village-level characteristics, X_{iv} is a vector of individual-specific characteristics, detailed above, encompassing the social, economic, and demographic factors that could determine electoral participation, V_v are village fixed-effects, and ε_{iv} is the random error term.

The average age of the 25,995 voters, referred to above,[3] was 42 years, 80 % were married, and the division by gender was almost equal with 51 % male and 49 % female voters. It is worth emphasising that the division of the sample is by social group: *SC*, *ST. OBC*, and *UC*. Each of these groups can contain persons of different religions. So, for example, the *SC* could comprise Hindus, Christians, and Buddhists while the *OBC* and the *UC* could contain both Hindus (mostly) and Muslims (as a minority). Although this study does not explicitly study the voting behaviour of Muslims in Indian villages it is worth saying something about this as Muslims comprise about 15 % of India's population. In our own study—which does not explicitly examine the voting behaviour of Muslims—it was found that 31 % of Muslim respondents, compared to 24 % of Hindu respondents, did not vote and further that this difference between the two groups was statistically significant.[4]

---

[3]To recapitulate, these were voters who answered whether they had voted in the *period* covering the (i) current panchayat election (ii) the previous panchayat election, and (iii) the previous to previous panchayat election and the level of election at which they had voted.

[4]For academic studies of the political participation of Muslims see Rowley and Smith (2009), Potrafke (2010), and Hanusch (2013).

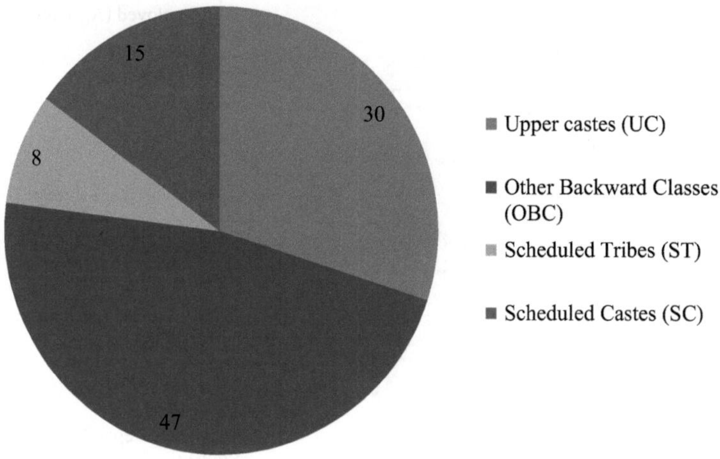

Fig. 1 Social group of the voters (%)

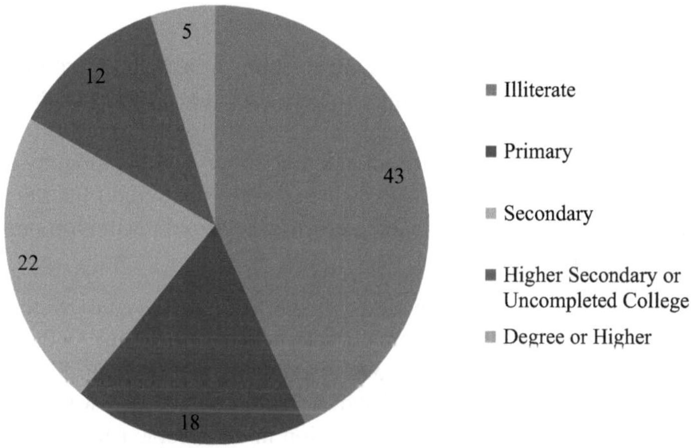

Fig. 2 Educational level of voters (%)

Figures 1, 2 and 3 show salient features of the voters in terms of their social group, educational level, and occupation.

The elections considered in the study could be distinguished by *election level* and by *election period*:

1. The election level referred to the difference between 'national' and 'local' elections. National Elections were defined as elections to the State Assembly or to the National Parliament; and 'Local Elections' were elections at the village panchayat level, either of the *gram pradhan* (village president) or a ward member. The 'national election effect' was captured by a variable *NE* which took the value 1 if the election was for the state Assembly or national Parliament and zero otherwise.

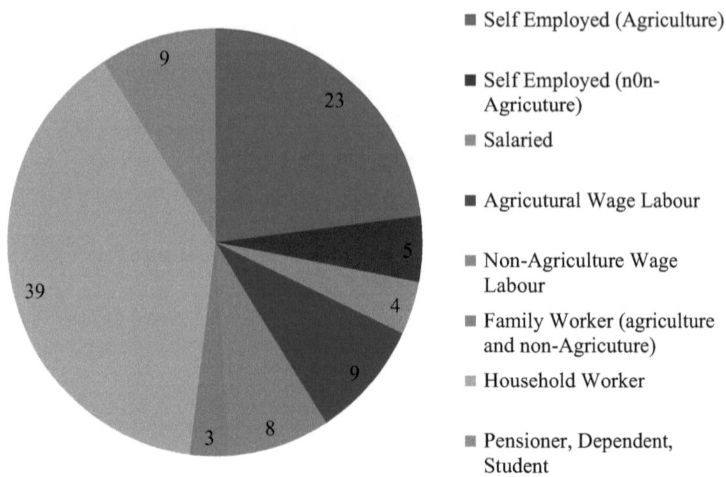

Fig. 3 Occupations of the voters (%)

2. The election period referred to when the elections were held. 'Current' Elections are elections that were held during the period of the *current* panchayat. 'Past' elections are elections that were held during the life of the *previous* (or *previous to previous*) panchayat. The 'current election effect' was captured by a variable *CE* which took the value 1 if the decision to vote occurred during the period of the current panchayat and the value zero if it occurred during the previous (or previous to previous) panchayat.

So, in total there were 12 elections in the villages covered by the sample: Parliamentary and Assembly (collectively referred to as 'national') × three election periods (current, previous, and previous to previous *panchayats*). Since the *panchayat* periods are not specifically defined, we assumed that they were of 5–7 years duration so that the earliest *panchayat* election in the sample (the 'previous to the previous' *panchayat*) was held around (approximately) 1994.

A person is eligible to vote in India at the age of 18 years. So, only those persons in the sample who were 18 years old in 1994—and, therefore at least 30 years of age in the survey of 2006—would have been eligible to vote in *all* 12 elections. So, from the from 25,995 *individuals* who answered the voting question, we chose the 18,322 persons who, by virtue of being older than 30 years at the time of the survey, *could* have voted in all 12 elections. On average, these persons voted in 9.2 of the 12 elections in which they *could* have voted, yielding an average participation rate of 77 %. There were 199,087 *responses* from these 18,322 voters to the "did you vote in election X?" question and, of these 199,087 responses, 85 % were positive.

Table 1 shows the results of estimating a logit model, for respondents above 30 years age, in which the dependent variable, *y*, took the value 1 if the person *i*, $i = 1, \ldots N$, voted ($y_i = 1$) in a particular election and zero if he/she did not ($y_i = 0$).

Table 1 Predicted and marginal probabilities of voting

1	2	3	4	5	6
Conditioning variable	Probability	Marginal probability	SE	z value	Pr > |z|
Scheduled Caste (SC)	0.8599	0.0106	0.003	3.75	0.00
Scheduled Tribe (ST)	0.8509	0.0016	0.005	0.34	0.74
Other Backward Classes (OBC)	0.8472	−0.0021	0.002	−0.92	0.36
Upper Castes (UC) [Reference]	0.8493				
Females	0.8460	−0.0084	0.003	−2.60	0.01
Males [Reference]	0.8543				
Married	0.8517	0.0137	0.003	4.99	0.00
Unmarried [Reference]	0.8380				
Illiterate (ILT)	0.8488	0.0058	0.004	1.30	0.19
Primary (PRM)	0.8582	0.0153	0.004	3.44	0.00
Secondary (SEC)	0.8479	0.0049	0.004	1.16	0.25
Higher Secondary (HSEC)	0.8490	0.0061	0.005	1.28	0.20
Graduate (GRD) [Reference]	0.8429				
Self-employed agriculture (SEA)	0.8593	0.0213	0.004	4.85	0.00
Self-employed non-agriculture (SEnA)	0.8572	0.0192	0.005	3.68	0.00
Salaried (SAL)	0.8292	−0.0089	0.006	−1.53	0.13
Agriculture wage labour (AWL)	0.8639	0.0258	0.005	5.21	0.00
Non-agriculture wage labour (NAWL)	0.8552	0.0171	0.005	3.37	0.00
Family worker (FWK)	0.8271	−0.0110	0.007	−1.49	0.14
Household worker (HWK)	0.8461	0.0080	0.005	1.73	0.08
Pensioner, dependent, student [Reference]	0.8381				
National election	0.9220	0.1434	0.002	89.30	0.00
Local election	0.7866				
Current election	0.88447	0.06024	0.0015552	38.74	0.00
Past election	0.82423				
Age at mean	0.8681	0.0028	0.000	33.06	0.00

Interaction effects were used to model whether the effect of one conditioning variable varied according to values of another variable. In the context of this study, a natural question to ask is whether the effects of some of the conditioning variables (social group, age, gender, marital status, education, and occupation) on the decision to vote varied according to whether the election was 'national' or local and also according to whether it was a current or a past election. In order to answer this question we estimated a general model in which the conditioning variables were allowed to interact with the national/local election variable (*NE*) and, also, separately with the current/past election variable (*CE*). By virtue of this characteristic, this model is hereinafter referred to as the *general interaction model* (GIM).

3 Model Estimation and Predicted Probabilities

The GIM was estimated on 181,556 responses which was the number of responses which had *non-missing values* associated with *all* the conditioning variables. The coefficient estimates, in terms of the odds ratios, are shown in an Appendix to this paper; these estimates are employed in the body of the paper to make predictions about the probability of voting under various scenarios relating to the values of the conditioning variables. Following Long and Freese (2014), the method of model interpretation used in this paper is based upon predicted probabilities rather than on the odds-ratios shown in Table 9 of the Appendix.

Overall, the GIM predicted that, $y_i = 1$ for 85.4 % of the 181,556 responses with a 95 % confidence interval of [85.2 %, 85.6 %].[5] This prediction was based upon using the equation estimates in conjunction with the observed values of the conditioning variables to compute $Pr[y_i = 1]$ for each response and, then to average over these 181,556 predicted probabilities to obtain 85.4 %. An alternative method of prediction is to hold the values of the conditioning variables at their mean values and to use the equation to predict the probability of voting. Under this scenario, $Pr[y_i = 1] = 91.9\,\%$ suggesting that there is a difference between the "average probability over all persons" (85.4 %) and the "probability of the average person".

The specific results from the estimated GIM are shown in Table 1 in terms of probabilities (column 2) and the marginal probabilities (column 3) of voting. Column 2 shows that the predicted probability of a *SC* response being positive is 85.99 %. This probability was obtained by setting $SC = 1$ for all the 181,556 cases but leaving the values of the other variables for each case unchanged (that is, as observed in the sample). Applying the equation estimates (shown in Table 9 of the Appendix) to these revised values yields a predicted probability of 85.99 %. It is important to emphasise that, in computing this probability, all the interaction effects (the interactions of *SC* with *NE* and with *CE*) are taken into account. The predicted probability of voting of the *ST*, *OBC*, and the *UC* are also computed similarly.

The *marginal probability* associated with a variable refers to the *change* in the outcome probability consequent upon a unit change in the value of the variable, *the values of the other variables remaining unchanged.* For discrete variables (as,

[5]That is, the probability of a randomly chosen response being positive will, with 95 % probability, be between 85.2 and 85.5 %.

indeed, are, except for age, all the variables reported above), an unit change in the value of a variable refers to a move *from the reference category to the category in question*, the values of the other variables remaining unchanged. So, the *marginal probability* associated with the *SC* is defined as the *difference* between the *SC* and the (group) reference category in their predicted probabilities of voting. Since, in this study, the *UC* are the reference category, the marginal probability associated with the *SC* is 85.99–84.93 % = 1.06 *percentage points*. This is shown in column 3 (against the *SC* row) as 0.0106. Dividing this marginal probability (in column 3) by its standard error (column 4) yields the z-value associated with this marginal probability (column 5). For the *SC* this is 3.75 and, as the *p*-value in column 6 suggests, this marginal probability is significantly different from zero. The marginal probabilities associated with the *ST* and the *OBC* are, however, *not* significantly different from zero.

Similarly, we predict the probabilities of the responses associated with the different educational responses being positive. Column 2 shows that the predicted probability of responses from persons with primary level of education being positive is 85.82 %. This probability was obtained by setting *PRM* = *1* for all the 181,556 cases but leaving the values of the other variables for each case unchanged (that is, as observed in the sample). Applying the equation estimates (shown in Table 9 of the Appendix) to these revised values yields a predicted probability of 85.82 %. [Again it is important to emphasise that, in computing this probability, all the interaction effects (the interactions of *PRM* with *NE* and with *CE*) are taken into account]. The predicted probabilities of voting of the other educational categories (*ILT, SEC, HSEC, GRD*) are also computed. Since *GRD* is the reference category, the marginal probabilities for education are defined as difference between the other educational categories and the *GRD* category in their probabilities of a positive response. The marginal probability for the *PRM* category is 85.22 %–84.29 = 1.53 percentage points; this is reported in column 3 as 0.0153 and the z value in column 5, in conjunction with the *p*-value of column 6, shows that this change is significantly different from zero. The marginal probabilities associated with the other educational categories are, however, *not* significantly different from zero.

Lastly, one can turn to the probabilities associated with national versus local and current versus past elections. Column 2 shows that the predicted probability of voting, when elections were national, was 92.2 % compared to 77.86 % when they were local. Similarly, the predicted probability of voting, when elections were held in the current panchayat period, was 88.45 % compared to 77.86 % when they were in past panchayat periods. These probabilities were obtained by, respectively, setting *NE* = *1* and *CE* = *1* for all the 181,556 cases but leaving the values of the other variables for each case unchanged (that is, as observed in the sample). The changes in these probabilities are the marginal probabilities associated with national and current elections: respectively, 14.34 and 6.02 points. As the z-values in column 5 show, these changes were significantly different from zero. Once again, it is important to emphasise that, in computing this probability, all the interaction effects (in this case, the interactions of *NE* and *CE* with all the other conditioning variables) are taken into account.

Table 1 allows one to identify the variables whose associated marginal probabilities were significantly different from zero:

1. Scheduled Castes versus the Upper Castes: the probability change from the reference category (upper castes) is positive and significant.
2. Women versus men: the probability change from the reference category (men) is negative and significant.
3. Married versus unmarried: the probability change from the reference category (unmarried) is positive and significant.
4. Primary education versus Graduates: the probability change from the reference category (graduates) is positive and significant.
5. Self-employed in agriculture versus pensioners, dependents, students: the probability change from the reference category (pensioners, dependents, students) is positive and significant.
6. Self-employed in non-agriculture versus pensioners, dependents, students: the probability change from the reference category (pensioners, dependents, students) is positive and significant.
7. Agricultural wage labourers versus pensioners, dependents, students: the probability change from the reference category (pensioners, dependents, students) is positive and significant.
8. Non-Agricultural wage labourers versus pensioners, dependents, students: the probability change from the reference category (pensioners, dependents, students) is positive and significant.
9. National versus local elections: the probability change from the reference category (local elections) is positive and significant.
10. Current versus past elections: the probability change from the reference category (past elections) is positive and significant.

The high probability of voting in elections (92 % in national elections and 79 % in local elections) flies in the face of the rational choice model of voting which weighs the costs of voting against its expected benefits. However, if one considers group-based based voting (Geys 2006) then turnout could be stimulated by the enforcement of group-based social norms. According to Grossman and Helpman (2001), three elements are likely to be particularly important for the existence of, and the ease of enforcing, such norms. First, there is the frequency of interaction between group members. Second, social norms will be more binding the greater the danger of social isolation if these norms are flouted. Third, enforcement is easier if actions are observable. All these conditions are likely to be particularly important in the context of the close proximity in which residents of an Indian village live Indeed, as Akerlof (1976) in his paper on caste has observed, the threat of ostracism plays a big role in enforcing caste norms.

4 The Basis for Choosing Candidates

Given that a person voted for a candidate/party, a further question is on what basis did he/she chose his/her preferred candidate/party? The REDS asked voters this question by offering them a range of possibilities. In the context of India's political economy, three of these questions are of interest.

The first concerns the *autonomy* of the women's vote: do women in rural India vote according to their own preferences or according to their husbands' preferences? In this context, voters were asked if the reason they voted for a candidate/party was because they "were told to do so by their spouse": of the 47,640 *male* responses to this question, only 8 % replied in the affirmative; however, of the 49,297 *female* responses to the same question, 69 % replied that what had determined their vote was their spouses' instructions.[6]

The second question relates to the *caste basis* for voting: when voting, do voters primarily vote for candidates who are of their caste? In this context, of the 201,999 responses to this question, only 17 % admitted to their vote having been determined by the candidates' caste.[7]

The third question relates to *candidate merit*: do voters choose candidates with a reputation for honesty and fairness? Of the 202,946 responses to the 'honesty' question, 60.8 % said that they voted on the basis of the candidates' reputation for honesty.[8]

[6]Autonomy, in general, refers to the control that women have over their lives—the ability of women to obtain information and to use that as the basis for making decisions both about themselves and their intimates (Dyson and Moore 1983). Jeejeebhoy and Sathar (2001) in their discussion of women's autonomy in India observe that "the cultures of South Asia are gender-stratified characterised by hierarchical relations… in which the patriarch or his relatives have control over family members." In her ethnographic study of Indian elections, Banerjee (2014) notes that it is "mainly men who conduct public discussions of politic because venues where these discussions occur are traditionally masculine places. These discussions then filtered back into people's homes as men brought back news of the day [and] women, who were often missing from public discussion of politics, often asked questions of their men requiring them to clarify points" (p. 87–88).

[7]The importance of caste as a determinant of electoral outcomes in India cannot be overemphasised: see Chandra (2004).

[8]Corruption in Indian public life has emerged as a salient feature of the country's political debate. In 2012, India ranked 94th out of 176 countries in Transparency International's Corruption Perception Index and, in practical terms, corruption has ramifications for almost every aspect of life in India (Witsoe 2012; Borooah 2012). Consequently, it is likely that a reputation for honesty and fairness might be an important consideration in evaluating candidates. Indeed, the desire on the part of Indian voters to address corruption in Indian public life has spawned an entirely new party—the *Aam Aadmi* Party—which came to power in the state of Delhi and also won a number of seats in the 2014 Indian parliamentary elections.

4.1 Women's Autonomy

In order to throw light on the women's autonomy question, we estimated a logit equation in which the dependent variable took the value 1 if the married woman said the reason she voted for a candidate/party was because she "was told to do so by their spouse", and took the value 0 otherwise. (It is important to emphasise that a particular woman did not necessarily *always* vote according to formula—she may well have recorded a value of 1 for some elections and 0 for others). As in the previous section, in order to answer this question we estimated a general model in which the relevant conditioning variables (social group, age, education, and occupation) were allowed to interact with the national/local election variable (*NE*) and, also, separately with the current/past election variable (*CE*).

Estimated over 38,033 responses from married women who were at least 30 years of age at the time of the survey, this model predicted that after all interaction effects had been accounted for, 69.3 % of women would have voted according to spousal instructions but, if the women's attributes had been held at the mean values, this would have risen to 78.3 %.[9] In other words, *on average* 69 % of the votes of married women (who were at least 30 years of age) were awarded according to spousal instructions but there was a 79 % chance that the *average woman* would vote as her husband told her.

The specific results from the estimated GIM are shown in Table 2 in terms of probabilities (column 2) and the marginal probabilities (column 3) of voting. Column 2 shows that the predicted probability of a *SC* female response being positive (that is, she voted according to her spouse's instructions) was 67.77 % while the equivalent *UC* (the reference category) response was 68.74 % yielding a marginal probability of 0.97 percentage points which, as the associated *z* value shows, was not significantly different from zero. Women from the *ST* and the *OBC* were, however, significantly more likely to vote according their husbands' wishes than *UC* (and *ipso facto SC*) women. Their marginal probabilities—that is, the difference between their probabilities (respectively, 72.78 % and 70.9 %) that of UC women (68.74 %)—were significantly different from zero. So, women's autonomy was *highest* among the *SC* and the *UC* and *lowest* among the *ST* and the *OBC*.

Interestingly, there did not appear to be any difference between women of different educational levels in their propensity to vote as their husbands asked. To illustrate this point, the likelihood of women graduates and of illiterate women voting according to spousal wishes was, respectively, 68.99 % and 70.41 % yielding a marginal probability 1.41 percentage points which, as the accompanying *z* value shows, was not significantly different from zero. So, the estimated model does *not* find support for the hypothesis that education liberates women from patriarchal control, at least as far as voting is concerned.

[9]The estimated coefficients from this, and the subsequent, models are not shown but may be obtained on request.

Table 2 Predicted, and marginal. Probabilities of the probability of women voting according to spouses' instructions

1	2	3	4	5	6
Conditioning variable	Probability	Marginal probability	SE	z value	Pr > |z|
Scheduled Caste (SC)	0.6777	−0.0097	0.007	−1.35	0.18
Scheduled Tribe (ST)	0.7278	0.0404	0.012	3.24	0.00
Other Backward Classes (OBC)	0.7090	0.0216	0.006	3.66	0.00
Upper Castes (UC) [Reference]	0.6874				
Illiterate (ILT)	0.7041	0.0141	0.015	0.96	0.34
Primary (PRM)	0.6978	0.0078	0.015	0.53	0.60
Secondary (SEC)	0.6823	−0.0077	0.015	−0.53	0.60
Higher Secondary (HSEC)	0.6860	−0.0039	0.016	−0.24	0.81
Graduate (GRD) [Reference]	0.6899				
Self-employed agriculture (SEA)	0.6736	−0.0220	0.018	−1.22	0.22
Self-employed non-agriculture (SEnA)	0.6086	−0.0870	0.029	−2.95	0.00
Salaried (SAL)	0.5847	−0.1109	0.025	−4.49	0.00
Agriculture wage labour (AWL)	0.6756	−0.0200	0.019	−1.07	0.28
Non-agriculture wage labour (NAWL)	0.5850	−0.1106	0.045	−2.44	0.01
Family worker (FWK)	0.6234	−0.0721	0.035	−2.06	0.04
Household worker (HWK)	0.7046	0.0091	0.015	0.59	0.55
Pensioner, dependent, student [Reference]	0.6956				
National election	0.6811	−0.0465	0.005	−10.29	0.00
Local election	0.7275				
Current election	0.6912	−0.0112	0.004	−2.49	0.01
Past election	0.7024				
Age at mean	0.6984	0.0001	0.000	0.52	0.60

There were strong occupational effects associated with the probability of women's vote being determined by her husband. The probability of women from the reference occupational category (pensioners, dependents, students) voting according to their husbands' instructions was 69.56 % and this was *significantly higher* than the corresponding probabilities for women who were self-employed in non-agriculture (60.86 %), salaried workers (58.47 %), non-agricultural wage labourers (58.5 %), and family workers (62.34 %). On the other hand, compared to the reference group, the probability of voting according to their husbands' wishes was *not* significantly different for women who were self-employed in agriculture (67.36 %), agricultural wage labourers (67.56 %), and household workers (70.46 %). So, in contrast to education, at least as far as voting was concerned, there was support for the hypothesis that being gainfully employed in non-agricultural activities, to a significant degree, liberated women from patriarchal control.

Lastly, a lack of women's autonomy, as measured by the probability of voting by reference to their husbands' instructions was significantly higher in local elections, than in national, elections (72.75 versus 68.11 %) and was significantly higher in 'past', than in current, elections (70.24 versus 69.12 %). Compared to national elections, the outcomes of local elections were more closely tied with the welfare of households and hence gave more reason for husbands to control their wives' votes. Once again, it is important to emphasise that, in computing these probabilities, all the interaction effects (in this case, the interactions of *NE* and *CE* with all the other conditioning variables) were taken into account.

4.2 The Caste Basis of Voting

In order to investigate the importance of caste in voters' candidate selection, we estimated a logit equation in which the dependent variable took the value 1 if the voter's response was that the candidate's caste determined his/her choice, 0 if it did not. (It is important to emphasise that a particular person did not necessarily *always* vote according to caste—he/she may well have recorded a value of 1 for some elections and 0 for others). As in the previous section, in order to answer this question we estimated a general model in which the relevant conditioning variables (social group, age, gender, marital status, education, and occupation) were allowed to interact with the national/local election variable (*NE*) and, also, separately with the current/past election variable (*CE*). By virtue of this characteristic, this model is referred to in the paper as the general interaction model (GIM) *for caste-based voting*. Estimated over 154,191 responses from persons who were at least 30 years of age at the time of the survey, this model predicted that after all interaction effects had been accounted for, 17.2 % of the responses would have voted according to caste but that if the respondent's attributes had been held at the mean values this would have fallen to 10.6 %. In other words, *on average* 17 % of votes by persons (who were at least 30 years of age) were on a caste basis but there was only a 10 % chance that the *average person* would vote on the basis of caste.

The specific results from the estimated GIM are shown in Table 3 in terms of probabilities (column 2) and the marginal probabilities (column 3) of voting. The first point to note is that compared to reference group of the *UC* (from which only 15.39 % of the responses chose candidates on the basis of caste), the likelihood of responses from the other caste groups, claiming to choose candidates on a caste-basis, was *significantly* higher: 16.16 % for the *SC*, 18.02 % for the *ST*, and 18.53 % for the *OBC*. Indeed, the predicted proportion of *ST* and *OBC* responses claiming

Table 3 Predicted and marginal probabilities of caste-based voting

1	2	3	4	5	6
Conditioning variable	Probability	Marginal probability	SE	z value	Pr > |z|
Scheduled Caste (SC)	0.1616	0.0077	0.003	2.55	0.01
Scheduled Tribe (ST)	0.1802	0.0263	0.006	4.32	0.00
Other Backward Classes (OBC)	0.1853	0.0314	0.003	11.60	0.00
Upper Castes (UC) [Reference]	0.1539				
Females	0.1760	0.0077	0.003	2.34	0.02
Males [Reference]	0.1683				
Married	0.1725	0.0045	0.003	1.54	0.12
Unmarried [Reference]	0.1679				
Illiterate (ILT)	0.1747	−0.0122	0.005	−2.28	0.02
Primary (PRM)	0.1631	−0.0239	0.005	−4.43	0.00
Secondary (SEC)	0.1628	−0.0242	0.005	−4.59	0.00
Higher Secondary (HSEC)	0.1867	−0.0003	0.006	−0.05	0.96
Graduate (GRD) [Reference]	0.1870				
Self-employed agriculture (SEA)	0.1813	−0.0049	0.005	−0.99	0.32
Self-employed non-agriculture (SEnA)	0.1580	−0.0282	0.006	−4.63	0.00
Salaried (SAL)	0.1742	−0.0119	0.007	−1.79	0.07
Agriculture wage labour (AWL)	0.1637	−0.0224	0.005	−4.08	0.00
Non-agriculture wage labour (NAWL)	0.1543	−0.0319	0.006	−5.40	0.00
Family worker (FWK)	0.1705	−0.0157	0.008	−1.96	0.05
Household worker (HWK)	0.1703	−0.0159	0.005	−3.11	0.00
Pensioner, dependent, student [Reference]	0.1862				
National election	0.1317	−0.0868	0.002	−45.46	0.00
Local election	0.2185				
Current election	0.1631	−0.0152	0.002	−8.04	0.00
Past election	0.1782				
Age at mean	0.1735	0.0000	0.000	−0.43	0.67

caste-based voting (respectively, 18.02 % and 18.53 %) was significantly higher than that for the *SC* (16.16 %).

It is interesting that persons from the OBC had the largest propensity to vote along caste lines. Jaffrelot (2003) points out that India has undergone a "silent revolution" as lower-status groups increasingly captured political office and used political power to alter the balance of power between the upper and the lower castes in the countryside. Foremost among these lower caste groups—who originally were mobilised by the upper caste Congress Party but who now mobilised themselves *against* the Congress—were the *OBC*. These were castes that were not forward—in the sense of belonging to the Brahmin, Kshatriya, or Vaishya *varnas*—but who, unlike the *SC*, were not considered 'untouchable'. In the context of Indian politics, the *OBC* is a useful electoral category encapsulating the lower castes *above the pollution line* who have tried, by voting along caste lines, to carve out a political space for themselves.

Interestingly, education level and the propensity to caste-based voting had a U-shaped distribution. The predicted probability of responses claiming caste-based voting fell from 17.47 % for illiterate persons to around 16.3 % for persons with primary and secondary educational levels before rising to 18.7 % for graduates and higher secondary responses. In consequence, the predicted probability of graduates claiming caste-based voting was *significantly higher* than the corresponding probabilities for responses from illiterate persons or persons educated to primary or secondary levels. In turn, the predicted probability for responses from illiterate persons was *significantly higher* than the corresponding probabilities for responses from persons educated to primary or secondary levels.

In terms of occupations, the propensity for caste based voting was highest for the occupational reference group of pensioners, dependents, students (18.62 %) and this was significantly higher than that for the other occupations. The lowest predicted probability of voting along caste lines emanated from those who were non-agricultural wage labourers (15.43 %) or self-employed in non-agricultural activities (15.8 %). Lastly the predicted likelihood of caste-based voting was significantly lower in national (13.17 %) compared to local (21.85 %) elections and significantly lower for elections conducted during the current panchayat period (16.31 %) compared to elections conducted during the past panchayat periods (17.82 %).

4.3 Candidate Merit

In order to investigate the importance of a candidate's merit as a determinant of voters' candidate selection, we estimated a logit equation in which the dependent variable took the value 1 if the voter's response was that the candidate's *reputation for honesty and fairness* determined his/her choice, 0 if it did not. (As before, it is important to emphasise that a particular person did not necessarily *always* vote according to merit—he/she may well have recorded a value of 1 for some elections and 0 for others). As in the previous section, in order to answer this question we estimated a general model in which the relevant conditioning variables (social group, age, gender, marital status, education, and occupation) were allowed to interact with the national/local election variable (*NE*) and, also, separately with the current/past election variable (*CE*). By virtue of this characteristic, this model is referred to in the paper as the general interaction model (GIM) *for merit-based voting*. Estimated over 156,325 responses from persons who were at least 30 years of age at the time of the survey, this model predicted that after all interaction effects had been accounted for, 60.3 % of the responses would have voted according to merit (honesty and fairness) but that if the respondent's attributes had been held at the mean values this would have risen to 63.8 %. In other words, *on average* 60.3 % of votes by persons (who were at least 30 years of age) were on a merit basis but 63.8 % of votes from the *average person* were on the basis of merit.

The specific results from the estimated GIM are shown in Table 4 in terms of the probabilities (column 2) and the marginal probabilities (column 3) of voting. The first point to note is that compared to reference group of the *UC* (from which 60.58 % of the responses chose candidates on the basis of merit), the likelihood of responses from the other caste groups, claiming to choose candidates on a merit basis, was not *significantly* different: 60.71 % for the *SC*, 61.71 % for the *ST*, and 59.7 % for the *OBC*.

In terms of the educational level of voters, there was a positive relationship between education and the propensity to vote on the basis of candidate merit. The predicted probability of responses being in favour of choosing on the basis of a reputation for honesty and fairness was highest for graduates (63.48 %) and lowest for illiterates (59.07 %). For all educational levels the difference in the predicted probabilities of merit-based voting between persons at the four lowest educational levels and persons who were graduates (the reference group) was significantly different from zero.

In terms of occupations, responses from persons who were self-employed in non-agricultural activities, and from non-agricultural wage labourers, predicted significantly *higher* probabilities (respectively, 63.28 % and 62.66 %) of merit-based voting—and responses from persons engaged in household work predicted a significantly *lower* probability (59.59 %)—compared to responses from the reference category of pensioners, dependents, and students (61.07 %). For the other occupations there was no significant difference between their predicted probabilities and that of the reference group.

Lastly, the honesty and fairness issue was less important as a voting issue in national compared to local elections—56.41 versus 64.45 % of positive responses—and less of an issue in elections conducted during the present panchayat period compared to those conducted in past periods.

Combining these results leads to some interesting implications. First, since household welfare is more directly affected by the outcome of local, compared to national, elections, candidates' honesty and fairness mattered more in the former than in the latter. Second, since agriculturists were more likely to dominate the *Gram Sabha* than non-agriculturists, it was more important for the latter that their position should be safeguarded through the election of candidates with a reputation for honesty and fairness. Lastly, it is perhaps a sad comment on the direction of Indian politics that the importance of honesty in candidates has, in the minds of voters, devalued over time.

Table 4 Predicted and marginal probabilities of merit-based voting

1	2	3	4	5	6
Conditioning variable	Probability	Marginal probability	SE	z value	Pr > |z|
Scheduled Caste (SC)	0.6071	0.0014	0.004	0.34	0.74
Scheduled Tribe (ST)	0.6171	0.0113	0.007	1.62	0.11
Other Backward Classes (OBC)	0.5970	−0.0088	0.006	−1.47	0.01
Upper Castes (UC) [Reference]	0.6058				
Females	0.5693	−0.0664	0.005	−13.94	0.00
Males [Reference]	0.6357				
Married	0.6021	−0.0053	0.004	−1.42	0.16
Unmarried [Reference]	0.6074				
Illiterate (ILT)	0.5907	−0.0441	0.007	−6.73	0.00
Primary (PRM)	0.6107	−0.0242	0.007	−3.64	0.00
Secondary (SEC)	0.6184	−0.0164	0.006	−2.57	0.01
Higher Secondary (HSEC)	0.6092	−0.0256	0.007	−3.63	0.00
Graduate (GRD) [Reference]	0.6348				
Self-employed agriculture (SEA)	0.6135	0.0028	0.006	0.46	0.65
Self-employed non-agriculture (SEnA)	0.6328	0.0221	0.007	2.97	0.00
Salaried (SAL)	0.6134	0.0026	0.008	0.33	0.74
Agriculture wage labour (AWL)	0.6194	0.0087	0.007	1.21	0.23
Non-agriculture wage labour (NAWL)	0.6266	0.0159	0.007	2.22	0.03
Family worker (FWK)	0.5959	−0.0148	0.010	−1.54	0.12
Household worker (HWK)	0.5827	−0.0281	0.006	−4.42	0.00
Pensioner, dependent, student [Reference]	0.6107				
National election	0.5641	−0.0804	0.002	−33.65	0.00
Local election	0.6445				
Current election	0.5811	−0.0344	0.002	−14.06	0.00
Past election	0.6155				
Age at mean	0.6040	0.0006	0.000	5.81	0.00

5 Attendance and Participation at *Gram Sabha* Meetings

Voting is one form of political involvement; *attendance* at, and *participation* in, *Gram Sabha* (GS) meetings is an alternative form of representation in local government. In this section, we consider attendance and participation in *Gram Sabha* meetings and study it in the context of similar factors that were hypothesized to influence electoral involvement. The average number of *Gram Sabha* meetings held across panchayat periods is approximately 7.6, and shows a decreasing trend, with an average of approximately 9 meetings in the previous-to-previous panchayat period to 6 meetings taking place in the current period.

Persons were regarded as having 'participated' in a Gram Sabha meeting which they attended if they answered yes to the question: "when you attend *Gram Sabha* meetings, do you participate actively, presenting issues, raising questions, and voicing your opinion?" They were regarded as not having participated if they answered this question in the negative. In total, there were 72,617 responses to this question from 8,586 respondents. This subsample only contains data on those individuals for whom voting data was also available. The total participation rate in *Gram Sabha* meetings stood at 46.3 % across all panchayat periods: 37 % of all persons belonging to the *SC* participated in Gram Sabha meetings at least once compared to 32 % for members of the *ST*. There were significant differences in participation rates in *Gram Sabha* meetings between Hindus and Muslims (as well as between the *SC* and the *UC*) across all panchayat periods. Members of the *UC* had a significantly higher participation rate relative to members of the *SC*.

If electoral participation and participation in Gram Sabha meetings are to be seen as two complementary dimensions of involvement in the process of local governance, then it is of interest to ask how respondents chose between these two dimensions. Table 5 shows the percentage of individuals who voted vis-à-vis the percentage of individuals who took part in GS meetings.

It was hypothesised that a person's decision of how many *Gram Sabha* meetings to attend and, then, whether to participate in the meeting would *inter alia* depend upon the same conditioning variables factors employed in the earlier sections on voting along with some additional factors. These were:

a. The notice period available to household members about the *Gram Sabha* meeting.
b. The total number of *Gram Sabha* meetings held in that particular period and it's square (since the effect may not be linear).
c. To test the effect of participation in the current panchayat period, we also include a dummy for *Gram Sabha* meetings held in the current period.

In the case of participation in GS meetings, two more variables were hypothesised to have an impact. These were:

i. The average length of meetings.
ii. Whether the person knew in advance of the topics to be discussed at the meeting.

Table 5 Participation in *Gram Sabha* meetings and voting participation in *Gram Sabha* meetings

		Yes	No
Voted	Yes	45.9	31.5
	No	20.2	13.3

N = 8586 individuals

5.1 Attendance at Gram Sabha Meetings

We used an ordinary-least squares (OLS) regression to estimate the impact of various factors on the *number* of *Gram Sabha* meetings attended. For this sample, the number of meetings attended ranged from 0 to 42 for each panchayat period. The average number of meetings attended was 5.08, whereas the median number of meetings attended was 3. The estimates from the model, over 41,453 observations may be obtained on request from the authors; the results presented in Table 6 are in terms of the *predicted number of meetings attended.*

Table 6 shows that the predicted number of meetings attended at 4.97 was *significantly* lower than the 5.1 meetings attended by men. The difference between women and men in the average number of meetings attended is, the estimated regression coefficient on the *FEM* variable in the OLS regression. Similarly, the predicted average number of meetings attended by married persons (5.08) was significantly higher than the predicted average for unmarried persons (4.99) where, again, the difference between married and unmarried persons in the average number of meetings attended is the estimated regression coefficient on the *MAR* variable in the OLS estimates.

There were no significant differences between the social groups in the average number of meetings attended by their members and, except for the fact that persons with secondary level education attended significantly more meetings (5.23) than persons with other educational levels, variations in the level of education did not significantly affect the number of meetings attended: illiterate persons were predicted to attend as many meetings as graduates (5.05).

There were, however, significant occupational effects. Compared to the number of meetings attended by persons from the reference group of pensioners, dependents, and students (5.21), a significantly smaller number of meetings were attended by those who were: salaried workers (4.82), agricultural labourers (4.79), non-agricultural labourers (4.91), and household workers (5.0). With the category of employment, it was self-employed persons who were more interested in attending than those who were employees.

There was no significant difference in the predicted number of meetings attended during the current panchayat (5.09) and past panchayats (5.07). The predicted number of meetings attended at the mean number of meetings held (8.6 over the three *panchayat* periods) was 4.73 and it was predicted that every additional meeting would increase attendance by 0.45 meetings. Similarly, the predicted number of meetings attended at the mean age of the respondents (48.8 years) was 5.18 and it was predicted that every additional year of age would increase attendance by 0.014 meetings.

Table 6 Predicted and marginal number of Gram Sabha meetings attended

1	2	3	4	5	6
Conditioning variable	Number attended	Marginal probability	SE	t value	Pr > |t|
Females	4.97	−0.14	0.06	−2.33	0.02
Males [Reference]	5.10				
Married	5.08	0.10	0.05	2.04	0.04
Unmarried [Reference]	4.99				
Scheduled Caste (SC)	5.12	0.07	0.04	1.59	0.11
Scheduled Tribe (ST)	5.12	0.07	0.07	0.92	0.36
Other Backward Classes (OBC)	5.07	0.02	0.04	0.45	0.65
Upper Castes (UC) [Reference]	5.05				
Illiterate (ILT)	5.05	0.00	0.07	−0.01	0.99
Primary (PRM)	5.02	−0.03	0.07	−0.42	0.68
Secondary (SEC)	5.23	0.18	0.07	2.72	0.01
Higher Secondary (HSEC)	5.10	0.05	0.07	0.77	0.44
Graduate (GRD) [Reference]	5.05				
Self-employed agriculture (SEA)	5.26	0.05	0.07	0.73	0.46
Self-employed non-agriculture (SEnA)	5.09	−0.12	0.08	−1.52	0.13
Salaried (SAL)	4.82	−0.39	0.09	−4.48	0.00
Agriculture wage labour (AWL)	4.79	−0.42	0.07	−5.76	0.00
Non-agriculture wage labour (NAWL)	4.91	−0.30	0.08	−3.82	0.00
Family worker (FWK)	5.11	−0.10	0.12	−0.83	0.41
Household worker (HWK)	5.00	−0.21	0.09	−2.41	0.02
Pensioner, dependent, student [Reference]	5.21				
Current Panchayat	5.09	0.03	0.03	1.08	0.28
Past Panchayat	5.07				
Advance notice >1 week	5.12	0.36	0.05	7.65	0.00
Advance notice <1 week	4.75				
Number of meetings held (at mean = 8.6)	4.73	0.45	0.00	139.43	0.00
Age (at mean = 48.8)	5.18	0.014	0.00	11.98	0.00
Number of meetings held (at mean = 8.6)	4.73	0.4517	0.003	139.47	0.00

5.2 Participation in Gram Sabha Meetings

In order to investigate the factors underlying participation in Gram Sabha meetings, we estimated a logit equation in which the dependent variable was coded 1 if the person answered affirmatively to the following question: "when you attend *Gram Sabha* meetings, do you participate actively, presenting issues, raising questions, and voicing your opinion?" If the answer to this question was a 'yes', the variable was coded 1, and was coded 0 if the answer was 'no'. (It is important to emphasise that a particular person did not necessarily *always* participate or not participate—he/she may well have recorded a value of 1 for some meetings and 0 for others). The participation equation was estimated over 33,757 responses from persons who were at least 30 years of age at the time of the survey and it predicted that 55.7 % of the responses would have said that they had 'participated'. Hereafter, this referred to as the 'participation rate'. If, however, the respondent's attributes had been held at the mean values this participation rate would have been 57.1 %. In other words, there was not much difference between the *average* participation rate (55.7 %) and the participation rate of the *average person* (57.1 %).

The specific results from the estimated equation are shown in Table 7 in terms of the probabilities (column 2) and the marginal probabilities (column 3) of voting. The first point to note is that compared to the male participation rate of 59.61 %, the female rate was significantly and considerably lower at 41.45 %. Worryingly, even when women attend *Gram Sabha* meetings, their voice was much less likely to be heard than that of men.

The participation rate for married persons (55.59 %) was slightly, but significantly, below that of unmarried persons (57.48 %). Compared to the 57.05 % participation rate of persons from the (reference group of) *UC*, it was only the participation rate of OBC persons (54.63 %) that was significantly different; other than that, social group did not affect participation.

The participation rate rose with the educational status of persons. The reference group of graduates had the highest participation rate (63.3 %); compared to that, the participation rate of persons with lesser educational qualifications was significantly lower with illiterate persons having the lowest participation rate (52.52 %).

In terms of occupation, there was no statistical difference between the participation rates of persons in the reference category (pensioners, dependents, students) and that of salaried workers, and those in agricultural self-employment: respectively, 60.33 %, 59.74 %, and 59.65 %. However, the participation rates for the other groups were significantly lower with the participation rate being lowest for household workers (47.71 %).

There was a significant difference in the predicted participation rates during the current panchayat (58.71 %) and past panchayats (53.72 %). Each additional meeting held increased the participation rate by 0.3 points.

Table 7 Predicted and marginal probabilities of participating in Gram Sabha meetings

1	2	3	4	5	6
Conditioning variable	Probability	Marginal probability	SE	t value	Pr > |t|
Females	0.4145	−0.1816	0.011	−15.89	0.00
Males [Reference]	0.5961				
Married	0.5559	−0.0190	0.009	−2.23	0.03
Unmarried [Reference]	0.5748				
Scheduled Caste (SC)	0.5664	−0.0041	0.008	−0.53	0.60
Scheduled Tribe (ST)	0.5519	−0.0186	0.013	−1.46	0.15
Other Backward Classes (OBC)	0.5463	−0.0242	0.007	−3.69	0.00
Upper Castes (UC) [Reference]	0.5705				
Illiterate (ILT)	0.5252	−0.1078	0.012	−8.91	0.00
Primary (PRM)	0.5619	−0.0711	0.012	−6.03	0.00
Secondary (SEC)	0.5891	−0.0440	0.012	−3.74	0.00
Higher Secondary (HSEC)	0.5797	−0.0534	0.012	−4.35	0.00
Graduate (GRD) [Reference]	0.6330				
Self-employed agriculture (SEA)	0.5965	−0.0069	0.013	−0.54	0.59
Self-employed non-agriculture (SEnA)	0.5315	−0.0718	0.015	−4.88	0.00
Salaried (SAL)	0.5974	−0.0059	0.016	−0.37	0.71
Agriculture wage labour (AWL)	0.5396	−0.0638	0.014	−4.56	0.00
Non-agriculture wage labour (NAWL)	0.5227	−0.0807	0.015	−5.43	0.00
Family worker (FWK)	0.5603	−0.0431	0.025	−1.75	0.08
Household worker (HWK)	0.4771	−0.1262	0.017	−7.48	0.00
Pensioner, dependent, student [Reference]	0.6033				
Current Panchayat	0.5871	0.0499	0.005	10.04	0.00
Past Panchayat	0.5372				
Advance notice >1 week	0.5701	0.1038	0.009	11.73	0.00
Advance notice <1 week	0.4663				
Agenda known in advance	0.6002	0.1212	0.005	22.72	0.00
Agenda not known in advance	0.4790				
Number of meetings held (at mean = 8.6)	0.5505	0.0031	0.001	3.92	0.00
Number of meetings attended (at mean = 4.66	0.5583	0.0053	0.001	5.52	0.00
Age (at mean = 48.8)	0.5574	0.014	0.00	11.98	0.00

6 Ideal Types

The predicted probabilities from Table 1 allowed one to identify "ideal types" where ideal types represent *hypothetical* cases with *specified* characteristics. For example, the voter *most* likely to vote would be an older *SC* married man, educated up to primary level, and working as an agricultural wage labourer (Ideal Type *A*); conversely, the voter who would be *least* likely to vote would be a young, illiterate, unmarried *ST* woman who was a dependent (Ideal Type *B*).

Similarly, from Table 2, we can identify the types of women *most* likely (Type *A*) and *least* likely (Type *B*). A type *A* woman would be an unmarried, dependent, illiterate, ST woman who was 30 years old. A type *B* woman would be a 60 year old, graduate, *SC* woman working in a salaried job. Again, one can compute the probability of voting of each of these types and test whether the difference between the probabilities of Cases A and B is statistically significant.

Table 3 allows one to identify the person type most likely (Type *A*) and least likely (Type *B*) to vote along caste lines. The former was an *OBC*, 60 year old, graduate, married woman who was either a pensioner or a dependent; the latter was a 30 year old, *UC*, unmarried male who was educated to secondary level.

Table 4 tells us that the person *most* likely to vote on the basis of a candidate's reputation for honesty and fairness (Type *A*) would be a 30 year old, unmarried, graduate *ST* man who was self-employed in non-agriculture. Conversely, the person *least* likely to vote on the basis of a candidate's reputation for honesty and fairness would be a 60 year old, married, *OBC* woman who was illiterate and did household work.

According to Table 6, the person *most* likely to attend *Gram Sabha* meetings would be a 60 year old *SC* male, educated to secondary level and self-employed in agriculture (Type *A*); the person least likely to attend these meetings would be an illiterate, 30 year old unmarried, *UC* woman working as an agricultural wage labourer (Type *B*).

Lastly, Table 7 suggests that the person most likely to participate at *Gram Sabha* meetings would be a 60 year old SC married man who was educated up to secondary level and was self-employed in agriculture (Type *A*). Conversely, the person least likely to participate at *Gram Sabha* meetings would be a 30 year old *UC* unmarried woman who was illiterate and worked as an agricultural wage labourer (Type *B*).

After identifying the 'ideal types', such that the probability of observing the relevant outcome was highest for Type *A* and lowest for Type *B*, one can proceed to computing the probability of the event for each of these types, *A* and *B*, and then to test whether the difference between their probabilities was statistically significant.

Table 8, which reports the results of this exercise, shows that, for all the probabilistic outcomes, there was a considerable difference between the probabilities of Type *A* (highest probability) and Type *B* (lowest probability) and that, in terms of attendance, there was also a marked difference between the meetings attended by Type *A* and Type *B* persons. Furthermore, as the results of the statistical tests show, these differences were all significantly different from zero.

Table 8 Outcome probabilities for 'ideal types'

	Probabilities (%)		Difference	Test statistics		
	Type A	Type B	Type A–Type B	SE	Z value	Pr > |z|
Voting	92.6	75.1	17.5	0.01	15.4	0.0
Voting by spouse's instructions	73.0	55.4	17.6	0.03	5.6	0.0
Voting by caste	21.5	12.1	9.4	0.01	9.1	0.0
Voting by candidate honesty	70.1	53.6	16.5	0.01	15.3	0.0
Participation in *Gram Sabha* meetings	69.3	33.8	35.5	0.02	19.1	0.0
	Meetings attended		Difference	SE	Z	Pr > |z|
Attendance at *Gram Sabha* meetings	5.7	4.2	1.5	0.1	14.5	0.0

7 Conclusions

The issue of voting on the basis of one's social identity, as opposed to voting as an individual, has recently attracted attention in the literature. Ben-Bassat and Dahan (2012), using data on Arab communities, examined the effect of social affiliation on actual voter turnout in local elections in Israel. They tested whether voters with a particular last name, which serves as a proxy for *hamula* (or clan) affiliation, were more likely to vote for a candidate with the same last name, as compared to other candidates, and found strong-evidence for *hamula*-based voting behaviour.[10] They also tested whether individuals who felt part of a group were more likely to participate in elections and found that that voter turnout in Arab localities is significantly higher than in Jewish localities—which have social structures more in common with European communities—controlling for the standard list of explanatory variables. This result is in line with the notion that communities with stronger senses of social attachment (Arab localities) are more likely to participate in elections.

[10]In the Palestinian territories, clans (locally called hamulas) have become a focus of political activity and major hubs of local power.

These ideas resonate very clearly in the Indian political context. It is a fact of Indian political life that voter turnout among the poor is greater than among the rich. One explanation for this is that the poor are organised into vote banks in terms of their social identity (for example, lower castes, Muslims) and vote because there is material benefit associated with voting for their group. As we argued in the introduction, the evidence is that the importance of vote banks based on the *quid pro quo* of material benefits to groups has declined. Instead, it is more reasonable to view the high voter turnout by the poor as an expression of *identity* and *presence*. This identity may be social, defined either in caste or religious terms, but presence may relate to a general desire to flex one's political muscles by reminding the governing classes of the folly of neglecting a significant portion of the electorate.

In the last 20 years Indian politics has changed in three important ways. Perhaps the most dramatic has been the fragmentation of politics as the lower castes have left the Congress party's upper-caste dominated 'big tent' to set up their own parties in opposition to the Congress. As Jodhka (2012) observes, there is a weakening of traditional caste relations based on status and hierarchy and this has been facilitated by India's lower classes rising to challenge, at the ballot box, the traditional political hegemony of India's upper castes (Jaffrelot 2003).

The second important change is that, as a consequence of political fragmentation, national governments, following the general elections of 1999, 2004, and 2009, have been formed by alliances comprising a cluster of regional parties led by a national party—the BJP-led National Democratic Alliance of 1999 and the Congress-led United Progressive Alliance of 2004 and 2009. (Ruparelia 2011). For alliances formed before the election this has meant seat sharing with the result that traditional workers and supporters of Party X have suddenly had to shift their allegiance, not always successfully or with enthusiasm, to Party X.[11] In addition to the reasons cited in the introduction, this factor too has contributed to the decline of 'vote bank' politics as the presence of alien candidates has strained traditional party loyalties (Banerjee 2014, pp. 78–79).

The third aspect of change has been village level elections under the auspices of the *Panchayati Raj* brought into being by the 73rd Constitution Amendment Act of 1993 with the accompanying provision that one-third of the total number of positions of *gram pradhan* would be held by women with another proportion held by the SC/ST. This has engaged a tranche of persons in political activity that previously had no experience or, indeed, the opportunity, of participating in public life (Krishna 2010; Corbridge et al. 2013).

[11]For example, the AIDMK-CPM and the DMK-Congress alliances in Tamil Nadu meant that traditional AIDMK supporters had to support CPM candidates and traditional DMK supporters had to support Congress candidates.

These three aspects justify the emphasis in this paper on political participation in terms of the individual-citizen (rather than by purely group loyalties) albeit constrained by considerations of gender and caste. The unique feature of this study was that it provided a *quantitative* analysis of political participation in rural India with respect to voting and to attendance/participation in *Gram Sabha* meetings. This analysis was conducted in terms of a common set of explanatory variables—social group, gender, age, marital status, education, and occupation. A novel twist was provided by allowing each of these variables to interact with whether the election was a 'national' or a 'local' election and with whether the election was conducted during the current or past panchayat periods. The estimated equations permitted predicted probabilities to be computed under a variety of scenarios and, from these scenarios, it was possible to cull 'ideal types' of persons—those with the highest and lowest probabilities of experiencing a particular outcome.

A worrisome feature of the results was the high proportion of married women reporting that they voted according to their husbands' instructions and further that, this proportion was impervious to the education level of the women. Women's education would not appear, from these results, to reduce the power of patriarchy. However, the fact that a secret ballot can drive a wedge between professed and actual actions might serve to ameliorate this.

Another source of anxiety was the gender gap in the proportion of men and women who took part in *Gram Sabha* discussions. This would suggest that the reservation of village panchayat positions (including that of *panchayat pradhan*, or village president) for women was a step in the right direction for the empowerment of women. In contrast, there were no inter-social group differences in participation in *Gram Sabha* meetings.

The paper suggests several avenues for further research based on the data from REDS. First, there is the question of the consequences of political participation in terms of good village governance and levels of village development. Second, there is the question of differences in political participation between the upper (the 'creamy layer') and lower echelons of the lower castes and it is possible to address this because the REDS data also provides information on household sub-caste. Third, but by no means last, is the question of the level of village level conflict in the wake of the 73rd amendment which, by establishing *Gram Sabhas*, has diluted the oligarchic hegemony of the upper castes in public policy matters pertaining to the village.

Appendix

See Table 9.

Table 9 Estimation results from the logit voting model with interactions on election type and election period

$Y_i = 1$, if voted	Odds ratio	Std. Err.	z	P>z
National election (NE)	0.278	0.060	−5.88	0.00
Social group				
Scheduled Caste (SC)	1.204	0.048	4.62	0.00
Scheduled Tribe (ST)	1.096	0.065	1.55	0.12
Other Backward Classes (OBC)	1.147	0.034	4.58	0.00
Reference group: upper classes				
Interaction of NE and group				
NE × SC	0.645	0.036	−7.83	0.00
NE × ST	0.853	0.057	−2.37	0.02
NE × OBC	0.625	0.024	−12.12	0.00
Current election (CE)	30.587	6.664	15.70	0.00
Interaction of CE and group				
CE × SC	1.151	0.063	2.59	0.01
CE × ST	0.921	0.058	−1.31	0.19
CE × OBC	0.960	0.035	−1.12	0.26
Female	0.874	0.043	−2.75	0.01
Interaction of NE and female				
NE × female	0.872	0.058	−2.06	0.04
Interaction of CE and female				
CE × female	1.303	0.085	4.06	0.00
Age	1.108	0.007	16.99	0.00
Age^2	0.999	0.000	−14.04	0.00
Interaction of NE and age				
NE × age	1.122	0.009	13.92	0.00
Interaction of NE and age^2				
NE × age^2	0.999	0.000	−11.88	0.00
Interaction of CE and age				
CE × age	0.912	0.008	−11.10	0.00
Interaction of CE and age^2				
CE × age^2	1.001	0.000	8.99	0.00
Married	1.148	0.045	3.52	0.00
Interaction of NE and married				
NE × married	1.078	0.060	1.35	0.18
Interaction of CE and married				
CE × married	0.910	0.049	−1.77	0.08
Occupation				
Self-employed agriculture (SEA)	1.306	0.082	4.25	0.00
Self-employed non-agriculture (SEnA)	1.115	0.085	1.43	0.15
Salaried (SAL)	0.933	0.074	−0.87	0.38
Agriculture wage labour (AWL)	1.278	0.094	3.34	0.00
Non-agriculture wage labour (NAWL)	1.093	0.080	1.21	0.23

(continued)

Table 9 (continued)

$Y_i = 1$, if voted	Odds ratio	Std. Err.	z	P>z
Family worker (FWK)	0.908	0.090	−0.98	0.33
Household worker (HWK)	1.087	0.072	1.27	0.21
Reference category: pensioner, dependent, student				
Interaction of NE and occupation				
NE × SEA	0.922	0.086	−0.87	0.38
NE × SEnA	1.005	0.114	0.05	0.96
NE × SAL	0.830	0.096	−1.61	0.11
NE × AWL	0.840	0.089	−1.65	0.10
NE × NAWL	1.139	0.125	1.19	0.23
NE × FWK	0.841	0.120	−1.22	0.22
NE × HWK	0.932	0.089	−0.74	0.46
Interaction of CE and occupation				
CE × SEA	0.899	0.076	−1.27	0.21
CE × SEnA	1.220	0.128	1.90	0.06
CE × SAL	1.152	0.126	1.29	0.20
CE × AWL	1.176	0.115	1.65	0.10
CE × NAWL	1.098	0.110	0.93	0.35
CE × FWK	1.166	0.162	1.10	0.27
CE × HWK	1.034	0.092	0.38	0.71
Education				
Illiterate (ILT)	1.324	0.084	4.45	0.00
Primary (PRM)	1.263	0.081	3.62	0.00
Secondary (SEC)	0.996	0.062	−0.06	0.95
Higher secondary (HSEC)	1.265	0.088	3.39	0.00
Reference category: degree or higher				
Interaction of NE and education				
NE × ILT	0.851	0.075	−1.83	0.07
NE × PRM	0.973	0.089	−0.30	0.76
NE × SEC	1.095	0.097	1.02	0.31
NE × HSEC	0.749	0.073	−2.97	0.00
Interaction of NE and education				
CE × ILT	0.613	0.053	−5.61	0.00
CE × PRM	0.800	0.072	−2.48	0.01
CE × SEC	1.071	0.094	0.78	0.44
CE × HSEC	0.783	0.076	−2.51	0.01

Number of observations	181,556
LR chi2 (284)	29,012.19
Prob > chi2	0.00
Pseudo R^2	0.19
Log likelihood	−62,191.732

References

Akerlof, G. (1976). The economics of caste and of the rat race and other woeful tales. *The Quarterly Journal of Economics, 90*(4), 599–617.

Banerjee, M. (2014). *Why India votes?* New Delhi: Routledge.

Ben-Bassat, A., & Dahan, M. (2012). Social identity and voting behaviour. *Public Choice, 151*(1), 193–214.

Besley, T., Pande, R., & Rao, V. (2012). Just rewards? Local politics and public resource allocation in south India. *World Bank Economic Review, 26*(2), 191–216.

Borooah, V. K. (2012). Corruption in India: A quantitative analysis. *Economic and Political Weekly, 47*(28), 23–25.

Breeding, M. E. (2011). The micro-politics of vote banks in Karnataka. *Economic and Political Weekly, 46*(14), 71–77.

Brennan, G., & Lomasky, L. (1993). *Democracy and decision: The pure theory of electoral preference*. New York, NY: Cambridge University Press.

Chandra, K. (2004). *Why ethnic parties succeed: Patronage and ethnic head counts in India.* New York, NY: Cambridge University Press.

Corbridge, S., Harriss, J., & Jeffrey, C. (2013). *India today: Economy, politics and society.* Cambridge: Polity Press.

Downs, A. (1957). *An economic theory of democracy*. New York, NY: Harper and Row.

Dyson, T., & Moore, M. (1983). On kinship structure, female autonomy, and demographic behaviour in India. *Population and Development Review, 9*(1), 35–60.

Geys, B. (2006). 'Rational' theories of voter turnout: A review. *Political Studies Review, 4*(1), 16–35.

Grossman, G. M., & Helpman, E. (2001). *Special interest politics*. Cambridge, MA: MIT Press.

Hamlin, A., & Jennings, C. (2011). Expressive political behaviour: Foundations, scope and implications. *British Journal of Political Science, 41*(3), 645–670.

Hanusch, M. (2013). Islam and democracy: A response. *Public Choice* 154: 315–321.

Inglehart, R. (2000). Culture and democracy. In L. E. Harrison & S. P. Huntington (Eds.), *Culture matters* (pp. 80–97). New York, NY: Basic Books.

Jaffrelot, C. (2003). *India's silent revolution: The rise of the lower castes in northern India.* New York, NY: Columbia University Press.

Jeejeebhoy, S. J., & Sathar, Z. A. (2001). Women's autonomy in India and Pakistan: The role of religion and region. *Population and Development Review, 27*(4), 687–712.

Jodhka, S. S. (2012, May). *The problem.* Paper presented at the Symposium #633 on Caste matters: Inequalities, identities, and hierarchies in India.

Krishna, A. (2010). Local politics. In N. Jayal & P. B. Mehta (Eds.), *The Oxford companion to politics in India*. New Delhi: Oxford University Press.

Long, J. S., & Freese, J. (2014). *Regression models for categorical dependent variables using Stata*. College Station, TX: Stata Press.

Potrafke, N. (2012), Islam and democracy. *Public Choice* 151: 185–192.

Rowley, C. K., & Smith, N. (2009), Islam's democracy paradox: Muslims claim to like democracy, so why do they have so little? *Public Choice, 139*(3–4), 273–299.

Ruparelia, S. (2011). Expanding India's democracy: The paradox of the third force. In S. Ruparelia, S. Reddy, J. Harriss, & S. Corbridge (Eds.), *Understanding India's new political economy: A great transformation* (pp. 186–203). London: Routledge.

Schedler, A., & Schaffer, F. C. (2007). What is vote buying? In F. C. Schaffer (Ed.), *Elections for sale: The causes and consequences of vote buying* (pp. 17–30). London: Lynne Rienner Publishers.

Sen, A. K. (1977). Rational fools: A critique of the behavioral foundations of economic theory. *Philosophy and Public Affairs, 6*, 317–344.

Shaffer, F. C. (Ed.). (2007). *Elections for sale: The causes and consequences of vote buying.* Boulder, CO: Lynne Rienner Publishers.

Srinivas, M. N. (1955). The social structure of life in a Mysore village. In M. Marriott (Ed.), *Village India*. Chicago, IL: Chicago University Press.

Witsoe, J. (2012). Everyday corruption and the political mediation of the Indian state: An ethnographic exploration of brokers in Bihar. *Economic and Political Weekly, 47*(6), 47–54.

Elections with International Relations Dominance

Jan Klingelhöfer

1 Introduction

Under what conditions is international cooperation possible when the participating countries have incentives to deviate from their promises? With the current problems in the governance of the European Union this important question has new relevance not only for political scientists, but also for economists who have to understand what type of economic cooperation is politically sustainable even in the face of adverse shocks.

McGillivray and Smith (2000, 2008) develop a theory of international cooperation using a repeated prisoner's dilemma setup. They show that the fact that countries are run by elected politicians who are agents of the voters gives credibility to international cooperation where it would not be an equilibrium without elections. The reason is that a country's leader can be punished with the loss of his office what is often a much harder punishment for a politician than the loss of the advantages of a continuation of international cooperation. Voters, who are in McGillivray and Smith (2000) indifferent between potential *prime ministers*, have the incentive to punish their leaders to restore international cooperation even when these leaders defection is actually in the voters interest when it occurs.

I present a model of international cooperation that allows not only for the punishment of deviating leaders, but also to reward leaders that cooperate internationally. This makes only sense because the representative voters are not indifferent between the *prime minister* and his challenger. Consequently, the representative voter has to pay a price for rewarding incumbents for international cooperation: They cannot elect their favorite candidates to the job of *prime minister* any longer and thus

J. Klingelhöfer (✉)
RWTH Aachen University, Aachen, Germany
e-mail: klingelhoefer@vwl1.rwth-aachen.de

N. Schofield, G. Caballero (eds.), *State, Institutions and Democracy*,
Studies in Political Economy, DOI 10.1007/978-3-319-44582-3_8

lose control over domestic policies. Nonetheless, they can be better off as long as international cooperation is of great importance relative to domestic policies.

2 The Model

There are two countries $j = 1, 2$ that cooperate with each other. The decision about each country's contribution to this international cooperation is made by its respective *prime minister*. The *prime minister* of a country is challenged in an election by an alternative candidate whom I refer to as the *challenger* in every period t of the game. The intertemporal utility function of all (potential) *prime ministers* is:

$$u_j^{pm} = \sum_{t=0}^{\infty} \beta^t (p_{j,t} + v \cdot o_{j,t}^{pm}) \text{ with } j = 1, 2.$$

Potential *prime ministers* enjoy the benefits of international cooperation and receive a payoff $p_{j,t}$ in every period (even when not in power). The exact determination of $p_{j,t}$ is explained below. In addition, the variable $o_{j,t}^{pm}$ takes the value 1 if the potential *prime minister* is *prime minister* of country j in period t. Otherwise, it takes the value 0. Thus, potential *prime ministers* benefit from holding office and receive the additional utility v in every period in which they serve as *prime minister*. We can think of an infinite pool of potential challengers from which one is drawn randomly before every election but rule out that former *prime ministers* become candidates again. The result of the election of the *prime minister* is determined by the decision of a representative voter with the following intertemporal utility function:

$$u_j^{v} = \sum_{t=0}^{\infty} \beta^t (p_{j,t} + b \cdot f_{j,t}) \text{ with } j = 1, 2,$$

where $\beta \in (0, 1)$ is the discount factor and $p_{j,t}$ the payoff from international cooperation that country j receives in period t. Thus, a representative voter benefits from international cooperation exactly in the same way as the *prime minister* of her country. The variable $f_{j,t}$ takes the value 1 if the candidate preferred by the representative voter (her favorite) in country j wins the election in period t, otherwise it takes the value 0. Thus, $b \geq 0$ is a payoff that voter receives in every period in which her favorite candidate is in power.

In every period in both countries the probability that the voter prefers the incumbent to the *challenger* is given by $\alpha \in (0, 1)$. The preference for a *prime minister* or his *challenger* is not correlated between countries or over time. While b could be interpreted as differences in ideology, the most convincing interpretation are differences in competence on matters of domestic policy or a combination of ideology and competence. This explains why the preferences of the representative voter change over time as she learns more about the competence of the incumbent.

Payoffs from International Cooperation The payoffs from international cooperation in country *j* given the contribution by the country itself (c_j) and the contribution by the other country (c_k) in any period are given by:

$$p_j(c_j, c_k) = c_j + \sqrt{c_j} + c_k + \sqrt{c_k} - (2c_j + \sqrt{c_j}) = c_k - c_j + \sqrt{c_k},$$

with $j, k = 1, 2$ and $j \neq k$. $c_j + \sqrt{c_j} + c_k + \sqrt{c_k}$ can be interpreted the benefit from an (international) public good that both countries enjoy to the same degree.[1] In this interpretation, $2c_j + \sqrt{c_j}$ is the cost for country *j* of providing the public good and c_j its contribution to the international public goods net of the benefits accruing to itself, for brevity called the contribution of country *j*.

Given the payoff function $p_j(c_j, c_k)$ in a one-shot game the best reply of the *prime minister* in country *j* against any c_k is always given by $c_j = 0$. However, if both *prime ministers* can somehow commit to provide a combination of c_1, c_2 for which $p_1(c_1, c_2) > 0$ and $p_2(c_2, c_1) > 0$ in a period of the game they are both better off. Agreeing on such a combination of payoffs is not credible in a one-shot game because the countries face a prisoner dilemma situation: Both *prime ministers* have a dominant strategy to contribute 0 independently of what they expect the other country to do.

There is a highest possible contribution level $c_j^{\max}$ with $j = 1, 2$ for both countries because any country is naturally limited in the amount of resources that it can provide for international cooperation.[2] Given the functional form, the international welfare maximizing contributions are given by $c_1^{\max}$ and $c_2^{\max}$. For notational convenience, I assume the that the largest possible contribution is in both countries larger than the largest sustainable contribution in any of the equilibria presented below. Consequently, the largest possible levels of contribution can be ignored in the presentation of the equilibria below.

The Order of Moves In every period t :

1. The level of contribution to international cooperation is decided simultaneously by the *prime ministers* in both countries.
2. Nature chooses the identity of the *challenger* to the *prime ministers* in both countries. In both countries, with probability α the representative voter prefers the incumbent *prime minister* to his *challenger*.
3. Elections take place simultaneously in both countries and the representative voter in country $j = 1, 2$ decides which of the two candidates becomes or remains

[1] It would be slightly more precise but also more cumbersome to use a subscripts t to make clear that the payoff refers to a specific period t and denote $p_{j,t}(c_{j,t}, c_{k,t})$ instead of using the notation in the text.

[2] This is a reasonable assumption given that the resources of a country are finite. Moreover, it allows us to use standard results for showing subgame perfection of the equilibria we present and rules out subgame perfect equilibria that are supported by ever-growing contributions.

prime minister. A replaced *prime minister* will not become the *challenger* to the *prime minister* in any future period.
4. All players receive their per-period utility for period t.

After the described 4 steps period t is over period $t + 1$ begins. Whoever is the *prime minister* at the end of period t in a country has this function also in the beginning of period $t + 1$.

3 Solving the Model

The standard game theory of cooperation in an repeated prisoner's dilemma setting shows that cooperation is possible if the prisoner's dilemma stage game is repeated infinitely many periods as long as the future is valued sufficiently by the players. Consequently, even when the voters ignore international cooperation in their voting decisions, it can nonetheless be rational for *prime ministers* of different countries to agree on some cooperation. This idea of modelling international cooperation as a repeated prisoner's dilemma goes back to Axelrod and Keohane (1985).

While this stage is not formalized, the most straightforward interpretation of the model is that the leaders of the two countries can negotiate (without cost) with each other before the game begins and in this way coordinate on the most desirable equilibrium.

3.1 Some More Notation

Because I focus on symmetric equilibria in which both countries provide the same amount of contributions, it is helpful to use the notation $p^{cc}(c) = p_j(c, c)$ to denote the payoffs when both countries provide a contribution of size c. The superscript cc denotes that both country play cooperatively given that c is the minimum level of cooperation that is understood to be cooperative behavior. Consequently, I use $p^{dc}(c) = p_j(0, c)$ to denote the payoff of country j that plays the best reply 0 against the cooperative level c and $p^{dd}(c) = p_j(0, 0)$ the payoff of both country playing noncooperatively.

3.2 Finding Subgame Perfect Equilibria

We have an infinite-horizon multi-stage game with observable actions and payoffs are the discounted sum of uniformly bounded per-period payoffs. From this it follows that a strategy profile is a subgame perfect equilibrium if and only if no player who can improve her payoff by only deviating in one subgame.[3] Thus, all we have to do is to establish a subgame perfect Nash equilibrium that in a strategic profile none of the player has a deviation in only one subgame what would make her better off. I present three types of subgame perfect equilibria of the game. In the first one, the *country specific grim trigger equilibrium*, domestic policies in the democracy play no role for international cooperation. Given the assumption on the payoffs from international cooperation, such an equilibrium always exists. The second equilibrium with *leader specific punishment* is (in a different setup) already known from McGillivray and Smith (2000). For this equilibrium to exist, payoffs from international cooperation must be relatively important compared to the payoffs from domestic politics. The *international dominance equilibrium* contributes a new idea to the literature: Besides using the stick of punishment for a deviation on the international level, there is also the carrot of reelecting a candidate who would not win an election otherwise. Again, this is consistent with equilibrium if the advantages of international cooperation are large enough. In this equilibrium voters pay a price for sustaining international cooperation even when the game is in equilibrium. In return, they can also sustain a higher level of cooperation than with purely leader specific punishment. Consequently, this equilibrium is not necessarily more difficult to sustain than in an equilibrium with *leader specific punishment.* While in the equilibrium with *leader specific punishment* domestic policies are only influenced off the equilibrium path of the game, here the influence on international politics becomes the only function of elections along the equilibrium path of the game. Voters do not choose the more able candidate as *prime minister* because that would lead to the breakdown of international cooperation.

3.3 International Cooperation with Country Specific Grim Trigger Strategies

The standard theory not only of international cooperation, but of all forms of cooperation in an repeated prisoner's dilemma setting shows that cooperation is possible if the prisoner's dilemma stage game is repeated infinitely many periods and the future is valued sufficiently (that is if β is large) even without any principal-agent relationship between politicians and voters or party members. Consequently, it is not surprising that if voters and party members ignore international cooperation in their decision-making, it is nonetheless rational for *prime ministers* of different countries to agree on some cooperation. The basic idea goes back to Axelrod and Keohane (1985).

[3]For a proof of this well-known result see for example Theorem 4.2 in Fudenberg and Tirole (1991).

Phases of the Game We divide the game in two phases to facilitate the description of the strategies of the players. The phases are *cooperation* and *punishment*. The game begins in phase *cooperation* and switches to *punishment* as soon as one of the *prime ministers* offers a level of cooperation below a threshold level c_{cs}. Once the game has entered the *punishment* phase there is no return to the *cooperation* phase.

The Strategy of the *Prime Ministers* Both *prime ministers* contribute $c_{j,t} = c_{cs}$ for $j = 1, 2$ as long as t is part of the cooperative phase. In phase *punishment*, they contribute $c_{j,t} = 0$ for $j = 1, 2$ if period t is in a noncooperative phase. This type of strategy is also known as grim trigger strategy. One of its appeals is that it is simple.[4]

The Strategy of the Representative Voters The representative voters in both countries always elect the candidate they prefer.

Largest Sustainable Level of Cooperation with Country Specific Grim Trigger Strategies Given the strategy of the *prime ministers*, voters have no influence on the level of international cooperation. Consequently, by deviating from the given equilibrium strategy they would only end up with a *prime minister* they do not favor and be worse off. The only condition that has to hold for a country specific grim trigger strategy to be consistent with equilibrium is that for a *prime minister* the gain from a deviation in cooperative phase ($p^{dc}(c_{cs}) - p^{cc}(c_{cs})$) is not larger than the *punishment* of Nash reversion forever (the *punishment* phase, receiving $p^{dd}(c_{cs})$ forever instead of $p^{cc}(c_{cs})$ before):

$$p^{dc}(c_{cs}) - p^{cc}(c_{cs}) \leq \frac{\beta}{1-\beta}(p^{cc}(c_{cs}) - p^{dd}(c_{cs})),$$

or, given the functional form we assumed:

$$c_{cs} + \sqrt{c_{cs}} - \sqrt{c_{cs}} \leq \frac{\beta}{1-\beta}\sqrt{c_{cs}}.$$

Solving for c_{cs}^*, the highest level of cooperation achievable with country specific grim trigger gives: $c_{cs}^* = \left(\frac{\beta}{1-\beta}\right)^2$.

The *punishment* phase is trivially consistent with a subgame perfect Nash equilibrium because the Nash equilibrium of the one-shot game is played in every period.

[4] However, a common point of critique is that it is not renegotiation proof in the sense of Bernheim and Ray (1989) and Farrell and Maskin (1989).

3.4 Leader Specific Punishment Equilibrium

The idea behind leader (or more general agent) specific punishment goes back to McGillivray and Smith (2000) and is thoroughly discussed in McGillivray and Smith (2008). If a *prime minister* deviates, cooperation is resumed if he is replaced by a different leader as *prime minister*. But as long as a *prime minister* has any political or private benefits from office, losing it constitutes a punishment that is potentially more severe than the damage to international cooperation in the future would be.

Phases of the Game There are now three phases of the game. The first phase is *cooperation*, the second phase *cheat* and the third phase *punishment*. Again, the only function of the phases is to facilitate the description of the strategies of the players. The game begins in phase *cooperation*. The game stays in phase *cooperation* as long as none of the *prime ministers* provides less than a threshold level c_{ls} of contributions to international cooperation. As soon as a *prime minister* provides less, the game switches to the phase *cheat*. If the game is in phase *cheat* and all leaders who deviated in phase *cooperation* are replaced by the representative voters in their respective countries, the game switches back from *cheat* to *cooperation*. Otherwise, the game switches from *cheat* to *punishment* and stays in phase *punishment* forever. If the game is in phase *cooperation* or in phase *punishment* when the parties decide if they should replace their leaders, it stays there independently of the decision of the parties. Once in phase *punishment* is reached the game never switches to a different phase again.

The Strategy of the *Prime Ministers* The *prime ministers* play cooperate by providing the lowest level of contributions accepted as cooperative, denoted by c_{ls}, as long as the game is in phase *cooperation*. They provide a contribution of 0 when the game is in the *punishment* phase.

The Strategy of the Representative Voters The representative voters elects the candidate whom she prefers to become *prime minister* for domestic reasons with one exception: Whenever a prime minster has deviated by offering a level of cooperation lower than c_{ls} in phase *cooperation*, he is replaced in the election by the *challenger* even if the representative voter prefers him.

Existence of Equilibrium and Size of Possible Cooperation Now punishment for the *prime minister* is of a different nature compared to the country specific grim trigger equilibrium: Because voters always replace *prime ministers* who have not cooperated internationally, the punishment for a *prime minister* consists now of losing his job for sure (instead of losing it only with probability $1 - \alpha$). On the other hand, the *prime minister* does not suffer from any damage to international relations because they go on untainted after he is replaced. Thus, the first condition that has to hold is that deviating can not make a *prime minister* better off. By cooperating in any period the *prime minister* has a change of α of staying in office because with probability α he will be preferred by the representative voter in his country.[5] On the other hand, if a *prime minister* deviates by providing a level of cooperation that is lower than what is perceived as cooperative, he loses office for sure given the strategy of the representative voter. Consequently, the expected loss in utility from deviating by providing less cooperation than c_{ls} is given by $\sum_{i=0}^{\infty} \alpha^{i+1} \beta^i v = \alpha \sum_{i=0}^{\infty} \alpha^i \beta^i v = \frac{\alpha v}{1-\beta\alpha}$. Because given our functional form for international cooperation we have $p^{dc}(c_{ls}) - p^{cc}(c_{ls}) = c_{ls}$, the largest possible level of cooperation consistent with equilibrium is given by $c_{ls}^* = \frac{\alpha v}{1-\beta\alpha}$.

For a voter there are two situations conceivable after a deviation. If the voter prefers the *challenger* anyway she has obviously no reason not to replace the *prime minister* and in this way to restore international cooperation. On the other hand, if the *prime minister* turns out to be her favorite in the election, she pays a price of b for replacing him. This is consistent with equilibrium as long as the one time cost of b is smaller than the discounted value of future international cooperation in all future periods:

$$b \leq \frac{\beta}{1-\beta}\sqrt{c_{ls}^*} = \frac{\beta}{1-\beta}\sqrt{\frac{\alpha v}{1-\beta\alpha}}$$

and thus the price the representative voter is paying for future cooperation is smaller than the discounted value of future international cooperation. On the other hand, if domestic policy considerations are too important because $b > \frac{\beta}{1-\beta}\sqrt{\frac{\alpha v}{1-\beta\alpha}}$, a leader specific punishment equilibrium does not exist. Again, the *punishment* phase of the game is trivially consistent with a subgame perfect Nash equilibrium because the Nash equilibrium of the one-shot game is played in every period.

3.5 International Dominance

Now we come to the main contribution of this paper. While McGillivray and Smith (2000) introduced the idea of leader specific punishment to the literature (the stick), there is also the possibility to incentivize politicians with keeping them in office that they would otherwise lose for domestic policy reasons (the carrot).

Again, I distinguish between 3 phases of the game, *cooperation, cheat* and *punishment*. As before, the game begins in phase *cooperation*. If the game is in phase *cooperation* and both leaders play cooperate, the game stays in phase *cooperation*. Otherwise, the game switches to the phase *cheat*. If it was in phase *punishment* the game stays in phase *punishment*. If the game is in phase *cooperation* and one or both of the *prime ministers* are replaced in an election the game enters the phase *punishment*. If the game is in phase cheat and either a *prime minister*

[5]His chance of surviving one more time after that are α^2 in period $t+1$ and so on as long as the game follows the equilibrium path.

who has cooperated in the last period is not reelected or a *prime minister* who has not cooperated in the last period is reelected the game enters the phase *punishment*. Otherwise, the game switches from *cheat* to *cooperation*.

The Strategy of the *Prime Ministers* The *prime ministers* play cooperate as long as the game is in phase *cooperation* and play punishment in phase *punishment*.

The Strategy of the Representative Voters In phase *cooperation*, the representative voters reelect the incumbent *prime minister*. In phase *cheat*, the voters vote against the incumbent if the incumbent has not cooperated in the current period. In phase *punishment*, the representative voters always elect their preferred candidates.

Existence of Equilibrium and Size of Possible Cooperation The gain from a deviation for a *prime minister* in phase *cooperation* is, if the level of contributions accepted as cooperations is c_{id}: $p^{dc}(c_{id}) - p^{cc}(c_{id}) = c_{id}$.

The loss is now given by the present value of losing office forever instead of keeping it forever is:

$$\frac{v}{1-\beta}.$$

A *prime minister* is consequently now willing to play *cooperate* as long as:

$$p^{dc} - p^{cc} \leq \frac{v}{1-\beta}$$

Consequently, the highest level of cooperation achievable with party specific punishment and international dominance is, given the assumed functional form:

$$c_{id}^{*} = \frac{v}{1-\beta}.$$

Conditions for Representative Voters Now a representative voter can be in two different situations in the cooperative phase and the cheat phase: She is either required to vote in favour of the candidate she prefers for domestic policy reason or to vote against him. Obviously, the tougher condition must be to vote against a favorite candidate for *prime minister*. Also, compared to the situation with leader specific punishment, now a voter does not only lose in future periods by deviating: Once the game is in the *punishment* phase the representative voter will enjoy optimal domestic politics forever, while by staying in the cooperative phase she has only a chance of α in every future period. Consequently, she will be willing to replace an otherwise preferred leader who has not provided a sufficient contribution to international cooperation if:

$$b + (1-\alpha)b\frac{\beta}{1-\beta} \leq \frac{\beta}{1-\beta}\sqrt{c_{id}^{*}}$$

$$\iff b \leq \frac{\beta}{1-\alpha\beta}\sqrt{\frac{v}{1-\beta}}.$$

It is noteworthy that this condition is not necessarily harder to meet than the condition for the *leader specific punishment* equilibrium which was given by $b \leq \frac{\beta}{1-\beta}\sqrt{\frac{\alpha v}{1-\beta\alpha}}$. The reason is that while the representative voter pays a larger price when reelecting a candidate she does not prefer than in the *leader specific punishment* equilibrium, she also is rewarded with more cooperation in the future for doing so than in the *leader specific punishment* equilibrium. Which effect is more important depends on the discount factor. As long as $\beta \leq \frac{1}{\alpha+1}$, the condition is less severe for the *international dominance equilibrium.*

3.6 Comparison of the Three Equilibria and Welfare Analysis

As mentioned before, the grim trigger equilibrium is always possible, while the two other equilibria are only feasible if domestic policies are not too important. It is easy to compare with the country specific grim trigger equilibrium and the equilibrium with leader specific punishment from a welfare perspective because the only difference in outcomes along the equilibrium path is the possible level of international cooperation. The representative voter obviously prefers the equilibrium with the higher level of international cooperation and prefers the leader specific punishment equilibrium as long as $c^*_{cs} \geq c^*_{ls} \iff \left(\frac{\beta}{1-\beta}\right)^2 \geq \frac{\alpha v}{1-\beta\alpha}$. While c^*_{cs} depends only on the discount factor, c^*_{ls} increases also in the value of office and the probability of reelection of an incumbent.

The comparison with the result of international dominance is less straightforward. With international dominance, voters have to pay a price for by giving up all control over domestic policies. Thus, compared to both other equilibria, they give up $(1-\alpha)\frac{b}{1-\beta}$ in expectations before the game begins. This cost is obviously increasing in the importance of the choice of the right *prime minister* given by b. The difference in gains from international cooperation compared to the equilibrium with *leader specific punishment* is given by: $\frac{\beta}{1-\beta}\sqrt{\frac{v}{1-\beta}} - \frac{\beta}{1-\beta}\sqrt{\frac{\alpha v}{1-\beta\alpha}}$, what is decreasing in α. When there is a large incumbency advantage (α close to 1), the additional reward of being reelected for international cooperation becomes relatively unimportant.

3.7 Conclusion

The most obvious criticism of the international dominance equilibrium is the seemingly unrealistic feature that a *prime minister* is reelected forever. This becomes less implausible if we reinterpret the fact that the future is discounted by β as at least partly the result of the possibility that there is a fundamental change in world affairs that lets bygones be bygones. Such a fundamental change would lead to new negotiations about international relations independently of what has happened in the past. If this were the case we could alternatively write the discount factor as the product of standard discounting of the future $\beta_f \in (0, 1)$ and a probability of $\beta_g \in (0, 1)$ that the world is going on as before without fundamental change. Consequently, future payoffs would be discounted by all players by the discount factor $\beta = \beta_f \cdot \beta_g$. Such a reset could for example happen if the leader of a country dies in office or international relations are put on a totally new basis. The end of the cold war would be one example for such a fundamental change.

References

Axelrod, R., & Keohane, R. O. (1985). Achieving cooperation under anarchy: Strategies and institutions. *World Politics 38*(1), 226–255.

Bernheim, B. D., & Ray, D. (1989). Collective dynamic consistency in repeated games. *Games and Economics Behavior 1*(4), 295–326.

Farrell, J., & Maskin, E. (1989). Renegotiation in repeated games. *Games and Economics Behavior 1*(4), 327–360.

Fudenberg, D., & Tirole, J. (1991). *Game theory*. Cambridge, MA: MIT Press.

McGillivray, F., & Smith, A. (2000). Trust and cooperation through agent specific punishment. *International Organization 54*(04), 809–824.

McGillivray, F., & Smith, A. (2008). *Punishing the prince: A theory of interstate relations, political institutions, and leader change*. Princeton: Princeton University Press.

Electoral Rules and Proportionality in Spain: Estimating the Impact of some Swedish Rules Through the 2011 Electoral Data

Jose M. Pavia and Fernando Toboso

1 Introduction

In democratic countries policy making is always framed by many procedures and rules. Some of these rules are particularly critical for allowing more or less proportionality in legislative chambers, though the behavior of political actors also matter as we are going to mention next. The rules used for technically converting votes into political representatives often exercise such an important role in western countries (Lijphart 1994, 2003; Sartori 2005). Examples are rules defining the number of constituencies, the number of representatives elected in each constituency, the size of the representative body, the electoral threshold (the minimum amount of support required to obtain representation), as well as the d'Hondt rule that is used in Spain as opposed to the *winner takes all rule* employed in majoritarian systems such as those in place in UK or USA.

This conflict or tension between more or less proportionality exists in all electoral systems (Powell 2000; Ortega 2004; Pavía and Toboso 2015). In fact, in those parliamentary democracies in which the executive is indirectly elected by a majority of Parliament, as is the case in Spain, these rules are even more influential. So, it is not surprising that a recurrent political debate arises after each election between those endorsing rules that tend to favor the emergence of stable majorities at expenses of proportionality and those endorsing rules that favor political pluralism with many more political parties being in the parliament.

In the Spanish case, complaining voices are particularly recurrent among those political parties underrepresented, but also in the academia, pointing out that these rules tend to favor the main big political groups as well as those regionalist-nationalist parties which present candidates only in some provinces, and impairs the

J.M. Pavia • F. Toboso (✉)
GIPEyOP, Department of Applied Economics, Universitat de València, Valencia, Spain
e-mail: Fernando.Toboso@uv.es

N. Schofield, G. Caballero (eds.), *State, Institutions and Democracy*, Studies in Political Economy, DOI 10.1007/978-3-319-44582-3_9

results of small parties that compete in all districts (Capo Giol 1999; Casarramona 2009; Martínez-Pujalte 2008). Some authors have been even more critical with the Spanish system (Urdanoz 2008; EFE 2008).

This non-proportionality bias has traditionally resulted in quite stable central governments in Spain with absolute majorities on several occasions. The under-representation has usually affected those nationwide parties at third position or lower (Ocaña and Oñate 1999; Pavía-Miralles 2011). This is why various suggestions have been made over the past decades in an attempt to reduce this degree of non-proportionality, for example, by adopting a single constituency for all Spain, by modifying the algorithm used for allocating seats (the d'Hondt rule), by replacing the provinces for the autonomous communities as districts, by keeping the d'Hondt rule and the provinces as districts but reducing the minimum seats assigned to provinces from two to one, etc.

Although these proposals are interesting, many face the problem of requiring a constitutional reform to be implemented, which no doubt undermines their chances of success (Colomer 2003). Moreover, if a proposal requires the reforming of the LOREG (Organic Law 5/1985 of 19 June on the General Electoral System), this reform must not violate the limits imposed by the Constitution. Therefore, to reform the electoral system in Spain is not an easy task even if we set aside consideration of the other difficulties derived from reaching the necessary consensus.

Because the Swedish system is known as a quite proportional system that could also be implemented in Spain without reforming the Spanish Constitution, we have chosen some of its basic electoral rules for performing our estimations. More specifically, the purpose of the paper is that of estimating, based on real electoral data, how much the share of seats that resulted from the 2011 Spanish general elections gets changed if we apply some of these Swedish rules for converting votes into seats, instead of the Spanish rules that were in fact used. Does proportionality between votes and seats increase when we implement such an estimate?

Of course, this means focusing on the so-called mechanical effects of electoral rules and electoral reforms. Or, let us say it differently, we will perform a standard comparative statics exercise for estimating the potential impacts of institutional reforms under the usual ceteris paribus assumption (Schmid 1987, 2004; Toboso 2013). This is an important issue to be mentioned here in order to avoid any misinterpretation of the purposes of the present chapter. Therefore, our research purpose is not that of obtaining "predictions" in a real case situation after an electoral reform has been made. For so doing we should take into account the many other influential variables not considered in our research exercise. Particularly, this is the case of the changes in behavior and strategies of voters and politicians that would surely follow in Spanish politics if the above mentioned changes were implemented, as many authors have stressed by referring to the psychological impacts of electoral rules and rules changing. It is evident that these psychological impacts greatly affect coordination, persuasion and mobilization strategies by political parties

$$Discrepancy(s) = \sum_{i=1}^{k} |p_i - e_i(s)|$$

Fig. 1 Comparative degree of proportionality between votes sharing and seats sharing

(Cox 2008, 2015).[1] Some rules may induce, for example, the making of pre-electoral coalitions or may systematically tend to direct more campaign efforts by a political party to those districts where the leaders estimate that winning a new seat is more likely or there is greater danger of losing one already hold (Gallego et al. 2012; García-Viñuela 2016).

We must also mention in these introductory comments that, of course, electoral results and seats sharing also depend on many other institutional and non-institutional factors besides those electoral ones mentioned above (Scartascini et al. 2013; Holm-Hadullaa et al. 2012; Schofield and Caballero 2011; Schofield et al. 2013). Similarly, it must be taken into account that in Spain there are many legislative chambers under a complex multilevel political system that in fact works as a federal system. Therefore, the many interdependencies arising from the overall institutional configuration of the country also influence, no doubt, electoral results and the final share of seats, as well as the emerging public policies (Pallarés and Keating 2003; Sanguinetti and Tomassi 2004; Rodden 2002; Toboso 2005, 2006; Knutsen 2011).

For comparing the different degrees of proportionality that result from our estimations we are going to use the formulae indicated in Fig. 1. Discrepancy's value is calculated as the difference between the distribution of the various votes percentages obtained by the parties and the distribution of seats percentages among parties that result from a specific electoral system of rules "s" applied for the allocation of seats. The p_i variable is the percentage of votes obtained by the i-th party in the election. The $e_i(s)$ variable is the percentage of seats obtained by the i-th party as a result of applying the electoral system "s". Finally, k is the number of political parties considered. When discrepancy ratio is zero this means perfect correspondence between the resulting share of seats and the real share of votes.

For accomplishing our research purposes, the paper first explains the main characteristics of the Spanish electoral system from which the above mentioned disproportionality mainly emerges (Sect. 2). Then we explain the above mentioned basic Swedish alternative rules for converting votes into seats that will be used for our quantitative comparative statics exercise (Sect. 3). In Sect. 4 several estimates are provided of how much the share of seats that resulted from the 2011 Spanish general elections would change if we apply the chosen basic Swedish rules, though considering several alternatives. Finally, in the concluding section some comparisons and conclusions are provided.

[1]See the classic contributions by Duverger (1954) and Cox (1997, 1999a, b).

2 The Spanish Electoral System: Basic Constitutional Principles and Legislation Rules for Converting Votes into Seats

The 1978 Spanish Constitution explicitly declares that the "proportionally principle" must play a key role in Spanish political elections.[2] However, the subsequent legislation passed on the already mentioned electoral rules (LOREG—*Organic Law 5/1985 of 19 June on the General Electoral System*) for making such a principle operative did not define a pure proportional system but opted for a(n) hybrid one, mainly due to the fact that the provinces were chosen as districts, that a threshold rule was established and that the d'Hondt rule was adopted for all electoral competition processes at central, regional-state and local levels of government.

Regarding the central legislative chamber in Spain (*Congreso de los Diputados*), articles 68.1, 68.2 y 68.3 of the Constitution establish that (1) "The Congress consists of a minimum of 300 and a maximum of 400 deputies elected by universal, free, equal, direct and secret suffrage, under the terms established by a future Law."; (2) "The electoral constituency is the province. The cities of Ceuta and Melilla are each represented by a deputy. The total number of deputies will be allocated by Law among districts, assigning a minimum initial representation to each district and distributing the remainder in proportion to the population."; and (3) "The election in each constituency will have to take place according to criteria of proportional representation." As we are going to show in the next section, there would be no need to reform the Constitution for applying, in this case, the Swedish electoral rules examined here.

Moreover, it was through the said LOREG that those principles were made operative. It is in articles 162 and 163 of the LOREG where the following specifications are made. First, the number of members of Congress was settled in 350. Second, an initial number of two seats were assigned to each province, except for Ceuta and Melilla where only one was settled. Third, the remaining 248 seats must be allocated proportionally to the legal population in each province[3] using the

[2]Article 68.2 state that seats must be assigned among constituencies in proportion to their population; article 68.3 states that in each district the assignment of seats should have to be based on criteria of proportional representation. More specifically, in article 69.6 the Constitution indicates that for the election of the number of senators that each regional parliament can propose-choose, it must be ensure an adequate proportional representation; in 78.1 the Constitution insists on the idea of proportionality when setting the Standing Committee of the Central Congress; and, in Article 152.1 is discussed, referring to the organs of the regions-states (CC.AA.), that "… the political organization of the region-state will be based on a Legislative Assembly elected by universal suffrage under a system of proportional representation that also ensure representation of the various villages-areas of the territory … ".

[3]Note that the legal population includes all residents of the province (regardless of nationality and age) and excludes non-resident voters, which, however, are part of the electoral body. For each election, the distribution of deputies among the provinces is done using the latest legal population published by the National Statistics Institute prior to the elections call.

so-called Hamilton rule or Vinton rule. There is an electoral threshold or barrier of 3 % of valid votes. And the d'Hondt rule is used to distribute seats in each district among political parties or coalitions that pass the 3 % barrier.

Regarding the Hamilton (or Vinton) method, popularized by Alexander Hamilton (the first US treasury secretary and assistant to George Washington), it must be briefly stated for our purpose here that it serves to distribute the available seats among the districts according to, as much as possible, their population quota. Specifically, as settled in Spanish legislation (BOE 1985), the method comprises the following steps: (i) by dividing the legal population of all provinces between the number of deputies or seats to be distributed we obtain the so-called sharing quota, (ii) then, by dividing the legal population of each province by the population quota we get the number of deputies of each district according to whole numbers, without decimal (iii) then, the remaining seats are distributed by assigning one to each of the provinces whose quota, obtained under the rules of the preceding paragraph, has a bigger decimal fraction. Hamilton's rule, however, presents a major drawback, known as the paradox of Alabama[4], which is inherent to all methods of allocation based on natural quotas (Balinski and Young 2001). Because of the paradox of Alabama this method was abandoned in US in 1911, after being in force since 1852 (Neubauer and Zeitlin 2003). Currently, the method used in US is that of equal proportions or Huntington–Hill, whose details, as well as those of some alternatives such as Jefferson or Webster, can be consulted in Balinski and Young (2001).

Concerning the d'Hondt rule, which was popularized Victor D'Hondt though invented by Thomas Jefferson nearly a century ago, we must briefly remember for our purpose here that this is a method that tends to favor the major parties in each district to the detriment of the smaller ones (Pavía-Miralles 2005; Pavía et al. 2016) and that has a significant tendency to produce majorities (Lijphart 1994, 2003, 2012). This allocation algorithm is slightly different from the one that is used in Sweden as we are going to see next. As known, it requires elaborating a table with a raw for each party or coalitions that overcomes the threshold and the same number of columns than seats are available for distribution. And then to fill up the cells with the result of dividing the number of votes obtained by each party by the serial 1, 2, 3, etc. up to the number of seats available which coincide with the number of columns. Finally, the seats are assigned sequentially to the parties that have the highest division ratio, so that whenever a party receives one seat the division ratio used gets canceled.

[4]The paradox of Alabama refers to the possibility that even when the sizes of provincial population may remain constant, a constituency could lose seats due to an increase in the number of deputies to be shared.

3 The Swedish Electoral Rules and How Could They Be Adapted to the Spanish Case

If we turn now to the basic electoral Swedish rules that attract our interest, it must be stated, first of all, that the Swedish Parliament consists of 349 deputies (*riksdagsledamöter*), who are elected every 4 years. For this election, the country is divided into 29 constituencies. Of the 349 deputies, 310 seats (permanent seats) are ex-ante allocated by Law among the districts in proportion to the number of electors in each constituency. The remaining 39 seats (adjustment seats) are distributed among the constituencies depending on the votes each party obtains upon the rules and procedures we are going to explain next.

As in Spain, the Swedish electoral system includes a threshold or barrier to exclude minority options. To participate in the allocation of permanent seats, political parties must at least obtain 4 % of the total votes in the country. Those who do not reach that percentage still may participate in the distribution of permanent seats in those constituencies where their share of valid votes exceeds 12 % (Valmyndigheten 2006).

Regarding the allocation of seats, the Swedish system proceeds in two stages. First, after elections, for those parties that gain over the 4 % of the national vote, or gain over 12 % in one or more constituencies, the permanent seats of each constituency are allocated by using the so-called modified Sainte-Laguë method. Basically, this method is similar to the above mentioned d'Hondt rule though instead of using the 1, 2, 3, 4 etc. series it uses the following: 1.4, 3, 5, 7 etc. as dividers.

In a second stage, the Swedish rules have the explicit purpose of compensating those political parties that obtain a lower share in permanent seats than the number they might have obtained if only a national district existed and a pure proportional allocation formula had been used. Therefore, the purpose is trying to increase the final proportionality between votes and seats. So, the rules require estimating a difference (A_j) between the *estimated* number of permanent seats under a pure national proportional assignment for each party (N_j) and the real number of permanent seats obtained (P_j).

If all parties get a non-negative A_j difference ($A_j = N_j - P_j$), they all have the right to participate in the said compensation process of adjustment seats allocation (39 seats available). This is done by a sequential allocation process using only the Sainte-Laguë table quotients that were not employed for the allocation of permanent seats, starting with the party whose remaining (constituency) quotient is greater. Once a divide coefficient is used it gets canceled. Likewise, as soon as a party reaches the maximum number of adjustment seats to which is has right to, its quotients are no longer taken into account in the allocation process. This sequential process ends with all parties reaching its maximum number of adjustment seats.

By contrast, if any political party has really obtained more seats than the said estimated national proportional number of seats (that is, if its A_j difference is negative) it does not lose any permanent seat but gets excluded from this second round together with the amount of popular votes it received. This requires to re-estimate again which is the pure national proportional distribution of the remaining seats among the remaining parties and proceeding as in previous paragraph but considering just those parties.[5]

Could these basic rules and procedures be adapted to comply with constitutional requirement and subsequent legislation in Spain? The straightforward answer is yes, because no constitutional reform would be needed if we keep the provinces as districts. For adding 50 more extra adjustment seats to the central parliament and implementing all or some of the said Swedish rules and procedures only some minor changes in the LOREG would be sufficient.

As we are going to see, these basic Swedish rules for converting votes into seats represent an imaginative solution to increase proportionality that takes into account the *estimated* national pure proportional results in order to reduce the differences between the share of votes and the final share of seats political parties obtain, at the same time that the procedure used for the compensation is not an arbitrary one but dependent on the comparative results obtained by political parties in each district, in each province in the case of Spain.

Let's now to explicitly indicate which of these rules are going to be used for our estimations and then check how the sharing of seats gets altered in the 2011 Spanish elections if we apply the said adapted version of these rules and procedures, ceteris paribus. We must emphasize again, that ceteris paribus means "all the remaining aspects not being considered being equal", which is unlikely, as mentioned in the introductory comments of this paper. If electoral rules had been different it is quite likely that many behaviors and strategies would have been different too.

4 Applying the Adapted Swedish Rules to the 2011 Spanish General Elections

As mentioned, in order to check whether the above mentioned basic Swedish rules might help to increase proportionality in Spanish general elections we need to decide which ones are going to be used in our estimations and how can they be adapted in case.

First of all, we need to choose how many extra adjustment seats are going to be added to the Spanish central parliament. As the constitution allows for a maximum of 400 seats, by a simple reform of the LOREG up to 50 more adjustment seats could be added to the current 350 ones, which could therefore be defined as permanent seats. Of course, <50 extra seats could be added. A second change that also requires reforming the LOREG might consist of not imposing any minimum national barrier, instead of the 3 % district threshold that is now in place according to the LOREG.

All the remaining Spanish constitutional principles and LOREG rules and procedures could be maintained because instead of using the modified Sainte-Lagüe

[5]For more details on the Swedish system see, for example, Valmyndigheten (2006).

one that characterizes the Swedish system we might keep the d'Hondt rule that is used in Spain, and this is how we have proceed in our research exercise. And for simplicity, we have not used the Swedish rule by which whenever a party gets a negative A_j difference adjustment seat calculations are remade for each of the remaining parties or coalitions under the new scenario. This entails that the sequential process ends with not all the parties reaching its maximum number of adjustment seats. It should be noted, however, that applying this rule would likely increase proportionality of the Spanish estimations a little bit more though.

For comparative purposes we are going to also estimate how the 350 permanent seats and the 50 adjustment ones would be allocated among political parties in three more scenarios according to 2011 voting raw percentages really obtained. First scenario: under the Spanish exact current system now in place, which includes a 3 % district barrier. Second: under the Spanish current system, but changing the provincial district by only one national district, and including a 3 % national barrier. Third: under the Spanish current system but changing the provincial district by only one national district, and with no barrier. Estimations are provided in the last three columns of the tables.

All those real vote shares and estimated seats allocations are provided in Tables 1 and 2. For interpreting results we must again emphasize that these are just simulations based on the usual ceteris paribus clause. Of course, if electoral rules in 2011 had been different all actors might have adapted their behavior and strategies, particularly political agents but also many voters. So, of course, we are not concluding that if the said electoral changes had been made election results would have been exactly those ones estimated here. An example of this adapted political behavior can be shown by pointing to what often happens in Spain when political parties compete for seats in the European Parliament where only one district exists. Regional political parties, even from different ideological backgrounds, often form coalitions to achieve the required national threshold of votes that enable them to gain representation.

Looking at the figures provided in Tables 1 and 2, several straightforward considerations can be made. First, the adapted Swedish system with a barrier would provide, under the assumptions already mentioned regarding the psychological impacts of electoral rules, a very similar distribution of seats than the current Spanish system if applied to a Congress with 400 deputies. The proportionality of results, as measured by our discrepancy statistic, is comparatively lower than some of the alternatives also estimated as discrepancies are the highest ones, as shown in Table 2 (19.80 and 24.85 respectively).

Second, if we apply the adapted Swedish rules but settle no barrier, the proportionality of results increase if compared with alternative cases. The two main parties reduce their share in votes, some smaller parties get representatives, and two statewide parties (IU and UPyD) significantly increase their shares in the Central Congress, with discrepancy ratios being 8.31. As mentioned, for implementing the Swedish rules for converting the Spanish Congress in a chamber with 350 permanent deputies and 50 adjustment ones no constitutional reform is needed. This requires reforming the LOREG only.

Table 1 2011 Spanish General Elections: allocation of seats under different rules[a]

Party	Actual % of votes[b]	(350) Seats on current system	(400) Seats on current system[c]	(400) Seats on Sweedish system[d]		(400) Seats based on current system but national district[e]	
				No barrier	With barrier	No barrier	With barrier
PP	44.63	186	213	186	201	186	201
PSOE	28.76	110	125	120	129	120	129
IU-LV	6.92	11	13	29	19	29	31
UPyD	4.70	5	5	19	11	19	21
CiU	4.17	16	20	17	18	17	18
AMAIUR	1.37	7	7	7	7	5	0
EAJ-PNV	1.33	5	6	5	5	5	0
COMPROMIS-Q + EQUO	1.40	1	1	4	1	5	0
ESQUERRA	1.06	3	3	4	3	4	0
BNG	0.76	2	2	3	2	3	0
CC-NC-PNC	0.59	2	3	2	2	2	0
PACMA	0.42	0	0	0	0	1	0
FAC	0.41	1	1	1	1	1	0
Eb	0.40	0	0	1	0	1	0
PA	0.32	0	0	0	0	1	0
PxC	0.25	0	0	1	0	1	0

(continued)

Table 1 (continued)

Party	Actual % of votes[b]	(350) Seats on current system	(400) Seats on current system[c]	(400) Seats on Sweedish system[d]		(400) Seats based on current system but national district[e]	
				No barrier	With barrier	No barrier	With barrier
P.R.C.	0.18	0	0	0	0	0	0
GBAI	0.17	1	1	1	1	0	0
Resto	2.16	0	0	0	0	0	0

Source: INE (2011), Ministerio del Interior (2012), and own made

[a] In all cases the d'Hondt rule is used

[b] Percentage of votes obtained by each party as compared with total valid votes

[c] LOREG rules are applied, except regarding the number of seats that are 400

[d] 350 permanent seats and 50 adjustment seats with a 3 % provincial barrier always settled in both cases, plus a 3 % national barrier of total valid votes when indicated

[e] Only one district equivalent to the whole country, plus a 3 % national barrier of total valid votes when indicated

Table 2 2011 Spanish General Elections: sharing percentages under different rules[a]

Party	Actual % of votes[b]	(350) Seats on current system	(400) Seats on current system[c]	(400) Seats on Sweedish system[d]		(400) Seats based on current system but national district[e]	
				No barrier	With barrier	No barrier	With barrier
PP	44.63	53.14	53.25	46.50	50.25	46.50	50.25
PSOE	28.76	31.43	31.25	30.00	32.25	30.00	32.25
IU-LV	6.92	3.14	3.25	7.25	4.75	7.25	7.75
UPyD	4.7	1.43	1.25	4.75	2.75	4.75	5.25
CiU	4.17	4.57	5.00	4.25	4.50	4.25	4.50
AMAIUR	1.37	2.00	1.75	1.75	1.75	1.25	0.00
EAJ-PNV	1.33	1.43	1.50	1.25	1.25	1.25	0.00
COMPR + EQUO	1.4	0.29	0.25	1.00	0.25	1.25	0.00
ESQUERRA	1.06	0.86	0.75	1.00	0.75	1.00	0.00
BNG	0.76	0.57	0.50	0.75	0.50	0.75	0.00
CC-NC-PNC	0.59	0.57	0.75	0.50	0.50	0.50	0.00
PACMA	0.42	0.00	0.00	0.00	0.00	0.25	0.00
FAC	0.41	0.29	0.25	0.25	0.25	0.25	0.00
Eb	0.4	0.00	0.00	0.00	0.00	0.00	0.00
PA	0.32	0.00	0.00	0.00	0.00	0.25	0.00
PxC	0.25	0.00	0.00	0.25	0.00	0.25	0.00
P.R.C.	0.18	0.00	0.00	0.00	0.00	0.00	0.00

(continued)

Table 2 (continued)

Party	Actual % of votes[b]	(350) Seats on current system	(400) Seats on current system[c]	(400) Seats on Sweedish system[d]		(400) Seats based on current system but national district[e]	
				No barrier	With barrier	No barrier	With barrier
GBAI	0.17	0.29	0.25	0.25	0.25	0.00	0.00
Resto	2.16	0.00	0.00	0.00	0.00	0.00	0.00
Discrepancy	–	24.85	25.46	8.31	19.80	7.39	21.64

Source: INE (2011), Ministerio del Interior (2012), and own made

[a] In all cases the d'Hondt rule is used

[b] Percentage of votes obtained by each party as compared with total valid votes

[c] LOREG rules are applied, except regarding the number of seats that are 400

[d] 350 permanent seats and 50 adjustment seats with a 3 % provincial barrier always settled in both cases, plus a 3 % national barrier of total valid votes when indicated

[e] Only one district equivalent to the whole country, plus a 3 % national barrier of total valid votes when indicated

Third, results also show that if provinces were replaced by a sole district and no barrier was settled, the share of seats would also present greater proportionality too (7.39). However, this option is more complicated to get it implemented in Spain as it requires a Constitutional reform for replacing the provinces as districts and no consensus among current political parties is expected.

If we consider how the extra 50 adjustment seats are allocated among provinces, our estimates indicate that the adapted Swedish rules tend to assign more seats to the most populated provinces that are in fact underrepresented in the current Spanish system due to the allocation of a minimum of two seats to each province.

If no barrier is applied the provincial allocation of the said 50 seats that results is: Madrid (18), Barcelona (11), Sevilla (3), Alicante, Malaga, Coruña and Murcia (2), Cadiz, Cordoba, Granada and Asturias (1). If the 3 % barrier is settled, only one more province enters the list (Pontevedra, 1), but several others as A Coruña, Granada, Malaga, Murcia and Asturias loose one seat, and Granada drops, if compared with the no barrier results. Madrid wins two more seats (18 + 2) and Sevilla wins one more too (3 + 1). Barcelona also loses one seat if compared with the no barrier case (11–1).

Finally, regarding the ideological distribution of seats in the Parliament significant changes toward a more leftist legislature have resulted in our estimations. This is mainly due to the share increase obtained by the leftist IU party, though the more centered UPyD also increases its share substantially. And also because the right-wing PP is the party whose share decreases more if we compare estimations of a 400-seats parliament with the current Spanish rules and those of a 400-seats parliament with the said adapted Swedish rules and no barrier. The PP share of seats goes from 53.25 to 46.50 in our 2011 estimations (from 213 to 186 seats). By contrast, IU goes from 3.25 to 7.25 (13 to 29 seats).

Of course, the estimations obtained would slightly change if we fixed the barrier at a different percentage level, or the number of permanent and adjustment deputies were different, or the total number of deputies was lower than 400, for example. And, as previously mentioned, if competition strategies by political parties under the new rules also changed and this impacted upon the share of votes, the estimations here provided might also change. Some small parties might in this case be left aside or be included into the elected chamber, affecting proportionality.

Therefore, once again, our estimations should not be interpreted as predictions but as potential influences that might come up if the considered electoral rules were reformed in one direction or another. Of course, the behavior of political agents is also important, as well as the several other factors we mentioned in the introductory section of the chapter. What our study serves to emphasize is that rules and institutions matter, so they deserve attention by the researchers. Though this is obvious among political scientists, it is no so evident among economic researchers if we exclude those with an institutional/political economy approach.

5 Concluding Remarks

As mentioned, in all electoral processes the sharing of seats among political parties tends to be influenced, in part, by the electoral system in place. This means that electoral rules and procedures matter, though the behavior of voters and political parties also matter and their strategies are not totally independent of the electoral rules in place. The number and size of constituencies, the size of Parliament, the formulas used for allocating seats between parties and between constituencies, the settled barrier to entry, the ballot structure or the vote system are examples of these factors that greatly influence who controls legislative chambers and executives as well as policy making in democratic countries.

In the case of Spain, the high number of provincial districts that characterize the Spanish electoral system, the minimum allocation of two deputies per province and the d'Hondt rules used for allocating seats in each district have traditionally favored those main political parties that present candidates in all districts. They have also favored some regionalist and nationalist small parties that only present candidates in a few provinces in which they are electorally predominant. On the other hand, this slightly majoritarian bias has traditionally affected negatively small statewide parties such as IU or UPyD, as mentioned in the paper. Even if the constitution proclaims that proportionality should be a key principle in all political processes, a slightly majoritarian bias is nevertheless introduced in the Spanish electoral system through the above mentioned key rules and procedures.

Given this non-proportionality bias and the traditional complaints that recurrently emerge, in the present paper we have performed a comparative statics exercise for estimating the so-called mechanical impacts of institutional reforms. In our case for estimating how the share of seats that resulted from the 2011 general elections in Spain change if we apply some key rules for converting votes into seats from the Swedish electoral system, ceteris paribus.

No constitutional reform would be needed to add the Central Parliament 50 more seats, considered as adjustment seats as indicated, to the current 350 ones, which could be considered permanent seats, and allocate all of them following the adapted Swedish rules as indicated in the chapter. For so doing, just some minor reforms in the LOREG would be needed. Therefore, the differentiation between permanent seats and adjustment seats has been the key aspects considered in our estimates, besides taking into account the possibility of establishing or not a threshold or minimum barrier. Instead of using the so-called modified Sainte-Laguë rule employed in Sweden, we have maintained for estimation the very similar d'Hondt rule required in the Spanish legislation (LOREG). We have also adapted the sequential procedure established in the Swedish system for allocating the adjustment seats. In the Spanish case we have just allocated all extra adjustment seats to all parties as indicated in the chapter.

As shown in previous tables, the scenario that provides greater degree of proportionality, as measured by our discrepancy statistic, is one in which the adapted Swedish rules are applied with no minimum national barrier. In this case, the two main parties reduce their share in seats, some more small parties get represented in the Central Congress, and two statewide parties (IU and UPyD) significantly increase their shares if compared with alternative estimated scenarios. Regarding the comparative ideological distribution of seats, significant changes toward a more leftist legislature have resulted in our estimations. This is mainly due to the share increase obtained by the leftist IU party and to the fact that the right-wing PP is the party whose share decreases more if we compare estimations of a 400-seats parliament with the Spanish current rules and those of a 400-seats parliament with the said adapted Swedish rules and no threshold.

It must also be stressed that adopting these rules in an attempt to increase proportionality in Spain may, nevertheless, diminish the likelihood that a single party gets a majority in the Central parliament or a stable coalition gets formed, then increasing the need of negotiations and the possibility that more governmental crises appear, with more frequent elections, etc., particularly if no barrier is settled.

Of course, all estimations here provided would have been slightly different if the barriers considered or the number of permanent and adjustment deputies or the total number of deputies that were tested had been different. Therefore, our estimates must not be interpreted as predictions but as potential influences that might come up if the considered electoral rules were reformed in one direction or another, all remaining things being equal. And again, our comparative statics analysis has focused on the mechanical effects of institutional reforms under the usual ceteris paribus clause. We cannot end these final comments without emphasizing again that electoral reforms usually affect the behavior and strategies of political actors as well as voters. The making, or not, of some pre-electoral coalitions is a straightforward way in which political parties often adapt themselves to the changing rules, as is the case of Spain regarding EU elections in which the provinces are not the districts.

What our study reveals is, once more, that rules and institutions matter not only in the economy and its many markets but also in the polity with its many political processes, legislative chambers and executives. If rules matter they deserve attention by the researchers, as papers and book by political scholars show. So, we wonder why so many economic scholars doing research on economic policy issues, macroeconomic policies, or public sector economic issues often disregard the fact that institutional-organizational aspects matter. Institutionalists as well as political economy scholars are exceptions, as mentioned.

Finally, we cannot end this paper without emphasizing that the electoral laws, and the rules and procedures they contain, are examples of particularly rigid legislation as these legislations often tend to favor the major parties whose approval is necessary to reform them. Our analysis and estimations should be considered only as a contribution for a deeper examination and informed discussion about the strengths and weaknesses of the current system.

Acknowledgements We wish to thank Tor Lundberg and Henrik Hannebo (Swedish Election Authority, Valmyndigheten) for their help in answering all our questions about the Swedish electoral system. Any responsibility resides, however, on the authors. This work benefited from the support received by the Spanish Ministry of Economics and Competitiveness under grant CSO2013-43054-R.

References

Balinski, M. L., & Young, H. P. (2001). *Fair representation: Meeting the ideal of one man, one vote*. Washington, DC: Brookings Institute.

BOE. (1985, June 20). Ley Orgánica 5/1985, de 19 de junio, del Régimen Electoral General. *Boletín Oficial del Estado, 147*, 19110–19134.

Capo Giol, J. (1999). Sistema electoral y gobernabilidad española. *Revista Española de Ciencia Política, 1*, 55–80.

Casarramona, T. (2009). El sesgo de participación en el sistema electoral español. *Revista Española de Investigaciones Sociológicas, 126*, 107–125.

Colomer, J. M. (2003). Son los partidos los que eligen los sistemas electorales (O las leyes de Duverger cabeza abajo). *Revista Española de Ciencia Política, 9*, 39–63.

Cox, G. W. (1997). *Making votes count: Strategic coordination in the world's electoral systems*. Cambridge: Cambridge University Press.

Cox, G. W. (1999a). Electoral rules and the calculus of mobilization. *Legislative Studies Quarterly, 24*, 387–419.

Cox, G. W. (1999b). Electoral rules and electoral coordination. *Annual Review of Political Science, 2*(1), 145–161.

Cox, G. W. (2008). Electoral institutions and political competition: Coordination, persuasion and mobilization. In Chapter 4 in Menard and Shirley, *Handbook of new institutional economics* (pp. 69–89). Berlin, Heidelberg: Springer.

Cox, G. W. (2015). Electoral rules, mobilization, and turnout. *Annual Review of Political Science, 18*, 49–68.

Duverger, M. (1954). *Political parties*. London: Methuen.

EFE. (2008, de Marzo de 14). IU presenta una denuncia contra la Ley Electoral por considerarla anticonstitucional. *El País*.

Gallego, A., Guillem Rico, E. A. (2012, March). Disproportionality and voter turnout in new and old democracies. *Electoral Studies, 31*(1), 159–169.

García-Viñuela, E. (2016). Allocating campaign effort in Spain: Evidence from four general elections. *South European Society & Politics, 21*(2), 243–262.

Holm-Hadullaa, F., Hauptmeiera, S., & Rothera, P. (2012). The impact of expenditure rules on budgetary discipline over the cycle. *Applied Economics, 44*(25), 3287–3296.

INE. (2009). *Population broken down by provinces 2008*. Spanish Municipal Register. Instituto Nacional de Estadística. Last checked January 9, 2016, from http://goo.gl/oIZll1

INE. (2011) *Population broken down by provinces 2010*. Spanish Municipal Register. Instituto Nacional de Estadística. Last checked January 9, 2016, from http://goo.gl/oIZll1

Knutsen, C. H. (2011). Which democracies prosper? Electoral rules, form of government and economic growth. *Electoral Studies, 30*(1), 83–90.

Lijphart, A. (1994). *Electoral systems and party systems. A study of twenty-seven democracies 1945–1990*. New York, NY: Oxford University Press.

Lijphart, A. (2003). Degrees of proportionality of proportional representation formulas. In B. Grofman & A. Lijphart (Eds.), *Electoral laws and their political consequences* (Agathon series on representation, Vol. 1, pp. 170–179). New York, NY: Algora Publishing.

Lijphart. (2012). *Patterns of democracy. Government forms and performance in thirty-six countries* (2nd ed.). New Haven: Yale Univ Press (Ariel 2000).

Martínez-Pujalte, A. L. (2008, Junio). El sistema electoral español: Contribución a un debate. *FUNCIVAnews, Reflexión y Debate*, 1–23.

Ministerio del Interior. (2012). *Resultados Elecciones Generales 2011*. http://www.infoelectoral.interior.es/min/

Neubauer, M. G., & Zeitlin, J. (2003). Outcomes of presidential elections and the house size. *Political Science and Politics, 36*, 721–725.

Ocaña, F. A., & Oñate, P. (1999). ´indice e indicadores del sistema electoral y del sistema de partidos. Una propuesta informática para su cálculo. *Revista Española de Investigaciones Sociológicas, 86*, 223–245.

Ortega, C. (2004). *Los sistemas de voto preferencial Un estudio de 16 democracias: Reflexiones sobre el sistema electoral español. Colección Monografías*. Madrid: Centro de Investigaciones Sociológicas.

Pallarés, F., & Keating, M. (2003). Multi-level electoral competition regional elections and party systems in Spain. *European Urban and Regional Studies, 10*(3), 239–255.

Pavía, J. M., García-Cárceles, B., & Badal, E. (2016). Estimating representatives from election poll proportions: The Spanish case. *Statistica Applicata—Italian Journal of Applied Statistics* (Election Forecasting Techniques Special Issue), *25*(3), 325–340.

Pavía, J. M., & Toboso, F. (2015). Federalism, proportionality, and popular will in US Presidential Elections: Did Colorado have the right idea? In N. Schofield & G. Caballero (Eds.), *The political economy of governance. Institutions, political performance and elections* (pp. 377–393). Cham: Springer.

Pavía-Miralles, J. M. (2005). Forecasts from non-random samples: The election night case. *Journal of the American Statistical Association, 100*, 1113–1122.

Pavía-Miralles, J. M. (2011). Tamaño del Congreso y Resultados Electorales. *Cuadernos 'Manuel Giménez Abab', 2*, 84–96.

Powell, G. B. (2000). *Elections as instruments of democracy: Majoritarian and proportional visions*. New Haven, CT and London: Yale University Press.

Rodden, J. A. (2002). The dilemmas of fiscal federalism: Grants and fiscal performance around the world. *American Journal of Political Science, 46*(3), 670–687.

Sanguinetti, J., & Tomassi, M. (2004). Intergovernmental transfers and fiscal behavior. Insurance versus aggregate discipline. *Journal of International Economics, 62*(1), 149–170.

Sartori, G. (2005). *Parties and party systems. A framework for analysis*. Essex: ECPRclassics.

Scartascini, C., Stein, E., & Tommasi, M. (2013). Political institutions, intertemporal cooperation, and the quality of public policies. *Journal of Applied Economics, 16*(1), 1–32.

Schmid, A. A. (1987). *Property, power, and public choice*. New York, NY: Praeger.

Schmid, A. A. (2004). *Conflict and cooperation. Institutional and behavioral economics*. Oxford: Blackwell.

Schofield, N., & Caballero, G. (Eds.). (2011). *Political economy of institutions, democracy and voting*. New York, NY: Springer.

Schofield, N., McAlister, K., & Jeong, J. (2013). Modeling elections with varying party bundles: Applications to the 2004 Canadian Election. In Schofield et al. (Eds.), *Advances in political economy* (pp. 289–316). Berlin: Springer.

Toboso, F. (2005). Institutional change and economic growth in Spain since democratic transition in 1978: Regulating regional governments as a key factor. In M. Oppenheimer & N. Mercuro (Eds.), *Law and economics: Alternative economic approaches to legal and regulatory issues* (pp. 293–427). New York, NY: M.E. Sharpe.

Toboso, F. (2006, December). Key organizational choices for financing regional governments in democratic Spain. *Revista de Análisis Económico*, *2*, 61–82.

Toboso, F. (2013). The distributional impacts of institutional reforms. *Investigacion Economica, LXXII*(286), 3–34.

Urdánoz G. J. (2008). El maquiavélico sistema electoral español. El País, 35.

Valmyndigheten. (2006). *Elections in Sweden. The way it's done!* http://www.val.se/

Part III
State and Public Services

Is There a Doctor in the House?

Jani-Petri Laamanen, Mikko Poutanen, and Katri Sieberg

1 Introduction

What is the most efficient type of healthcare system? This questions resonates globally, as governments seek to ensure that their citizens are provided with adequate care while simultaneously attempting to control costs. A vast literature addresses the various advantages and disadvantages of private versus public systems in meeting these two goals. Summers (1989) suggests that an optimal system would combine a public system—to ensure universal coverage—with some a private alterative, so that those who were willing and able to pay for extra services would be able to use their resources to provide a better fit to their wants and needs. Appealing to the benefits of a simple economic model, and using the case of Finland as an example, our paper examines this option.

The effects of a hybrid public–private health care system on patient choice are discussed in a paper by Poutanen et al. (2016). The authors found that the choice between the public and the private sector depends strongly on the level of care the public sector is capable of offering in comparison to the private sector. In usual circumstances this could stimulate healthy competition, but in a hybrid model where the private sector is subsidized by public funding, the competitive element has a tendency to undermine the capacity of the public sector by strengthening the private sector. The paper's model reveals a potential for resources in the public system to decrease over time, such that, at best, a two-class system develops, in which the wealthier patients select the private system, leaving the poorer patients in the public sector.

J.-P. Laamanen • M. Poutanen • K. Sieberg (✉)
Kanslerinrinne 1, 33014 University of Tampere, Tampere, Finland
e-mail: katri.sieberg@uta.fi

N. Schofield, G. Caballero (eds.), *State, Institutions and Democracy*,
Studies in Political Economy, DOI 10.1007/978-3-319-44582-3_10

This argument suggests that the demand of services by the consumers in the hybrid system will show a decrease in support and resources for the public system. This model was applied to the national context of Finland, a nation representing the general bloc of Nordic welfare systems (Esping-Andersen 1990). Drawing on the perception of freedom of choice, the demand of consumers in fact drives more market space for private health care providers at the expense of the public providers. The conclusion stated that—in line with existing research (Valtonen et al. 2014; Jäntti 2008)—public subsidies for private care increase the probability of choosing a private health provider. Thus, these consumer preferences create a *pulling* effect for private services through satisfaction, and a *pushing* effect from public services through dissatisfaction.

The authors further hypothesized that, given that public basic-level health care services are the highest utilized service, this is the area in which the most customer dissatisfaction is also statistically located (Fredriksson and Martikainen 2008). Their findings indicated that problems of the public sector such as long waiting lines (the highest reason for dissatisfaction: ibid. 58–59) are at least in part caused by a decrease in resources for the public sector, combined with an increasing share of care—and thus resource—intensive patients.

Expanding upon the above results, we note that a care service that is tight on resources is predictably not only a negative customer experience, but also a negative employment position. Thus the degree of consumer dissatisfaction can correlate with the level of employee (i.e., health care professional) dissatisfaction with working in the public sector (Kankaanranta et al. 2007 show data indicating that job satisfaction tended to decrease physicians' desires to switch from the public to private sector in Finland and also, surprisingly, that job dissatisfaction did not tend to increase the desire to switch.). At the least, a private sector with more resources should be able to offer better wages and working conditions in order to tempt doctors to move from the public to the private sector. We employ a model in this paper to see what potential impact the presence of a hybrid system has on the supply of skilled professionals to the various sectors.

Poutanen et al.'s (2016) research on demand already suggests that consumer preference in the current hybrid system entails trends that can create a two-tiered system between the legally mandated public sector care (for poorer and sicker consumers) and a private sector alternative for those with the means to finance their consumption. We expand upon this previous model of consumer preferences to include the impact of wage or working condition differentials on the abilities of the various sectors to affect the choices of employees of that system—doctors—regarding employment in the public system or to opt for private health care providers as alternate employers.

Observing only the demand model would give us an imperfect understanding of the overall pressures facing the institution of public health care provision. For example, even if customer satisfaction improves, it is not guaranteed to improve job satisfaction or increased desirability of the public sector as an employer for the doctors. Thus a separate model is necessary to outline the effect of resource differentials on the employees of the health care sector to see whether their employment choices could alleviate or exacerbate the pressures of the demand model. In the model presented in this paper we find that employee choices in fact exacerbate the pressures, leading to a similar push-and-pull model as described for consumers; the financial preferences create a *pulling* effect for private services and a *pushing* effect from public services through satisfaction with resources and/or working conditions, and/or dissatisfaction thereof respectively.

The Finnish Medical Association (FMA) in Finland, whose members are restricted to doctors, operates as the labor union for doctors. Given the Association's relative strength, its positions regarding the supply of doctors to the labor pool also partially thus determine the incentives available to the doctors.[1] We examine the distribution of doctors to the private and public sector, and also other elements affecting their position in the labor pool. We note, for example, that the high degree of specialization among Finnish doctors is also financially incentivized in the private sector, as it allows for the doctors—or rather the private care providers that employ them—to charge more in terms of public subsidies. A similar incentive does not exist in the public sector.

Within this paper we also offer some comments regarding how private health care providers have operated in Finland in the context of their finances. This is an important consideration in understanding the financial environment in which public and private systems compete; if private companies are capable of minimizing their tax burden, for example, they can offer services in the market at a lower cost. The public sector has arguably less room to maneuver, and thus can compete poorly. While one could argue that the public sector should not compete in terms of customers (regardless, customers/patients do make preferential choices between the two: Poutanen et al. 2016), it has to compete in terms of health care professionals (namely doctors). As a consequence, we argue that the private sector in the Finnish hybrid system is actually moving beyond its planned role as supplementing public care (the ideal of the hybrid system is expressed both in official ministry documents and research, see STM 2013 and Mattila 2011, respectively) into a superseding one.

2 Hybrid Systems

Hybrid systems are a subject of interest in the healthcare literature. Theoretically, as suggested by Summers (1989), these systems have the potential to provide everything that public or private systems individually cannot. Public systems are frequently credited with ensuring universal coverage but may be subject to waste, inefficiencies or politics (Hsiao 1995; Reinhardt 2007). Public systems also have drawbacks in terms of restricting ability for the wealthier members of society to use their resources to purchase better services (Besley et al. 1999; Epple and Romano 1996). In contrast, many (Sieberg and Shvetsova 2012; Besley et al.

[1] All relevant information provided in Finnish has been translated into English by the authors.

1999; Besley and Gouveia 1994; Hsiao 1995) argue that private health insurance, without regulation, will not provide universal coverage and frequently leads to higher overall costs. The hybrid public–private system, however, is not without its potential downsides. Propper (2000) demonstrates that the presence of a private sector alongside a public sector can create problems including a decline in the availability of doctors in the public sector, which can lead to the emergence of quality differences. She notes, additionally, that those who make use of the private sector may have less support for—and willingness to pay taxes to fund—the public sector.

This concern is echoed in the research of Epple and Romano (1996). These authors examine the voting decisions of a population that has a public system supplemented by a private alternative. They note the potential for differential equilibria to arise. In one case, majority rule voting means that the median voter is pivotal, and the public system continues to receive support. In another—their famous "ends against the middle"—the middle class is opposed by the wealthy, who prefer to use the private system and do not wish to spend tax money to support the public one, and by the poor, who vote for lower support for the system in an attempt to lower their own taxes.

As noted above, Poutanen et al. (2016) examine the hybrid system from the perspective of need and use of medical services. They find that the presence of a subsidized private system, alongside the public system, can lead to a decrease in resources and eventually support for the public sector. This paper extends their model to examine the effect of a hybrid system on doctor supply in the various sectors.

3 Demand Model and Results

The model in Poutanen et al. (2016) uses tools of evolutionary game theory to expand on a model from Besley et al. (1999) that addressed the choice between public and private healthcare.

The model depicts a society of N individuals, in which individuals face a probability $\theta \in [0, 1]$ of needing care, requiring one unit of medical care. The care has varying levels of quality, $q \in \left[\underline{q},\ \overline{q}\right]$.

The quality of care in the public sector is Q, and is financed by general taxation. In the private sector, an individual can purchase insurance for any level, q, that he wants. The authors assume moral hazard: the consumer who pays a premium π for health insurance will purchase the highest possible level $q = \overline{q}$, and the insurance company will provide it.

The health insurance premium is: $\pi = \beta\theta p\overline{q}$, a combination of a price, p, and a factor β, and probability of needing medical care, θ, (subsidized purchase when $\beta < 1$, or additional costs if $\beta > 1$). The utility for a sick and insured individual is

$u(\overline{q},\ y-\beta\theta p\overline{q})$, and the utility for a healthy and insured individual is $u(y-\beta\theta p\overline{q})$. Utility increases in y and q.

The utility from purchasing insurance is $V^I(\theta, p, \overline{q}, y, \beta) = \theta u(\overline{q}, y-\beta\theta p\overline{q}) + (1-\theta)U(y-\beta\theta p\overline{q})$.[2]

And the utility from being covered by public insurance alone is:

$$V^p(\theta, Q, y) = \theta u(Q, y) + (1-\theta)U(y)$$

Besley et al. (1999) find that, given these factors, if there exists a value of income $\widehat{y} \in \left\lfloor \underline{y}, \overline{y} \right\rfloor$ at which an individual is indifferent between purchasing private insurance and using the public sector, then all individuals above that income will purchase.

Poutanen et al. (2016) show that if healthcare subsidies are drawn from the total healthcare budget, *T*, such that the remainder goes to the public sector, and if the quality of care[3] depends on total resources for the public sector over the number of patients in the public sector, then 3½ cases can occur:

Case 1: If $\frac{T-\sum_{i=1}^{m_t}\beta_i}{N-m_t} > \frac{T}{N}$ then the number of people *m* at time *t* exiting the public sector for the private sector improve efficiency by freeing resources for the public sector. This situation is fragile. If one too many persons leaves the public sector, taking subsidies with him/her, then the situation changes to that in Case 2.

Case 2: If $\frac{T-\sum_{i=1}^{m_t}\beta_i}{N-m_t} = \frac{T}{N}$, then the situation will be static. This equilibrium is also fragile. If one too many persons leaves the public sector, taking subsidies with him/her, then the situation changes to that in Case 3.

Case 3: If $\frac{T-\sum_{i=1}^{m}\beta_i}{N-m} < \frac{T}{N}$ then the level of quality Q_1 will be lower than Q_0.

Case 3.½: If, again, $\frac{T-\sum_{i=1}^{m_t}\beta_i}{N-m_t} < \frac{T}{N}$ then the level of quality Q_1 will be lower than Q_0. If, additionally, $\overline{q}\left(\frac{e+m_t p}{m_t}\right)$ where maintaining the level of quality $\overline{q}$ in the private sector depends on any initial endowment, e and on the premiums paid by the m_t customers, over the number of customers at time t, then the number of customers in the private sector will increase until the next customer, in time t + 1, would decrease the quality. In this situation, the two sectors will be static, with a low level of quality Q_{t+1} in the public sector.

The authors argue that, given that cases 1 and 2 represent very fragile equilibria, the latter scenarios are more likely, and the policy of subsidizing the purchase of private health insurance will lead, at best, to two sectors—one well-funded, and the other a low quality service for the poor.

---

[2]Note that in these utility functions, an individual is assumed to consume healthcare only when un-healthy. Thus, the consumption of any healthcare q or Q is left out of the utility function when healthy.

[3]Here, following Besley et al. and others in the healthcare literature, quality of care is vaguely defined and is most visible in terms of waiting times.

Poutanen et al. expand their model to include health outcomes as a variable, such that health in increasing in quality of care, and income is increasing in health. They show that as the price for private healthcare increases, sick individuals will have to choose public healthcare, despite the lower quality. Taken together, the models imply that the public sector risks becoming relegated to the sick and the poor (Poutanen et al. 2016).

3.1 Exclusion and Costs

As noted, Poutanen et al. (2016) demonstrated that if income depends on health, then a situation can emerge in which the sickest and poorest individuals choose the public sector, whereas the more healthy ones choose private care. This result relied purely on individual choice and ignores the well-known problem of adverse selection in insurance. If private insurance companies are allowed to exclude the sicker (more costly) individuals, through refusing coverage to cases in which the health status is known to be poor and/or by imposing lifetime limits on coverage to avoid attracting mainly riskier patients, this bifurcation emerges more starkly.

Here, assume that of the total population of N people, z of them have sufficiently low current and expected healthcare needs that the private sector is willing to provide care for them. The remaining N-z will be refused service by the private sector and must seek care in the public sector. Given the costs related to the purchase of private care services, only k_t of these z people will opt to purchase care at time t.[4,5]

What happens to patients in the public sector depends strongly on resources and politics. If the public sector faces a tight budget constraint, then it is likely that the costs of the most expensive patients will exceed resources and, as a result, some patients will be left untreated or undertreated. If, instead, the sector has a soft budget constraint, then the surplus costs must be financed through taxes. These taxes will be borne, in part, by people who are not using this service, and who are paying for (subsidized) private care. Thus, they are likely to face political resistance, at best.

3.2 Costs and Employment

The previous section noted that, via exclusion of the sickest patients, the private sector can ensure that it covers only the lowest cost patients. These savings can then either go into profit or can be used to affect quality differentials between the

[4]Note that the number k is used instead of m from the Poutanen, Sieberg and Kettunen paper, because, given the private sector's option to exclude costly patients, k can be smaller than m.

[5]The number z is kept the same for simplicity.

two sectors, to further lure healthy customers into purchasing private insurance. For simplicity, we assume here that the private firm will put all savings into the company, and that each sector works with a balanced budget in each period. This assumption holds if the private market is competitive.

Recall that the budget of the public sector was $T - \sum_{i=1}^{k_t} \beta_i$. To work within a balanced budget, the public sector must ensure that the sum of the labor costs and the (other) treatment costs is not larger than this amount.[6] Thus, this budget must be divided between labor costs for all doctors in the public sector, $w_p L_p$ and treatment costs for the $N - k_t$ public sector patients at time t. Here, we assume that the cost of treatment is a function of the number of patients covered at time t,[7] $c_p\,(N - k_t)$. It follows from private sector's incentive to expand by treating more patients in the low-cost end of the cost distribution that the marginal treatment cost is decreasing in the public sector. The total costs of the public sector can be expressed as $TC_p = c_p + w_p L_p$.

The budget for the private sector is $e + k_t p$ and, again to work with a balanced budget, this budget must be divided between labor costs for all doctors in the private sector, $w_I L_I$ and treatment costs for the k_t public sector patients at time t. Treatment costs for the private sector are also a function of the number of patients, (where the number of treatments depends on the population covered by the private sector) $c_I\,(k_t)$. The marginal treatment cost is increasing simply because it is most profitable to include the lowest-cost patients. The total costs of the private sector are, thus, $TC_I = c_I + w_I L_I$. In line with its exclusionary policies, the private sector will accept only patients from the z low-cost members of the population. Of these, given relative levels of quality between the sectors and given the price of private care, k_t of these z people will opt to purchase care at time t.

It is already given that average treatment cost is smaller in the private than in the public sector, that is $\frac{c_I(k_t)}{k_t} < \frac{c_p(N-k_t)}{N-k_t}$ Therefore, even if, at time t, $\frac{T-\sum_{i=1}^{k_t} \beta_i}{N-k_t} = \frac{e+k_t p}{k_t}$, the private sector would have more resources left over to hire doctors. This potential can affect employment, which can affect the supply of doctors to each sector. If we assume that any given doctor can see a maximum of b patients per day, with b decreasing in the need per patient $b(n)$, then differences in supply will have a strong effect on the quality levels in each sector.[8]

---

[6]Here, treatment costs involve the cost of treating patients and include input and other capital costs.

[7]The treatment cost function depends on the number of patients, where we assume that a patient with greater medical needs will have more treatments than a healthier patient.

[8]Given that, rather than profit maximization, our focus is on a balanced budget, and a situation in which sectors compete using relative levels of doctors, we do not include labor costs in a total cost function, but rather leave them as distinct.

3.3 Supply and Full Employment

It is illustrative to approach the problem of supply first through the effects on employment. A basic economic premise is if there is a pool of employees—here doctors—and two different places of employment, then if the salaries and other factors (benefits, working conditions, working hours, etc.) are equal, then we have no reason to expect any differences between the employees in each place.

For reasons discussed below, doctor's unemployment has been close to zero in Finland.[9] We use this fact to motivate the following analysis. Let the total number of, at this stage identifically qualified, employees in the labor market be fixed at D. In a situation of full employment and L_p employees demanded at the public sector. Then, all other things being held equal, we should, at the beginning, see L_p and L_I employees at each place. Assume that the number of workers LI is less than private sector would like to employ at the going wage. As differential budgets allow salaries and other factors of employment to change, the relative attractiveness of employment in the various sectors should change as well.

Ceteris paribus, if $w_I = w_P$ then sectors I and p may hire L_I and L_p employees, respectively. If $w_I > w_P$ then it will be more attractive for workers to work in sector I than in sector p. In a system of unlimited employees, this may not matter, but if, at least in the short run, the number, D of employees is limited, then sector I will take as many employees as it demands, leaving sector p with a potential shortage and a diminished capacity to rectify that shortage in a tight labour market. Thus, the public sector will have fewer employees, potentially leading to an insufficient number of employees to meet the needs of their patients. The same situation arises if salaries are held constant but benefits, hours, or other factors can vary.[10] Thus, by offering superior wages or working conditions, the private sector can cause the quality in the public sector to decrease, and can attract a greater number of healthy patients to purchase private coverage.[11]

[9]We do not claim that the level of unemployment for physicians in Finland is non-existent, but THL reports that it has been relatively small for a long time—approximately 0.7 % of the total labor pool. The persisting economic crisis has, however, the potential to affect that situation, mostly through layoffs in the public sector.

[10]Note here how the geographical variable of undesirability in terms of employment can play a role. When this problem confronts the public sector, which is less flexible in terms of wages. Mikkola (2009) notes a discernible preference on the part of the doctors to exact more control over their working conditions, when the labor market allows for it.

[11]Changes in quality are likely to have an effect on the labor costs and on the treatment cost functions in a variety of ways. At a minimum, a decrease in quality, indicated by a decrease in labor, will decrease labor costs, which could leave some additional resources to cover treatment costs. If, however, we maintain the assumption that doctors can see a maximum of b(n) patients per day, then the extra treatment resources may not be able to be used. Additionally, as discussed below, a decrease in quality will incentivize some of the z low-cost people that have stayed in the public sector to switch to the private sector, taking their subsidies with them. This change in patient base can have differential effects.

Competition strategies in this scenario will depend on the relative level of total employees D to the labor demands of each sector. Note, this particular market is not the competitive labor market described in Shapiro and Stiglitz (1984) in which any wage increase on the part of one firm will be matched by its competitors. In the private/public market, the public market, due to budget constraints, must respond more slowly. If the private sector wishes to employ the entire labor force D then with a fixed short term budget, the public sector will have to raise its wages to match that of the private sector, to avoid losing all employees, but will not be able to hire as many as the private sector. Given now tighter budget constraints, the public sector will not be able to treat as many patients. Thus, Q, in the model, will decrease, creating incentives for customers to exit the public sector.

To examine the dynamics of the system, assume that in time 0, the public sector has a starting budget $T - \sum_{i=1}^{k_0} \beta_i$. Recall that because of the ability to exclude the sickest (most costly) patients, the private sector has fewer costs for provision per patient.

The public sector has $\left(T - \sum_{i=1}^{k_0} \beta_i\right) - c_p\,(N - k_0)$ in funds to hire doctors. Given full employment, the public sector will have funds of $w_P\,(D - L_I)$ to hire.

$(e + k_O p) > c_I(k_O) + w_I L_I$ such that at time 0, private sector would like to hire more employees to increase profits. These differences are affected by the differences in costs in treating patients. The evolution of the system will be affected by the wage and hiring choices of the private firm.

Decision 1: The firm keeps labor in the private firm equal to what it was in time 0 (L_I), and offers a higher wage, $w_I > w_P$.

In this case, given identical qualities of doctors, then all other things held equal, no patient has an incentive to leave or join the public system, and the system remains static. Because the L_I employees are willing to work for the private firm already at the going wage, increasing the wage without increasing the number of employees is, of course, not rational for a profit maximising firm.

Decision 2: The private sector offers a slightly higher wage, $w_I > w_P$ and hires more employees.

The second decisions is likely because making it gives firm more profits, given that it results in getting more patients.

In time 1, given a shortage of doctors, the quality, Q_1 of the public system has fallen below Q_0. In this case, following the model in Poutanen et al. (2016), some h patients leave the public system for the private one, taking their subsidies with them.

The public system's revenues are decreased from $\left(T - \sum_{i=1}^{k_0} \beta_i\right)$ to $\left(T - \sum_{i=1}^{k_1} \beta_i\right)$ by the h patients leaving, but the costs of treatment are also decreased to $c_p\,(N - k_1)$, and there is also a reduction in personnel costs. Three possibilities arise:

- If $\left(T-\sum_{i=1}^{k_0}\beta_i\right)-\left(T-\sum_{i=1}^{k_1}\beta_i\right)<c_p\,(N-k_0)-c_p\,(N-k_1)+w_pL_{p0}-w_pL_{p1}$, where $k_1=k_0+h$, then the public firm saves more from the exit of the h patients and L_{p0}–L_{p1} doctors than from the loss of their subsidies, and the public funds after treatment costs will be larger in time 1. Note that this budget difference will depend on the size of the subsidy for private care β_i and on the share of the costs of treatment for the h patients. Given that these patients have the option to purchase private care, their costs must be low enough to prevent them from being excluded. This means that for this condition to hold, the level of subsidy, β_i must also be low.
- If $\left(T-\sum_{i=1}^{k_0}\beta_i\right)-\left(T-\sum_{i=1}^{k_1}\beta_i\right)=c_p\,(N-k_0)-c_p\,(N-k_1)+w_pL_{p1}-w_pL_{p0}$, then the public firm saves as much from the exit of the h patients and L_{p0}–L_{p1} doctors as it loses from the subtraction of their subsidies, and the public budget is equal in time 1.
- If $\left(T-\sum_{i=1}^{k_0}\beta_i\right)-\left(T-\sum_{i=1}^{k_1}\beta_i\right)>c_p\,(N-k_0)-c_p\,(N-k_1)+w_pL_{p1}-w_pL_{p0}$, then the public firm loses more in subsidies than it saves in costs, and its budget is smaller in time 1. With a smaller budget, the public firm will either offer a lower wage or hire a lower number of employees in time 1. Looking ahead, the quality in time 2 will be lower still.

It can be seen that how the situation evolves depend crucially on costs of treatment and the sizes of the subsidies. It should be noted that there is a potentially important additional element driving the public sector to the direction of having a shortage of labor. If the private firms provide higher quality, such as shorter waiting times, via more doctors per patient, doctors switching to the private sector do not cause a proportionate number of patients to follow, and the costs of treating those who remain are borne by the public sector.

3.4 *Quality*

3.4.1 Perfect Information

We can complicate the situation to create two different types: say "High ability" and "Low ability" employees. Again, if all salaries, benefits, etc. are the same, we have no reason to expect vastly different distributions of high and low quality employees between the two places of employment.

If we allow differences in conditions between the two places, then simple economic logic shows that we should expect some differences. If salaries differ between the private and public sectors, and the employee types differ in such a way that they can be identified, then the higher salary sector will attract the "high ability" types, leaving lower ability types to the lower salary sector. This assumption draws from Kotakorpi and Laamanen (2010) who state,

> We believe that, rather than being axiomatically unhelpful, extra money has potential to improve aspects of care quality such as effectiveness, patient satisfaction or access to care. These positive outcomes can be attained by using monetary resources to, for example, hire more or better-suited personnel, train personnel, buy better equipment or improve facilities.

Let L^{A+} be the number of high ability employees in the population, L^{A-} be the number of low ability doctors in the population and $L^{A+} + L^{A-} = D$.

For sector I, w_{IH} is the wage offered to high ability doctors and w_{IL} is the wage offered to low ability doctors.

Likewise, for sector p, w_{pH} is the wage offered to high ability doctors and w_{pL} is the wage offered to low ability doctors. Here, to make the model a better match with the system analyzed, we assume that sector p (the public sector) has—at least in the short run—less ability to alter wages. Thus, the primary decision makers in the short run are sector I and the employees.

Assume, at first, full employment and labor demand of the private sector being less than L^{A+}.

Sector I offers $w_{IH} > w_{pH}$ and attracts only high quality employees. The public sector has the remaining high ability employees, but mostly low ability ones.[12]

In the case of private sector labor demand larger than or equal to the number of high ability employees, sector p obtains only low ability employees. Sector I offers $w_{IH} > w_{pH}$ and attracts all of the high ability employees, and offers $w_{IL} = w_{pL}$ to attract the remaining employees needed.

Again, note that the ability for sector I (the private alternative) to have more flexibility to offer higher salaries in the short term leads to a potential dearth or absence of high ability employees for sector p.

If the labor market is tight, then the firm offering the higher salary will benefit, leaving the lower salary firm with lower ability workers, and a potential shortage of workers altogether. Note that we have ruled out unemployment as negligible in our model. If there were unemployment in the market, especially if there were more high ability workers available that sector I demands, then sector p would have a better chance of attracting some high ability workers.

If types cannot be identified, game theory has a host of tools to entice "low ability" types to prefer to accept a lower salary, allowing the higher paying center to attract only high ability employees.

The last major adjustment to physician salaries in the public sector followed their strike in 2001. Since then the salaries in the public sector have mostly followed the normal trends of wages across most public sector workers. In statistical analysis

[12]This assumption and the ones that follow ignore the very real fact that there are doctors who see public service as "a calling" and are thus willing to sacrifice some increase in wages for the utility of providing work to the public sector. However, as data, below, shows, this number is not sufficient to slow the trend towards private employment.

conducted by the Finnish Medical Association, it appears that the private sector has a markedly higher salary cap (and relative high lowest salary point) compared to the public sector (FMA 2014). This would be in line with our expectations.

3.4.2 Additional Costs

Aside from attracting away patients, private companies can use the dearth of public doctors to secure even more funds from the public sector by leasing doctor services at a fee. This type of situation is the best of both worlds for the private sector, because they make money treating public sector patients without bearing any long-term responsibility for their care. As an example, in 2003, companies offering doctors to municipalities made about 20 million euros in sales, and in 2008 it had grown to almost 200 million euros (Mikkola 2009: 17). In other words, the growth of private health care providers within the sphere of public municipal health care has increased funding outflow from the public sector.

It is interesting to note that in the long term, with a more flexible budget, the public sector can avoid the shortage by increasing wages and still hiring a sufficient number of workers, thus the introduction of a private alternative in a tight labour market can lead to an increase in costs, in terms of higher overall salaries. Given that visits to private health providers seem to favour in the specialist care (private sector covers some 16 % of primary health consultations, but 25–30 % of specialist consultations: Valtonen et al. 2014: 10), the growing trend in terms of salaried annual remuneration (NCU) seems predictable (Figs. 1 and 2).

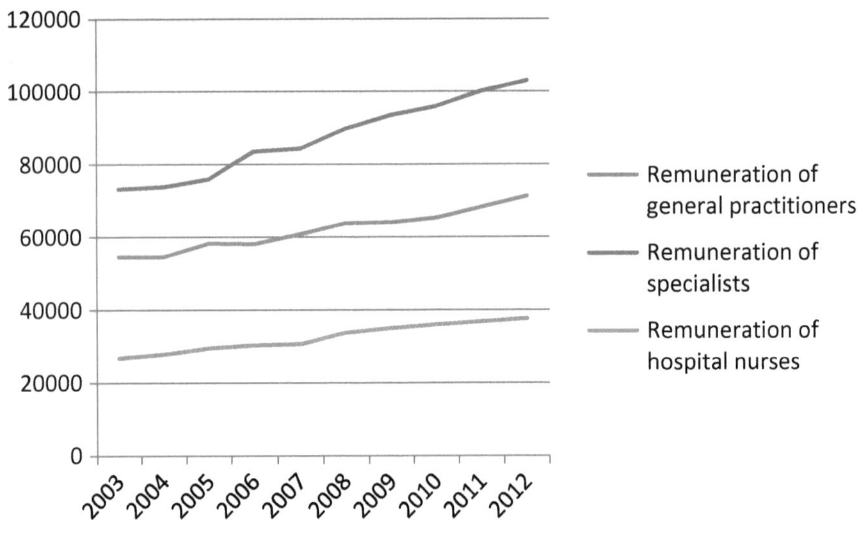

Fig. 1 Renumeration, *Source*: OECD 2014 Health statistics Finland

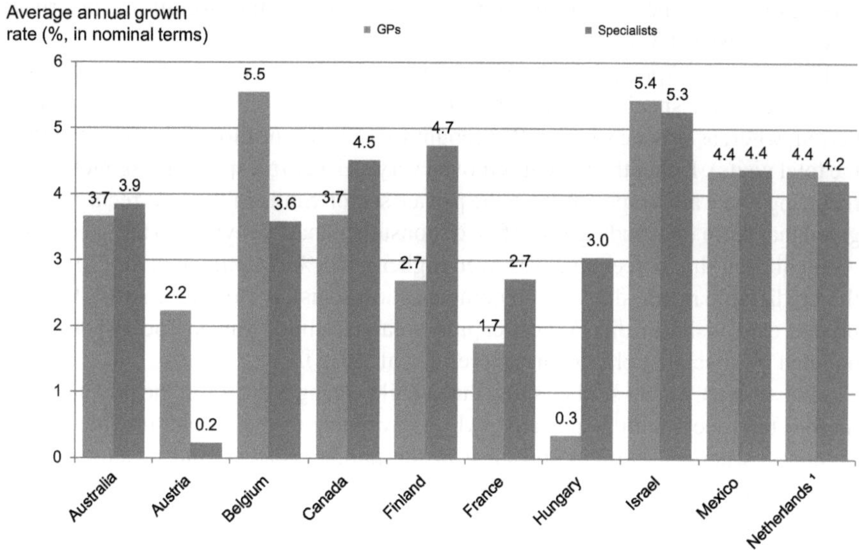

Fig. 2 Average annual growth rate of doctors. Growth in the remuneration of GPs and specialists, 2005–2011 (or nearest year): OECD (2013)

Comparing these trends to the growth of average wages also shows they are not only determined by inflation either: inflation-levels in Finland have remained at roughly 2 % or less annually during the time of observation.

The OECD (2013: 74–75) has noted that the growing gap in Finland between general practitioners and specialists which can be seen to decrease the financial attractiveness of general practice.[13] The Finnish Medical Association—FMA (Suomen Lääkäriliitto)—calculated that in the 2015 statistical survey some 65 % of Finnish doctors have received specialization (FMA 2015). The number is somewhat higher when considering private physicians only, at 70 % (FMA 2014: 26).

While we should note that specialization is not *only* financially incentivized, we must equally maintain that in the private sector it nevertheless *is* financially incentivized. As discussed earlier in Poutanen et al. (2016), we should also note that the Finnish Social Insurance Institution (KELA) subsidizes private care to the order of 20–30 %, depending on the nature of the procedure (Valtonen et al. 2014; Mikkola and Virta 2012). At the same time, specialist care is allowed a 50 % increase in tariff rates, as determined by the SII, meaning that if the customer opts for, or is given access to, the services of a specialist physician in the private sector, that service is subsidized even further. Accordingly, Miettinen et al. (2013) note that in their research three fifths (58 %) of insured individuals have used private *specialist*

[13]GPs tend to remain in the public sector, the private sector provides specialists. Alternatively, if the public sector cannot acquire GPs, they will have to be purchased as a service from the private sector (Mikkola 2009).

services at least once during the study period, whereas the overall use of private medical access is 63 %.

Furthermore, Appendix 1 in Miettinen et al. (2013) further shows that visits to private sector specialists account for some 15.9 million visits during the study period, whereas private sector GPs account for only 4.1 million visits (i.e., a fifth of the total visits). Either the patient is moved very quickly to a specialist, or most of the recurring visits are to specialists in the private sector. Some of this was recurring use, given that from one study group 46 % of consumers had 4+ visits to the specialists, with children this percentage was even higher at 61 % (Miettinen et al. (2013). As the predictable result, drawing on compensation statistics from KELA/SII, 90 % of private care visits in the Finnish capital area (Helsinki, Vantaa and Espoo) were handled by specialist physicians (Järvelin et al. 2015).

And, indeed, recent studies show that a child seeing a doctor in the private sector more often meets with a specialist, who is available at the private provider's own premises, whereas seeing a specialist in the public sector would mean a transfer from the health care center to a hospital (Järvelin et al. 2015; Paulavaara 2015). The FMA has also noted that many Finns receive their primary care through private and occupational care, where the number of specialists is statistically higher, and that the changes in the structures of health services influence both the attractiveness of specialization and the availability of the specialists (Ruskoaho et al. 2015; FMA 2014). FMA (2014) further notes that the rate of physicians seeing patients in private practice has overtaken physicians (seeing patients) in public sector (e.g., 91 % of private practitioners work full time, whereas 88 % of health centre physicians listed patient work as their primary occupation).

This is some cause for concern on two points: first, the concentration of specialists into private care will decrease the availability of public sector specialists, or at the very least require more visits to the hospital. At worst, highly specialized private sector staff treats healthier children, while sicker children have to wait for public access (Järvelin et al. 2015), and thus will be included in the queues if their situation deteriorates to the point that they need longer care. Second, due to preference for private care, physicians in the public sector can gain less experience from specialized care patients, and arguably colleagues in the work environment. This could also cause deterioration in terms of care quality in the public sector (ibid.).

It is thus perhaps unsurprising that the subsidies either through either health insurance payments or occupational health care to private care providers make up a significant portion of the income of these companies. According to the investigative reporting of *MOT* (Skön 2015). For example, the two largest private health care providers in Finland, Terveystalo and Mehiläinen (both parts of a larger web of multinational holding companies and similar constructs of convoluted investment structures), grossed 108 and 78 million euros respectively *only in 2013*, *only* from care subsidies from the SII (Skön 2015).[14] For Terveystalo this subsidy constituted

[14]The data has also been made fully available through a Creative Commons license at https://www.avoindata.fi/data/fi/dataset/kelan-sairaanhoitovakuutuksen-suorakorvaukset-2011-2014

approximately a third of their entire turnover. However, in a recent study (Hiltunen et al. 2015), interviewed representatives of private care providers tended to stress how little income they derive from the subsidies.

4 Supply in Terms of Skilled Labor

Doctors in Finland are all trained through the public sector (i.e., university education) which is currently tuition-free. Doctors are also expected to conduct their internship primarily in the public sector, where they will get first-hand experiences both of their profession, but also of the working conditions of the public sector, for better or for worse. The public sector (through e.g., municipalities) is still the primary employer of 70 % of Finnish physicians (FMA 2014).

The degree of unionization in Finland in terms of doctors is exceptionally high: according to 2015 statistics, some 93 % of all doctors are members of the Finnish Medical Association (FMA 2015). The level of unionization has remained high in recent years, and membership in the union is actively advertised and recommended to medical students. This suggests a relatively high degree of control exerted by the union on the labor supply. Accordingly, the FMA also often argues in its own journal (Suomen Lääkärilehti) that the current number of doctors, both in employment and under training, is sufficient for Finnish needs, regardless of demographic changes (e.g., Parmanne et al. 2014). The current plan of the Finnish government is to increase the number of medical students to 750 annually by 2016, a 10 % increase from 678 in 2014 (Parmanne et al. 2014). While this has been accepted, historically speaking the union has resisted—successfully or not—increases in medical student intake (see e.g., YLE Uutiset 2009). In other words, the union is, as Olson (1965) would hypothesize, acting to avoid expansion of the labor pool.[15]

In a relatively restricted domestic labor pool, THL reports a clear increase in terms of personnel for the private sector of all health care workers from 11 % in 2000 to 20 % in 2013. Based on the employer's status (private–public–other non-profit organizations) there has been an increase of staff overall by 10 % for public, but a sizable 105 % for private care in Finland between 2000 and 2013 (see Fig. 3). As can be seen from Fig. 4, the increase of importance of the private sector is most pronounced in outpatient care that involves physicians' services (the numbers include inpatient care in public health centers). In this care category, the number of employees showed a 9 % decrease for public health providers, and an increase of 78 % for private health providers. Further, the employment share of private providers is much higher in outpatient care (26 %) than in the case of hospitals (4 %), mostly because private hospitals are still rare in Finland.

[15]An injection of non-Finnish physicians to the labor pool is also modest according to THL and FMA statistics.

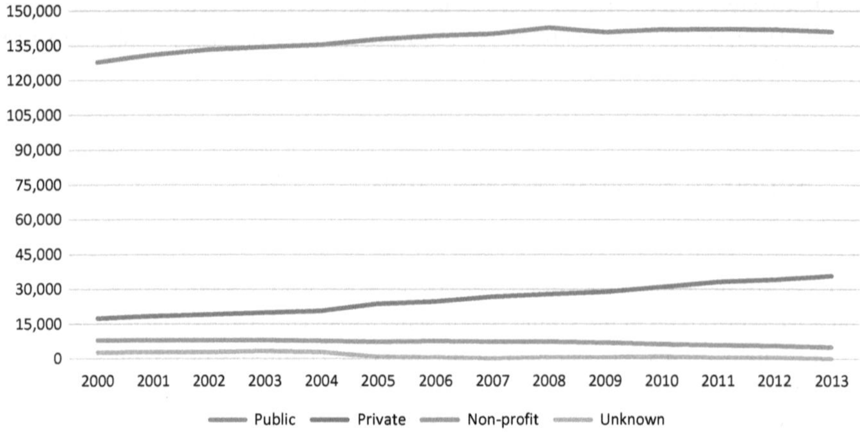

Fig. 3 Employees in health care by sector. *Source*: National Institute for Health and Welfare

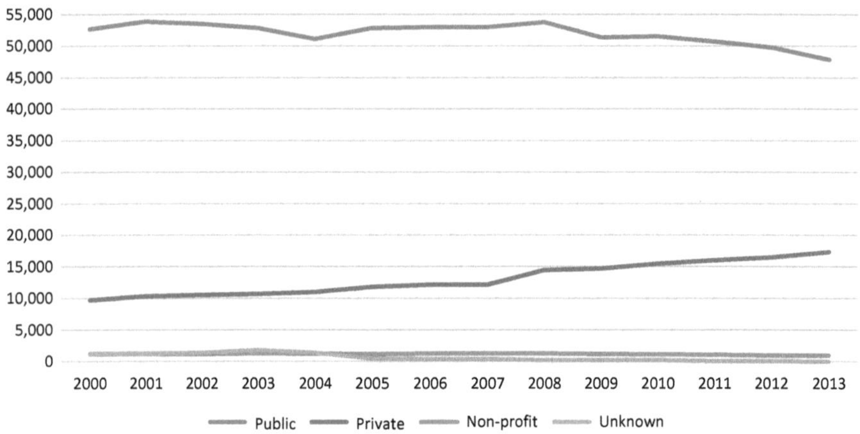

Fig. 4 Employees in health care involving physicians by sector. *Source*: National Institute for Health and Welfare

The figures also include a total increase of some 26,000 people working in health care in Finland within the same time period. The increase of the number of employees in private provision of some 18,000 is notable because it outnumbers the increase in public provision of some 13,000. At the same time, other non-profit organizations have experienced a fall of about 3000. In other words, the overall growth of health care work has correlated with an increasing market share of private providers.

5 Private Incentives: Mergers and Taxes

Finally, we wish to draw attention to the incentives and profit-mechanics of private health care providers in Finland. When public and private sector are placed side by side, it stands to reason that their position in a competitive environment is highly dependent on several external factors. The state, for example, can, through restrictions or heavy bureaucracy, favour the public option, making the private measure too costly in terms of effort or availability. In the Finnish case, however, we call attention to the fact that private health care services in Finland are subsidized (see Poutanen et al. 2016), so customers of private services do not bear the full price.

Further inefficiencies are introduced, because private health care services do not operate according to free market expectations. Many of the companies are fairly large in size and have expanded aggressively through acquisitions (Mikkola 2009: 20–21). Instead of competing amongst themselves, the consolidation of successful companies with large market shares (Mikkola 2009: 18) can actually lead to the competitive positioning to form between public and private care provision, rather than between private companies (Hiltunen et al. 2015).[16] Entering a deregulated market can still be costly, and thus companies with external backing (i.e., newly founded subsidiaries or larger multinational companies) can enter the market—even at a high cost—if they can be confident enough that their strategy will guarantee them a sufficiently dominant position in the market. This hypothesis seems to fit with the current maneuverings in the Finnish health care sector (Holttari and Vanhanen 2013).

The theoretical model noted the impact of different costs of patients, between the public and private sectors in terms of their remaining budgets and abilities to hire additional doctors. Private firms have another advantage in terms of net costs. Private companies operating with multinational subsidiaries have the possibility—and in terms of cost management of entering a market, the incentive—to engage in what has been charitably called "tax planning". In its simplest form, the consortium to which the private care provider belong to can "recycle" its finances through more favourable locations in terms of corporate taxation, engaging in and settling intra-consortium loans and other measures to manipulate the bookkeeping though holding companies and similar structures (Hänninen 2012a).

For example, according to reports in the leading Finnish newspaper Helsingin Sanomat (Hänninen 2012a), many privately held health care providing companies have managed to cut their corporate tax rate effectively to <14 %, when the standard rate is 24.5–26 %. The report further describes how borrowed money used to expand the business is at the same time declared as costs to cut the effective tax rate down.[17]

[16]Light (1995: 147–148) notes that often mergers to "increase competitiveness" in actual fact achieve, from the social perspective, exactly the opposite.

[17]We should also note that this is not merely a Finnish issue, but a global one. Indeed, one might hypothesize that globalized financial services that have spearheaded successful tax planning systems are at an advantage when implementing these systems into new markets. Their existing

In so doing the provider may avoid paying its full allocated tax burden in the country (and municipality) in which it operates, effectively decreasing the tax income of that country and contributing to the budgetary pressures of its public sector health care.[18]

Thus private care providers can arguably manage their costs in terms of their tax burden very effectively, and have more leverage in cost management than the public sector without having to sacrifice working conditions or salaries. Furthermore, some private health care providers also offer tax planning advice to their physicians that would allow them to set up their own holding companies, effectively to decrease the income tax rates of these individual physicians (Hänninen 2012b). The financial incentives in the private sector far outstrip those in the public.[19]

6 Discussion

The above analysis suggests that a public and private mix of health care is not without problems. Private care providers are more or less engaged in competition not between themselves but with the public sector, given its considerable "market share", which can quite naturally guide the companies' strategic choices (Hiltunen et al. 2015). The public sector effectively partially finances its own competition. The seemingly benevolent idea of providing freedom of choice and multiple channels has its advantages but at the same time it has the potential to erode the basis of the system and create an inherently contradictory financing mechanism. The basic principle of the Scandinavian single payer system is that all services are universal. This justifies the relatively high level of taxation. A regulated system need not create this problem. Specifics can be left to design, but the basics can be explored here.

capital and financial know-how tilt the market in their favor. In Finland many other companies have engaged in this sort of action than just the health care sector, but the type of business the health care sector engages in makes it very susceptible to perceptions of unethical conduct. See e.g., Finnwatch report (Ylönen 2014: 21–24) on the dialogue between the organization and Terveystalo, the largest Finnish private health care provider.

[18]Raphael (2014) sees economic globalization as a considerable threat for the economic sustainability of the welfare state. The permeation of this new line of thinking is statistically visible in the Nordic countries: increases in income inequality and poverty rates—that coincide with the ramping down of (some aspects) of previously all-encompassing welfare policy—occur across virtually all nations, but these effects are most visible in Finland, Norway, and Sweden, where the relatively large size of the welfare state is decreasing (OECD 2011). The increased division of the health care sector into public and private in Finland is actually undermining the welfare state's *raison d'etre* as it is seen more as a potential burden to well-being (through high taxation), rather than enabling it universally (Raphael 2014). For companies this undermining means effectually increased business, so it tax planning would also from this perspective be in their best interests.

[19]While physicians working in the public sector can also set up their holding companies, this would require the public provider to outsource the care from this new private provider representing their doctors. In municipalities where there is a lack of physicians this might be an increasingly successful strategy.

What do the models mean in terms of having a private alternative to public health care? If unregulated, then with higher salaries or better working conditions (more attractive work hours, etc.) we should expect either that the private sector could attract away a large percentage of the doctors, or that it will attract the higher ability doctors, or both. Having a surplus of labor, in contrast, could ease some of these constraints, but this situation is unlikely; Olson (1965) among others notes the rational tendency for doctors to make efforts to tighten requirements—thereby reducing numbers and increasing salaries of the in-group.

The model explored in this paper provides suggestions as to how the relative qualities can be affected. It also highlights policy choices that could create potential improvements. First, as noted, a tight labor market creates greater potential for quality differences to arise. With full or tight employment, a higher paying firm can attract a greater number of employees, causing the quality of the competing firm to suffer. If we include this potential into the (Poutanen et al. 2016) consumer demand model, the difference in quality in one period is likely to cause exit from the public sector in following periods, creating possible further strains in terms of lost funding.

Indeed, in 2013 there were approximately 800 posts for doctors left unfilled in the Finnish public sector (Parmanne et al. 2014). Even if we would factor in the possibility that some of these posts wouldn't be actually filled even if applicants were available, this seems like a staggering number. Private health care providers or occupational health providers (which can also include public providers, but the business is kept separate from public service) have encountered no similar deficiencies in terms of labor. Instead the number of physicians in the occupational health sector is expected to continue growing—as the current trend would suggest—by a quarter (approximately 200 physicians) in the near future (Ruskoaho et al. 2015).

It seems doubtful that an increase of 70 doctors annually, mentioned above, can satisfy the increased demand for occupational health doctors. As such, we feel we should stress that the public sector is legally mandated and obligated to provide equal quality care, which makes the deficit of labor in their side even more alarming, especially so when the mechanics feeding into this deficit show no signs of abating.

This analysis suggests that, as part of a solution, it would be beneficial to the public sector to train a larger number of doctors. This would, as noted, be resisted by labor unions wanting to control the labor supply to retain control over their wages through choices between public and private employers. While a threat to the salary-range of doctors in Finland, increases in the amount of physicians accepted into medical schools could expand the potential labor pool. However, this is only a partial solution. The problem of quality differentials can still persist with an increased level of doctors. As seen, with higher salaries, the private sector can attract away the better doctors. Stricter training requirements may improve this problem, but may also lead back to the situation of insufficient numbers of doctors to meet demand.

To address this problem, policy could potentially be drafted that shares doctors between the sectors—for instance each doctor could be required to work a certain percentage of his or her time in the public sector, with possibly up to half of the time going to the public sector. This type of requirement (assuming it were well designed and enforced) could possibly help to reduce differences between the sectors. It could, however, also increase dissatisfaction among doctors feeling they have to work in the public sector against their will. Additionally, combining the two can have negative effects on perceptions of public employment. Kankaanranta et al. (2007) found that having a private practice outside of public employment increased the likelihood that a given doctor would seek to switch from the public to private sector. This concern is reflected by the FMA; in their 2012 review of a proposal of "forced employment" in the public sector for all graduating doctors, the FMA ruled that forced measures would not only decrease appreciation of public sector work, especially among the youngest physicians thus targeted,[20] but also equally decrease the appreciation of public sector care in the eyes of the customers (FMA 2012). Given the current state of customer preference in terms of health care provision, as found by Poutanen et al. (2016), the latter argument is not completely without merit. A further problem with this type of policy, is that doctors could use access to patients in the public sector to tempt them—using promises of shorter wait times, etc.—to become their patients in the private sector.[21]

Other options could involve rules to equalize salaries, hours, and other conditions between the sectors to remove currently standing preferences and incentives to favour private over public. These actions would also require rigorously tackling with tax planning systems of private companies to stop the outflow of capital from the public sector. These rules are based on the above discussion, but would be more difficult to implement, and would involve extensive (and predictably costly) monitoring.

Thus the role of income and health has become increasingly significant in the formation of care organizations for at least one portion of the public. Our simple economic logic reveals that an unregulated system with public health care and a private alternative may result in an upper and lower class system, where the upper class pays for services and the lower class must—at best—be resigned to wait longer for services due to a relative lack of doctors. At worst, the lower class will suffer from low quality doctors, even if the assumption is that in terms of clinical treatment the quality wouldn't differ (Paulavaara 2015).

This corresponds with the finding that in some demographically homogeneous urban municipalities[22] public provision for children's health services is left practically unused (as is in the case of Espoo: Järvelin et al. 2015). Over a half (57 %)

[20]We also note that according to FMA statistics (FMA 2014), young physicians (44 years old or younger) tend to work predominantly in the public sector. We can assume that only after they reach a certain level of seniority do they transfer to private practice; both the pushing and pulling elements can be seen to work here over time.

[21]We are grateful to Theis Theisen for reminding us of this potential.

[22]Fredriksson and Martikainen (2008) find that young urbanites view market-centered reforms and privatized services much more favorably than other demographics. Hypothetically this is so because the larger customer pool allows for a richer variety of this services to be present in their area.

of doctoral visits for children under 7 in the metropolitan area of Helsinki were to private providers (Paulavaara 2015). The results show that while private health insurance and private care providers were seen as a way to supplement the Finnish health care system, the private sector has instead begun to replace public services in some municipalities. Given that private providers increase their range, the decrease in customers will inevitably lead into cuts into the public provision as the ratio of doctors per patient—the issue already plaguing the image of public care—is adjusted according to efficiency principles.[23] The existence of a strong local market in private health care provision can be seen, then, to undermine the raison d'etre of public services.

When interviewed about the decreased attractiveness of public service providers the municipality doesn't see any point in competing for those customers who can afford to get treatment from the private sector with only a relatively small public subsidy (Paulavaara 2015).[24] In other words, the public sector doesn't (or cannot afford to) advertise for more patients. However, demographics can change, and municipalities who could have previously afforded to ramp down their public service might find themselves in a situation where they have to ramp up those services again.

Finnish municipalities have encountered problems in attracting doctors to more far-flung regions, whereas university-cities where doctors are trained have a degree of oversupply. Problems with supply, then, are highly regional in nature. The existence of the private sector, could be seen as an element that keeps physicians in centralized population centers, where demographics are also favourable for private practice, and decreases the supply to more peripheral areas. Efforts of public sector cost savings have also decreased the number of smaller regional (public) health centers (FMA 2014: 43).

As consequence, resorting to outsourced or privatized service provisions has become necessary in some outlying municipalities (Mikkola 2009). This forces the municipalities to attract physicians, often through private providers, with more lucrative contracts. Indeed, in a survey regarding the attitudes of chief physicians in managing position of municipal health care administration, Mikkola (2009: 30) found that most of the respondents (55 %) saw that outsourced services had increased costs somewhat, or considerably (28 %). Based on this the current

[23]Reports from Finnish health and social services sector have suggested that efficiency principles are poorly applicable, given that both the vehicle and target for treatment are human subjects. When pressed for time, professionals especially in the public sector feel they're not providing the best care they feel they could (Rönneberg 2013). Given that such statements are often publically reported, it is no wonder that both professionals not wishing to be rushed in an ethically unsustainable way or customers fearing they won't receive optimal care, have reservations about the public sector.

[24]Both private care providers and customers seem to find the subsidy too small: for care providers it is represented as too small to truly change the business environment (Hiltunen et al. 2015) while similarly customers feel they are too small to make a difference in the choose for care provision (when the compensation rate reaches 50 %, approximately doubling the current effective rate, it would, according to surveys, become a conscious factor in solicit care: Jäntti 2008).

dynamics of labor supply are arguably benefitting private care providers either through subsidies from or contracts with the public sector.

Indeed, the specialist-heavy formation of labor in the private sector should also be a cause for concern. Following Hiltunen et al. (2015) we also find that, while admittedly profitable in terms of the subsidized tariffs, specialized care utilizes lower levels of care poorly, which creates an inflated demand for specialist services and prevents allocating resources (also across sectors) efficiently. Some increased control over the labor pool could provide a solution, although as long as the incentives for specialization remain, professionals would prefer specialization both for personal qualifications and income-potential.

Moreover, we should note that emerging new service markets are fairly sought after by both national and international private service providers. As the Finnish health sector has been open for competing companies for some time, the same providers also show increasing interest in gaining a larger foothold in the field of social services (Seppälä and Pekurinen 2014: 26). As such, the current trend is towards increased erosion of public services, where private services are seen as increasingly substitutive, rather than complementing elements.

This is why it isn't sufficient to simply look at relative sizes of the public and private sector to determine the distribution of market opportunities; to do so would offer a very simplistic view. Instead of looking at pie charts that show X percentage of care being provided by public or private operators, we should pay more careful attention to the contents of each slice of this pie. If, for example, and as argued by Poutanen et al. (2016) the consumer preferences favor private providers, this defunds the public sector and undermines the standard of coverage. The type of patient that ends up in private or public care can be expected to have a significant impact on the costs of treatment.

As long as private health care provision continues be viewed as a supplementary element, the real social dynamics of the hybrid system can be misinterpreted. Furthermore, we should note that especially in occupational health, there is very little incentive for politicians to start problematizing the usage of private care, since occupational health relies on employer and employee payments. It would seem that any cut in public subsidies of the private sector would also have to include increased and efficacious funding for public services. In light of political expediency in terms of the image-difference between public and private services that doesn't seem very likely.

7 Conclusion

The growth of the private sector in the Finnish hybrid public–private healthcare system has been justified on the basis of offering increased 'choice' to patients and in terms of increased efficiency. Our analysis indicates that this policy fails in terms of both of these objectives. Rather than the emergence of a multitude of private healthcare services, the market tends to be dominated by a small number of large companies (as Sieberg and Shvetsova 2012 would predict). Furthermore, these companies operate at the expense of the public sector, over time making the public option a poor 'choice.' If budget constraints are tight (and/or if the population refuses to increase taxes to fund a service they do not use) then the public sector will either disappear or be a poorly funded service for the sick and the poor. With a softer budget constraint, the public sector can persist, but only at the cost of higher salaries—both for full time employees and for employees 'rented' from the private sector. Thus, instead of increasing efficiency, introduction of the private sector into the public market increases costs for everyone. Despite the promises offered, the creation of the hybrid model of healthcare seems to offer a more dismal future of mixed administrative and financing systems coupled with increased incentives for private sector preference.

Seppälä and Pekurinen (2014) note in the conclusions of their own study on the financing of Finnish social and health services that the current system of financing is highly complex and difficult to track. Overlapping financing systems make it harder to decipher the actual costs of the system or the cost–benefits derived from increased private care provision. Various actors have their own incentives that direct them to optimize their services and costs (incl. fees) to achieve the maximum benefits, as opposed to maximizing societal gains in health and social services. We argue that the costs of attempting to regulate and control a hybrid system combined with the noted added costs to the public system, outweigh any of the potential benefits gained through privatization. Rather than offer more 'choice,' a government that seeks to improve healthcare services should provide more resources to the public sector.

References

Besley, T., Hall, J., & Preston, I. (1999). The demand for private health insurance: Do waiting lists matter? *Journal of Public Economics, 72*, 155–181.

Besley, T., & Miguel, G. (1994). Alternative systems of health care provision, *Economic Policy, 19*: 199–258.

Epple, D., & Romano, R. E. (1996). Ends against the middle: Determining public service provision when there are private alternatives. *Journal of Public Economics, 62*, 297–325.

Esping-Andersen, G. (1990). *The three worlds of welfare capitalism*. Oxford: Polity Press.

FMA—Finnish Medical Association [Suomen Lääkäriliitto]. (2012, October 24). *Valmistuvien lääkärien velvoittaminen terveyskeskustyohon*.https://www.laakariliitto.fi/uutiset/jasenuutiset/valmistuvien-laakarien-velvoittaminen-terveyskeskustyohon/

FMA—Finnish Medical Association [Suomen Lääkäriliitto]. (2014). *Lääkärit Suomessa—Tilastotietoja lääkäreistä ja terveydenhuollosta 2014/Physicians in Finland—Statistics on physicians and the health care system 2014*.https://www.laakariliitto.fi/site/assets/files/1268/laakarit_suomessa_2014.pdf

FMA—Finnish Medical Association [Suomen Lääkäriliitto]. (2015). *Physicians 2015*. Annual statistics. http://www.laakariliitto.fi/site/assets/files/1011/vuositilastot_2015_en.pdf

Fredriksson, S., & Martikainen, T. (2008). *Julkista vai yksityistä—Kuntalaisten palveluita koskevat valinnat* (Kunnallisalan kehittämissäätiön Kunnat ja kilpailu—Sarjan julkaisu no. 6). Vammala: Vammalan Kirjapaino Oy.

Hänninen, J. (2012a, August 31). Kauas verot karkaavat. *Helsingin Sanomat*. http://www.hs.fi/talous/a1346293515810

Hänninen, J. (2012b, October 9). Attendo houkuttelee lääkäreitä veroneuvoilla. *Helsingin Sanomat*. http://www.hs.fi/talous/a1349666487040

Hiltunen, R., Mikkola, H., Halonen, J.-P., & Saarni, J. (2015). Sairaanhoitovakuutuksen korvausten merkitys lääkäripalveluyrityksille. *Suomen Lääkärilehti, 24*(70), 1751–1758.

Holttari, S. & Vanhanen, A. (2013, September 27). Seuraava rahastus alkaa. *Talouselämä* (Special report Terveystalous 2013), *34*.

Hsiao, W. C. (1995). Abnormal economics in the health sector. *Health Policy, 32*, 125–139.

Jäntti, S. (2008). *Kansalainen terveyspalveluja valitsemassa. Kolmivaiheinen valintamalli julkisissa ja yksityisissä lääkäripalveluissa* (E Yhteiskuntatieteet 154). Kuopio: Kuopion Yliopisto.

Järvelin, J., Virta, L., & Mikkola, H. (2015). Hoitoon yksityiselle vai julkiselle sektorille? *Suomen Lääkärilehti, 47*(70), 3199–3206.

Kankaanranta, T., Nummi, T., Vainiomäki, J., Halila, H., Hyppölä, H., Isokoski, M., Kujala, S., Kumpusalo, E., Mattila, K., Virjo, I., Vänskä, J., & Rissanen, P. (2007). The role of job satisfaction, job dissatisfaction and demographic factors on physicians' intentions to switch work sector from public to private. *Health Policy, 83*, 50–64.

Kotakorpi, K., & Laamanen, J.-P. (2010). Welfare state and life satisfaction: Evidence from public health care. *Economica, 77*, 565–583.

Light, D. W. (1995). Homo economicus: Escaping the traps of managed competition. *European Journal of Public Health, 5*(3), 145–154.

Mattila, Y. (2011). *Suuria käännekohtia vai tasaista kehitystä? Tutkimus Suomen terveydenhuollon suuntaviivoista* (Sosiaali- ja terveysturvan tutkimuksia 116). Helsinki: Kelan tutkimusosasto.

Miettinen, J., Tervola, J., Virta, L., Koskinen, H., Tuominen, U., Maljanen, T., & Mikkola, H. (2013). *Sairaanhoitovakuutuksen korvaamien yksityisten terveyspalvelujen käytön kehitys ja hintavertailu* (Työpapereita 45/2013). Helsinki: KELA, Kelan Tutkimusosasto.

Mikkola, H. (2009). *Toimiiko kilpailu lääkäripalveluissa?* (Kunnallisalan kehittämissäätiön Kunnat ja kilpailu—sarjan julkaisu no. 15). Sastamala: Vammalan kirjapaino Oy.

Mikkola, H., & Virta, L. (2012). Miten sairaanhoitovakuutus tulevaisuudessa korvaa lääkärinpalkkioita. In H. Mikkola, J. Blomgren, & H. Hiilamo (Eds.), *Kansallista vai Paikallista? Puheenvuoroja sosiaali- ja terveyshuollosta* (pp. 190–203). Helsinki: Kelan Tutkimusosasto.

OECD (2011) Geneva:OECD.

OECD (2012) Geneva:OECD.

OECD (2013) Geneva:OECD.

Olson, M. (1965). *The logic of collective action*. Boston, MA: Harvard University Press.

Parmanne, P., Vänskä, J., & Halila, H. (2014). Lääkärimäärä kasvaa eläköitymisaallosta huolimatta. *Suomen Lääkärilehti, 24*, 1181–1182. https://www.laakariliitto.fi/site/assets/files/1268/140610_sll24_lyhyesti_parmanne.pdf

Paulavaara, P. (2015, November 27). Pääkaupunkiseudulla jo puolet lasten lääkärikäynneistä tehdään yksityisellä—'Ei ole aikaa jonotella'. *Helsingin Sanomat*. http://www.hs.fi/kaupunki/a1448522811308

Poutanen, M., Sieberg, K. K., & Kettunen, P. (2016). *The use of an alternative private system in a public health care system—Critical viewpoints*. Unpublished Manuscript.

Propper, C. (2000). The demand for private health care in the UK. *Journal of Health Economics, 19*, 855–876.

Raphael, D. (2014). Challenges to promoting health in the modern welfare state: The case of the Nordic nations. *Scandinavian Journal of Public Health, 42*, 7–17.

Reinhardt, U. E. (2007). Keeping health care afloat: The United States versus Canada. *The Miliken Institute Review*, 36–43.

Rönneberg, A. (2013, November 21). Tehostaminen pahentaa hoitoalojen pahoinvointia. *Helsingin Sanomat*. http://www.hs.fi/mielipide/a1384934549084

Ruskoaho, J., Parmanne, P., & Vänskä, J. (2015). Erikoisalojen lääkärimäärät kehittyvät eri suuntiin. *Suomen Lääkärilehti, 21*, 1524–1525. Accessed December 14, 2015, from http://www.laakarilehti.fi/pdf/SLL212015-1524.pdf

Seppälä, T. T., & Pekurinen, M. (Eds.). (2014). *Sosiaali- ja terveydenhuollon keskeiset rahavirrat.* Raportti, 22. THL. Accessed December 22, 2015, from http://www.julkari.fi/bitstream/handle/10024/116653/THL_RAP022_2014verkko.pdf?sequence=1

Shapiro, C., & Stiglitz, J. E. (1984). Equilibrium unemployment as a worker discipline device. *The American Economic Review, 74*(3), 433–444.

Sieberg, K. K., & Shvetsova, O. (2012). Kustannustehokkuuden ja kattavuuden ongelmat Yhdysvaltain terveydenhuollossa (Efficiency and coverage problems in United States' Healthcare) Puheenvuoro. *Hallinnon Tutkimus (Administrative Studies).*

Skön, K. (2015, April 14). *Lääkärikeskukset lihovat Kela-korvauksilla.* YLE/MOT. http://yle.fi/aihe/artikkeli/2015/04/13/laakarikeskukset-lihovat-kela-korvauksilla

STM. (2013). *Sairaanhoitovakuutuksen rooli osana sosiaali- ja terveyspalvelujärjestelmää* (Sosiaali- ja terveysministeriön raportteja ja muistioita 2012:34). Helsinki. https://www.julkari.fi/bitstream/handle/10024/112115/URN%3ANBN%3Afi-fe201504226552.pdf?sequence=1

Summers, L. H. (1989). Some simple economics of mandated benefits. *The American Economic Review, 79*(2), 177–183.

Valtonen, H., Kempers, J., & Karttunen, A. (2014). *Supplementary health insurance in Finland consumer preferences and behaviour* (Working papers 65/2014). KELA.

YLE Uutiset. (2009, February 26). Lääkäriliitto torjuu aloituspaikkojen lisäämisen. http://yle.fi/uutiset/laakariliitto_torjuu_aloituspaikkojen_lisaamisen/5727867

Ylönen, M. (2014). Messinkilaattojen Suomi—Pöytälaatikkoyhtiöiden rooli suomalaisyritysten toiminnassa. *Finnwatch, 1.* http://www.finnwatch.org/images/vero_final.pdf

What Makes People Nursing Home Residents: Individual Need or Municipalities' Supply?

Theis Theisen

1 Introduction

The share of old and frail in the populations of many countries has in the last decades been increasing. This development will continue in the years to come, and raises the issue of how to care for those in need of long-term care (LTC). Researchers have increasingly turned their attention to how these people are cared for, but as noted inter alia by Grabowski (2008), research on long-term care is lagging behind research on the hospital and physician markets.

Chiswick (1976) and Nyman (1989), who both studied the demand for nursing home care, are early contributions to economists' research on long-term care. Scanlon (1980) offers a more comprehensive approach, by examining the use of nursing home care within a model containing the demand side of the market as well as the supply side. Scanlon's model covers a market where the supply side largely is driven by the profit motive. In many European countries, however, nursing homes belong to the public sector, or they are non-profit institutions. Moreover, entrance to nursing homes is in many countries strictly rationed. For such contexts we need to approach the issue of what makes an individual a nursing home resident in a way that differs from that of Scanlon (1980) and most of the other American contributions.

In countries where access to nursing homes is rationed through non-price mechanisms, decisions are usually taken in a step-wise manner. First, the capacities of nursing-homes are determined. Second, the allocation of this capacity to individuals is decided. In the present paper we focus on nursing home residents. To the best of my knowledge, there exists in the economics literature no widely accepted model of the nursing home sector in a context where admission to nursing homes is

T. Theisen (✉)
Department of Economics and Finance, School of Business and Law, University of Agder, PO Box 422, 4604 Kristiansand S, Norway
e-mail: Theis.Theisen@uia.no

N. Schofield, G. Caballero (eds.), *State, Institutions and Democracy*, Studies in Political Economy, DOI 10.1007/978-3-319-44582-3_11

rationed. Hence, in Sect. 3 we set up a theoretical model describing the selection of individuals to nursing homes in a system where admission is rationed. Before presenting the model we will, however, in Sect. 2 briefly describe the system of long-term care in Norway, the country from which our data come. In Sect. 4 we describe the empirical model, and Sect. 5 contains a brief account of the data. Empirical results are presented in Sect. 6 and Sect. 7 concludes the paper.

2 Long-Term Care in Norway

Formal long-term care is in Norway almost exclusively provided by municipalities. They allocate one third of their revenues to such care.[1] For-profit organizations play an insignificant role,[2] but informal care of spouses or other relatives of care-recipients living in their private homes constitutes an important supplement to publicly provided home care.

Formal LTC comes in two main forms: home care and care in nursing homes. Home care includes home nursing provided by professional nurses, and home help provided by less educated staff. In accordance with central government by-laws, home nursing is free of charge, while users of home help pay an income-dependent user fee with rates determined by the local government assembly. We include in the concept of nursing homes all institutions for long-term residence. Hence, the few old peoples' homes that still exist in some municipalities are subsumed under nursing homes. On the other hand, we do not include in our concept of nursing homes institutions where care-recipients who regularly receive home care may stay temporarily for a few days or weeks, for instance during an episode of illness, after discharge from a hospital, when informal care-givers are on vacation, etc.

[1] Another one third goes to education and kindergartens, and the last one third to the cultural sector, utilities, administration, etc. Municipalities obtain revenues to finance their expenditures mainly from central government block grants, and taxes on income and wealth. Incomes and wealth are in all Norwegian municipalities taxed at the maximum legal rates. Tax incomes from these sources, as well as block grants from the central government, can therefore be taken as exogenous to municipalities. The only components of revenues that to some extent can be influenced by municipalities themselves are the property tax and some user fees, but there are strict central government by-laws regulating these sources of revenues.

[2] There exist a few nursing homes that are run by private firms or non-profit organizations, but these operate on contracts with the municipality where they are located, and are financed by municipalities. Admissions to these nursing homes are handled by the municipalities, and user fees are the same as in a public sector nursing homes. There exist in some municipalities also a few private homemaking organizations. Most customers of these are, however, relatively young, they are active in the labor market, have high incomes, and pay the full costs for homemaking services.

Norwegian nursing homes provide high-quality care, as indicated by the fact that current costs per resident amount to about twice the average salary of a nurse, and by the fact that almost all nursing-home residents have their own private room with a bathroom. User fees for nursing homes follow an income-dependent schedule laid down in a central government by-law. The schedule is the same in all municipalities.[3] Even if nursing-home residents are charged 75–85 % of their after-tax incomes, these fees on average constitute merely 10–15 % of municipalities' current costs per nursing home resident. User fees are not allowed to exceed municipalities' current costs. Hence they do not cover capital costs, and the maximum fee is equal to current costs per nursing-home bed. Due to the heavily subsidized and income dependent user fees, all Norwegian citizens can afford to stay in a nursing home—even for a period of many years. Because of this, and because of the high quality of care, aggregate demand for nursing home care exceeds supply. Hence, access to nursing homes is rationed. The strictness of rationing varies, however, between Norwegian municipalities.

In the short run, the capacity of nursing homes can be taken as exogenous, determined by the previous decisions of local government assemblies to build nursing homes. Hence, the short-run question is whether the whole capacity should be used, and which individuals to admit to nursing-homes. Since nursing-home residents rarely are discharged, we concentrate on admissions. In order to address these questions, insight into the process governing the allocation of nursing home beds is necessary. The procedure for admitting residents to nursing homes differs somewhat between municipalities, but the admittance decision is commonly taken by an administrative unit operating separately from the nursing homes. Since the number of beds (rooms) in a nursing home in the short run is exogenously given, a bed usually becomes available because a resident dies. Very rarely, a bed may become available because a nursing home resident is transferred to a hospital for terminal care. Nursing home residents are almost never transferred to home care, except in the very few cases when they want to stay their last days of life at home. When a nursing home bed becomes available, it is in most municipalities supposed to be filled immediately, within a week or so, by the non-institutionalized person in highest "need". An application must be filed to be considered for admittance to a nursing home. The application may be filed by the applicant himself or herself, by employees in home care, by a medical doctor, or by relatives of the applicant. Municipalities are not allowed to have waiting lists for nursing homes.[4]

[3]User fees for nursing homes are deducted directly from the pension of nursing home residents. Since Norway has a mandatory public pension system covering all Norwegian citizens, municipalities have almost no problems with user fees that are not paid. Notice also that the wealth Norwegian nursing home residents have accumulated do not affect the user fee they pay, except through the interest income that this wealth may generate. This stands at sharp contrast to the user fee systems in some other European countries, the US, etc.

[4]A central government by-law states that municipalities are not allowed to have waiting lists for nursing homes. In every county there is a County Governor, appointed by the Central Government. The County Governor surveys that municipalities within the county adhere to Norwegian law

Nursing home residence is almost always offered to an individual who have received extensive home care, usually for an extended period of time. Hence, except in rare cases, the "allocation office" has substantial information about the "needs" of potential nursing-home residents.

3 Theoretical Model

3.1 The Demand for Nursing Home Care

Assume that users of long-term care are guided by a state-contingent utility function. There are two mutually exclusive states, corresponding to two living arrangements: residing in a private home or in a nursing home. The rationale behind the state-contingent utility-function is that the type of living arrangement may have a profound impact on the utility an individual derives from care and other goods, as well as from leisure. If residing in a nursing home, the utility function is $U_N(x_N^i, y_N^i, d_N^i, c_N^i, l_N^i; \alpha^i)$. If the individual lives in a private home, the utility function is $U_H(x_H^i, y_H^i, d_H^i, c_H^i, l_H^i; \alpha^i)$. Here c_j^i is the volume of care, x_j^i and y_j^i are the volumes of two composite goods, d_j^i is a vector of housing characteristics, l_j^i is leisure, and α^i is a vector of individual characteristics (j = H, N).[5]

For a nursing home resident, total care is $c_N^i = \overline{q}_N^i + \overline{z}_N^i + s_N^i$, where s_N^i is self-care, $\overline{z}_N^i$ is care provided by the nursing home, and $\overline{q}_N^i$ is informal care.[6] For self-care we assume the production function $\gamma^i G(t_N^i)$, where t_N^i is the individual's input of own time, and $\gamma^i > 0$ is an exogenous productivity factor. The G-function has the first and second-order derivatives $G_t > 0$ and $G_{tt} < 0$.[7] The individual's time budget is $T = l_N^i + t_N^i$, where T is total time. The monetary budget constraint for a nursing home resident is $r^i = x_N^i + p_N^i$, where r^i is the exogenous after-tax income, x_N^i is the numeraire good, with unit price 1, and p_N^i is the user fee for the nursing home. The user fee is payment for a bundle of goods including formal care services, housing in a nursing home, and a composite good provided

and central government by-laws. Some municipalities use, however, short-term places in nursing homes for taking care of those in need of nursing home care who cannot immediately be offered a permanent place.

[5]Ettner (1994) modelled the choice between care in a nursing home and in a private home in an alternative way. She introduced quality of care as a basic good in the utility function, and assumed separate production functions for quality of care at home and in a nursing home.

[6]Hoerger et al. (1996) abstract from informal care in nursing homes. The case for abstracting from informal care in nursing homes is likely to be much stronger in the case of Norway than in the US case considered by Hoerger et al. On the other hand, also nursing home residents receive some informal care. For instance, visitors may assist them at meals.

[7]Since we here consider only non-working individuals with larger or smaller functionality-problems, it seems natural to assume $\gamma^i G_t < 1$, but our results do not require such an assumption.

by the nursing home, i.e. the set $\left(\overline{z}_N^i, \overline{y}_N^i, \overline{d}_N^i\right)$, where the bars indicate that these variables are determined by the nursing home, and hence are exogenous to the resident. Notice that the charge a resident pays for staying in a Norwegian nursing home is independent of the volume of care-services received. In other words, once an individual is admitted to a nursing home, he or she is fully insured against additional expenditures due to low functionality, expensive drugs, etc. Inserting the monetary budget, the time constraint and the production function for self-care into the utility function we obtain $U_N\left(r^i - p_N^i, \overline{y}_N^i, \overline{d}_N^i, \overline{q}_N^i + \overline{z}_N^i + \gamma^i G\left(t_N^i\right), T - t_N^i; \alpha^i\right)$. Maximizing this w.r.t. t_N^i, yields the first-order condition $u_l^i/u_{c_N}^i = \gamma^i G_t^i$, which solves for the supply of time to self-care conditional on nursing-home residence: $t_N^i = f\left(r^i - p_N^i, \overline{y}_N^i, \overline{d}_N^i, \overline{q}_N^i + \overline{z}_N^i, \gamma^i, \alpha^i\right)$. Hence, we obtain the individual's indirect utility function conditional on living in a nursing home: $V_N\left(r^i - p_N^i, \overline{y}_N^i, \overline{d}_N^i, \overline{q}_N^i + \overline{z}_N^i, \gamma^i; \alpha^i\right)$.

For an individual living in a private home, the total volume of care is $c_H^i = \overline{z}_H^i + \overline{q}_H^i + s_H^i$, where $\overline{z}_H^i$ and $\overline{q}_H^i$ are care provided by formal and informal caregivers respectively. Formal and informal caregivers are both assumed to have productivity 1 in the production of care, and both of these forms of care are taken to be exogenous to the care-recipient, as indicated by the bar on the variables. Since the private market for home care in Norway is almost non-existent, we assume that formal care exclusively is provided by the municipality. Hence, the monetary budget is $r^i = x_H^i + w_H^i y_H^i + p_H^i \overline{z}_H^i + k_H^i \overline{d}_H^i$, with p_H^i, w_H^i and k_H^i being the user fee per hour of home care, the unit price of the y-good, and a unit price vector for housing characteristics. This implies $U_H\left(r^i - w_H^i y_H^i - p_H^i \overline{z}_H^i - k_H^i \overline{d}_H^i, y_H^i, \overline{d}_H^i, \overline{q}_H^i + \overline{z}_H^i + \gamma^i G\left(t_H^i\right), T - t_H^i; \alpha^i\right)$, where $\gamma^i G(t_H^i)$ is self-care. We assume that an individual who lives in a private home at the point of time when transfer to a nursing home becomes an option to consider will continue to live in the same dwelling as before he or she became frail, hence the bar on $\overline{d}_H^i$. In our view this is more realistic than assuming that housing also towards the end of life in the community is optimally chosen, like assumed inter alia by Hoerger et al. (1996). High transaction costs, and an expectation that the time to enjoy a more suitable dwelling might be short, may make it optimal not to adjust size and type of dwelling late in life. Maximizing individual utility w.r.t. t_H^i and y_H^i yields the first-order conditions $u_{l_H}^i/u_{c_H}^i = \gamma^i G_t^i$ and $u_{x_H}^i = u_{y_H}^i/w_H^i$, which together with the constraints solve for the individual's supply of time to self-care, and the demand for the two composite goods. From this we obtain the individual's indirect utility function conditional on residing in a private home: $V_H\left(r^i - p_H^i \overline{z}_H^i - k_H^i \overline{d}_H^i, \overline{d}_H^i, \overline{q}_H^i + \overline{z}_H^i, \gamma^i; \alpha^i\right)$.

An individual will demand nursing home care if the utility derived from such care exceeds the utility of receiving home care, i.e. if the following inequality is fulfilled:

$$\begin{aligned} &V_N\left(r^i - p_N^i, \overline{y}_N^i, \overline{d}_N^i, \overline{q}_N^i + \overline{z}_N^i, \gamma^i; \alpha^i\right) \\ &- V_H\left(r^i - p_H^i \overline{z}_H^i - k_H^i \overline{d}_H^i, \overline{d}_H^i, \overline{q}_H^i + \overline{z}_H^i, \gamma^i; \alpha^i\right) > 0, \end{aligned} \tag{1}$$

Through the provision of home care an individual is offered, the care-office may influence heavily the optimum choice of individuals. In particular, if the volume of home care provided by the municipality is very limited, a large number of frail individuals may increase their utility if they were transferred to a nursing home, and hence demand this form of care. Moreover, notice that a sudden drop in informal care, or in the productivity of self-care, may throw an individual into a situation where a nursing home may be the preferred living arrangement, in particular if the individual resides in a dwelling not suitable for a frail person.

3.2 *Admission to Nursing Homes*

Admissions of individuals to nursing homes are in Norway determined by the municipality in which people live. There is a step-wise decision-process. At the first stage, resources are allocated to broad sectors like long-term care, education, etc. Next, each municipality appropriates budgets to nursing homes and the home care sector.[8] Finally, nursing-home beds and hours of home care are allocated to individuals. We establish a descriptive (positive) model for this last step in this allocation process. In particular we want to explain which individuals become nursing home residents. Before turning to this issue we take, however, a brief look at the economic-political environment within which these decisions are taken.

Our starting point is that politicians in a democratic society must be responsive to the preferences of the electorate, as embedded in the individual utility functions. Local government politicians do not, however, possess detailed information on individuals. Their information is confined to aggregate indicators like the number of individuals in age-categories containing many in need of care, the number of school-aged children, etc. Based on such information, Aaberge et al. (2010), Strömberg (2006), and others examine how municipalities allocate funds to major sectors.[9]

[8]Usually there are, in each municipality, separate budgets for home nursing, home help, and for each nursing home. In order not to overload the model we assume, however, that there is only one home care sector (encompassing home help and home nursing), and only one nursing home in each municipality.

[9]Strömberg (2006) demonstrates that decisions at the political level of municipalities may be modelled in a median voter framework, and is explicit on the connection between political and individual choices. His model is particularly appropriate for the Scandinavian context, but

Theisen (2015) examines the additional step of how long-term care resources are allocated to nursing homes and home care, i.e. the how a municipality's nursing-home bed-capacity and the home care budget are determined.

We assume that local government politicians, in order to come around the problem that they have limited information on individuals' "need" for care, assign the responsibility for deciding which individuals to admit to a nursing home, and for allocating home care to those residing in private homes, to a separate administrative body, a Bureau-Of-Care (BOC).[10] The fact that the BOC is a pure administrative body, providing no care-services itself, and operating separately from the day-to-day management of nursing homes and home care, is important, as it sets aside much of the self-interest that might come into play if decisions on service allocation and actual service provision were handled by the same administrative body. We assume that the superiors of the BOC implement a reward-structure that contains incentives for the BOC-employees to act according to the assigned tasks. This reward-structure may contain implicit promises of wage-rises, and/or advancement to higher administrative positions in the municipality for BOC-employees that adhere to the goals assigned by their superiors. In order to further support the bureau's focus on the assigned tasks, notice that the municipality normally recruits care-professionals, like nurses, perhaps also with administrative experience, as BOC-employees. Through their education and work-experience, such employees are likely to have acquired care-based preferences.[11] Hence, we assume that BOC-employees obtain on-the-job utility from allocating care-recipients to what a health professional would consider to be the "right" form of care, and from allocating a "proper amount" of care to each care-recipient.

differs substantially from the traditional median voter model, and also from the vein of research originating from Barr and Davis (1966).

[10]The exact organization differs between municipalities. Hence, the assumption that there is a BOC should to some extent be interpreted as an *as-if* assumption. The assignment of narrow tasks seems, however, typical to public bureaus, presumably in order to secure political control with main priorities in the public sector, to reduce problems of monitoring, to facilitate implementation of incentives in the forms of a reward structure, and to promote team-behavior within each bureau.

[11]This corresponds well with the statement of Niskanen (1971, page 23) that "Bureaucrats are not "just folks" any more than ball players, businessmen, and bishops are "just folks". They have different latent and developed characteristics, just as individuals in other professions have different characteristics." Culyer (1970) has suggested that preferences of a similar kind may be relevant in higher education. In a discussion of university teachers' role in selecting students to be admitted to universities he argues that "In general, they (university teachers) may be expected as utility maximizers to choose those students from which they derive the most enjoyment in teaching, who have the best capacity for learning, who will subsequently reflect upon them to their professional credit and who will, perhaps, for various reasons have a good chance of holding powerful political positions later in life."

Based on these arguments, and in accordance with Theisen (1997) and Langørgen (2004), we assume that the BOC's preferences for nursing home care for an individual may be formalized through the assessment function $W_N(d_N^i; c_N^i, \alpha^i)$. Here, c_N^i is the sum of the formal care, $\overline{z}_N^i$, that the nursing home will provide, the self-care, $\overline{s}_N^i$, that the individual will produce in a nursing home environment, and the small amount of informal care, $\overline{q}_N^i$. Notice that $\overline{z}_N^i$ is a decision variable of the nursing home, while $\overline{s}_N^i$ is a decision variable of the individual, hence they are both exogenous to the BOC. We assume that the $\overline{z}_N^i$'s and $\overline{s}_N^i$'s for individuals in a nursing home are determined through a simultaneous full information non-cooperative Nash-game. Under reasonable assumptions, this game will have a unique and stable equilibrium. In equilibrium, the $\overline{z}_N^i$'s and $\overline{s}_N^i$'s will be functions of the manpower-budget of the nursing home, the productivity-parameters of the nursing home residents, and the volume of informal care they enjoy. Since the staff-residents ratio in Norwegian nursing homes is fairly standardized (due to central government regulations), we assume, however, that the $\overline{z}_N^i$'s and $\overline{s}_N^i$'s are determined only by the productivity parameters and informal care. Conditional on $d_N^i = 1$, the assessment function then gives the BOC's utility from allocating individual i to a nursing home as a function of the individual's self-care productivity and volume of informal care. The more care the individual is estimated to enjoy in a nursing home, the higher utility we assume that the BOC will obtain from allocating the individual to such care.

For home care we assume that the BOC's preferences may be formalized by the assessment function $W_H\left(c_H^i; \overline{d}_H^i, \alpha^i\right)$ where $\overline{d}_H^i$ is chosen by the individual prior to the time we now consider and hence is exogenous to the BOC. We assume that the first derivative of the assessment function for home-care with respect to care is non-negative and that the second derivative is non-positive: $W_H^{i\,\prime} \geq 0$ and $W_H^{i\,\prime\prime} \leq 0$. Moreover, we assume that the BOC gains no utility from those living in private homes but receiving no care, i.e. $W_H^i\left(0; \overline{d}_H^i, \alpha^i\right) = 0$.

Before proceeding one important caveat should be made. While the decentralization of care decisions may solve the problem that politicians have insufficient individual information, it may give rise to a new problem: Once the BOC is established, there clearly is a possibility that it may develop preferences different from those of local government politicians and the electorate. In particular, in accordance with the theory of Migué and Bélanger (1974) one might suspect the BOC to have preferences for slack. Through the budget system the superiors of the BOC may, however, more or less close the possibility for obtaining substantial slack. The trick is that the BOC's superiors impose three strictly separate budget constraints on the BOC. There is one budget constraint for the current expenditures of the office, one for home care, and one for nursing homes. The BOC neither has the permission nor the ability to transfer resources between these three budgets. Hence, it is only from the modest office-budget that the BOC may obtain slack. Since a slack from this source does not intervene with the allocation of individuals between home care and institutional care, and the allocation of home care, we here abstract from slack.

Assume now that the budget for home care is $B_H = \sum_{i=1}^{M} z^i$, and that the BOC's aggregate utility from home care is $\sum_{i=1}^{M} W_H\left(c_H^i; \overline{d}_H^i, \alpha^i\right)$.[12] The BOC's optimal allocation of home care will then be the solution to:

$$\underbrace{Max}_{z_H^1 \ldots z_H^M} \left\{\sum_{i=1}^{M} W_H\left(c_H^i; \overline{d}_H^i, \alpha^i\right)\right\} \text{ s.t } B_H = \sum_{i=1}^{M} z^i, \text{ and } \overline{q}_H^i, \overline{s}_H^i, \forall i. \quad (2)$$

The solution to this problem is the BOC's allotment functions for home care:

$$z_H^i = \begin{cases} 0 & \text{for } W_H^{i\,\prime} < \lambda \\ g^i\left(B_H, \overline{q}_H^1, .., \overline{q}_H^M, \overline{s}_H^1, .., \overline{s}_H^M, \overline{d}_H^1, .., \overline{d}_H^M\right) & \text{for } W_H^{i\,\prime} = \lambda \end{cases}, \forall i, \quad (3)$$

where λ is the BOC's marginal utility of home care. The allotment functions give the optimal allotment to each individual conditional on the individual's production of self-care and the informal care they receive. In order to see what the allotment functions imply, let us consider two individuals living in the same type of dwelling and with the same α^i. Assume that both individuals receive home care. Individual A receives in optimum 2 units of formal home care, 2 units of informal care, self-supplies 2 units of self-care, and hence enjoys in total 6 units of home care. Individual B receives only 1 unit of informal care, and supplies 1 unit of self-care. In optimum individual B will then be provided 4 units of formal home care. In other words, within the group of home-care users, initial differences in total care will be fully compensated by the BOC. This is a direct consequence of our assumption that the assessment functions are general, i.e. not individual-specific. Total care enjoyed by those who receive formal home care will, however, fall short of total (self and informal) care enjoyed by individuals who receive no formal care, i.e. those for whom $W_H^{i\,\prime} < \lambda$. In other words, the BOC in effect functions as an insurance mechanism where all individuals receiving home care enjoy the same volume of total care, but there is not full insurance against loss of self-care productivity or access to informal care. The difference between full and actual insurance in our allotment model has a counterpart in the concept of "*unmet need*" frequently used in the nursing literature. Furthermore, notice that there in our allotment model is no insurance against differences in individual's use of own time. Finally, there is—through the BOC—no insurance against the economic consequences that different use of home care gives rise to. If the two individuals here considered have different incomes, however, the income-dependent user fees give a partial insurance against *economic* consequences of different allotments. We will argue that the kind of insurance implied by the BOC's allotment behavior is

[12] Since we in the empirical part of this paper have no information on differences in unit costs of care between different individuals, we abstract from this possibility also in the theoretical model.

likely to be in good accordance with the preferences of the electorate and the local government politicians.

The allotment functions give the optimal allotment to each individual conditional on the individual's access to informal care and self-supply of care. Similarly, the individual's optimal choice of self-care is conditional on its access to informal care and the BOC's provision of formal home care. The interaction between the BOC and individuals may therefore be modelled as a simultaneous full information non-cooperative Nash-game.[13] Under reasonable assumptions this game has a unique stable equilibrium. In equilibrium, the use of home care for each individual will be a function of this individual's informal care received, its self-care productivity, income, consumption of housing and the home care budget in the municipality. Since we mainly are interested in which individuals that become nursing home residents, we abstain from discussing in more detail the allocation of home care.

Consider now the BOC's choice of individuals to direct to nursing home residence. Assume that nursing-home residents cannot be discharged.[14] The death of a nursing home resident is then the only way that a nursing home bed may become available for a new person. Furthermore, assume that the BOC is instructed by its superiors to allocate a new individual from home care to the nursing home as soon as a bed in a nursing home becomes available.[15] The question is who the BOC will allocate to the available nursing home bed. The problem can be formalized as follows: Pick the individual that will give the BOC the highest increase in utility, i.e. the individual for whom, with $d_N^i = 1$ inserted, the following expression is maximal:

$$\begin{aligned} \Delta W^i = {} & W_N\left(\overline{q}_N^i + \overline{z}_N^i + \overline{s}_N^i; d_N^i, \alpha_i\right) \\ & - W_H\left(\overline{q}_H^i + \overline{z}_H^i + \overline{s}_H^i; \overline{d}_H^i, \alpha_i\right) + \lambda \overline{z}_H^i \end{aligned}, \quad \forall i, \tag{4}$$

[13]Perhaps needless to say, the assumption that the game is a full information game represents a simplification. Notice, however, that the BOC has substantial information on heavy home care users, since these usually have been within "the system" for a long time period. Information on marginal home care users may be more limited. For an analysis of how uncertainty of individual characteristics may affect allotments, see Theisen (1997).

[14]An exception may be cases when the individual itself, and/or his or her relatives, explicitly wants it. There are very few such cases, though. Also the BOC itself is likely to have self-interest in adhering to the guideline that nursing home residents cannot be discharged. The reason is that discharge of a nursing home resident most likely would give rise to strong conflicts with nursing home residents and their relatives, as well as with politicians.

[15]There is a simple rationale behind the assumption that the BOC's superiors instruct the BOC that the bed-capacity of nursing homes should be utilized 100 %: In a nursing home, capital costs, the bulk of the wage costs, and also several additional current expenditures like cleaning the buildings, heating, etc. are not affected by leaving a small share of the capacity unused for a short period of time. Taken together cost components that in the short run are fixed amount to more than 90 % of total nursing home costs. Moreover, the small costs that might be saved in the short run if not utilizing the nursing home capacity fully are likely to fall considerably short of the costs of providing home care to a heavy home-care user. Consequently, we assume that the care-office operates under the hard budget constraint that nursing home capacity has to be fully used.

The two first terms on the r.h.s. give the BOC's net increase in utility from transferring individual i form home care to a nursing home. The last term, where λ is the BOC's marginal utility of home care, gives the utility that the BOC may gain from re-allocating the home care resources initially provided to individual i to other home care users. From our previous analysis, we have that W_N is a function of the self-care productivity and informal care, W_H is a function of self-care productivity, informal care received, income, consumption of housing and the home care budget. Finally, for a given municipality $\lambda \bar{z}_H^i$, is a function of the same factors as W_H.

To complete our model one more element must be added: in municipalities' with a large nursing home budget relative to the aggregate "needs" of the population, the BOC's marginal utility of home care will be lower than in municipalities where nursing-home beds are more scarce. In other words, λ will be a function of the number of nursing home beds relative to the needs of the population.

Two exogenous factors are likely to be very important for whether an individual is admitted to a nursing home. The first is a drop in the individual's productivity in self-care, which usually will lead to a substantial drop in the volume of self-care. The second is a drop in informal care, for instance due to the death of a spouse for those living in a private home. If it would take a large increase in publicly provided home care to compensate for such exogenous changes, the BOC will, in our model, give this individual high priority when it comes to admission to the nursing home.

Notice that in a period when many places in the nursing home sector of a municipality become available, the threshold for admission to a nursing home may be lower. Moreover, if we consider the individuals residing in a nursing home at a specific point in time, their self-care productivity may have developed differently since they were admitted. Consequently, we expect that there may be considerable variation in the functionality-level of those who are in nursing homes at a specific point in time. Moreover, the constraint that no individual will be discharged from a nursing home implies that full re-optimization at every point of time is disregarded from. Hence, it should be no surprise if we at a specific point in time may find some individuals living in their private homes with a lower level of self-care productivity and/or lower access to informal care than some nursing home residents. These would, however, be strong candidates for admission to nursing homes.

4 Empirical Model

The probability that an individual will be observed as a nursing home resident is the product of the probability that the individual demands nursing home care, and the probability that the individual is allotted nursing-home care, conditional on having demanded such care. Ideally, we would like to estimate both of these probabilities. This is, however, very challenging. Hence, like Scanlon (1980) and most other researchers we delimit ourselves to estimate the joint probability that an individual who demand nursing home care is also allotted such care.

Specifically, we use a logit model to estimate the probability that an individual resides in a nursing home at a specific point of time. From the previous section, it follows that the probability that an individual is admitted to a nursing home depends on self-care productivity, informal care received, individual income, the pre-determined consumption of housing, the home care budget, and the number of nursing home beds available. These factors are also assumed to determine the probability that an individual will be a nursing home resident at a specific point in time.

We assume that an individual's self-care productivity is a function of its age, functionality, and gender. Age is almost always included among the explanatory variables in studies of which individuals that enter or reside in a nursing home. Presumably, age may have a non-linear impact on the probability of being a nursing home resident. To some extent this may be accounted for by the logit-function, but in order to examine whether age has a more complex impact, we will in addition to a plain age-variable consider age-class dummies and a spline function.

Our measure of self-care productivity is based on measures of individuals' functionality (ADL, IADL, etc.). There are 17 different functionality-measures at our disposal, but some of these may be of little relevance when it comes to whether an individual is a nursing home resident or not. Moreover, some of the functionality indicators are likely to be highly correlated. Consequently, we aggregate the functionality-measures into the four main categories that measure the individual's ability in doing housework, ability in providing self-care, cognitive and decision-making ability, and his or her mobility. Moreover, in order to facilitate the interpretation of the results within our theoretical model, we convert the original indicators to our productivity-indicator, γ^i. Our γ^i -indicators are contained in the interval $\gamma^i \in [0.2, 1.0]$, with 1.0 corresponding to full functionality, and 0.2 to very high need for assistance. Admittedly, the lower bound of γ^i is somewhat arbitrarily set, but since it seems natural to affiliate $\gamma^i = 0$ with a dead person, we have chosen the lower bound of γ^i somewhat larger than zero.

Since admission to nursing homes is rationed, the capacity of the nursing home sector is likely to be a decisive variable for the probability of residing in a nursing home. A straightforward measure of this capacity would be the number of beds in nursing homes per inhabitant in the municipality. It is more common, though, to use a measure like the number of beds per inhabitant above say 80 years of age, i.e. the bed-capacity relative to an aggregate measure of need. In our view it is, however, rather arbitrary to draw a sharp distinction between individuals below and above 80 years of age. In order to avoid such a dichotomy, we will instead measure the capacity of the nursing home sector in each municipality as the number of beds divided by the number of persons who can be expected to die within 1 year. This measure weighs together persons in all age-classes, but gives substantially higher weight to the very old than to the younger. Notice also that when we use national death-rates in weighing together the age-variables, our measure will not be a measure of population age (distance from birth), but of distance to death. Since a large share of the population die as nursing home residents, this measure seems appropriate. Zweifel et al. (1999) argue strongly that distance to death is likely to be a more relevant variable than calendar age for explaining individuals' use of health care services. In my view, the argument for emphasizing distance to death is even stronger in the case of admittance to nursing homes.

In line with our theoretical model, we also include a measure of the capacity of the home-care sector, measured as the total number of home care hours per individual who are expected to die in the course of 1 year. Finally, we include the supply of sheltered dwellings, measured as the total number of such dwellings per individual expected to die in the course of 1 year. Sheltered dwellings are housing units that are meant to be occupied by individuals in need of care, and may be organized as rental dwellings owned by municipalities, co-operative dwellings, or dwellings owned by the residents. Sheltered dwellings are often located close to a nursing home or a home-care center. Hence, residents in sheltered dwellings often have better access to home care than those living in ordinary dwellings. Presumably, the more sheltered dwellings there is in a municipality, the lower will be the probability that an individual becomes a nursing home resident.[16] Our dummy variable for sheltered dwellings is the only measure we have that represent $\overline{d}_H^i$ in our theoretical model.

According to our theoretical model, we should also include a measure of individual incomes among the independent variables of our empirical model. We have not had access to income data, but in our view this is not very problematic. Firstly, notice that within our theoretical model, it is income net of expenditures on rationed goods and the predetermined housing goods that matter. Due to the income dependent user fees and the presumption that rich households have much higher expenditures on housing, the relevant income measure differs much less between household than do the full after tax income. Secondly, in our theoretical model income mainly affects the allocation of the two composite commodities. The allocation of time, which in our context is most important, is less affected by income. Finally, in their empirical analysis, Øien et al. (2012) found that individual incomes had no impact on municipalities' allocation between home care and nursing home care.

5 Data and Descriptive Statistics

Our sample is drawn from the administrative register IPLOS, which contains all Norwegian residents who have applied for and/or used at least one of 22 different publicly provided long-term care services or benefits. In this paper we delimit the

[16]Residents in rental sheltered dwellings pay a rent equal to the full cost of this living arrangement, and those who live in co-operative sheltered dwellings also carry the full costs of their housing arrangement. Through the State Housing Bank construction of sheltered dwellings may receive a subsidy of maximum 20 % of the building costs. This benefit is supposed to be transferred to the occupants of sheltered housing. Moreover, residents in sheltered dwellings pay exactly the same for home care as those living in ordinary private homes.

Table 1 Variable definitions

Variable	Definition
Nursing home	Binary variable equal to 1 if the individual is in a long-term nursing home at the end of the year 2010, 0 if not.
Age	Age of the individual at the end of the year 2010.
Age_S45	Age_S45 = (Age −45) if Age ≥ 45, equal to 0 if Age < 45.
Age Ω	Binary variable equal to 1 if the individual is in the 5-year age class Ω_t, otherwise 0, with Ω = 5 for age class 5–9, Ω = 10 for age class 10–14, … Ω = 105 for age class above 105. Age class 0 (0–4) is the left our category.
Male	Binary variable equal to 1 if male, otherwise 0.
Housework	Average productivity in (1) general housework, (2) preparation of meals, measured on a scale 0.2–1.0.
Self-care	Average productivity in (1) taking care of own health, (2) personal hygiene, (3) dressing/undressing, (4) eating, (5) toilet function; measured on a scale 0.2–1.0.
Cognitive	Average ability in (1) cognitive matters, (2) taking decisions in daily life, measured on a scale 0–1.0.
Mobility	Average ability in (1) indoors mobility, and (2) outdoors mobility, measured on a scale 0.2–1.0.
Inf_Ψ	Binary variable equal to 1 if weekly hours of informal care is in the interval Ψ, where Ψ = 0_3 denotes the interval (0, 3), Ψ = 3_9 the interval (3, 9), Ψ = 9_15 the interval, (9, 15), Ψ = 15+ the interval above 15, Ψ = *UNK* if informal care is received in unknown volume.
NursingCap.	The number of nursing home beds in the municipality, divided by the number of individuals in the municipality that are expected to die in the course of 2010.
ShelterCap.	The number of sheltered dwellings in the municipality, divided by the number of individuals in the municipality that are expected to die in the course of 2010.
HomeCap.	Total home care hours provided by the municipality, divided by the number of individuals in the municipality that are expected to die in the course of 2010.

sample to the subset of 262 932 individuals who *at the end of 2010* were included in the register. This sample constitutes roughly 5 % of the total Norwegian population, and somewhat more than 9 % of the individuals in the sample were permanent residents in long-term care institutions. We have linked the individual data from the IPLOS-register with municipality-level data for the capacity of the nursing home sector, the capacity of sheltered dwellings, and the capacity of the home care sector in each municipality in the same year.[17] Table 1 provides precise definitions of all variables we use in the empirical analysis, and Table 2 contains descriptive statistics for these variables. Figures 1, 2 and 3 provide additional distributional information on the variables.

[17]We downloaded municipality-level data from the data base KOSTRA, which is available from Statistics Norway.

Table 2 Descriptive statistics

Variable	Mean	Standard dev.	Minimum	Maximum
Nursing home	0.0919	0.2888	0	1
Age	67.1643	24.0936	0	109
Male	0.3668	0.4819	0	1
Housework	0.6933	0.2675	0.2	1
Self-care	0.8067	0.2053	0.2	1
Cognitive	0.8183	0.2282	0.2	1
Mobility	0.8027	0.2322	0.2	1
Inf_0_3	0.2151	0.4109	0	1
Inf_3_9	0.0858	0.2801	0	1
Inf_9_15	0.0230	0.1499	0	1
Inf_15+	0.0589	0.2354	0	1
Inf_UKN	0.1386	0.3456	0	1
NursingCap.	1.0524	0.2743	0.2854	4.3071
ShelterCap.	0.7101	0.3487	0.0747	2.7719
HomeCap.	53.3379	17.2190	3.0138	216.4667

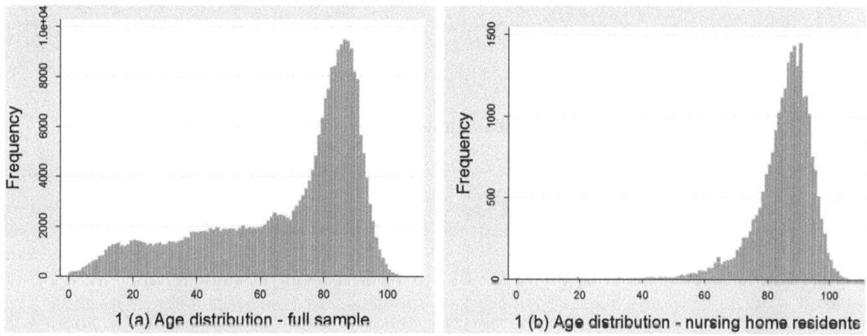

Fig. 1 Age distributions

6 Empirical Results

Table 3 presents the results from estimating three different specifications of the logit-equation. The specifications differ only in how age is accounted for. In all specifications, most of the independent variables have a statistically significant impact on the probability of being a nursing home resident. Moreover, as seen from McFadden's pseudo R-sq. statistic, the fit of all estimated specifications is good and at the same level.

Consider first the results for the age-variable in Specification A, where age is measured by a set of dummy variables. The results show clearly that age has no impact on the probability of nursing home residence for individuals below 45–50 years, a fact that also can be seen from Fig. 1(b). As soon as an individual's age

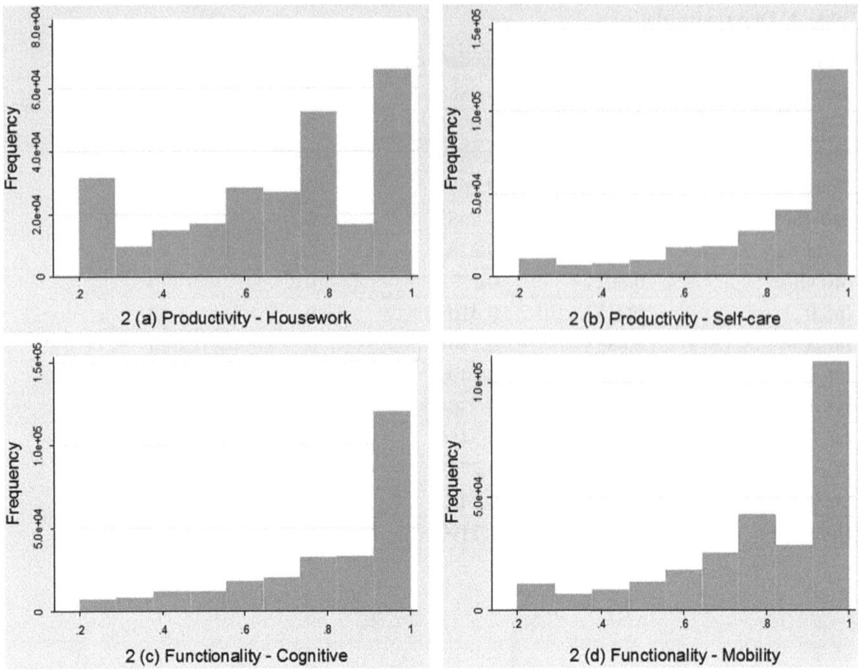

Fig. 2 Productivity and functionality distributions

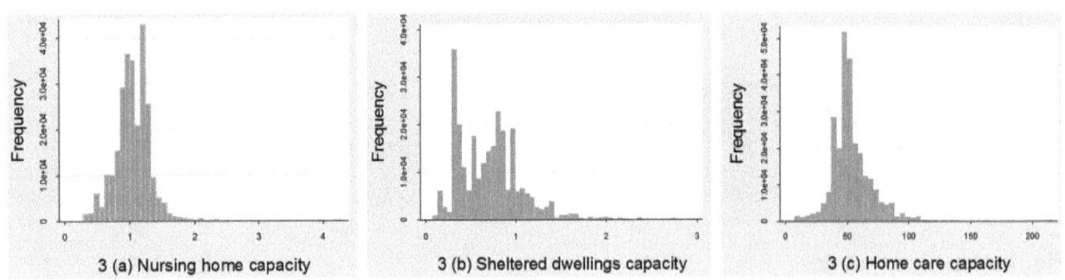

Fig. 3 Capacity distributions for nursing homes, sheltered dwellings and home care

exceeds 45, the probability of nursing home residence increases, however, and the higher the age, the higher is the probability of nursing home residence. Since the estimated coefficients affiliated with the age-dummies increase surprisingly linearly with age above 50, we have in Specification B replaced the age-dummies with a plain age-variable, and in Specification C with a spline-function where only age above 45 counts. The coefficient of the age-variable in Specification C is estimated with greater precision than the corresponding coefficient in Specification B, while the estimates and precision of the other coefficients are little affected. The overall fit of the three equations also differ little. Hence, Specification C is our preferred specification.

Table 3 Estimation results. *Dependent*: Nursing home, N = 262 932, t-values in parentheses

	Specification A		Specification B		Specification C	
Age 5	−1.7028	(−2.36)				
Age 10	−0.5299	(1.05)				
Age 15	0.2828	(0.61)				
Age 20	−0.7701	(−1.56)				
Age 25	−0.5396	(−1.10)				
Age 30	−0.0538	(−0.12)				
Age 35	0.0505	(0.11)				
Age 40	0.2044	(0.45)				
Age 45	0.2238	(0.50)				
Age 50	0.8310	(1.89)				
Age 55	1.5039	(3.47)				
Age 60	2.2314	(5.18)				
Age 65	2.5004	(5.81)				
Age 70	3.1216	(7.28)				
Age 75	3.3920	(7.92)				
Age 80	3.5322	(8.26)				
Age 85	3.7782	(8.84)				
Age 90	4.0938	(9.57)				
Age 95	4.4828	(10.45)				
Age 100	5.0092	(11.33)				
Age 105	4.8477	(6.91)				
Age			0.0689	(82.75)		
Age_S45					0.0770	(89.33)
Male	−0.2077	(−9.82)	−0.1858	(−8.84)	−0.1701	(−8.09)
Housework	−0.3355	(−7.94)	−0.3197	(−7.56)	−0.3410	(−8.09)
Self-care	−3.7480	(−42.54)	−3.7848	(−43.12)	−3.7800	(−43.05)
Cognitive	−3.4393	(−67.33)	−3.4094	(−66.93)	−3.4050	(−66.73)
Mobility	−0.4028	(−6.57)	−0.3802	(−6.22)	−0.3643	(−5.97)
Inf_0_3	−1.0291	(−39.62)	−1.0298	(−39.67)	−1.0365	(−39.87)
Inf_3_9	−1.6694	(−37.63)	−1.6668	(−37.56)	−1.6792	(−37.78)
Inf_9_15	−1.9138	(−22.30)	−1.9012	(−22.14)	−1.9203	(−22.37)
Inf_15_m	−2.1606	(−36.03)	−2.1110	(−35.20)	−2.1685	(−36.44)
Inf_UKN	−1.4790	(−40.18)	−1.4634	(−39.75)	−1.4817	(−40.28)
NursingCap	1.3035	(37.15)	1.3119	(37.42)	1.3161	(37.57)
ShelterCap	−0.3565	(−12.27)	−0.3511	(−12.11)	−0.3466	(−11.96)
HomeCap.	−0.0021	(−3.71)	−0.0021	(−3.78)	−0.0020	(−3.56)
Constant	−0.6051	(−1.40)	−2.7922	(−29.79)	−0.0431	(−0.61)
Pseudo-Rsq.	0.5115		0.5099		0.5087	
Log-likelih.	−392045		−39333		−39425	
Iterations	7		6		6	

High productivity in self-care and high cognitive ability have a strong, and statistically significant, negative impact on the probability of nursing home residence. By contrast, high housework productivity and high mobility have only a small negative impact on the probability that the person is in a nursing home. As to the results for housework productivity, the likely explanation is that low housework productivity quite easily may be compensated for through the provision of home help, thereby precluding institutionalization. The likely explanation why mobility has so small impact on the probability of being in a nursing home is that there in our sample are a number of young wheel-chair users. Presumably, these neither demand nursing home residence, nor do they have substantial problems managing in their private homes. A similar case occurs for individuals who do not hear well or who do not see well. Even if many in these categories are deaf or blind, they do not want to be in a nursing home, and neither are they assessed to need such care. We have estimated Specification C also with functionality-variables for seeing and hearing, and but these variables did not have a significant impact and were hence not included in the final specification.

Perhaps a little surprising, males have a lower probability of being nursing home residents than have females. The magnitude of the estimated coefficient is, however, modest. To get a feeling of how important gender is, let us compare the estimated coefficients for variables Male and Housework. The maximum magnitude of both of these variables is 1, and the estimated coefficient for Housework is −0.34, while it for Male is −0.17. This implies that full productivity in housework reduces the probability of nursing home residence by twice as much as being a man rather than a woman. Hence, men are only marginally less likely to be in a nursing home than women of the same age, self-care productivity etc. The main reason why men are somewhat less likely to live in a nursing home is that the majority of old men still live together with their wife. The wife is usually somewhat younger than the man, and often also in a better health condition. Moreover, when a man and a woman live together in a private home they may provide informal care services to each other. In principle, this should be picked up by our informal care variables, but there may be gains from exploiting comparative advantages in two-person households that are not fully captured by the informal care variables. Such effects are picked up by our Male-variable.

The estimated coefficients of the informal-variables are, as expected, negative and highly significant, and the magnitudes of the estimated coefficients are substantial. Hence, individuals who receive informal care are much less likely to be nursing home residents.

Those who live in municipalities with a high nursing home capacity are, as expected, much more likely to be nursing home residents. That is, an individual of a given age, sex, a given productivity in self-care and housework, a given cognitive and mobility ability, and a given volume of informal care, is more likely to be in a nursing home if the nursing home capacity in the municipality is high. By contrast, a high capacity of sheltered dwellings have an opposite effect, but of much smaller magnitude. The interpretation is that nursing home residence may be reduced by establishing more sheltered dwellings.

Living in a municipality with high home care capacity has a negative, and statistically significant, but not very strong, impact on the probability that an individual of a given age, sex, etc. is a nursing home resident. A likely reason for the small impact of this variable is that a larger home care budget—within our theoretical model—will lead to the same increase in home care to all individuals who initially received such care, and also an extension of home care to individuals who initially did not receive such care. Hence, the increased home care will not be targeted towards those who are closest to become nursing-home residents.

7 Concluding Remarks

We developed a theoretical model describing the allocation of individuals to nursing homes, in a setting where admissions to nursing homes are strictly rationed. Rationing decisions are in our model taken by a separate bureau of care in each municipality. Using a national sample of the total Norwegian "care-population" we examined empirically the impact on the rationing decision of as well individual characteristics as characteristics of the municipalities in which individuals live.

Low productivity in self-care, low cognitive ability, and high age, has a strong positive impact on the probability of becoming a nursing home resident. Low productivity in housework and low mobility also has a positive impact on the probability of becoming a nursing home resident, but the impact of these factors is not very strong. Individuals who receive informal care are less likely to be nursing home residents. Moreover, males are, ceteris paribus, marginally less likely to be nursing-home residents than are females.

In municipalities with a high nursing-home capacity, the incidence of nursing home residence is clearly higher than in municipalities with few nursing-home beds. By contrast, in municipalities with many sheltered dwellings, the incidence of nursing home residence is lower than in municipalities with less access to sheltered dwellings. The capacity of the home care sector has, however, in itself only a small negative impact on the probability that an individual is a nursing home resident. If a municipality wants to reduce the capacity of nursing homes, it should simultaneously increase the capacity of sheltered dwellings and the capacity of the home care sector. The impact of such a change in the structure of care on the municipality's total costs of long-term care, and on the utility of care-recipients, will depend very much on the relative capacity of nursing homes, home care and sheltered dwellings before the change is implemented.

Acknowledgements This paper is part of the project Care for the needy, financed by the Research Council of Norway.

References

Aaberge, R., Bhuller, M., Langørgen, A., & Mogstad, M. (2010). The distributional impact of public services when needs differ. *Journal of Public Economics, 94*(9–10), 549–562.

Barr, J. L., & Davis, O. A. (1966). An elementary political and economic theory of the expenditures of local governments. *Southern Economic Journal, 33*(2), 149–165.

Chiswick, B. R. (1976). The demand for nursing home care: An analysis of the substitution between institutional and non-institutional care. *Journal of Human Resources, 11*(3), 295–316.

Culyer, A. J. (1970). A utility-maximising view of universities. *Scottish Journal of Political Economy, 17*(3), 349–368.

Ettner, S. L. (1994). The effect of the Medicaid home care benefit on long-term care choices of the elderly. *Economic Inquiry, 32*(1), 103–127.

Grabowski, D. C. (2008). The market for long-term care services. *Inquiry, 45*(1), 58–74.

Hoerger, T. J., Picone, G. A., & Sloan, F. A. (1996). Public subsidies, private provision of care and living arrangements of the elderly. *Review of Economics & Statistics, 78*(3), 428–440.

Langørgen, A. (2004). Needs, economic constraints, and the distribution of public home-care. *Applied Economics, 36*(5), 485–496.

Migué, J.-L., & Bélanger, G. (1974). Towards a general theory of managerial discretion. *Public Choice, 17*, 27–47.

Niskanen, W. A., Jr. (1971). *Bureaucracy and representative government*. Chicago: Aldine-Aderthon.

Nyman, J. A. (1989). The private demand for nursing home care. *Journal of Health Economics, 8*(2), 209–231.

Øien, H., Karlsson, M., & Iversen, T. (2012). The impact of financial incentives on the composition of long-term care in Norway. *Applied Economic Perspectives & Policy, 34*(2), 258–274.

Scanlon, W. J. (1980). A theory of the nursing home market. *Inquiry: A Journal of Medical Care Organization, Provision and Financing, 17*(1), 25–41.

Strömberg, D. (2006). *Demography, voting, and public expenditures: Theory and evidence from Swedish municipalities*. Working paper, Stockholm University.

Theisen, T. (1997). Uncertainty and systematic bias in provision of social benefits by a public bureaucracy. *European Journal of Political Economy, 13*(3), 639–659.

Theisen, T. (2015). Municipalities' decision to care: at home or in a nursing home. Paper presented at the 30th Annual Congress of the European Economic Association, Mannheim, August 24–27, 2015.

Zweifel, P., Felder, S., & Meiers, M. (1999). Ageing of population and health care expenditure: A red herring? *Health Economics, 8*(6), 485–496.

Civil Service and the Crisis: A Comparative Analysis of Iberian Countries (2008–2013)

Enrique José Varela-Álvarez, Joaquim Filipe Ferraz Esteves de Araújo, and Óscar Briones Gamarra

1 Introduction

Recent decades have been hard times for civil servants in western countries which systems were under pressure for personnel reforms. The Global Financial Crisis (GFC) brought in an extreme stresses for changes and cutback management in the civil service. These were particularly deep in European Southern countries like Portugal and Spain where governments are introducing budgets cuts and private sector practices in the management of public services to reduce the payroll. As a consequence, many areas of public services have lost their uniqueness and become quite similar to the general employment system. The aim of this chapter is to do a comparative analysis of the changes in Portuguese and Spanish public services in recent years. The research is approached from a qualitative perspective, drawing on the analysis of the legal, historical and political changes.

The current crisis in public administration that erupted abruptly towards the beginning of 2008 mainly due to the international financial crisis has sent shock waves through the countries of Southern Europe, affecting with particular intensity Portugal and Spain (Ramió 2011, 2013, 2015; DGAEP 2013). The impact has been felt in practically all spheres of civil society and in the functions and services

E.J. Varela-Álvarez (✉) • Ó. Briones Gamarra
University of Vigo, Vigo, Spain
e-mail: evalvarez@uvigo.es; oscarbriones@uvigo.es

J.F.F.E. de Araújo
University of Minho, Minho, Portugal
e-mail: jfilipe@eeg.uminho.pt

N. Schofield, G. Caballero (eds.), *State, Institutions and Democracy*,
Studies in Political Economy, DOI 10.1007/978-3-319-44582-3_12

provided by the States for the welfare of citizens[1]. One key area where governments have implemented radical policy reforms has been the human capital of their own organizations. Notwithstanding, these policies have been adopted without any ostensible evidence attesting they enhance the performance or outcomes of public administration or serve to resolve disputes concerning the values and efficiency of the public sector (Echevarría 2010; Arenilla and Delgado 2014).

The aim of this paper was to assess the changing working conditions of public employees in order to shed some light on controversial issues concerning public employment models of central government in Spain and Portugal. The trends and reforms have been analysed to assess the theoretical and ideological approaches underpinning policy reform implemented until the year 2013. In short, the aim of this study was to answer the question: Are reforms implemented due to the international financial crisis simply reforms and cuts in public employment, or do these changes entail a widespread far-reaching transformation in the current public employment models of the two Iberian States? Should the answer be the latter, this would signal the death of the civil servant as key actor the human resource management model of the central government in Spain and Portugal.

To answer this question, the array and impact of political-administrative reforms in human resource management (HRM), according to the terminology used by Yntema (1996), Coleman (2010) and OECD (2013a, b), that have been rushed through by both States (Gorriti 2012) have been analysed to determine if they undermine the principle of good governance in public sector industrial relations, which have prevailed to the present date[2].

Moreover, different types of public employment in the central government of Spain and Portugal, which share similar models of public employment, were analysed as well as the evolutionary trends experienced by both countries in contrast to the diversity that predominates across Europe (Adomonis 2008). Besides comparing central administration of both Iberian states, the data was compared with the figures for the other member states of the Organization for Economic Cooperation and Development (OECD), and the European Union (EU). Data from other territorial tiers of government e.g., regional (autonomous communities as is the case in Spanish) or local administration were not included for study.

[1]If this were not so, one is compelled to ask why there is such controversy concerning the number of public employees in Spain in 2013 ("Are there many public employees in Spain?" Arenilla and Delgado 2014). Moreover, some of the most prominent members of the Academy of Law in Spain have voiced their doubts regarding the performance and outcomes of administrative modernization programs ("We are doing something wrong", stated the daily El País, 20 February 2014, García and Esteve).

[2]In addition to the reforms brought on by the ongoing crisis, Portugal began to significantly modify its civil service management system and enforce extensive public sector cuts as from the year 2005 (Nunes 2008; OECD 2013a, b), with some of these changes occurring a decade before the broad process of administrative modernization (Bouzas and Varela 2005; Rocha and Araújo 2007); which were less austere for civil service management in Spain.

This study is approached from a qualitative perspective in the analysis of the judicial, historical, and socio-political context in order to obtain a descriptive analysis that will serve to elucidate the repercussions of public employment reforms in both Iberian countries during the global economic recession (2008–2013). The comparative method was employed to broaden and maximize the explicative powers of this study, and the limitations inherent to this type of analysis were also in mind (Parrado 2002; Román and Láiz 2003; Brans 2010; Porta 2013). In order to complete the descriptive analysis and to further explore the impact of the global economic recession on public employment system in both Iberian states, particularly since this is one of the first systematic comparative analysis, a quantitative analysis was undertaken of data obtained from secondary sources such as the Organization for Economic Cooperation and Development (OECD 2013a, b), and data from the Ministries responsible for public employment in both countries (MAP 2012; DGAEP 2013).

Data was gathered on public employment reforms, human resource management, and several broad categories[3] to assess aspects such the overall impact on remuneration, working conditions, and other reforms affecting the entire scope of industrial relations in public sector. These categories were derived from the wide array of public expenditure cuts, and in particular those affecting public employees and their working conditions, which have become so crucial that they have become a key element in the strategy of public expenditure cuts. Moreover, the analysis of these data will enable us to determine if these measures were designed to balance budgets and reduce the public debt, and/or if we are witnessing the implementation of major reforms in public employment models that are aligned with the postulates of the New Public Management (NPM) (Hood 1996; Pollitt 1993; Araújo 2002), and the OECD (2008).

However, ideological aspects regarding the beginning of the global economic downturn have been consciously excluded from the study. Thus, the degree to which the current crisis may have been "fabricated" or not by capitalism or neoliberalism, as suggested (Vahid et al. 2011), is an interesting aspect that goes beyond the scope of this study. Many of the policies referred to in this study are in line with the proposals of what Nunes and Castro (2010), and Thompson (2010) have termed "New Public Human Resource Management", that is, the specific academic current of thought on human resource management that embraces the philosophy of NPM[4].

[3]In relation to the categories selected for empirical analysis, one must take into account the problem of generalization of concepts observed in the legislation analysed such as austerity, efficiency, rationalization, and optimization, which are not precise because of the political discourse. A good example, of these, which will not be the object of analysis in this study given its general character, is the *rationalization of bodies and scales of civil servants* as outlined in the public employment legislation introduced by the Spanish Government (Orden PRE/824/2009).

[4]Without carrying out an in-depth analysis on this point, it should be noted that from its very inception in the early 70s of the previous century, New Public Management has always included as part of its discourse policies that are currently being implemented. For instance, the elimination of permanent positions, deteriorating conditions of pay which are subject to criteria of measurable

Furthermore, it is worth noting the "tabula rasa" of the cuts or cut uniformly that have been implemented (Gorriti 2012). Regardless as to whether it is the urgent measures imposed by the "Troika", as politicians from different states claim, or the ideological standpoint as some authors such as Thompson (2010) or even the OECD itself claim (OECD 2013a, b), the fact is that the homogeneous or "lineal" implementation of the cuts is most striking considering the precise timing in which the opposite axiom—performance-based contracting (Heinrich 2010)—had begun to enjoy a certain degree of general political consensus[5]. Underlying these changes is a set of ideas and theories developed by western countries which have had a substantial impact on the public sector.

2 Sources of Change in Civil Service

Recent decades have seen hard times for civil servants in western countries who have come under pressure for labour reforms. The pressures for reforming the labour market brought on by the financial crisis are not new. The deteriorated financial situation of governments coupled with increased demand for better services were major contributors for change in many western countries. The first version of NPM in the 80s of the last century expounded a doctrine of economic rationalism within the political framework of neo-liberalism (Silvestre 2010; Pollitt and Bouckaert 2011). The first principle of NPM is "managerialism", defined by Pollitt (1993) as involving: continued increased efficiency, the use of "ever-more-sophisticated" technologies, a labour force disciplined towards productivity, clear implementation of the professional management role and managers being given the right to manage. NPM regards some features of civil servants, like tenure, career appointment, and promotion through qualifications and seniority as inhibiting greater responsiveness and efficiency.

The introduction of market-based public service management breaks with the notion of the traditional civil service system, and the axiom that public sector organizations are governed through formalized internal management and rule-based modes of actions. Governments elsewhere, for the first time, have questioned the traditional values of public services and the expected value qualifications of public managers (Virtanen 2000; Pollitt 1993; Greener 2009). In many countries the private sector has become the standard to be attained. The goal of NPM reforms was to reduce the distinction between the public sector and the private sector employment (Hood

---

efficiency, eliminating trade union opposition, and bringing the working conditions of public employees in line with the private sector have always been "prescriptions" of this current of thought on public management (Hood 1997).

[5]The initial unpublished research results obtained from the Observatory of Governance of the University of Vigo arrive at the same conclusion i.e., corroborating this consensus on the need for further in-depth analysis of the results on public management, both on a collective and individual level.

1998). Under the influence of NPM some governments have employed private sector analyses of civil service deficiencies with an emphasis on budget allocation and financial management as key priorities. This was the argument used by politicians to initiate reforms to ensure a more flexible, responsive, and performance based public administration (Pollitt and Bouckaert 2011) at a time when the world of government was 'a more anxious and treacherous place' (Peters 1988). In addition, the disaggregation of units in the public sector and quantitative performance controls turned implementation closer to that of management activities (Araújo 2013). Public organizations were considered similar to private organizations, and many of the changes radically influenced the civil service rules, training, and working conditions. It required staff to work to performance targets, indicators and output objectives (performance management); shifting the basis of public employment from permanency and standard national pay and conditions towards team contracts, management related pay, local determination on pay and conditions; and increasing emphasis on service 'quality', standard setting and 'customer responsiveness'.

Finances and economics overshadowed the role of law, political science, philosophy and other long-standing contributors to the theory and practice of public administration. After years of pressures for change endorsed by the NPM and driven by "a group of administrative doctrines that figured prominently in the agenda for bureaucratic reform in OECD countries" (Hood 1996), the 2008 Global Financial Crisis (GFC) brought with it enormous pressure for change and cutback management. These changes challenged even the political-institutional context within which top civil servants work, and undermined the traditional ethos of top civil servants on their own career paths. The dichotomy between private sector management and public administration seems to be "obsolete". This has blurred the traditional boundary between the public and private sectors. The global financial and fiscal crisis has completely altered the agenda of the debate on public services, and increased the impression of a widening gap between 'main street' and political classes (and even the media), which has eroded public confidence in politics in taking the moral lead in guiding us through these turbulent times. In countries like Portugal and Spain, governments have applied management principles to the management of public employees in order to reduce the costs of public employment. Consequently, many areas of public employment have lost their uniqueness and have become quite similar to private sector employment systems. In the next sections we made a comparative analysis of the changes in civil service systems in Portugal and Spain.

3 Public Employment Models in Spain and Portugal

The link between employment and the public sector varies according to the political and cultural philosophy of the public service of each state (OECD 2008, 2013a, b). Nevertheless, public expenditure in European countries comes close to 50 %

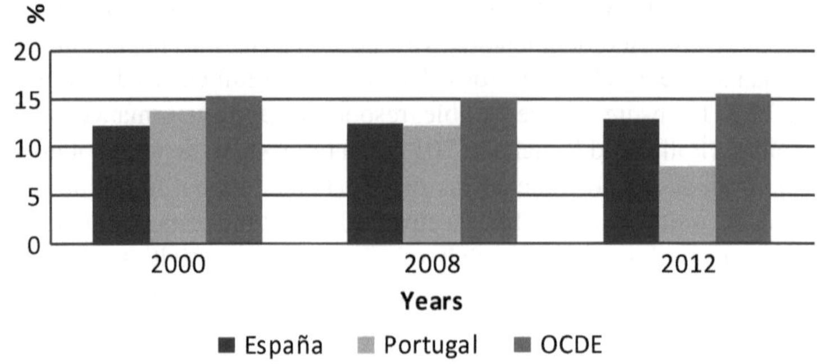

Graphic 1 Percentage of public employees in relation to the working population. *Source*: http://www.oecd.org/gov/pem/publicemploymentkeyfigures.htm

of GNP, regardless of the political party in power[6]. Moreover, public employment accounted for 13.2 % of the total working population in Spain (EPA 2012; Arenilla and Delgado 2014)[7], and 9.5 % of the labour force in Portugal (OECD 2013a, b; SIEP 2013), both figures being below the mean (15.1 %) for OECD countries (OECD 2013a, b). Thus, neither country has a disproportionate number of public employees as compared to other European countries, and both have a middle ranking according the OECD (2008: 20), Gómez et al. (2009), and Bouzas (2011)[8].

As for the proportion of civil servant and contracted labour (or statutory employment and contractual employment which are the types of public employment in both countries), the Spanish central administration had 581.861 workers in 2012 (MAP 2012), of which 2/3 were civil servants, and the remaining 1/3 were public employees hired under contract. In comparison, Portugal that introduced the "individual employment contract" enshrined in labour law in 2004[9] (Araújo

[6]Notwithstanding, the current budgetary tightening is objectively distancing Spain from the OECD mean, particularly considering public expenditure fell by 40 % of GNP in the 2013 budget (OECD 2013a, b). The figures for Portugal are somewhat more conservative on this point i.e., maximum public expenditure reached 33.4 % of GNP in the year 2011 under the government of José Socrates (DGAEP 2013: 7).

[7]The Spanish President, Mariano Rajoy, recently admitted in a speech on the presentation of the CORA Report (2013) (Commission para la Organization and Rationalization of the Administration), that Spain lags behind the OECD mean in terms of the number of public employees per inhabitants.

[8]As the OECD (2008: 20) has pointed out, Spain and Portugal have dramatically increased levels of public employment in the last 25 years in order to compensate for the extraordinarily low number of public employees that left both countries lagging well behind most EU countries (Rocha and Araújo 2007: 587; Gómez et al. 2009: 16; 39). Thus, there has been a strong process of convergence with other neighbouring European countries, and the "accelerated" incorporation of new public functions (França 2003).

[9]This type of employment, which is not applied to activities involving the exercise of power or authority or the exercise of sovereign power, ensures staff are hired through a transparent and simplified recruitment and selection process that safeguards the principles of publicity and

2005; Bouzas and Varela 2005), reported a slightly lower number of 563.595 public employees in December 2013 (SIEP 2013), a figure similar to Spain, though in Portugal there has been a steady decline in the number of public employees since 2005 onwards (Nunes 2008; SIEP 2013), partly due to a process of agencification (OECD 2013a, b; Araújo 2013).

The factor centralization/decentralization is essential for understanding the data of this study i.e., Spain is considered to be a very decentralized state with the setting up of "autonomous communities" and the substantial transfer of competences and human resources management to other administrative tiers, mostly autonomous communities. On the other hand, the Portuguese State is characterised in the literature as a highly centralized state (Barreto 1996; Varela 2003)[10], with a larger apparatus and greater resources i.e., 80 % of civil servants belong to central administration (DGAEP 2013: 10) in comparison to 25 % in Spain (MAP 2013).

This runs counter to one of the main tenets of NPM for reducing the number of public employees and downsizing oversized public-sector employment (Navarro 2009). There is no evidence, study or official report, which has reported any data substantiating any oversizing in Spanish or Portuguese central Administration[11] despite such claims are politically motivated (Ramió 2011, 2013)[12]. As for the problem of duplicity (Morón 2013), due to uncontrolled expansion in certain specific sectors (Longo 2012), or deficiencies in the internal allocation of public employees (Palomar 2013), these shortcomings can be overcome through reallocation, mobility or replacements, fostering the generation of innovative ideas in the field of HRM and allow for possible deficiencies to be corrected.

---

impartiality has been highlighted in relation to the Resolution of the Council of Ministers 53/2004 that introduced the individual employment contract.

[10]This process was accelerated by Portugal entry into the EU (Rocha and Araújo 2007: 594).

[11]Notwithstanding, even if one holds the opinion that there is an excessive number of public employees regardless of the data obtained, one must also take into account the factor highlighted by Mauri (2012) concerning the proximity of these employees to the age of retirement. Accordingly, recent data from a survey of the working population for the third quarter of 2011, found more than 600.000 civil servants were aged 55 years or older. A third of these (214.000) were aged between 60 to 64 years, which means that many will retire in the next 3 years. If we further add the 100.000 passive civil servants aged between 50 to 59 years, who are entitled to early-retirement at the age of 60 years so long as they have contributed to social security payments for 35 years or more, the number of employees who might retire from the civil service in the coming years may be around 315.000. Obviously, these figures are estimates based on the condition that there will be strict compliance with the age of retirement at the age of 65 years, and that the number of civil servants remains frozen. In fact, the "Plan for the rationalization and youth employment in the state administration", designed by the Spanish Ministry of Public Administrations in 2005 has been implemented.

[12]For example, we may refer to the public comments of Juan Rosell, President of the Spanish Confederation of Business Organizations, arguing the case for the need to fire civil servants as there were too many in the Spanish public sector (*Expansión newspaper,* 16/12/2011). Moreover, they have been concerted campaigns in the Spanish and Portuguese press claiming there are too many public employees e.g., "Civil Servants", *El País*, Cataluña, 17/06/2009); or "The number of civil servants is coming close to the number of entrepreneurs", *El Periódico*, 15/06/2009).

In theoretical terms, bearing in mind the crucial connection between administrative and judicial traditions of a country and its model of public employment, Spain and Portugal belong to the "Mediterranean" tradition, in line with the categories established by Demmke et al. (2008) and Kuperus and Rode (2010) who have underscored the low status assigned to public employees and their functions, and the high degree of political intervention in public administration[13]. Nevertheless, the similarities or "parallel paths" of the Spanish and Portuguese models have not arisen from a phenomenon of "self-referential mimetic", but rather to quite the contrary i.e., both countries have historically ignored each other (Varela 2003; Bouzas and Varela 2005).

In terms of governmental decisions on public employment, nowadays HRM is merely an economic instrument aimed at tackling the public deficit (Bouzas and Varela 2005). In structural terms, HRM has distanced itself from its own dynamics as an instrument of public management, which has been transferred to the Treasury and Finance Ministry, a symbolic structural change. This runs counter to strategic nature of HRM, in favour of an economic approach to public employment that is hegemonic in this stage of the crisis. As for the implementation of HRM by the relevant Ministries, that is, who is responsible for the HRM strategies in their respective central government, according to the OECD Report (2013a) the similarity between Spain and Portugal is entirely limited to the fact that the central HRM body is responsible for the budget allocated to wages and other expenses.

In relation to the implementation of HRM in Spain and Portugal, the assignation of functions and tasks differ in that the Portuguese model is more homogeneous and reliant on the central administration than the Spanish one. For instance, the characteristics of the public employment model in both countries exhibit predominantly the characteristics of a career-based system[14] (França 2003; OECD 2013a, b). Features or components of the "position-based employment model" are progressively incorporated (Bouzas and Varela 2005), particularly in "functional administration" (Ramió 2009) e.g., agencies and public bodies, eventually constitute a truly "hybrid model" (Adomonis 2008; Nunes and Castro 2010).

These characteristics of the prevailing career model, based on the French model (Arenilla 2005), are linked to the notion of permanent and stable "lifelong" employment in the public sector as a basic principle of all bureaucratic organizations (Vázquez 2007), as well as the prevalence of the principle of hierarchy, the allocation of employees to professional bodies instead of to specific positions, an intense socialization process of "corporate identity" (Crozier 1993), high degree of geographical and functional immobility (Mayntz 1985; Morón 2013), professionalism, objectivity, and impartiality (Law 7/2007, Article 1.3.e); and a "career" almost

[13]We should bear in mind the numerous viewpoint of the doctrine criticising the politicized model due to the abusive use of freely designated officials which is open to political manipulation and the high degree of political interference in the Spanish public administration (Morón 2013).

[14]Demmke et al. (2008) even claim that traditional career models no longer exist in their "pure" state in the new millennium.

inevitably[15] according to the principle of "seniority" (Arenilla 1996), as opposed to the principle of merit and skills in the recruitment and successive provisioning processes, and a degree excessive officialdom and bureaucracy (Araújo 2013). The final outcome is an overwhelmingly complex and rigid personnel management model (Ramió 2009: 38; Longo 2012; Morón 2013).

Alternatively, the other major public employment model, the employment model or "position-based system", a good example being the United States [16] and other countries such as Austria, Belgium, Denmark, and Canada, among others (Cardona 2006; Recio 2011), is characterized by a situation where the position is the key component in designing the entire organizational system. In this contractual system there is neither the legal right of preference to occupy other posts, nor the right to "tenure"; consequently, a public employee holds a post whilst both parties consider it mutually convenient. Thus the overriding criteria is the idealness of a candidate for a particular post (including merits in a broad sense), which underscores the need for carrying out a detailed analysis and job description of public employee positions. This analysis is based on the criteria for correctly selecting candidates, which is by definition individualized, on more practical than theoretical assessment criteria, and on the merits awarded to previous experience (Cardona 2006). Moreover, the remuneration subsystem is linked to the work performance, which fosters the view that public employment should not be understood as a profession, but rather as individuals applying their competences and skills to specific needs, which may eventually become permanent in the public sector (Table 1).

With regard to the OECD countries (2013a)[17], Spanish and Portuguese public employment models share similar characteristics, as well as significant differences given that the human resource management model is more strategic and professional in Portugal (Bilhim and Soriano 2013), an inexistent aspects in the Spanish model (Palomar 2013) which is conditioned by several characteristics such as a more politicized model due to the abusive use of freely designated officials, discretion in the personal choice of managers, and the lack of accountability of managers (Jiménez 2009). In any case, both models are excessively complex in terms of the classification of careers and categories or groups of public employees (Nunes 2008; Del Pino and Villoria 2009).

[15]Nevertheless, it is worth noting, as Irujo (1993 cited by Briones 2014:158) has pointed out, career options are so limited in small administrations—such as in many local councils—that in reality the civil service career bears greater resemblance with the employment or open system than the career system itself.

[16]Though the US is one of the best example of the open system, Hood (1997) has highlighted the gradual incorporation of the "contract by merits", which entails the apolitical selection of most of the federal civil servants.

[17]An example of these "strategic practices" is the implementation of an integrated performance-based evaluation system in public administration (SIADAP) since 2004, and promoting a system of management by objectives (Araújo 2005).

Table 1 Comparison of the two main public employment models

Career model	Employment model
Stability and permanenceLifelong employment	Working relationship according to organizational needs
Emphasis on formal merits and professional diplomas and certificates	Emphasis on employee's overall experience and qualifications
Public law (administrative)	Private law (labour law)
Principle of hierarchy	Principle of achievement and performance
Focused on professional bodies	Focused on specific positions
High geographical-functional immobility	High geographical and functional mobility
Career system "quasi-automatically" regulated according to seniority. Limited general mobility	Career according to organizational needs. Many possibilities for general mobility
Principle of merit and skills in staff recruitment and provision as a formal process	Principle of merit and skills attenuated by "idealness" as informal process
Statutory pay according to seniority	Negotiated pay according to outcomes/performance without considering seniority
Legislation for specific collective bargaining	Legislation for general collective bargaining

Source: Adapted from OECD (2008) and Adomonis (2008)

4 Main Evolutionary Trends

In recent decades, the main evolutionary trends in the public employment models of the countries analysed in this study ranged from the career model to the employment model[18], and as Bouzas and Varela (2005) have pointed out the tendency is to adopt the proposals of the European Union and the OECD (OECD 2013a, b) i.e., to adopt an employment model similar to the model in United Kingdom or Holland, instead of the current career regime (Bordogna 2008). This entails a certain dismantling of the career model in Portugal (Nunes 2008), possibly as a consequence of the project "*Revisão do Sistema de Carreiras*[19]" promoted by the Portuguese government in 2005 (Rocha and Araújo 2007: 591; Bilhim and Soriano 2013). As for Spain,

[18]However, owing to the 2007–2008 crisis that has profoundly affected the entire public sector, it is possible to introduce a third trend, incipient but real for those states that have adopted the strategy of cuts in public services and employees: "de-civil servicing" through measures such as reducing the possibility of professional careers through internal promotion, reducing perks and other complements, flexibility in the models of functional and territorial mobility, reinforcing the skills of public managers with the intention of reducing the labour force, and increasing the workload of public employees. These measures and others (discourage new staff; the aging of the workforce and the rate of staff repositioning, undermining the role of trade unions in the management of industrial relations in public sector), as stipulated by recent Spanish legislation reforming the labour laws that undoubtedly affect the public sector, introduce a new dimension, supported by the OECD (2013a, b), under the concept of "delegated HRM").

[19]Resolution of the Council of Ministers 109/2005, 30th June.

Cantero (2013) has underscored the need for clarifying the classification of public employees in terms of the figure of the civil servant and contractually employed workers.

Though the dominant trend is to adopt the employment model some scholars (Adomonis 2008) have moderated such claims by suggesting it is perhaps best to speak of "mix model" or "hybrid model" (Christensen and Laegreid 2010; Parrado 2013), in which the career system is coming closer to the employment model in international scenario, characterised by the heterogeneity of existing employment models in terms of institutional and legislative complexity (Adomonis 2008).

Nonetheless, one cannot claim that the move towards an employment model necessary entails a trend towards a labour model of the civil service as has occurred in Italy. Martínez and Arufe (2013) assert that the transition to an employment model is perhaps simpler from a statutory or career model, in which collective bargaining is not predominant and legal litigation are referred to an administrative appeals to courts, which are much slower and less favourable towards the employees.

In Spain these trends towards an employment model have been, until the outbreak of the current international financial crisis, more tenuous than in Portugal and the modernization process and reforms undertaken during the 1980s and 1990s in Spain, have failed to alter in essence the traditional model of the public administration (Bouzas and Varela 2005).

In Portugal this process has been geared towards an employment model since the last quarter of the past century, when NPM made its mark with the managerialist approach operationalized through an intense process of agentification that has progressively changed the prevailing philosophy (Araújo 2013). In addition to the previous managerial processes of the twenty-one century, the delicate Portuguese economy, prior to the current international crisis, provoked in the preceding years, in particular 2004–2005, a strong drive to bring the public employment model closer to private sector regimes (DGAEP 2013; Araújo 2005; Bouzas and Varela 2005), which was implemented under the guise of "budget consolidation", rather than as a fundamental change to the model itself (Nunes 2008). The theoretical basis for bringing about change in the employment model is management by objectives, and the unprecedented distinction between civil servants with permanent positions and responsibilities in the sovereign functions of the state, and employees who have no lifelong public service employment.

There is a current of thought that seek to drive public employment models towards private-sector employment models (Hood 1998; Bordogna 2008), by employing concepts such as employability, and the overall flexibility of the model (Hughes 1994; Coleman 2010; Thompson 2010), which have been expediently implemented (Nunes and Castro 2010; Rojas 2013), or the ability to adapt to the circumstances in a permanently changing world. In addition to these constructive measures, both countries have sponsored negative press campaigns that intended to undermine the productivity of public employees, their "special" status and their number.

Thus, the emphasis on controlling productivity and improving efficiency (the SIADAP in Portugal), the reduction in wages, reviewing nearly every aspects of working conditions (working hours, sick leave, free days off work, holidays, conciliation), the increased mobility of public employees (functional and/or geographic) (Nunes 2008), and perhaps the most effective measure of them all, the provisions for dismissing public employees in Spain (*Ley* 3/2012 and the *Real Decreto de desarrollo* 1483/2012), and even laying-off civil service staff, in the case of the Portuguese Law (*Lei n° 59/2008, de 11 de Setembro; Lei n° 12-A/2008, de 27 de Fevereiro, Lei 53/2006, de 7 de Dezembro*).

This model coheres with many of the postulates of NPM adopted by most OECD countries from the late 1970s onwards (Hughes 1994), with the political underpinning of the new right. In line with these postulates, an ongoing process is underway of "slimming" down the public functions carried out by the state (Nunes and Castro 2010). Though lacking any well-defined ideology (Clifton et al. 2006)—in spite of the neoliberal undertones—new forms of recruitment and provision have been implemented ranging from public-private partnerships or the outsourcing of services under public ownership and control (Cantero 2011), to the privatization of services with no public ownership or control (Rodríguez 2011). Hence, the transfer of public functions to the private sector is gradually increasing in both states, with a fall in public employment particularly from 2005 onwards (DGAEP 2013; OECD 2013a, b), and a reduction in the functions and services provided by the state (Bordogna 2008).

Moreover, attempts at achieving the presumed flexibility of HRM in the private sector have "overlooked" the basic pillars of Public Administration in the direct management of services provided by the state (Bouzas 2011). The HRM model was originally designed to enhance objectivity, professionalism and legal certainty for public employees in exercising their public duties and functions that in turn fuel a healthy democratic system. Historically, public administration and its employees has been the instrument for implementing democratically legitimized public policy, and a tool for supervising the legality of the political function itself.

Thus, the trend is towards a HRM model with an emphasis on flexibility, adaptability, simplicity, and cost-cutting (Adomonis 2008; Nunes and Castro 2010), but with voids in conception, values, transparency, and even instances of "clientelism" such as those described by Rocha and Araújo (2007) as a consequence of this process of flexibility. Fairness, objectivity, professionalism, impartiality, legal certainty, public participation in public administration, and the eradication of corruption[20], are values well consolidated in the judicial-administrative culture of citizens in both states, who have been systematically exposed to the ongoing debates on the future of public sector employment. Besides the "conventional" values of the previous model of public administration, there appears to be the alarming prospect of a relationship of negative dependency—described by Propper

[20]In relation to the variable salary and the number of cases of corruption, the work of di Tella and Schargrodsky (2003), has corroborated a relationship of negative dependency between salary range and the cases of corruption in the hospital public health sector i.e., the lower the salary the more the corruption.

and van Reenen (2010) in the public health sector—between cuts and the quality of public services. Severe cuts in the conditions of public employment invariably leading to deterioration in the quality of public services.

5 Effects of the Crisis on Public Employment in Spain and Portugal

Changes produced on the work force in the public sector in Spain and Portugal has been evident, at least along the period that goes from the beginning of the financial crisis in Europe until 2013. The tables below shows two main impacts (two major factors) in relation to the human resources in the public sector. The first one (Table 2) is related to the number of persons that work for the public sector in percentage of GDP. The second (Table 3) is related with the evolution (decreasing, in this case) of the number of public employees, by level of governments (central and subnational) for the period of 2008–2013.

Table 2 Compensation of general government employees in percentage of GDP

	2008	2009	2010	2011	2012	2013
Portugal	13.13	14.03	13.68	12.84	11.69	12.52
Spain	10.58	11.64	11.55	11.45	10.92	11.12
OECD—Average	10.34	11.08	10.86	10.70	10.66	10.65

Source: OECD (2016)

Table 3 Evolution of the number of civil servants in Portugal and Spain

	2008	2009	2010	2011	2012	2013
Portugal						
Central administration	523,117	522,925	512,424	458,951	437,081	419,406
Regional and local administration	124,357	134,912	135,888	153,615	148,519	144,333
Total	647,474	657,837	648,312	612,566	585,600	563,739
Spain						
Central administration	561,551	575,021	591,559	592,813	581,861	570,691
Regional and local administration	1,923,446	1,962,349	2,006,397	1,989,773	1,949,095	1,857,150
Total	2,484,997	2,537,370	2,597,956	2,582,586	2,530,956	2,427,841

Source: DGAEP (2011, 2013, 2014a, b) and MAP (2008, 2009, 2010, 2011, 2012, 2013, 2014) (statistical bulletin of public employment)

In both cases, the argument that the crisis has kept the "status quo" of public employees is easily refuted, albeit with differences between the Spanish and Portuguese case. In Spain, public employment increased its weight in percentage of the GDP, despite the decline in the period 2008–2013, mainly due to the rising unemployment in the private sector. Portugal's case is different because there was a decrease of the weight of public employment in percentage of the GDP for the same period. In any case, both countries have a weight of public employment above the OECD average for the period 2008–2013.

Beyond the macro data on employment, the measures implemented by the Spanish and Portuguese governments have left their mark not only in the number of public employees, but also on their working conditions present and future. To understand the impact of these labor conditions change in both countries, we will analyse the remuneration measures, the measures on employment conditions and the measures on industrial relations in the public sector and collective bargaining.

5.1 Remuneration Measures

Of the measures affecting the working conditions of public employees, within the framework of what has been termed working relations, a large number these directly concern the pay conditions of public employees. Thus, in order to effectively compare the Spanish and Portuguese public administrations, the analyses have focused on measures that were similar, in addition to other measures that were peculiar to both States.

It should be noted that the previous context in both countries on this issue was different, and in any case both have lagged far behind in what the OECD refers to in its Report as "Performance and Skills-based Pay Systems" (OECD 2013a, b). In Spain the remuneration system was extremely rigid in concepts, and unequivocally adverse to Performance Pay Systems. In Portugal the remuneration system has been undergoing radical changes since 2005, particularly by implementing performance-based pay systems, and by redefining most of the remuneration concepts in an attempt to raise productivity (OECD 2013a, b).

Nevertheless, in 2010 the first cuts in the civil servants' pay will come into force (from 2 to 8 % in Spain and from 3.5 to 10 % in Portugal). The severity of these measures reside in that they are permanent and not temporary cuts implemented provisionally in response to the grave economic circumstances of both States. In Portugal the first cuts introduced by the social democrats were initially meant to be provisional, but eventually this proved not to be the case with the publication of the rates and scales of pay for all civil servants with the cuts combined, which in effect makes them statutory.

In addition to previous cutbacks, the wage freeze in 2011 was followed by further cuts in 2012 that suspended (but not eliminated) two extra pays in Portugal (holidays and December), and one extra pay in Spain (in December). Moreover, in Spain, contributions to pension funds were suspended, as was paid sick-leave with a 100 % of earnings in cases of common illness.

Finally, the year 2013 merely continued the trend of freezing wages, and implementing cuts. Both governments have had to publicly acknowledge that bearing in mind that net cutbacks were followed by freezing wages[21], public employees have lost on average 20 % of purchasing power, which varied according to rank in the hierarchy, the tier of territorial administration, and the country under study[22].

5.2 *Measures on Employment Conditions*

The Spanish Law (*Orden PRE/824/2009*) marks a turning point in the implementation of measures deteriorating the conditions of public employment with the introduction of important restrictions on employment such as ensuring that the number of posts left vacant never exceeds 8 % of the total number of positions, and the rationalization of civil servants into bodies and scales. These measures were included in our analysis in the section on "Measures on the conditions of employment", given that the management of vacancies and temporary staff inevitably affects the workload ratios and functions assigned to staff. Thus, according to the (OECD 2013a, b), Spain is predicted to be one of the countries with a decrease in the numbers of public employees as a result of the reforms that have been implemented.

Both States have adopted measures designed to reduce the number of public employees mainly by eliminating vacancies, dismissal temporary staff, and postponing the compulsory age of retirement to 65 in Spain and 66 in Portugal.

Notwithstanding, both countries should bear in mind that the large number of public employees on the point of retirement (3 years), as estimated for Spain by Majós (2012), with this problem being even more acute in the case of Portugal (França 2003; Nunes 2008), where the mean age of public employees is higher than for other OECD countries (OECD 2013a, b). In all likelihood, this trend will continue in the coming years with the Portuguese government announcing an annual

[21]It should be highlighted that wages have been frozen for four consecutive years spanning the 2011–2014 budgets.

[22]In the case of Spain the figures for the number of public employees of the central national administration in this study do not include 75 % of public employees from the other administrations of the Spanish State. Indeed, if one is to assess the full impact on public employment, the cuts of each autonomous or local administration affecting this 75 % of public employees from administrations with the cuts imposed by national governments. To sum up in just a few words: one does not have to wait long for a state to eliminate extra holiday pay for an autonomous government to immediately follow suit. This comment highlights that the cuts in the pay of public employees varies considerably according to the particular circumstances of each autonomous or local administration.

2 % fall (implemented de “facto” by the Spanish government) in the number of public employees until the year 2014.

Recent legislation in Spain (article 15 of the *Real Decreto 20/2012*), has once again brought to the forefront the concept of “forced worker mobility” by establishing mechanisms of “forced mobility” that allow public administrations to transfer civil servants according to the organizational needs of public services, even if this entails changing the worker’s place of residence.

A further impact of the public employment freezing is that it thwarts any possibility of pursuing a career in the civil service given that public services are no longer obliged to adopt a career employment model. The measure having the most direct impact on public employment is the extinction of any fixed formal working relationship between civil servants or public employees. This is the end of job security for civil servants or the tenure of public employees. In Spain, the focus has been primarily on the workforce with the labour legislation reform (*Ley 3/2012* and *Real Decreto de Desarrollo 1483/2012)* aimed at facilitating dismiss of employees according to the economic or organizational needs and circumstances. Public employees can be made redundant in spite of the time-honoured public sector principles of equality, merit, and skills. Perhaps due to the legal complexities (Martínez and Arufe 2013; Palomar 2013), the legislation on redundancies has rarely been used since it was approved in 2012, (Morón 2013)[23].

Portugal has gone one step further by legislating in 2013 that those civil servants—not only contracted staff as in Spain—may be deemed surplus labour (*excedentários)*. In this case they are part of the Mobility Program (*Programa de Mobilidade*) and can be reallocated in other public service. If they are not affected to a public service they are allocated to the ‘Requalification Program’ (*Programa de Requalificação*). In such program they must follow a training program and its salary is reduced to 60 %. After a year in this situation the salary is reduced again to 40 % for 1 year. After this period if the civil servant is not reallocated in a public service his/her employment contract finishes. In practice this is a smooth process to dismiss civil servants. Besides this measure strategies have been proposed to encourage voluntary dismiss in the public sector.

Finally, raising working hours, and reducing free days off work[24] has brought Spain and Portugal into line with other OECD countries, as both countries were above the OECD mean[25] (OECD 2013a, b).

---

[23]In fact, in the few public sector layoffs reviewed in this study, the Supreme Court of Andalusia (Tribunal Superior de Justicia de Andalucía) has overturned a previous ruling in favour of the Council of Jaen. The weakness of the Spanish law regulating layoffs mainly resides in that redundancies can’t be announced before determining the needs of public services, and that government itself is responsible for the economic hardship resulting from mass redundancies, which in turn leads to considerable legal uncertainty.

[24]This Portuguese Constitutional Court ruled in favour of these measures on the grounds that these measures do not violate the constitutional principle of equality.

[25]The OECD reported a total of 1622 working hours per annum for Portuguese public employees in comparison to the OECD mean of 1745 h.

5.3 Measures on Industrial Relations in Public Sector and Collective Bargaining

It would be advisable to review the background of both countries prior to analysing these measures.

In Spain, the right to collective bargaining enshrined in the law by the Spanish Constitutional Court has led to situation that has been described as benevolent, or even prone to "hyper-trade unionism" (Longo 2012; Morón 2013). Moreover, the favourable stance of governments open to collective bargaining in the public sector has been further enhanced—at least in theory—with the government's approval of the Basic Statute of Public Employees that fosters collective bargaining and a consensually agreed management of human resource (Palomar 2013).

Nonetheless, under the pretext of the current economic downturn, Decree-laws have been used extensively as an expedient way of sidestepping the legislation outlined in the Public Employee Basic Statute (EBEP-*Estatuto Básico del Empleado Público*) (Law, 7/2007 of 12 April). Majós (2012) and Palomar (2013) refer to the concerted efforts at "dynamiting" the right to collective bargaining (Morón 2013), which has been annulled by the Spanish government through Decree-laws and the restoration of statutory law which enables executives to manage and decide about the general interests of public administration (Morón 2013).

The point of departure of the Portuguese situation, however, is different since industrial relations in public sector, and the role of trade unions in collective bargaining have not been as vigorous as in Spain. Moreover, one of the requirements of the employment model has been met. Working conditions are negotiated in the same bargaining context as any other worker in the country (Economic and Social Council), without a specific framework for the collective bargaining of public employees as is the case of Spain where the career model prevails. In addition to these some of the measures of the Spanish and Portuguese governments have been directly aimed at undermining parties involved in collective bargaining. Thus, the Spanish government has reduced the resources and the number of paid trade union representative (*Real Decreto* 20/2012), which in practice has led to trimming down the number of trade union representatives and their organizational and functional powers.

Thus, there is a growing trend predicted by Bordogna (2008) towards a system of free collective bargaining, which is restricted, less formal and mandatory, and not as legally sanctioned as before. This breakdown has been further exacerbated by the trend of New Management Public towards the decentralization of collective bargaining (Hood 1998).

6 Conclusions

Portugal and Spain have shared similar models of public employment throughout their recent history with similar evolutionary trends regardless of the distinctive features that distinguish the two countries. Portugal's public employment model is more influenced by the doctrine of New Public Management, more strategic and professional in perspective, whilst Spain's model is more traditional and most adverse to the influence of New Public Management in the design of public employment programs.

This paper has assessed the changes implemented in the public administration of both Iberian countries following the international financial crisis of 2008, the outcomes of the measures imposed by the Troika, as well as the effects on the public employment systems of each central government. These measures consisted of horizontal cuts applied to all areas of government activity that have particular incidence on what is generically called the civil service.

Thus, change in the public services is being driven by NPM models, and in both cases without a clear strategy except for cuts in the national budget. This has led to a fall in the number of civil servants, the dismantling of the career system, which was more pervasive in Portugal, a significant deterioration in overall working conditions and benefits traditionally associated to public employment, and a fall in wages.

In Spain, as the effects of the crisis were felt later, the reforms in the civil service were similar to those adopted by Portugal. Thus, the financial crisis led to a significant fall in civil servants, and a convergence between public and private employment models. Undoubtedly, one of the most prominent changes in public administration is the dismantling of the career system which is gradually being replaced by private sector employment models.

It is perhaps too early to understand the full impact of these changes on the morale, values, and motivation of public employees in Spain and Portugal. Notwithstanding, there is a merger between public-sector and private-sector employment models that will undoubtedly entail serious challenges for both states: What values will prevail under working conditions comparable to private sector employment models? How to attract and retain qualified professionals in public administration when it offers little more than public ethics, the defence of the general interest, and the maintenance of social cohesion? In short, what does the future hold for public employment? Will there be civil servants or are we definitely heading for the hiring labour under work contracts, as appears to be the trend after the financial crisis of 2008? Thus, would it be right to speak in Spain and Portugal of the "death of the civil servant"?

References

Adomonis, V. (2008). *Structural elements of a law on civil service trends and fundamental choices.* Paper on SIGMA Programme.

Araújo, J. F. (2002). NPM and the change in Portuguese central government. *International Public Management Journal, 5–3*, 223–236.

Araújo, J. F. (2005). *A reforma administrativa em Portugal I: em busca de um novo paradigma.* NEAPP Working Paper, Universidade do Minho.

Araújo, J. F. (2013). Da Nova Gestão Pública à Nova Governação Pública: pressões emergentes da fragmentação das estruturas da Administração Pública. In Hugo Consciência Silvestre and Joaquim Filipe Araújo (Coords.), *Coletãnea em Administração Pública* (pp. 25–61). Lisboa: Escolar Editora.

Arenilla, M. (1996). *La implantación de la Nueva gestión Pública en el viejo continente: La experiencia anglosajona como modelo.* II Congreso Español de Ciencia Política y de la Administración (1996).

Arenilla, M. (2005). La vigencia de los modelos de gestión de los recursos humanos en las Administraciones Públicas. *Presupuesto y Gasto Público, 41*, 33–53.

Arenilla, M., & Delgado, D. (2014). ¿Hay muchos empleados públicos en España? Eficiencia y efectividad en el contexto de la OECD. *Revista de Administración Pública, 193*, 297–334.

Barreto, A. (1996). *A Situação Social em Portugal 1960–1995.* Lisboa: Impresa de Ciências Sociais.

Bilhim, J., & Soriano, J. E. (2013). La racionalidad política y técnica en la selección de la alta administración pública y gestión pública portuguesa: una experiencia útil para España. *El Cronista*, 38.

Bordogna, L. (2008). Moral hazard transaction costs and the reform of public service employment relations. *European Journal of Industrial Relations, 14*(4), 381–400.

Bouzas, R. (2011). Sector Público: Los recursos humanos en las Administraciones Públicas en España. In R. Gutiérrez & M. Martínez (Eds.), *Gestión de Recursos Humanos: Contexto y políticas.* Madrid: Thomson–Civitas.

Bouzas, R., & Varela, E. J. (2005). Caminos paralelos, deficiencias comunes: Aproximación a los modelos públicos de recursos humanos en España y Portugal. *Gestión y Análisis de Políticas Públicas, 32*, 61–78.

Brans, M. (2010). Administração Pública Comparativa: Da Teoría Geral a Estruturas Gerais. In B. Guy Peters & Jon Pierre (Coords.), *Administração pública* (pp. 419–446). Coletânea, São Paulo-Brasilia DF: ENAP and Editora UNESP.

Briones, O. (2014). *Factores determinantes en la construcción de la función de recursos humanos autonómica: Galicia 2000–2012.* Madrid: Instituto Nacional de Administración Pública.

Cantero, J. (2011). La decisión administrativa de externalizar y su repercusión en el empleo público. Límites y pautas para su adopción. In Luis Ortega (Dir.), *Crisis y Externalización en el Sector Público: ¿Solución o Problema?* (pp. 69–109). Madrid: INAP.

Cantero, J. (2013). Criterios para la clasificación del empleado público: ¿funcionario o laboral? *Revista Vasca de Gestión de Personas y Organizaciones Públicas, 5*, 82–99.

Cardona, F. (2006). *Tendencias en la gestión de la función pública. Países Unión Europea y OECD.* Santander: Universidad Internacional Menéndez Pelayo.

Christensen, T., & Laegreid, P. (2010). Complexity and hybrid public administration: Theoretical and empirical challenges. *Public Organizational Review,* doi: 10.1007/s11115-010-0141-4 (Accessed March 30, 2016).

Clifton, J., Comín, F., & Díaz, D. (2006). Explaining public enterprise privatization in the EU: ¿A European or British policy? *Revista de Economía Mundial, 15*, 121–153.

Coleman, S. (2010). Inovações e tendencias globais nas práticas de gestão de recursos humanos. In B. Guy Peters & Jon Pierre (Coords.), *Administração pública* (pp. 79–97). Coletânea São Paulo-Brasilia DF: ENAP and Editora UNESP.

Crozier, M. (1993). Datos elementales de un <<círculo vicioso>> burocrático. In C. Ramió & X. Ballart (Coords.), *Lecturas de Teoría de la Organización Vol. I. La evolución histórica del pensamiento organizativo. Los principales paradigmas teóricos* (pp. 411–421). Madrid: MAP.

Del Pino, E., & Villoria, M. (2009). *Dirección y gestión de recursos humanos en las Administraciones Públicas*. Madrid: Tecnos.

Demmke, C., Henökl, T., & Moilanen, T. (2008). What are public services good at? success of public services in the field of human resource management. *Report to the 50th Meeting of the Directors-General of Public Services of the Member States of the European Union. European Institute of Public Administration.*

DGAEP. (2011). *Quadros excel (BOEP n.° 5 e n.° 6).* Lisboa: Direção-Geral da Administração e do Emprego Público.

DGAEP. (2013). Análise da evoluçao das estruturas da administraçao pública central portuguesa decorrente do PRACE e do PREMAC. Direcção Geral da Administração e do Emprego Público.

DGAEP. (2014a). *Boletim estatístico do emprego público, No 10, Direção-Geral da Administração e do Emprego*. Lisboa: Público.

DGAEP. (2014b). *Síntese Estatística do Emprego Público: 1° Trimestre 2014, Direção-Geral da Administração e do Emprego*. Lisboa: Público.

di Tella, R. & Schargrodsky, E. (2003). The role of the wages and auditing during a crackdown on corruption in the city of Buenos Aires. *Journal of Laws and Economics, 46*(1), 269–292.

Echevarría, K. (2010). *Crisis y empleo público en España*. SUMAS.

EPA. (2012). *Encuesta de población activa española*. Accessed August 10, 2013, from www.ine.es/daco/daco42/daco4211/epa0413.pdf

França, J. A. (2003). Reforma e inovação em épocas de escassez aguda de recursos: a experiencia portuguesa em curso. *VIII Congreso Internacional del CLAD sobre la Reforma del Estado y de la Administración Pública.*

Gómez, S., Sánchez, J., Rivas, C., & Moreno, M. M. (2009). Análisis regional del empleo público en España: especial consideración de los empleados autonómicos. *XVI Encuentro de Economía Pública: "Crisis financiera y sector público". Granada.*

Gorriti, M. (2012). Un sistema de reforma del empleo público alternativo a los recortes. *Federación de Municipios de Cataluña, 4*, 8–23.

Greener, I. (2009). *Public management: A critical text*. Hampshire: Palgrave MacMillan.

Heinrich, C. J. (2010). Como avaliar o desempenho e a efetividade do setor público. In B. Guy Peters & Jon Pierre (Coords.), *Administração Pública* (pp. 53–75). Coletânea São Paulo-Brasilia DF: ENAP and Editora UNESP.

Hood, C. (1996). Exploring variations in public management reform of the 1980s. In H. A. G. Bekke, J. L. Perry, & T. A. J. Toonen (Eds.), *Civil service systems in comparative perspective* (pp. 268–287). Bloomington: Indiana University Press.

Hood, C. (1997). Which contract state? Four perspectives on over-outsourcing for public services. *Australian Journal of Public Administration, 56*(3), 120–131.

Hood, C. (1998). *The art of the state: Culture, rethoric and public management*. Oxford: Oxford University Press.

Hughes, O. (1994). *Public management & administration: An introduction*. New York: Palgrave.

Jiménez, R. (2009). La dirección profesional: Perspectiva comparada y diagnostic de la situación en España. In R. Jiménez, A. Palomar, & M. Villoria (Eds.), *La dirección pública profesional en España*. Madrid: Instituto Vasco de Administración Pública and Marcial Pons.

Kuperus, H., & Rode, A. (2010). More efficient services in times of economy recession and beyond: Can a flexisecurity approach help? *European Institute of Public Administration (EIPASCOPE), 2010*(1), 15–22.

Longo. (2012). *Less of the same is not reforming the administration* (article published in the newspaper El País 27th August, 2012 edition).

Majós, J. M. (2012). Gestionando la crisis. *Ponencia presentada al XII congreso sobre recursos humanos en el sector público*. Vitoria, Mimeo.

MAP. (2008). *Boletín estadístico del personal al servicio de las Administraciones Públicas*. Madrid: Ministerio de Administraciones Públicas.

MAP. (2009). *Boletín estadístico del personal al servicio de las Administraciones Públicas*. Madrid: Ministerio de Administraciones Públicas.

MAP. (2010). *Boletín estadístico del personal al servicio de las Administraciones Públicas*. Madrid: Ministerio de Administraciones Públicas.

MAP. (2011). *Boletín estadístico del personal al servicio de las Administraciones Públicas*. Madrid: Ministerio de Administraciones Públicas.

MAP. (2012). *Boletín estadístico del personal al servicio de las Administraciones Públicas*. Madrid: Ministerio de Administraciones Públicas.

MAP. (2013). *Boletín estadístico del personal al servicio de las Administraciones Públicas*. Madrid: Ministerio de Administraciones Públicas.

MAP. (2014). *Boletín estadístico del personal al servicio de las Administraciones Públicas*. Madrid: Ministerio de Administraciones Públicas.

Martínez, G. J., & Arufe, V. A. (2013). *El impacto sobre el empleo público de la ley 3/2012*. Santiago: Ponencia no curso EGAP monográfico sobre os retos e as perspectivas do emprego público.

Mauri, J. (2012). Gestionando la crisis. Ponencia presentada al XII Congreso sobre Recursos Humanos en el Sector Público, Mimeo, Vitoria

Mayntz, R. (1985). *Sociología de la Administración Pública*. Madrid: Alianza Universidad.

Morón, M. S. (2013). *Os axustes e as reformas no emprego público: a situación actual e as perspectivas: Curso sobre os retos e as perspectivas do emprego público*. Santiago de Compostela: EGAP (Xunta de Galicia).

Navarro, V. (2009). *Too many civil servants?* Article published in the Public newspaper in the 25th June, 2009 edition.

Nunes, P. (2008). Reforma do emprego público: breves considerações ás grandes reformas em curso em Portugal. *Revista de Estudos Politécnicos, VII-1*, 49–73.

Nunes, P., & Castro, C. (2010). Sistemas de emprego público no século XXI: Que significado? Uma sistematização. *Revista Chilena de Administración Pública, 15–16*, 191.

OECD. (2008). *The state of the public service*. Paris: OECD Publishing.

OECD. (2013a). *Estudio específico de perfiles de la gestión de recursos humanos por países*. Paris: OECD Publishing.

OECD. (2013b). *Panorama de las Administraciones Públicas 2011: Colección Estudios y Documentos INAP-OECD* (pp. 1–417). Madrid: INAP.

OECD. (2016). *Government production costs (indicator)*. Paris: OECD Publishing. 10.1787/44ec61e6-en (Accessed March 30, 2016).

Palomar, A. (2013). *A organización e o réxime do emprego público á luz da Constitución e da xurisprudencia constitucional: Curso sobre os retos e as perspectivas do emprego público*. Santiago de Compostela: EGAP (Xunta de Galicia).

Parrado, S. (2002). *Sistemas administrativos comparados*. Barcelona: Editorial Tecnos and Universitat Pompeu Fabra.

Parrado, S. (2013). La Función Pública. In S. Parrado, C. Colino, & J. A. Olmeda (Eds.), *Gobiernos y Administraciones Públicas en Perspectiva Comparada* (pp. 135–177). Tirant lo Blanch: Valencia.

Peters, G. (1988). *Comparing public bureaucracies: problems of theory and method*. Tuscaloosa: University of Alabama Press.

Pollitt, C. (1993). *Managerialism and the public service: The Anglo-American experience*. Oxford: Blackwell.

Pollitt, C., & Bouckaert, G. (2011). *Public management reform: A comparative analysis: New public management, governance, and the neo-weberian state*. Oxford: Oxford University Press.

Porta, D. D. (2013). Análisis comparativo: la investigación basada en casos frente a la investigación basada en variables. In D. Della Porta & M. Keating (Eds.), *Enfoques y metodologías de las ciencias sociales: Una perspectiva pluralista* (pp. 211–236). Tres Cantos (Madrid): Akal.

Propper, C., & Van Reenen, J. (2010). Can pay regulation kill? Panel data evidence on the effect of labor markets on hospital performance. *Journal of Political Economy, 118*(2), 222–273.

Ramió, C. (2009). Teoría y práctica del fenómeno de la externalización. In C. Ramió (Coord.), *La colaboración público privada y la creación de valor público* (pp. 57–80). Barcelona: Diputación de Barcelona.

Ramió, C. (2011). *La administración que se espera para después de la crisis*. (Working Papers 2011–02 GIGAPP-IUIOG), pp. 1–16.

Ramió, C. (2013). *Balance del impacto de la crisis económica, política, social e institucional sobre las administraciones públicas en España 2011–2013: Diagnóstico y propuestas*. (Working Papers 2013–28 GIGAPP-IUIOG), pp. 1–34.

Ramió, C. (2015). *Administración pública y crisis institucional: Estrategias de reforma e innovación para España y América Latina*. Madrid: Tecnos.

Recio, J. M. (2011). Nuevas perspectivas en los sistemas comparados de carrera funcionarial. *Revista Aragonesa de Administración Pública, 38*, 293–334.

Rocha, J. A. O., & Araújo, J. F. (2007). Administrative reform in Portugal: Problems and prospects. *International Review of Administrative Sciences, 73*, 583–596.

Rodríguez, S. (2011). Externalización y empleo público en régimen laboral. In L. Ortega (Dir.), *Crisis y Externalización en el Sector Público: ¿Solución o Problema?* (pp. 154–270). Madrid: INAP.

Rojas, G. (2013). La reforma laboral 2012 en las administraciones públicas. *Revista Vasca de Gestión de Personas y Organizaciones Públicas, 4*, 56–75.

Román, P., & Láiz, C. (2003). *Política Comparada*. Madrid: McGraw-Hill.

SIEP. (2013). *Síntese estatística do emprego público*. Direcção-Geral da Administração e do Emprego Público.

Silvestre, H. (2010). *Gestão Pública: Modelos de Prestação no Serviço Público*. Lisboa: Escolar Editora.

Thompson, J. R. (2010). Relação e parceria trabalho-gestão: elas foram reinventadas. In B. Guy Peters & Jon Pierre (Coords.), *Administração pública* (pp. 99–123). Coletânea, São Paulo-Brasilia DF: ENAP and Editora UNESP.

Vahid, F., Muntaner, C., Puig-Barrachina, V., & Benach, J. (2011). Recortes profundos que hay que cortar por lo sano. *Papeles de Relaciones Ecosociales y Cambio Global, 113*, 107–119.

Varela, E. J. (2003). *Las Administraciones Públicas Contemporáneas en España. Una Visión Multidisciplinar desde el Estado de las Autonomías*. Santiago de Compostela: Tórculo Edicións.

Vázquez, R. P. (2007). *Derecho del Empleo Público*. Madrid: Marcial Pons.

Virtanen, T. (2000). Changing competences of public managers: Tensions in commitment. *International Journal of Public Sector Management, 13–4*, 333–341.

Yntema, P. (1996). La gestión de los recursos humanos en el sector público. In Q. Brugué, & J. Subirats (Coords.), *Lecturas de Gestión Pública* (pp. 301–319). Madrid: INAP-BOE.

Part IV
Cases of Institutional Change

Congressional Negotiations with Costly Voting: Understanding the Reforms to PEMEX in 2006–2008

Gilles Serra

1 Introduction[1]

For decades until 2008, Pemex seemed impossible to reform. Petróleos Mexicanos (Pemex), the Mexican state-owned company in charge of all petrochemical activities in the country, started facing economic difficulties around three decades ago. In particular, the company struggled to maintain high levels of productivity; its production of oil started falling steeply from its peak in 2004; and oil reserves were being depleted. The stakes have been high for the Mexican people whose well-being is still linked to oil production. Although the Mexican industry has been able to diversify into producing many other goods and services, petroleum and its derivatives are still a fundamental part of the economy. Any decline in oil production can be expected to have a negative effect on growth and development. Furthermore, the government remains highly dependent on taxes levied on the oil industry, which still represent about one third of public revenue: for instance, in 2007, during the negotiations studied in this chapter, 32 % of the Federal Government's income came from royalties paid by Pemex. If production continued to decline at that pace, the

[1]This chapter grew out of a commission to explain the politics of energy reform in Mexico from the Baker Institute for Public Policy at Rice University. The research benefitted from being presented at UC Berkeley, Rice University, the University of Oxford, CIDE, and the annual meetings of American Political Science Association and the Midwest Political Science Association. I benefitted from insightful conversations with Allyson Benton, Carlos Elizondo, Raul Gonzalez, Miriam Grunstein, Gregg Johnson and Ignacio Marván. Cristian Puga provided excellent research assistance. All errors are my responsibility.

G. Serra (✉)
División de Estudios Politicos (DEP), Centro de Investigación y Docencia Económicas (CIDE), Carretera México-Toluca #3655, Col. Lomas de Santa Fe, Mexico City 01210, Mexico
e-mail: gilles.serra@cide.edu

N. Schofield, G. Caballero (eds.), *State, Institutions and Democracy*, Studies in Political Economy, DOI 10.1007/978-3-319-44582-3_13

government's fiscal balance would be in imminent jeopardy. The stakes have been high for the global market as well. Among oil companies in the world, Pemex is the eleventh largest overall, and the fifth largest state-owned company. Thus an absence of Mexican oil could lead to increases in international prices. This would be particularly hurtful to American consumers since the Unites States relies on oil supplies from its southern neighbor, which is one of its three largest suppliers.

Such being the stakes, it is worth asking why changes to the oil industry in Mexico had been so slow to come about. In spite of many attempts by a series of administrations, the Mexican government had not been able to enact a legal reform that significantly altered the functioning of Mexico's giant oil company. Political gridlock between parties in the Mexican Congress was a main obstacle. Note that any reform must be the product of legislative negotiations, so the crucial role of political elites and government institutions should not be underestimated. Therefore, a good understanding of the political process in Mexico is crucial for explaining the lack of reform for over two decades, as well as the success of the reforms of 2008, which is the focus of this chapter. Nevertheless, political studies of the Mexican oil industry are hard to find. In spite of an active debate in terms of policy recommendations, little analysis has been done about the political constraints. A lot of ink and paper is spent on advocacy, with pundits and politicians making passionate recommendations with varying degrees of expertise. But almost no academic writing can be found about the political negotiations to reform Pemex. More analytical and conceptual research is needed if we are to gain a deep understanding of these problems and their possible solutions.

The energy reforms of 2008 in Mexico are interesting to study for several reasons. First, the fact that they actually occurred is remarkable. Voices calling for deep structural changes had been heard at least since the 1980s, when it started to become evident that an overhaul of some kind was necessary. However, there has always been disagreement on specific proposals on this highly sensitive issue that polarizes Mexicans among ideological lines. Hence an impactful proposal revising the legal framework, management structure, or fiscal regime of Pemex was elusive. Low-impact reforms were passed in 1993 and 1995, but subsequent attempts to implement significant changes had largely failed. Several high-ranking politicians, including Presidents Ernesto Zedillo and Vicente Fox, sought to modernize the oil company but their attempts were ultimately unsuccessful as both presidents failed to pass energy reforms through Congress. So when President Calderón finally succeeded in passing meaningful legislation, he was able to claim with some veracity that "Mexico has accomplished an achievement that can be described as historic, as this is the most important reform in this matter since 1938, when the oil industry was nationalized."[2]

[2]As quoted by Elizondo (2011, p. 35).

Yet the reforms of 2006–2008 that ended up being approved in Congress were significantly watered-down versions of Calderón's initial proposals. So a second puzzle is why the enacted reforms were not more profound. As I will document later, there were conditions for much deeper reforms. In fact, a far-reaching initiative was very close to being approved, but unexpected events blocked this initiative in surprising ways that deserve better understanding. Another set of reasons making these reforms interesting is their positive impact. At the economic level, while being considered insufficient, these reforms succeeded in slowing down the fast decline in Pemex's productivity. Official figures show some stability since 2009, which has been partly attributed to the positive effects of previous legal reforms. At the political level, the negotiations of 2008 can be given significant credit for the success of a subsequent series of profound reforms in 2013 by laying the ground for these new negotiations.

A final reason for studying these reforms is theoretical. I will propose a general analytical framework that will shed light on some of the very complex dynamics occurring in legislative negotiations of the kind seen in Mexico during 2006–2008. I use traditional concepts from the *spatial theory of voting*, which characterizes policy issues as linear dimensions, and depicts ideological positions as points in those dimensions. In particular, I will propose a way to analyze the formation of congressional coalitions in Mexico based on specific graphs to visualize the positions of different political actors. I pay special attention to the main stakeholders, their interests, and their ideologies, all of which influenced their negotiations in the legislature. To this traditional framework, I will add a non-standard element that I believe serves to complement the theory in realistic ways: I propose that legislators face costs and benefits from voting a certain way, independently of their ideology. As will be illustrated below, this simple addition can go a long way in explaining certain decisions by politicians that would otherwise look puzzling.

In sum, the contribution of this chapter will be fourfold. First, I identify the main issues of contention that systematically arise in debates and negotiations to reform Pemex. I claim that three issues create the most tension between the main political actors: the involvement of private capital in the oil industry; the transparency of Pemex's economic transactions; and the fiscal burden on Pemex. Second, I identify the positions of the main stakeholders on those issues. Political parties, the Executive Branch, and other key players have strong preferences on those three dimensions that will determine the type of commitments they are willing to agree to. Third, I study the types of coalitions that were formed in 2006–2008 to pass new legislation. The need for coalitions, and the type of coalitions that can be formed, hinge on the structure of Congress and the specific lawmaking rules in Mexico. And fourth, I illustrate how the theoretical concepts proposed in this chapter, in particular the existence of voting costs and benefits independent of ideology, help explain the outcomes of these important negotiations. The analysis in this chapter will also suggest the general usefulness of applying this spatial voting framework to other congressional reforms in Mexico and elsewhere.

2 The Economic and Political Context in 2006–2008

In recent history, Pemex has faced several hurdles. The challenges facing the beleaguered oil company have been geological, managerial, economic and political. In previous research I described in more detail the situation of the oil industry during Felipe Calderón's administration, while he launched his reform processes (see Serra 2011). Here I summarize it succinctly before focusing on the congressional negotiations that are the topic of this chapter.

2.1 Geological Challenges

By the mid 2000s, the situation was pessimistic: some experts even believed that Mexico would become a net oil *importer* the following decade (Medlock and Soligo 2011). The decline in oil production was mainly a consequence of new geological constraints. The easy reserves to be found and exploited were becoming rare; and the areas that were known or suspected to have large reserves were difficult to explore and exploit. Much oil is suspected to exist in the Gulf of Mexico, underneath 5000 feet of water. But those reserves are hard to reach as they require modern technology for deep-water exploration. The Mexican government has always lacked the technology and the expertise to explore beyond shallow waters. Hence, for those ventures to be viable they require partnering with other oil companies. However, the Mexican regulation used to be one of the most restrictive in the world as it precluded most types of joint ventures with any type of private or foreign firms (Grunstein 2010).

2.2 Managerial Inefficiencies

In addition to these geological challenges, Pemex faced a number or structural problems making its operation far from efficient. Pemex has a powerful union that exerts much influence in the company's management. Employees are nearly impossible to layoff, and the union serves as gatekeeper for new hiring (de la Calle 2007). Another source of inefficiency is the degree of clientelism that pervades the company. Many of its economic activities are captured by interest groups and rent seekers of different sorts. Corruption is common both in downstream activities, such as transportation, and upstream activities, such as exploration, where juicy contracts are granted in less than transparent ways (Elizondo 2011). On top of its internal problems, the government imposed a large tax levy on the company. Royalties and sales taxes have tended to deplete Pemex's revenues leaving little scope for reinvestment and recapitalization. Hence reformers had to confront highly mobilized groups whose interests would be affected by changes in the status quo.

2.3 Legal Restrictions

Regarding the oil industry, any substantive change would require passing new legislation. The statues that needed modification prior to 2006 were well known. Negotiations about Pemex and the oil industry have usually been spurred by two kinds of initiatives: fiscal initiatives and energy initiatives. Some possible changes required modifying ordinary laws; other options required amending the Constitution. Either way, difficult negotiations and major concessions were needed. Changes to an ordinary law require a simple majority in Congress, namely 50 % of the votes cast. In contrast, changes to the Constitution require a supermajority of votes in Congress, namely two thirds of the votes in each chamber plus the approval by simple majority of a majority of state legislatures. It follows that changing the Constitution is more difficult than changing ordinary laws, a fact that must be taken into account by those who wish to initiate any reform.

The oil industry is regulated at both levels. At the Constitutional level, a strict ownership of petroleum and other natural resources was granted to the State. More importantly, the Constitution had put the State *exclusively* in charge of the economic activities deemed strategic. The strategic areas include petroleum and all other hydrocarbons as well as basic petrochemicals. In effect, these Constitutional articles established a state-monopoly in most activities related to oil. At the ordinary-law level, the statutes accompanying the Constitution reinforced the State's monopoly in oil-related activities. Reformers always need to choose their goals carefully: a legal battle to change the Constitution would presumably be more meaningful, but tougher, than changing ordinary laws. In 2008, President Calderón chose the latter: he explicitly ruled out any Constitutional amendments, and therefore the initiative he sent to Congress pertained only to statutory laws. Indeed, he calculated this was the only kind of reform that could get past the major political parties in Congress (Farfán and García 2009).

2.4 Congress

Congressional gridlock had been one of the major obstacles for any structural reform in Mexico, including energy reform. The Executive is quite limited in what it can accomplish on its own, given that changing the regulatory framework requires passing new legislation through Congress. The government is divided in three independent branches: Executive, Legislative and Judicial. The legislative branch has two chambers: the Senate, i.e. the Upper House, and the Chamber of Deputies, i.e. the Lower House. Importantly, legislators are not allowed to seek reelection in consecutive terms. Hence, they must find a different appointment at the end of each term. This implies that Senators and Deputies are highly dependent on their parties for subsequent promotions. This no-reelection rule is one of the sources of the exceptional discipline that party leaders can exert on their delegates in Congress.

Legislative bills can be initiated by Congress or the Executive, and they usually need to be approved in both chambers.

2.5 Political Parties

Mexico had three main political parties at the time: the National Action Party (PAN), the Party of the Democratic Revolution (PRD), and the Party of the Institutional Revolution (PRI). In general terms, the PAN is viewed as right-of-center, the PRD is viewed as left-of-center, and the PRI claims to hold the middle ground. In 2008, there were other smaller parties represented in congress. In particular, two leftist parties had made a close alliance with the PRD.[3] Two other small parties were closely allied with the PRI and the PAN during oil negotiations.[4] I describe the ideologies and preferences of those parties in more detail later, especially in regards to oil issues.

These three parties are strong, well defined, and hierarchical. They have large memberships and large bases of support. Such is their dominance of politics that together they are often referred to as a "partyarchy" (Serra 2012). In particular, they tend to be exceptionally disciplined in Congress, meaning that all the legislators nearly always vote the party line. (Interestingly, as we will see, the 2008 energy reforms were an exception where parties faced internal divisions.) In the past two decades, all three parties have held solid shares of seats in Congress. Figure 1 shows the configuration of the legislatures following the 2006 presidential election.

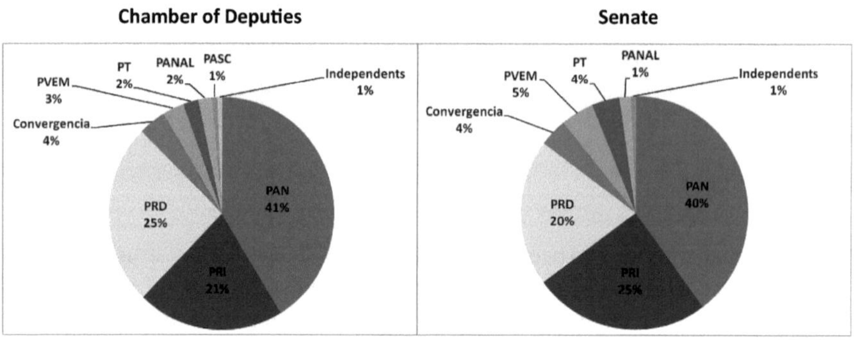

Fig. 1 Parties' share of seats in the LX Legislature, 2006–2009 *Source*: Secretaría de Gobernación, Sistema de Información Legislativa http://sil.gobernacion.gob.mx/portal

[3]The Workers Party (PT) and the party *Convergencia*. Together, the three leftist parties were referred to as the Ample Progressive Front (FAP).

[4]The Green Ecological Party of Mexico (PVEM) and the New Alliance Party (PANAL).

As we can tell from the figure, in 2008, no party had more than 50 % of the seats in Congress. We can also see that the governing PAN could make a coalition with either of the big parties to reach a majority of votes for changing ordinary laws. In theory, the PAN could also make a coalition with one big party and several small parties to reach the two-thirds supermajority needed to change the Constitution. As I describe later, both strategies were attempted in order to reform Pemex.

2.6 *Political Polarization*

The presidential election held in July 2006 posed an unprecedented challenge to Mexican democracy. The PAN candidate, Felipe Calderón, came in first place while the PRD candidates came in second; but the margin of victory was breathtakingly narrow. The official tally yielded a difference of barely 0.6 % between the first-place and second-place candidates (the PRI candidate came in a distant third). The PRD always claimed they had been robbed of their victory by a conspiracy of conservative groups that orchestrated a fraudulent election. López Obrador proclaimed himself the true winner, calling Calderón an "illegitimate" or "spurious" president. Conservative and progressive forces were more polarized in 2006 than they had ever been in modern Mexican history.[5]

Such being the institutional context for an eventual energy reform, now I analyze its possible substance. What are the main issues that parties could bargain over in Congressional negotiations?

3 Issue Dimensions

The topic of oil production is complex, with countless implications and ramifications. Its regulation is also complex; the Mexican law includes many statutes and clauses relating to the energy sector with a wide array of consequences. However, when it comes to fundamental reforms, only a few key issues tend to dominate the discussions. This is certainly the case in the public debate: among the numerous facets of the oil industry, the public debate has tended to focus mostly on a few hot buttons. We can observe that the media, for example, tends to comment on topics that create passion while ignoring topics that are less sensational. Political parties, for ideological and practical reasons, also tend to take strong positions on only certain topics but not others. Likewise, ordinary citizens tend to form an opinion on broad problems, such as corruption, rather than forming an opinion on detailed

[5]For more details on the 2006 post-election crisis and how it influenced legislation in Congress, see Serra (2012).

minutiae, such as specific extraction technologies. For empirical accuracy it is thus pertinent to identify the issues that are usually most salient in the public debate.

I am also interested in pointing out the issues that are most divisive among political actors. Upon studying past energy reforms, it is apparent that politicians spend most of their time debating a few sticking points. To be precise, I postulate that most of the contentious points of oil reform in Mexico can be organized in three broad dimensions. (1) The degree to which private capital can and should participate in exploration and other economic activities of Pemex. I call this dimension *Private Investment*. (2) The degree of benefits and influence granted to the union leaders, clientelistic contractors and other non-accountable rent-seekers. I call this dimension *Accountability*. And (3), the amount of income that Pemex should be allowed to keep rather than being transferred to the government, as well as the freedom granted to Pemex to manage its funds. I call this dimension *Fiscal Autonomy*. Those three topics have created the most tension among political actors in past negotiations to reform Pemex, including the ones from 2006 until 2008 which are the focus of this chapter.

In Serra (2011) I described these three issues at length—the reader could refer to that paper as a complement to this chapter. In that research I showed that all three issues entail a wide spectrum of possibilities that allow us to think of them as continuous dimensions. For instance, the law could specify any degree of fiscal autonomy. It could go from complete control of Pemex's expenditure and complete taxation of its income (i.e. no autonomy) to complete freedom to use its resources (i.e. full autonomy). The law could also specify any degree of private participation. It could go from assigning every single stage of the production process exclusively to the state without allowing any delegation to external providers (i.e. no private participation) to complete freedom for other companies to partner or compete with Pemex (i.e. full private participation). Finally, the law could specify any degree of accountability. It could go from leaving large voids by being completely ambiguous in its regulation (i.e. no accountability) to being extremely precise and forceful in its monitoring of economic transactions (i.e. full accountability). In Serra (2011) I describe the moderate, intermediate and extreme states that those three dimensions could possibly take.

Taken together, those three topics serve as the conceptual framework for my analysis. I refer to each of those topics as an "issue-dimension" or a "policy-dimension" because they neatly separate the positions of different political actors as distinct points on a continuous line. I will show how this "spatial" framework can help analyze energy reforms. It should be noted, however, that these three issues are not usually negotiated together. In fact, the first two issues, private investment and accountability, are usually negotiated jointly as part of an energy bill while the third issue, fiscal autonomy, is usually negotiated as part of a fiscal bill. Such was the case between 2006 and 2008, which means that we must analyze two sets of negotiations separately.

4 The Main Actors and Their Policy Positions in 2006–2008

The next step in understanding the reform process is to identify the actors that were most influential. The legislative process in Mexico is usually dominated by a few individuals and organizations who act as the main dealmakers in Congress. My goal is to identify them and describe their preferences on the main dimensions of energy reform. Legal initiatives of this magnitude need to be spearheaded by a determined leader. In this period, it was President Calderón who designed and sent the relevant initiatives. Once received, it was up to the major political parties to decide whether to approve, reject or amend the initiatives. Given the pivotal influence they have in passing any reform, those are the main agents to consider: the president, the PAN, the PRD and the PRI.

4.1 The Executive Branch and the President

Felipe Calderón is a lifelong *panista*—his father was one of the founders of the PAN and he joined the party when he was 19. As president, he did not have full control of his party, however. Calderón was closely identified with a certain faction within his party, but he had differences with other members. In particular, he made enemies by sidelining those cadres that were not particularly loyal to him. Thus, to garner support for his initiatives, the President had to engage in internal negotiations within his party in addition to the external negotiations with the other parties. Regarding Pemex, Calderón was very familiar with its challenges since he served as Energy Secretary in the previous administration of Vicente Fox. His preferred solutions very clearly involved liberalizing the oil industry although he was always realistic in how much he could push for. To simplify the analysis, in terms of policy preferences, I will assume that the president was perfectly represented in Congress by one of the dominant factions within his party, but other legislators in the same party were represented by a second faction. I describe such factions within the PAN below.

4.2 The PAN

In general terms, the PAN is a center-right party with a long tradition of advocating economically liberal policies. For most of the twentieth century, the PAN was the most prominent opposition to the hegemonic PRI. After democratic reforms in the 1990s that leveled the playing field in elections, the PAN routed the PRI by winning the 2000 election with Vicente Fox as its candidate. The PAN won the presidency again in the subsequent election of 2006, granting office to Felipe Calderón until 2012. We should keep in mind that Mexico does not allow the reelection of presidents, which implies that all administrations can only last for one term.

Compared to the other major parties, the PAN has traditionally been the most homogenous ideologically. Opposing factions exist, but their discrepancies seem to come from loyalties to different leaders and preferences for different political tactics, rather than fundamental ideological disagreements. Hence conflict between factions tends to arise from power struggles to dominate the party rather than ideological struggles to advocate different policies. In addition, these conflicts have often been resolved internally such that a unified front can be presented in congressional negotiations. This was patent while preparing the energy reform of 2008. To be sure, it was reported that some ideological divisions existed within the PAN and the government. More specifically, there was an "entrepreneurial" faction who wanted more liberalization than President Calderón considered prudent to fight for at that point in time. On the other hand, there was another faction called the "humanists" who shared the more pragmatic strategy of the President (Farfán and García 2009). Ultimately, all factions rallied behind the Executive's initiative, at least publicly.[6]

On the issue of private investment, the PAN has insisted on the need for Pemex to partner with big transnational companies to carry out deepwater exploration and other upstream activities for which Pemex lacks expertise. For this purpose, it has advocated for more flexible contracts that include economic incentives to service providers, such as risk-sharing or production-sharing contracts. Moreover, consistent with its traditional market-friendly ideology, the PAN would also prefer to delegate to the private sector the construction of refineries, ducts, storage, and other downstream activities.

On the issue of accountability, *panistas* shared the view of many technocrats that Pemex would be better off if the union was weakened. According to this view, the strong grip that union leaders had on the company was preventing its modernization—consequently the union should be forced to make serious concessions. It should be noted, however, that in spite of such views, both President Fox and President Calderón were unwilling to confront the union directly fearing a possible retaliation. PAN presidents were unwilling to push this issue by themselves: only a large coalition of partners that included the PRI was likely to challenge the union's interests. Regarding economic clienteles profiting from doing business with Pemex, the PAN was eager to introduce more transparency in those economic transactions. It should be noted that prominent members of the PAN had themselves been embroiled in high-level scandals of corruption for their lucrative dealings in the oil industry.[7] But as an institution, the PAN wished to be consistent with its traditional stance for honesty and transparency.

[6]The negotiations did encounter some trouble due to enmities of PAN members with the president, which seemed to stem from personal vendettas rather than fundamental ideological differences (Starr 2009, p. 146).

[7]See the many examples described in Elizondo (2011, fn 73).

On the issue of fiscal autonomy, the Calderón administration had mixed motivations. On one hand, its entrepreneurial instincts would normally be to decrease the tax burden on Pemex allowing it to operate as a rational profit-maximizing firm. On the other hand, the PAN was running the federal government, thus needing to raise fiscal funds to carry out its program. In the end, its ideological views were dwarfed by the very pragmatic desire to have fiscal funds throughout the administration. Hence the Secretary of the Treasury endeavored to quell the sustained pressure from opposition parties to let Pemex keep more of its income. The conjecture in this chapter is that incumbency will trump ideology, such that any incumbent party will tend to oppose a large reduction in tax income.

4.3 The PRD

The PRD was born in the late 1980s out of a broad alliance of leftist groups that ranged from left-of-center dissidents of the PRI all the way to smaller communist organizations. So from birth, the party has served as an umbrella organization for a number of diverse subgroups, sometimes referred to as "the PRD tribes," which have occasionally engaged in damaging strife. In 2008, two large factions dominated the party. The first one, which was officially called *Nueva Izquierda*, commanded most of the bureaucratic positions in the PRD, including the Chairman position. It also commanded the loyalty of a majority of PRD legislators in Congress. *Nueva Izquierda* was considered the moderate faction within the party because they were the most willing to engage with President Calderón and the other parties in legislative negotiations (Starr 2007).

On the other hand, the second dominant faction had explicitly ruled out any communication with the government. This faction was loyal to Andrés Manuel López Obrador, who was a presidential candidate in 2006. López Obrador never accepted his defeat. Since the election, he used his influence to dissuade the PRD and other left-wing parties from cooperating in any way with the Calderón administration. His faction was more radical than *Nueva Izquierda* both in terms of ideology and tactics (Langston and Pérez 2009, p. 497). Among PRD legislators, López Obrador had a sizeable number of self-identified loyalists, but not a majority. However, as I explain later, he still wielded considerable influence on the totality of PRD politicians given his tremendous popularity with the leftist base of voters. In addition, López Obrador could count on the unconditional support of the other two small parties in the left-wing alliance.

The PRD generally supports socially liberal issues, and it advocates distributive policies in favor of the most vulnerable groups in the population. On the issue of private investment, the PRD espoused the nationalistic view that oil should be exploited exclusively by the State. In a way, the PRD was in competition with the PRI to be the most patriotic defender of strategic resources. For most of the twentieth century there was no doubt that such nationalistic banners were politically owned by the PRI, especially given that it was a PRI president, Lázaro

Cárdenas, who initially nationalized the oil industry from foreign firms. But then the ownership of the nationalistic banner was very much in doubt with the PRD rising as the fiercest defender of national sovereignty. This was especially true of López Obrador's faction which organized massive street demonstrations to stop the 2008 energy reforms, as I describe later. Even symbolically, the party has claims over the historic nationalization of the oil industry given that Lázaro Cárdenas' prodigal son, Cuauhtémoc, was the founder of the PRD.

Consequently, the PRD's position was that private firms should not be allowed in strategic activities such as transportation, storage and transformation of hydrocarbons. Moreover, contracts with service providers should not have any privatizing undertones. In particular, contracts should not be tied to the price, quantity or quality of the oil extracted. Service providers should not be allowed to speculate with the rent from oil, and they should certainly not be allowed to add Mexican reserves to their books. And most crucially, Pemex should never sell shares of stock, or be otherwise privatized. The PRD position in 2008 could be summarized in a few words: No more changes to the Constitution. In fact, many in the PRD felt that recent policies had already violated the spirit of the Constitution, and that PEMEX had already moved too far in the direction of privatization. They pointed out that PEMEX engineers used to conduct most exploration endeavors, while later many tasks were outsourced to private contractors. So we can safely say that some *perredistas* in 2008 were to the left of the status quo.

Regarding Pemex's labor union, the PRD's position was surprisingly close to the PAN. Given its progressive nature, the PRD is naturally pro-worker. But that does not mean it was pro-union in the case of Pemex. The union had a tainted reputation, which contradicted the PRD's desire for more transparency. In addition, the selection of union leaders was not exactly democratic, which fed the PRD's demands for more accountability. Importantly, the union remained highly loyal to the PRI. Therefore the PRD was relatively supportive of decreasing the power of the union. On the issue of accountability, the party was even also clearly against corrupt practices among rent-seeking entrepreneurs doing business with Pemex.

Regarding the fiscal burden on Pemex, the PRD has long argued that it should be drastically reduced. As a matter of fact, such is the main solution it has proposed to rescue the oil industry. In response to the crisis in production that Pemex was going through, the PRD's proposal was to increase public investment. More public funds should be devoted to exploration. More spending should also be devoted to scientific research done by Mexican engineers. Pemex mostly needed to keep a larger share of its income rather than paying such high royalties. In addition to its ideology, the PRD also had political incentives to advocate for a lower tax burden. First, it was a popular issue with voters. And second, the PRD is an opposition party and, as I argued above, opposition parties have fewer incentives to protect government revenues.

4.4 The PRI

The PRI is the party issued from the Mexican revolution. It governed Mexico since 1929 until 2000, at which point it lost power to the PAN's candidate, Vicente Fox. It failed again to gain power in 2006, when it came a distant third behind the PAN and the PRD. However, the PRI had garnered significant momentum since 2006, being the best positioned party to win the 2012 presidential election. A large part of the PRI's renewed popularity was due to the mediating role it had taken during the Calderón administration. Ideologically it presented itself as the moderate party between the rightist PAN and the leftist PRD. It blossomed in the role of ultimate power-broker in a political ambience that was extremely polarized.

The PRI membership covers a wide political spectrum. So it is no surprise that ideological divisions exist within its large structure. In 2008, two factions emerged as the most influential in discussing the oil industry. One faction consisted of the technocrats within the party. It was often referred to as the "neoliberal" faction for its association with economics-trained presidents Carlos Salinas and Ernesto Zedillo. This faction was ideologically close to the PAN, and was willing to consider a partial liberalization of the oil industry. The members of the other faction called themselves the "nationalists." They opposed any reform with privatizing undertones. They were quick to recall that it was a PRI president who nationalized the oil industry back in 1938. Indeed, the PRI has a strong claim over the symbolism surrounding Mexican oil. Pemex in particular, which has become a symbol of Mexican sovereignty in the struggle to overcome foreign imperialism, is strongly identified with that party. Hence many traditional "priístas" spoke publicly against the PAN initiative of 2008, and implicitly sided with the PRD in trying to block it.

On the issue of accountability, the PRI was the most opposed in Congress to changing the status quo. As with other trade unions, the PRI has a very close link to the Pemex one. During its period in power, the PRI gave ample autonomy to trade unions to manage their funds without oversight, and it ensured that union leaders were recurrently reelected undemocratically. In exchange, the party has enjoyed the trade unions' political and economic support during elections. A blatant example occurred in 2000 when the Pemex union channeled massive amounts of illegal funds to the presidential campaign of the PRI's candidate. Given their relationship of mutual support, the PRI served as the union's ally in Congress, opposing any measure that affected the union's interests. In fact, such was a prerequisite to support the PAN's legislative initiative in 2008: the PRI requested that labor privileges be kept out of the negotiations (Farfán and García 2009).

Regarding transparency, the PRI's position is further complicated by the close ties it has with service providers. The PRI is known to have a clientelistic relationship with trucking companies transporting gasoline and gas, as well as other entrenched rent-seekers (Elizondo 2011). For that reason, in 2008 the PRI opposed the clauses that would have increased transparency in contracting. They also opposed opening transport, storage, distribution and other downstream activities to market competition.

On the issue of fiscal autonomy, the PRI advocated for lower taxes on the oil industry. Its reasons were similar to those of the PRD described above: an ideological preference for strengthening state-owned companies rather than strengthening private competitors; and a high tolerance to reducing the government's income because it was an opposition party.

4.5 Other Actors

There are of course several other actors that tried to influence the process. These include: the small parties[8] and the independent legislators represented in Congress; the Pemex labor union; oil companies and the oil industry around the world; public opinion; the media; pundits; intellectuals; experts and academics. I consider those actors to be secondary in my analysis because their influence was either smaller (as with small parties), or they do not directly vote in Congress in spite of having a strong indirect influence (as with the labor union).

4.6 Multiparty Negotiations

We are now in a position to analyze the negotiation process. How could we expect energy reforms to unfold in the Mexican Congress of 2006? So far, I have described the players, i.e. the political actors, and the rules of the game, i.e. the legislative institutions. Given this setup, the next section describes the type of coalitions that needed to be made in order to achieve a reform. I do so by constructing some useful graphs depicting the political parties and their positions on different issues. Such graphs will serve as visual aids to help identify the types of coalitions that could have been formed, and the types of outcomes that each coalition could bring about. This type of graphical analysis of coalition-making is common in "spatial voting theory," as mentioned in previous sections. While my presentation here will be heuristic and intuitive, the reader can read the appendix to this chapter for a more formal presentation of these theoretical ideas.

Before proceeding I need to distinguish two different types of Congressional negotiations that relate to Pemex. As it turns out, there are two separate types of agendas where issues about Pemex can be included. One type of agenda encompasses fiscal and budgetary issues, which is where Pemex's fiscal burden would be discussed. Such discussions typically take place in the context of a *budget law* or a *fiscal reform* of the kind that President Calderón initiated in 2006 and 2007 respectively. A second type of agenda encompasses the issues of private investment and accountability. The set of laws regulating those two issues can be discussed

[8]PVEM, PANAL, PT, *Convergencia*, PASC.

together, particularly in the context of a comprehensive *energy reform* such as the one of 2008. Given that those two types of agendas are fairly independent of each other, I will study them separately.

5 The Negotiations for a Fiscal Reform of Pemex in 2006 and 2007

One of the most important concerns regarding Pemex is its fiscal health. Several measures can increase the fiscal independence of Pemex such as allowing the company to acquire more debt—but the most direct measure would be to decrease its tax burden. As I mentioned above, the royalties and other levies on Pemex are very high, preventing the company to reinvest its income in research and exploration. So it is no surprise that reducing those taxes is a frequent proposal among politicians who wish to save Pemex from bankruptcy. Accordingly, I focus my analysis on whether taxes on Pemex can be decreased as the result of a Congressional negotiation. How did it occur at the end of 2006 and then again in 2007? The finances of Pemex tend to be discussed in the context of budget and fiscal negotiations. For example, during the Calderón administration, the finances of Pemex were first discussed during the budget law at the end of 2006, and then again during the fiscal reform of 2007. In those negotiations, the taxation of Pemex was pitched against all other taxes to determine an overall level of government revenues. Indeed, Mexico's government is in a tight fiscal situation: it has the lowest tax revenue as a percentage of GDP among all the OECD countries. So any reduction on Pemex's levy would need to be compensated by other sources income.

My goal now is to construct a graph that will help us visualize the type of discussions that take place in fiscal and budget negotiations in Congress. In accordance with the theoretical framework that I present in the appendix, I will interpret the possible policy outcomes as a two-dimensional space. In this case, the two dimensions correspond to the following two policy instruments: first, the amount of taxes levied on Pemex; and second, the amount of all other non-Pemex taxes. Each of those two policy instruments will be interpreted as a continuous line, where different points represent different levels of taxation. I do this in Fig. 2. The horizontal line, meaning the x axis, represents the amount taxes and royalties levied on Pemex, and the vertical line, meaning the y axis, represents the amount of taxes from all other sources. I also aim to depict the positions of all three major political parties during the Calderón administration, according to their ideological preferences on those two dimensions along with their costs and benefits from supporting the government's initiatives.

It turns out that the PAN, being an incumbent party, was willing to entertain a small reduction in Pemex royalties but not a large one since it needed resources to carry out its program. It also wanted to increase other taxes given that Mexico's tax revenue was so small. This led to the paradoxical situation where the most

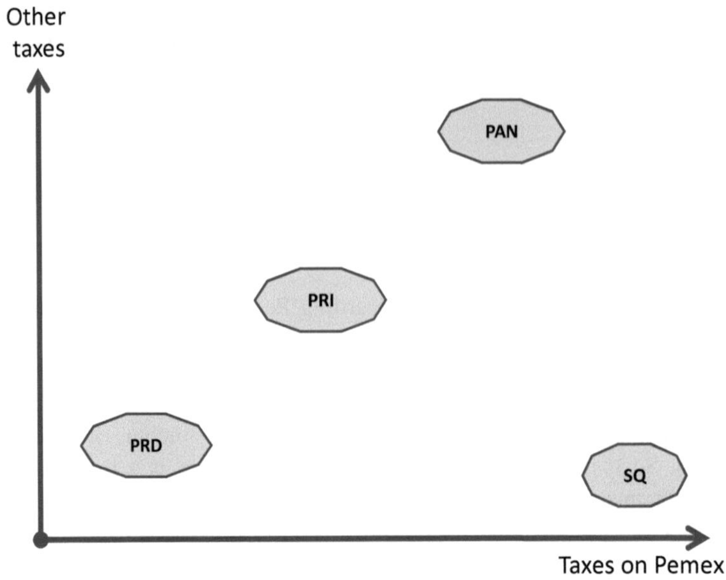

Fig. 2 The agenda to decrease the fiscal burden on Pemex during Felipe Calderón's administration

conservative and market-oriented party in Mexico, the PAN, was resisting a decrease in Pemex taxes and fighting for higher taxes on all other possible items. On the other hand, the opposition parties could afford to advocate for tax cuts, and more so if they did not expect to win the presidency in the short run.

This political logic led the PRD to adopt some surprising positions. It advocated for significantly decreasing the royalties on Pemex, which was consistent with its traditional position. But what about other taxes? Naturally enough, the PRD was against some ostensibly regressive taxes proposed by the PAN, such as increasing the VAT and the gasoline levy. However, paradoxically, the PRD also opposed many of the progressive taxes proposed by Calderón, which included a large corporate tax in addition to closing loopholes on the income tax. In principle, many PRD legislators were ideologically in favor of these progressive measures. Yet, as I will narrate below, they decided to oppose them for several reasons. One reason was purely electoral: the PRD wanted to earn points with businessmen in the middle class. Another important reason was the pressure from López Obrador. Here is how Pamela Starr, professor at ITAM and senior consultant at Eurasia Group at the time, described this dynamic:

> My personal conversations with PRD members show that PRD legislators, both Senators and Deputies, are unwilling to defy the spirit of López Obrador's order not to have any contact with the Calderón administration. The left continues to believe that López Obrador lost the 2006 presidential election as a consequence of political machinations, and López Obrador thus continues to insist that the left have nothing to do with a "spurious" president who reached office illegally and unfairly. PRD legislators, however, want to do their job;

> they want to exploit the left's control of nearly a third of congressional seats to legislate and thereby to advance some of the left's traditional policy demands. This implies working with the government to a certain degree and thus defying López Obrador. Their ability or willingness to do so, however, is limited allowing López Obrador to act like a break on their actions in the legislature. López Obrador controls the heart of the PRD's electoral base. These voters continue to look upon López Obrador as their champion. This influence with the base gives López Obrador the ability to impose limits of acceptable political behavior on most PRD politicians. If López Obrador concludes that his movement has been betrayed by a particular PRD politician, he can denounce that legislator as a traitor to the cause and rally his supporters to defeat that politician. Nor is this an unfounded fear. In July 2006, López Obrador's supporters successfully challenged the Governor of Zacatecas [of the PRD], who openly defied López Obrador, by defeating most of her candidates to the state legislature [by supporting candidates from other leftist parties]. (Starr 2007, p. 15–16).

The PRI was striking a different balance. This party actually had notable chances of winning the presidency the following election. So it had to strike a trade-off between advocating for low taxes, which was immediately popular with voters, and high taxes, which would be useful if it won the presidency in 2012. For these reasons, I believe its ideal point was placed approximately midway between the PAN's and the PRD's ideal points. Figure 2 depicts the ideal points of the three main parties, and also includes a fourth point corresponding to the level of taxation at the time, labeled Status Quo. With these graphs we can see the types of coalitions that could have been formed to decrease the level of taxation on Pemex.

5.1 The Budget Negotiations of 2006

One possible scenario was a broad coalition including all the major parties: the incumbent and the whole opposition. Such coalition can be seen in Fig. 3 below. Because it includes the three large parties, I call it a "consensus coalition."

This was the scenario at the end of 2006 during negotiations to approve the following year's budget. It was the first big negotiation between political parties following Calderón's highly contested election in July. The political atmosphere was still acrimonious, especially with the many followers of López Obrador. Calderón was eager to legitimize his narrow election with some early victories as president. He knew that approval of his first budget in Congress would go a long way in proving to the Mexican people that his administration could get things done. In addition to being a seasoned politician, Calderón had recently returned from studying a mid-career master's degree at the Harvard Kennedy School where he met many of his future policy advisors. He also took courses from the well-known *Program on Negotiation* where he learned the importance of earning the trust of his negotiation partners early on.[9] He was also advised that a sequence of negotiations

[9] I briefly overlapped with Felipe Calderón while taking similar courses in graduate school.

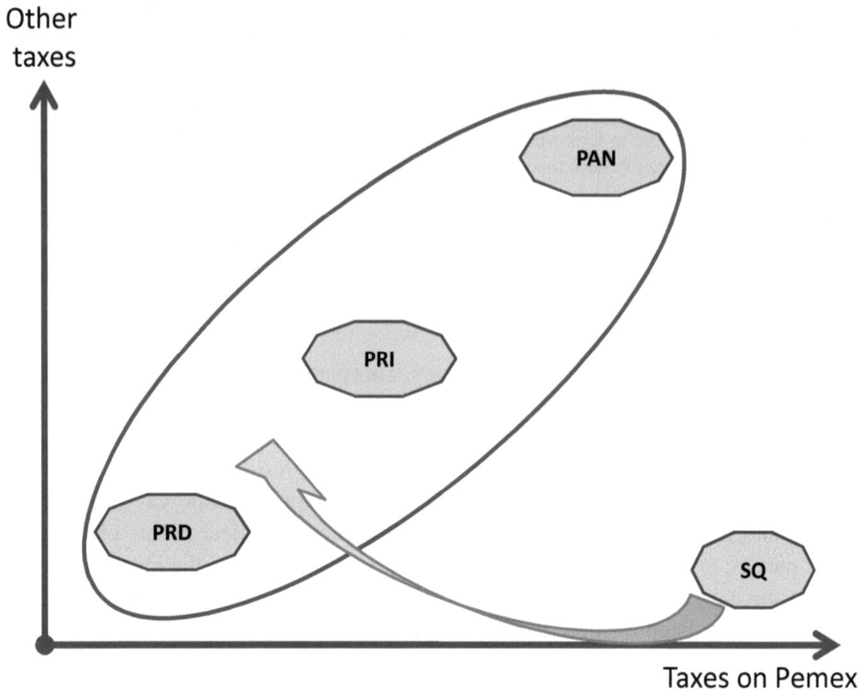

Fig. 3 Budget negotiations in 2006: A consensus coalition

should start with the easy ones, leaving the hardest ones at the end. Calderón heeded those lessons assiduously.

The PAN administration could have chosen to negotiate exclusively with the PRI, which was the opposition party with closest interests; but it did not. Calderón was eager to show that he was able to build a large consensus, and thus he endeavored to include the PRD as well as the PRI in his first major political bargain. By compromising on all fronts, the administration was able to get a smooth approval at the end of 2006. The budget for 2007 was quickly passed on a nearly unanimous vote by enticing (in effect buying) opposition support by including several key PRD budget priorities and increasing federal transfers to the states, which were governed in their majority by the opposition (Starr 2009, 140).

Insisting on a large coalition came at a cost to the government, however, as it included a larger-than-expected reduction on Pemex's tax burden requested jointly by the opposition parties. The PRD requested to include additional items in exchange for their vote. In terms of increasing subsidies, they requested higher old-age pensions for seniors in rural areas. This was a core PRD issue that helped the party justify why it was supporting a president it had so intensely scorned. It coincided with a temporary weakness in López Obrador's political power due to the erosion of his public image following the long street protests he had organized in

2006 trying to prevent the president-elect from taking office. To sweeten the deal, Calderón offered to broker the early exit of the electoral institute's staff, which had become anathema to the left for supposedly carrying out a fraud against the PRD. All this translated in low costs and high benefits for the PRD of supporting the budget. The result was a virtually unanimous vote from all parties in favor of the budget law in 2006.[10]

5.2 *The Fiscal Negotiations of 2007*

Another possible coalition with a sufficient number of votes was between the PAN and the PRI only. Such a coalition is depicted in Fig. 4 below. Because it only includes enough parties to get the bill approved while excluding other unnecessary parties, I call it a "minimum winning coalition."

This scenario occurred during the fiscal reform of 2007. The PAN proposed the creation of several new taxes, including a corporate tax (the IETU) and eliminating several deductions from the income tax. The government initially considered increasing another important tax, the VAT, which would have helped its finances;

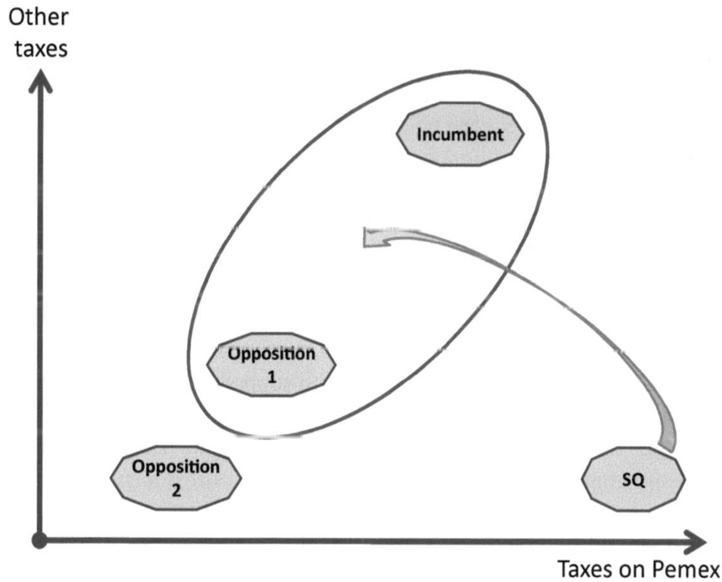

Fig. 4 Fiscal negotiations in 2007: A minimum winning coalition

[10]Technically, there were two laws that needed approval: an income law and an expenditures law, both of which were approved nearly unanimously (Castellanos et al. 2009, p. 157).

but this tax was highly unpopular. So the government eventually eschewed the VAT, focusing on more progressive taxes instead. In his continued attempt to lure left-wing voters, Calderón chose to propose the IETU which would be levied on corporations, not on individuals. Calderón also promised to devote most of the revenue to his successful poverty alleviation programs. As explained by Magar et al. (2009):

> The executive went public to persuade citizens that government resources were insufficient to deepen redistributive programs. This was an odd strategy for a center-right party whose bases of support are mostly in the middle and upper classes, but the framing succeeded in leaving left parties without strong arguments against the reform. (Magar et al. 2009, p. 73).

The PRD (i.e. the farthest opposition party) was in favor of reducing taxes on Pemex but decided to take a public stance against any tax raise. In contradiction with its leftist ideology, the PRD even voted against the corporate tax IETU. Many of its legislators were supporting this tax in private but refused to do so publicly (Castellanos et al. 2009, p. 165). It is widely believed they were bowing to strong pressure from López Obrador. This is how Starr (2007) explained this political pressure:

> Supporting this legislation was simply a bridge too far—fiscal reform was Calderón's central legislative goal for 2007 and the key to many of his policy objectives. As such, supporting fiscal reform would weaken López Obrador's strategy of weakening the Calderón presidency through a policy of non-recognition; López Obrador would thus not countenance that level of PRD collaboration with *el espurio*. (Starr 2007, p. 16).

So it became eventually clear that the PRD would not support the fiscal reform of 2007, even though it included measures to increase business taxes and income taxes to finance social programs for the poor. To their chagrin, many PRD legislators had to vote against their own preferences.

At this point the PRI (i.e. the closest opposition) became the only viable partner to the PAN for this vote in Congress. Yet the PRI feared being labeled a puppet of the president for repeatedly supporting his reforms. To avoid this cost, it preferred including the PRD in the negotiations to serve as political cover (Starr 2009, p. 141). When the PRD withheld its support for the bill, the PRI demanded higher concessions to stay on board. Being a pivotal player gave the PRI ample scope for its demands. Concretely, the PRI only agreed to support a watered down version of those taxes, namely a lower IETU. The party also conditioned its support of the fiscal package on the inclusion of substantive modifications to the fiscal regime of Pemex, which the government had not contemplated at all. As a side-payment, the party also requested fiscal decentralization by significantly increasing federal transfers to the states. It should be noted, of course, that the large majority of states had PRI governors.

In addition, the PRI also engaged in logrolling with the PAN, whereby the former would support a *fiscal* reform in exchange for the latter supporting an *election* reform. This led to the creation of highly controversial legislation known as the "2007 electoral reform." This law was in large part designed by PRI senators. It included major requests from the PRI, such as removing most of the staff of the national electoral institute, which was later replaced with new staff that allegedly had a slant in favor of the PRI. Another controversial measure designed by PRI senators was the prohibition of negative campaigning. In effect, the new law prohibited candidates from critiquing each other freely, as they could be accused of slander.[11] It can be conjectured that old-school party bosses from the PRI had the most to benefit from a ban on public critiques, so this measure can be interpreted as a side payment to PRI leaders. Confirming that logrolling was indeed taking place, both reforms, the fiscal one and the electoral one, were voted on the same day in Congress (Castellanos et al. 2009, pp. 154–155).

The fiscal reform passed on September 14, 2007, with the votes of the PAN and the PRI but without the full support of the PRD.[12] The assessment from authors like Magar, Romero and Timmons is consistent with the analysis in this section:

> The resulting changes improved the country's fiscal structure; however, it is still far from meeting the country's needs. Moreover, many amendments were side-payments to opposition parties, such as increasing spending decentralization, giving more resources to governors. That is why we deem the reform as partially successful with respect to the limited change over the status quo. (Magar et al. 2009, p. 75).

6 The 2008 Negotiations for an Energy Reform

President Calderón's most salient legacy in terms of economic reform is undoubtedly the 2008 energy bill. His initiative was introduced in April and was discussed throughout the summer until it was voted in October of that year, becoming law on November 28th. I claim that two broad dimensions can subsume the most important issues that were discussed: the degree of participation of private and foreign firms in the Mexican oil industry; and the degree to which economic transactions would become transparent in detriment of entrenched rent seeking groups. In accordance with the framework laid out above, I will respectively call those two dimensions *private investment* and *accountability*.

My goal is to construct a graph that will depict the positions of all parties on the two issues at hand—in a bi-dimensional graph I will place each political actor according to its preferences, along with the status quo according to the situation of Pemex and the oil industry in 2008. Figure 5 depicts this policy space. The horizontal line, meaning the x axis, corresponds to the level of private investment in the economic activities of Pemex. The vertical line, meaning the y axis, corresponds to the level of accountability of the Pemex labor union and service providers. In this space I have placed six important political groups according to the levels of private investment and accountability that they are expected to advocate for. Those

[11] A detailed critique of these measures from the 2007 electoral reform can be found in Serra (2012).

[12] According to Castellanos et al. (2009), the PRD legislators voted in favor of some pieces of the legislation, such as decreasing Pemex royalties, which were going to pass anyway. Rhetorically, though, the PRD came out against the fiscal package in full.

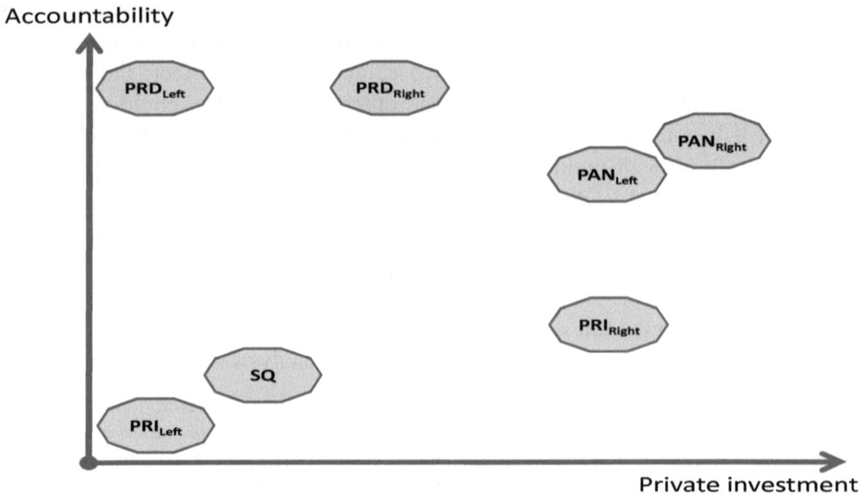

Fig. 5 The agenda to increase private investment and accountability

six groups are the left-wing faction and the right-wing faction of the three major parties, the PAN, the PRD, and the PRI, as I described in Sect. 4 above. I labeled those factions PAN_{Left}, PAN_{Right}, PRD_{Left}, PRD_{Right}, PRI_{Left}, and PRI_{Right}. The figure has a seventh point corresponding to the status quo at the time.

This two-dimensional space allows studying the possible coalitions that could be formed to implement a reform. What are the coalitions of party factions that were willing and able to move the status quo to a different location? How was reform possible in 2008, and what kind of reform was it? We should recall that changing an ordinary law requires 50 % of the votes in Congress. So the PAN by itself did not have enough votes to change the law (see the shares of seats in Fig. 1). It needed to make a coalition with some of the factions represented in Congress.

6.1 First Round: The PAN-PRI Coalition

One possible coalition was an alliance of the PAN and the PRI. Such a coalition is depicted in Fig. 6 below. This alliance was best suited to liberalize the legal restrictions on private investments in the oil industry. In fact, this was exactly the coalition that was initially formed: since the beginning of his administration in 2007, President Calderón started talks with top leaders of the PRI to discuss a possible liberalization of the petroleum industry. While PRI leaders belonged largely to the "technocratic" wing of their party, they insisted on limits on such liberalization to avoid a fracture with their "nationalist" wing. Two immediate requests from the PRI was that any reform should be restricted to ordinary laws instead of the

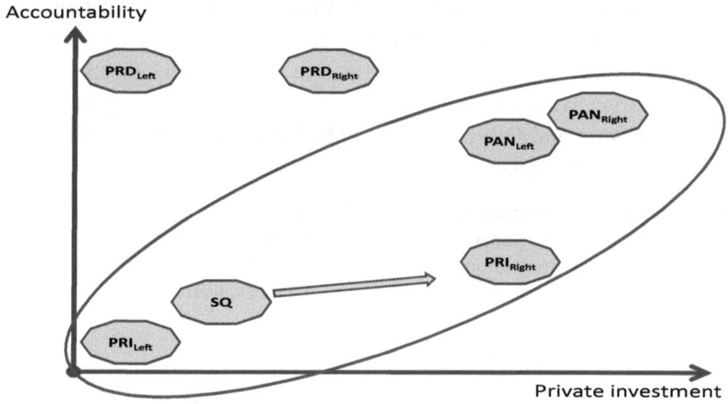

Fig. 6 The first attempt: a PAN-PRI coalition

constitutional laws; and to avoid any changes that would significantly affect the labor union's interests (Farfán and García 2009, p. 326). The PRI was also opposed to liberalizing the transport of oil products, presumably because it controlled most of the truck drivers through a patronage network (Elizondo 2011, p. 23).

It should be noted that liberalization was quite unpopular with the population at large. Public opinion was still oblivious to the trend of oil reserves being depleted and the risk of Pemex going bankrupt. So to reduce the political costs of supporting these changes, the PRI requested the government to initiate a public campaign informing Mexicans of the dire situation of the oil industry. As part of this campaign, President Calderón famously told the public that Mexico's existing reserves could only last nine more years.[13] Calderón's dramatic statement succeeded in creating a sense of urgency. The PRI also insisted that the PAN should be the one introducing their bill in Congress, as it was understood that whoever introduced the bill would pay the highest political cost.

Calderón had some early overtures to the PRD, trying to include at least its moderate legislators in the negotiations, but it became clear that such participation was out of the question at this stage. Since early 2008, when the government announced its plan to discuss a reform to Pemex, opponents had been organizing massive mobilizations against it. López Obrador had positioned himself as the undisputed leader of those opposed to any liberalization of the oil industry, and he was in effect the ultimate organizer of street protests against Calderon's initiatives. His goal with these mass mobilizations was not only to get the media's attention, but also to put enormous pressure on PRD legislators to oppose the reforms in Congress.

López Obrador also found a rhetorical device to raise the costs of voting in favor of Calderón's reform. He and his followers cleverly framed the proposed

[13]Strictly speaking, Calderón's remark was correct only considering *proved* reserves. If we add the *probable* and *possible* reserves, Mexico had enough oil until the year 2035 (Alberro 2007).

private-public ventures as a full-blown "privatization of Pemex." This accusation was factually incorrect, since the actual initiative was not proposing the sale of any assets or stocks of Pemex. But it was effective in triggering fear in the Mexican population at large, which saw the state-owned firm as a dear part of their own patrimony (Langston and Pérez 2009, p. 493). Here is how Starr (2009) explained the effects of these strategies.

> With Lopez Obrador setting the tone of the debate, PRD moderates were cornered. Some had toyed with the idea of supporting limited private investment outside of Pemex's core activities (exploration, production, and sales), but the political consequences of supporting what was now clearly labeled as a privatization of Pemex were suddenly much greater. (Starr 2009, p. 146).

Consequently PAN and PRI leaders met privately to broker a deal without the PRD. Together, they finally agreed on a legislative agenda that would allow more flexible service contracts to create partnerships with other oil companies and private service providers. Their major achievement was designing a new type of partnership that Pemex could strike with service providers in the exploration of oil fields. Instead of paying a flat fee to contractors irrespective of their results, as used to be done previously, now Pemex would be allowed to pay contractors in accordance to their performance, namely, in proportion to the quantity of oil they found. This so-called "incentivized contract" was the crown-jewel of Calderón's deal with the PRI. In addition, the two parties agreed on allowing private investment in the construction and management of oil refineries. Such plans, they claimed, did not require changes to the Constitution; they only involved changes to ordinary laws, so the PRI-PAN coalition had enough seats in Congress to get the bill approved. Initially, the PAN along with the technocratic leaders of the PRI were able exert enough pressure on the nationalist faction of the PRI to accept those changes without major complaints. President Calderón sent his initiative to Congress on April 9, 2008, with the presumed goal of carrying out a surprise approval the following days before the PRD could react (Farfán and García 2009). In the event, this master plan for a fast-track approval of a meaningful liberalization of the oil industry was thwarted.

6.2 The Shocks That Changed the Game

The PRI-PAN initiative did not move forward in Congress as expected, as the PRD and the other leftist parties that felt excluded from the process found a way to stop it cold. For different reasons, all the left-wing factions were determined to prevent the energy bill from being approved. The moderate wing of the PRD wanted to influence any subsequent negotiations by including some of its demands; while the more radical factions wanted to block any attempts to change the status quo. However, they all knew the bill would pass if a vote took place since they did not hold enough seats to reach a simple majority. Their only chance was to prevent the vote altogether. So, reacting quickly to rumors that the PAN and the PRI were planning a fast-track approval, the PRD and its allies stormed both houses of Congress to occupy their precincts, effectively preventing any vote from taking place. The left-wing legislators physically seized the pulpits, and then blocked access to the Senate floor with chairs and tables.

In tandem with their occupation of Congress, the leftist parties also flooded several streets and public spaces with thousands of protesters—and López Obrador's calls for civil disobedience intensified. According to some observers, this new assertiveness of leftist parties motivated the left-wing faction in the PRI to be more assertive as well:

> Lopez Obrador's discourse strengthened the position of nationalists within the PRI. They began to speak out more loudly and aggressively against the kind of reform favored by Calderon and made it politically much more costly for the PRI legislative leadership to support the President's initiative. Starr (2009, p. 146).

By closing down Congress and taking to the streets, the leftist parties were hoping to prevent Calderón's initiative from being approved. They made several requests in order to vacate the premises: the current bill on the floor should be definitely tabled; new negotiations should start in which they would be included; there should be a ten-week period of broad public debates with academics and the media; and a new vote had to take place after those debates.

Their plan worked. Legally, Congress could have simply selected an alternative venue to take the vote where the PAN and the PRI would have approved their bill. But politically it had become too costly. Emboldened by the PRD's actions, the nationalist faction of the PRI (namely PRI_{Left}) threatened to rebel against its technocratic leadership (namely PRI_{Right}). The nationalist *priístas* repudiated the bill as much as the *perredistas*, so they took this opportunity to express their ideological differences with the top brass. In defiance of their leaders, the nationalist wing of the PRI sided with the PRD demanding the postponement of the vote until a new debate took place. In addition to their ideology, it should be noted that nationalist *priístas* had other reasons for dissent. As argued by Elizondo (2011, p. 33), these legislators probably wanted to flex their muscles in order to extract side payments such as monetary rewards for supporting the government's bill.

At this point, the previous agreement between PAN and PRI leaders ceased to be viable. The PRI leadership was forced to back out of its previous compromises with the PAN. Bowing to political reality, Calderón agreed to withdraw his initiative allowing a broad national debate leading to new negotiations for a different bill. The Senate organized a series of talks in its precinct, inviting academics, oil experts and public intellectuals of all stripes. Following 71 days of inclusive, diverse and publicized debates, a new bill was negotiated and written by the government and the opposition, this time including many PRD legislators.

6.3 Second Round: The PAN-PRI-PRD Coalition

A second type of coalition that could be formed in this context would include a super-majority of legislators from the three major parties, the PAN, the PRI and the PRD. Such a coalition would have more seats than were actually needed to pass legislation, but would include all veto players such as left-wing legislators who had achieved in becoming politically indispensable. Without them, the PAN and the PRI were now too vulnerable to public accusations of being sold to big American corporations and other private interests. The PRI also risked fracture if its leaders did not heed the nationalistic demands. Hence a super-majoritarian coalition was formed in the fall of 2008, when the PAN and the PRI reluctantly agreed to include the PRD as a full negotiating partner.

The so-called radicals within the PRD, along with the two smaller leftist parties were still unwilling to engage in any conversation with Calderón, hence excluding themselves from the bargaining table. But the so-called moderates within the PRD were eager to participate in the negotiations to promote leftist viewpoints. By this time, their political costs and benefits from engaging with the government were pointing in new directions. The no-recognition strategy espoused by López Obrador was seriously backfiring as he and his followers were losing popularity. Even some of his prominent sympathizers, such as leftist intellectuals, started critiquing his lack of engagement complaining that he had not designed an alternative proposal to pitch against the president's one (Farfán and García 2009, p. 333). According to several observers, López Obrador was starting to look like a "subversive politician" with personal interests rather than an earnest defender of the beloved oil company Langston and Pérez (2009, p. 494). His detractors in the PRD, on the other hand, felt the need to show voters their capacity to influence legislation. Those in the PRD wishing to exert their power in the legislature were numerous—and they were increasingly willing to defy López Obrador by engaging in talks with the PRI and the PAN.

Accordingly, a new bill was jointly designed by the PAN, the PRI, and the moderate wing of the PRD. Such a coalition is depicted in Fig. 7 below.

As we can tell from comparing Figs. 6 and 7, a three-way coalition was expected to lead to a more modest bill than a two-way coalition. The reason is that more parties needed to agree to this bill. This was indeed the outcome when the PAN and the PRI were forced to include the *Nueva Izquierda* faction of the PRD in their negotiations. In terms of private participation in the oil sector, the ensuing legislation was a watered down version of the April initiative. In particular, a number of restrictions were explicitly imposed on the new "incentivized contracts" to safeguard against the private appropriation of rents from oil exploration. The contractor should be only paid with currency, never with oil barrels; the price paid per found barrel should be fixed ex-ante to prevent the contractor from trying to influence the market price ex-post (i.e. speculation); and barrels found should under no circumstances be included in the books of the contractor as its property. PRD legislators claimed credit for these safeguards, although some observers believe they

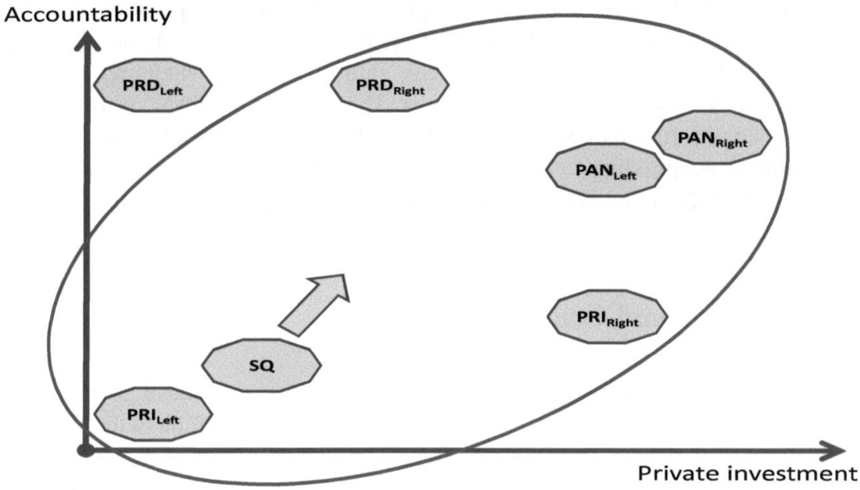

Fig. 7 The second attempt: a PAN-PRI-PRD coalition

had actually been brokered by the nationalist wing of the PRI (Farfán and García 2009, p. 337).

On the other hand, this type of coalition was better suited to move along the accountability dimension. When the PRD was included, the PAN gained an ally for pressuring the PRI into weakening the union and other rent-seeking groups. For instance, the PRD insisted that all contracts signed by Pemex should be made publicly available on the internet. It also insisted that contracts should be audited before being enacted. And it insisted on strengthening the regulatory agency in charge of overseeing oil activities. All three requests were supported by the PAN and made into law (Farfán and García 2009, fn. 21).

The PAN and the PRD also sought to weaken the presence of the union in the firm's administrative board. First they proposed to reduce the number of union members on the board, which the PRI vehemently opposed. Then it was proposed to increase the number of non-union members in the board, which the PRI approved. To be concrete, four so-called "professional counselors" would now be added to the administrative board of Pemex. These professional counselors should be external businessmen and industry experts who should take control of some of the responsibilities that union representatives would have liked to keep for themselves. It is likely that the creation of these four external counselors was intended as side payment to the PRI for allowing some weakening of the labor union. Indeed, their selection mechanism seems to be designed as a perk to this party—they need to be named by the Executive and ratified by the Senate, giving the PRI tremendous leverage to staff these four positions with loyalists. Elizondo (2011) believes that these new members of the administrative council were used as a bargaining chip in negotiations with *priístas*.

On October 28, 2008, Mexico's Congress finally passed legislation intended to modernize the state-oil company, Petróleos Mexicanos, and boost declining production. Approval of the energy sector reform was overwhelming: 93 % of senators and 83 % of deputies were in favor. The PRI and the PAN voted in favor. The two small leftist parties voted against it. The PRD legislators were divided: a majority corresponding to the *Nueva Izquierda* wing voted in favor, while the minority of hard-core loyalists of López Obrador voted against it.

7 Discussion and Conclusions

The historical nationalization of the oil industry in 1938 is a source of great pride to many Mexicans. To date, Pemex continues to symbolize the triumph of the Mexican State over private greed and foreign imperialism. Any mention of reform arouses passions, both among the political elite and ordinary citizens. Accordingly, there has been much ideological resistance to changing the legal framework regulating this highly symbolic industry. For decades, reformers and policymakers failed to pass any profound reforms that would modernize Pemex. In addition to an ideological opposition to reform, there also exists an entrenched class of interest groups who oppose any changes to the status quo. For those reasons, many administrations avoided a battle to change the legislation of the oil industry. Reformers hesitated to touch Pemex for fear of committing political suicide. In the jargon of political science, we would call it a "third rail" issue, meaning an issue that is so politically sensitive that it will electrocute anyone touching it. I suggest that Pemex used to be the third rail of Mexican politics.

Yet, significant changes were achieved in the administration of Felipe Calderón. In particular, President Calderón was successful in getting the approval of a government budget in 2006, a fiscal reform in 2007 and an energy reform in 2008 that provided Pemex with fresh resources and tools to operate the following few years. These reforms also laid the ground for a new series of profound reforms carried out by the subsequent administration under President Enrique Peña Nieto. The 2008 reforms were criticized by many analysts, however. Some said the reforms went too far, while others said they did not go far enough. It is clear that any change will leave important groups unsatisfied, but such is the nature of political negotiations in a democracy: all parties have to compromise. The interesting question to ask is: Why were some specific compromises reached and not others?

The goal of my chapter was to develop an analytical framework to study those questions. I did so by studying the politics of energy reform as they occur in the Mexican Congress. The conceptual framework in this chapter was based on the following elements: postulating the main issues regarding Pemex; identifying the main political agents in charge of reform; and locating the positions of these agents on those issues. The analysis was aided by a series of original graphs that helped us visualize the kind of coalitions that are conducive to change. I claimed that three issues tended to dominate the debate: private investment, accountability, and fiscal autonomy. I also identified the agents that were pivotal in creating a new legislation: the Chief Executive; the three major parties, namely the PAN, the PRD, and the PRI; and the internal factions within each of those parties.

The graphical analysis showed that several coalitions could have implemented changes. On the fiscal side, a three-party coalition of all major parties was formed at the end of 2006; it fail to expand the overall tax base, but it was conducive to a reduction on the taxes levied on Pemex. In 2007, a two-party coalition between the incumbent PAN and its closest ally, the PRI, resulted in a modest reduction on Pemex's tax burden in exchange for some new taxes from other sources. In terms of the comprehensive energy bill that was discussed in 2008, a PAN-PRI coalition was best suited to create more flexible contracts for joint explorations with other international oil companies (IOCs) or national oil companies (NOCs). Yet this coalition could not be sustained as some politicians in the left who were radically opposed to these reforms found effective ways to stop them. Once moderate elements of the PRD were included in a new coalition, the resulting liberalization was milder. In particular, the contracts designed for private investors were less flexible. However, the labor union and service contractors were forced to become somewhat more accountable: once the PRD was on board, the PAN had an ally to force the PRI to weaken these rentier groups.

The appendix presented these theoretical ideas more formally, in particular the idea that the ideological preferences of Congress members should be complemented by the costs and benefits from supporting a bill. I believe such framework can be pushed beyond the analysis provided in this chapter. In particular, the same tools from spatial voting could be applied to other important reforms in Mexico's Congress and other parliaments. It can also serve to speculate about future energy reforms, as I attempted in a companion paper (Serra 2011). This chapter hopefully illustrated the usefulness of such theoretical tools in analyzing important congressional negotiations that seem in principle complex and puzzling.

Appendix: A Theory of Legislative Preferences With Costs and Benefits of Supporting a Bill

The theory of spatial voting postulates that policymaking takes place in a "policy space," by which we understand a series of dimensions where different policies are located. For instance let us assume that a given policy can be represented with a single dimension that we will call x, where x is a number larger than zero. Our assumption is that different policies can be represented by different values of x. This would be the case of a tax levied on Pemex. If the tax rate in the *status quo* is 79 % as it was around 2006, we can say that $x_{SQ} = 79$. Three different tax rates, x', x'' and x''' can be ordered along the tax policy line, for example if $x' < x'' < x'''$. A given legislator i will have a preferred policy in this dimension, which we call the legislators "ideal point" and we denote by x_i. For example, if the legislator belongs to the incumbent party, she might prefer a fairly high tax rate of 85 %, such as $x_i = 85$. The theory assumes that legislators are increasingly unhappy with policies that are increasingly farther from their ideal point. In other words, legislator i would want to minimized the distance between a given policy proposal x and her ideal point, which is given by $|x_i - x|$.

Now assume that a given legislative bill has two dimensions that we will call x and y, where x and y are numbers larger than zero. For example, this would be the case of an energy bill introduced in Congress that affects the state-owned firm Pemex on two issues: private investment and accountability. Each bill is then defined by a point called (x, y) in this two-dimensional graph. Three different bills, called (x', y'), (x'', y'') and (x''', y'''), can be placed in a two-dimensional graph with axes x and y, where x', x'', x''' are the amounts of private participation and y', y'', y''' are the amounts of transparency that each bill is proposing for the state-owned firm, respectively. A given legislator i will have a preferred policy in this two-dimensional space, which we call the legislators "ideal point" and we denote by (x_i, y_i). As I said above, the theory assumes that legislators are increasingly unhappy with policies that are increasingly farther from their ideal point. In other words, legislator i would want to minimize the distance between a given policy proposal (x, y) and her ideal point, which is given by $\sqrt{}[(x_i - x)^2 + (y_i - y)^2]$.

This framework is standard in political science and political economy (see for example Chapter 5 in Shepsle 2010). To this traditional framework I would like to add some elements that will be useful in understanding the type of congressional negotiations that I study in the chapter. In many circumstances, it is quite clear that legislators have payoffs from supporting a bill irrespective of their ideological preferences for this bill. There are several types of costs and benefits, punishments and rewards, to a legislator for voting in favor of a given initiative. For example, if a powerful political boss repudiates a bill, he might be able to punish legislators who support it by jeopardizing their future political careers. On the other hand, if a certain initiative is popular with the electorate at large, anyone supporting it will gain points with public opinion. I will assume that this type of payoffs may exist for certain legislators in the negotiations studied in this chapter. For a given legislator i, we call b_i and c_i the benefit and the cost she would incur if she voted in favor of the bill being discussed.

To sum up the theory that will be guiding this chapter, I will assume that each legislator would like to minimize the distance between her ideal point and the policy in being discussed, while at the same trying to obtain the benefit and avoiding the cost of supporting this policy. If the bill being negotiated is not accepted, then the status quo (SQ) will remain in place. These preferences can be summarized as follows.

Consider a bill (x', y') that involves two policy dimensions, x and y.

1. If the bill passes, legislator i would receive the following payoff:
   $\sqrt{[(x_i - x')^2 + (y_i - y')^2]}$ if she votes against the bill
   $\sqrt{[(x_i - x')^2 + (y_i - y')^2]} + b_i - c_i$ if she votes for the bill
2. Otherwise, if the bill does not pass, legislator i would receive the following payoff:
   $\sqrt{[(x_i - x_{SQ})^2 + (y_i - y_{SQ})^2]}$ if she votes against the bill
   $\sqrt{[(x_i - x_{SQ})^2 + (y_i - y_{SQ})^2]} + b_i - c_i$ if she votes for the bill

With this theoretical framework in mind, the chapter analyzes the negotiations to reform Pemex between 2006 and 2008.

References

Alberro, J. L. (2007). Mexico's oil: Who needs it? In *Oil as a strategic resource in Mexico?* Washington, DC: Woodrow Wilson Center, Mexico Institute.

Castellanos, R., Suárez, C., & Montalvo, V. (2009). La Reforma Fiscal (2008). In M. Hernández, J. del Tronco, & G. Sánchez (Eds.), *Un Congreso Sin Mayorías: Mejores Prácticas de Negociación y Construcción de Acuerdos*. Mexico City, Mexico: Facultad Latinoamericana de Ciencias Sociales FLACSO.

de la Calle, L. (2007). Saving pemex or a new energy policy in Mexico. In *Oil as a strategic resource in Mexico*. Washington, DC: Woodrow Wilson Center, Mexico Institute.

Elizondo, C. (2011). Stuck in the mud: The politics of constitutional reform in the oil sector in Mexico. In *The future of oil in Mexico*. Houston, TX: The James A. Baker III Institute for Public Policy, Rice University.

Farfán Mares, G., & García Briones, A. L. (2009). De la confrontación nació el acuerdo: la reforma de petróleos mexicanos 2008. In M. Hernández, J. del Tronco, & G. Sánchez (Eds.), *Un Congreso Sin Mayorías: Mejores Prácticas de Negociación y Construcción de Acuerdos*. Mexico City, Mexico: Facultad Latinoamericana de Ciencias Sociales FLACSO.

Grunstein, M. (2010). *De la Caverna al Mercado: Una Vuelta al Mundo de la Negociaciones Petrolera*. Mexico City, México: Centro de Investigación para el Desarrollo, A.C. (CIDAC).

Langston, J., & Pérez, B. (2009). Mexico 2008: The year of living dangerously. *Revista de Ciencia Política, 29*(2), 491–513.

Magar, E., Romero, V., & Timmons, J. F. (2009). The political economy of fiscal reforms in latin America. Mexico. Available at SSRN 1963863, http://dx.doi.org/10.2139/ssrn.1963863

Medlock, K. B., & Ronald, S. (2011). Scenarios for oil supply, demand and net exports for Mexico. In *The future of oil in Mexico*. Houston, TX: The James A. Baker III Institute for Public Policy, Rice University.

Serra, G. (2011, November). *How could pemex be reformed? an analytical framework based on congressional politics*. CIDE Working Papers DTEP-233.

Serra, G. (2012). The risk of partyarchy and democratic backsliding: Mexico's 2007 electoral reform. *Taiwan Journal of Democracy, 8*(1), 93–118.

Shepsle, K. (2010). *Analyzing politics: Rationality, behavior, and institutions* (2nd ed.). New York: W.W. Norton.

Starr, P. (2007). Energy reforms in the short and long term. In *Oil as a strategic resource in Mexico?* Washington, DC: Woodrow Wilson Center, Mexico Institute.

Starr, P. (2009). Neither populism nor the rule of law: The future of market reform in Mexico. *Law & Business Review of the Americas, 15*, 127–151.

Institutional Change, Specific Investments and Photovoltaic Power Plants: The Empirical Effects of the Energy Policy of "Solar Farms" in Spain

Marcos Álvarez-Díaz, Raquel Fernández-González, and Gonzalo Caballero

1 Introduction

The Spanish economy has historically relied heavily on oil as a source of energy, and this has led to a political and economic debate on the Spanish energy model. This is particularly evident in the twenty first century when efforts have been made by Spanish political decision-makers to contain such strong dependence and furthermore try to develop renewable energies in order to have a more diverse, sustainable and cleaner energy model. Therefore, the Spanish government introduced a bonus policy for installation and exploitation of photovoltaic solar energy, which produced a strong sectoral increase and gave rise to a cumulative installed power rating of 4651 MW up to 2014. However, the institutional framework and the incentive policies for the sector were unstable between 2007 and 2014, and led to a substantial change in bonus policies applied by the different governments to the sector. Therefore, while Royal Decree no. 661/2007 established a special scheme that actually managed to increase photovoltaic installations in Spain through a bonus system, later the passing of several decrees and rules led to an institutional change that resulted in a reduction and cancellation of such bonuses and to a downfall of the sector.

There was an exponential increase in the amount of energy produced by solar plants thanks to existing bonus policies (prior to 2007, the cumulative solar power rating in Spain was 152 MW and in 2010 the figure reached 3842 MW). However, these bonus policies came at a high cost to the public treasury. The severe economic

M. Álvarez-Díaz (✉) • R. Fernández-González • G. Caballero
University of Vigo, Vigo, Spain
e-mail: marcos.alvarez@uvigo.es

N. Schofield, G. Caballero (eds.), *State, Institutions and Democracy*,
Studies in Political Economy, DOI 10.1007/978-3-319-44582-3_14

crisis that struck Spain and the ensuing limitation of public resources explain the change in bonus policies for the sector. Consequently, the returns to solar energy investors plummeted when such bonus policies were withdrawn and these investments had serious uncertainties for amortising capital and obtaining the minimum expected return on investment.

This chapter analyses the process of institutional change and of bonus policies in the Spanish solar energy sector from the point of view of New Institutional Economics, by performing an empirical analysis on the effects of an energy policy that first announced and established public bonuses for solar parks but which later eliminated them unilaterally. These changes in energy policy had a significant impact on return for investors who had made irreversible investments in solar parks. Moreover, the analysis of this paper is a new contribution in the literature about institutional change in Spain (Caballero 2004, 2008; Caballero and Álvarez-Díaz 2015).

Section 2 introduces the theoretical foundations for institutional analysis. Section 3 presents how bonuses were established and their effects. Section 4 focuses on the institutional change that eliminated the bonuses. Section 5 provides an empirical study on the evolution of solar energy installation and production in Spain during these years. Section 6 analyses the legal actions initiated in Spain against elimination of the bonuses. Section 7 presents the conclusions.

2 Incomplete Contracts, Specific Assets and Political Hold-Up in Policy-Making: A New Institutional Approach

The New Institutional Economics (NIE) has included Transaction Cost Economics in its research program (North 1990a). Therefore, the NIE has studied issues related to transactions and governance structures in the third level of social analysis that was proposed by Williamson (2000). Transaction Cost Economics has traditionally been dedicated to the study of transactions in a firm, based on the central contribution of Coase (1937). This study program has likewise assumed a contractual role in which the contract is considered as the unit of analysis, and any incompleteness of the contracts is construed as a main reason for the presence of transaction costs. This is so because transactions between economic agents can be construed as implicit or explicit contractual relationships and the contracts ensuing from such relations are incomplete, i.e., they do not contain full details of the contractual relationship or all possible contingencies. This is the usual scenario that occurs in a world with positive transaction costs (Coase 1937, 1960).

In Transaction Cost Economics, Joskow (1985) defined the "hold-up problem" that might exist between a coal mine and a coal-fired power plant. An electricity generation company benefits maximally if it is located nearest to the coal mine, however, such proximal location to the mine is an irreversible investment. This is because, after making the investment, the electricity company becomes trapped in its contractual relationship with the coal mine. That is to say, in its commercial relationship, the electric company would find that the mine can set a very high price for coal which is even higher than the market price. In view of this risk, which would be a kind of "seizure" or "hold-up" of the irreversible investment made by the company, it is likely that the company would choose to be located in a geographical location that offers several different possibilities for business with several mining companies and thus retain its power to act in the market. Another traditional solution to this problem lies in vertical integration, wherein the electric company and the mine are integrated into a single ownership structure so that it can make investments without risk of "hold-up" or "seizure". In this world of positive transaction costs and incomplete contracts, whoever owns and controls the ex-post assets becomes relevant when a scenario occurs that was not contemplated in the contract: control of ex-post rights may determine the possibilities of decision making on the resource, in an unexpected setting (Epstein and O'Halloran 1999).

Incomplete contracts, irreversible investments and the risk of "hold-up" in contractual relations are an outstanding argument within the program of Transaction Cost Economics. Likewise, transaction cost policies have applied the progress made in the NIE, and more specifically in transaction cost economics, to study political phenomena (North 1990b; Dixit 1996; Caballero and Arias 2003, 2013). In particular, transactional political analysis also uses the approach of incomplete contracts, irreversible investments and "political hold-ups" to study the relationships between political actors, on the one hand and those between politicians and citizens, on the other hand. The case study of this chapter looks into this latter type of relationship.

If incomplete contracts and the risk of "hold-up" of irreversible investments are relevant in the economic theory of a firm, these issues have an even greater impact on political or political-private relationships. This is so because contracts in the world of politics are especially complex, incomplete, and difficult to implement and affect multiple actors. Therefore a scenario of higher transaction costs in political activity is projected. Among other aspects, there are political contracts that are not guaranteed through third-party enforcement (for example, the major election promises made by candidates to gain votes, or the political agreement that permits several parties to form a coalition government). Furthermore, legislators can pass laws at a certain time but can change them at a later date, thus, the inter-temporal component of public policies is quite important in policy-making (Weingast and Marshall 1988; Spiller and Tommasi 2009). Whenever a law is changed, we are faced with centralised institutional change (Kingston and Caballero 2009; Caballero and Soto 2015). And when these laws change incentives for certain types of investments, this affects the productive sector and the behaviour of economic agents.

According to the rule of law, legislators must respect the non-retroactive nature of their decisions, i.e., that the rules or legal instruments adopted today are not applied to facts that occurred in the past. However, the future return on investment will depend on the evolution of the institutional framework over the next few decades, and legislators can regulate the future, thereby changing the institutional environment that economic agents had envisaged. In the case of irreversible investments made in the past, any change of institutional rules can affect the future yield of the investment, and investors find themselves trapped in earlier investments. The Constitutional Courts and the general Courts of Justice may be able to resolve legal claims that arise due to conflicts of interests and thus ensure the rule of law.

3 The Spanish Institutional Framework for Expansion of Solar Farms and Photovoltaic Energy in Spain

Solar energy is produced by solar panels made up of photovoltaic cells that transform the sun's rays into electrical power. The process starts when photons that make up sunlight are incident on certain types of materials to produce electricity. This is what happens when sunlight is incident on solar panels composed of two conductive layers (the top layer is made of silicon crystal with phosphorus impurities while the bottom one is made of silicon-crystal with boron impurities) to generate electricity (UNESA 1998). Solar power farms are made up of photovoltaic panels installed in certain agricultural areas to produce alternating current which is subsequently marketed by the electric companies that purchase it (Espejo Marín 2004). Figure 1 shows the evolution of the price of the photovoltaic cells and modules.

Weather conditions in Spain provide the country with potential for establishment of solar power farms. However, there are three major zones classified at present depending upon the level of incident solar radiation: Low radiation area (Heliophany ≤ 2000 h annually); Intermediate radiation area (2000 < Heliophany ≥ 2600 h); High radiation area (Heliophany > 2600 h annually).

In Spain, the Electricity Sector Act of 1997 established the basis for the solar power generation support policy, and subsequently Royal Decree no. 2818/1998, of 23 December 1998, concerning "Electricity Production by facilities fed by resources

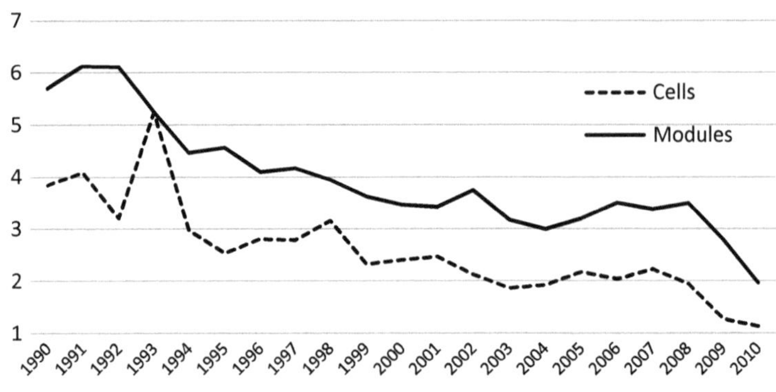

Fig. 1 Price of photovoltaic cells and modules in dollars per Watt peak. *Source*: U.S. Energy Information Administration (EIA)

or renewable energy sources, waste and co-generation", attempted to create a climate that was conducive to investment in renewable energies. To that end, the Decree made a distinction between the different types of renewable energies and created a stimulus package to boost the presence of renewable energies (Espejo Marín 2005). In particular, it contained bonuses for solar energy which varied in line with their power ratings (Lorenzo 2005). Producers could choose between two forms of remuneration for their electricity: market price plus a bonus or a fixed fee. The two options were updated every year but the second one permitted producers to know their remuneration in advance and not depend on the price of electricity (Del Rio Gonzalo 2009). This was how photovoltaic installations were encouraged to share connection points to the power grid and the union of small power plants was generally coined as solar power farms. Royal Decree no. 436/2004 established rates as a percentage of the average power tariff or reference paid by subscribers, and maintained the possibility of the existence of the solar power farms (Mir 2012).

Later, a relevant institutional change for the development of the sector was Royal Decree no. 661/2007, of 25 May 2007, which established that the initial tariff was fixed and that its amount, for already authorised plants, would be updated each year in line with inflation. The combination of a well-known tariff and an unambiguous and easy to implement updating method, together with a long-term guarantee, provided great return stability and security for investors in solar photovoltaic plants. This Royal Decree established that the remuneration framework would be reviewed in 2010, and thereafter every 4 years. Other important features were: (a) the Decree provided a partial lowering of the rate after 25 years, which was a long-term horizon; (b) It had a 371 MW installed power ceiling, and rates would be reviewed upon reaching 85 % of this amount. Since the production of photovoltaic energy had increased by about 204 MW in the year prior to the entry into force of Royal Decree no. 661/2007, in May 2007, production had already reached 71 % of the ceiling figure (371 MW) (Mir 2012).

The installed power rating increased during autumn and winter 2007, and mention must be made of the huge rise during the central months of 2008, such that at the end of September 2008, the registered capacity stood at 3116 MW. Investors had found a possibility for safe and profitable investment in this sector within the context of a Spanish economic crisis (incipient stage), with banks willing to finance these projects, which resulted in a total investment of approximately €20 billion, in the more than 50,000 existing photovoltaic plants. It is estimated that about €15 billion were provided by Spanish or foreign banks (Mir 2012). Figure 2 shows the percentage growth of the power rating with respect to the previous year: growth in 2006, 2007 and 2008 was explosive.

Mir (2012) states that the "Spanish photovoltaic boom was unprecedented and surprised the entire world". The bonus policy which enabled high performance and recovery of investments in solar power parks was, beyond any doubt, the key factor for expansion of the sector, but there were other factors, such as the availability of financing through banks and the low import costs of photovoltaic panels, which also boosted this trend.

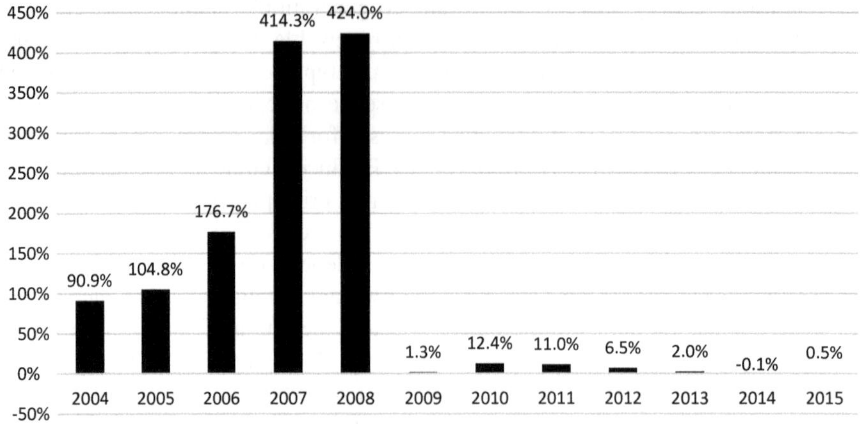

Fig. 2 Annual growth rate of the Spanish solar photovoltaic power. *Source*: CNMC

4 Institutional Change: Reduction and Elimination of Bonuses

On 26 September 2008, the socialist government, in the light of the economic situation and the explosive evolution of the photovoltaic sector, passed Royal Decree no. 1578/2008, on "remuneration for photovoltaic solar technology power production parks after the expiry of the deadline for maintaining remuneration as per Royal Decree no. 661/2007". This Decree sought to control growth in the sector and created the pre-allocation registry for compensation in order to control the allocated installed power rating, and implied an inter-annual 10 % fall in rates. In relation to the pre-allocation registry for compensation, the Decree likewise established that "facilities connecting at the same point in the distribution or supply grid or those with a common evacuation line are to be considered as belonging to a single project, and their power rating will be the sum of the individual facilities". This Decree resulted in the cessation of new investments in the sector.

Interruption in the granting of new licenses and stagnation in the photovoltaic industry resulted in a sector decline and was quickly reflected in the number of sector jobs. Figure 3 shows the sharp fall in number of employees in the Spanish photovoltaic sector since 2008.

The process of change of rules concerning bonuses for the production of photovoltaic energy was consolidated through Royal Decree no. 1003/2010, passed on 5 August 2010, which regulated the elimination of the special bonuses scheme to facilities producing electrical energy using photovoltaic technology. The introduction of this new regulation meant that solar park owners had to certify the date on which their plant began operations, and depending on this date, they would be entitled to collect one or the other bonus. Therefore, a special sub-section was created in the "State Special Scheme Register" to include facilities which could

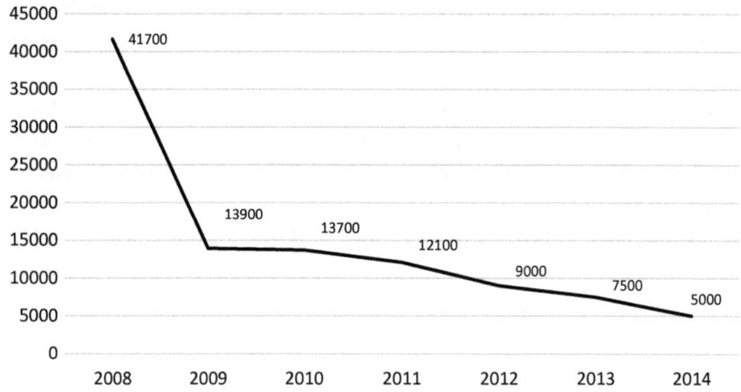

Fig. 3 The evolution of the direct photovoltaic employment in Spain. *Source*: UNEF 2015

continue operations but which were not entitled to receive a bonus. The State had to introduce inspection and control mechanisms due to cases of cheating and administrative fraud attempts by plant owners.

The costs of "enforcement" were quite high and favoured the implementation of an amnesty policy. The presence of a number of illegal facilities meant that the authorities permitted a sizeable part of them to continue operations if they voluntarily declared their illegal situation, even though this would lead to an elimination of bonus or a reduction of the same. Thus, Royal Decree no. 1003/10 permitted facilities that openly acknowledged their defaults, to be able to continue to receive a bonus. This represented a 30 % decrease over that fixed by Royal Decree no. 661/2007, and was the same as that established in Royal Decree no. 1578/08 for the first call in 2009: 0.32€/kWh (ASIF 2011). In the light of the above, 907 facilities (64.56 MW) welcomed this amnesty and saved €17 million/year (ASIF 2011).

Subsequently, in November 2010, Royal Decree no. 1565/2010, of 19 November 2010, regulating and modifying certain power production activity aspects under the special scheme revised certain aspects of Royal Decree no. 661/2007. This new Decree established technical innovations that photovoltaic plants must incorporate in line with their power rating, as well as deadlines for implementing the same. This Decree provoked many protests from the photovoltaic energy producer associations because they felt that the photovoltaic energy sector was unfairly treated as compared to the other energy sectors.

The reduction of subsidies also had significant economic effects on the sector, and affected all segments of the solar market: subsidies for new installations were reduced by 5 % for buildings with power rating of up to 20 kW, and by 25 % for buildings with rating between 20 kW and 2 MW and by 45 % for ground-based installations. In this case, savings were estimated to be €141.5 million in 2011, €202.3 million in 2012 and €263.4 million in 2013. It is estimated that photovoltaic rates fell by 70 % from 2007 to 2011.

Royal Decree Law no. 14/2010, of 23 December 2010, established urgent measures for correction of the tariff deficit in the electricity sector. The measures adopted in this Decree were even more restrictive for return on investment in photovoltaic energy. One of the measures stated that producers would have to pay a toll for access to the grid (EUR 0.5/MW), which in the case of installations in buildings, represents a reduction in income of 0.3 % and for ground-based plants of 0.2 % (ASIF 2011).

However, the most controversial measure in Royal Decree Law no. 14/2010 for the photovoltaic industry was the one that reduced the equivalent hours of operation for eligibility to receive the photovoltaic tariff. On the one hand, the country was divided into five climatic zones as specified in RD no. 314/2006, and a limit of equivalent hours was set for each zone for facilities to receive a bonus. Furthermore, this Royal Decree Law also implemented another time restriction which came into effect only in 2011, 2012 and 2013, on facilities affected by Royal Decree no. 661/2007, and the intention was that the government would be able to reduce spending on bonuses by 30 % with this measure.

This reduction meant an even higher decline of profits. Producers therefore suffered hardships to repay the funding acquired for their investments. A large part of the solar power plants had not yet been fully amortised, and many owners were doomed to renegotiate their debt with banks.

Law 2/2011 on Sustainable Economy (2011) tried to change the trend after the bonus rebates in the photovoltaic energy sector, and tried to compensate the sector with various measures. It included several measures for the sector but did not substantially change the cuts in bonuses. Subsequently, Royal Decree no. 1544/2011, passed on 31 October 2011, established an economic toll of 0.5€/MWh on producer companies for the use of the transport and distribution grids. These new rates resulted in an increase in the cost of photovoltaic plants.

Moreover, Royal Decree no. 1699/2011, passed on 18 November 2011, regulated the connection to the grid, of production facilities with low power ratings. This Decree eliminated the administrative authorisation required for facilities of less than 100 kW rating and intended to encourage facilities with low power ratings.

Later, Royal Decree Law no. 1/2012, passed on 27 January 2012, by urgent procedure, on the grounds that it was important to take measures in the light of an increase in tariff deficit, established the indefinite interruption of rates, bonuses and allowances on efficiency and on reactive power. This measure affects all facilities which on 28 January 2012 had not yet been registered in the Pre-allocation Registry for compensation. Furthermore, the photovoltaic quota was deleted from 2012 onwards (the quota was 550 MW in 2012). The impact of this Decree on the photovoltaic sector employment was very detrimental, and nearly 40 % of the jobs in the sector were destroyed between 2012 and 2013.

Law 15/2012, passed on 27 December 2012, on "tax measures for energy sustainability" established a tax of 7 % per kilowatt generated. This tax was especially damaging for photovoltaic energy because it had a fixed price and this increase could not be passed on to the consumer and thus had to be assumed by the producer.

Royal Decree Law no. 2/2013 on "urgent measures in the electricity system and in the financial sector", passed on 1 February 2013, applied the same criteria to all renewable energy generation technologies and thus eliminated the choice option between the two previously existing remuneration mechanisms (access market or receive a compensatory bonus when the price could not cover the generation costs). After the adoption of this Decree Law, producers had to exclusively choose the one system. The immediate consequence of this measure was that the entire set of renewable energy producers assumed the full value of the tax (7 % per kilowatt generated) for production of electrical energy.

Royal Decree Law no. 9/2013, on "urgent measures to ensure the financial stability of the electricity system", passed on 12 July 2013, attempted to reduce the energy sector deficit of €26 billion. The measures affected all operators in the sector, but the most relevant measure for the photovoltaic sector was the one that triggered the "specific emoluments scheme".

The legislative change scenario also implied that Law 15/2013, passed on 17 October 2013, was repealed on 3 December of the same year.

Finally, Royal Decree no. 413/2014 and Order IET/1045/2014 clarified and defined the final text of Royal Decree Law no. 9/2013. Royal Decree no. 413/2014 was passed on 6 June 2014, and it finally replaced the regulated tariff system introduced by RD no. 661/2007 and established the specific emoluments scheme based on two features: remuneration for investment per unit of power (Rinv); remuneration for operation per unit of energy generated (Ro).

All photovoltaic plants that had embraced Royal Decrees 661/2007 and 1578/2008, i.e. those that had used the earlier bonus scheme, would have to accept a nominal power rating and not the peak power rating (which is higher).

The rise and fall of the Spanish photovoltaic sector is showed too in a comparative analysis. Figure 4 shows the five first producers in Europe for different years.

5 Empirical Analysis

In order to carry out a statistical analysis of the photovoltaic energy in Spain, we have data of two variables: the *Amount of Energy Sold* (E) and the *Power Installed* (P) during the period that goes from January 2006 to September 2015. In total, we collect 117 monthly observations. The data were obtained from the CNMC ("Comisión Nacional de Mercados y Competencia") through its web page. Royal Decree no. 661/2007, of 25 May 2007, and Royal Decree no. 1578/2008, of 26 September 2008, allowed us to divide the whole sample into three subsamples. The first one, named as sub-sample 1, spans from January 2006 to May 2007. The second sub-sample covers from June 2007 to September 2008. The third period starts in October 2008, month in which the incentives started to disappear, and finishes in September 2015, the last date available at the time of doing this study.

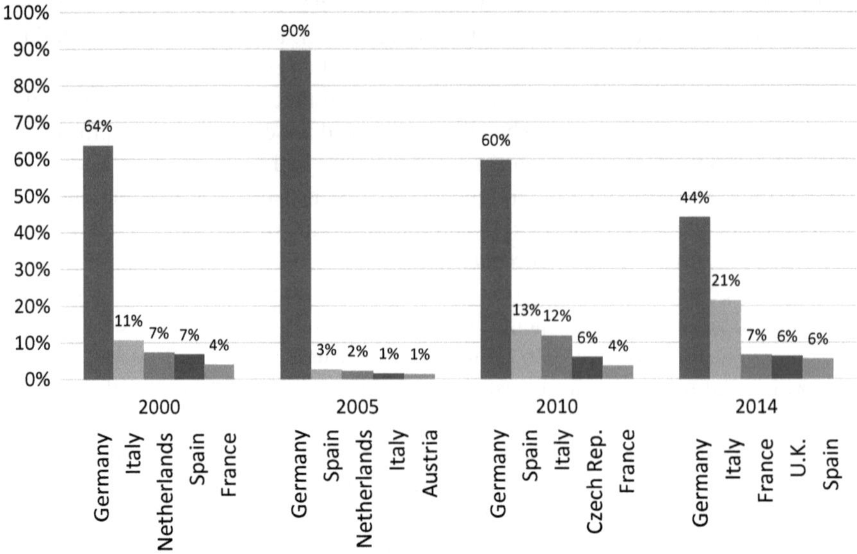

Fig. 4 Top 5 European countries by photovoltaic production (2000–2014)

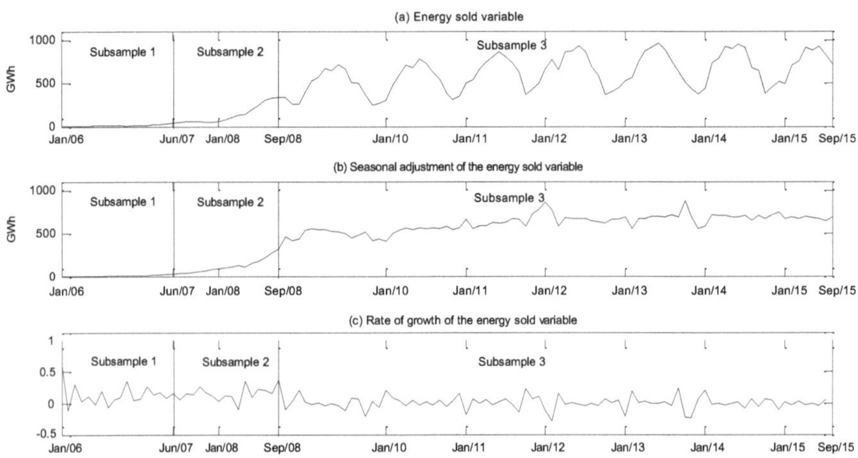

Fig. 5 Energy sold, seasonal adjustment and rate of growth. (**a**) Energy sold variable. (**b**) seasonal adjustment of the energy sold variable. (**c**) Rate of growth of the energy sold variable

Figures 5 and 6 describe the dynamic evolution and the sample division for both time series.

Regarding the variable that computes the amount of photovoltaic energy sold in Spain (E), the most remarkable characteristic of this series is the existence of a seasonal pattern. This fact is clearly observed in Fig. 5a where a peak is perceived for the summer months. Figure 5b represents the same variable but without this

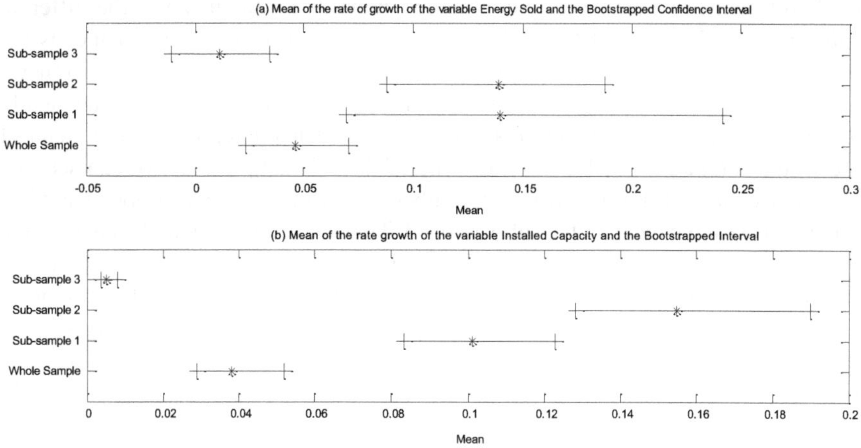

Fig. 6 Mean of the rate growth of the variables and the bootstrapped confidence intervals. (**a**) Mean of the rate growth of the variables energy sold and the bootstrapped confidence intervals. (**b**) Mean of the rate growth of the variables installed capacity and the bootstrapped intervals

Table 1 Main descriptive statistics of the variable energy sold

	Rate of growth of the variable installed capacity			
	Sample	Sub-sample 1	Sub-sample 2	Sub-sample 3
Mean	0.0462	0.1393	0.1388	0.0108
Median	0.0344	0.1011	0.1281	0.0056
Maximum	0.5821	0.5821	0.3516	0.3705
Minimum	−0.2859	−0.1156	−0.1033	−0.2859
Std. Dev.	0.1309	0.1743	0.1025	0.1084
Jarque-Bera (p-value)	30.8374(0.00)	2.72(0.07)	0.6128(0.50)	8.7632(0.02)

seasonal component, which was extracted by using the Census X-12 method. As usual in time series analysis, the seasonal adjusted series was transformed in the following way:

$$\Delta LE_t = \log(E_t) - \log(E_{t-1}) \quad (1)$$

where E_t is the seasonal adjusted amount of energy sold in Spain at month t, ΔLE_t is its logarithm first difference. This transformed variable has some interesting statistical properties; basically, we get stationary which is a statistical requirement to statistically study time series. Moreover, this transformed series can be understood as the rate of growth of the original variable. The evolution of this transformed variable is depicted in Fig. 5c. Table 1 offers the main descriptive statistics for the whole sample, and for the different sub-samples defined in the study.

At this point, it is interesting to check if the calculated mean of the variable ΔE_t is statistically different for the different sub-samples. To do so, we use the bootstrap method to construct empirically confidence intervals for the mean of the different sub-samples[1]. If the bootstrapped intervals associated to the different means are overlapped, then we have arguments to say that there are no statistical differences; otherwise, if the intervals are not overlapped, then the means are statistically different. Figure 6a reflects the bootstrapped confidence intervals for the mean of the whole sample, as well as for each one of the sub-samples. As we can see, the confidence intervals for the mean of the sub-samples 1 and 2 are overlapped, but it is not the case for the mean of the sub-sample 3. This result implies that the mean of the growth rate of the sub-sample 3 is statistically different from those obtained in the sub-sample 1 and 2. This fact is also supported by the non-parametric Kolmogorov-Smirnov test. The values of this test reveal that we cannot reject the null hypothesis that the data in sub-sample 1 and 2 are from the same continuous distribution (K-S test = 0.25, p-value = 0.63). However, this test allow us to reject that the data in sub-sample 1 and 2 have the same empirical distribution as the data in sub-sample 3 (K-S test = 0.68, p-value = 0.00). It seems, therefore, that the amount of photovoltaic energy sold in Spain shows a different pattern since September 2008.

A similar analysis for the case of the variable that represents the photovoltaic power installed in Spain (P) confirms that the elimination of the incentives since October 2008 had a statistically significant impact on this variable. Figure 7a depicts the evolution of the variable over the sample period. Figure 7b represents the rate of growth of the variable calculated similarly to that described in (1). It is visually clear in this case the negative effect of having abolished the incentives. After September 2008, the power installed does not practically show any growth. Table 2 displays the main descriptive statistics of the rate of growth of this variable for the whole sample and for the different sub-samples. The mean of the growth rate for the subsample 2 is 0.1548, which is similar to that observed in subsample 1 (0.1010) and much higher than the mean when incentives disappear (0.0049). Figure 7 also represents the bootstrapped confidence intervals for the mean of the growth rate of the photovoltaic installed capacity. As we can see, none of the intervals overlap. This implies that the mean of the different subsamples are statistically different. The value of the Kolmogorov-Smirnov tells us that there are evidences that the data in sub-sample 1, 2 and 3 come from different distributions[2].

[1]The bootstrapping used in this study was based on the accelerated bias-corrected interval (Bca), and the interval confidence was 95 %. It has been demonstrated that the BCa method performs better under a wider variety of assumptions (Briggs et al. 1997), and it has been recommended for general use (Efron and Tibshirani 1998). In our study, we have also considered other methods such as the normal approximation method and the percentile method. The resulting intervals were quite similar among all them. These results are not reported in this study, but they can be sent by request.

[2]Specifically, the values of the Kolmogorov-Smirnov test were the following for the different comparisons between subsamples: K-S test = 0.50 (p-value = 0.02) for the comparison between subsamples 1 and 2; K-S test = 0.99 (p-value = 0.00) for the subsamples 1 and 3 and K-S test = 1 (p-value = 0.00) for the subsamples 2 and 3.

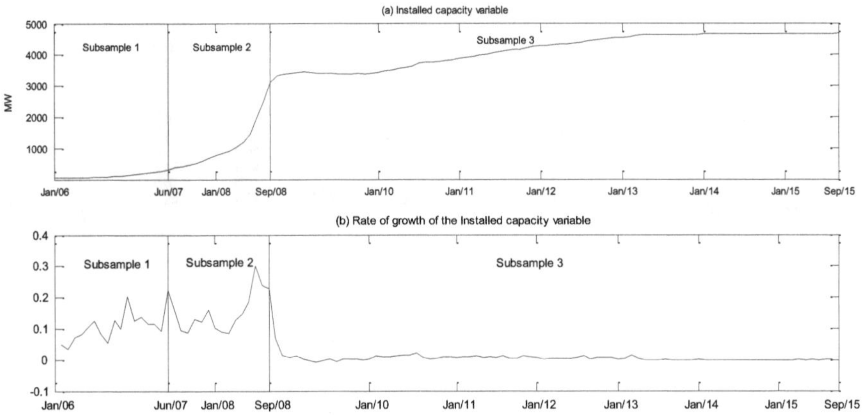

Fig. 7 Installed capacity and rate of growth. (**a**) Installed capacity variable. (**b**) Rate of growth of the installed capacity variable

Table 2 Main descriptive statistics of the variable installed capacity

	Rate of growth of the variable installed capacity			
	Sample	Sub-sample 1	Sub-sample 2	Sub-sample 3
Mean	0.038	0.1010	0.1548	0.0049
Median	0.007	0.1010	0.1384	0.0022
Maximum	0.3005	0.2031	0.3005	0.0689
Minimum	−0.0077	0.0344	0.0844	−0.0077
Std. Dev.	0.0637	0.0407	0.0644	0.0088
Jarque-Bera (p-value)	109.04(0.00)	1.3252(0.23)	1.76(0.13)	3.86(0.00)

A common and simple method used in science research to describe the existing interrelationships between two time series X and Y is to estimate the sample cross-correlation coefficients

$$\widehat{\rho}_{X,Y}(l) = \frac{Cov\,(X_t, Y_{t-l})}{S_{X_t} \cdot S_{Y_{t-l}}} \tag{2}$$

where Cov is the covariance and S is the standard deviation. The values of the cross-correlation coefficients range from −1 and 1; and they give us information about the intensity and direction of the relationship between both variables at lag l. Specifically, a value of zero means no-relationship, a value close to −1 implies a strong negative relationship, and a value near to 1 involves a strong positive relationship. This statistical tool is employed to discover the existence of a statistical connection between the amount of photovoltaic energy sold and the photovoltaic power installed. There is no doubt that the cross-correlation analysis can be a very useful tool to detect statistical connections between these two variables, but it is also important to underline the existence of a problem: if each one of the analyzed

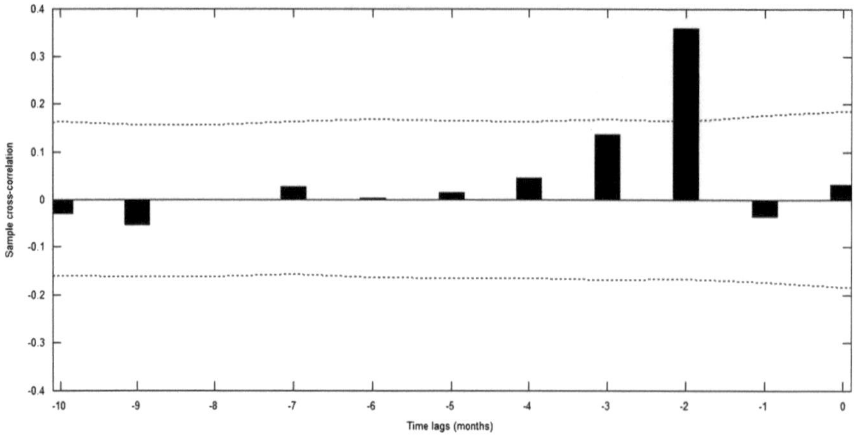

Fig. 8 Sample cross-correlation between the variables photovoltaic installed power and photovoltaic energy sold

series has a very high degree of autocorrelation, then the nonzero values of the cross-correlation function do not necessarily imply a true relationship between the two time series (Katz 1988). This means that the presence of autocorrelation can generate a spurious statistical relationship between the variables. The consequence would be that the cross-correlation analysis would not be a valid tool. In order to avoid possible fictitious relationship in our cross-correlation analysis, we have bleached our series by using and autoregressive model. This procedure of whitening is explained in Katz (1988) and was already applied in several studies (see, for example, Álvarez-Díaz et al. 2015). Figure 8 shows the sample cross-correlation coefficients between the bleached series, where the intervals of confidence associated to each cross-correlation coefficient were empirically constructed by means of a Montecarlo simulation[3]. These intervals are used to determine the statistical significance of the cross-correlation coefficients. As we can see, the variable photovoltaic energy sold shows a positive and statistically significant co-movement with the variable power installed at lag $l = 2$, and no significant cross-correlations are detected to other lags. It seems that the photovoltaic installed power has a significant positive impact on the energy sold two periods ahead.

There is no doubt about the usefulness of the sample cross-correlation analysis, but the existence of a significant cross-correlation coefficient does not necessarily imply a relationship of causation. It only allows us to know if two time series are

[3]Specifically, the Montecarlo experiment was carried out as follows: we generate randomly 5000 time series with the same characteristics as a random white variable and with the same standard deviation as the variable e_t. Then, each one of these artificial variables was cross-correlated with the residual series of the variable w_t. An empirical distribution of each cross-correlation coefficient for each lag was computed. Using this empirical distribution, a confidence interval with a specific significant level is built and, in this case, the significance was determined to be 95 %.

Table 3 Results of the Granger causality test

Null hypothesis	Lags	F-statistic	p-value
Installed capacity does not Granger cause energy sold	5	10.9	0.00

Note: The lag length is based on the Akaike information criterion. The residuals show no serial autocorrelation

related only in terms of co-movements. For that reason we also perform the Granger causality test (Granger 1969). This test checks the causality between two variables by means of the construction of a simple causal model

$$\Delta LE_t = \alpha_0 + \alpha_1 \cdot \Delta LE_{t-1} + \ldots\ldots. + \alpha_p \cdot \Delta LE_{t-p} + \beta_1 \cdot \Delta LP_{t-1} + \ldots\ldots. + \beta_p \cdot \Delta LP_{t-p} + \varepsilon_t \quad (3)$$

where ε_t is assumed to be a white-noise error term. The optimal number of lags (p) for the equation is chosen according to a specific information criterion such as the Akaike Information Criterion. The Eq. (3) says that the growth rate of the variable Energy Sold at time t (ΔLE_t) can be represented as a function of its own past $(\Delta LE_{t-1}, \ldots, \Delta LE_{t-p})$, and of the past of the growth rate of the variable Installed Power $(\Delta LP_{t-1}, \ldots, \Delta LP_{t-p})$. According to this test, we are able to say that the variable P_t has a casual effect on E_t in the sense of Granger if some parameter β_i is statistically nonzero. The null hypothesis is $H_0 : \beta_1 = \beta_2 = \ldots\ldots. = \beta_p = 0$. Put in other words, the null hypothesis to be contrasted tells us if the photovoltaic Installed Power does not have a causal effect on the photovoltaic Energy Sold in Spain. Table 3 shows the null hypothesis and the results of the statistical hypothesis testing. Specifically, the F-statistic associated to the hypothesis testing has a value of 10.90 (p-value = 0.02). As a consequence, we have statistical arguments to reject the null hypothesis at 1 % level of significance. Therefore, and according to any coherent economic reasoning, the Installed Power has a causal effect on the Energy Sold, at least a causation effect in the sense of Granger. This is normal because energy sold and energy produced are very inter-related because the market of energy is very intervened and the bonuses were key in these solar markets.

6 Legal Actions

The change in bonus policies in the photovoltaic sector was a "hold-up" problem due to the specific investments made, and resulted in a great number of appeals and lawsuits. The sectors that considered their rights violated looked at the several possible action routes to seek "third-party enforcement" in order to claim their rights to the bonuses. The two main arguments used by investors for the claims were: (a) the approved rules involved an improper retroactivity; (b) the change of rules was an "infringement of the legitimate expectation" of investors on the commitments undertaken by the administration. In addition to these two arguments, the claimants affirmed that such institutional change lowered profitability to below that of the minimally acceptable rate of return to cover payment of capital.

The Spanish Constitutional Court, the Spanish ordinary courts, foreign courts and international agencies such as the ICSID (International Centre for Settlement of Investment Disputes, which is the world's leading institution devoted to international investment dispute settlement), were the third-parties to which claimants basically resorted to for their grievance against Law 14/2010, and also against other regulations and Royal Decrees that eliminated the bonus model.

Therefore, in 2011, several Autonomous Communities, such as Murcia, Castilla-La Mancha and Valencia, presented appeals of unconstitutionality against Law 14/2010. These were regions with considerable investment in solar parks and with many affected parties, and therefore the autonomous governments agreed to represent their interests (besides, these regional governments were in the hands of the main opposition party).

The National Association of Producers and Investors in Renewable Energies (Anpier) also filed a lawsuit against Royal Decree no. 1565/2010. In particular, it complained about the 30 year maximum period limit for receiving bonuses, claiming that the Royal Decree constituted an expropriation of rights and violated the principles of legal certainty, legitimate expectation, equality and proportionality of administrative action. The Supreme Court in July 2012 dismissed this claim under the argument that the limit set on years for bonus collection did not affect the "reasonable return" of plants, and because it did not appreciate any expropriation of rights in Royal Decree no. 1565/2010 as claimed by the association.

Furthermore, the Photovoltaic Industry Association (ASIF) filed an appeal under the administrative and contentious procedure before the Supreme Court against Royal Decree no. 1565/2010, based on the assumption that the regulatory changes brought about by the Royal Decree could have disastrous effects, and cause economic bankruptcy to many facilities. Finally, the Supreme Court dismissed the appeal just like on other occasions against similar claims. The Photovoltaic Legal Platform (PLF), which includes a part of the producers affected by the reduction of bonuses, then filed an appeal before the Supreme Court of Spain.

In view of the poor success obtained in the claims, the four main photovoltaic associations (AEF, Anpier, Appa-Fotovoltaica, Asif) decided to merge into a single cluster: UNEF (Spanish Photovoltaic Union). The UNEF carried out several legal actions against the cut back in bonuses and even won the support of certain political parties to take the matter before the Constitutional Court.

This cutback in bonuses not only adversely affected Spanish producers but also groups of international investors and therefore joint lawsuits were filed in other judicial instances. Thus, in February 2011, a set of companies that had invested more than €21.569 million in the Spanish renewable sector sued the Spanish Government before a London court for damages caused by the retroactive measures arising from Royal Decree no. 14/2010. To that end, they sought support in the "Energy Charter Treaty", which seeks to protect foreign direct investments in energy whenever they are affected by a breach of contract. There were indeed more lawsuits based on this treaty.

The claims did not end with the passing of Law 15/2013, Royal Decree No. 413/2014 and Order EIT/1045/2014. Moreover, claims were also submitted before the ICSID, which is the arbitration body within the World Bank. At the end of 2013, several international funds and investors filed their first lawsuits seeking the international arbitration of the ICSID. In total there were 22 lawsuits against Spain before the ICSID.

After the entry into force of Royal Decree Law no. 1/2012, claims against the Government measures were filed not only by private institutions but also by the Autonomous Communities of Galicia, Extremadura and the Canary Islands by appealing against the Decree before the Constitutional Court. Murcia, Valencia and Castilla-La Mancha also appealed against Royal Decree Law no. 14/2010, as previously mentioned. In March 2013, Andalusia filed a joint appeal that encompassed several regulations. Royal Decree Law no. 2/2013 was also the subject of an unconstitutionality appeal made before the Constitutional Court by the regional government of Extremadura, which justified its request arguing that the change in legislation on bonuses led to insecurity among investors and modified the expected profitability. However, in January 2016, the Constitutional Court ratified the constitutionality of Royal Decree no. 9/2013 that had reduced the bonuses, and denied any violation of the principles of legal certainty and non-retroactivity. The Court argued that the Government used the urgency procedure due to the "unforeseen" increase in tariff deficit caused by the crisis.

Furthermore, in January 2016, the Spanish Supreme Court dismissed the first five appeals filed by the photovoltaic companies against the decision of the Council of Ministers which refused to pay for damages derived from cut backs in bonuses to solar power plants in 2010. The Supreme Court felt that the income reduction arising from a reduction of bonus was subsequently compensated with other provisions made by the government, and considered the profitability of about 8 % per annum of the plants as "reasonable", and therefore excluded the presence of any real, unlawful and compensable damage. According to the Supreme Court judgement, the investors in photovoltaic companies did not acquire an "unlimited right" to receive bonuses, and "the nature, the amount, the extent and duration of the incentives granted to the photovoltaic installations cannot be petrified through the initial regulation, but they are susceptible to the relevant adaptations to the new circumstances", such as technological development and the changing economic scenario. It therefore denied the compensation claimed in the first four lawsuits that were resolved, indicating that the judgement establishes criteria that will also be crucial for the appeals presented by the other 150 companies (Fig. 9).

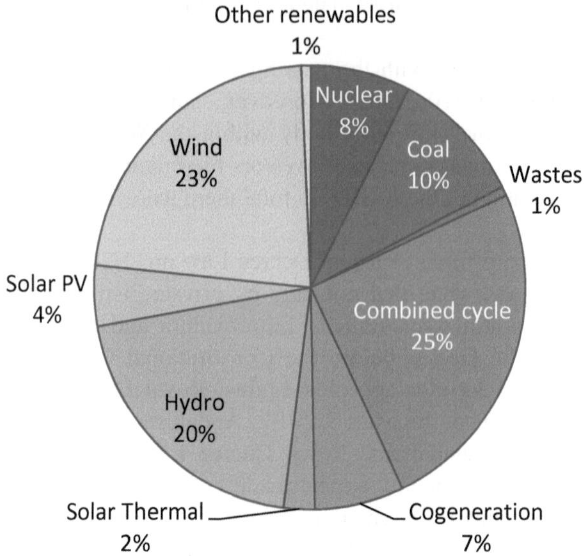

Fig. 9 Spain's installed electricity capacity by fuel (2015). *Source*: REE

7 Conclusions

Institutional change is a roadmap that determines the evolution of the rules (of the game) which establish incentives for economic agents. The theories of institutional change can be grouped into four main approaches (Kingston and Caballero 2009), and the process of institutional change in the present case study corresponds to an institutional change marked by the Government's political action and the parliament's legislative action, and therefore is a centralised "top down" institutional change produced by collective action, resulting in concrete laws and Royal Decrees.

Institutional change studies how the different rules result in different types of economic operations: the institutional scenario of bonuses produced expansion of the sector through large investments but the subsequent change of policy paralysed investments and considerably reduced the return on investments.

The institutional analysis performed throughout this chapter portrays how an institutional change in incentives and bonus policies for the photovoltaic sector led to an expansion and a posterior shrinkage of the sector. Indeed, the institutional framework defined by Royal Decree no. 661/2007, established a system of bonuses and incentives which led to the creation of a photovoltaic energy sector bubble, principally due to government interest in energy diversification through promotion of renewable energies, and to an expansive economic situation where the public treasury reached surplus. The Spanish government decided to take advantage of the buoyant situation in the national economy experienced since the mid-1990s to promote a change in the energy model.

However, the government did not adequately take into account the cost of the bonuses for the public treasury and neither did it contemplate the changing macroeconomic scenario derived from the great recession since 2008. In fact, the same Socialist government that had introduced the bonus policy in the photovoltaic sector rectified later and proceeded towards cancellation and elimination of that policy, for example through Royal Decree 1578/2008 and Royal Decree Law no. 14/2010 which limited the hours of photovoltaic installations for bonus eligibility. This trend was subsequently also continued by the conservative government elected in the 2011 general elections. Empirical analysis shows that since September 2008 the growth of the sector was stopped. One must bear in mind that the renewable energies bubble which involved the solar thermal and photovoltaic energy sectors received State aid for an amount of more than €2.5 billion in 2009.

The study of endogenous institutional change tries to explain the causes of institutional change. The problems of public sector financing, the sky-rocketing cost of bonus policies and abuse of existing bonus systems forced legislators to stop bonus policies for solar farms. It should likewise be noted that large electric companies criticised the bonus policy for solar farms by highlighting its high cost, and demanded elimination of the same.

The change of solar farms policy should be understood in a context of general change in the economic policy. In fact, the change in the economic cycle induced a rectification of the Spanish economic policy in May 2010, and the socialist government, when faced with market uncertainties and pressure from the European institutions, was obliged to reduce the salary of civil servants, freeze pensions and cancel baby aid. Within this scenario of turnaround in economic policy guidelines, the government was induced to amend its energy policy, which had already experienced problems due to an unexpected rapid expansion.

From an investors' point of view, once an investment is made and the photovoltaic panels are installed, such investment becomes an irreversible investment and revenues from such investment lie in the hands of the other contracting party, which in this case is the government. The government maintains its right to control bonuses over time, and the government can change the bonus amount after the investor has made investments ("a hold-up problem"). Hence, this type of transaction relation reveals the importance of the inter-temporal component in political transactions, which implies that payments or benefits for one of the contracting parties may change over time (Spiller and Tommasi 2009). This is the situation described in this case study, wherein investors invest in solar parks at a particular moment in time but the bonuses for energy produced are received as future revenues and in which the legislator must take decisions continuously.

Weingast and Marshall (1988), in their lead article on the American Congress, pointed to the presence of non-contemporary benefit flows in existing political transactions. This implies that the duration of revenues from projects interchanged can differ, and in this case, Weingast and Marshall (1988) suggest the possibility that one of the parties, after achieving its objective, could curb the other's project if its application is slower. In our case study, the Government, after obtaining investments in renewable energies, withdrew bonuses and thus stopped guaranteeing the yields expected by investors. Whether such change in energy policy is legal or not is another issue altogether and therefore investors have resorted to the courts of justice.

In the light of the legal changes, both domestic and international investors made their grievance public. According to the AEF, €20 billion from international banks, investment funds and foreign individuals have been invested in photovoltaic farms and therefore these companies are essential for the Spanish photovoltaic sector.

With the change of system rules, the affected investors resorted to legal action, arguing that the policy change punished their investments, since it infringed their legitimate expectations and they furthermore questioned the legitimacy of the "alleged" retroactivity of bonus policies. Appeals were lodged before the Spanish Supreme Court, the Constitutional Court, other foreign courts and the International Centre for Settlement of Investment Disputes, against the supposed "hold-up" carried out by the Spanish State by eliminating the existing bonuses. However, as has been analysed in detail above, the judgements issued until January 2016 concluded that the photovoltaic sector investors did not have an "unlimited right" to receive bonuses and that the Government could legitimately change the incentive system for solar energy due to the new circumstances in the country. In this way, the government was able to assure its ex-post rights to act with a certain degree of freedom in its energy policy.

Acknowledgement The authors acknowledge the support provided by the projects of the Spanish Ministry of Economic Affairs (HAR2013-40760-R; ECO2014-52412-R) and Xunta de Galicia (GRC2014/022; ECOBAS AGRUP-2015/08).

References

Álvarez-Díaz, M., Caballero, G., Manzano, B., & Martin-Moreno, J. M. (2015). Assessment of political situation over the business cycle in Spain: A time series analysis. *Hacienda Pública Española, 213*, 41–62.

ASIF. (2011). *Hacia el crecimiento sostenido de la fotovoltaica en España. Informe Anual 2011*. Asociación de la Industria Fotovoltaica. Available in www.asif.org. Madrid.

Briggs, A. H., Wonderling, D. E., & Mooney, C. Z. (1997). Pulling cost-effectiveness analysis up by its bootstraps: A non-parametric approach to confidence interval estimation. *Health Economics, 6*, 327–340.

Caballero, G. (2004). De la jerarquía al mercado: la reforma financiera española desde la nueva economía institucional. *Papeles de Economía Española, 101*, 64–79.

Caballero, G. (2008). El cambio institucional de la economía española del franquismo a la democracia: un análisis histórico institucional. *Política y Gobierno, XV*(2), 353–402.

Caballero, G., & Álvarez-Díaz, M. (2015). Institutional change in Spain from francoism to democracy: The effects of the great recession. In N. Schofield & G. Caballero (Eds.), *the political economy of governance: Institutions political performance and elections*. Heidelberg: Springer.

Caballero, G., & Arias, X. C. (2003). Una reorientación teórica de la economía política: el análisis político de costes de transacción. *Revista Española de Ciencia Política, 8*, 131–164.

Caballero, G., & Arias, X. C. (2013). Transaction cost politics in the map of the new institutionalism. In N. Schofield, G. Caballero, & D. Kselman (Eds.), *Advances in political economy: Institutions, modeling and empirical analysis* (pp. 3–31). Heidelberg: Springer.

Caballero, G., & Soto, D. (2015). The diversity and rapprochement of theories of institutional change: Original institutionalism and new institutional economics. *Journal of Economic Issues, 49*(4), 947–977.
Coase, R. H. (1937). The nature of the firm. *Economica, 4*, 386–405.
Coase, R. H. (1960). The problem of social cost. *Journal of Law and Economics, 3*(1), 1–44.
Del Rio Gonzalo, P. (2009). La promoción de la electricidad renovable en España en el contexto europeo. *Información Comercial Español: Revista de economía, 847*, 59–74.
Dixit, A. (1996). *The making of economic policy: A transaction-cost politics perspective*. Cambridge, MA: The MIT Press.
Efron, B., & Tibshirani, R. (1998). *An introduction to the bootstrap*. Boca Raton, Fla: Chapman & Hall/CRC.
Epstein, D., & O'Halloran, S. (1999). *Delegating powers: A transaction cost politics approach to policy making under separate powers*. Cambridge: Cambridge University Press.
Espejo Marín, C. (2004). La energía solar fotovoltaica en España. *Revista Nimbus, 13–14*, 5–31.
Espejo Marín, C. (2005). *La producción de electricidad en régimen especial en España*. Murcia: Universidad de Murcia. Homenaje al Profesor Antonio Roldán Pérez.
Granger, C. W. J. (1969). Investigating causal relations by econometrics models and cross spectral methods. *Econometrica, 37*, 424–438.
Joskow, P. L. (1985). Vertical integration and long term contracts: The case of coal-burning electric generating stations. *Journal of Law, Economics and Organization, 1*, 33–80.
Katz, R. W. (1988). Use of cross correlation in the search for teleconnections. *International Journal of Climatology, 8*, 241–253.
Kingston, C., & Caballero, G. (2009). Comparing theories of institutional change. *Journal of Institutional Economics, 5*(2), 151–180.
Lorenzo, E. (2005). Retratos de la conexión fotovoltaica a la red (V): de la AIE a los inversores. *Era Solar: Energías renovables, 126*, 52–59.
Mir, P. (2012). La regulación fotovoltaica y solar termoeléctrica en España. *Cuadernos económicos de ICE, 83*, 185–205.
North, D. C. (1990a). *Institutions institutional change and economic performance*. Cambridge: Cambridge University Press.
North, D. C. (1990b). A transaction cost theory of politics. *Journal of Theoretical Politics, 2*(4), 355–367.
Spiller, P. T., & Tommasi, M. (2009). *The institutional foundations of public policy in Argentina: A transaction cost approach*. Cambridge: Cambridge University Press.
UNESA. (1998). *Centrales eléctricas*. Madrid.
Weingast, B. R., & Marshall, W. J. (1988). The industrial organization of congress; or, why legislatures, like firms, are not organized as markets. *Journal of Political Economy, 96*(1), 132–163.
Williamson, O. E. (2000). The new institutional economics: Taking stock looking ahead. *Journal of Economic Literature, 38*, 595–613.

The Economic Effects of the Implementation of the Greek Adjustment Plan in the Great Recession

Inmaculada Carrasco, Carmen Córcoles, and John McCombie

1 Introduction

With many European economies in "fiscal consolidation mode" (paraphrasing Blanchard and Leigh 2013: 3), the debate concerning the effects on income and economic growth and the accuracy of economic forecasts becomes of great importance. It is generally accepted that when economies move into a deep recession, stabilization and adjustment reforms become an imperative. Following Nayyar (2008), the debate is about how this is to be accomplished. The orthodox approach focuses on inflation and deficits while the Keynesian perspective concentrates more on unemployment and stagnation.

Related to this debate, inequality and poverty are recognised as a barrier to stability and economic growth. In his recent work, Atkinson (2015) argues that in order to reduce present levels of inequality and poverty, economic and political orthodoxies should be abandoned. There should be return to a more progressive rate of income tax and an increase in unemployment benefit. Even a minimum level of income for all should be implemented. Considering the market distribution of income, salary levels should also be addressed to avoid workers living in poverty, even when they are employed. Countries are not passive agents, but they can choose their own path in the global economy. However, as also pointed out by Atkinson (2014), at a time of austerity, how much should spending be cut and by how much should taxes be raised? His answer is that even if, at first glance, there seems to be only one solution, there are always other options, as not all austerity plans are the same. Consequently, in current fiscal austerity programmes, policy makers should

I. Carrasco (✉) • C. Córcoles
Castilla-La Mancha University, Albacete, Spain
e-mail: Inmaculada.Carrasco@uclm.es

J. McCombie
Cambridge University, Cambridge, UK

N. Schofield, G. Caballero (eds.), *State, Institutions and Democracy*,
Studies in Political Economy, DOI 10.1007/978-3-319-44582-3_15

consider the balance between cutting spending and raising taxes, and the key role of public investment. This should be all undertaken in the context of the *Idea of Justice* for public policy (Atkinson 2012).

The second question is: what can a country do when vicious circles appear? Following Kotios et al. (2015), when a country is in a deep recession (with adverse economic, political and social effects), there are five vicious circles in operation at the same time. These are what might be termed the fiscal, the internal devaluation, the financial, the psychological, and the socio-political vicious circles. In this situation, the orthodox suggestion of international institutions such as the IMF is to restore fiscal equilibrium and implement structural reforms. There is also the need to design bailout plans for the banking systems, which will require the financial support of external institutions. Other authors, such as Alesina and Perotti (1997) show that the composition of fiscal adjustment plans can be important in determining their success in terms of a long-term deficit reduction. If fiscal multipliers are higher than assumed, major errors in the forecast of the rate of growth of economic activity can occur. This is the case in the recent crisis in the advanced economies, where greater planned fiscal consolidation has led to a lower rate of growth than that which had been projected (Blanchard and Leigh 2013; Charles et al. 2014). This showed that, especially in the Eurozone, the values of Keynesian multipliers are higher than expected, so that austerity policies led to deeper recession than was originally anticipated.

In the case of Greece, Christodoulakis (2013) explains that fiscal cuts did not result in just a temporary minor downturn. Now that the failure of the consolidation programme for Greece is confirmed, policies should focus on improving growth and allowing the multipliers to raise activity by relaxing fiscal targets. This is the only route to ensure an escape from stagnation and to guarantee debt sustainability. Greece provides a good case study as it is the EMU country that has suffered one of the greatest debt and deficit crises. It has implemented some variations in the tax and expenditure-reduction policies as well as debt-consolidation policies. This has been undertaken in a highly unstable political environment, and Greece has had to accept three bailout programmes.

The aim of this essay is to evaluate the first Greek adjustment plan in the context of the financial crisis and global recession. To achieve this goal, an input–output methodology is applied to the case of Greece, based on data from WIOD (2010). This methodology and the multiregional database that we have used, allow us to know the effects of the adjustment measures in all economic sectors as well as the effects in the European Union (EU) and the Rest of the World (RW) (Miller and Blair 1985; Cadarso et al. 2010; Dejuán et al. 2013; Timmer et al. 2015).

The paper is structured as follows: after this introduction, the second section is devoted to contextualizing the current economic and political situation in Greece. The third section presents data, methodology and results and the fourth sets out conclusions and policy implications.

2 A Commentary on the Chronology of Events Regarding the Recent Crisis in Greece

2.1 *From Integration in the Eurozone to the Financial Meltdown*

To understand the present problems in Greece, we have to go back to the years before it joined the Eurozone. At this time there was tendency for Greece to increase the public deficit beyond all reasonable sustainable levels. After adopting the euro, the public deficit rose more sharply than the average of the other EU countries. The goal of maintaining a balanced budgetary position has never been reached. The primary balance has never been below 3 % of GDP. Between 2000 and 2009, the size of the public sector rose from 44 % to about 50 % of GDP. Social transfers and the compensation of public employees increased from about 25 % of GDP to about 34 % over this period. Events such as 2004 Athens Olympics led to a large increase in debt. General government net borrowing reached 7.5 % of GDP in this year, crowding-out private sector borrowing. An effort to reduce public debt reduced net public borrowing to 3.6 % of GDP in 2006. However, from then on it grew massively until 2009 when it 13.6 % of GDP (European Commission 2010).

These fiscal imbalances were produced by an unsustainable rate of economic growth, endemic immoral private behaviour (reflected in, for example, widespread tax evasion) and over-optimistic tax projections. On average, Greece grew about 2 percentage points more than the euro-area average from 2000 to 2009. This reduced the GDP gap by 15 percentage points (from 25 to 10 % below the EU average) (European Commission 2010). However, this growth was led by drivers such as private consumption and residential investment that were unsustainable. These drivers were encouraged by the growth in real wages and the expansion of credit, resulting from liberalization of the financial sector and a phase of expansion in European monetary policy. Commentators such as Borooah (2014) argue that the European crisis is a result of private sector overspending, which existed before the 2008 recession began. This was unobserved by the European monetary authorities, providing evidence of the lack of automatic signals in the Euro-regime to indicate that there was overspending in the private economy.

Monetary policy can sometimes be spatially asymmetric (Angeloni and Ehrmann 2004; Angeloni et al. 2003; Claussen and Hayo 2006) It cannot avoid becoming pro-cyclical when specific economies act counter-cyclically with respect to the European average or there exist other institutional or structural reasons such as different consumption patterns and rigidity in certain markets. Greece had an inflation rate that was higher than the average of the Eurozone countries. But it was not a notable exception. Portugal, Ireland, Spain and Italy also had to confront problems resulting from asymmetries in European Monetary Policy (Angeloni and Ehrmann 2004).

In these situations, there is a high risk of financial bubbles and governments need to be watchful in order to avoid excessive public expenditure exacerbating the situation. But when local problems of unemployment are seen to be more important than those of high local inflation, governments, locked into short-term political cycles, can be tempted to try to reduce unemployment below historical rates. By doing so, they overlook the fact that these policy drivers lead to unsustainable economic growth and the creation of stock market bubbles.

Furthermore, Greece's external competitiveness decreased as a consequence of wage increases that exceed that of labour productivity. In a context of growing internal demand, the deterioration of external competitiveness led to a rapidly worsening current account deficit, peaking at 14 % of GDP in 2008 (European Commission 2010).

In addition to this, problems with the efficiency of the accounting and statistical methods used in Greece imposed a delay in the identification of these problems. This led to a delay in the implementation of the eventual necessary political and economic measures. The substantial revision of the estimate of the budget deficit (from 2 % of GDP reported in the 2009 budget to the 12.7 % in the October notification and from 12.7 % of GDP of 2010 budget to 13.6 % in the April notification) appeared at the time of the worst of the international financial crisis. It had immediate consequences for Greek sovereign bonds, which were downgraded by the rating agencies to junk status. Spreads of credit default swaps (CDS) also increased sharply in 2009. In the context of international financial markets that had frozen, with resulting serious difficulties of international borrowing, the financial situation in Greece was unsustainable. The country could not access the private international financial markets. Consequently, after an official request for international financial assistance, a mission comprising members of the European Central Bank, the European Commission and the International Monetary Fund visited Athens in April, 2010.

2.2 *From the First Bailout to the Present*

On 2 May 2010, in order to avoid the sovereign default of Greece, the mission agreed a €110 billion financing package: €80 billion coming from the European Union (more particularly, from the EU countries joining the euro); €30 billion from the IMF and the rest from some extraordinary financial measures taken by ECB. The IMF took the lead and determined much of the deficit targeting and policy restructuring reforms suggested to Greece. This is because the IMF was the institution set up to lend money to a country in serious financial difficulties and it has with a great deal of experience in the implementation of bailouts. Finally, the European Central Bank, abandoning its orthodox policies, began to buy Greek bonds with a view to calming financial markets and to reduce Greece's risk premium.

The programme aimed to restore macroeconomic stability and install the drivers for sustainable long-term growth. With a wide range of short-term and structural measures, a package of fiscal policies was also agreed. In addition to the strict fiscal measures already implemented in 2010, estimated at 5.5 % of GDP (European Commission 2010), the new measures sought a reduction in the fiscal balance below

3 % in 2014 (a reduction of almost 11 percentage points in the period 2010–2014). Fiscal consolidation aimed not only for expenditure cuts but also for tax revenue increases. Tax measures were centred on indirect taxation and the battle against tax evasion. Other measures included nominal wages and pension cuts (abolishing the Easter, Summer and Christmas bonuses, which were replaced by a flat bonus for salaries and pensions at a certain rate), an increase in VAT, and efficiency savings from the reform of local governments. Complementary to these efforts was the €10 billion allocated to the Financial Stabilisation Fund devoted to restore banking system solvency. The residual amount (€10 billion in 2010; €40 billion in 2011; €24 billion in 2012 and €8 billion in 2013) would be used to cover the financing needs of the public sector. The intention was that this would prevent the need for Greece to tap the international bond markets for 18 months. Up until 2012, €73 billion had been disbursed in international assistance.

In change, Greece took the compromise of reducing public expenditure: €1080 billion in pharmacy expenditure; €50 billion in medical expenditure; €300 billion in purchase of military equipment; a reduction of central government and electoral expenditure by €30 billion and €270 billion; €190 billion reduction in grants and subsidies; €300 billion in pensions; €205 billion in salaries. In total, €2425 billion reduction.

Until 2012, the compliance with policy conditionality was partially observed in the policy towards the financial sector. In terms of fiscal policy, consolidation measures were partially implemented and the stock of arrears to suppliers at the end of 2011 was higher.

This programme was possibly too ambitious. Perhaps the estimates were mistaken or possibly the international financial crisis was too complicated to implement the planned reforms. Furthermore, political instability, the state of social tension and perhaps the lack of administrative capacity made it extremely difficult to achieve the planned goals. It was impossible for Greece to return to market financing. A new programme was needed.

However, the new scenario was worse than the previous one. The goals were the same, but now the Greek economy was shrinking and it was expected that there was little capacity for short-term growth. As noted in the European Commission report (2012a), all the main components of domestic demand shrank in 2011. A negative mind-set took over Greek businesses and households. There were credit restrictions, higher unemployment, delays in the implementation of political reforms, and a mixture of external and debt problems. All of these led to greater uncertainty, which gave rise to the idea Greece might leave the eurozone. This last factor complicated the situation even more, as the interest-rate dynamics reflected not only the default risk but also the exchange-rate risk (i.e., the risk that the sovereign debt could be paid back in a currency other than the euro). In February 2012 a new agreement was reached and in March 2012 a large-scale debt restructuring operation was carried out. This involved an agreement with private sovereign-debt holders to lengthen repayment periods, reduce interest rates and it assumed a 53.5 % decrease in nominal value of the debt. In this new programme, fiscal targets were revised and a new disbursements were agreed: the remaining €37.2 billion plus €130 billion in the period 2012–2014; the European Financial Stability Fund (EFCF) and the IMF would cover those quantities. Greece committed itself to a new policy package aimed at reducing structural expenditure by €325 million in order to balance the fiscal situation. In the long-term, the government set a target of raising €50 billion by the privatisation of assets and the reallocation of land. The delayed tax reforms were to be enacted and combating tax evasion was now made a priority.

A heated electoral climate arose as doubts emerged in the international markets about whether Greece would be able to implement the necessary fiscal consolidation and structural reforms. Following the European Commission report (2013a: 1) there were "signs of a lack of commitment by the Greek government, administration and population, while a large amount of financial assistance was being provided to the country". Later, in its third review report (European Commission 2013b), the Commission highlighted the delays in the reforms (especially in the health sector) which it considered limited Greece's capacity to achieve the fiscal targets for 2013 and 2014. This was even though it also recognised important progress that had been made in public finances, the recapitalisation of the core banks, the improvements in the business environment, and the broadening and acceleration of product market reforms. It also recognised that weak economic growth in the Euro area was undermining Greek fiscal consolidation. It raised concerns about the ability of the Greek administration to efficiently collect income tax and suggested implementing a privatisation programme. Despite this, the Commission recommended the disbursement of the third tranche (Q3) of EFSF funds to be made in October 2013.

The Fourth Revision (European Commission 2014) showed a slight improvement in some of Greece's macroeconomic indicators, such as the primary deficit which was now in net surplus. In this apparently advantageous environment, the government decided to call parliamentary elections in December 2014. For the first time in Greek history, Syriza, a left-wing radical coalition won the elections (with only two seats short of an absolute majority). It was able to form a government in coalition with ANEL, the Independent Greeks Party. Syriza proposed to renegotiate the major reduction in the nominal value of Greek debt and not to respect the terms of the previous agreement.

In this environment, the Eurogroup gave a 4-month extension to the Greek bailout programme, making the last payment conditional on its renegotiation with the new government before April. Some attempts to achieve a new agreement were made until the end of June. A cessation of payments would imply applying capital controls to avoid the collapse of the financial system and could put Greece on the brink of a more than likely exit from the euro. Growing liquidity restrictions could also lead to great difficulties in paying pensions and public salaries.

Following the official Euro group (2015) declaration (which Greece did not sign), the Greek government unilaterally broke off the negotiations. Consequently, the Troika revoked the remaining programmed aid (as the current agreement technically expired on 30 June). The interruption of financial aid caused an unexpected liquidity crisis in both the Greek public and financial sectors. Interest rates on Greek debt rose once again, making it nearly impossible for the public administration to access the private financial markets.

Some hours after his statement on the breakdown of negotiations, Prime Minister Tsipras announced on 25 June 2015, a referendum on whether or not to accept the terms of the proposal offered by the Troika. This was in order for the Greek population to have its say on the second bailout agreement. The government publicly defended the No option, in accord with its anti-austerity philosophy. Some analysts and the opposition parties demanded a political U-turn that would cause the supply of money to dry up.

On Sunday 5 July 2015 the Greeks voted against accepting the Troika's new plan that would have ensured further financing for Greece. Then, according to a source from the Kremlin, mentioned in the press, Tsipras met with the Russian Prime Minister Putin, who expressed his wish to help Greece. He indicated Russia's willingness to purchase Greek assets in sectors such as communication infrastructures (ports, airports, railways) or energy, if they were privatized. However, Russia was not likely to make any loans to Greece. Three days after the referendum, Tsipras unexpectedly and officially made a new demand for financial support. On this occasion, it was directed to the European Commission, not the ECB and IMF. More specifically, he presented Greece's third request for a bailout to the European Stability Mechanism (ESM). He requested €50 billion, while committing the Greek government to implementing the postponed fiscal reform and the remaining structural adjustments.

The Euro group countries agreed an €86 billion bailout, payable over 3 years. The parliaments of seven Euro group countries (Greece included) voted on giving their governments a mandate to negotiate a new attempt (the last, according to the German Federal Minister of Finance, Schäuble) for Europe to resolve the Greek crisis. The Greek Parliament also voted in favour of the proposal.

On the same day, Friday 17 July 2015, 28 European Union countries authorised an urgent loan of €7.1 billion in order to enable the Greek government to meet previous agreements with the ECB and IMF. Immediately, the financial markets reacted positively and S&P upgraded the rating of Greek bonds two notches (from CCC− to CCC+). A New Memorandum of Understanding (MoU) was signed in, 2015.

3 An Input–Output Estimation of the Effects of Austerity Plan on a Regional Economy: The Case of Greece

Taking into account the social, political and economic situation described above, the aim of this paper is to investigate the sectorial effects on Greek and European economies of the adjustment policy in Greece. In order to meet this objective, we will develop an input–output analysis. The input–output analysis allows us to identify the multiplier effects of an expansion (or a contraction) in autonomous demand. The main advantages of this methodology are that on the one hand, we can identify these effects broken down by sector, and on the other hand, we can calculate not only the direct, but also, the indirect effects that autonomous expenditure has on all sectors of the economy (Miller and Blair 1985).

This type of analysis is currently being used in many areas of economics in a global context, for example, in environmental and sector studies (Timmer et al. 2015). It has the advantage that it permits the interpretation of inter-country effects, which are so important in a globalised world. See Dejuán et al. (2013) for some extensions to this model.

3.1 Data and Methodology

This empirical study uses data from the WIOD (World input–output database), a database offering input–output tables of 40 countries[1] from 1995 until 2011 broken down into 35 manufacturing sectors (Timmer 2012). WIOD provides data in the context of a multiregional model, bringing together the inter-sectorial relations in an input–output table for the 40 countries. It includes a 1435×1435,[2] dimension matrix of intermediate inputs presenting all the purchases and sales between all the sectors and in all the countries. For example, if we consider a country such as Greece, in each column we find the inputs required from each of 41 countries and in each of 35 sectors for production in the column sector. In each row we can see the sales of each sector to all considered sectors of different countries As in all input–output tables, there is also information about primary inputs (added value and output, basically) and final demand (such as private final consumption, government consumption, exports, etc.).

The model is based on Leontief's input–output analysis (Leontief 1973). The main equation of which is:

$$X = AX + Y \tag{1}$$

where:

X = output sectorial vector.

A = technical coefficients matrix, each element of this matrix, a_{ij}, tells us direct inputs of sector i that sector j needs for its production.

Y = final demand sector.

[1]The 40 countries are: 27 EU countries (all excepting Croatia), and Australia, Brazil, Canada, China, Indonesia, India, Japan, Korea, México, Russia, Turkey, Taiwan and USA.

[2]This matrix includes information on intermediate inputs for 40 countries with 35 sectors in each one, and another country, referred to as rest of world, whose part has not been included in the countries considered.

From Eq. (1) we can derive:

$$MT = [I - A]^{-1} Y \tag{2}$$

where:

$[I–A]^{-1}$ is Leontief's inverse matrix, each element, m_{ij}, indicates direct and indirect inputs of sector i required in the production of one unit in sector j. So, aggregating sector j column, we obtain the multiplier in this sector, indicating direct and indirect requirements of all sectors in order to produce one unit in sector j.

Y is the final demand sector.

From the WIOD dataset[3] we have obtained Leontief's matrix[4] for Greece and its relations, on the one hand, with other European Union countries (EU), and on the other, with the rest of the countries (RW). In this matrix, each column shows the direct and indirect inputs that Greek sectors need from each sector in each country to produce one unit. We have aggregated the EU and RW requirements. The sectors with the largest multiplier effects are those with higher values in the sum of their columns, because these sectors need more quantity from the other sectors in order to produce their outputs.

To calculate the final effects of fiscal consolidation in Greece, we have constructed a final demand vector, summarising the different public expenditure policy measures taken in all the sectors. The product of this vector by the Leontief's inverse matrix gives us the final effect of the policy.

To test this methodology, we have considered the different reductions in expenditure in the 2012 adjustment plan, mentioned in Sect. 2.

3.2 *Results and Discussion*

If we assign these expenditures to the industrial sectors of Greece, we can use Eq. (1) and obtain the effects of this reduction on Greece's public expenditure, in all sectors and in all countries considered in the WIOD.

Table 1 summarizes the multiplier effects of these policies in the Greek, European and Rest of World economies.

The total multiplier effect of the contraction in Greek public sector, as we can see from Table 1, is a reduction of €3200 billion in domestic production, €506 billion in the UE and €359 billion in the other countries. The largest effects for Greece are in sectors 33 and 31 (Health and Social Work and Public Administration and Defence; Compulsory Social Security) as these sectors are responsible for a

[3]Generally, the elaboration of input–output tables by direct surveys is done each 5 years. Between these years the tables are updated. We have used WIOD-2010 because this is the last published matrix.

[4]This matrix has been calculated using Matlab computing software.

Table 1 Multiplier effects of reduction in Greece's public sector 2012 adjustment plan (€ billions)

		Greece	EU	RW
Agriculture, hunting, forestry and fishing	c1	−2.00	−2.54	−4.51
Mining and quarrying	c2	−7.19	−4.12	−48.46
Food, beverages and tobacco	c3	−15.66	−5.45	−4.66
Textiles and textile products	c4	−2.42	−2.20	−3.94
Leather, leather and footwear	c5	−0.13	−0.23	−0.33
Wood and products of wood and cork	c6	−0.83	−1.87	−1.48
Pulp, paper, paper, printing and publishing	c7	−12.62	−10.14	−6.47
Coke, refined petroleum and nuclear fuel	c8	−14.45	−13.04	−15.56
Chemicals and chemical products	c9	−39.10	−131.92	−57.31
Rubber and plastics	c10	−1.50	−8.22	−6.22
Other non-metallic mineral	c11	−4.97	−3.69	−2.53
Basic metals and fabricated metal	c12	−15.74	−33.08	−25.29
Machinery, nec	c13	−9.61	−51.83	−17.61
Electrical and optical equipment	c14	−20.87	−45.32	−27.95
Transport equipment	c15	−5.97	−21.15	−10.35
Manufacturing, nec; recycling	c16	−0.82	−3.35	−2.10
Electricity, gas and water supply	c17	−59.77	−12.87	−9.51
Construction	c18	−31.31	−5.53	−5.24
Sale, maintenance and repair of motor vehicles and motorcycles; retail sale of fuel	c19	−38.16	−4.88	−1.06
Wholesale trade and commission trade, except of motor vehicles and motorcycles	c20	−106.68	−23.33	−13.89
Retail trade, except of motor vehicles and motorcycles; repair of household goods	c21	−70.73	−14.43	−4.79
Hotels and restaurants	c22	−11.28	−2.23	−2.49
Inland transport	c23	−12.26	−9.17	−11.22
Water transport	c24	−0.12	−1.08	−1.91
Air transport	c25	−0.92	−1.66	−2.74
Other supporting and auxiliary transport activities; activities of travel agencies	c26	−0.38	−8.72	−4.14
Post and telecommunications	c27	−40.28	−5.51	−7.06
Financial intermediation	c28	−91.94	−13.66	−15.32
Real estate activities	c29	−49.00	−7.60	−6.60
Renting of M&Eq and other business activities	c30	−78.22	−47.20	−24.21
Public admin and defence; compulsory social security	c31	−1107.74	−1.53	−1.32
Education	c32	−3.27	−1.45	−1.74
Health and social work	c33	−1136.99	−1.18	−1.41
Other community, social and personal services	c34	−207.12	−5.59	−9.59
Private households with employed persons	c35	0.00	0.00	−0.02
Total		−3200	−506	−359

Source: Own elaboration from WIOD

large volume of direct expenditure. But we can also see the significant impact on other sectors such as sector 20 (Wholesale trade and Commission Trade, Except for Motor Vehicles and Motorcycles), sector 30 (Financial Intermediation) or sector 17 (Electricity, Gas and Water Supply). We can also highlight the contractionary effects in EU and RW countries: the most important effects are in sector 9 (Chemical and Chemical Products) for EU countries and in sector 2 (Mining and Quarrying) for RW countries.

The results show that the total multiplier is 1.32 that fits with IMF's total multiplier estimated values, IMF (2012) and Blanchard and Leigh (2013) say that multipliers have been in the 0.9–1.7 range since the Great Recession. Corsetti et al. (2012); Batini et al. (2012), Christiano et al. (2010) also confirm that during the recession, fiscal multipliers are higher.

We can also calculate the multiplier effects in each sector (resulting from an increase in one production unit) by adding columns in the Leontief's inverse matrix. Results for the Greek case are presented in Table 2.

Table 2 shows which sectors in Greece have the largest effect on the rest of the economy. They are, in general, the industrial sectors (with multiplier effects higher than 2) and the sectors that need more inputs from other sectors for production. Across the public sector, education has a smaller multiplier effect than the others. Although the results are more relevant in Greece, we can see that contractionary multiplier effects can also be serious in EU and RW countries. This depends on the sector (for example, in the RW, Greece has more direct and indirect requirements in the textile sector).

These results confirm that all adjustment measures are contractionary in the short term and that cuts affecting industrial sectors have a more negative impact, not only because the reduction of income is immediate, but also due to the effects on the drivers of future economic growth. This idea is consistent with the theory proposed by Alesina and Perotti (1997) which explains that fiscal adjustments which rely primarily on tax increases and cuts in public investment tend not to last and are contractionary. It also confirms the approach of Atkinson (2014), who highlights the key role of public investment in the economy. Consequently, policy makers should consider this outcome when designing public expenditure cuts, since they do not all have the same impact on every economy.

4 Conclusions

Greece faces a difficult social, political and economic situation characterised by serious disequilibria in key macroeconomic variables, political instability, and growing social discontent and loss of faith in its public institutions. In such an adverse situation, there is a debate on what measures should be implemented. From a theoretical point of view, two main alternative approaches emerge. One focuses on solving the deficit and debt problems, and the other considers problems of unemployment and economic growth.

Table 2 Multipliers in Greece-MT (Leontief's inverse matrix—columns added)

		Total	Greece	EU	RW
Agriculture, hunting, forestry and fishing	c1	1.77841	1.43816	0.14903	0.19121
Mining and quarrying	c2	1.78948	1.46590	0.12739	0.19619
Food, beverages and tobacco	c3	2.03976	1.66972	0.17388	0.19616
Textiles and textile products	c4	1.90750	1.42922	0.17256	0.30572
Leather, leather and footwear	c5	1.96953	1.61871	0.18114	0.16968
Wood and products of wood and cork	c6	1.99601	1.58028	0.24016	0.17558
Pulp, paper, paper, printing and publishing	c7	2.00541	1.56707	0.25413	0.18422
Coke, refined petroleum and nuclear fuel	c8	2.42860	1.15321	0.06821	1.20718
Chemicals and chemical products	c9	2.22362	1.54512	0.38069	0.29781
Rubber and plastics	c10	2.07632	1.46149	0.36211	0.25272
Other non-metallic mineral	c11	2.04224	1.70217	0.15305	0.18702
Basic metals and fabricated metal	c12	2.52434	1.73597	0.34647	0.44190
Machinery, nec	c13	2.07290	1.43161	0.32293	0.31836
Electrical and optical equipment	c14	2.28701	1.62751	0.30213	0.35738
Transport equipment	c15	2.05134	1.40166	0.16988	0.47981
Manufacturing, nec; recycling	c16	2.11211	1.62901	0.25931	0.22379
Electricity, gas and water supply	c17	1.63527	1.41183	0.06523	0.15821
Construction	c18	2.13538	1.66920	0.21521	0.25097
Sale, maintenance and repair of motor vehicles and motorcycles; retail sale of fuel	c19	1.38224	1.27974	0.04444	0.05806
Wholesale trade and commission trade, except of motor vehicles and motorcycles	c20	1.57150	1.35506	0.09552	0.12092
Retail trade, except of motor vehicles and motorcycles; repair of household goods	c21	1.46607	1.31360	0.06372	0.08875
Hotels and restaurants	c22	1.66061	1.44420	0.10450	0.11192
Inland transport	c23	1.90113	1.42930	0.12956	0.34226
Water transport	c24	1.68113	1.15623	0.23434	0.29056
Air transport	c25	2.10091	1.37607	0.29245	0.43239
Other supporting and auxiliary transport activities; activities of travel agencies	c26	1.56078	1.34668	0.07417	0.13993
Post and telecommunications	c27	1.26403	1.17191	0.03765	0.05448
Financial intermediation	c28	1.47846	1.36161	0.03685	0.08001
Real estate activities	c29	1.19576	1.14304	0.01648	0.03623
Renting of M&Eq and other business activities	c30	1.83975	1.59815	0.07836	0.16324
Public admin and defence; compulsory social security	c31	1.58222	1.32586	0.14437	0.11198
Education	c32	1.13889	1.09566	0.01780	0.02543
Health and social work	c33	1.77441	1.29190	0.29473	0.18778
Other community, social and personal services	c34	1.63882	1.44795	0.06935	0.12152
Private households with employed persons	c35	1.00000	1.00000	0.00000	0.00000

Source: Own elaboration from WIOD

In this paper, our intention is not to enter the debate about the applicability of adjustment plans, but to determine how the different composition of fiscal adjustment plans can affect the outcome. The goal of this article is to evaluate the first Adjustment Plan for Greece in the context of the debate between different positions on fiscal consolidation measures. To achieve this goal, an input–output model was developed.

Our results demonstrate the notable effects of the adjustment plan on the contraction of the Greek economy and also in the economies of Europe and the rest of the World. Furthermore, the methodology applied enables us to identify the effects by sector. The sectors bearing the greatest impact are Health and Social Work (33) and the sector Public Administration and Defence; Compulsory Social Security (31). These sectors account for a major part of direct expenditure. However, we can also see the significant impact on other sectors such as Wholesale Trade and Commission Trade, except of Motor Vehicles and Motorcycles (20), Financial Intermediation (30) and Electricity, Gas and Water Supply (17). We can also highlight the contractionary effects in EU and RW countries: the largest effects are in the sector of Chemical and Chemical Products (9) for EU countries and in Mining and Quarrying (2) for RW countries.

Our results also confirm that all adjustment measures are contractionary in the short term and that the cuts affecting industrial sectors have a more negative impact, not only because the reduction in income is immediate, but also due to the effects on the drivers of future economic growth.

Bibliography

Alesina, A., & Perotti, R. (1997). Fiscal adjustments in OECD countries: Composition and macroeconomic effects. *IMF Staff Papers, 44*(2), 210–248.

Angeloni, I., & Ehrmann, M. (2004). *Euro area inflation differentials*. (Working Paper, n. 388), European Central Bank.

Angeloni, I., Kashyap, A., Mojo, B., & Terlizzese, D. (2003). *Monetary policy transmission in the euro area*. Cambridge: Cambridge University Press.

Atkinson, A. B. (2012). Public economics after the idea of justice. *Journal of Human Development and Capabilities, 13*(4), 1–16. doi:10.1080/19452829.2012.703171.

Atkinson, A. (2014). *Public economics in an age of austerity*. New York: Routledge.

Atkinson, A. (2015). *Inequality: What can be done?* Oxford: Oxford University Press.

Batini, N., Callegari, G., & Melina, G. (2012). *Succesful austerity in the Unites States, Europe and Japan*. (IMF Working Paper, WP/12/190).

Blanchard, O., & Leigh, D. (2013). Growth forecast errors and fiscal multipliers. *También se ha publicado en American Economic Review, 103*, 117–120. IMF Working Papers, WP/13/I, January.

Borooah, V. K. (2014). *Europe in an age of austerity*. New York: Palgrave Macmillan.

Cadarso, M. A., Gómez, N., López, L. A., & Tobarra, M. A. (2010). CO_2 emissions of international freight transport and offshoring: Measurement and allocation. *Ecological Economics, 69*(8), 1682–1694.

Charles, S., Dallery, T., & Marie, J. (2014). *Why are Keynesian multipliers bigger in hard times? A Palley-Aftalion-Pasinetti explanation*. http://www.academia.edu/9704418/ Why are Keynesian Multipliers Bigger in . . .

Christiano, L., Eichenbaum, M., & Rebelo, S. (2010, December). *When is the government spending multiplier large*. Northwestern University.

Christodoulakis, N. (2013). From grexit to growth: On fiscal multipliers and how to end recession in Greece. *National Institute Economic Review, 224*, 66–76.

Claussen, V., & Hayo, B. (2006). Assymmetric monetary policy effects in EMU. *Applied Economics, 38*, 1123–1134.

Corsetti, G., Meier, A., & Müller, G. J. (2012). *What determines government spending multipliers*. (IMF Working Paper, WP/12/150).

Dejuán, O., López, L. A., Tobarra, M. A., & Zafrilla, J. (2013). A post-Keynesian AGE model to forecast energy demand in Spain. *Economic Systems Research, 25*(3), 321–340.

Euro group. (2015). *Euro group statement on Greece*. Press Release 532/15, 27/06/2015d.

European Commission. (2010, May). *The economic adjustment programme for Greece*. Occasional Papers, n. 61, Directorate-General for Economic and Financial Affairs.

European Commission. (2012a, March). *The second economic adjustment programme for Greece*. Occasional Papers, n. 94. Directorate-General for Economic and Financial Affairs.

European Commission. (2012b, December). *The second economic adjustment programme for Greece*. Fist Review-December 2012. Occasional Papers, n. 123, Directorate-General for Economic and Financial Affairs.

European Commission. (2013a, May). *The Second economic adjustment programme for Greece*. Second Review-May 2013, Occasional Papers, n. 148, Directorate-General for Economic and Financial Affairs.

European Commission. (2013b, July). *The second economic adjustment programme for Greece*. Third Review-July 2013, Occasional Papers, n. 159, Directorate-General for Economic and Financial Affairs.

European Commission. (2014, April). *The second economic adjustment programme for Greece*. Fourth Review-April 2014, *Occasional Papers*, n. 192, Directorate-General for Economic and Financial Affairs.

International Monetary Fund. (2012). *World economic outlook: growth resuming, dangers remain*. Washington, DC: IMF.

Kotios, A., Galanos, G., Plymakis, S., & Roukanas, S. (2015). The vicious circles of recession and development prospects. *Procedia Economics and Finance, 19*, 63–68.

Leontief, W. (1973). *Análisis económico input–output*. Barcelona: Ariel.

Miller, R. E., & Blair, P. D. (1985). *Input–output analysis*. Cambridge: Cambridge University Press.

Nayyar, D. (2008). Macroeconomics of structural adjustment and public finances in developing countries: A heterodox perspective. *International Journal of Development Issues, 7*(1), 4–28.

Timmer, M. (2012). *The World Input–output Database (WIOD): Contents, sources and methods*. Accessed in www.wiod.org

Timmer, M. P., Dierzenbacher, E., Los, B., Stehren, R., & De Vries, G. J. (2015). An illustrated user guide to world input–output database: The case of global automotive production. *Review of International Economics, 23*, 575–605.

WIOD. (2010). In Timmer, M. (Ed.), *The World Input-output Database (WIOD): Contents, sources and methods*. Accessed in www.wiod.org

E-Procurement and Innovation in the Portuguese Municipalities: When Change Is Mandatory

Luís Soares and Adão Carvalho

1 Introduction

The electronic public procurement (e-procurement) refers to the use of electronic communications and transaction processing by government institutions and other public sector organisations when buying supplies and services or tendering public works (European Commission 2010c). Today, the creation of a European e-procurement single market is a mission of the European Commission (and of the EU Member States) to explore the potential advantages (in terms of transparency, efficiency, competition, innovation, speed of the process, etc.) that the electronic public procurement has to offer. The e-procurement is part of the Digital Agenda for Europe, which is one of the flagship initiatives under the Europe 2020 strategy to reverse the European Union's declining competitiveness. The creation of the European e-procurement single market is an ambitious goal of the EU in view of the complexity of extending e-procurement to all stages of the procurement process, the required interoperability of all e-procurement platforms across Europe and the sense of urgency of the EU.

Often public policies have objectives that involve significant organizational changes in public institutions to be effective. Sometimes the implementation of public policies, such as e-procurement, require major organizational changes that force public institutions to a process of radical innovation. It is common, however, that such organizational impacts are not properly anticipated (Mota and Filho

L. Soares (✉)
Câmara Municipal de Castro Verde, Praça do Município, 7780-217 Castro Verde, Portugal
e-mail: lso4res@gmail.com

A. Carvalho
Departamento de Economia, Escola de Ciências Sociais, CEFAGE, Universidade de Évora, Largo dos Colegiais 2, 7000-803 Évora, Portugal
e-mail: acarvalho@uevora.pt

N. Schofield, G. Caballero (eds.), *State, Institutions and Democracy*,
Studies in Political Economy, DOI 10.1007/978-3-319-44582-3_16

2011). Moving to e-procurement is a lot more than a mere replacement of paper with electronic files in the procurement process, since it involves major organizational changes, breaking up of traditional processes and practices, obsolescence of knowledge and skills. It also requires new technological, organizational and legal competencies for dealing with the procurement process, managing of information and interacting with economic operators and e-procurement platforms. In 2009, Portugal went beyond the European Commission's recommendations and pioneered in making e-procurement mandatory in the pre-award phase to all purchases of goods and services and tender works above a threshold amount. Portugal did it in a prevailing context of voluntary adoption of e-procurement (by countries, public institutions and companies) and autonomy of the EU Member States in designing their e-procurement policies. Portugal took a bold step forward by making e-procurement mandatory in a EU context of a "kaleidoscope of results" and lack of interoperability of e-procurement platforms. It implicitly assumed that all the Portuguese contracting authorities (and economic operators) were receptive to adopt e-procurement and prepared to cope with the organizational changes (thus reaching the policy objectives).

Six years on, the e-procurement law in Portugal is about to be changed to accommodate the Directive 2014/24/EU[1] and no study is known that has thoroughly analysed the impacts and outcomes of the e-procurement policy. There are a number of studies that have examined extensively the implications and the impact of this innovation in the specific context of its application, but only a small proportion of these studies focused on the innovation implications in public contracting authorities (and particularly in a mandatory e-procurement context). Prior research on e-procurement relies heavily on case studies, with a bias towards the analysis of the drivers, benefits and implications of e-procurement in business firms. This study looks at the relationship between e-procurement and innovation in a subset—municipalities—of the thousands of Portuguese contracting authorities that were required by law to change to e-procurement. It tries to understand the extent into which the adoption of e-procurement has embraced a real organizational change for the municipalities or, on the other hand, if it has represented a mere adaptation of the usual procurement practices. To answer this question, we conducted an electronic survey of all municipalities in mainland Portugal, designed with three main objectives in mind: to understand the main implications of the change to the electronic paradigm; to identify traits of behaviour of contracting authorities to help us understand the extent to which they are committed to this paradigm; and, to analyse the receptivity of municipalities to the idea of making e-procurement a strategic tool for decision-making support. The survey reached a response rate of 53.2 %. A descriptive analysis of the data shows that municipalities have an unbalanced perception of the innovation dimensions of e-procurement, claim a significant increase in transparency and are receptive to a new tool for assisting the management

[1]Of the European Parliament and of the Council of 26 February 2014 on public procurement and repealing Directive 2004/18/EC.

of procurement processes. The findings are important for the legislative change underway in Portugal and for the construction of the European e-procurement single market. The exploratory nature of the study will hopefully stimulate the debate on the relationship between public policy and public organization innovation.

The study is organized as follows. Section 2 discusses the theoretical background of e-procurement, its importance in the European Union and the link between e-procurement and innovation. Section 3 details the methodology used in this study. Section 4 examines the empirical data along three dimensions: organizational innovation and paradigm shift; traits of behaviour in the e-procurement era; and the challenges of the future. Some conclusions close the paper.

2 E-Procurement: A Radical Change in the Name of Progress and Transparency

2.1 A Mission of the European Union

The recent evolution of information and communication technologies (ICT) has supported much of the ongoing revolution in the economy and society, with increasing impact on business, at work, at play, in communication and in all sectors and activities. This revolution is also taking place for some years now in public procurement, which falls within the broader area of electronic government (e-government), that is, the use of information and communication technologies to improve the activities of public sector organizations and their agents (UN 2008: 126). In the Manchester Declaration in 2005, the ministers of the European Union Member States, accession states and candidate countries and EFTA countries have recognized that electronic public procurement (e-procurement) is a proven high-impact service capable of producing benefits for both the administrations and companies, having the potential to improve markets, competition and stimulate innovation (Manchester 2005). Today, e-procurement is an important part of the Digital Agenda for Europe (European Commission 2010a), which is one of the flagship initiatives of the Europe 2020 strategy to pull Europe out of its lethargic state. A digital single market based on ultra-fast internet and interoperable applications is the vision of the European Union for delivering sustainable economic and social benefits.

E-procurement has become a mission for the European Union! A mission to create a European e-procurement single market and make e-procurement "the rule rather than the exception" in 2016 (European Commission 2012b), with the ultimate goal of processing electronically all phases of the procurement process, from notification (e-notification) to payment (e-payment)[2] (European Commission

[2]The procurement process comprises two major phases: (i) the pre-award phase, which comprises all the sub-phases of procurement until the award of the contract (publication of notices, access to

2012a). Sometimes Governments define "indiscriminate goals" (Tonkin 2003), such as "By 2010 all public administrations across Europe will have the capability of carrying out 100 % of their procurement electronically, where legally permissible..." (Manchester 2005), on the assumption that the mere availability of public services online is beneficial in itself (Tonkin 2003) and the potential benefits of that policy might thus be achieved. The European Union has defined a legal framework and a plan of action in order to achieve the indiscriminate and ambitious e-procurement objectives set for 2010, but each member state had the freedom to define and implement the e-procurement policy that best suited its interests or vision. Such flexibility in dealing with e-procurement ended up in a "kaleidoscope of approaches and results" (European Commission 2010b), with some EU countries making e-procurement mandatory (in varying degrees) and others leaving to contracting authorities the decision to change to e-procurement. The implementation of public e-procurement at an organizational level "requires a broad and complex process of change" (Fernandes and Vieira 2015), and more so if extended to all phases of the procurement process. Adding to this the existence of "too many standards" (European Commission 2010b), the perceived risk of (voluntarily) moving to e-procurement increases substantially. In this context, the mere availability of technological solutions (if incompatible or when in presence of network effects) is insufficient for the wide adoption of an innovation. Unless adoption is mandatory.[3]

When public e-procurement has become a priority over a decade ago, the EU policy makers seem to have largely overlooked the fact that the change would represent a "profound organizational innovation" (Cattaneo 2012) with large network and technology effects. On a first stage, they have set indiscriminate goals and identified potential benefits for the contracting authorities, the state and the economy, assuming that e-procurement technology was in a mature state and, being highly beneficial, would be gradually adopted by all the EU member states and contracting authorities. At this stage, the policy goals and potential advantages of the change prevailed over (perhaps, overshadowed) the "complexity of the change required and the inherent challenges in moving towards electronic systems" (European Commission 2010b). Only on a second stage the EU policymakers started to pay due attention to the complexity and implications of the innovation process

tender documents, submission of bids, evaluation of the proposals and the award of the contract); (ii) the post-award phase, which comprises all the sub-phases of procurement after the award of the contract (ordering, invoicing and payment) (European Commission 2012a: 3). See also McConnell (2009).

[3]There is an extensive body of literature on diffusion of innovations and the phenomenon is analysed from a range of disciplines. It is mainly developed for and applied to the private sector (Huntgeburth et al. 2012), generally in a context of voluntary adoption. See, for instance, Rogers (2003) for a sociological view and Tidd (2010a, b) for a managerial perspective. According to (Huntgeburth et al. 2012), the [voluntary] adoption of e-procurement in the public sector is studied by researchers from two perspectives: (i) the success factors of regional or national e-procurement initiatives; (ii) the contextual factors that influence the adoption of e-procurement.

by setting policies and creating instruments (e.g., the PEPPOL—Pan-European Public Procurement On-Line in 2008) in an attempt to fix structural problems already apparent, such as the lack of interoperability between platforms of different countries, multiplicity of technical standards, market fragmentation and information not standardized. This is a concern of the European Commission's Green Paper (2010c). As compared to the paper based model, e-procurement is likely to produce several types of benefits which are important at different levels and for different actors[4], but the benefits alone are not enough for the widespread adoption of this innovation by public contracting authorities and economic operators. The advantages of e-procurement is a major line of research in this area of study, but most empirical studies have looked at it from the private sector organizations perspective (McConnell 2009: 33) and only a few studies have examined the benefits that public sector organisations gain from e-procurement (Johnson 2011).[5] This is likely so because the lack of evaluation research is a common occurrence for most e-government initiatives and it should be far less surprising when looking specifically at e-procurement initiatives (McCue and Roman 2012: 224). According to Cattaneo (2012), the Public Administration has three main reasons do adopt e-procurement: to reduce process costs; to save money and improve control of their spending; and, when it is legally obliged to do so.

2.2 Portugal: Pointing a Way Forward

Going beyond the European Commission's recommendations, in 2009 Portugal was the first EU country to make e-procurement mandatory in the pre-award phase (European Commission 2010b), a bold step on an unclear European path and in a European context where 50 % of the public entities were against mandatory e-procurement (European Commission 2010d). This decision, however, is consistent with the then Government's objective of dematerialization and de-bureaucratization of the public administration, and the Technological Plan[6] 2005 in which the Government set the goal to "make available in a single Internet site all tenders for the acquisition of goods and services of the central and local governments" (MCTES

[4]The European Commission (2010b, c) has identified multiple potential benefits of e-procurement, ranging from more competition between suppliers, reduced administrative costs and procurement times, more efficient management of contracts, economies of scale and scope, integration in a European electronic contracting market to reduce distance barriers. For a recent review of the literature see, for example, Khorana et al. (2014).

[5]For a review of the literature on benefits and barriers of e-procurement in private enterprises see, for example, Croom and Brandon-Jones (2005), Trkman and McCormack (2010), Hassan (2013) and Toktaş-Palut et al. (2014).

[6]The "Plano Tecnológico" (Technological Plan) was a growth strategy based on knowledge, technology and innovation of the former Portuguese Government (2005–2009) (http://www.presidencia.pt/archive/doc/PlanoTecnologico.pdf).

2005). Besides that, Portugal has other pioneering experiences in e-government since it was the first country to offer the possibility of online income tax form submission in 1996 (Neves 2007), and was a leading European nation in terms of full online availability and sophistication of the 20 basic services (European Commission 2009).

By making e-procurement mandatory for all public purchases of goods, services and tender works above a threshold amount, the Portuguese Government: (i) forces contracting authorities to a radical innovation of the procurement process; (ii) assumes that all contracting authorities are prepared to make the transition to the electronic model (or that the transition could be done in a year's time, period during which both models were in operation); (iii) forces all public suppliers (economic operators) to adopt the e-procurement model; and, (iv) assumes that the chosen model is the one that best serves the country's domestic (e.g., preventing the co-existence of incompatible e-procurement platforms) and external (e.g., assuring platform interoperability across the European Union) interests.[7]

Mandatory e-procurement has a positive side. For Moon (2005), "implementing e-procurement requires strong policy leadership and a managerial willingness to innovate", believing that strong leadership and centralized authority are important aspects of a successful e-procurement policy. Since "the adoption of e-procurement tools does not necessarily ensure their effective or extensive utilization", the government's challenges "may not be technical, but organizational and managerial" (Moon 2005), thus justifying the option for mandatory e-procurement. Cattaneo (2012) finds it effective to overcome the barriers to innovation and intensify the change, being those a combination of organizational inertia, resistance to change (mostly) by public institutions and legal restrictions (electronic signature and multiple platforms). This is also a way that policy makers have to set a country-wide e-procurement model and avoid the negative consequences of the coexistence of incompatible standards (electronic platforms), as in the case of Costa Rica (Barahona and Elizondo 2014) and the European Union. The "Evaluation of the 2004 Action Plan for Electronic Public Procurement" concludes that there were "too many standards" and a "kaleidoscope of perspectives and results", estimating the EU average use of e-procurement around 5 % of total value but nearly 100 % in Portugal (European Commission 2010b).

[7]For example, the choice of sophisticated systems such as those requiring qualified signatures (as in Portugal) was considered an obstacle to the desired systems interoperability across the EU, as still there is no capacity in all countries for mutual recognition of critical elements of e-procurement as authentication (European Commission 2010b).

Moving from a paper-based to an electronic model of public procurement involves innovation mainly of two types, process and organizational innovation (OECD 2005)[8]. It is entering into a world of electronic files instead of paper documents, dematerialized procedures, timestamps, electronic signatures, technological platforms, interaction with economic operators through electronic means instead of personal contacts, new entities to report information like BASE[9], and a new and complex legal framework. But this topic has not yet received much attention from researchers, even evaluation research from Governments. Most empirical studies on public e-procurement examine specific case studies in contexts of voluntary adoption. Recent research has addressed issues such as the implications of running two incompatible electronic platforms simultaneously in Costa Rica (Barahona and Elizondo 2014); the duality of e-procurement technology on two levels of government in Brazil which are located in the same context (Mota and Filho 2011); the factors affecting the adoption of e-procurement by central and regional public organizations in the UK (McConnell 2009); the introduction of e-procurement in a local unit of the Italian healthcare system (Federici 2009); the acceptance of e-procurement systems by employees of a large Australian municipality (Rahim 2008); the adoption of e-procurement in seven UK Government's central departments (Croom and Brandon-Jones 2005). As for surveys: the study of McCue and Roman (2012) is based on 499 responses from 2269 procurement professionals from national public bodies and local government who were asked to assess the status of e-procurement in the USA and Canada; the study of Tavares et al. (2011) assesses the impacts induced by e-procurement after the first year of mandatory operation in Portugal, from a survey of 2033 companies (102 responses) and 2894 contracting authorities (224 responses); Costa et al. (2013) compare the situation of e-procurement in Portugal before and 1 year after it becoming mandatory.

Not much is known about the innovation process occurring in public institutions subject to mandatory adoption of e-procurement, or their expectations about the strategic use of these new technologies to support decision-making. Vaidya (2007) recognized the need to look beyond the (voluntary) decision of adoption and analyse the relationship between "innovation assimilation and the environmental factors". But the issue of innovation in public sector organizations has not even been considered relevant to the Green Paper on the expansion of e-procurement in the EU (European Commission 2010c), suggesting that the European authorities were not

[8]This follows the concept of innovation of the Oslo Manual (OECD 2005), with the necessary adaptations to public sector organisations: a process innovation is the implementation of a new or significantly improved production or delivery method. This includes significant changes in techniques, equipment and/or software; an organizational innovation is the implementation of a new organizational method in the firm's business practices, workplace organization or external relations.

[9]BASE is the Portuguese national website (http://www.base.gov.pt/Base/pt/Homepage) where the information on all public contracts under the Public Contracts Code is reported and stored. Currently, there are seven electronic platforms (run by private firms) certified to provide e-procurement services.

sufficiently aware of the relationship between public policy and public organization innovation. McCue and Roman (2012: 228) observe, however, that the management and monitoring of e-procurement systems emphasize different skill sets and relationship constructs that are not witnessed in traditional public procurement practices. Vaidya et al. (2006) study identifies as the most important success factor the need for training of professionals in the practices and tools of e-procurement and the identification of the skills required for these professionals. Cattaneo (2012) points out that public employees need a different mix of skills "involving knowledge of technologies, administrative processes and core administration competencies". Costa et al. (2013) stress that training is crucial in the implementation of e-procurement and normally organizations get it from external experts. Mota and Filho (2011) conclude that, despite the huge investments that countries make in the electronic government, so far it has been given more attention to the purpose or intended use than to the context in which e-procurement occurs, being common the occurrence of unanticipated organizational impacts due to neglecting the importance of human and contextual aspects.

3 Methods and Data

Of the thousands of Portuguese public institutions of different types (hospitals, universities, municipalities, etc.) for which e-procurement is mandatory since 2009 for the acquisition of goods, services and tender works (Article 2 of the Public Contracts Code)[10], the empirical analysis of this study focuses on a subset of those institutions—Municipalities—to ensure greater consistency and representativeness of results. The Portuguese public administration comprises two levels: (i) the central Government; (ii) and the local administration, on the responsibility of the Municipalities. A considerable amount of competencies, responsibilities and financial means are committed to the Municipalities, which accomplish a large number of acquisitions of goods, services and works every year.

This study was conducted through a web-based survey to all 278 municipalities in mainland Portugal, based on a questionnaire with 21 closed questions. The municipalities of Azores and Madeira islands were excluded from the study since these autonomous regions have specific rules for public procurement and e-procurement is not mandatory. A web-based survey is a convenient and effective way to quickly and relatively cheaply reach a large number of potential respondents (Jansen et al. 2007) dispersed across a country, being an appropriate way to reach all the Portuguese municipalities and obtain the data for the study. The online survey was implemented

[10]The Public Contracts Code (hereinafter PCC), approved by Decree-Law no. 18/2008 of 29th of January, is the Portuguese e-procurement law which gathered in a major piece of legislation all scattered and sectoral legislation and integrated into the national law the Directive 2004/18/EC and Directive 2004/17/EC.

between February 9 and March 9 2015 using the survey management application LimeSurvey (www.limesurvey.org). The questionnaire was submitted to a pre-test with four capital district municipalities from different geographic areas (two inland and two coastal). We sent an email to the email contact[11] of all municipalities inviting them to participate in the survey, a strategy that proved unsuccessful since most invitations did not reach the target recipients (e-procurement professional) quickly enough or were lost in the bureaucracy of the institutions. A follow-up email reminder did not produce relevant results which led us to change the strategy. Midway through the data collection period, we conducted around 270 telephone calls in order to get the email contact of all e-procurement professionals from the municipalities in order to resend the invitation. A final follow-up email reminder just days before the end of the response period concluded the survey administration procedures. An Excel database was used to process the data.

148 municipalities answered the survey, representing 53.2 % of the total (278). About 55 % of respondents are in the age range of 41–55 years, and other 43 % are in the range of 26–40 years old. The overwhelming majority of the respondents' activity is the e-procurement area and over 53 % of them hold a university degree. Analysing by district (each comprising several municipalities), stand out Beja, Santarém and Guarda with the highest response rate (71.4 %); the districts of Viana do Castelo (40.0 %), Porto (33.3 %), Braga (28.6 %) and Castelo Branco (18.2 %) obtained the lowest response rate (Table 1). According to Carvalho et al. (2013) classification, the size of respondents is as follows: 92 (56.8 %) out of 162 are small municipalities (<20,000 inhabitants), 46 (49.5 %) out of 93 are medium-sized municipalities (between 20,000 and 100,000 inhabitants) and 10 (43.5 %) out of 23 are large municipalities (>100,000 inhabitants). The structure of the sample is rather similar to the structure of the whole population under analysis (in brackets): 6.8 % (8.3 %) of large municipalities, 31.1 % (33.5 %) of medium-sized municipalities and 62.2 % (58.3 %) of small municipalities.

Due to the nature of the data and the study the analysis is mainly descriptive and exploratory, using basic statistics and graph analysis. It makes a critical analysis and interpretation of the empirical data aiming at better understanding the implications of mandatory e-procurement for organizational innovation at the municipality level. The study provides some valuable insights on this matter but the generalization of results to other public institutions should be done with caution.

[11]The contact information (emails and telephone numbers) of all municipalities have been collected from the "Portal Autárquico" webpage (http://www.anmp.pt/munp/mun/mun10111.php?cod=20140110).

Table 1 Response rate by district

District	Municipalities	Respondents	%	District	Municipalities	Respondents	%
Aveiro	19	11	57.9	Leiria	16	10	62.5
Beja	14	10	71.4	Lisboa	16	9	56.3
Braga	14	4	28.6	Portalegre	15	5	33.3
Bragança	12	7	58.3	Porto	18	6	33.3
Castelo Branco	11	2	18.2	Santarém	21	15	71.4
Coimbra	17	10	58.8	Setúbal	13	7	53.8
Évora	14	8	57.1	Viana do Castelo	10	4	40.0
Faro	16	10	62.5	Vila Real	14	7	50.0
Guarda	14	10	71.4	Viseu	24	13	54.2

Source: Authors' survey data

4 E-Procurement in the Municipalities: Mere Adaptation or Real Organizational Change?

4.1 The Change: Dynamics of the Innovation Process

4.1.1 Few Pioneers

The diffusion process of e-procurement in Portugal lasted nearly 24 months and comprised four main stages of different duration, from the pre-presentation of the new legislation—the Public Contracts Code (PCC)—to its entry into force (Table 2). In the first year—stages 1–3—the public institutions (contracting authorities) could voluntarily adopt e-procurement by choosing one of the electronic platforms available on the market. In the second year—stage 4—the contracting authorities had to adopt e-procurement, but both procurement processes (paper based and electronic) were simultaneously in operation. We attempt to capture the diffusion process of e-procurement among the municipalities in two different ways: first, by asking municipalities at which stage they have changed to e-procurement (Fig. 1), it is possible to know of many of them decided for e-procurement before the mandatory stage, that is the innovator ones; second, in the mandatory stage, by collecting information about the publication date of the first public contract reported to the BASE portal for the 278 municipalities, it is possible to make the diffusion curve in a context of mandatory adoption of an innovation.

According to Fig. 1, only 7.4 % (11) of the municipalities changed to the electronic procurement in stage 1 and might be called innovators (pioneers), since they adopted the new technology early in the process, in a moment of scarce information and higher uncertainty about the electronic platforms, the procurement process and the organizational implications of the change. Of these, 4 (36.3 %) were large

Table 2 Implementation stages of the Public Contracts Code (PCC)

Stage (time period)	Observations
1. Pre-presentation (31-07-2007 to 29-01-2008)	- Few (not certified) electronic platforms provided e-procurement services; - No requirement to report information on contracts to the BASE portal (not in operation);
2. Public presentation (30-01-2008 to 16-03-2008)	
3. Debriefing sessions (17-03-2008 to 29-07-2008)	
4. Entry into force of the PCC (30-07-2008)	- Both procurement systems (paper and electronic) were in operation for 1 year; - Mandatory reporting of information to the BASE website;

Source: Authors

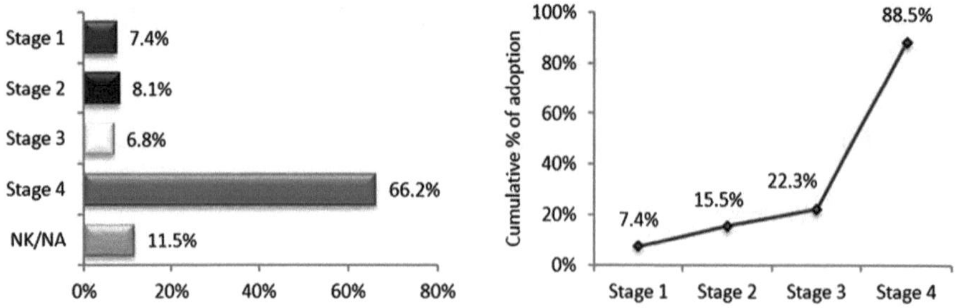

Fig. 1 Diffusion curve of e-procurement. *Source*: Authors' survey data. NK/NA = Not know/No answer

municipalities and 7 (63.6 %) small (geographically dispersed across the country). Another 22 municipalities adopted e-procurement in stages 2 and 3 and might be called early innovators according to Rogers (2003). Taking together stages 1, 2 and 3—before entry into force of the PCC—only 33 out of 148 respondents moved to the electronic model, being 21.2 % large municipalities, 18.2 % medium-sized and 60.6 % small. Being the adoption mandatory, and a schedule for its implementation known, it is somewhat surprising that the great majority of municipalities opted to "wait and see", adopting e-procurement only in stage 4.[12] Figure 2 shows two important things. First, the almost perfect s-shaped diffusion curve is consistent with the diffusion of innovation theory (Rogers 2003) and it is no different than what other empirical studies have found in voluntary adoption contexts. Second, perhaps surprisingly given the results above, the cumulative percentage of adoption exceeded 80 % in the first 4 months after the PCC entering into force. The fact that all the municipalities have formally moved to e-procurement in stage 4 does not say much about the degree of organizational change occurred.

There are many barriers to the widespread adoption of an innovation, including economic (costs, benefits, incentives), behavioural (motivations, inertia, propensity for change), organizational (routines, power and influence, culture) and structural (infrastructure, governance) barriers (Tidd 2010a). The results suggest that early innovation (stages 1–3) is not related to economic or structural factors, but the decision not to innovate was influenced by behavioural and organizational factors. It is reasonable to admit that many municipalities have decided to adopt e-procurement in stage 4 in order to gather more information about the new process, including experiences of the early adopters, to better accommodate the transition to the electronic paradigm. However, resistance to change is also likely to be an important factor

[12]According to Rogers (2003), the rate of diffusion is explained by five attributes of an innovation. In the case of e-procurement: Fig. 5 below shows that it has "relative advantages" over the paper based process, though not critical; there is no "compatibility" with existing values and past experiences; its "complexity" comes from the fact that it is a radical innovation; municipalities had a 1 year "trialability" period plus the period of stages 1–3; "observability" likely explains much of the adoption rate of stage 4.

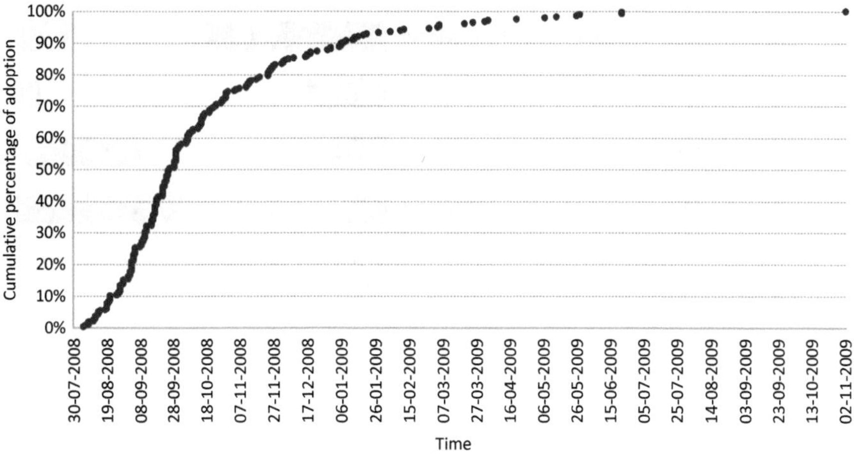

Fig. 2 Diffusion curve of e-procurement (stage 4; 278 municipalities). *Source*: Authors. Data collected from the BASE portal (http://www.base.gov.pt/Base/pt/Homepage)

to take into consideration, since it is a mandatory change and many municipalities were not receptive to it considering that public procurement "represents one of the main sources of power and influence of public administrations" (Cattaneo 2012). In the Tavares et al. (2011)[13] study, 38 % of the Portuguese contracting authorities (against 7 % of companies) considered resistance to change a relevant or very relevant difficulty of e-procurement.

4.1.2 Perception of Changes and Barriers Introduced by the PCC

Imposing mandatory e-procurement to public institutions with a weak culture of innovation and not enthusiastic about the change increases the risk of failure. Firstly, the contracting authorities need to understand what organizational changes they should perform when adopting e-procurement, those required by the PCC and those they are supposed to do if a real change is to occur. The perception of the changes determines the way the municipalities get involved with e-procurement and ultimately the degree to which the policy objectives are achieved. Figure 3 shows the respondents' perception about the importance of four key changes, two explicit changes related to key policy instruments (electronic platform and new legislation), and two implicit changes related to the organization's adaptation to the new paradigm (organizational structure and collaborative networks). The explicit changes are part of the e-procurement implementation process itself, but the implicit

[13]The Tavares et al. (2011) survey was carried out a year after the mandatory use of e-procurement in Portugal and included companies (suppliers) and public institutions of different types (not just municipalities).

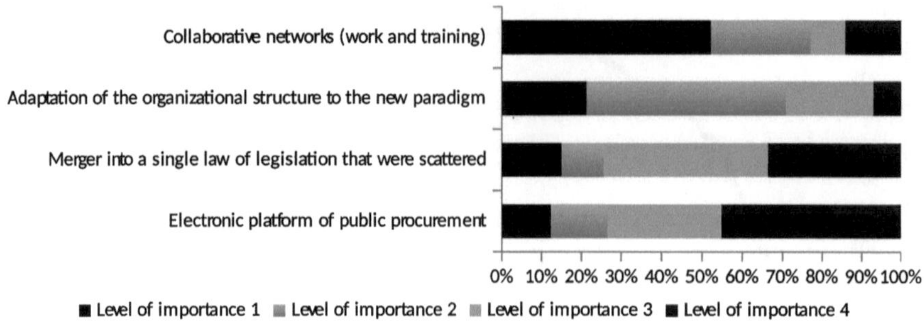

Fig. 3 Perception of the importance of innovation. *Source*: Authors' survey data. Valid responses n = 113

changes depend on the innovative capability, vision and interest of the municipalities to innovate. The respondents ranked these four changes in ascending order of importance using a 1–4 scale.

The perception about the relative importance of each type of change varies widely among municipalities, but a pattern emerges from the data: the explicit changes are generally considered rather more important than the implicit changes. The electronic platform is considered the most important change to 45.1 % of the municipalities, increasing to 73.4 % by adding the answers of levels 3 and 4. The new legislation is the most important change to 33.6 % (level 4) and 74.3 % (levels 3 and 4) of the municipalities. On the other hand, organizational changes are not much important for 70.8 % of the respondents, despite being at the core of the innovation process. 52.2 % of respondents understand that collaborative networks are relatively unimportant, ignoring the effects of e-procurement on the "internal and external relational linkages" (Croom and Brandon-Jones 2005). Apparently, most respondents do not attach much importance to the implicit changes of e-procurement related to the management of Knowledge and information, networking and relational linkages. However, 81 % of the respondents in Tavares et al. (2011) study took training on e-procurement and the PCC. Not many respondents seem to agree that e-procurement requires a "profound organizational innovation" since only 8 (7.1 %) of them consider that the adaptation of the organizational structure is the most important factor of innovation. It increases to just below 30 % by adding the answers of levels 3 and 4. Interesting enough, 5 (62.5 %) out of those 8 are small size municipalities, 2 are of large size and 1 is medium-sized. Overall, the results suggest that most municipalities do not have a clear understanding of the innovative scope (depth and diversity) implied by the e-procurement model made mandatory.

Figure 4 shows how the respondents ranked the importance of four potential barriers to innovation related to the complexity of legislation, access to specialized training, implicit interdisciplinary of the PCC and the electronic platform. Respondents ranked these four barriers of innovation in ascending order of importance using a 1–4 scale. The electronic platform is one of the most important changes of e-procurement (Fig. 3), but it is much less important as a barrier to innovation

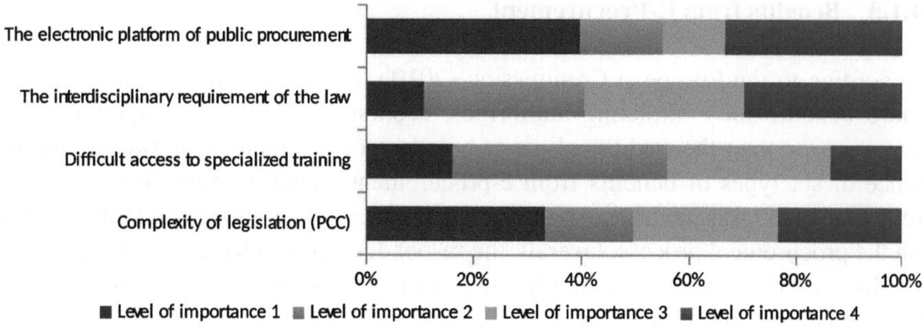

Fig. 4 Importance of four barriers to innovation. *Source*: Authors' survey data. Valid responses n = 111

(Fig. 4). The results are mixed: for 39.6 % of the respondents the electronic platform is the less important barrier to innovation, but for 33.3 % other respondents it is the most important. In comparison with the results of Fig. 3, the former increased around 27 percentage points (from 12.4 to 39.6 %) and the latter decreased around 12 percentage points (falling from 45.1 to 33.3 %). For most municipalities, the electronic platform is relatively more important as an innovation than as a barrier to innovation. The conclusion is analogous for legislation, since 74.3 % of the respondents believe the PCC is an important innovation but only 50.4 % consider it to be an important barrier to innovation. This also suggests that half of the municipalities have access to appropriate legal advice and the PCC application does not raise major concerns.

An interesting result from Fig. 4 is that the municipalities seem to have easy access to knowledge and/or resources for specialized training. Only 13.5 % of them regard the access to specialized training as the major barrier to innovation, while other 56 % believe it is not an important barrier. In the Tavares et al. (2011) study, the lack of training and lack of human resources were considered relevant or very relevant difficulties to implementation of e-procurement for 44 % and 36 % of the contracting authorities, respectively. Training was a very important difficulty for 22 % of the contracting authorities. The differences between studies may be explained by methodological issues (this study focuses only on municipalities) and the elapsed time (most of the initial difficulties may have already been settled or even forgotten). The interdisciplinary perspective implied in the legislation has a balanced distribution of responses, being an important barrier to innovation for about 60 % (levels 3 and 4) of the municipalities. It helps to explain the need for training and qualified people referred to above and the organizational implications of e-procurement.

4.1.3 Benefits from E-Procurement

According to the European Commission (2010b, c), public e-procurement carries more benefits for contracting authorities, economic operators, competition and transparency than the traditional paper based process. Figure 5 shows the importance of six types of benefits from e-procurement related to paper consumption, redundancy of tasks, mailing expenses, transparency, process speed and information on the procurement process. Overall, the respondents recognize that e-procurement produces all those benefits, and only a few of them think otherwise. For the majority of respondents, "more transparency in the procurement process" is the most obvious benefit from e-procurement as compared to the paper based process, which is also one of the most important objectives of the PCC and the Government. Indeed, 86 (58.11 %) respondents rated "more transparency" as "very important" and 134 (90.54 %) as "important" or "very important". Equally interesting is that for 76.4 % (113) of the respondents the procurement process is now faster and a staggering 88.5 % (131) of them agree that there is more information available. There is more and better information available on procurement processes because it becomes available to all economic operators at the same time and all of them have access to the same pieces of information. The reduction of mailing expenses (and related processing costs) is also an important benefit of e-procurement recognised by 3 in 4 municipalities.

Surprisingly, the "reduction of paper archive" and the "reduction of redundant administrative tasks" show less impressive benefits, suggesting that in some municipalities the paradigm shift has not yet occurred. Around 39 % of the respondents recognize that there was at most a marginal reduction of the paper archive or no reduction at all (9.5 %), and other 32.5 % admit that the reduction of redundant administrative tasks has been unimportant or slightly important. Despite formally adopting e-procurement, many municipalities seem to maintain a parallel paper

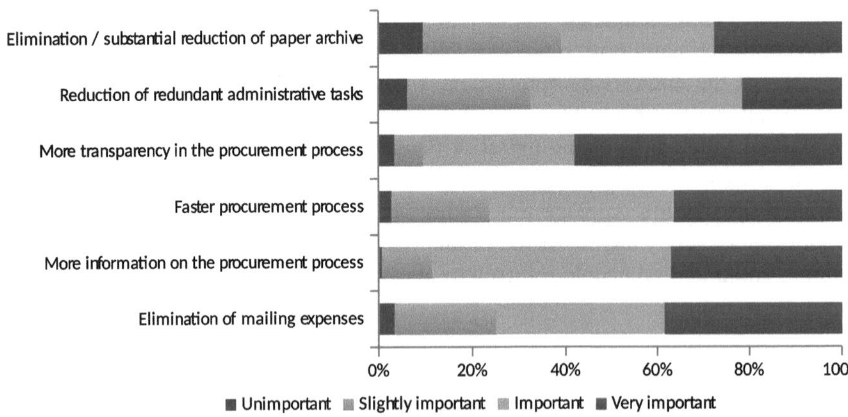

Fig. 5 Benefits from e-procurement. *Source*: Authors' survey data. Valid responses n = 148

based procurement procedure. Or, perhaps the current state of affairs in Portugal does not allow the full dematerialization of the procurement process. Indeed, both of them. On the one hand, it is a symptom that represents the resistance to change; on the other, the ability of municipalities to fully dematerialize the procurement process is constrained by external factors. Let us take the example of a public tender subject to prior inspection by the Portuguese Court of Auditors. The whole process in the pre-award phase is processed electronically by the contracting authority (municipality). After awarding and signing the contract, a paper copy of the process is sent to the Court of Auditors for inspection and validation, because the procedures of this court are still paper-based. As Cattaneo (2012) says, "in each country there seems to be some little step of the procurement process that is still not really aligned with digital technologies", causing an increase in costs, additional administrative workload and inefficiencies in the e-procurement process.

4.2 The Commitment: Enthusiasm as Needed

4.2.1 Phases of the Procurement Process

The legislation (CPP) identifies four main phases of the procurement process, which are briefly the following: Phase 1 involves the definition of objectives and scope of the contract for the acquisition of a good, service or work; Phase 2 comprises the setting of tender specifications and evaluation criteria, sub-criteria, descriptors and weighting coefficients; Phase 3 concerns the running of the competitive process, analysis of tenders, award and contract signing; Phase 4 relates to the execution of the contract, ex-post evaluation and reporting. The phases 1 and 4 are of a strategic nature (acquisition should be based on a real need to avoid "useless initiatives" (Tavares 2008), and management of contract is an essential task), while phases 2 and 3 are operational. Currently, for each public procurement process, contracting authorities are only required to make available information on the electronic platform about phases 2 and 3. To what extent each person in the organization is aware of all these phases? Does any procurement process follows these four steps? The municipalities were asked to rank the four phases of the procurement process in increasing order of importance on a 1–4 scale (Fig. 6).

The results of Fig. 6 may give rise to consideration. The response distribution of phase 1 suggests that many respondents do not think that phase 1 is of critical importance. Perhaps their contribution is not required for phase 1 or they ignore the rationale behind the procurement decision. For 40 (34.5 %) respondents phase 1 is relatively unimportant and for other 28 (24.1 %) it is just slightly important. This does not seem to make sense for any public acquisition whose decision is based on a cost-benefit analysis. It should not be a surprise that many of the public initiatives that later on turn out to be useless are motivated by the possibility of obtaining non-recoverable funding from any EU/national funding instrument. It is understandable the response distribution of phase 2. The operational nature of this phase makes it

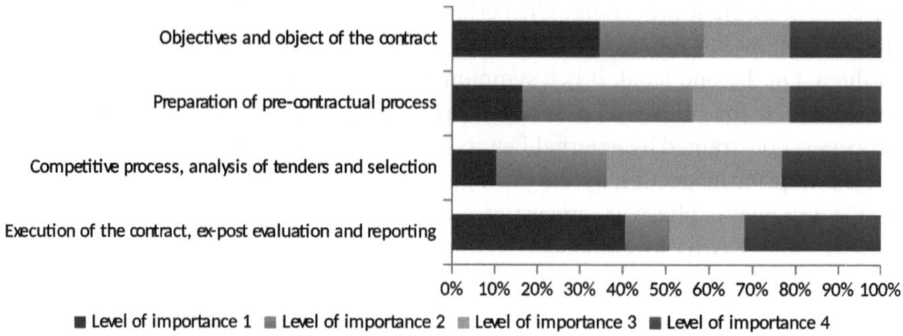

Fig. 6 Main phases of the procurement process. *Source*: Authors' survey data. Valid responses n = 116

less relevant to the procurement process, but the existence of errors or shortcomings in the terms of reference and in the evaluation parameters may give rise to important problems in phase 4 (contract execution).

It is also meaningful that 63.8 % (74) of the respondents understand that phase 3 is worth a score of 3 or 4. It is hard to explain why phase 3 is so important to so many municipalities since it is likely the most operational of all the phases (invitation to tender, selection of proposals, . . .), being its successful accomplishment more the consequence of good practice in phases 1 and 2. The outcome of phase 4 is also surprising and deserves reflection, as more than half (50.8 %) of the municipalities assign it marginal importance. The responses of phase 4 are of extremes: 40.5 % of the respondents believe this is the less important phase in the procurement process, while other 31.9 % believe it is the most important phase. For 31.9 % of the municipalities, the monitoring and evaluation of contracts is extremely important and must be part of the organization's core. For 40.5 % of the municipalities, the monitoring and evaluation of contracts is not important. And yet, evaluation is fundamental to support decision making.

4.2.2 Contract Administration and Supplier Performance Assessment

The fulfilment of the terms of reference is assessed in phase 4, an important procedure that requires the attention from the contracting authority. The absence of implemented procedures for the systematic monitoring of contract execution and assessment of supplier performance represents an information gap with potential undesirable consequences. According to Fig. 7, of the 148 municipalities under analysis, only 38 (25.7 %) have implemented procedures for a systematic assessment of contracts and performance of suppliers. Other 35 (22.6 %) municipalities say the assessment is carried out sporadically and not systematically, while another 51 (34.5 %) municipalities say they have not implemented any form of evaluation of procurement contracts and suppliers. Excluding the "Not know/No answer" answers and recalculating the figures, the percentage of municipalities that have

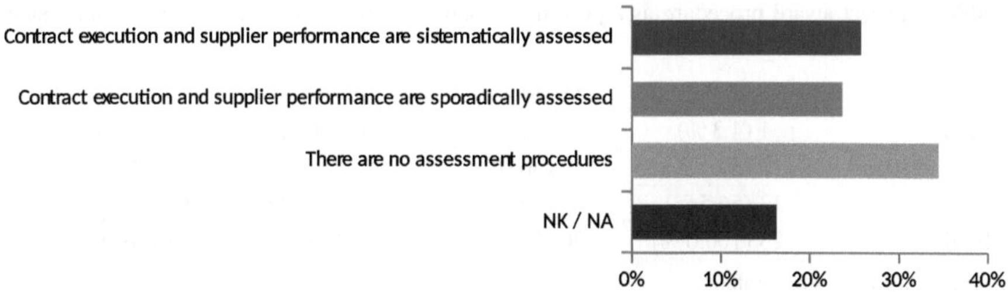

Fig. 7 Contract execution and supplier performance assessment. *Source*: Authors' survey data. Valid responses n = 148

no assessment procedures raises to 41.1 %. This unexpected result makes us wondering about the reasons leading the municipalities to not implement assessment procedures since it is mandatory to produce contract execution reports. In any case, this is consistent with the number of respondents who have considered phase 4 unimportant (Fig. 6).

When notified by InCI[14] in 2013 to deliver the overdue contract execution reports, only 46 (31.1 %) municipalities were not overdue. The other 102 (68.9 %) municipalities were in situation of nonconformity with the legislation in force, 32 (21 %) of them claiming the electronic platform is not prepared to produce such reports, 8 (5.4 %) assuming the management and monitoring of contracts is not of primary importance, 20 (13.5 %) claiming for other reasons and 43 (29.1 %) choosing the "not know/no answer" option. In a workshop on public procurement in October 2014, InCI estimated that about 80 % of the final execution reports were not being delivered. Of the many reasons for not delivering the reports, including refusal or inability, the results point to a symptom of no adaptation to the electronic paradigm of many municipalities, but also reveals that there is no appropriate software tool available to produce these reports in a standardized and easy manner. In other words, all the municipalities have implemented procedures to comply with the requirements of the electronic procurement process (phases 2 and 3), but a great many of them appear to have not changed much the internal procedures for collecting and processing information about phases 1 and 4. Apparently, all municipalities are committed to the explicit changes required by e-procurement, but many of them are not that committed to the explicit changes discussed above.

4.2.3 Use (and Abuse) of the Direct Award Procedure

The direct award (*Ajuste Direto*, in Portuguese) is one of the five ways foreseen by the law (PCC) to award a public contract. It is different from the other procedures

[14]IcNI (Instituto da Construção e do Imobiliário) is the public institution responsible for operating the BASE portal.

Table 3 Direct award procedure as a percent of total number of contracts by municipality size, 2013

Size/weight	71–80 %	81–90 %	≥91 %	Total
Large	1 (4.3 %)	1 (3.3 %)	3 (7.9 %)	5 (5.5 %)
Medium-sized	9 (39.1 %)	9 (30.0 %)	8 (21.1 %)	26 (28.6 %)
Small	13 (56.5 %)	20 (66.7 %)	27 (71.1 %)	60 (65.9 %)
Total	23 (100.0 %)	30 (100.0 %)	38 (100.0 %)	91 (100.0 %)

Source: Authors' survey data

because "the contracting authority invites one or several entities to present a proposal and freely negotiate aspects from the execution of the contract" (Tavares 2011).[15] The direct award procedure allows for greater freedom of decision-making in public procurement and, consequently, it is also the procedure that offers greater resistance to change. We asked municipalities how often they used the direct award procedure in 2013 as a percentage of the total number of public contracts awarded that year. Of the 148 municipalities under analysis, 38 (25.7 %) admit the direct award procedure accounted for between 91 and 100% of all contracts in 2013. For 68 (45.9 %) municipalities it accounted for above 80 % of the contracts, while for 91 (61.5 %) municipalities it accounted for above 70%.[16] Excluding the 23 "Not know/No answer" answers, these percentages (between brackets) increase to 30.4 %, 54.4 % and 72.8 %, respectively. Only for 6 (4.1 %) municipalities the direct award procedure accounted for less than 10% of all contracts in 2013, and for 7 (4.8 %) of them less than 20 %. 21 (15.5 %) of the municipalities did not answer the question, despite the fact that this information has to be reported to the BASE and published in the Municipality's Management Account report.

Table 3 shows the relationship between the municipality size and the use of direct award procedure for percentages above 70%. Size seems to matter: smaller municipalities tend to use direct award procedures more often than the larger ones. More than 71 % of the municipalities that reported direct award procedure rates above 90 % are of small size, which is way above the relative weight of small municipalities in the sample (62.2 %) and the total number of municipalities (58.3 %). Do small municipalities have better information systems? Maybe not.

[15]According to the PCC the contracting authorities may choose the direct award procedure in case the contract value falls below: 150,000€ for public works contracts, 1,000,000€ for public works contracts (for some entities), 75,000€ for supply or services contracts, 193,000€ for supply or services contracts (for some entities), 25,000€ in case of plans, projects or conceptual creations acquisitions contracts on the architecture or engineering domain by public entities, 100,000€ for any other contracts with the exception of public works concessions, public services concession and company contracts (Tavares 2011).

[16]It is likely the real numbers are much higher. Information on all public contracts since 2009 is freely available on the BASE website. A quick search for the public contracts between 2009 and 2015 of a few municipalities randomly chosen has shown rates over 95 %. This is an issue for further research.

There are at least two factors that certainly help to explain the phenomenon: first, the awarding of public contracts to local economic operators is a way of protecting the local economy; second, the cost of timestamps and using the electronic platform is significant for public contracts of small value and for small businesses.

There remains the question as to whether the systematic use of direct award procedure goes into contradiction with the great increase of transparency shown in Fig. 5. Or, whether there has been a great increase of transparency in public procurement despite the systematic use of direct award procedure. It looks like as if e-procurement has exposed the symptom of "institutionalized ideas (which are) difficult or even impossible to change" (Faridian 2015). There certainly are many reasons for choosing the direct award procedure, but the fact that it is used so often raises questions about the quality of transparency and the effectiveness of the e-procurement system (law and technological platform) to promote transparency in public procurement. The electronic platform is not the only means of communication used by municipalities in direct award procedures[17]: 10.8 % of the municipalities never use the electronic platform and other 12.2 % use it very rarely; 14.2 % always use the email and other 23.7 % use it frequently; yet other municipalities use the fax and other means of communication. The lack of interoperability of the electronic platforms requires that all the invited companies to submit a proposal for a tender have to be registered with the same electronic platform of the contracting authority. The cost of timestamps, the low value of some contracts and the fact that some (small) firms are not registered with any electronic platform are other reasons to explain the behaviour of municipalities. On the other hand, the data suggest that this is also the way that municipalities have found to explore the loopholes of the PCC. The direct award procedure appears to be a paradigmatic example of resistance to change that makes it difficult for municipalities to meet the innovation challenge posed by e-procurement.

4.3 *The Challenge: Making E-Procurement a Tool to Support Decision-Making*

The European Union aims to reach the ultimate objective of making e-procurement the rule rather than the exception in all phases of the procurement process. It is a path of no return and the public sector organizations have no better choice but to try to take the maximum benefits from the e-procurement paradigm. Some important benefits relate to the quality and availability of information on all phases of the procurement process, from the launching of the tender up to the award of the contract, to the ex-post evaluation reports. There are different types of benefits,

[17]Contracting authorities may use other means of communication (email, fax...) besides the electronic platform in direct award procedures, but the information on these contracts has to be reported to the BASE portal.

including organizational benefits (related to the coordination, systematization and no duplication of information production processes and storage), economic benefits (related to the production costs, redundancy of tasks and activities, storage, access and quality of information to support decision-making), and decision-making benefits (related to the reliability, accuracy and accessibility of information). A passive adaptation to e-procurement or even resistance to change may delay or even compromise the opportunity to get those benefits. According to Cattaneo (2012: 18), the most frequent situation (and risk) when adopting e-procurement by public institutions is that the management team tends to maintain a double process, paper-based and digital, which substantially raises costs. There is some evidence that this appears to be the case in an unquantified percentage of municipalities in Portugal.

Is the current Portuguese e-procurement model designed to be used as a tool to support decision-making by contracting authorities? Hardly, for some reasons. First, information on public procurement is partial and incomplete. Contracting authorities are not required to provide information on all the four phases of the procurement process, which does stimulate them to improve the internal information system and make the required organizational changes. Second, the process of reporting information. The information about any public procurement procedure is made available on the electronic platform in PDF files and there are no standardized templates for data collection. The electronic platforms are not designed for collecting basic input data on each public contract (data of phase 1) for monitoring and reporting purposes (phase 4), for computing and statistical analysis, for historical data analysis, etc. Third, there is no platform interoperability. The certified electronic platforms cannot communicate to each other for the exchange of basis information on public contracts, contracting authorities and economic operators, being not possible for an economic operator registered with one platform to respond to a call for tenders in another platform. Four, the post-award phase is not mandatory. E-procurement is not mandatory in the post-award phase and there is no software tool (integrated into the existing electronic platforms or complementary to it) to manage the information on contract execution. These aspects reduce the potential benefits that contracting authorities can get from the electronic paradigm and hinders the transition from paper to digital. Therefore, it is difficult to fully agree with Faridian (2015) assertion that "today, it is safe to assume public e-procurement as a solid innovation in public management".

Figure 8 shows the receptiveness of a new software tool, complementary to the existing electronic platform, for timely monitoring and reporting of the contracts execution. A tool for collecting and processing data on public procurement and supporting decision-making. The results show great receptiveness to such a solution and the existence of a market need. 109 out of 148 municipalities, 73.6 %, believe such a software would make a significant contribution to increase the quality of information on public procurement. 37 (25 %) believe it would make a very important contribution and seem to be the ones that better understand the potential benefits of the electronic paradigm. Of these, 13.5 % are large municipalities, 37.5 % average-sized and 48.6 % small. In comparison with the structure of the sample, this new tool is considered relatively more important the larger the municipality.

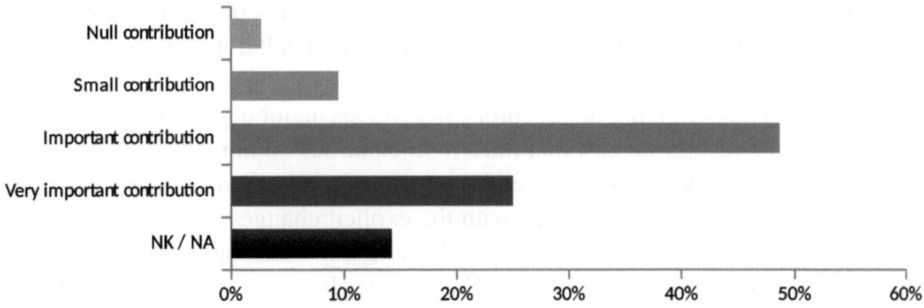

Fig. 8 Contribution of a new tool for monitoring and reporting of contracts execution. *Source*: Authors' survey data. Valid responses n = 148

The respondents were asked about the importance of five possible functionalities: real-time access to the BASE website to report on contract execution; access to awarded contracts via electronic platform; information on supplier purchase history; communication base with suppliers; and, activity planning (to support decision making). All these functionalities have been considered important by the great majority of respondents and unimportant by less than 2.7 % of them. The "real-time connection to Base portal to report on the contract execution" and "supplier purchase history" are the two most interesting features, being important or very important for 89.2 % and 86.4 % of the respondents, respectively. The former is very important for 45.9 % of the respondents. The other three functionalities were somewhat less appreciated, but nevertheless important for between 75 and 80 % of the municipalities. About 17.6 % of the respondents scored "very important" 4 or 5 of the five functionalities, while 25 % scored "very important" at least three.

Most respondents recognize de advantages of a new software application to assist contract management and support efficient and timely decision-making. But how many municipalities are preparing the next stage of innovation, knowing that the great majority of the respondents do not have policy-level responsibilities in the municipality? What influence do they have? About 50 % of the municipalities have introduced improvements in the procurement process since 2009 and the vast majority (82.4 %) of the proposals for improvement came from within the organization, 70 % of them suggested by operational personnel.

5 Conclusion

In 2009, Portugal made e-procurement mandatory in a EU context of multiple technical standards and lack of interoperability of electronic platforms. Changing the traditional pattern of public procurement for an electronic paradigm involves a profound organizational innovation and the Portuguese legislator assumed that all public sector organizations were prepared to do so. This study discusses the relationship between e-procurement and innovation in the Portuguese municipalities aiming to understand the extent into which the adoption of e-procurement has embraced a real organizational change or, on the other hand, if it represented a mere adaptation of the usual procurement practices.

The paradigm shift in public procurement involves major organizational changes but, overall, the results suggest that most municipalities do not have a clear understanding of the innovative scope (depth and diversity) implied by e-procurement. They are more aware and concerned with the explicit changes (electronic platform and new legislation) than with the less visible and implicit changes (organizational structure and collaborative networks). The former changes are determined by the law (the PCC), while the latter depend more on the innovative capability, vision and interest of the municipalities to carry out changes in the organization. This unbalanced perception of the innovation dimensions has influenced the implementation of e-procurement and the degree of organizational change. The e-procurement has benefits over the paper based process, including more and better information, faster procurement procedures, reduction of administrative costs and greater transparency on the procurement process. The reduction of redundant administrative tasks and paper archive are generally rated among the less important benefits from e-procurement, which might be a symptom of poor adaptation to the electronic paradigm of many municipalities, but also the consequence of external factors to the procurement process which are not aligned with the digital environment.

The municipalities show an enthusiasm as needed with e-procurement. They have implemented the necessary procedures to comply with the requirements of the electronic procurement process, but a great many of them are not paying the same attention to the implicit changes they were supposed to carry out to take advantage of the e-procurement paradigm. It appears that in many cases the adoption of e-procurement boils down to comply with the law, but the internal procedures and practices for managing information on public procurement have not changed much, being common the absence of implemented procedures for a systematic assessment of contract execution and supplier performance. The frequency with which the municipalities use the direct award procedure suggests that this is a way they have found to get round the PCC requirements and reach their own objectives. It also shows the PCC limitations and raises questions about the greatest benefit from e-procurement—transparency.

The vast majority of the respondents are receptive to a new software tool, complementary to the existing electronic platform, for assisting the management of the procurement process and supporting decision-making.

Acknowledgments The authors would like to thank the Municipality of Castro Verde and the Department of Economics of the University of Evora for the financial support provided.

References

Barahona, J. C., & Elizondo, A. M. (2014). Introducing a disruptive service innovation: A national dilemma in e-procurement. *Management Decision, 52*(9), 1782–1800.

Carvalho, J. B., Fernandes, M. J., Camões, P. J., & Jorge, S. M. (2013). *Anuário Financeiro dos Municípios Portugueses 2011 e 2012*. Lisboa: Ordem dos Técnicos Oficiais de Contas.

Cattaneo, G. (2012). *The case of e-procurement: No more excuses: Will public administrations overcome their own inertia before EC mandatory regulation will force them to?* 1st International EIBURS-TAIPS TAIPS conference on "Innovation in the public sector and the development of e-services", University of Urbino, April 19–20.

Costa, A. A., Arantes, A., & Tavares, L. V. (2013). Evidence of the impacts of public e-procurement: The Portuguese experience. *Journal of Purchasing and Supply Management, 19*(4), 238–246.

Croom, S. R., & Brandon-Jones, A. (2005). Key issues in e-procurement: Procurement implementation and operation in the public sector. *Journal of Public Procurement, 5*(3), 367–387.

European Commission. (2009). *Smarter, faster, better eGovernment: 8th benchmark measurement*. European Commission, Directorate General Information Society and Media.

European Commission. (2010a). *A digital agenda for Europe*. European Commission, COM(2010) 245.

European Commission. (2010b). *Evaluation of the 2004 action plan for electronic public procurement*. Accompanying document to the green paper on expanding the use of e-Procurement in the EU. European Commission, SEC(2010) 1214 final.

European Commission. (2010c). *Green paper: On expanding the use of e-procurement in the EU*. European Commission, COM(2010) 571.

European Commission. (2010d). *Summary of the responses to the green paper on expanding the use of e-procurement in the EU* (DG MARKT Services working document). European Commission. http://ec.europa.eu/internal_market/consultations/docs/2010/e-procurement/synthesis_en.pdf

European Commission. (2012a). *A strategy for e-procurement*. European Commission, COM(2012) 179 final.

European Commission. (2012b). *Delivering savings for Europe: Moving to full e-procurement for all public purchases by 2016*. Press release IP/12/389.

Faridian, P. H. (2015). Innovation in public management: Is public e-procurement a wave of the future? A theoretical and exploratory analysis. *International Journal of Public Administration, 38*(9), 654–662.

Federici, T. (2009). Introducing e-procurement in a local healthcare agency. In A. Scupola (Ed.), *Cases on managing e-services*. Denmark: Roskilde University, IGI.

Fernandes, T., & Vieira, V. (2015). Public e-procurement impacts in small- and medium-enterprises. *International Journal of Procurement Management, 8*(5), 587–607.

Huntgeburth, J. C., Steininger, D. M., Parasie, N. P., & Veit, D. J. (2012). Increasing the adoption of e-procurement services at the municipal level. *e-Service Journal, 8*(3), 3–23.

Hassan, H. (2013). *Factors affecting the extent of e-procurement use in small and medium enterprises in New Zealand*. Ph.D thesis, Massey University. http://muir.massey.ac.nz/bitstream/handle/10179/4701/02_whole.pdf?sequence=1

Jansen, K. J., Corley, K. G., & Jansen, B. J. (2007). E-survey methodology. In R. A. Reynolds, R. Woods, & J. D. Baker (Eds.), *Handbook of research on electronic surveys and measurements*. Hershev and London: IGI Global. Chap. I.

Johnson, M. (2011). Public sector e-procurement: A study of benefits from e-markets in the local government sector. *International Journal of Services Technology and Management, 16*(1), 1–27.

Khorana, S., Ferguson-Boucher, K., & Kerr, W. A. (2014). Governance issues in the EU's e-procurement framework. *Journal of Common Market Studies, 53*(2), 292–310.

Manchester Declaration. (2005). *Ministerial declaration*. Approved unanimously on 24 November 2005. Manchester, UK.

McCue, C., & Roman, A. V. (2012). E-procurement: Myth or reality? *Journal of Public Procurement, 12*(2), 221–248.

McConnell, D. J. (2009). *An analysis into the factors affecting the uptake of applications of e-procurement, within the UK public sector*. Ph.D thesis, Loughborough University.

MCTES. (2005). *Ligar Portugal—Um programa de acção integrado no Plano Tecnológico do XVII Governo: mobilizar a Sociedade de Informação e do Conhecimento*. Lisboa: Ministério da Ciência, Tecnologia e Ensino Superior.

Moon, M. J. (2005). E-Procurement management in state governments: Diffusion of e-procurement practices and its determinants. *Journal of Public Procurement, 12*(2), 212–238.

Mota, F. P. B., & Filho, J. R. (2011). Public e-procurement and the duality of technology: A comparative study in the context of Brazil and of the state of Paraíba. *Journal of Information Systems and Technology Management, 8*(2), 315–330.

Neves, B. B. (2007). *Inovação, modernização e competitividade na administração pública: o exemplo do governo electrónico em Portugal, Espanha e Irlanda*. Communication presented at the "XII Congresso da CLAD", Santo Domingo, Dominican Republic, October-November 2007.

OECD. (2005). *Oslo manual: Guidelines for collecting and interpreting innovation data* (3rd ed.). Paris: OECD.

Rahim, M. (2008). Identifying factors affecting acceptance of e-procurement systems: An initial qualitative study at an Australian city council. *Communications of the IBIMA, 3*, 7–17.

Rogers, E. M. (2003). *Diffusion of innovations* (5th ed.). New York: The Free Press.

Tavares, L. (2008). *A gestão das aquisições públicas: guia de aplicação do Código dos Contratos Públicos—Decreto-Lei 18/2008—Empreitadas, Bens e Serviços*. Lisboa: OPET.

Tavares, G. G. (2011). Portugal. In Global Legal Group (Ed.), *The international comparative legal guide to: Public procurement 2011: A practical cross-border insight into public procurement*. London: GLG. Chap. 26.

Tavares, L., Rosa, M., Graça P., Costa, A., & Tavares, T. (2011). *2° inquérito nacional de contratação pública electrónica. Relatório final*. APMEP: Associação Portuguesa dos Mercados Públicos.

Tidd, J. (2010a). From models to the management of diffusion. In J. Tidd (Ed.), *Gaining momentum: Managing the diffusion of innovations*. Series on technology management (Vol. 15). London: Imperial College Press.

Tidd, J. (Ed.) (2010b). *Gaining momentum: Managing the diffusion of innovations*. Series on technology management (Vol. 15). London: Imperial College Press.

Toktaş-Palut, P., Baylav, E., Teoman, S., & Altunbey, M. (2014). The impact of barriers and benefits of e-procurement on its adoption decision: An empirical analysis. *International Journal of Production Economics, 158*, 77–90.

Tonkin, C. (2003). E-procurement in the public sector: story, myth and legend. Working Paper, The Policy Institute, Trinity College Dublin.

Trkman, P., & McCormack, K. (2010). Estimating the benefits and risks of implementing e-procurement.*IEEE Transactions on Engineering Management, 57*(2), 338–349.

UN. (2008). *UN e-Government Survey 2008: From e-government to connected governance*. United Nations. http://unpan1.un.org/intradoc/groups/public/documents/UN/UNPAN028607.pdf

Vaidya, K., Sajeev, A. S. M., & Callender, G. (2006). Critical factors that influence e-procurement implementation success in the public sector. *Journal of Public Procurement, 6*(1&3), 70–99.

Vaidya, K. (2007). Organizational assimilation of e-procurement: An institutional perspective and the research model. In A. K. Pani & A. Agrahari (Eds.), *E-procurement in emerging economies: Theory and cases* (Chap. II). Hershey and London: IGI Global.

MIX
Papier aus verantwortungsvollen Quellen
Paper from responsible sources
FSC® C105338

If you have any concerns about our products,
you can contact us on
ProductSafety@springernature.com

In case Publisher is established outside the EU,
the EU authorized representative is:
Springer Nature Customer Service Center GmbH
Europaplatz 3, 69115 Heidelberg, Germany

Printed by Libri Plureos GmbH
in Hamburg, Germany